PREFACE

The aim of this book is to provide a treatment of media law which will be of use to students and practitioners. Media law is an area which evolves and develops with great rapidity. As ideas and technology changes, so our conception of the media and of the role which it plays changes also. The courts are continually asked to assess the implications of new developments: some involving the application of traditional principles in a new context; others requiring a reconsideration of those traditional principles themselves. Legislation, both Irish and European, is introduced to regulate new forms of media activity, to address new concerns that emerge as media practices change, or, indeed, to reform legislative policies that have been overtaken by events.

The experience in recent years in Ireland has been testament to the fluid nature of media law. In the last decade or so, the Irish courts have made extensive efforts to flesh out and refine our constitutional jurisprudence on freedom of expression. This book charts these changes with a particular focus on what they mean for the place of the media in Ireland's constitutional order. The influence of the European Convention on Human Rights and recent developments in the Strasbourg courts are also discussed. The establishment of a Press Council and Press Ombudsman, and the complex and emerging caselaw on the protection of a right to privacy under the Irish Constitution and under the ECHR have had a notable impact on the regulation and activities of the media in recent years. Recent legislative developments meanwhile have included the passage of the Defamation Act 2009, the Broadcasting Act 2009 and the adoption of the Audiovisual Media Services Directive. These have changed the legal landscape significantly and this book attempts to provide a guide to the legislation which will hopefully provide a useful reference point for the core aspects of these reforms.

As this brief overview indicates, the pace and scope of developments means that it is difficult to provide anything more than a snapshot of the developing jurisprudence at any particular moment in time. Analysis may be made and prognostications offered but these are always liable to be overtaken by events. Even in the few short weeks between finalising the manuscript and it being typeset, several decisions were handed down by the High Court that required a re-working of some of the chapters. We have endeavoured to state the law as at 31 July 2010 while making some references to subsequent developments also.

The ever-shifting nature of the media environment also means that it is difficult to identify precisely what a text on media law should contain. The media, in its widest sense, could include all forms of communications technology, through which companies may deliver services or products, or through which individuals may express views, access information, or exchange material, either in written, oral, or electronic form. In that sense, media law could cover laws on data protection, copyright, postal or courier services, net neutrality, and so on. As communications technology develops, so might this range of potential legal issues expand to include a multitude of other areas. This is an area in which any legal work is particularly susceptible to being overtaken by events – and by newly emerging technologies in particular.

By contrast, this book confines itself to a discussion of the law as it impacts upon the media in its more traditional sense – the broadcasters, editors and journalists who have been regarded for decades as occupying a critically important democratic and constitutional role as the 'Fourth Estate'. There is no question but that these traditional forms of media organisation and activity are under pressure. Commerical pressures, together with competition from online commentators whose work often blurs the boundaries between expression, comment and news, threaten traditional techniques of newsgathering and reporting. The migration from a print and analogue broadcast environment to the new multi-channel, multi-form digital reality further obliges the media to change the way in which it does business. Quite what form these changes will take is currently unclear. What this will means for approach adopted by the law, therefore, is even more uncertain. It seems likely that any future editions will be considering a very altered media environment with – quite possibly – consequential changes in the way in which the law conceives of freedom of expression and of the media itself. At present, however, the uncertain future for the media – and the notable lack of significant legislative efforts in Ireland to address the implications of any of these issues – means that it would be premature to consider such matters in detail in a practically-focused text such as this.

We have been fortunate to have the generous assistance of several colleagues in producing this work. We are grateful to our editor Amy Hayes for her patience and support, and Marie Armah-Kwantreng for her tremendous work on typesetting the text. Eva Nagle BL provided very helpful research assistance, which was generously funded by a research award from UCD School of Law. Our thanks also to Paul O'Higgins SC, David Keane SC, Natalie McDonnell BL, Bernadette Quigley BL, Ronan Lupton BL, Ray Ryan BL and John O'Dowd of UCD School of Law for taking the time to read drafts of this work and for their helpful comments and suggestions, as appropriate. Any mistakes or omissions are our own.

Bluehaven,

November, 2010.

CONTENTS

TABLE OF AUTHORITIES

Ireland

United Kingdom

European Union

European Court and Commission of Human Rights

Other Jurisdictions

TABLE OF STATUTES

Irish Legislation

United Kingdom, Pre 1922 and Other Nations' Legislation

TABLE OF STATUTORY INSTRUMENTS

TABLE OF EU LEGISLATION

TABLE OF TREATIES AND CONVENTIONS

TABLE OF CONSTITUTIONS

Chapter 1

THEORIES OF FREEDOM OF EXPRESSION AND THE MEDIA

INTRODUCTION

[1.01] This chapter explores the various theories that have been identified as underlying freedom of expression and assesses their relevance to the regulation of media expression. Much academic ink has been spilt in this area. The purpose of this chapter is not to reproduce in full the nuanced analyses and critiques that appear in works dedicated to the finer points of free speech theory. Such an exercise would be outside the scope of this work and of limited practical assistance to the reader. Instead, this chapter provides an account of the main issues that arise when attempting to theorise about media expression and in so doing provides a philosophical backdrop for the remainder of this book.

FREEDOM OF EXPRESSION – A FUNDAMENTAL VALUE

[1.02] Freedom of expression of the media is generally accepted to be a crucial feature of most constitutional democracies. It has been included as a core value in a variety of international conventions and other instruments including the European Convention on Human Rights and Fundamental Freedoms[1] (the ECHR) and the United Nations Universal Declaration of Human Rights.[2] It is widely recognised across constitutional democracies as a key constitutional protection and interference with 'freedom of press' is often viewed as the hallmark of a totalitarian regime.

[1.03] The recognition of the importance of freedom of media expression is as old as the media itself. Written centuries before the development of the modern media as we now know it, Milton's *Areopagitica* emerged in the seventeenth century against a background of what would nowadays be referred to as prior restraint of the press. Milton's pamphlet was published in 1644 by way of reaction to the licensing order passed by the British Parliament the previous year.[3] The licensing order created a number of official censors to whom authors were required to submit their work prior to publication. Milton, arguing for the repeal of the licensing order, argued strongly that suppression of ideas was wrong because it is only through the clash of ideas that truth is confirmed or discovered. In one of the best-known passages of the pamphlet, Milton wrote:

> And though all the winds of doctrine were let loose to play upon the earth, so
> Truth be in the field, we do injuriously by licensing and prohibiting to misdoubt

---

1. ECHR, Art 10.
2. United Nations Universal Declaration of Human Rights, Art 19. See also the International Covenant on Civil and Political Rights, Art 19.
3. Licensing Order of 16 June, 1643.

her strength. Let her and Falsehood grapple; who ever knew Truth put to the worse in a free and open encounter? Her confuting is the best and surest suppressing.[4]

The primary purpose of Milton's pamphlet was to argue for free publication of coverage of parliamentary proceedings.[5] As Hallam wrote, 'the liberty of the press consists, in a strict sense, merely in an exemption from the superintendence of a licensor'.[6] Such a narrow view of press freedom is at odds with the current views on freedom of expression which assume a much more broadly based protection for the media, the rationales for which are discussed below.

[1.04] There is now, it is fair to say, a general liberal consensus that freedom of expression should be protected and that the protection of the media is particularly important.[7] Public and legal discourse about freedom of expression tends, therefore, to focus on the parameters of appropriate restriction of speech rather than questioning the importance of freedom of the press as a key constitutional value.[8] Cases which come before the courts in Ireland and elsewhere tend to deal with the dividing line between permissible and impermissible restrictions of freedom of media expression. This generally involves a balancing act of sorts. Some cases require the balance of freedom of media expression against a competing public interest. Restrictions on the basis of national security, the protection of the authority and impartiality of the judiciary fall into this category. Some restrictions seem aimed at both the public interest and the private interests of certain individuals or groups who may be offended (or some might argue harmed) by particular types of speech. Thus the courts and the legislature have had to balance laws regulating obscene expression, blasphemy and speech which incites hatred against the general public interest in a free press. Other cases give rise to a more direct clash of freedom of expression with private interests, reputation and privacy being two such examples.

---

4.   Milton, *Areopagitica* (1644).

5.   The primary purpose of Milton's pamphlet was to argue for free publication of coverage of parliamentary proceedings. While subsequently lauded as a general plea for freedom of expression, the pamphlet does not seem to have had any great practical impact at the time of its publication. As Hallam noted in his *Constitutional History of England*: 'We read the noble apology of Milton for the freedom of the press with admiration; but it had little influence on the Parliament to which it was addressed.'

6.   Hallam, *Constitutional History of England* (2nd edn, 1829).

7.   The general acceptance, at least rhetorically, of a broad conception of freedom of expression is a relatively recent phenomenon. The original draft of the United States Constitution contained no provision for freedom of expression. It was at the insistence of the states that the First Amendment was added and there is little doubt that this request was inspired in part by the colonial history of the newly independent states. See discussion in Blom-Cooper, 'Press Freedom: constitutional right or cultural assumption?' [2008] Public Law 260.

8.   There is, however, a debate as to the precise status of freedom of expression as a constitutional value and whether, for example, it necessarily trumps competing interests which might also be entrenched at a constitutional level. See discussion of a putative 'free speech principle' in Barendt, *Freedom of Speech* (2nd edn, OUP, 2005), 6–7.

[1.05] Clashes of these interests can arise when individuals speak or when the media speaks. The subject matter of this book is concerned primarily with the latter situation. In this context, it seems important to explore the theoretical bases for the protection of freedom of media expression and the extent to which it may differ from individual expression. The consequences of such differing bases are of more than merely academic interest. As will be illustrated in the discussion of the case law in the remainder of this book, they may have a significant impact on the way in which the case law treats media expression.

THEORISING MEDIA EXPRESSION

Free speech – an instrumental or deontological principle?

[1.06] Freedom of expression has been justified on various philosophical grounds. While the area has spawned a plethora of academic articles and arguably an unnecessarily complicated analytical framework, there are essentially two categories of rationale for protecting free speech. These can be usefully described as the deontological and instrumental categories of justification. A deontological theory of freedom of expression values speech as a fundamental aspect of one's individuality. This approach has the advantage of capturing certain types of expression which may not easily be accommodated within a more utilitarian, instrumental framework. Instrumental justifications for protecting freedom of expression, on the other hand, seem more suited to accommodating the role of the media in expression.

Instrumental theories of freedom of expression

[1.07] There are a number of ways in which the protection of freedom of expression can be seen as having an instrumental value. The most common approaches can be summarised as the Millian concept of the pursuit of truth, the commitment to a marketplace of ideas, the need to restrain government to protect the autonomy of the citizen and the narrower conception of speech as being crucial to participatory democracy.

Mill and the pursuit of truth

[1.08] One of the oldest and enduring rationales for protecting freedom of expression has been the importance of free exchanges of ideas to the discovery of truth. This idea is usually identified with the work of Milton in the seventeenth century[9] and John Stuart Mill[10] in the mid-nineteenth century.

[1.09] Mill wrote that:

> The time, it is to be hoped, is gone by when any defence would be necessary of the 'liberty of the press' as one of the securities against corrupt or tyrannical government. No argument, we may suppose, can now be needed, against

---

9.   Milton, *Areopagitica: A Speech for the Liberty of Unlicensed Printing* (1644).
10.   Mill, *On Liberty* (1859).

permitting a legislature or an executive, not identified in interest with the people, to prescribe opinions to them, and determine what doctrines or what arguments they shall be allowed to hear.[11]

[1.10] Mill's famous essay, *On Liberty*, takes as its starting position the view that the soundest judgment is reached by considering all of the facts and opinions about a proposition. Individuals are flawed in their prejudices, emotions and personal interest and limited in their viewpoint. By allowing the free circulation of ideas and opinions, it is more likely that truth will be revealed. One should not preclude the circulation of unproven ideas because human understanding is a continuous process. Even some of the most seemingly obvious truths can be rejected and no opinion should enjoy immunity from challenge. Government cannot identify and prohibit false speech because to do so assumes infallibility on the part of government and risks tyranny.

[1.11] Such an approach risks the circulation of ideas which are false. However, from this perspective, even where speech is false it must be permitted because the promulgation of false ideas performs the function of forcing those who hold the truth to defend their views. Suppression of ideas and information prevents individuals from reaching the most rational judgment and blocks the evolution of human understanding. Even where an opinion or idea is in error, its circulation fulfils a vital function in that it compels a rethinking of accepted opinions. This results in a deeper appreciation of the reasons for holding the opinion and avoids a situation where accepted views, going unchallenged, become 'held as a dead dogma, not a living truth'.[12]

[1.12] Mill's view of the role of freedom of expression is not without its critics. It is a fundamentally optimistic projection of the likely outcome of absolutely unfettered free speech. It assumes that the process of the free exchange of ideas will have a positive outcome. In fact, the dissemination of false ideas may well find a receptive audience, at least for a time. To borrow a military euphemism, the 'collateral damage' caused by false speech to private and public interests of the type described above is ignored. Mill's response would presumably be that the long-term interest in constant and uninhibited debate outweighs the short-term damage that may be caused by the temporary acceptance of false ideas. A theory which requires the sacrifice of current interests in such an open-ended manner and which leaves no room for protecting other values is unsurprisingly not reflected wholesale in the law's approach to media expression.

[1.13] Another weakness of Mill's theory is that it is underinclusive as it does not seem to explain the protection of expression which lacks an educative function in the quest for truth, such as certain artistic or emotional expression. It is also difficult to fit into Mill's theory disciplines such as mathematics which claim to have a methodology for verifying facts and which in their internal discourse simply cannot accommodate notions of constantly shifting truths.

---

11.   Mill, *On Liberty* (1859), Ch II.
12.   *Ibid.*

The 'marketplace of ideas'

[1.14] While no legal system has ever managed to import Mill's theory and all its consequences completely, the central idea behind Mill's defence of freedom of expression has attracted extensive judicial approval. Perhaps the best known of the judicial statements of this libertarian approach to free speech derives from the US Supreme Court case of *Abrams v United States*,[13] where Justice Oliver Wendall Holmes gave a famous dissenting judgment in which he stated that:

> Persecution for the expression of opinions seems to me perfectly logical. If you have no doubt of your premises or your power and want a certain result with all your heart you naturally express your wishes in law and sweep away all opposition. To allow opposition by speech seems to indicate that you think the speech impotent, as when a man says that he has squared the circle, or that you do not care whole heartedly for the result, or that you doubt either your power or your premises. But when men have realized that time has upset many fighting faiths, they may come to believe even more than they believe the very foundations of their own conduct that the ultimate good desired is better reached by free trade in ideas – that the best test of truth is the power of the thought to get itself accepted in the competition of the market, and that truth is the only ground upon which their wishes safely can be carried out.[14]

[1.15] The phrase 'marketplace of ideas' is often used as a shorthand description of this enduring rationale for freedom of expression.[15] Holmes's economic metaphor of the 'free trade in ideas' has been highly influential. In subsequent opinions of the US Supreme Court, the concept of the free marketplace of ideas has been relied on to defend allegedly obscene material[16] and to impose a requirement that a plaintiff suing for intentional infliction of emotional distress arising from a parody prove actual malice.[17] Holmes J's dissent has also met with judicial approval in the House of Lords in the United Kingdom,[18] the Supreme Court of Canada[19] and the Irish High Court.[20]

[1.16] The rhetorical adoption of this metaphor in the case law belies its problematic foundations. There are a number of critiques of Holmes's justification for protecting freedom of expression. Perhaps the most common is that Holmes J's statement in *Abrams* can be read as adopting a relativist conception of truth in which no core truths can ever triumph. Whatever is for the time being accepted as truth (whatever ideas have

---

13.   *Abrams v United States* (1919) 250 US 616.
14.   *Abrams v United States* (1919) 250 US 616, 630–631.
15.   In fact, the phrase 'marketplace of ideas' does not appear in Justice Holmes's opinion.
16.   *Smith v United States* 431 US 291 (1977), Stevens J, dissenting, fn 24.
17.   *Hustler Magazine v Falwell* 485 US 46 (1988).
18.   *R v Secretary of State for the Home Department, ex parte, Simms* [2002] 2 AC 115.
19.   *Retail, Wholesale and Department Store Union v Dolphin Delivery* [1986] 2 SCR 573, para 14.
20.   *Mahon v Post Publications* [2005] IEHC 307, HC, Kelly J, 4 October 2004; *Holland v Governor of Portlaoise Prison* [2004] 2 IR 573, 605. The European Court of Human Rights tends not to use the phrase 'marketplace of ideas' itself although see the dissenting opinion of Klecker J in the European Commission of Human Rights decision in *Arrowsmith v United Kingdom* (1981) 3 EHRR 218, para 10.

won the current competition) constitute truth. The impossibility of discovering truth is a pessimistic proposition and one which does not convincingly justify the restriction of government from interfering with freedom of expression.[21]

[1.17] Further, the analogy with the market raises a problem in that the marketplace of ideas is far from an idealised competitive market. As Bork pointed out, '[t]he market for ideas has few of the self-correcting features of the market for goods and services.'[22] Furthermore, not everyone has access to the market. The analogy with healthy competition in the economic sphere seems particularly problematic when applied to the media expression. In *Australian Broadcasting Corporation v Lenah Game Meats Pty Ltd*,[23] Callinan J of the High Court of Australia noted that:

> The expression 'marketplace of ideas' has been used as a justification for 'free speech', as if the two expressions were synonymous. The concept of a marketplace is of a place to which access is readily available to everyone. The notion of a 'marketplace of ideas' conveys an idea of an opportunity for everyone with ideas to put these into currency for entry into the public domain, and for them to be exchanged for other ideas. The concentration of media control and the absence of rights of reply to which I have referred deny these opportunities in practice.[24]

[1.18] The criticism has also been made that the media set the agenda for public debate and this may exclude some ideas which are not newsworthy. The selection by the media of what to cover and not cover is likely to be based on what will be profitable. It has been suggested that 'any truth argument assumes attitudes on the part of the speaker of sincerity and truthfulness'[25] so that this profit motivation detracts from the value of the speech contributed by the media. One possible response to this is that access to the marketplace of ideas has expanded exponentially with the increased use of the internet. It is now possible for individuals and organisations of limited resources to circulate ideas and arguments to a broader audience than ever before. However, even here the extent to which an idea that is expressed online attracts widespread attention or support may be influenced by the action or omissions of the limited number of internet services (such as Google's search engine rankings) that exert a level of control over web traffic.

[1.19] As indicated above, Holmes J's famous quote is redolent of free market theory in the economic sphere. As in the economic version, however, it is generally recognised that some regulation of the market is desirable to avoid harm. Few, for example, would take issue with the regulation of commercial advertising so as to protect the consumer from out-and-out fraud. Furthermore, it may be argued that the effective communication of expression requires some state intervention to avoid a cacophony of clashing voices.

---

21.   Schauer, *Free Speech: A Philosophical Enquiry* (Cambridge University Press, 1982), 19–21.
22.   Bork, 'Adversary Jurisprudence', *The New Criterion* (May 2002), 7.
23.   *Australian Broadcasting Corporation v Lenah Game Meats Pty Ltd* (2001) 76 ALJR 1.
24.   *Australian Broadcasting Corporation v Lenah Game Meats Pty Ltd* (2001) 76 ALJR 1, 55.
25.   Barendt, *Freedom of Speech*, (2nd edn, OUP, 2005), 12.

Broadcasting regulation is aimed at this. If these restrictions are accepted (and it seems in most constitutional democracies that they are), it seems that the marketplace of ideas, while an attractive metaphor, is inadequate to fully explain the modern doctrine of freedom of the press.

Speech and democracy

[1.20] While there may be debate over the protection of some forms of expression, such as commercial advertising, pornographic material etc, there appears to be a general consensus across Western democracies that political expression is deserving of protection. Alexander Meiklejohn's work[26] sees the main function of the First Amendment to the US Constitution as being inherently connected with the democratic process. Expression is protected because it facilitates citizens in understanding political issues and thus in participating effectively in democracy.[27]

[1.21] The principal objection to this theory of free speech is that it is underinclusive. By viewing expression as a purely instrumental means of safeguarding the effectiveness of democracy, the theory ignores speech which does not contribute to that goal. Forms of expression which lack a political dimension are left out. Further, speech which advocates eg the overthrow of the democratic system may not be deserving of protection according to this theory.[28]

Another problem is that identified by Schauer, namely that 'the very notion of popular sovereignty supporting the argument from democracy argues against any limitation on that sovereignty, and thereby argues against recognition of an independent principle of freedom of speech'.[29] Such a majoritarian approach to constitutional principles runs counter to the more modern understanding of the democratic state and the role of constitutional principles such as free speech. One modern conception of the democratic state views it as one in which political and legal institutions must respect the right of all citizens to be treated with equal respect and concern.[30] The majority is thus seen as a temporary one, subject to change depending on the outcome of the political process. If this view is taken, then the right to free speech is too fundamental to be subject to the whims of the elected majority. The right of everyone to participate in society through the exercise of free speech rights is part of the foundation of democracy itself.

---

26. Meiklejohn, *Free Speech and its Relation to Self-Government* (Harper and Brothers, 1948).
27. This was the basis upon which the High Court of Australia conferred protection on freedom of expression in political matters. See *Nationwide News Pty Ltd v Walls* (1992) 177 CLR 1; *ACT Pty Ltd v Commonwealth* (1992) 177 CLR 106.
28. See Bork, 'Neutral Principles and Some First Amendment Problems' (1971) 47 Indiana Law Journal 1.
29. Schauer, *Free Speech: A Philosophical Enquiry* (Cambridge University Press, 1982).
30. Dworkin (edn), *The Philosophy of Law* (Oxford University Press, 1977), 15–26.

A deontological theory of freedom of expression

Expression and autonomy

[1.22] One of the most influential contributors to the debate about the theoretical foundations of freedom of expression is Thomas Scanlon. Coming from a libertarian perspective, he bases the protection of speech on the principle of autonomy and the need to restrain governmental incursion on the individual. According to Scanlon:

> [T]he legitimate powers of government are limited to those that can be defended on grounds compatible with the autonomy of its citizens – compatible, that is, with the idea that each citizen is sovereign in deciding what to believe and in weighing reasons for action.[31]

[1.23] Autonomy requires the freedom to weigh for oneself the arguments for propositions and to choose how to act. The State cannot restrict speech on the basis that it might cause individuals to form harmful beliefs or to commit harmful acts on the basis of those beliefs.

[1.24] As has been pointed out by Eric Barendt,[32] one of the difficulties of such an autonomy-based justification for freedom of expression is that it is difficult to separate from other autonomy-based rights. For example, is the right to view pornography justified by a free speech principle or by some other autonomy-based principle such as sexual or moral autonomy?[33]

[1.25] The United States Supreme Court has arguably used the First Amendment to encompass a general right to personal autonomy which has little connection with freedom of expression as a distinct value. For example, the right to contribute financially to political causes is protected under the umbrella of free speech by the characterisation of money as speech on the basis that restrictions on such contributions reduce the volume of speech.[34] It seems odd to describe the act of political donation as 'speech'. Such a broad, 'house-that-Jack-built',[35] approach to identifying speech seems to stretch the First Amendment beyond what most observers would recognise as a guarantee of freedom of expression.

[1.26] Scanlon's contribution to free speech theory, as with the approach taken by Mill and Holmes, focuses on listener autonomy ie the interests of the audience rather than the speaker. In so doing, it can be criticised for ignoring the self-fulfilment of the speaker as a key product of individual expression. Much speech may be more intuitively defended by reference to the speaker as opposed to the audience. The artistic expression of

---

31.   Scanlon, *A Theory of Freedom of Expression* (1977) 1 Phil & Pub Aff 204, 215.
32.   See discussion in Barendt, *Freedom of Speech* (2nd edn, OUP 2007), 14–15.
33.   Dworkin refers in this context to a broad freedom of moral independence: R Dworkin, 'Is there a Right to Pornography?' (1981) 1 OJLS 177.
34.   *Buckley v Valeo* 424 US 1 (1976). This approach can also be seen as endorsing an instrumental theory of freedom of expression linking it to the democratic process.
35.   The phrase is borrowed from Justice White's dissent in *Federal Election Commission v National Conservative Political Action Committee* 470 US 480 (1985), 508.

dubious taste is an example of expression which may be of limited interest to an audience but which may be of fundamental importance to the speaker. Over-emphasising listener autonomy and the value of speech to the marketplace of ideas runs the risk of ignoring the importance of speech in reinforcing the autonomy of the speaker.[36]

[1.27] To explain freedom of expression as a deontological principle is to recognise it as what we in modern parlance might call a 'human right'. From this perspective, expression is valued because it is an inherent aspect of one's status as a human being. The ability to express oneself freely is an important freedom because it facilitates personal development.[37] The act of self-expression is an act of self-realisation. The advantage of this approach to freedom of expression is that it captures the importance of speech to the speaker regardless of its value to the audience. A speaker-centred approach to freedom of expression has the added potential to protect speakers and speech which may not be adequately accommodated in an instrumental theory of freedom of expression.

[1.28] Artistic and creative expression, for example, is first and foremost an act of self-expression. Of course, some art is overtly political and can fall within both frameworks. Even art which is not ostensibly political may be seen as indivisible from the cultural milieu which makes up public discourse. The fact remains that to ignore the self-expressive function of creative endeavours is to disregard an important dimension to this type of expression.[38]

[1.29] A deontological view of free speech also provides a basis for protecting the expression rights of individuals whose speech may not be valued under a more instrumental conception of expression. Expression by young children, for example, might be more difficult to accommodate in a framework which values speech solely for its instrumental value.[39] Similarly, protecting expression by the mentally ill seems more

---

36.   The distinction drawn at one stage by some judges between the right to communicate and freedom of expression may recognise this. See *AG v Paperlink* [1984] ILRM 373 which seems attuned intuitively to this distinction.

37.   It is possible to view this approach to freedom of expression as instrumental in that it facilitates personal development. This is true of most human rights but the distinction being drawn here is between utilitarian understandings of speech and protection based purely on the connection between speech and human personality.

38.   See Weinstein, Review of 'The Irony of Free Speech' by Owen Fiss [1998] Law & Philosophy 159, 169–170:

   Some art, of course, is highly political. Moreover, as Lenin observed, everything is connected to everything else. Since art is connected to culture and culture is connected to politics, it is possible to view all art as political. But doing so denies art's essence, which has more to do with aesthetics than politics, with self-realisation than collective self-determination.

39.   Although see discussion in S Langlaude, 'On how to build a positive understanding of the child's right to freedom of expression' [2010] Human Rights Law Review 33 which suggests that such accommodation is not impossible.

adequately safeguarded as a human right.[40] This is not to suggest that the speech of children and the mentally ill offers nothing of instrumental value to public discourse. It does, however, recognise that the protection of such speech is an aspect of the respect for human dignity to which all individuals are entitled by virtue of their humanity.

[1.30] This approach to freedom of expression rarely emerges in the legal discourse about freedom of expression. Rhetorical references to the 'marketplace of ideas' have been wholeheartedly endorsed by the judiciary, no doubt attracted by the seductive (if inevitably reductive) simplicity of this concept. For example, in *Müller v Switzerland*,[41] the European Court of Human Rights reiterated that the guarantee of freedom of expression under Article 10 of the European Convention on Human Rights 'constitutes one of the essential foundations of a democratic society, indeed one of the basic conditions for its progress and for the self-fulfilment of the individual'.[42] In considering whether the confiscation of the art work in question was necessary in a democratic society, however, the court reverted to a purely instrumental attitude to artistic works, stating that:

> Those who create, perform, distribute or exhibit works of art contribute to the exchange of ideas and opinions which is essential for a democratic society. Hence the obligation on the State not to encroach unduly on their freedom of expression.[43]

[1.31] Similarly, in *Otto-Preminger-Institut v Austria*,[44] the court discussed the duties and responsibilities in Article 10(2) of the Convention and noted that:

> Amongst them – in the context of religious opinions and beliefs – may legitimately be included an obligation to avoid as far as possible expressions that are gratuitously offensive to others and thus an infringement of their rights, and which therefore do not contribute to any form of public debate capable of furthering progress in human affairs.[45]

[1.32] A singular focus on the instrumental value of speech sidelines the human dimension of expression and is thus an incomplete theory of free speech.[46]

The media and an autonomy-based theory of expression

[1.33] As far as the media is concerned, however, a defence of freedom of expression based on speaker autonomy seems likely to be of limited application. The fact that the

---

40.   See discussion in Peonidis, 'Freedom of Expression, autonomy and defamation' [1998] Law & Philosophy 1, 3–4.
41.   *Müller v Switzerland* (1988) 13 EHRR 212.
42.   *Müller v Switzerland* (1988) 13 EHRR 212, para 33.
43.   *Müller v Switzerland* (1988) 13 EHRR 212, para 33.
44.   *Otto-Preminger-Institut v Austria* (1995) 19 EHRR 34. See also *Wingrove v United Kingdom* (1997) 24 EHRR 1.
45.   *Otto-Preminger-Institut v Austria* (1995) 19 EHRR 34, para 49.
46.   Dworkin (edn), *The Philosophy of Law* (Oxford University Press, 1977), 14–16.

media generally takes corporate form adds a layer of complication to [1.36]
freedom of expression justified on the basis of self-expression.

[1.34] There is a school of thought epitomised by Dicey's view of tl
press[47] which suggests that the justifications for media expression are i ~~ ~~ uuose
for individual expression. Freedom of the press, from this perspective, means freedom
of the owners, writers and editors. A similar approach was taken by Barrington J
referring to the protection of freedom of expression under the Irish Constitution where
he noted that:

> Article 40.6.1°(i) is unique in conferring rights and liberties upon the 'organs of
> public opinion'. 'Organs' are not capable of having rights so this reference must
> be taken to mean a reference to those persons whether natural or artificial (such as
> the applicants in the present action) who control the organs of public opinion.[48]

Dicey's approach has certain advantages. It avoids the need to define 'the media' and
does not need to address whether certain forms of mass communication fall within the
meaning of that phrase. There may be some egalitarian merit in treating individuals and
the media equally when it comes to freedom of expression.

On the other hand, it seems unavoidably artificial to ascribe to the owner of a media
corporation the 'speech' of that corporation. The approach makes little sense if the self-
realisation of the speaker is seen as a fundamental aspect of free speech. In what sense
can the investor in a media company be said to be fulfilling herself as an autonomous
human being by merely contributing to (and hopefully profiting from) the sales of
newspapers or the profits from broadcasting? Similarly, who is to say that the writer or
editor of a piece is expressing their individuality by performing the duties of their
employment? Such speech may not in fact represent the uncensored views of the writer
at all but rather their views as expressed through the restrictions of editorial policy. It
thus seems that the protection of media expression is best characterised as an
instrumental mechanism, the primary purpose of which is to further the interests of the
audience or, as the European Court of Human Rights would emphasise, the functioning
of a healthy democracy.[49]

TREATING THE MEDIA DIFFERENTLY?

[1.35] Accepting that an instrumental conception of free speech seems a more solid
foundation for protecting the media does not necessarily resolve the issue of the
appropriate level of protection for the media relative to that accorded to individuals. It is
not uncommon for constitutional provisions to refer specifically to freedom of the press.
This is the case in Ireland and it suggests that the framers of the Constitution saw the
media as having a different role to the individual in this context. The media arguably

---

47.   Dicey, *Introduction to the Study of the Law of the Constitution* (10th edn, Macmillan, 1959).
48.   [1998] 1 IR 359, 404–405.
49.   See further Carolan, 'A Democratic Model of Media Freedom' (2006) 11 Bar Review 147;
       O'Neill, 'Corporate Freedom of Expression' (2005) 27 DJLS 185.

perform an important constitutional role that is qualitatively different to individuals expressing themselves.

[1.36] If this special role is recognised then we can see freedom of the press as a means of safeguarding the institutions of the media so as to ensure they can continue to act as a check on governmental power. This approach[50] could be used to justify greater protection for the media which might even extend beyond freedom of expression and into other areas of privilege such as access rights that might not be available to the public.[51] The idea that the media are entitled to special access can be criticised for ignoring others who may also justifiably demand access, eg campaigning groups.[52] Also, if the reason for privileging the media is its role in the broad dissemination of ideas and information then the capacity of individuals to do so via the internet cannot be ignored.

[1.37] It is also important to separate the free speech function of the media from its commercial activities. For example, claims by the press to be free from the rigours of merger law could result in an over-concentration of media ownership and a consequent loss of plurality of views.[53] Such claims are really based in property rights rather than expression rights and should be recognised as such.

[1.38] Another approach would be to recognise that the media enjoy the right to free speech only on the instrumental basis that they assist in the spread of ideas and information. From this perspective, the media enjoys protection because of what it contributes to the marketplace of ideas or, more specifically, to the functioning of a democracy. This approach has been rejected by the US Supreme Court, which has reiterated that the media and individuals enjoy the same free speech protection in the context of libel actions[54] and that, for example, journalists are not entitled to protect

---

50.　Stewart, 'Or of the Press' (1975) 26 Hastings Law Journal 631.

51.　There are some indications that the European Court of Human Rights may be heading in this direction. See discussion of the embryonic development of a right of access to information under Art 10 discussed in **Ch 2**.

52.　Although the extension of privileges to such groups is consistent with an approach which protects media expression on the basis of its contribution to the functioning of democracy. See *Tarsasag a Szabadsagjogokert v Hungary* (Application No 37374/05) 14 April 2009 (Second Section) discussed in **Ch 2** at **[2.107]–[2.110]**.

53.　See **Ch 10**.

54.　*Dun & Bradstreet Inc v Greenmoss Builders Inc* 472 US 749 (1985). See also the concurring opinion of Burger CJ in *First National Bank v Bellotti* 435 US 765, 795–802 (1978). Although see also *Miami Herald v Tornillo* 418 US 241 (1974) where the court recognised the First Amendment right of a newspaper editor to refuse to publish a reply to a personal attack. In *Grosjean v American Press* 297 US 233 (1936) it was held that taxation of newspapers is unconstitutional where its purpose is to penalise a particular viewpoint. Non-discriminatory taxation is not a violation of the First Amendment – *Leathers, Commissioner of Revenues of Arkansas v Medlock* 499 US 439 (1991). (Although see also *Minneapolis Star & Tribune v Minnesota Commissioners of Revenue* 460 US 575 (1983) where a non-discriminatory tax measure was found to be unconstitutional).

their sources.[55] The European Court of Human Rights, on the other hand, has recognised the special role of journalists who may not be subject to punishment for the dissemination of racist views during interviews[56] and who may protect their sources.[57]

[1.39] It seems, from an analysis of the Irish case law, that freedom of media expression is given a higher level of protection where it performs the function of contributing to the democratic functioning of the State. Such an approach does not mean that other forms of media expression – such as commercial and artistic expression – are unprotected. Recognising freedom of expression as a foundational democratic value means that all media expression is prima facie protected under Article 40.6.1°(i). What it does mean, however, is that some media speech may be more highly protected than other speech. That the content and context of media speech should be relevant to its level of protection is recognised by the European Court of Human Rights. Despite absolutist rhetoric regarding the free marketplace of ideas, the US Supreme Court eventually recognised differing levels of protection under the First Amendment for eg commercial speech.[58] The calibration of protection according to the function of the speech is an approach which arguably leads, in the long run, to greater protection for freedom of speech and the liberal values underlying its protection. The insistence of the US Supreme Court, for example, on absolute protection for all forms of expression, forced it into a position where it had to leave some forms of expression, such as hard core pornography, outside the First Amendment altogether.[59] By way of contrast, the European Court of Human Rights has included almost all speech within the coverage of Article 10, albeit applying varying levels of review depending on the context.[60] Recent case law from the European Court of Human Rights has focused on the extent to which journalists have complied with journalistic ethics, including verification of sources, as a relevant factor to consider when balancing freedom of the press against other values.[61] Such an approach takes seriously the notion of the role of the press in contributing to the functioning of democracy.

The case law from the Irish and Strasbourg courts explaining their approaches to freedom of media expression are considered in the next chapter.

---

55.   *Branzberg v Hayes* 408 US 665 (1972).

56.   *Jersild v Denmark* (1995) 19 EHRR 1.

57.   *Goodwin v United Kingdom* (1996) 22 EHRR 123. See the dissent by Walsh J arguing that journalists should not be entitled to any more protection than individuals. See also *Mahon and Keena* [2009] 2 ILRM 373 and *Financial Times Ltd v United Kingdom* (Application No 821/03) 15 December 2009 (Fourth Section). These cases are discussed in **Ch 5**.

58.   *Central Hudson Gas & Electric Corp v Public Service Commission* 447 US 557 (1980); *Lorillard Tobacco Co v Reilly* 533 US 525 (2001).

59.   *Roth v United States* 354 US 476 (1957); *Miller v California* 413 US 15 (1973).

60.   *Wingrove v UK* (1996) 24 EHRR 1.

61.   See **[2.77]–[2.105]**.

ONLINE PUBLICATION

[1.40] Questions are raised for the theories of individual and media expression set out above by the relatively recent phenomenon of online expression. The emergence of the internet has had a radically democratising effect by providing individuals with the opportunity, in principle, to reach a similar or equivalent audience to traditional media organisations. In fact, the global nature of the internet means that the expression of individuals can spread further than would ever have been possible in the era of the print or broadcast media alone.

[1.41] What does this mean for theories of media expression? In particular, what does it mean for our understanding of what represents the media? One argument is that, by lowering the barriers to entry so substantially, the emergence of the internet has created the conditions for a truly free marketplace of ideas in which the quality of the idea, rather than the level of access which it enjoys to a media platform, will determine its success. This could mean that traditional media should be subject to no more regulation than online publishers on the basis that, as media audiences and markets further fragment, these traditional operations are likely to lose their current positions of influence as the 'organs of public opinion'.

[1.42] On the other hand, it might also be argued that the rise of an unfettered online marketplace of ideas increases the need for regulation of the media so as to ensure that comment which has the potential to influence public opinion is accurate, reliable and responsible. This seems to have been the view adopted by the European Court of Human Rights in *Stoll v Switzerland* (discussed further in **Ch 2**) when it referred to the growing proliferation of publishers as support for its conclusion that reliability and accuracy in media expression is more important than ever in the modern world.

[1.43] However, subjecting traditional media to higher standards of objectivity and reliability carries with it the risk that it may increasingly lose market share to the more opinionated, prurient or salacious voices online. This seems to have been the experience in the United States where the figures demonstrate that more people now get their news from online (and often partisan) sources than from the traditional press who, in America in particular, have taken the journalistic duty of objectivity very seriously. This raises the question of whether it is better for society in the long run to insist on more responsible journalism from the traditional press, or rather allow them more latitude to compete as the lesser of two subjective or sensationalist evils.

[1.44] Alternatively, it might be argued that the solution in this situation is not to engage in a race to the partisan bottom but to expand our conception of the 'media' to include such online publishers. One consequence of this, as discussed above, is that the democratic theory of media freedom would suggest that these online 'media' outlets might also be permissibly subject to some degree of regulation. This would raise complex questions of how to distinguish between online media expression that contributes to democratic debate and online individual expression that represents a form of self-actualisation. Online phenomena like personal blogs that express political views blur the lines between these two categories.

[1.45] It would also give rise to practical problems of how such r‹
enforced. However, in this regard it may be instructive to note tha
internet as a diverse and untameable marketplace of ideas is being c
recent technological developments. It is already the case that, while ‹
express themselves online, it remains much more difficult to attract ‹
Certain core websites, from search engines to the most popular sites, have a significant
influence on patterns of online traffic. The successes of companies like Apple in recent
years with so-called 'walled garden' products which limit access to a restricted number
of sites and applications has also shown that many users are content to use services that
do not provide them with unfettered access to the online marketplace.

[1.46] With technology and trends still evolving, it is difficult at present to conclude
what the final implications of this will be for our understanding of the media or of media
freedom. Where the internet once appeared to represent a return to a perceived golden
age of media expression when any individual with a printer could create a freesheet for
distribution to the public, there are signs in more recent times of a growing
centralisation and homogeneity online. As a limited number of powerful corporations
and opinion-formers exercise increasing control over the internet, the issue for theories
of regulation and freedom of expression may not be the originally obvious one of how to
respond to a cacophony of countless voices online but the more mundane and familiar
one of how to value and deal with the expression interests of a small number of
influential actors.

Chapter 2

FREEDOM OF MEDIA EXPRESSION UNDER THE CONSTITUTION AND THE CONVENTION

INTRODUCTION

[2.01] There was a time when the Irish courts, seeking inspiration from abroad for the interpretation of the Constitution, would reach across the Atlantic to borrow from the case law of the United States Supreme Court. Given the First Amendment's terse and absolutist protection of freedom of expression, that practice has had less of an impact on the development of Irish jurisprudence in the context of freedom of expression than in other areas of constitutional interpretation.[1] The Irish constitutional text is far more nuanced and presents freedom of expression as a value that requires balancing against other values. In fact, the text of Article 40.6.1°(i) has always been far more closely related to Article 10 of the European Convention on Human Rights than the First Amendment of the US Constitution.

[2.02] As Denham J observed in *O'Brien v Mirror Group Newspapers Ltd*:[2]

> The right to communicate, the right to information and the right to freedom of expression, guaranteed by Article 40.3.1° and 40.6.1°(i) of the Constitution of Ireland, are similar to the right of freedom of expression guaranteed by Article 10 of the European Convention on Human Rights. The rights guaranteed in the Irish Constitution are not absolute, neither are the rights of the European Convention. Both documents require that a balance be achieved and that balance going to matters of reputation, information, communication and the freedom of expression is a matter of importance in a democracy and is of public interest.[3]

[2.03] Both the Constitution and the Convention have been interpreted as recognising freedom of expression of the media, the Irish text making an explicit reference to the 'organs of public opinion' in Article 40.6.1°(i). Both have also justified press freedom

---

1.   The First Amendment to the United States Constitution states that: 'Congress shall make no law abridging the freedom of speech, or of the press ...' The case law from the US Supreme Court has been more influential in areas such as the right to a fair trial and the provisions relating to private property, although Fennelly J recently referred to the US case law concerning the protection of journalists' sources in *Mahon v Keena* [2009] 2 ILRM 373. The Strasbourg jurisprudence, however, was found to be of more guidance in that case.

2.   *O'Brien v Mirror Group Newspapers Ltd* [2001] 1 IR 1.

3.   *O'Brien v Mirror Group Newspapers Ltd* [2001] 1 IR 1, 32–33. For comments to the effect that the provisions protecting free speech under the Constitution are analogous to those under the Convention, see, Denham J in *De Rossa v Independent Newspapers* [1999] 4 IR 432 and *Hunter v Duckworth* [2003] IEHC 81, where O'Caoimh J similarly observed that 'no essential difference exists between the provisions of the Convention and the provisions of Art 40.6.1 of the Constitution'.

primarily on the instrumental basis that freedom of the press is a foundational principle in a democratic society.

[2.04] This chapter provides an overview of the approach taken by the European Court of Human Rights and the Irish courts to media expression and identifies some common themes between the two streams of jurisprudence. In so doing, it provides a background for much of the discussion in subsequent chapters. Before exploring the case law, the next section explains briefly the legal status of the Convention in Irish law.

THE EUROPEAN CONVENTION ON HUMAN RIGHTS ACT 2003 AND THE INFLUENCE OF CONVENTION CASE LAW

[2.05] The European Convention on Human Rights has been incorporated into the domestic law of the State by the European Convention on Human Rights Act 2003. This provides that Irish courts have an obligation to interpret the law in accordance with its provisions, including the guarantee of freedom of expression in Article 10.[4] Judges are also required to take judicial notice of the case law of the European Court of Human Rights.[5] In the event that a law is incompatible with the Convention, the High Court and the Supreme Court may make a declaration of incompatibility with the Convention as a remedy of last resort.[6] While the remedial provisions of the Act have not proved very significant in practice,[7] the interpretive obligation has encouraged increasing citation of and references to Strasbourg case law and an increasing cross-fertilisation of Irish and Strasbourg jurisprudence.[8]

[2.06] Thus in *Mahon v Keena*,[9] the Divisional High Court in addressing the question of the protection of journalists' sources as an aspect of the constitutional protection of freedom of the press did so by reference to the case law on this point from the European Court of Human Rights. The court referred to a number of decisions of the Strasbourg Court in support of its ruling (contrary to an earlier decision of the Court of Criminal Appeal)[10] that the identity of journalists' sources would generally be protected by the courts. That the court felt able to consider this issue from a primarily Article 10 perspective indicates the extent to which the Convention has supplemented the

---

4.   European Convention on Human Rights Act 2003, s 2.
5.   European Convention on Human Rights Act 2003, s 4.
6.   European Convention on Human Rights Act 2003, s 5.
7.   Only one declaration of incompatibility has been made and there are relatively few cases in which the Convention has led directly to a remedy.
8.   It should be noted that the practice of referring to the case law under the Convention was established before 2003. While the Convention was not part of Irish law as such at that time, it was referred to as source of inspiration in the interpretation of Irish constitutional guarantee. See O'Connell, Commiskey, Meeneghan and O'Connell, *ECHR Act 2003: preliminary impact* (Dublin Bar and Solicitors Association and Law Society of Ireland, 2006).
9.   *Mahon v Keena* [2009] 2 ILRM 373.
10.   *Re Kevin O'Kelly* (1974) 108 ILTR 97.

protection available under Article 40.6.1°. The Irish courts now effectively treat the two provisions as complementary and co-extensive guarantees of media freedom.

[2.07] One significant impact that the Convention has had on Irish free speech law is to encourage the adoption in Ireland of the sort of proportionality analysis favoured by the European Court of Human Rights. This doctrine has been regularly applied by Irish courts in their interpretation of Article 40.6.1°.[11]

[2.08] The judgment of Kelly J in *Mahon v Post Publications*[12] is a prime example of the use of the proportionality doctrine in this context. Having referred to the 'cardinal importance of press freedom', the judge held that '[a]ny restriction on it must be proportionate and no more than is necessary to promote the legitimate object of the restriction.' Fennelly J expressly approved of this approach on appeal, acknowledging that it 'is, and has been recognised by this Court to be, closely comparable to that adopted by the European Court of Human Rights'.

Media Freedom of Expression under the Irish Constitution

The text of Article 40.6.1°(i)

[2.09] Article 40.6.1°(i) of the Constitution provides as follows:

1. The State guarantees liberty for the exercise of the following rights, subject to public order and morality:

    (i)   The right of the citizens to express freely their convictions and opinions.

    The education of public opinion being, however, a matter of such grave import to the common good, the State shall endeavour to ensure that organs of public opinion, such as the radio, the press, the cinema, while preserving their rightful liberty of expression, including criticism of Government policy, shall not be used to undermine public order or morality or the authority of the State.

    The publication or utterance of blasphemous, seditious, or indecent matter is an offence which shall be punishable in accordance with law.

[2.10] Article 40.6.1°(i) clearly recognises media freedom of expression. The specific reference to criticism of government policy suggests an understanding of the media as playing an important role in the constitutional democracy established by the 1937 Constitution.

There are a number of observations which can be made about the text of Article 40.6.1°(i) itself. One of its idiosyncrasies is that the text subjects media freedom of expression to the requirements of public order and morality not once, but twice. Notably, the text also provides that the media may not be used to undermine the

---

11.   See, for example, *Murphy v IRTC* [1999] 1 IR 12; *Desmond v Moriarty* [2004] 1 IR 334; *Mahon v Keena* [2009] 2 ILRM 373.

12.   *Mahon v Post Publications* [2007] 3 IR 338.

authority of the State, a limitation which does not appear to apply to the 'citizens' referred to in the first paragraph.[13]

[2.11] As for the positive recognition of the role of the media, the illustrative references to 'the radio, the press, the cinema' have not precluded the recognition of television as a protected 'organ of public opinion'[14] and the list seems capable of further addition as advances in technology increase the means by which ideas may be disseminated to a mass audience:[15]

> The reference to the 'education of public opinion' which is considered by the Constitution to be 'a matter of ... grave import to the common good' indicates that media freedom of expression is protected primarily for its contribution to debate on matters of public interest.

The effect of the separate reference to the media in the text on the level of protection of media expression has been debated. On the one hand, it might be thought to justify a lower protection of media expression given the additional caveats that accompany it.[16] It has been argued that these specific references to the media speech, which is always public, may justify granting it a higher level of protection than that of individual citizens.[17] It is more useful to consider the context of the speech and the competing interests that may clash with it in a given case rather then developing a rule that one

---

13.   The case law concerning this is dealt with in **Ch 4**.
14.   *State (Lynch) v Cooney* [1982] IR 337.
15.   For the view that the provision includes the internet, see Hogan and Whyte, eds, *Kelly; The Irish Constitution* (4th edn, Bloomsbury Professional, 2003), 1729. At one stage, the reference in the text to 'convictions and opinions' was interpreted by the courts as confining the application of Article 40. 6.1(i) to circumstances in which beliefs rather than information was being conveyed. The communication of information was held to be protected by the guarantee of personal rights under Article 40.3. See, for example, *AG v Paperlink* [1984] ILRM 373; *SPUC v Grogan* (No 5) [1988] 4 IR 434; *Carrigaline Community Television v Minister for Transport, Energy and Communications (No 2)* [1997] 1 ILRM 241; *Murphy v IRTC* [1997] 2 ILRM 467 (High Court). This issue was clarified by the Supreme Court in *Irish Times v Ireland* and in *Murphy v IRTC* when it held that Article 40.6 1. covers the communication of information as well as ideas. Fennelly J appeared to raise some fresh doubts in this area in *Mahon v Post Publications* when he remarked (at para 51) that '[i]t matters little, at least for present purposes, which Article of the Constitution expresses the guarantee'. It seems, however, that the matter was settled by the earlier Supreme Court decisions so that expressions of factual matters as well as opinions come within the guarantee. In any case, if the media are covered by the second paragraph rather than the first, the distinction seems unlikely to apply to them. It can hardly be the case that the framers intended the media to educate public opinion without publishing factual material.
16.   Hogan and Whyte, eds, *Kelly; The Irish Constitution* (4th edn, Bloomsbury Professional, 2003), 1729; Law Reform Commission, *Report on the Civil Law of Defamation* (Law Reform Commission, 1991), 116–120.
17.   McDonald, 'Defamation Report – a Response to the LRC Report' (1992) *Irish Law Times* 70. The Law Reform Commission considered the issue in its *Report on the Civil Law of Defamation* and rejected the idea that the media should enjoy greater protection than the citizenry without much discussion. *Report on the Civil Law of Defamation* (Law Reform Commission, 1991), 118–120. See also Casey *Constitutional Law in Ireland* (3rd edn, Round Hall Sweet and Maxwell, 2000), 545.

speaker's voice is always to be more highly protected than another's and this is the approach that has been taken by the Irish courts.

Theories of media expression and the Irish Constitution

Democracy and media expression

[2.12] As noted in the previous chapter, there are a number of theories upon which the protection of media expression may be justified. It was argued in that chapter that media expression may be most persuasively justified on instrumental grounds including, in particular, the central contribution which the may make to a functioning democratic polity.

That this is the rationale under the Irish Constitution seems apparent from the references in the text to the function of the organs of public opinion.[18] This appears to acknowledge the media's as fulfilling an educational or informational function. This conception of media expression as an instrumental democracy-oriented value seems to derive support from an analysis of the Irish case law, which indicates media expression tends to enjoy given a higher level of protection where it performs the function of contributing to the democratic functioning of the State.

[2.13] That does not necessarily mean that other forms of media expression – commercial advertising being one example[19] – are necessarily unprotected. As freedom of expression is a foundational democratic value, all media expression is prima facie protected under Article 40.6.1°(i) and its restriction requires a justification. What it does mean, however, is that some media speech may be more highly protected than other speech. That the content and context of media speech should be relevant to its level of protection has long been recognised by the European Court of Human Rights.

[2.14] Despite its absolutist rhetoric regarding the free marketplace of ideas, the US Supreme Court eventually ended up recognising differing levels of protection under the First Amendment for some forms of speech.[20] Free speech purists would no doubt object that such an approach allows for content-based restriction of speech, an anathema to an

---

18.   The *Report of the Constitution Review Group*, Stationery Office, 1996 seemed to prefer a similar approach to freedom of media expression, noting that:

   [T]he print and electronic media exercise an important role in the formation and development of public discourse in contemporary society. They occupy a central position, not only in informing, but also in creating and interpreting events, and in prioritising particular events and issues over others as worthy of public transmission and attention …. While 'freedom of expression' for media-related institutions is undoubtedly essential for such democratic guardianship, the latter is also dependent on the value accorded to democratic principles by the media itself, and by the procedures in operation for making the media accountable to democratic principles (p 271).

19.   See *Murphy v IRTC* [1999] 1 IR 12, 24–25.

20.   *Valentine v Chrestensen* 316 US 52 (1942); *Virginia State Pharmacy Board v Virginia Citizens Consumer Council* 425 US 748 (1976); *Central Hudson Gas & Electric Corp v Public Service Commission* 447 US 557 (1980); *Lorillard Tobacco Co v Reilly* 533 US 525 (2001).

absolutist approach to freedom of expression. The calibration of protection according to the function of the speech is, however, an approach which arguably leads to greater protection for freedom of speech and the liberal values underlying its protection in the long run. The insistence of the US Supreme Court, for example, on absolute protection for all forms of expression, effectively forced it into a position where it had to leave some forms of expression outside the First Amendment altogether.[21] By way of contrast, the European Court of Human Rights has included almost all speech within the coverage of Article 10, albeit applying varying levels of review depending on the context.[22]

Media expression in the Irish courts: an instrumental value?

[2.15] In recent decades, the Irish courts have consistently emphasised the importance of media freedom of expression. In *Cullen v Toibin*[23] O'Higgins CJ set out the principle that 'the freedom of the press ... which is guaranteed by the Constitution ... cannot be lightly curtailed.'[24] The Supreme Court has confirmed that Article 40.6.1°(i) guarantees freedom of the press in a number of decisions.[25]

[2.16] The case law on Article 40.6.1°(i) emphasises the relationship between freedom of media expression and democratic government. In *Irish Times Ltd v Ireland*,[26] for example, the Supreme Court emphasised the educative function of media free speech in reporting on court proceedings.[27] Hamilton CJ referred to the 'public administration of justice and the right of the wider public to be informed by the media of what is taking place [as] matters of the greatest importance.'[28] Similarly, O'Flaherty J noted that 'the press are entitled to report, and the public to know, that the administration of justice is being conducted fairly and properly'.[29] Denham J noted that the case involved a balancing between 'the freedom of expression of the community, a freedom of expression central to democratic government, to enable democracy to function [and] the freedom of expression of the press.'[30] Thus, 'any curtailment of the press must be viewed as a curtailment of the access of the people to the administration of justice'.[31]

---

21.   *Roth v United States* 354 US 476 (1957); *Miller v California* 413 US 15 (1973). Cf *Simon & Schuster Inc v Members of the New York State Crime Victims Board* 502 US 105 (1991), 127.
22.   *Wingrove v UK* (1996) 24 EHRR 1. Although the court has also indicated that speech which subverts the democratic values which underlie the Convention rights may not be deserving of protection.
23.   *Cullen v Toibin* [1984] ILRM 577.
24.   *Cullen v Toibin* [1984] ILRM 577, 582. Cited by O'Flaherty J in *Irish Times Ltd v Ireland* [1998] 1 IR 359, 396. See also Barrington J at 405.
25.   Examples of recent cases confirming this include *Irish Times v Ireland* [1998] 1 IR 359; *Kelly v O'Neill* [2000] 1 IR 354; *O'Brien v Mirror Group Newspapers* [2001] 1 IR 1; *Jonathan v Ireland* [2002] IEHC 59.
26.   *Irish Times Ltd v Ireland* [1998] 1 IR 359. See O'Flaherty J at 395, Denham J at 399 and Barrington J at 405.
27.   Paras **[2.17]** and **[5.02]**.
28.   *Irish Times Ltd v Ireland* [1998] 1 IR 359, 383.
29.   *Irish Times Ltd v Ireland* [1998] 1 IR 359, 396.
30.   *Irish Times Ltd v Ireland* [1998] 1 IR 359, 399.
31.   *Irish Times Ltd v Ireland* [1998] 1 IR 359, 398.

[2.17] As Keane J observed, the freedom of expression of the media is essential if the constitutional purpose of educating and informing the public is to be fulfilled. It was, in his view:

> ... imperative that the media should have the widest possible freedom to report what happens in court ... In modern conditions, the media are the eyes and ears of the public and the ordinary citizen is almost entirely dependent on them for his knowledge of what goes on in court. Justice must be administered in public, not in order to satisfy the merely prurient or mindlessly inquisitive, but because, if it were not, an essential feature of a truly democratic society would be missing. Such a society could not tolerate the huge void that would be left if the public had to rely on what might be seen or heard by casual observers, rather than on a detailed daily commentary by press, radio and television. The most benign climate for the growth of corruption and abuse of powers, whether by the judiciary or members of the legal profession, is one of secrecy.[32]

[2.18] A similar approach was taken by Clarke J in *Cogley v RTÉ*[33] where, considering an application to restrain the broadcast of a television programme on privacy grounds, he held that:

> [T]he Constitution ... recognises the need for a vigorous and informed public debate on issues of importance ... The form of parliamentary democracy enshrined in the Constitution requires that there be a vigorous and informed public debate on issues of importance. Any measures which would impose an excessive or unreasonable interference with the conditions necessary for such debate would require very substantial justification.[34]

These decisions connect the protection of media expression with the interests of the public in being educated and informed about matters of public interest. They thus reflect an instrumental view of media freedom. Media expression is socially valuable because of the contribution it makes to the democratic process.[35] It is protected because of what it does, rather than because of what it is. This suggests that 'the particular protection given to media companies is primarily due to the interest of the public in hearing expression rather than the interests of the companies themselves'.[36]

The distinction between individual and public expression

[2.19] Chapter 1 outlined in brief the broad distinction that exists between instrumental and deontological theories of media expression. The Irish courts have found that the text

---

32. *Irish Times Ltd v Ireland* [1998] 1 IR 359, 409. Keane J, unlike the other members of the court, saw the role of the media in reporting on the administration of justice as a matter deriving from Art 34.1 rather than Art 40.6.1°(i). The taxonomy notwithstanding, his judgment supports the idea that the media contribute to the functioning of democracy, in this instance by the exposition of the administration of justice.
33. *Cogley v RTÉ* [2005] 4 IR 79.
34. *Cogley v RTÉ* [2005] 4 IR 79, 94.
35. Carolan, 'A democratic model of media freedom?' (2006) 11 Bar Review 147.
36. O'Neill, 'Corporate Freedom of Expression' (2005) 27 DULJ 184 at 184.

of the Constitution also tracks this distinction with the effect that private or personal instances of expression are protected under Article 40.3.1° with public expression protected under Article 40.6.1°(i).

This analysis of the constitutional text was first advanced by Barrington J in *Irish Times v Ireland*,[37] and was endorsed by the Supreme Court as a whole in *Murphy v IRTC*.[38] In *Irish Times v Ireland*, Barrington J underlined the importance of the context of Article 40.6.1.°(i):

> [I]t is important to look at the context in which the right of the citizens to express freely their convictions and opinions is placed in the Constitution. Article 40.6.1° deals with three rights, the right of the citizens to express freely their convictions and opinions, the right of the citizens to assemble peaceably and without arms and the right of the citizens to form associations and unions. All of these relate to the public activities of the citizens and to the practical workings of a democratic society. They are part of the dynamics of political change. They are at once both vitally important to the success of a democracy and potentially a source of political instability. That is why the Constitution and the European Convention both assert and circumscribe them.[39]

[2.20] He repeated this analysis in *Murphy*, pointing out that Article 40.6.1°(i) was designed to secure the conditions in which democracy could flourish:

> Article 40.6.1° ... is concerned with the public activities of the citizen in a democratic society. That is why ... the framers grouped the right to freedom of expression, the right to free assembly and the right to form associations and unions in the one sub-section. All three rights relate to the practical running of a democratic society.[40]

This underlines the fact that Article 40.6.1°(i) is directed towards the 'public activities of the citizen in a democratic society'.[41]

[2.21] Article 40.3.1°, on the other hand, protected in his view the individual's basic entitlement as an autonomous human being to engage in expressive or communicative conduct. It ensures the individual of the freedom to 'convey ... needs and emotions' as well as to participate in 'rational discourse'. This, for the Court, 'must be one of the most basic rights of man'.[42] This right is not, therefore, protected for instrumentalist reasons. Article 40.3 does not protect expression only where it aims to achieve a socially valuable purpose. Rather, expression is protected because of the importance of communication as a fundamental human need. This is why it is a protected as an aspect of the citizen's 'personal rights'.[43]

---

37.   *Irish Times v Ireland* [1998] 1 IR 359.
38.   *Murphy v IRTC* [1999] 1 IR 12.
39.   *Irish Times v Ireland* [1998] 1 IR 359, at 404.
40.   *Murphy v IRTC* [1999] 1 IR 12, 24.
41.   *Murphy v IRTC* [1999] 1 IR 12, 24. See also *Hunter v Duckworth* [2003] IEHC 81, O'Caoimh J.
42.   *Murphy v IRTC* [1999] 1 IR 12, 24.
43.   *Murphy v IRTC* [1999] 1 IR 12, 24.

[2.22] This is an important distinction for a number of reasons. For one, it does not suffer from the conceptual and practical difficulties which often arose in relation to the distinction which had previously been drawn in the Irish jurisprudence between communication and expression.[44] Most notably, distinguishing in this way between the rights that are protected under Article 40.3.1.° and Article 40.6.1.°(i) provides the court with a clear and intellectually coherent mechanism for examining freedom of expression issues. It treats expression as an autonomy interest under the personal rights guarantee of Article 40.3.1° while also providing protection for expression that is instrumentally valuable because of the contribution it makes to democratic and public discourse.

[2.23] The distinction is a flexible and context-sensitive one which takes seriously the differences between different theories and forms of expression, thereby eschewing the all-or-nothing absolutism that has frequently caused difficulties for American constitutional jurisprudence in this area. As Barrington J explained in *Murphy*, although the two rights may overlap in practice, they are derived from 'different philosophical systems'.[45] This allows the Irish courts to accurately identify and assess the nature of the freedom of expression issues that arise in a particular case. As Chapter 1 indicated, the basis upon which the protection of expression is justified can affect the way in which that protection applies in a particular case. As McKechnie J noted in *Holland v Governor of Portlaoise Prison*,[46] this means that the courts must have regard to the particular circumstances of an individual case in determining which Article(s) are engaged in that specific situation.

[2.24] As against this, it should be noted that Fennelly J described the rights under Art 40.3.1° and Article 40.6.1.°(i) in *Mahon v Post Communications*[47] as 'inseparable'. This would appear to cast some doubt on the distinction. However, it is arguable that this would read too much into that comment. Fennelly J's decision was directed only to the facts of that case, as indicated by his acknowledgement that '[i]t matters little, *at least for present purposes,* which Article of the Constitution expresses the guarantee'.[48] That he cited Barrington J's decision in *Murphy* without dissent suggests that the distinction endorsed by the Supreme Court in that case continues to apply as a matter of Irish constitutional law.

[2.25] This raises the question of what this distinction means for the theory of media freedom of expression under the Constitution. Do the media enjoy rights under both Articles or are they confined to relying on Article 40.6.1.°(i)? This is unclear at present. However, the fact that the Constitution's express references to the media appear in Article 40.6.1°(i), when taken together with the emphasis on the instrumental value of the media for democracy in the Irish caselaw and the difficulties associated with

---

44.   See, *AG v Paperlink* [1984] ILRM 373. Barrington J. effectively rejected this distinction in *Irish Times v Ireland* and in *Murphy v IRTC*.
45.   *Murphy v IRTC* [1999] 1 IR 12, 25.
46.   *Holland v Governor of Portlaoise Prison* [2004] 2 IR 573.
47.   *Mahon v Post Communications* [2007] 3 IR 338.
48.   *Mahon v Post Communications* [2007] 3 IR 338 (emphasis added).

justifying media expression on autonomy grounds, indicate that it is arguable that the Irish Constitution's protection of media expression may be predominantly (if not exclusively) provided for in Article 40.6.1.°(i).

Content restrictions on media expression

[2.26] The protection of freedom of expression of the media being based primarily on a conception of freedom of expression as a democratic ideal, the question arises whether all media expression is protected to the same degree. There are some indications in the case law of a blanket protection for all media expression to the same level. Such statements are often premised on the notion that to differentiate between types of expression on the basis of content is a dangerous exercise which inevitably subverts freedom of expression.

[2.27] That view is implicit in the judgment given by O'Hanlon J in *M v Drury*[49] where, considering an application to restrain publication based on the privacy interest of the applicant,[50] he referred with approval to Hoffman LJ's warning in *R v Central Independent Television plc*[51] against the regular use of the courts' powers to restrain media publications:

> [A] freedom which is restricted to what judges think to be responsible or in the public interest is no freedom. Freedom means the right to publish things which government and judges, however well motivated, think should not be published. It means the right to say things which right-thinking people regard as dangerous or irresponsible.[52]

O'Hanlon J therefore held that, in light of the 'strongly-expressed guarantees in favour of freedom of expression' in the Constitution, the courts would only be required to intervene to protect a plaintiff's right to privacy in 'extreme cases'.[53]

[2.28] More recently, Fennelly J in his majority judgment in *Mahon v Post Publications*[54] refused to countenance value judgments on the content of media expression:

> The courts do not pass judgment on whether any particular exercise of the right of freedom of expression is in the public interest. The media are not required to justify publication by reference to any public interest other than that of freedom of expression itself. They are free to publish material which is not in the public interest. I have no doubt that much of the material which appears in the news media serves no public interest whatever. I have equally no doubt that much of it is motivated, and perfectly permissibly so, by the pursuit of profit. Publication may indeed be prompted by less noble motives. So far as the facts of the present case

---

49. *M v Drury* [1994] 2 IR 8.
50. See **Ch 7** for a discussion of privacy and media expression.
51. *R v Central Independent Television plc* [1994] 3 WLR 20.
52. *R v Central Independent Television plc* [1994] 3 WLR 20, 30.
53. *Ibid.*
54. *Mahon v Post Publications* [2007] 2 ILRM 1.

are concerned, the decision of Mr O'Kelly to publish the names of three TD's in direct defiance of the wishes of the Tribunal was disgraceful and served no identifiable public interest. On the other hand, that does not mean that it was unlawful. The right of freedom of expression extends the same protection to worthless, prurient and meretricious publication as it does to worthy, serious and socially valuable works. The undoubted fact that news media frequently and implausibly invoke the public interest to cloak worthless and even offensive material does not affect the principle.[55]

While the judgment describes freedom of media expression in a manner similar to the free marketplace of ideas approach considered in the previous chapter,[56] it has been argued elsewhere that the context in which the passage appears limits its application as a general principle.[57] The court in that case was considering whether a statutory tribunal could render the publication of certain information unlawful by bestowing on it a legally binding requirement of confidentiality. Speech is permitted unless some specific rule of law prohibits it. To find that it was not within the tribunal's powers to restrain expression does not necessarily mean that all media expression is entitled to the same level of protection regardless of the public interest involved.

[2.29] The subsequent decision of Dunne J in *Herrity v Independent Newspapers*[58] noted that the statement by Fennelly J reproduced above constituted 'a powerful expression of the right to freedom of expression'.[59] She went on to state:

> It is not authority however for saying that the right to freedom of expression is more significant than the right to privacy ... the freedom is subject to clearly defined exceptions laid down by common law or statute. It is in that context that the constitutional right to privacy comes into the equation. Accordingly it seems to me that there is a balancing exercise engaged in circumstances where the right to freedom of expression conflicts with the right to privacy. It is clear that newspapers are free to publish all sorts of matters regardless of public interest and questions of good taste but, as is the case with the right to privacy, the right to freedom of expression is not an unqualified right.[60]

[2.30] Exceptions to the general principle of freedom of expression must be set down clearly in statute or be clearly discernible common law rules. As Dunne J pointed out, where expression comes into conflict with some other constitutional value such as privacy, the absence of a 'clear, demonstrable public interest'[61] in publication will affect the balancing exercise undertaken by the court.

---

55.   *Mahon v Post Publications* [2007] 2 ILRM 1, 13–14.
56.   Para **[1.17]**–**[1.19]**
57.   See discussion in Carolan and Delany, *Privacy Law in Ireland* (Thomson Round Hall, 2008), 76.
58.   *Herrity v Independent Newspapers* [2009] 1 IR 316.
59.   *Herrity v Independent Newspapers* [2009] 1 IR 316, 339.
60.   *Herrity v Independent Newspapers* [2009] 1 IR 316, 339.
61.   *Herrity v Independent Newspapers* [2009] 1 IR 316, 340.

[2.31] The relevance of the public interest was also explored by Clarke J in *Cogley v RTÉ*.[62] In that case, the plaintiffs sought an injunction to preclude the broadcast of a television programme which they claimed would infringe their right to privacy. The defendants argued that the subject matter of the programme was a matter of public interest. After finding that the programme involved a prima facie interference with the plaintiff's privacy rights, Clarke J specifically considered the question of the public interest in the broadcasting of the programme, finding that 'the issues raised in the programme are those of the highest public interest and that, therefore, a very significant weight indeed needs to be attached to those matters in weighing the rights and values involved at this stage.'[63]

Penalisation of speech after the event

[2.32] The common law and statute alike provide for a variety of rules which penalise publication after the fact. Where the media breach laws such as those relating to defamation, privacy, confidentiality and official secrecy, the courts may intervene to compensate an injured party or to penalise the publication. In either case, the danger of a deterrent effect on media freedom of expression arises.

[2.33] O'Caoimh J referred to the 'chill effect' of defamation law in *Hunter v Duckworth*[64] and seemed to approve of the approach of the House of Lords in *Reynolds v Sunday Times Newspapers*,[65] where it developed a defence of publication in the public interest to protect the media from libel actions.

The responsibilities of the media under the Irish Constitution

[2.34] The *Reynolds* defence was also expressly approved by Charleton J in *Leech v Independent Newspapers Ltd*.[66] In that case, Charleton J drew a distinction between matters in which the public might be interested and matters which could be said to concern the public interest generally as follows:

> Being interested in matters, it seems to me, would refer to matters which are merely titillating or salacious or gossipy. Matters which are of public interest, on the other hand, have to be matters which affect the public in terms of the governance of the country, their safety, their security, and their right to judge their public representatives fairly on the basis of real information.

He also went on to hold that:

> [A] public interest defence can arise where the subject matter of a publication, be it an article or radio or television report, considered as a whole, was a matter of public interest ... I would rule as well that there is a professional duty on the part

62. *Cogley v RTÉ* [2005] 4 IR 79.
63. See also further discussion of this case in the context of prior restraint below at **[2.40]**.
64. *Hunter v Duckworth* [2003] IEHC 81, O'Caoimh J.
65. *Reynolds v Sunday Times Newspapers* [2002] 2 AC 127.
66. *Leech v Independent Newspapers Ltd* [2007] IEHC 223.

of journalists to both seek out information that is of public interest and to impart it to the public and that while that is a matter of professional skill and training, that it is also a matter of responsibility. And once a public interest is established in terms of the information the subject matter of the article, there is a second test to be met, which is as to whether on the evidence the steps taken to gather and publish the information were responsible and fair. The question may need to be put as to whether a newspaper, or a television channel or radio channel, on the evidence behaved fairly and responsibly in gathering and publishing the information. And that may indeed take into account ... whether the article contained the gist of the Plaintiff's side of the story, and whether the Plaintiff was contacted for comment.

Charleton J also emphasised that in assessing journalistic responsibility, regard must be had 'to the practical realities of news gathering' given that 'urgency can be a matter of importance in news reporting, which is, of course, dealing with a perishable commodity.'

Prior restraint under Article 40.6.1°(i)

[2.35] The 'perishable' nature of news reporting has also been adverted to in the context of attempts to restrain speech before it is disseminated as opposed to punishing it after the event. Such measures have been seen as particularly restrictive of speech and the Irish courts have been reluctant to grant injunctions in this context, particularly in advance of a full hearing. In *AG for England and Wales v Brandon Book Publishers Ltd*,[67] where an injunction was sought to prevent the publication in Ireland of a book containing information about the British Secret Service, Carroll J refused the order, referring to, 'the very important constitutional right to communicate now and not in a year or so when the case has worked its way up through the courts'.[68]

[2.36] As Irvine J noted in *Murray v Newsgroup*:[69]

Time and time again the courts have referred to the dangers inherent in granting what are described as prior restraint orders and have determined that such orders should only be made following a close and penetrating examination of the factual justification for the restraint sought.

[2.37] The usual test[70] in considering whether to grant an interlocutory injunction requires a plaintiff to show the existence of a serious question to be tried, the inadequacy of damages, and that the balance of convenience lies in favour of the grant of the injunction. Where an injunction seeks to restrain freedom of expression of the media, however, a different test is applied and a plaintiff must 'demonstrate, by proper

---

67. *AG for England and Wales v Brandon Book Publishers Ltd* [1986] IR 587; [1987] ILRM 135.
68. *AG for England and Wales v Brandon Book Publishers Ltd* [1986] IR 587; [1987] ILRM 135, 138.
69. *Murray v Newsgroup* (18 June 2010, unreported), HC, Irvine J.
70. *Campus Oil v Minister for Industry and Energy (No 2)* [1983] IR 88.

evidence, a convincing case to bring about a curtailment of the freedom of expression of the press'.[71]

[2.38] Kelly J pointed out in *Foley v Sunday Newspapers Ltd* that[72] 'save in truly exceptional circumstances a court will not impose a prior restraint on publication unless it is clear that no defence will succeed at trial.'[73] He referred to the decision of the Court of Appeal in *Bonnard v Perryman*, where Lord Coleridge CJ had explained the rationale for this approach in the context of libel as follows:

> The right of free speech is one which it is for the public interest that individuals should possess, and, indeed, that they should exercise without impediment, so long as no wrongful act is done; and, unless an alleged libel is untrue, there is no wrong committed; but, on the contrary, often a very wholesome act is performed in the publication and repetition of an alleged libel. Until it is clear that an alleged libel is untrue, it is not clear that any right at all has been infringed; and the importance of leaving free speech unfettered is a strong reason in cases of libel for dealing most cautiously and warily with the granting of interim injunctions.[74]

[2.39] The plaintiff in the *Foley* case sought to restrain publication of material which he claimed was putting his right to life and bodily integrity at risk and which the defendant stated was true. Kelly J noted that none of the material exhorted anyone to violence against the plaintiff. He held that:

> In this country we have a free press. The right to freedom of expression is provided for in Article 40 of the Constitution and Article 10 of the European Convention on Human Rights. It is an important right and one which the courts must be extremely circumspect about curtailing particularly at the interlocutory stage of a proceeding. Important as it is however, it cannot equal or be more important than the right to life. If therefore the evidence established a real likelihood that repetition of the material in question would infringe the plaintiff's right to life, the court would have to give effect to such a right.[75]

[2.40] Similarly, in *Cogley v RTÉ*[76] Clarke J, having referred to the obligation on Irish courts to have regard to the approach taken by European Court of Human Rights, held

---

71.   *Foley v Sunday Newspapers Ltd* [2005] 1 IR 88, 102. See also the judgment of Irvine J in *Murray v Newsgroup Newspapers Ltd & Ors* (18 June 2010, unreported), HC.
72.   *Foley v Sunday Newspapers Ltd* [2005] 1 IR 88.
73.   [1891] 2 Ch 269 and *Sinclair v Gogarty* [1937] IR 377.
74.   *Bonnard v Perryman* [2005] 1 IR 88, 98–99. As Kelly J noted, this test was approved by the Supreme Court in *Sinclair v Gogarty* [1937] IR 377.
75.   *Bonnard v Perryman* [2005] 1 IR 88, 101. While the latter part of this extract from the judgment suggests a balance that is weighted against free speech, this is presumably due to the nature of the underlying complaint by the plaintiff that his right to life was potentially threatened. Unlike the situation where an injunction is sought to restrain alleged defamatory publication, speech which threatens one's right to life is not amenable to the vindication by the ex post facto remedy of an award of damages.
76.   *Cogley v RTÉ* [2005] 4 IR 79.

that the media should generally be given an opportunity to defend applications to restrain publication pending trial of an issue and that 'a court should be reluctant to grant interim orders which would have the effect of restraining in advance, publication in circumstances where the intended publisher has not had an opportunity to be heard':[77]

> It should be noted that one of the underlying reasons for the reluctance of the courts in this jurisdiction to grant injunctions at an interlocutory stage in relation to defamation stems from the fact that if the traditional basis for the grant of an interlocutory injunction (ie that the plaintiff had established a fair issue to be tried) was sufficient for the grant of an injunction in defamation proceedings public debate on very many issues would be largely stifled. In a great number of publications or broadcasts which deal with important public issues persons or bodies will necessarily be criticised. There will frequently be some basis for some such persons or bodies to at least suggest that what is said of them is unfair to the point of being defamatory. If it were necessary only to establish the possibility of such an outcome in order that the publication or broadcast would be restrained then a disproportionate effect on the conduct of public debate on issues of importance would occur. In that regard it is important to note that both the constitution itself and the law generally recognises the need for a vigorous and informed public debate on issues of importance. Thus the constitution confers absolute privilege on the debates of Dáil and Seanad Éireann. The form of parliamentary democracy enshrined in the constitution requires that there be a vigorous and informed public debate on issues of importance. Any measures which would impose an excessive or unreasonable interference with the conditions necessary for such debate would require very substantial justification. Thus the reluctance of the courts in this jurisdiction (and also the European Court of Human Rights) to justify prior restraint save in unusual circumstances and after careful scrutiny.[78]

However, it has also been argued that the courts' firm reluctance to countenance issuing a prior restraint order except in exceptional circumstances may be subject to some degree of modification in the context of applications to prevent the disclosure of private information. This is discussed in more detail in **Ch 7**.

THE MEDIA UNDER ARTICLE 10 OF THE EUROPEAN CONVENTION ON HUMAN RIGHTS

[2.41] Freedom of expression is protected under Article 10 of the European Convention on Human Rights. Article 10(1) sets out the guarantee of freedom of expression and Article 10(2) describes a range of circumstances in which the freedom may be subject to regulation or restriction:

> (1) Everyone has the right to freedom of expression. This right shall include freedom to hold opinions and to receive and impart information and ideas without

---

77.   *Cogley v RTÉ* [2005] 4 IR 79, 82.
78.   *Cogley v RTÉ* [2005] 4 IR 79, 94. See also Fennelly J in *Mahon v Post Publications Ltd* [2007] 3 IR 338 where he held that the court must scrutinise an application for an injunction seeking prior restraint of a publication 'with particular care'. *Mahon v Post Publications Ltd* [2007] 3 IR 338, 381.

interference by public authority and regardless of frontiers. This Article shall not prevent States from requiring the licensing of broadcasting, television or cinema enterprises.

(2) The exercise of these freedoms, since it carries with it duties and responsibilities, may be subject to such formalities, conditions, restrictions or penalties as are prescribed by law and are necessary in a democratic society, in the interests of national security, territorial integrity or public safety, for the prevention of disorder or crime, for the protection of health or morals, for the protection of the reputation or rights of others, for preventing the disclosure of information received in confidence, or for maintaining the authority and impartiality of the judiciary.

[2.42] In one of its early and seminal judgments on Article 10, *Handyside v United Kingdom*,[79] the European Court of Human Rights stated that:

> The Court's supervisory functions oblige it to pay the utmost attention to the principles characterising a 'democratic society'. Freedom of expression constitutes one of the essential foundations of such a society, one of the basic conditions for its progress and for the development of every man. Subject to paragraph 2 of Article 10, it is applicable not only to 'information' or 'ideas' that are favourably received or regarded as inoffensive or as a matter of indifference, but also to those that offend, shock or disturb the State or any sector of the population. Such are the demands of that pluralism, tolerance and broadmindedness without which there is no 'democratic society'.[80]

[2.43] The European Court of Human Rights has consistently affirmed the critical importance of media expression to democracy. In *Jersild v Denmark*[81] the court explained that:

> [F]reedom of expression constitutes one of the essential foundations of a democratic society and … the safeguards to be afforded to the press are of particular importance … it is … incumbent on it to impart information and ideas of public interest. Not only does the press have the task of imparting such information and ideas: the public also has a right to receive them. Were it otherwise, the press would be unable to play its vital role of 'public watchdog'.[82]

The court, in assessing claims that Article 10 has been violated by a respondent state, engages in a structured analysis which typically follows a similar pattern. The next section sets out and explains that structure and gives examples of its application in the context of media expression in particular.

---

79.   *Handyside v United Kingdom* (1979–1980) 1 EHRR 737.

80.   *Handyside v United Kingdom* (1979–1980) 1 EHRR 737, para 49.

81.   *Jersild v Denmark* (1995) 19 EHRR 1.

82.   *Jersild v Denmark* (1995) 19 EHRR 1, para 31.

The structured analysis of the European Court of Human Rights

[2.44] In assessing whether an impugned state measure violates Article 10, the court engages in a structured analysis which can be broken down into a number of parts. These usually follow the sequence set out below. While the first two elements are generally considered distinctly, there is greater interplay between the latter two. As well as this structured analysis, the court has developed a doctrine it describes as the 'margin of appreciation'. The function of this is discussed below also.

Whether there has been an interference with freedom of expression

[2.45] The first step in any given case is for the court to ask whether there has been an interference with the rights set out in Article 10(1). Article 10(2) refers to 'formalities, conditions, restrictions or penalties' and any of these will constitute an interference with freedom of expression. This threshold requirement is generally quite easily met in freedom of expression cases. The court has held that there is an interference with freedom of expression where there is prior restraint of publication[83] or confiscation of published material.[84] It has also found that measures taken post publication may constitute an interference with the freedom of the press where they have a potential chilling effect on expression.[85] Thus the court has found that criminal sanctions[86] and damages in a civil action[87] are interferences with speech. Less direct interferences which nonetheless have a general chilling effect on media expression are also considered to interfere with Article 10 and this includes measures requiring the disclosure of journalists' sources.[88]

On the basis of the above, national laws on matters such as defamation, privacy, contempt of court, official secrecy and the protection of journalists' sources have all been analysed as measures which interfere with freedom of the press.

Whether the measure was prescribed by law

[2.46] The next stage in the court's analysis is to consider whether the measure was 'prescribed by law'. This involves a number of elements. First, the measure must have

---

83.   *Sunday Times v United Kingdom* (1979) 2 EHRR 245; *Observer and Guardian v UK* (1991) 14 EHRR 153.

84.   *Vereniging Weekblad Bluf! v Netherlands* (1995) 20 EHRR 189.

85.   In *Lingens v Austria* (1986) 8 EHRR 407, the court noted that while the penalty for criminal libel had been imposed after publication of the offending article in that case, it was nonetheless 'liable to hamper the press in performing its task as purveyor of information and public watchdog' (1986) 8 EHRR 407, para 44.

86.   *Zana v Turkey* (1999) 27 EHRR 667.

87.   *Tolstoy v Miloslavsky v United Kingdom* (1995) 20 EHRR 442. See also *Independent News and Media and Independent Newspapers Ireland Limited v Ireland* (Application No 55120/00) 16 September 2005 (Third Section).

88.   *Goodwin v United Kingdom* (1996) 22 EHRR 123; *Financial Times Ltd v United Kingdom* (Application No 821/03) 15 December 2009 (Fourth Section).

been authorised under the law of the respondent state. As well as this formal requirement, the court held in *Sunday Times v United Kingdom*[89] that there were two further requirements implied by the words 'prescribed by law':

> Firstly, the law must be adequately accessible: the citizen must be able to have an indication that is adequate in the circumstances of the legal rules applicable to a given case. Secondly, a norm cannot be regarded as a 'law' unless it is formulated with sufficient precision to enable the citizen to regulate his conduct: he must be able – if need be with appropriate advice – to foresee, to a degree that is reasonable in the circumstances, the consequences which a given action may entail. Those consequences need not be foreseeable with absolute certainty: experience shows this to be unattainable. Again, whilst certainty is highly desirable, it may bring in its train excessive rigidity and the law must be able to keep pace with changing circumstances. Accordingly, many laws are inevitably couched in terms which, to a greater or lesser extent, are vague and whose interpretation and application are questions of practice.[90]

Despite this strong statement of principle, the European Court of Human Rights has frequently held that a variety of arcane and vague laws interfering with freedom of expression meet the test.[91] Thus interferences with expression based on vague laws relating to blasphemy,[92] obscenity[93] and indecency[94] have been held to be 'prescribed by law'.

Whether the measures had a legitimate aim

[2.47] The court also considers whether the interferences with expression had a legitimate aim. Aims which are considered to be legitimate in this regard are listed out in Article 10(2). Common restrictions on speech will usually fall within Article 10(2). Thus, for example, defamation law protects 'the reputation or rights of others',[95] the law on contempt of court seeks to 'maintain the authority and impartiality of the judiciary'[96] and obscenity laws are for the 'protection of ... morals'.[97]

---

89.   *Sunday Times v United Kingdom* (1979) 2 EHRR 245.

90.   *Sunday Times v United Kingdom* (1979) 2 EHRR 245.

91.   For a rare example of a finding that a measure which interfered with speech rights was not prescribed by law, see *Hashman and Harrup v UK* (2000) EHRR 24 where the applicants (hunt protesters) had been bound over to keep the peace for conduct contra bones mores.

92.   *Wingrove v UK* (1996) 24 EHRR 1. Compare with *Corway v Independent Newspapers (Ireland) Ltd* [1999] 4 IR 484, [1997] 1 ILRM 432 (HC), [1999] 4 IR 485, [2000] 1 ILRM 426 where the Irish Supreme Court found that the offence of blasphemy referred to in Art 40.6.1°(i) of the Constitution was too vague to form the basis of a private criminal prosecution.

93.   *Handyside v UK* (1976) 1 EHRR 737; *Perrin v UK* (Application No 5446/03) 18 October 2005 (Fourth Section), decision on admissibility.

94.   *S and G v United Kingdom* (Application No 17634/91) 2 September 1991.

95.   *Lingens v Austria* (1986) 8 EHRR 407 – criminal libel.

96.   *Sunday Times v United Kingdom* (1979) 2 EHRR 245.

97.   *Muller v Switzerland* (1989) 13 EHRR 212.

[2.48] Article 10(2) also refers to the 'protection of the ... rights of others'. The court has, on occasion, referred to other Convention provisions as supporting an argument that a measure which restricts speech pursued a legitimate aim. Thus the requirements of a fair trial in Article 6 of the Convention means that measures which restrain speech that might prejudice the fairness of a trial have a legitimate aim.[98] Similarly, the protection of the privacy rights protected under Article 8 of the Convention lends support to arguments that a measure which restrains expression to protect privacy is one which has a legitimate aim.[99]

[2.49] As well as the above, the court has also held that it may be legitimate to restrict Convention rights where the restriction is necessary to prevent the destruction of the rights and freedoms set out in the Convention itself. This limitation is placed on the exercise of Convention rights by the text of Article 17.[100]

Whether the interference is 'necessary in a democratic society'

[2.50] Most of the analysis in Article 10 cases thus falls to be considered under the final limb of the test applied by the court which is whether the measure is 'necessary in a democratic society'. In *Handyside v United Kingdom*,[101] the court held that:

> [W]hile the adjective 'necessary' .... is not synonymous with 'indispensable', neither has it the flexibility of such expressions as 'admissible', 'ordinary'. 'useful', 'reasonable' or 'desirable'.[102]

[2.51] The court has developed a requirement of proportionality against which to measure state interferences with Convention rights. In *Olsson v Sweden*,[103] the court described the approach as follows:

> According to the Court's well-established case-law, the notion of necessity implies that an interference corresponds to a pressing social need and, in particular, that it is proportionate to the legitimate aim pursued.[104]

In this context, the court has emphasised that what is 'necessary' is to be judged against the requirements of a democratic society. In the context of Article 10, this has led the court to emphasise the particular contribution of political expression to the functioning of a democracy as well as the role of the media.

---

98.   *Worm v Austria* (1998) 25 EHRR 454; see also *Ribemont v France* (1995) 20 EHRR 557.
99.   *Von Hannover v Germany* (2006) 43 EHRR 7.
100. European Convention on Human Rights, Art 17 provides that:
      Nothing in this Convention may be interpreted as implying for any State, group or person any right to engage in any activity or perform any act aimed at the destruction on any of the rights and freedoms set forth herein or at their limitation to a greater extent than is provided for in the Convention.
101. *Handyside v United Kingdom* (1979–1980) 1 EHRR 737.
102. *Handyside v United Kingdom* (1979–1980) 1 EHRR 737, para 48.
103. *Olsson v Sweden* (1988) 11 EHRR 259.
104. *Olsson v Sweden* (1988) 11 EHRR 259, para 67.

[2.52] The court has also emphasised the extent of any penalty in assessing whether an interference oversteps the boundaries of a proportionality. Thus the amount of a fine imposed may be relevant to the proportionality of a measure found to interfere with expression.[105] Even where a fine is small, the fact of a criminal conviction itself – albeit for a minor offence – is viewed by the court as having a potentially inhibiting effect on the media.[106] On the other hand, where speech infringes the rights of others in a very damaging way, its punishment by means of a custodial sentence will not necessarily violate Article 10.[107]

[2.53] The court also has indicated on a number of occasions that, as a matter of principle, unpredictably large damages awards in civil cases are considered capable of having a chilling effect on press expression and therefore require 'the most careful scrutiny'.[108] In *Tolstoy Miloslavsky v United Kingdom*,[109] the court indicated that 'under the Convention, an award of damages for defamation must bear a reasonable relationship of proportionality to the injury to reputation suffered.'[110] The court accepted in that case that there was an inevitable level of unpredictability surrounding damages awards in such cases. It held that, in assessing whether a large award of damages was disproportionate for the purposes of the Convention, it would have regard to both the amount of any damages awarded and the safeguards in the domestic legal system permitting the review of excessively large awards. In the *Tolstoy* case the award was disproportionate both on the basis of its size and the lack of safeguards under English libel law which would have enabled judicial revision of the figure.[111]

[2.54] While the court indicated in *Tolstoy* that it was willing to review the amount of damages awards as part of its proportionality analysis, the approach taken in *Independent News and Media and Independent Newspapers Ireland Limited v Ireland*,[112] seemed to place more emphasis on examining the safeguards in the domestic legal system. The case arose in the context of a large damages award made by a jury in a High Court libel case which had been the subject of an appeal to the Irish Supreme Court.

---

105. See *Kwiecien v Poland* (9 April 2007, unreported), ECtHR where the court pointed out that the penalty imposed was 16 times the average monthly wage.
106. *Oberschlick v Austria (No 2)* (1997) 25 EHRR 357 and *Stoll v Switzerland* (2007) 44 EHRR 53, discussed below at **[2.81]**–**[2.826]** and **[2.93]**–**[2.106]**.
107. See *Fatullayev v Azerbaijan* (Application No 40984/07) 22 April 2010 (First Section).
108. *Bladet Tromso v Norway* (1999) 29 EHRR 125; *Tolstoy v Miloslavsky v United Kingdom* (1995) 20 EHRR 442.
109. *Tolstoy v Miloslavsky v United Kingdom* (1995) 20 EHRR 442.
110. *Tolstoy v Miloslavsky v United Kingdom* (1995) 20 EHRR 442, para 49.
111. As the European Court of Human Rights noted, the Court of Appeal had indicated in a case arising after the *Tolstoy* case reached Strasbourg that the scope of review of such awards would be greater bearing in the mind the requirements of Art 10. *Rantzen v Mirror Group Newspapers Ltd* [1993] 4 AER 975, referred to by the European Court of Human Rights in *Tolstoy v Miloslavsky v United Kingdom* (1995) 20 EHRR 442, 50.
112. *Independent News and Media and Independent Newspapers Ireland Limited v Ireland* (Application No 55120/00), 16 September 2005 (Third Section).

That appeal[113] had resulted in a reduction of the award from IR£300,000 to IR£150,000. The Irish court had rejected the submission made by the applicant that juries should be given guidelines in respect of damages, by virtue of the 'unusual and emphatic sanctity' of the jury's role in defamation proceedings.[114]

[2.55] The European Court of Human Rights referred back to its decision in *Tolstoy* and noted that:

> ... while the defamation was undoubtedly serious, the present award was three times more than the highest libel award ever previously approved by the Supreme Court and the Government have not pointed to a 'comparable award' made since then.[115]

Ultimately, however, the court accepted that the level of review applied to the award by the Irish Supreme Court indicated that there were sufficient safeguards in place to ensure that a proportionality analysis was applied to damages awards in libel cases. The shift in emphasis from the amount of damages to the process for reviewing them was heavily criticised in a dissenting judgment delivered by Judge Cabral Barretto.

[2.56] In cases where the media are restrained from publication, the court will assess the scope of any injunction carefully to ensure that it does not go further than is merited in the context of the expression concerned. In *News Verlags v Austria*,[116] the applicant news company had published a photograph of a right wing extremist accused of sending letter bombs during a political campaign. The text beside the photo accused him of being the perpetrator of the attacks. The domestic courts had granted injunctions which precluded further publication of any photographs of the individual concerned. The European Court of Human Rights accepted that these measures had the legitimate aim of protecting the individual from defamation and insult and of protecting his right to a fair trial. The court found, however, that the injunction was a disproportionate interference with the applicant's freedom of expression as it imposed an absolute prohibition on publishing a picture of the individual concerned in circumstances where the objectionable aspect of the publication was the juxtaposition of the photograph with allegations of guilt.

[2.57] The European Court of Human Rights is particularly suspicious of measures involving prior restraint of media expression because they deprive the public of information. While the court has found that such restraint can be permissible under

---

113. *De Rossa v Independent Newspapers* [1999] 4 IR 432.
114. Denham J dissented strongly on this point *De Rossa v Independent Newspapers* [1999] 4 IR 432, 471–483. The issue came before the Supreme Court again in *O'Brien v Mirror Group Newspapers* [2001] 1 IR 1 where the court was asked to reconsider its approach. The majority refused to do so (Denham J dissented again) but finding the award of IR£250,000 overly high, they remitted the matter back to the High Court for a further jury determination. The second jury award was a record breaking €750,000. See (2006) *Irish Times*, 23 November. The Defamation Act 2009 fundamentally altered Irish law on damages in defamation actions. See **Ch 8**.
115. *Independent News and Media and Independent Newspapers Ireland Limited v Ireland* (Application No 55120/00) 16 September 2005 (Third Section), para 116.
116. *News Verlags v Austria* (2001) 31 EHRR 8.

Article 10,[117] the court will subject prior restraint of expression to 'careful scrutiny'. In *Observer and Guardian v UK*,[118] the court held that:

> [T]he dangers inherent in prior restraints are such that they call for the most careful scrutiny on the part of the Court. This is especially so as far as the press is concerned, for news is a perishable commodity and to delay its publication, even for a short period, may well deprive it of all its value and interest.[119]

The margin of appreciation

[2.58] The court frequently refers in its decisions to the margin of appreciation. The statement of the court in *Handyside v United Kingdom*[120] is often repeated in this context:

> By reason of their direct and continuous contact with the vital forces of their countries, State authorities are in principle in a better position than the international judge to give an opinion on the exact content of these requirements as well as on the 'necessity' of a 'restriction' or 'penalty' intended to meet them.[121]

The margin of appreciation is perhaps best understood as the degree of discretion states enjoy.[122] It is recognised as applying to both the legislature and to bodies, judicial and others, that are called upon to interpret and apply the laws in force.[123]

[2.59] Referring to this doctrine, the court may defer to the views of the national authorities as to whether it was in fact 'necessary' to interfere with freedom of expression to protect one of the interests in Article 10(2) and also in respect of the choice of means of so doing. The doctrine facilitates the court in allowing for diversity of approaches in the signatory states. The margin of appreciation is thus typically greater in cases which raise controversial or culturally sensitive issues on which there is no pan-European consensus.

---

117. The text of the Article itself indicates that this is possible in its references to 'conditions', 'restrictions', 'preventing' and 'prevention' – see *Ekin Association v France* (2002) 35 EHRR 1207, para 56. See also *Sunday Times v UK (No 1)* (1979) 2 EHRR 245. For the view that Art 10 completely excludes prior restraint measures, see the dissenting judgment of Judge de Meyer in *Wingrove v UK* (1996) 24 EHRR 1, 36. Judge de Meyer's approach is close to that taken by the United States Supreme Court in *Near v Minnesota* 283 US 697 (1931). See also *New York Times v US and Washington Post v US* 403 US 713 (1971), the 'Pentagon Papers' case.
118. *Observer and Guardian v UK* (1991) 14 EHRR 153.
119. *Observer and Guardian v UK* (1991) 14 EHRR 153, para 60.
120. *Handyside v United Kingdom* (1979–1980) 1 EHRR 737.
121. *Handyside v United Kingdom* (1979–1980) 1 EHRR 737, para 48.
122. For a full discussion of the rationale behind the margin of appreciation, see Arai-Takahati, *The Margin of Appreciation Doctrine and the Principles of Proportionality in the jurisprudence of the ECHR* (Intersentia, 2002). See also Letsas, 'Two Concepts of the Margin of Appreciation' [2006] Oxford Journal of Legal Studies 705.
123. *Engel* 8 June 1976 (Series A No 22), 41–42.

[2.60] While it is frequently mentioned separately in the judgments of the court, the margin of appreciation is arguably not a free-standing concept. It has been observed[124] that it often signifies the standard of review applied by the court in different types of case. Where the margin is wide, the necessity/proportionality analysis is shallow. Where the margin is narrow, a more searching analysis of state justifications for measures is engaged in.

[2.61] The extent of the margin of appreciation in Article 10 cases is often affected by the type of speech concerned. As noted above, the court has developed a hierarchical approach to free speech in which political speech is particularly highly valued for its contribution to democracy. Thus, in cases involving such speech, the standard of review applied to the relevant state measure is high.

[2.62] The important role of the media in this context is also recognised by the court so that:

> [T]he Court closely scrutinizes any interference with speech and associated activities (particularly those of the press and broadcasters) which may advance democratic participation or accountability or the free market of ideas.[125]

Thus in cases where the media report matters of public interest relating to politicians, the margin is very narrow.[126] On the other hand, despite the insistence that Article 10 covers expression which offends or disturbs, the court has consistently given Member States a wide margin of discretion in cases involving controversial areas such as religious advertising, blasphemy, and obscenity.[127]

ARTICLE 10 AND THE SPECIAL ROLE OF THE MEDIA

[2.63] Article 10(1) does not refer specifically to the media, recognising simply that '[e]veryone' enjoys the right described therein. The court has, however, recognised 'the pre-eminent role of the press in a State governed by the rule of law.'[128] This is seen by the court as a crucial feature of a democracy and the court has stated that the margin of appreciation is particularly narrow in situations where the media contributes to debate on matters of public concern including, but not limited to, political affairs.[129]

[2.64] This approach was set out by the court in the case of *Sunday Times v UK*,[130] one of its early and seminal judgments on press freedom under Article 10. In that case, the

---

124. Fenwick and Phillipson, *Media Freedom under the Human Rights Act* (2006, Oxford University Press), 48–50.
125. Feldman, 'Content Neutrality' in Loveland (ed), *Importing the First Amendment* (2nd edn, Hart Publishing, 1998), 147.
126. See *Flux (No 4) v Moldova* (Application No 17294/04) 12 February 2008 (Fourth Section).
127. See **Ch 3**.
128. *Castells v Spain* (1992) 14 EHRR 445, para 43
129. See *Thorgeirson v Iceland* (1992) 14 EHRR 843, 64.
130. *Sunday Times v UK* (1979) 2 EHRR 245.

court undertook a robust analysis of the respondent state's justification for interfering with the freedom of the press.

[2.65] The case arose when the applicant newspaper was prevented by an injunction from publishing any further stories regarding a matter of public controversy. The *Sunday Times* had been covering the Thalidomide controversy, in which a sedative drug was found to cause severe harm to fetuses when taken by pregnant women. A large number of legal actions were taken against the drug company responsible for producing the drug. Those proceedings were still the subject of lengthy settlement negotiations which had been going on for several years when the *Sunday Times* published an article which was generally critical of the law relating to compensation by drug companies and which called on the drug company responsible for Thalidomide to 'think again' about the amount of compensation it had offered to the affected women. The drug company complained that this was prejudicial to it.

[2.66] The *Sunday Times* subsequently produced another article which contained an argument supported by some evidence that the drug company had failed to carry out proper tests as to the safety of Thalidomide. The newspaper sent this article to the Attorney-General, seeking reassurance that it would not be prosecuted for contempt of court if the article was published. The Attorney-General obtained an injunction preventing the publication of the article and any other article that prejudged the issue of negligence or dealt with evidence relevant to the issues between the parties to the litigation. The injunction was appealed up through the UK courts and finally approved by the House of Lords, following which the *Sunday Times* brought the case to Strasbourg.

[2.67] The *Sunday Times* argued that the injunction breached its rights under Article 10. The European Court of Human Rights found that the injunction had a 'legitimate aim' – to protect the authority of the judiciary. It also found that it was 'prescribed by law'. By a narrow majority, however, the court held that it did not meet the test of being 'necessary in a democratic society'. The minority judgments used a weak standard of review, seeing the issue as being whether the State had 'exercised its discretion reasonably, carefully and in good faith'.[131] The majority judgment took a more rigorous approach, which looked behind the State's justification for the measure and included its own assessment of the facts of the situation. The court held that:

> The thalidomide disaster was a matter of undisputed public concern. It posed the question whether the powerful company which had marketed the drug bore legal or moral responsibility towards hundreds of individuals experiencing an appalling personal tragedy or whether the victims could demand or hope for indemnification only from the community as a whole; fundamental issues concerning protection against and compensation for injuries resulting from scientific developments were raised and many facets of the existing law on these subjects were called in question.

---

131. *Sunday Times v UK* (1979) 2 EHRR 245, para 48.

> As the Court has already observed, Article 10 guarantees not only the freedom of the press to inform the public but also the right of the public to be properly informed …
>
> In the present case, the families of numerous victims of the tragedy, who were unaware of the legal difficulties involved, had a vital interest in knowing all the underlying facts and the various possible solutions. They could be deprived of this information, which was crucially important for them, only if it appeared absolutely certain that its diffusion would have presented a threat to the 'authority of the judiciary'.[132]

The court reviewed the argument put forward by the State that the article might have pressured the drug company to settle out of court on better terms. It took the view that this was not factually likely at the time the injunction was granted and was even less likely by the time the House of Lords approved the injunction.[133]

[2.68] In considering whether the aim of protecting the authority of the judiciary outweighed the free speech interest, the court found that while the courts are the forum for settling legal disputes, the newspapers are not excluded from engaging in discussion before a case. It noted that the article in question was moderate in its language and approached the issues in a balanced way. The court also found that the injunction was overly broad in its terms as it precluded all discussion of the issues forming the background to the case.

[2.69] The court has also held on a number of occasions that expression concerning political matters is particularly strongly protected under the Convention. Interferences which affect the media's role in commenting on matters pertaining to political affairs thus require particularly careful review to ensure their compatibility with Article 10.

[2.70] This was made clear by the court in its decision in *Lingens v Austria*.[134] The applicant in that case was a journalist and editor of a magazine. He had published two articles which accused the Austrian Chancellor of protecting and helping former Nazi SS officers for political reasons. The Chancellor took a successful private prosecution of the applicant for criminal defamation. Following an appeal, the applicant was fined 15,000 schillings and required to publish the appeal judgment in the magazine.

[2.71] The court accepted that the protection of the Chancellor's reputation was a legitimate aim. It repeated the quotation from *Handyside* regarding the protection of ideas that offend, shock or disturb and went on to state that the principles set out in that statement were 'of particular importance as far as the press is concerned'.[135] It pointed out that:

> Whilst the press must not overstep the bounds set, inter alia, for the 'protection of the reputation of others', it is nevertheless incumbent on it to impart information

---

132. *Sunday Times v UK* (1979) 2 EHRR 245, para 66.
133. *Sunday Times v UK* (1979) 2 EHRR 245, para 63.
134. *Lingens v Austria* (1986) 8 EHRR 407.
135. *Lingens v Austria* (1986) 8 EHRR 407, para 41.

and ideas on political issues just as on those in other areas of public interest. Not only does the press have the task of imparting such information and ideas: the public also has a right to receive them.[136]

[2.72] In a classic passage which has been repeated in several subsequent judgments of the court, it held that:

> Freedom of the press furthermore affords the public one of the best means of discovering and forming an opinion of the ideas and attitudes of political leaders. More generally, freedom of political debate is at the very core of the concept of a democratic society which prevails throughout the Convention.
>
> The limits of acceptable criticism are accordingly wider as regards a politician as such than as regards a private individual. Unlike the latter, the former inevitably and knowingly lays himself open to close scrutiny of his every word and deed by both journalists and the public at large, and he must consequently display a greater degree of tolerance. No doubt Article 10 para 2 enables the reputation of others – that is to say, of all individuals – to be protected, and this protection extends to politicians too, even when they are not acting in their private capacity; but in such cases the requirements of such protection have to be weighed in relation to the interests of open discussion of political issues.[137]

[2.73] In the *Lingens* case, the background to the publication of the article was a highly charged political controversy in which the President of the Austrian Liberal Party had been identified as a former SS officer by a Jewish pressure group a few days after a general election had taken place. The Chancellor gave a television interview a few hours after ruling out forming a coalition with the Liberals in which he compared the Jewish pressure group to the 'mafia'. The court emphasised the importance of the context in which the statements had been made, noting that 'in this struggle each used the weapons at his disposal; and these were in no way unusual in the hard-fought tussles of politics.'[138]

[2.74] The court was also critical of the defence available to criminal libel under the Austrian law. This required the accused to establish the truth of his statements. The Austrian courts had found that while the facts stated in the article were accurate, the behaviour of the Chancellor was open to a number of different interpretations so that the value judgment contained in the article could not be said to be 'true'. The European Court of Human Rights found that the defence was impossible to establish in respect of value judgments and that this infringed 'freedom of opinion' which was a crucial aspect of the right to freedom of expression.[139]

---

136. The court also rejected the view of the Vienna Court of Appeal, to the effect that the task of the press was to impart information, the interpretation of which had to be left primarily to the reader.
137. *Lingens v Austria* (1986) 8 EHRR 407, para 42.
138. *Lingens v Austria* (1986) 8 EHRR 407, para 43.
139. See also *Oberschlick v Austria (No 1)* (1991) 19 EHRR 389.

[2.75] The court has also pointed out in *Von Hannover v Germany*[140] that in situations where the media's entitlement under Article 10 clashes with the individual's right to privacy under Article 8, the balancing between the two interests will focus on whether the publication can be said to be on a matter of public interest. Thus in that case, where coverage of a public figure going about her daily life was published, the court assessed the Article 10 value of the speech based on the 'contribution that the published articles and photos make to a debate of general interest'.[141]

The court has thus developed in its case law a 'special standard of tolerance'[142] for media expression which concerns a matter of public interest.

Polemic speech

[2.76] The *Lingens* case remains a touchstone statement of the court's approach to political expression and the role of the media therein. One of the points that was made by the court was that the use of polemic language may have to be tolerated in the context of political expression. This principle was strongly reiterated by the court in two cases, *Oberschlick v Austria (No 1)*[143] and *Oberschlick v Austria (No 2)*.[144]

[2.77] In *Oberschlick v Austria (No 1)*, the applicant, who was a journalist and editor of a review, was convicted of criminal defamation following a private prosecution. The conviction related to the publication of the text of a 'criminal information' which he and other persons had laid against a politician. In the course of an election campaign, this politician had made certain public statements, reported in a television programme, that the family allowances for Austrian women should be increased by 50% in order to obviate their seeking abortions for financial reasons, whilst those paid to immigrant mothers should be reduced to 50% of their current levels. The applicant had expressed the opinion, set out in the criminal information, that this proposal corresponded to the philosophy and the aims of National Socialism as stated in the NSDAP Manifesto of 1920.

[2.78] The court noted that the applicant had been unable to defend the prosecution under Austrian law because to do so would require proof of the truth of the value judgments contained in the publication – a feature of Austrian defamation law which it had criticised in the *Lingens* case.

[2.79] The court noted that the publication contributed to public debate on an important political issue, noting that 'the issue of different treatment of nationals and foreigners in

---

140. *Von Hannover v Germany* (2005) 40 EHRR 1.
141. *Von Hannover v Germany* (2005) 40 EHRR 1, para 60. See also *Radio Twist AS v Slovakia* (Application No 62202/00) (19 December 2006, unreported), ECtHR.
142. *Radio Twist AS v Slovakia* (Application No 62202/00) (19 December 2006, unreported), ECtHR, para 58. See also *Kwiecien v Poland* (9 April 2007, unreported), ECtHR.
143. *Oberschlick v Austria (No 1)* (1991) 19 EHRR 389.
144. *Oberschlick v Austria (No 2)* (1997) 25 EHRR 357.

the social field has given rise to considerable discussion not only in Austria but also in other member States of the Council of Europe.'[145]

[2.80] Importantly, the court pointed out that:

> Mr Oberschlick's criticisms ... sought to draw the public's attention in a provocative manner to a proposal made by a politician which was likely to shock many people. A politician who expresses himself in such terms exposes himself to a strong reaction on the part of journalists and the public.[146]

The court also refused to find fault with the form the publication took 'given the importance of the issue at stake'.[147]

[2.81] In *Oberschlick v Austria (No 2)*,[148] the applicant was convicted of the criminal offence of insult and fined a small sum. He had published a report of a speech by a politician under a headline that read, 'PS: "Idiot" instead of "Nazi".' In the speech, the politician had praised the Austrian soldiers who fought in WWII including those in the SS and Wehrmacht for their contribution to Austria's prosperous democracy. The court reiterated what it had said in *Oberschlick (No 1)* about the criticism of politicians and noted that the speech reported in the article was 'intended to be provocative and consequently to arouse strong reactions.'[149]

[2.82] The court found that the conviction of the applicant for insult was not necessary in a democratic society, noting that:

> It is true that calling a politician a Trottel in public may offend him. In the instant case, however, the word does not seem disproportionate to the indignation knowingly aroused by Mr Haider. As to the polemical tone of the article, which the Court should not be taken to approve, it must be remembered that article 10 protects not only the substance of the ideas and information expressed but also the form in which they are conveyed.[150]

Thus the media appeared from these cases[151] to enjoy a significant degree of latitude in terms of the tone used in the coverage of political affairs. The approach of the court has,

---

145. *Oberschlick v Austria (No 1)* (1991) 19 EHRR 389, para 61.
146. *Oberschlick v Austria (No 1)* (1991) 19 EHRR 389, para 61.
147. *Oberschlick v Austria (No 1)* (1991) 19 EHRR 389, para 63.
148. *Oberschlick v Austria (No 2)* (1997) 25 EHRR 357.
149. *Oberschlick v Austria (No 2)* (1997) 25 EHRR 357, para 31.
150. *Oberschlick v Austria (No 2)* (1997) 25 EHRR 357, para 34. See also *Dehaes and Gijsels v Belgium* (1997) 25 EHRR 1 where the court found that an article with a 'polemical and even aggressive tone' accusing judges of bias was protected under Art 10. *Oberschlick v Austria (No 2)* (1997) 25 EHRR 357, para 48.
151. See also *Dehaes and Gijsels v Belgium* (1997) 25 EHRR 1, para 48. A degree of exaggeration and provocation is permissible when discussing political issues, *Ibrahim Aksoy v Turkey* (Application Nos 28635/95, 30171/96 and 34535/97) 10 October 2000, para 52. (French text only).

however, altered slightly. In *Stoll v Switzerland*,[152] in particular, the court was critical of what it saw as sensationalist and reductive coverage of a matter of public interest.[153]

JOURNALISTIC ETHICS – A DOUBLE-EDGED SWORD

[2.83] While earlier cases repeatedly emphasise the need to protect the media due to their important function in a democracy, more recent case law from the European Court of Human Rights suggests a more nuanced approach which focuses on the responsibilities of the media. This approach, while it may seem less protective of media expression, is consistent with the court's underlying rationale for protecting the media's expression rights. That rationale does not require that the media be given carte blanche to publish irresponsibly. On the contrary, the protection of media expression on the basis of its function in contributing to political debate justifies some review of the accuracy and reliability of publication. It might be argued that the danger of this is that too nuanced an approach might have a chilling effect on robust media comment. In the *Stoll* case, considered below, the court's reliance on the findings of the Swiss Press Council illustrate an attempt to circumvent this issue. By relying on the findings of a self-regulatory body such as the Press Council, the court was on relatively safe ground. In later cases, however, the court has taken it upon itself to assess the quality of media output in a much more direct way.

[2.84] The court made reference to the question of journalistic ethics in *Goodwin v United Kingdom*,[154] where it held that:

> Protection of journalistic sources is one of the basic conditions for press freedom, as is reflected in the laws and the professional codes of conduct in a number of Contracting States and is affirmed in several international instruments on journalistic freedoms[155] … Without such protection, sources may be deterred from assisting the press in informing the public on matters of public interest. As a result the vital public-watchdog role of the press may be undermined and the ability of the press to provide accurate and reliable information may be adversely affected. Having regard to the importance of the protection of journalistic sources for press freedom in a democratic society and the potentially chilling effect an order of source disclosure has on the exercise of that freedom, such a measure cannot be compatible with Article 10 of the Convention unless it is justified by an overriding requirement in the public interest.[156]

---

152. *Stoll v Switzerland* (2007) 44 EHRR 53. Discussed further below **[2.93]–[2.106]**.
153. *Ibid.*
154. *Goodwin v United Kingdom* (1996) 22 EHRR 123.
155. The court referred to the Resolution on Journalistic Freedoms and Human Rights, adopted at the 4th European Ministerial Conference on Mass Media Policy (Prague, 7–8 December 1994) and Resolution on the Confidentiality of Journalists' Sources by the European Parliament, 18 January 1994, OJ C 44/34).
156. *Goodwin v United Kingdom* (1996) 22 EHRR 123, para 39.

While the case law on journalists' sources[157] refers to professional ethics to protect the media, the court has also relied on codes of practice as a source of standards by which to review media responsibility. This development was preceded by case law in which the court suggested that Article 10 protection required responsible journalism in the form of fact checking and source verification.[158]

[2.85] In *Bladet Tromso v Norway*,[159] the court emphasised a degree of latitude on the part of the media in this regard. The applicants in this case (a newspaper and its editor) had published a number of articles on seal hunting in a local newspaper which was circulated in an area of Norway where seal hunting had been the subject of considerable controversy. One article alleged breaches of seal hunting regulations on board a particular vessel. The article had relied on a report carried out on behalf of the Minister for Fisheries which made those allegations. The report had not been released to the public at that time but had been sent to the newspaper by the individual responsible for producing it. It later transpired that the report was inaccurate in relation to the allegations of illegality. The applicants were sued by crew members of the vessel concerned and were found to have defamed them.

[2.86] The court considered whether the award of damages was necessary in a democratic society. It emphasised the fact that the article was part of a series of articles on a matter of public interest which, taken as a whole, had presented a balanced view of the issues. The court found that it was reasonable for *Bladet Tromso* to rely on the report that had been sent to it without seeking to further verify the information contained therein. The fact that the report was later found to have been inaccurate was not relevant. The court also emphasised the fact that the potential damage to reputations was ameliorated by the fact that the article did not name individual crew members. The court also noted that the paper had acted in good faith.

[2.87] The emphasis placed by the court on the fact that individuals were neither named nor readily identifiable is interesting in that the court seemed to suggest that if it were otherwise, a more rigorous approach to the source of the allegations might have been required.

[2.88] In *Radio Twist AS v Slovakia*,[160] the court indicated that Article 10 protects the media in their use of sources which are themselves unlawful. In that case, the court held that the respondent state had violated Article 10 of the Convention by permitting a civil action against the applicant in respect of the broadcasting of telephone conversations between two high-ranking politicians which a third party had unlawfully obtained.

---

157. See also *Financial Times Ltd v United Kingdom* (Application No 821/03) 15 December 2009 (Fourth Section). The case law on the protection of sources is considered further at **[5.94]–[5.118]**.

158. See in an Irish context, the judgment of Charleton J in *Leech v Independent Newspapers Ltd* [2007] IEHC 223 discussing a live radio broadcast in which a allegedly defamatory statement was made on air by an unidentified caller.

159. *Bladet Tromso v Norway* (1999) 29 EHRR 125.

160. *Radio Twist AS v Slovakia* (Application No 62202/00) (19 December 2006, unreported), ECtHR.

[2.89] The court noted that:

> [T]he applicant company was penalised mainly for the mere fact of having
> broadcast information which someone else had obtained illegally. The Court is
> however not convinced that the mere fact that the recording had been obtained by
> a third person, contrary to law, can deprive the applicant company of the
> protection of Article 10 of the Convention.[161]

Furthermore, the court observed that there was:

> ...no indication that the journalists from the applicant company acted in bad faith
> or that they pursued any purpose other than reporting on matters which they felt
> obliged to make available to the public.[162]

The court in that case placed considerable emphasis on the content of the broadcast
which was 'clearly political' and lacked a 'private life dimension'[163] so that finding by
the national court that the recording ought not to have been broadcast was inconsistent
with the protection of the media under Article 10.

[2.90] In *Tonsbergs & Blad A/S v Norway*,[164] the court noted that:

> [P]rotection of the right of journalists to impart information on issues of general
> interest requires that they should act in good faith and on an accurate factual basis
> and provide 'reliable and precise' information in accordance with the ethics of
> journalism ... Under the terms of paragraph 2 of Article 10 of the Convention,
> freedom of expression carries with it 'duties and responsibilities', which also
> apply to the media even with respect to matters of serious public concern. These
> 'duties and responsibilities' are significant when there is a question of attacking
> the reputation of a named individual and infringing the 'rights of others'. Thus,
> special grounds are required before the media can be dispensed from their
> ordinary obligation to verify factual statements that are defamatory of private
> individuals. Whether such grounds exist depends in particular on the nature and
> degree of the defamation in question and the extent to which the media can
> reasonably regard their sources as reliable with respect to the allegations ...[165]

That case concerned an award of damages for defamation given by domestic courts in
respect of an article published in a newspaper to the effect that a prominent businessman
in Norway appeared on a list drawn up by a municipality, of persons considered to have
breached the permanent residence requirements. The applicants had relied on an
anonymous source for the allegation. The national courts had held that where the media
relied on an anonymous source 'a stricter duty of care applied and that it would largely

---

161. *Radio Twist AS v Slovakia* (Application No 62202/00) (19 December 2006, unreported), ECtHR,
para 62.
162. *Radio Twist AS v Slovakia* (Application No 62202/00) (19 December 2006, unreported), ECtHR,
para 63.
163. *Radio Twist AS v Slovakia* (Application No 62202/00) (19 December 2006, unreported), ECtHR,
para 58.
164. *Tonsbergs & Blad A/S v Norway* (Application No 510/04) (1 March 2007, unreported), ECHR.
165. *Tonsbergs & Blad A/S v Norway* (Application No 510/04) (1 March 2007, unreported), ECHR,
para 89.

be the risk of the newspaper if factual information originating from such sources were false'.[166] The European Court of Human Rights agreed with that approach, stating that it saw 'no special grounds for dispensing the newspaper from its ordinary obligation to verify factual statements that are defamatory of private individuals.'[167]

[2.91] The court went on to find that in the circumstances of the case there had been 'substantial evidence to corroborate the newspaper's contention' and emphasised that the issue was one 'that should be determined in the light of the situation as it presented itself to *Tønsberg Blad* then, rather than with the benefit of hindsight'.[168]

[2.92] Echoing its approach in *Bladet Tromso*, the court emphasised the balance between the impact of the publication on an individual's rights and the requirements of responsible fact checking, noting that:

> [H]aving regard to the relatively minor nature and limited degree of the defamation at issue and the important public interests involved, the Court is satisfied that the newspaper took sufficient steps to verify the truth of the disputed allegation and acted in good faith.[169]

[2.93] In *Stoll v Switzerland*,[170] the applicant journalist had obtained a copy of a confidential document drawn up by the Swiss ambassador to the United States dealing with negotiations that were being conducted between, among others, the World Jewish Congress and Swiss banks concerning compensation due to Holocaust victims for unclaimed assets deposited in Swiss bank accounts. A Zürich Sunday newspaper, *Sonntags-Zeitung*, published two articles by the applicant under the headings 'Carlo Jagmetti [the author of the leaked document] insults the Jews' and 'The ambassador in bathrobe and climbing boots puts his foot in it again', accompanied by extracts from the document in question. The next day, two daily newspapers reproduced extensive extracts from it. The applicant was convicted of breaching the Swiss Criminal Code by publishing secret official deliberations and fined 800 francs. The Press Council subsequently upheld a complaint against the applicant on the basis that the articles had represented the ambassador in terms that were sensational and shocking.

[2.94] The applicant argued that his conviction and fine were contrary to Article 10. The Grand Chamber found that the conviction had the legitimate aim of protecting information received in confidence and was prescribed by law. In determining whether

---

166. *Tonsbergs & Blad A/S v Norway* (Application No 510/04) (1 March 2007, unreported), ECHR, para 95, referring to the decision of the Supreme Court of Norway.
167. *Tonsbergs & Blad A/S v Norway* (Application No 510/04) (1 March 2007, unreported), ECHR, para 95.
168. *Tonsbergs & Blad A/S v Norway* (Application No 510/04) (1 March 2007, unreported), ECHR, para 99.
169. *Tonsbergs & Blad A/S v Norway* (Application No 510/04) (1 March 2007, unreported), ECHR, para 101.
170. *Stoll v Switzerland* (2007) 44 EHRR 53. Discussed further below **[2.93]**–**[2.106]**.

the interference was necessary in a democratic society, the court accepted that the aim was to protect the disclosure of information in confidence.[171]

[2.95] The judgment of the court started by repeating some of the traditional Convention principles which have become akin to a judicial mantra in the court's free speech jurisprudence. Thus, the court noted that there was a narrow margin of appreciation where press freedom was at issue[172] and that interferences with press freedom in the context of political affairs would be carefully reviewed where there was a risk that it might have a chilling effect on press participation in debates over matters of legitimate public concern.[173]

[2.96] The court went on, however, to sound a new note in the tune on press freedom. It commented that such press freedom was not absolute and that there was no principle under Article 10 which required the press to be exempt from the criminal law. It also pointed out that there could be limitations on press freedom of political expression.[174] Importantly, it held that:

> [T]he safeguard afforded by Article 10 to journalists in relation to reporting on issues of general interest is subject to the proviso that they are acting in good faith and on an accurate factual basis and provide 'reliable and precise' information in accordance with the ethics of journalism.[175]

[2.97] The importance of reliable journalism was underlined by the power wielded by the media. The court, referring to the strong influence of the modern media, commented that:

> [N]ot only do they inform, they can also suggest by the way in which they present the information how it is to be assessed. In a world in which the individual is confronted with vast quantities of information circulated via traditional and electronic media and involving an ever-growing number of players, monitoring compliance with journalistic ethics takes on added importance.[176]

The court also expressed suspicion of official secrecy laws of the type at issue in the case, noting that '[p]ress freedom assumes even greater importance in circumstances in which State activities and decisions escape democratic or judicial scrutiny on account of their confidential or secret nature.'[177] It noted that the conviction of a journalist for

---

171. The court rejected the argument that the interference had the aim of protecting national security or public safety, pointing out that those exemptions were to be interpreted restrictively (para 54). The argument that the interference sought to protect the rights of others, ie the reputation of the ambassador was also rejected as no proceedings were taken in respect of same (para 55).
172. *Stoll v Switzerland* (2007) 44 EHRR 53, para 105
173. *Stoll v Switzerland* (2007) 44 EHRR 53, para 106.
174. *Stoll v Switzerland* (2007) 44 EHRR 53, para 103.
175. *Stoll v Switzerland* (2007) 44 EHRR 53, para 103.
176. *Stoll v Switzerland* (2007) 44 EHRR 53, para 104.
177. *Stoll v Switzerland* (2007) 44 EHRR 53, para 110.

revealing secret information could discourage the press from performing 'its vital role as 'public watchdog'.[178]

[2.98] Significantly, the court examined the content of the articles to assess whether they 'were capable of contributing to the public debate'.[179] It found that the focus of the articles was 'almost exclusively' on the ambassador's personality and individual style but that it was possible to argue that there was a public interest in the strong languages used by the ambassador.[180] The court took the view that the articles were thus capable of contributing to the public debate on the issue of unclaimed assets.[181]

[2.99] According to the court, the fact that the material in the articles had been derived from a leak was not particularly important to its assessment of journalistic ethics.[182] Instead, the court placed great emphasis on the opinion of the Swiss Press Council[183] which had identified a number of flaws in the articles under the relevant code of practice. The court set out in detail what it saw as the shortcomings of the articles in question. These included the 'reductive and truncated' content, and 'the fact that the articles quoted at times isolated extracts from the report in question, taken out of context'. The court compared the articles unfavourably with other articles which subsequently appeared in other newspapers which had included the full text of the leaked report, thus allowing readers to form their own view. [184]

[2.100] The court also noted that the vocabulary used by the applicant suggested that the comments by the ambassador were anti-Semitic. While reiterating that 'freedom of the press covers possible recourse to a degree of exaggeration, or even provocation', the court went on to note that:

> [T]he applicant, in capricious fashion, started a rumour which related directly to one of the very phenomena at the root of the issue of unclaimed assets, namely the atrocities committed against the Jewish community during the Second World War. The Court reiterates the need to deal firmly with allegations and/or insinuations of that nature.[185]

---

178. *Stoll v Switzerland* (2007) 44 EHRR 53, para 110. The court also referred to the Council of Europe and Inter-American Commission on Human Rights at para 111 to support its view of official secrecy measures.
179. *Stoll v Switzerland* (2007) 44 EHRR 53, para 121.
180. *Stoll v Switzerland* (2007) 44 EHRR 53, para 123.
181. *Stoll v Switzerland* (2007) 44 EHRR 53, para 124.
182. Cf *Mahon v Keena* [2009] 2 ILRM 373.
183. *Stoll v Switzerland* (2007) 44 EHRR 53, para 145.
184. The editor's arguments that it would have been virtually impossible to add another page to the newspaper at the time and that plans to publish the full text on the internet were abandoned owing to technical problems were rejected by the court: *Stoll v Switzerland* (2007) 44 EHRR 53, para 147.
185. *Stoll v Switzerland* (2007) 44 EHRR 53, para 148. The court also noted that the rumour had likely contributed to the ambassador's resignation.

[2.101] The third flaw identified by the court was in respect of the editing of the article. In a scathing comment, the judgment noted that:

> [T]he way in which the articles were edited seems hardly fitting for a subject as important and serious as that of the unclaimed funds. The sensationalist style of the headings and sub-headings is particularly striking.[186]

[2.102] It noted that a picture which accompanied the second article, which showed the ambassador in bathrobe and climbing boots, confirmed:

> '... the trivial nature of the applicant's articles, in clear contrast to the seriousness of the subject matter. Moreover, the headings, sub-headings and picture in question have no obvious link to the subject matter but have the effect of reinforcing the reader's impression of someone ill-fitted to hold diplomatic office.'[187]

[2.103] Finally, the court pointed out that the articles were 'inaccurate and likely to mislead the reader by virtue of the fact that they did not make the timing of the events sufficiently clear.'[188]

For all of these reasons, the court held that the conviction of the applicant was not a disproportionate interference with media freedom of expression.

SENSATIONALISM, EDITORIAL DISCRETION AND ARTICLE 10

[2.104] The judgment of the court in *Stoll* was not endorsed by all the members of the Grand Chamber who heard the case. A strident dissenting judgment was delivered by Judge Zagerbelsky[189] who argued that the 'real reason' for the majority's decision was the 'form of the articles'.

[2.105] The dissenting judgment accuses the majority of contradicting itself:

> The judgment reiterates that Article 10 protects the substance of the ideas and information expressed and the form in which they are conveyed. 'Consequently, it is not for this Court, nor for the national courts for that matter, to substitute their own views for those of the press as to what technique of reporting should be adopted by journalists' (see paragraph 146 of the judgment). Having said that, the majority seems to me to contradict itself by stating in the following paragraph: 'Nevertheless, like the Press Council, the Court observes a number of shortcomings in the form of the published articles'. The judgment does not give any reason for this surprising 'nevertheless', which introduces an element of

---

186. *Stoll v Switzerland* (2007) 44 EHRR 53, para 149. Interestingly, the court did not think it significant whether the headings were chosen by the applicant himself or the editors. These included 'Ambassador Jagmetti insults the Jews – Secret document: Our adversaries are not to be trusted' and 'The ambassador in bathrobe and climbing boots puts his foot in it – Swiss Ambassador Carlo Jagmetti's diplomatic blunderings'.
187. *Stoll v Switzerland* (2007) 44 EHRR 53, para 149.
188. *Stoll v Switzerland* (2007) 44 EHRR 53.
189. Joined by Judges Lorenzen, Fura-Sandström, Jaeger and Popovi.

censure regarding the form chosen by the journalist and leads the Court to endorse the wholly different position of a private body concerned with journalistic ethics.

The dissent noted also that the judgment of the majority 'falls into a trap' by focusing on personal nature of the comments about the ambassador which, as the dissent pointed out, were never the subject of defamation proceedings. The criticism made by the majority of the form of the articles was described by the dissent as 'unduly harsh' and 'not relevant from the Court's perspective'.

[2.106] The approach of the majority judges of the Grand Chamber in *Stoll* suggests a willingness to critically analyse the exercise of editorial discretion and the presentation of published material. It also saw the court relying on the self-regulatory codes of practice used by the media in order to assess the compliance of the media with their responsibilities as regards reporting.[190] A similar approach has been taken in a number of other cases.

[2.107] In *Tonsbergs & Blad A/S v Norway*,[191] the First Section of the court gave a judgment in which it too engaged in an analysis of the manner in which a news story was presented. It noted that the story in question, while 'presented in a somewhat sensationalist style', did not give an 'overall impression' that it was 'inviting the reader to reach any foregone conclusion' about whether the individual who was the subject of the story had breached permanent residence requirements. The court found that the tone of the article was such that 'it raised question marks with respect to both whether he had breached the said requirements and whether those requirements should be maintained, modified or repealed.' Thus, although the news item 'was sensationalist in style, it was balanced overall.'[192]

[2.108] In *Eerikäinen v Finland*,[193] the court considered a complaint relating to a successful privacy action which resulted in an award of damages of approximately €3,000. The applicant had published an article about an individual who was at the time facing a criminal trial. The article was entitled 'It seemed legal, but ... a woman entrepreneur cheated to obtain a pension of over 2 million marks?'. The woman concerned was not named in the main body of the article but her first name appeared in the table of contents of the magazine and included a reproduction of an article written several years previously about her with two photographs, one of which was taken of the applicant inside her home. The earlier article had related to an entirely different matter. It had appeared in another magazine and had given her full name.

---

190. See Carolan, 'The Changing Face of Media Freedom' (2008) Bar Review.
191. *Tonsbergs & Blad A/S v Norway* (Application No 510/04) (1 March 2007, unreported), ECHR.
192. *Tonsbergs & Blad A/S v Norway* (Application No 510/04) (1 March 2007, unreported), ECHR, para 92. See also *Ustun v Turkey* (10 May 2007, unreported), ECHR where the court held that the conviction and sentencing of the applicant for publishing a book about the life and political views of a left wing revolutionary cinema artist violated Art 10 of the Convention, despite the 'hostile tone' of the narrative (para 32).
193. *Eerikäinen v Finland* (Application No 3514/02) 10 February 2009 (Fourth Section).

[2.109] Again, echoing the approach taken in *Stoll*, the court paid significant attention to the Finnish Guidelines for Journalists issued by the Finnish Union of Journalists as part of a self-regulatory regime. Noting that these provided that suspects in criminal cases ought not usually to be identified in advance of a trial, the court also referred to an updated version of the guidelines issued after the article in question was published which emphasised respect for privacy of suspects. The European Federation of Journalists intervened as a third party in the case, giving an overview of the position relating to identification of suspects across a number of Contracting States. The court examined the content of the article carefully and noted the phrasing of the headline to the article as a question rather than a statement of guilt. In respect of the use made of the earlier article and in particular the reproduction of the photographs in it, the court noted that its subject matter had not been a matter of public debate but that the individual concerned had given her consent to its publication at the time. Demonstrating a reluctance to challenge editorial decisions, which contrasts strongly with the approach taken in *Stoll*, the court held that:

> The 1997 article must be considered to have reproduced an article which was irrelevant to the subject under discussion, giving X's name and picture, which were thereby expressly communicated to the general public. It is however not for this Court, any more than it is for the national courts, to substitute its own views for those of the press as to what techniques of reporting should be adopted by journalists ... For the sake of clarity, it is not the initial publication of that article which is before the Court but its use as an illustration in the 1997 article.[194]

The court found that the award of damages in the case had not been necessary in a democratic society.

[2.110] The intervention of the European Federation of Journalists is an interesting development in this case. The court appears to be increasingly willing to rely on the professional codes of conduct of the media in its assessment of whether media expression has been produced responsibly. While the *Stoll* case may seem to come dangerously close to interfering with editorial discretion, it is noteworthy that the court was explicit in *Eerikäinen* in stating that this was not the role of the court.[195]

[2.111] The willingness of the court to review the process by which the media generates its output is consistent with its view of the important role the media plays in contributing to debate about public affairs. As the recent cases demonstrate, this important role brings with it certain responsibilities. Another recent development in the approach of the court to media expression has been its embryonic recognition of special privileges for the media in terms of access to information, discussed below.

---

194. *Eerikäinen v Finland* (Application No 3514/02) 10 February 2009 (Fourth Section), para 65.
195. See also *Tuomela v Finland* (Application No 25711/04), 6 April 2010; *Flinkkilä v Finland* (Application No 25576/04) 6 April 2010; *Jokitaipale v Finland* (Application No 43349/05) 6 April 2010; *Iltalehti and Karhuvaara v Finland* (Application No 6372/06) 6 April 2010; *Soila v Finland* (Application No 6806/06) (Fourth Section).

SPECIAL ACCESS FOR THE MEDIA – A POSITIVE OBLIGATION UNDER ARTICLE 10?

[2.112] The European Court of Human Rights has held in a number of cases that there can be circumstances in which the provisions of the Convention confer positive obligations on the State.[196] Thus in *Ozgur Gundem v Turkey*,[197] where the premises and staff of a newspaper had been subject to serious attacks and harassment including bombs, armed attacks and the killing of a number of individuals connected to the paper, the court held that the State had a positive obligation to take measures to protect the applicants.

[2.113] While the above case arose against an unusual and extreme factual background, there have been attempts to assert positive obligations under Article 10 in more benign social conditions.[198] The decision of the court in *Tarsasag a Szabadsagjogokert v Hungary*[199] seems to indicate a willingness to consider claims relating to access to information. The applicant in the case was a non-governmental organisation which was active in the field of drug policy. It alleged that the decisions of the Hungarian courts denying it access to the details of a parliamentarian's complaint challenging the constitutionality of criminal legislation concerning drug-related offences pending before the Constitutional Court had amounted to a breach of its right to have access to information of public interest. The Constitutional Court had denied the request without having consulted the MP, explaining that a complaint pending before it could not be made available to outsiders without the approval of its author.

[2.114] The European Court of Human Rights considered whether there had been an interference with Article 10 arising from the facts and held that:

> The Court has consistently recognised that the public has a right to receive information of general interest. Its case law in this field has been developed in relation to press freedom which serves to impart information and ideas on such matters ... In this connection, the most careful scrutiny on the part of the Court is

---

196. See *X and Y v The Netherlands* (1986) 8 EHRR 235.
197. *Ozgur Gundem v Turkey* (Application No 23144/93) 16 March 2000 (Fourth Section).
198. In the context of political activism and Art 10, see *Appleby v UK* (Application No 44306/98) 6 May 2003 (Fourth Section). The applicants sought to gain access to a privately owned shopping and office complex that formed the town centre of the relevant area. They sought this access to publicise their opposition to the proposed development of a public park in another part of the town. The company that owned the complex refused them access, stating that it had a policy of maintaining neutrality concerning political issues. The applicants argued that Art 10 placed a positive obligation on the State to secure their right to freedom of expression in the complex. The court refused to find that Art 10 extended to such a positive obligation in that case, while not ruling out the possibility that such an obligation could arise. As the court noted, the applicants were not completely excluded from their expressive activity – they remained free to seek access from individual businesses, to distribute pamphlets from the public paths leading up to the complex and to use other channels of expression such as calling door to door. It suggested that a different approach might be taken if, for example, the entire town had been controlled by a private body.
199. *Tarsasag a Szabadsagjogokert v Hungary* (Application No 37374/05) 14 April 2009 (Second Section).

called for when the measures taken by the national authority are capable of discouraging the participation of the press, one of society's 'watchdogs', in the public debate on matters of legitimate public concern … even measures which merely make access to information more cumbersome.[200]

The court went on to note that, because of the matters protected by Article 10:

[T]he law cannot allow arbitrary restrictions which may become a form of indirect censorship should the authorities create obstacles to the gathering of information. For example, the latter activity is an essential preparatory step in journalism and is an inherent, protected part of press freedom …[201]

The subject matter of the instant dispute was the constitutionality of criminal legislation concerning drug-related offences. In the Court's view, the submission of an application for an *a posteriori* abstract review of this legislation, especially by a Member of Parliament, undoubtedly constituted a matter of public interest. Consequently, the Court finds that the applicant was involved in the legitimate gathering of information on a matter of public importance. It observes that the authorities interfered in the preparatory stage of this process by creating an administrative obstacle. The Constitutional Court's monopoly of information thus amounted to a form of censorship. Furthermore, given that the applicant's intention was to impart to the public the information gathered from the constitutional complaint in question, and thereby to contribute to the public debate concerning legislation on drug-related offences, its right to impart information was clearly impaired.[202]

[2.115] The court considered that the restrictions had a legitimate aim – to protect the rights of the Minister under data protection law – and that they were prescribed by law. The court referred to a number of its earlier decisions which suggested that the reference in Article 10 to freedom to receive information did not entail a right of access to documents or an obligation on the government to provide them.[203] It went on to indicate a change in policy in this area, declaring its willingness to develop a right of access to information.[204]

[2.116] The court's judgment went on to characterise the case as one involving a restriction on the right to receive information under Article 10:

[T]he present case essentially concerns an interference – by virtue of the censorial power of an information monopoly – with the exercise of the functions of a social watchdog, like the press, rather than a denial of a general right of access to official

---

200. *Tarsasag a Szabadsagjogokert v Hungary* (Application No 37374/05) 14 April 2009 (Second Section), para 26.
201. *Tarsasag a Szabadsagjogokert v Hungary* (Application No 37374/05) 14 April 2009 (Second Section), para 27.
202. *Tarsasag a Szabadsagjogokert v Hungary* (Application No 37374/05) 14 April 2009 (Second Section), para 28.
203. The court referred to *Leander v Sweden* [1987] ECHR 9248/81, para 74 and *Loiseau v France* (Application No 46809/99) ECHR 2003–XII.
204. *Tarsasag a Szabadsagjogokert v Hungary* (Application No 37374/05) 14 April 2009 (Second Section), para 35.

documents. In this connection, a comparison can be drawn with the Court's previous concerns that preliminary obstacles created by the authorities in the way of press functions call for the most careful scrutiny ... Moreover, the State's obligations in matters of freedom of the press include the elimination of barriers to the exercise of press functions where, in issues of public interest, such barriers exist solely because of an information monopoly held by the authorities. The Court notes at this juncture that the information sought by the applicant in the present case was ready and available ... and did not require the collection of any data by the Government. Therefore, the Court considers that the State had an obligation not to impede the flow of information sought by the applicant.[205]

The court went on to relate its decision in the case to the role of the media under Article 10, noting that:

[O]bstacles created in order to hinder access to information of public interest may discourage those working in the media or related fields from pursuing such matters. As a result, they may no longer be able to play their vital role as 'public watchdogs' and their ability to provide accurate and reliable information may be adversely affected.[206]

While the court's judgment is framed as being concerned with a restriction on freedom of access to information, this is mere semantics. The case refers to a positive obligation on states to eliminate barriers which hinder media access to information. This positive obligation is justified by the court on the basis of the vital role of the media as public watchdogs which might otherwise be impeded. The court has been heavily suspicious in other cases of measures which provide for a state monopoly on information and the case seems to open up the possibility of carving out special access privileges for the media, if not for the general public.[207]

---

205. *Tarsasag a Szabadsagjogokert v Hungary* (Application No 37374/05) 14 April 2009 (Second Section), para 36.
206. *Tarsasag a Szabadsagjogokert v Hungary* (Application No 37374/05) 14 April 2009 (Second Section), para 38.
207. See also *Kenidi v Hungary* (Application No 31475/05) 26 May 2009 (Second Section) which suggests a similar privilege may be extended to academic researchers.

Chapter 3
CENSORSHIP AND PUBLIC MORALITY

INTRODUCTION

[3.01] Article 40.6.1°(i) of the Irish Constitution twice refers to freedom of expression being subject to 'public order and morality'. The second reference refers to the State's role in ensuring that the 'organs of public opinion' do not undermine public order and morality. The censorious tone of the provision is continued in the second sub paragraph of Article 40.6.1°(i) which provides that:

> The publication or utterance of blasphemous, seditious, or indecent matter is an offence which shall be punishable in accordance with law.

The contrast with the First Amendment to the US Constitution's bald statement in favour of freedom of the press could not be greater, but even in that jurisdiction some restrictions are permissible on moral grounds.[1] Article 10(2) of the European Convention on Human Rights allows for restriction of free speech on the grounds of morality and despite the oft-repeated mantra that the Convention's protection of freedom of expression extends to ideas that 'offend, shock or disturb the State or any sector of the population,'[2] some of its proportionality analysis of state restrictions in this area has been less than searching.[3]

This chapter considers some of the forms of censorship of the media in Irish law including the law on blasphemy, the ban on religious advertising, censorship of violent material, taste and decency rules as well as incitement to hatred.[4]

BLASPHEMY
A constitutionally-mandated criminal offence

[3.02] While the Constitution specifically refers to an offence of uttering or publishing blasphemous material, there was no legislation defining the concept of blasphemy until the passage of the Defamation Act 2009. In *Corway v Independent Newspapers (Ireland) Ltd*,[5] the Supreme Court upheld the judgment of Geoghegan J in the High

---

1. *Butler v State of Michigan* 352 US 380 (1957); *Roth v US* 354 US 476 (1957).
2. *Handyside v United Kingdom* (1979–1980) 1 EHRR 737.
3. See case law discussed below.
4. The references to seditious matter, public order and the authority of the State are discussed in **Ch 4**.
5. *Corway v Independent Newspapers (Ireland) Ltd* [1999] 4 IR 484; [1997] 1 ILRM 432 (HC) [1999] 4 IR 485; [2000] 1 ILRM 426.

Court, refusing to grant the applicant leave to initiate a criminal prosecution for blasphemy against the respondent newspaper under s 8 of the Defamation Act 1961.[6]

[3.03] Section 13 of the Defamation Act 1961 provided for penalties for printing or publishing blasphemous libel as well as certain powers of search and seizure.The case arose in the context of the divorce referendum when the *Sunday Independent* newspaper published an article on the implications of the referendum which was accompanied by a cartoon. The cartoon showed three prominent politicians and a priest holding a communion wafer and a chalice. The priest appeared to be offering the politicians the Eucharist but they were depicted as turning away and were shown with their backs to him. The caption over the cartoon read '*Hello progress – bye bye Father?*' This was a reference to a campaign slogan used by some of those opposed to the referendum proposal to remove the constitutional ban on divorce.[7]

[3.04] The Supreme Court noted the lack of any definition of blasphemy in either the Constitution or statute. At common law, the House of Lords had confirmed in *Bowman v Secular Society Ltd*[8] that blasphemy was established only where there was an attack on the doctrines of the established Church (Anglicanism).[9]

[3.05] Barrington J, delivering judgment on behalf of the Supreme Court, referred to the more modern House of Lords decision in *Whitehouse v Lemon*,[10] where the House of Lords had considered the mens rea of the common law offence of blasphemy and found that it was satisfied where there was an intention to publish material which was blasphemous and that there was no additional requirement of a specific intention to blaspheme. Barrington J referred to the 'remarkable rationale' for the existence of the offence in the judgment of Lord Scarman in *Lemon* where he argued that it should be extended to cover multiple religions in modern society as it belonged 'to a group of criminal offences designed to safeguard the internal tranquillity of the kingdom.'

[3.06] Barrington J took the view that the Constitution of the Irish Free State in 1922 may not have carried forward the common law offence of blasphemy as it was a secular Constitution which recognised freedom of expression subject only to public order and morality and under which no one religion could have enjoyed greater legal protection than any other. He then considered the 1937 Constitution which had originally

---

6.   Defamation Act 1961, s 8 read as follows:

        No criminal prosecution shall be commenced against any proprietor, publisher, editor or any person responsible for the publication of a newspaper for any libel published therein without the order of a Judge of the High Court sitting in camera being first had and obtained, and every application for such order shall be made on notice to the person accused, who shall have an opportunity of being heard against the application'.

7.   The slogan used was 'Hello divorce – bye bye daddy'.

8.   *Bowman v Secular Society Ltd* [1917] AC 406.

9.   See also the earlier authorities of *R v Taylor* (1676) 1 Vent 293, 86 ER 189; *Gathercole's* Case (1838) 2 Lewin 237; *R v Ramsay and Foote* (1883) 15 Cox CC 231.

10.   *Whitehouse v Lemon* [1979] 1 All ER 898. In that case, the conviction of the editor and publisher of *Gay News* for blasphemy was upheld. *Gay News* had printed a poem depicting explicit homosexual acts with Christ's body after his death.

recognised particular denominations in Article 44.2–3 and had then removed the relevant paragraphs.[11] He noted that freedom of conscience and freedom to practise religion and equality were all guaranteed under the Constitution, which also placed a duty on the State to respect and honour religion as such but did not require the State to be the 'arbiter of religious truth', only to protect public order and morality. He found that the implications of this constitutional framework for the crime of blasphemy would have to be worked out in statute and noted that it was difficult to see how the common law offence, which was tied to an established Church and established religion could survive in that framework. He also commented that it was difficult to see how the common law offence as described in *Lemon* which found that there was no requirement of an intention to blaspheme could be reconciled with a Constitution guaranteeing freedom of conscience and the free practice and profession of religion.

[3.07] In rejecting the appeal, and confirming the High Court's refusal of leave to initiate a private prosecution, he concluded that the task of defining the offence of blasphemy was one for the legislature.

[3.08] The Law Reform Commission had noted in its *Consultation Paper and Report on Criminal Libel*[12] the lack of any statutory definition of blasphemy. Its existence was presumed in s 7(2) of the Censorship of Films Act 1923 and in s 13(1) of the Defamation Act 1961 but no attempt to set out the ingredients of this constitutional criminal offence had been made. The Oireachtas addressed this in the Defamation Act 2009 which provides for an offence of uttering or publishing blasphemous matter which carries with it a maximum fine of €25,000.

[3.09] Section 36 of the Defamation Act 2009 sets out the ingredients of the offence as requiring the utterance or publication of matter that is grossly abusive or insulting in relation to matters held sacred by any religion, thereby causing outrage among a substantial number of the adherents of that religion where the offender intends, by the publication or utterance of the matter concerned, to cause such outrage.[13] Thus, unlike the position at common law, there is a requirement that the offender intend to cause outrage.

---

11. Constitution of Ireland, Article 44 as originally enacted read as follows:
 1° 'The State acknowledges that the homage of public worship is due to Almighty God. It shall hold His Name in reverence, and shall respect and honour religion.
 2° The State recognises the special position of the Holy Catholic Apostolic and Roman Church as the guardian of the Faith professed by the great majority of the citizens.
 3° The State also recognises the Church of Ireland, the Presbyterian Church in Ireland, the Methodist Church in Ireland, the Religious Society of Friends in Ireland, as well as the Jewish Congregations and the other religious denominations existing in Ireland at the date of the coming into operation of this Constitution'.
 Paragraphs 2° and 3° were removed following a referendum in 1972 by the Fifth Amendment to the Constitution.
12. *Consultation Paper on the Crime of Libel* (August 1991), *Report on the Crime of Libel* (December 1991).
13. Defamation Act 2009, s 36(2).

[3.10] Significantly, there is also a statutory defence to the crime of blasphemy which attempts to balance this offence with the requirements of freedom of expression. Where a defendant can prove that a reasonable person would find genuine literary, artistic, political, scientific, or academic value in the matter to which the offence relates, this is a defence to a prosecution for blasphemy.[14]

[3.11] The Oireachtas, while significantly expanding the offence beyond its common law limitation to the Church of England, has defined religion to as to exclude certain organisations or cults.[15]

Blasphemy under the European Convention of Human Rights

[3.12] The interaction between blasphemy law and Article 10 of the European Convention on Human Rights has arisen in a number of cases.

[3.13] Following the granting of leave for a private prosecution in the *Lemon* case, the jury held that the editor and the publishing company were guilty of blasphemous libel. The convicted defendants brought proceedings under the European Convention on Human Rights. The European Commission on Human Rights ruled their application inadmissible.[16] Despite the difference of views among the Law Lords[17] on the mens rea of the offence, the Commission found that the law was clear enough and that the interpretation given by the Law Lords had been foreseeable with proper legal advice. The offence, in so far as it was interference with freedom of expression, was thus 'prescribed by law'. The Commission went on to consider whether the law had a legitimate aim. The UK government argued that the law of blasphemy aimed to prevent disorder, protect morals and protect the rights of others. The Commission rejected the first two of these arguments, noting that the UK government had not sought to prosecute the applicants. It found, however, that the protection of the rights of citizens not to be offended in their religious beliefs by publications was a legitimate aim. It went on to find that the law and the prosecution of the offence were 'necessary in a democratic society'. The Commission found that the strict liability nature of the offence did not render it disproportionate.

[3.14] The issue of blasphemy arose again in *Otto-Preminger-Institut v Austria*,[18] which concerned a public showing of a satirical film called 'Council of Heaven'. Prior to its premiere, the public prosecutor in Austria took criminal proceedings against the manager of the applicant institution and a court order for the seizure of the film was

---

14. Defamation Act 2009, s 36(3).
15. Defamation Act 2009, s 6(4) provides that 'religion' does not include any organisation or cult the principal object of which is making a profit or that employs oppressive psychological manipulation of its followers or for the purpose of gaining new followers.
16. *Gay News Ltd and Lemon v UK* (1982) 5 EHRR 123.
17. The House of Lords held by a 3:2 majority that that there was no requirement of an intention to blaspheme with four of the Law Lords agreeing that the state of the law on this point was unclear.
18. *Otto-Preminger-Institut v Austria* (1995) 19 EHRR 34. See discussion of this case in Pannick, 'Religious feelings and the European Court' [1995] Public Law 7.

made, followed by a forfeiture order. The Commission found by a majority that the seizure of the film and its forfeiture constituted violations of Article 10. The Commission found that the relevant Austrian law was aimed at protecting the rights of others and at preventing disorder by preserving religious peace. The court similarly emphasised the importance of religious freedom in a democratic society and stated that some methods of opposing or denying religious beliefs could inhibit persons holding those beliefs from expressing them. It also noted that respect for the religious feelings of believers – guaranteed by Article 9 of the Convention – could be violated by provocative portrayals of objects of religious veneration. The Commission took the view that the seizure was not necessary in a democratic society. It pointed out that the film was being shown late at night in an art-house cinema addressed to an interested audience, an admission fee was charged and there was a warning about the contents of the film. A majority of the Commission considered these conditions adequate to protect the rights of others by preventing the viewing of the film by children and anyone who might be offended. The complete ban by the State was disproportionate in these circumstances and the forfeiture was also disproportionate. A majority of the court took a different view, finding that both the seizure and the forfeiture were necessary in a democratic society to protect the rights of the majority of the population from gratuitous insults to religious feelings. The seizure of the film to ensure public peace was thus within the margin of appreciation of the Austrian State.

[3.15] In *Wingrove v UK*,[19] the European Court of Human Rights found that a refusal by the British Board of Film Classification (BBFC) to classify the film *Visions of Ecstasy* on the ground that it violated the criminal law of blasphemy was foreseeable. The BBFC was required to refuse to classify works which infringed the provisions of the criminal law and counsel had advised that the film in question was blasphemous. In *Wingrove*, the applicant argued that the rights of others proviso in Article 10 of the Convention referred only to an actual right not to be offended and that it could not include a hypothetical right of some individuals to avoid disturbance at the prospect of other people watching the work without being so shocked. The Commission and the court rejected this argument. The applicant argued that there was no pressing social need to ban the video work on the assumption that it would violate the law on blasphemy. The applicant pointed out that the alternative was to allow the circulation of the video and to prosecute post-distribution. He also argued that the ban was disproportionate to the aim pursued. The court found that the ban was necessary in a democratic society and that it was within the State's margin of appreciation. The court did acknowledge that some states had abolished the law of blasphemy and that there were arguments in favour of so doing. Overall, however, it found that there was insufficient evidence of a consensus in the legal and social orders of the Member States to find that the restriction of blasphemous material was unnecessary in a democratic society.

[3.16] In *IA v Turkey*,[20] the court considered the prosecution by the respondent state of the managing director of a publishing firm. The firm had published a novel containing

---

19.   *Wingrove v UK* (1996) 24 EHRR 1.
20.   *IA v Turkey* (2007) 45 EHRR 30.

offensive criticism of Mohammed and Islam. A majority of the court made reference to the judgment in *Handyside* to the effect that Article 10 protects speech which offends and shocks but went on to conclude that the conviction of the applicant was necessary in a democratic society on the basis of the mild nature of the sanction and the content of the expression at issue. The majority felt that the relevant parts of the novel went further than offending and shocking readers and included an abusive attack on the Prophet of Islam. The three dissenting judges[21] agreed that certain passages in the novel were deeply offensive to devout Muslims but disagreed with the approach of the majority which relied on these isolated passages as a justification for banning the entire novel and criminalising its publication. They also took issue with the majority's emphasis on the mildness of the sanction imposed on the basis that any sanction could have a chilling effect on free speech and encourage self-censorship. The dissenting judgments also noted that the decisions in *Otto-Preminger-Institut* and *Wingrove* were controversial at the time and that it might be time to 'revisit' this case law.

[3.17] A differently constituted chamber of the court considered the application of Article 10 to a conviction and fine for blasphemy in *Aydin Tatlav v Turkey*.[22] The penalties related to the publication of a book entitled 'The Reality of Islam.' The court took the view that the book was critical of Islam but not abusive or insulting in its tone so that the prosecution was not 'necessary in a democratic society'. The court noted that limited penalty but noted that the possibility of a conviction with potential for a custodial sentence could discourage publication of non-conformist views about religion which would hinder the protection of pluralism which was key to the healthy development of a democratic society.

[3.18] In *Klein v Slovakia*,[23] the court again considered the limits of Article 10 in the context of causing offence to religious sensibilities. In this case, a weekly magazine had published an article by the applicant (a journalist and film critic) in which he had criticised an archbishop for his televised appeal to withdraw the film *The People v Larry Flint* and the poster advertising it. The article contained colloquialisms and innuendos with oblique sexual connotations. It also alluded to the archbishop's alleged collusion with secret police under the former communist regime and invited members of the Catholic faith to leave their Church. The applicant was prosecuted for public defamation of a group of inhabitants of the republic for their belief and sentenced to a fine. The European Court of Human Rights found that the applicant's strongly worded opinion related only to the archbishop and the fact that some Catholics might have been offended by this and by his call to leave the Catholic Church did not alter this. The court found that despite the vulgar tone of the article, its publication did not interfere with the right to freedom of religion of others in such a way as to justify a criminal penalty. The court found that the interference with his freedom of expression did not correspond to a pressing social need and was not proportionate to the aim pursued. It is noteworthy that the court also found that the conviction 'pursued the legitimate aim of protection of the

---

21. Judges Coista, Cabral Barreto and Jungwiert.
22. *Aydin Tatlav v Turkey* (Application No 50692/99) 2 May 2006.
23. *Klein v Slovakia* (Application No 72208/01) 31 October 2006.

rights of other persons whose religious feelings, as the Slovak authorities concluded, had been offended by the applicant's article.'[24]

RELIGIOUS ADVERTISING

The statutory provisions

[3.19] Section 20(4) of the Broadcasting Act 1960 prohibited RTÉ from accepting any advertisement 'which is directed towards any religious or political end'[25] or which had 'any relation to an industrial dispute.' An identical obligation was placed on independent broadcasters by s 10(3) of the Radio and Television Act 1988. The Broadcasting Act 2001 relaxed the prohibition slightly, providing in s 65 that the provisions just described did not prevent 'the broadcasting of a notice of the fact that (a) a particular religious newspaper, magazine or periodical is available for sale or supply, or (b) any event or ceremony associated with any particular religion will take place' provide that the contents of the notice did 'not address the issue of the merits or otherwise of adhering to any religious faith or belief or of becoming a member of any religion or religious organisation.'

[3.20] The prohibition has been furthered narrowed by s 41(4) of the Broadcasting Act 2009 which prohibits the broadcast of 'an advertisement which addresses the issue of the merits or otherwise of adhering to any religious faith or belief or of becoming a member of any religion or religious organisation.' While this narrower prohibition, which seems to be targeted primarily at proselytising, is a lesser interference with freedom of expression, it is interesting to note that the earlier blanket ban on religious advertising was found to be constitutional by the Supreme Court in *Murphy v IRTC*.[26] Perhaps more surprisingly, it was also found to be 'necessary in a democratic society' by the European Court of Human Rights in *Murphy v Ireland*.[27]

The *Murphy* litigation

[3.21] *Murphy* arose when a pastor wished to advertise on the radio a screening of a video on the resurrection of Christ during Easter week in Dublin.[28] The IRTC rejected the advertisement on the basis of s 10(3) of the 1988 Act. The High Court upheld the decision, as did the Supreme Court, on appeal. Barrington J considered whether the

---

24. *Klein v Slovakia* (Application No 72208/01) 31 October 2006, para 45. The conviction was 'prescribed by law' as the relevant offence was set out in the Slovak Criminal Code, Art 198.
25. The issue of political advertising is considered in **Ch 4**.
26. *Murphy v IRTC* [1999] 1 IR 12.
27. *Murphy v Ireland* (2004) 38 EHRR 13.
28. The script for the advertisement was as follows: 'What think ye of Christ? Would you, like Peter, only say that he is the son of the living God? Have you ever exposed yourself to the historical facts about Christ?) The Irish Faith Centre are presenting for Easter week an hour long video by Dr Jean Scott PhD on the evidence of the resurrection from Monday 10th to Saturday 15th April every night at 8.30 and Easter Sunday at 11.30 and also live by satellite at 7.30pm.'

restriction imposed on freedom of expression by s 10(3) was proportionate to the aim which this prohibition pursued. He noted that it was:[29]

> ... clear from the foregoing analysis of the legislation that the Oireachtas wished to protect society from certain dangers which it perceived. The real question is whether the limitation imposed upon the various constitutional rights is proportionate to the purpose which the Oireachtas wished to achieve ...

> ... In the present case the limitation placed on the various constitutional rights is minimalist. The applicant has the right to advance his views in speech or by writing or by holding assemblies or associating with persons of like mind to himself. He has no lesser right than any other citizen to appear on radio or television. The only restriction placed upon his activities is that he cannot advance his views by a paid advertisement on radio or television ...[30]

[3.22] Describing the restriction in his rights as 'very slight', Barrington J went on to apply the proportionality test developed in *Heaney v Ireland*[31] as follows:[32]

> [I]t therefore appears to the Court that the ban on religious advertising contained in s 10(3) of the Act of 1988 is rationally connected to the objective of the legislation and is not arbitrary, unfair or based on irrational considerations. It does appear to impair the various constitutional rights referred to as little as possible and it does appear that its effects on those rights are proportional to the objective of the legislation.[33]

[3.23] The somewhat mechanical application of the *Heaney* proportionality test does not really engage with the constitutional requirements of free speech. The applicant argued

---

29. He also considered whether the prohibition was contrary to Article 44 of the Constitution which protects freedom to profess and practise religion.
30. Barrington J drew a distinction between the restriction in this case and that found to be disproportionate in *Cox v Ireland* [1992] 2 IR 503 where a person convicted of an offence could lose his job and be barred from resuming his profession as a teacher.
31. In *Heaney*, Costello J set out the test as follows:
> In considering whether a restriction on the exercise of rights is permitted by the Constitution, the courts in this country and elsewhere have found it helpful to apply the test of proportionality, a test which contains the notions of minimal restraint on the exercise of protected rights, and of the exigencies of the common good in a democratic society. This is a test frequently adopted by the European Court of Human Rights and has recently been formulated by the Supreme Court in Canada in the following terms. The objective of the impugned provision must be of sufficient importance to warrant over-riding a constitutionally protected right. It must relate to concerns pressing and substantial in a free and democratic society. The means chosen must pass a proportionality test. They must:
> (a) be rationally connected to the objective and not be arbitrary, unfair or based on irrational considerations,
> (b) impair the right as little as possible, and
> (c) be such that their effects on rights are proportional to the objective ...' *Heaney v Ireland* [1994] 3 IR 593, 607.
32. *Heaney v Ireland* [1994] 3 IR 593, 26.
33. *Heaney v Ireland* [1994] 3 IR 593, 27–28

that a selective ban targeting only offensive religious advertising would have had less of an impact on freedom of expression while achieving the same end. Barrington J accepted this but stated that:

> [T]he Oireachtas may well have decided that it would be inappropriate to involve agents of the State in deciding which advertisements, in this sensitive area would be likely to cause offence and which not. In any event, once the Statute is broadly within the area of the competence of the Oireachtas and the Oireachtas has respected the principle of proportionality, it is not for this Court to interfere simply because it might have made a different decision.[34]

[3.24] Barrington J noted that the ban on religious advertising was one of three:

> One can best glean the policy of the Act of 1988 by looking at the three kinds of prohibited advertisement collectively. One might get a false impression by singling out one kind of banned advertisement and ignoring the others. All three kinds of banned advertisement relate to matters which have proved extremely divisive in Irish society in the past. The Oireachtas was entitled to take the view that the citizens would resent having advertisements touching on these topics broadcast into their homes and that such advertisements, if permitted, might lead to unrest. Moreover the Oireachtas may well have thought that in relation to matters of such sensitivity, rich men should not be able to buy access to the airwaves to the detriment of their poorer rivals.[35]

[3.25] Following the dismissal of his appeal by the Supreme Court, the applicant in *Murphy* initiated proceedings in the European Court of Human Rights.[36] The court found, unsurprisingly, that there had been an interference with the applicant's rights. Referring back to its seminal judgment in *Handyside v United Kingdom*,[37] the court noted that 'even expression which could be considered offensive, shocking or disturbing to the religious sensitivities of others falls within the scope of the protection of Article 10'.[38] The parties accepted that this was prescribed by law and the court accepted the government's argument that the measures had a legitimate aim, which the court paraphrased as follows:

> ... that the prohibition sought to ensure respect for the religious doctrines and beliefs of others so that the aims of the impugned provision were public order and safety together with the protection of the rights and freedoms of others.[39]

[3.26] The court went on to consider whether the restriction was necessary in a democratic society. The judgment stated that while the margin of appreciation was narrow in the context of political speech, in matters pertaining to religion and personal

---

34. *Murphy v IRTC* [1999] 1 IR 12, 27.
35. *Murphy v IRTC* [1999] 1 IR 12, 22.
36. *Murphy v Ireland* (2004) 38 EHRR 13.
37. *Handyside v United Kingdom* (1979–1980) 1 EHRR 737.
38. *Murphy v Ireland* (2004) 38 EHRR 13, 61.
39. *Murphy v Ireland* (2004) 38 EHRR 13, 63. The court referred back to its decision in *Otto-Preminger-Institut v Austria* (1995) 19 EHRR 34.

morals, the Member States enjoyed a greater discretion.[40] The court specifically distinguished its earlier decision in *Vgt Verein gegen Tierfabriken v Switzerland* (*Tierfabriken I*)[41] where it had held that a similar ban on political advertising was disproportionate. The court held in *Murphy* that *Tierfabriken I* concerned an advertisement 'on a matter of public interest to which a reduced margin of appreciation applied'.[42]

[3.27] The court emphasised the importance of 'pluralism, tolerance and broad-mindedness' and stated that Article 10 did not 'as such, envisage that an individual is to be protected from exposure to a religious view simply because it is not his or her own'.[43] It went on to state that it was possible for expression which was not facially offensive to cause offence in certain circumstances. The judgment of the court placed great emphasis on the government's submissions regarding religious sensitivities in Ireland and the finding of the Supreme Court that the legislation addressed subjects that had been 'extremely divisive in Irish society in the past'. The European Court of Human Rights also emphasised the limited nature of the restrictions which applied only to broadcasting of advertisements and left open other possible means of expression. It accepted the submission by the government that broadcasting presented particular issues due to its potential impact on the audience. The applicant in the case argued that the aim of the legislation could be achieved through less invasive means. The court accepted the government's submission 'that the exclusion of all religious groupings from broadcasting advertisements generates less discomfort than any filtering of the amount and content of such expression by such groupings'.[44] Emphasising that there was a lack of consensus among the Member States on the issue of religious advertising, the court found that the government had established relevant and sufficient reasons to justify the interference with freedom of expression.

[3.28] The approach taken by the European Court of Human Rights in *Murphy* is consistent with its approach in *Otto Premiger* and *Wingrove* in that it allows the respondent state a wide margin of appreciation in the restriction of religious expression.[45] As can be seen from the post-*Murphy* case law from Strasbourg, considered above, the court may be moving away from that approach. It is noteworthy that both the Supreme Court and the European Court of Human Rights were prepared to accept that the absolute ban considered in *Murphy* was proportionate on the basis of the State's argument that a more selective measure would prove unworkable, partly because

---

40.   *Murphy v Ireland* (2004) 38 EHRR 13, para 67.
41.   *Vgt Verein gegen Tierfabriken v Switzerland* (*Tierfabriken I*) (2002) 34 EHRR 4.
42.   *Murphy v Ireland* (2004) 38 EHRR 13, para 67. See *Colgan v IRTC* [2000] 2 IR 490, which applied the decision of the Supreme Court in *Murphy* to the ban on political advertising. See discussion of the ban on political advertising in **Ch 4**.
43.   *Murphy v Ireland* (2004) 38 EHRR 13, para 72.
44.   *Murphy v Ireland* (2004) 38 EHRR 13, 77.
45.   For criticism of the decision of the European Court of Human Rights in *Murphy*, see Geddis, 'You can't say "God" on the radio: Freedom of expression, religious advertising and the broadcast media after *Murphy v Ireland*' [2004] 2 European Human Rights Law Review 2004, 181.

it would involve the State in adjudicating between different religions. The fact that the narrower ban in the Broadcasting Act 2009 requires precisely that exercise suggests that the old ban was never 'proportionate' at all. The point is of more than historical interest given the retention in the Broadcasting Act 2009 of the absolute ban on political advertising.[46]

INCITEMENT OF HATRED

[3.29] As well as the criminal offence of blasphemy, there is also a provision in the Video Recordings Act 1989[47] which permits the censor to refuse a certificate or to prohibit a video recording if the video 'would be likely to stir up hatred against a group of persons in the State or elsewhere on account of their … religion'. The Prohibition of Incitement to Hatred Act 1989 uses a similar definition in s 1.

[3.30] Apart from incitement of religious hatred, the Prohibition of Incitement to Hatred Act 1989 covers hatred against a group of persons in the State or elsewhere on account of their race, colour, nationality, religion, ethnic or national origins, membership of the travelling community or sexual orientation.[48] There is an exemption for fair and accurate reports of proceedings in the Oireachtas or of judicial proceedings in s 5.

[3.31] The Act prohibits the publication and distribution of written material and recorded material, including broadcasting thereof. It also makes it an offence to make, prepare or be in possession of material likely to stir up hatred.[49] The prohibition in respect of broadcasting has been imported into the Broadcasting Act 2009 by s 71(6) which contains a statutory clause for content provision contracts which allows the Broadcasting Authority of Ireland to end contract provision where a programme breaching the Prohibition of Incitement to Hatred Act 1989 is broadcast and requires it to do so where this has happened more than once in a six-month period.

[3.32] While the Act has potentially far-reaching consequences for freedom of expression, it has not led to a flood of prosecutions either for individuals or for the media[50] although a complaint was made about one journalist to Gardaí in 2008 arising from an article he had written in the *Irish Independent*.[51]

---

46.   See **Ch 8**.

47.   See Video Recordings Act 1989, s 3 (certification) and s 7 (prohibition orders). The Video Recordings Act 1989 is discussed further below.

48.   See the definition of 'hatred' in the Prohibition of Incitement to Hatred Act 1989, s 1.

49.   See Prohibition of Incitement to Hatred Act 1989, s 4.

50.   There have been only a few recorded prosecutions. In one it was held that the abusive language used was unlikely to incite hatred: (1999) *Irish Times,* 2 March, and (2001) *Irish Times*, 14 March 2001. In another, a successful prosecution was brought against an individual in the Dublin District Court for making racist remarks (2002) *Irish Times*, 5 July.

51.   The Immigrant Council of Ireland made a complaint to Gardaí concerning an article published by journalist Kevin Myers published in the *Irish Independent*. See (2008) *Irish Times*, 16 July.

[3.33] While the Prohibition of Incitement to Hatred Act 1989 is far-reaching in criminalising the making, preparation or possession of material likely to stir up hatred, the prohibitions on publication and broadcasting of such material is not an unusual feature of the law in many countries.[52] The US Constitution protects such speech and permits its criminalisation only where it makes imminent violence likely[53] but it is seemingly alone in this tolerance of such speech.

[3.34] The approach of the European Court of Human Rights has been twofold. In *Lehideaux and Isornia v France*,[54] the court stated that where material is directed at attacking the Convention's underlying values, it may fall outside the scope of protection of Article 10.[55] In *Glimmerveen and Hagenbeeck v Netherlands*,[56] Article 10(1) was held to cover speech which incited racial discrimination but the applicant's conviction for distributing leaflets expressing such sentiments was justified. The court in that case relied also on Article 17 of the Convention which provides that:

> Nothing in this Convention may be interpreted as implying for any State, group or person any right to engage in any activity or perform any act aimed at the destruction of any of the rights and freedoms set forth herein or at their limitation to a greater extent than is provided for in the Convention.

[3.35] As far as the Irish media are concerned, it is worth noting that the breadth of the Prohibition of Incitement to Hatred Act 1989 is such that it potentially catches reporting of extremist views. Prosecution of the media (as opposed to the person expressing the objectionable view) for such reporting has been found to be incompatible with Article 10. In *Jersild v Denmark*,[57] the European Court of Human Rights held that it was a

---

52. For a discussion of the justifications for such legislation, see Abel, *Speech and Respect* (Sweet and Maxwell, 1994); Hare and Weinstein, *Extreme Speech and Democracy* (Oxford University Press, 2009). See also Hare and Weinstein, 'Free Speech and Democracy' [2009] Entertainment Law Review 287.

53. See *Beauharnais v Illinois* 343 US 250 (1952); *National Socialist Party of America v Village of Skokie* 432 US 43 (1977); *RAV v City of Saint Paul* 505 US 377 (1992); *Virginia v Black* 538 US 343 (2003), See Schaeur, 'The Exceptional First Amendment' The Canadian Supreme Court's decision in *R v Keegstra* [1990] 3 SCR 697 takes an approach closer to that of the European Court of Human Rights. See also *R v Krymowski* [2005] 1 SCR 101. As recently as 2006, the UK enacted the Racial and Religious Hatred Act. This covers the media but only where the intention in publication or broadcast is to stir up religious hatred.

54. *Lehideaux and Isornia v France* (2000) 30 EHRR 665.

55. The material in that case supported a pro-National Socialist policy. Although see also Kuhnen v FRG (1988) 56 DR 205 where it was found that the conviction of the applicant for advocating the reinstitution of the Nazi Party was a matter which fell to be considered under Art 10(1), albeit one that was 'necessary in a democratic society' under Art 10(2). See also *Soulas v France* (Application No 15948/03) 10 July 2008 (French text only) and *Le Pen v France* (Application No 18788/09) 20 April 2010 (French text only).

56. *Glimmerveen and Hagenbeeck v Netherlands* (1979) 18 DR 187.

57. *Jersild v Denmark* (1994) 19 EHRR 1.

breach of Article 10 to convict a journalist in respect of racist views expressed in a pre-recorded radio programme by an extremist group.

OBSCENITY AND 'INDECENT MATTER'

[3.36] Censorship of the media on the grounds of obscenity, while seemingly a relic of a bygone era, is still a feature of the legal system. What constitutes obscenity is a problematically subjective determination and one prone to change over time and it has been said that:

> The problem of drawing a legal line between moral outrage and personal freedom has become intractable at a time when one person's obscenity is another person's moral outrage.[58]

[3.37] As Keane CJ noted in *Melton Enterprises Ltd v The Censorship of Publications Board Ireland*:[59]

> The history of obscenity laws in many countries affords eloquent testimony of just how subjective such determinations, whether made by judges, juries or other bodies, can be. It would, however, be difficult to find a more graphic illustration than the operations of the [Censorship of Publications] Board itself at an earlier stage of its history, when it prohibited the sale and distribution in Ireland of a vast range of books as being indecent or obscene, many of which would now be generally acknowledged to be masterpieces of 20th century literature.

[3.38] It is common case that censorship of material can be counterproductive in that it often generates publicity for the material concerned. Thus DH Lawrence's *Lady Chatterley's Lover* sold three million copies following its prosecution in 1961. *Inside Linda Lovelace* had sold a few thousand copies before facing a court case in 1976. Following its acquittal, 600,000 copies were sold within three weeks.[60] The internet has made attempts to censor the circulation of such material even less effective.

[3.39] That is not to say that there is no active censorship on moral grounds. The IFCO's recent decision to prohibit the DVD release of a film originally banned in 1978[61] indicates that views on some moral issues at least remain unchanged.[62]

---

58. Robertson and Nicol, *Media Law* (4th edn, Penguin Books, 2002), 154.
59. *Melton Enterprises Ltd v The Censorship of Publications Board Ireland* [2000] 3 IR 623.
60. Robertson and Nicol, *Media Law* (4th edn, Penguin Books, 2002), 155.
61. Zarchi's *I Spit on Your Grave* was banned by the IFCO in September 2010 on the basis that it depicts acts of gross violence and cruelty including torture towards humans. See (2010) *Irish Times*, 24 September, 'Ultimate video nasty stays banned in Ireland'.
62. Cf *EMI Records (Ireland) Ltd v Eircom Ltd* [2010] IEHC 108, High Court, Charleton J, 16 April 2010 where the judge referred to contractual arrangements in an internet service provision agreement which preclude the user from downloading obscene images and images in breach of copyright as 'a step taken in pursuance of a corporate policy that is no less than lawful and proper.' [2010] IEHC 108, para 29.

[3.40] The various statutory censorship regimes that apply to the print, film and broadcast media are considered below.[63] These include references to obscenity and indecency as well as other grounds for censorship. As well as specific censorship legislation, the media are also subject to a range of statutory and common law rules which make the publication of indecent or obscene material a criminal offence.

References to indecency and obscenity in the Constitution

[3.41] The Constitution refers specifically to 'indecent matter' in Article 40.6.1°(i). While there is no further guidance as to the meaning of the phrase in the Constitution, the Censorship of Publications Acts 1929 (the 1929 Act) provides in s 2 that 'the word 'indecent' shall be construed as including suggestive of, or inciting to sexual immorality or unnatural vice or likely in any other similar way to corrupt or deprave.'[64]

[3.42] The Constitution makes no reference to obscenity. At common law, there was a long recognised offence of obscene libel and this was supplemented in 1857 by the Obscene Publications Act which permitted magistrates to destroy immoral books within their jurisdiction.[65] The Act contained no definition of obscenity but the dictum of Lord Cockburn in *R v Hicklin*[66] encapsulates the common law definition as follows:

> I think the test of obscenity is this, whether the tendency of the matter charged as obscenity is to deprave and corrupt those whose minds are open to such immoral influences, and into whose hands a publication of this sort may fall.[67]

[3.43] The Constitution Review Group recommended that the publication or utterance of indecent matter should not be a constitutional offence and that these references should be taken out. It recommended their replacement with text providing for the regulation by law of obscene material to enable the legislature to balance freedom of expression against the public interest in prohibiting degrading portrayals of women and the need to protect children.[68]

Offence of obscene libel has been abolished

[3.44] Reference was made to the existence of the common law offence of obscene libel by Keane CJ in *Melton Enterprises Ltd v The Censorship of Publications Board Ireland*.[69] Section 13 of the Defamation Act 1961 also created a statutory offence of composing, printing or publishing obscene libel.[70] The statutory offence of obscene libel

---

63.   **[3.55]–[3.87]**.
64.   The same definition is repeated in the Censorship of Publications Act 1946, s 1.
65.   *R v Hicklin* (1868) LR 3 QB 360.
66.   *R v Hicklin* (1868) LR 3 QB 360.
67.   *R v Hicklin* (1868) LR 3 QB 360, 371.
68.   *Report of the Constitution Review Group* (1996), Pn 2632, 299–300.
69.   *Melton Enterprises Ltd v The Censorship of Publications Board Ireland* [2003] 3 IR 628.
70.   There was no statutory definition of what constituted obscenity in the context of the Defamation Act 1961. See Hogan and Whyte, *Kelly: The Irish Constitution* (4th edn, Bloomsbury Professional, 2003), 1754.

under the UK Obscene Publications Act 1959 has been held to be sufficiently clear in its components to be compatible with Article 7 of the European Convention on Human Rights.[71] Section 35 of the Defamation Act 2009 repeals both the statutory and common law offences in this jurisdiction.

Outraging public decency

[3.45] The common law recognises an offence of outraging public decency[72] which may still form part of Irish law. While the parameters of the offence are not entirely clear, it has been described as 'performing any indecent activity in such a place or way that more than one member of the public may witness and be disgusted by it'.[73] The modern case law requires two elements to be proved: first, that the act was of such a lewd character as to outrage public decency; and secondly, that the act took place in a public place and must have been capable of being seen by two or more persons who were actually present although those persons need not have actually seen it.[74]

[3.46] The offence has been applied in a range of other situations and was relied on in *R v Gibson and Sylveire*[75] to prosecute the defendants for the exhibition of a sculpture comprised of a human head with freeze-dried human fetuses as earrings.[76] A magazine publisher was prosecuted for conspiracy to outrage public decency in *Knuller (Publishing Printing and Promotions) Ltd v DPP*[77] arising from the publication of contact advertisements for homosexuals. The offence has survived challenge in the European Court of Human Rights[78] and is still prosecuted in the English courts.[79]

[3.47] The UK Law Commission is currently reviewing this area[80] and has provisionally recommended that the offence of outraging public decency be retained but that the mens rea required to prove the offence be clarified so that a person must intend to outrage public decency or be reckless as to same. The Commission took the view that this would address issues around artistic censorship on the basis that 'where the work is truly of

71. See *R v Perrin* (22 March 2002, unreported), Court of Appeal of England and Wales; *Perrin v UK* (Application No 5446/03) 18 October 2005 (Fourth Section), decision on admissibility.
72. *Knuller (Publishing Printing and Promotions) Ltd v DPP* [1973] AC 435; *R v Gibson* [1991] 1 AER 439.
73. Consultation Paper, para 3.1.
74. *R v Hamilton* [2008] QB 224, para 21.
75. *R v Gibson and Sylveire* [1991] 1 AER 439.
76. For criticism of the case, see Lewis, 'Human Earrings, Human Rights and Public Decency' [2002] Entertainment Law Review 50.
77. *Knuller (Publishing Printing and Promotions) Ltd v DPP* [1973] AC 435.
78. *S and G v United Kingdom* (Application No 17634/91) 2 September 1991.
79. See, for examples, *R v Pedley* (14 May 2009, unreported), Court of Appeal of England and Wales.
80. Consultation Paper, *Simplification of Criminal Law: Public Nuisance and Outraging Public Decency* (Law Commission, 2010). See www.lawcom.gov.uk/docs/cp193.pdf.

artistic importance, the jury can always find that, though the effect of outraging the public was foreseeable and indeed foreseen, the decision to take the risk was justified'.[81]

Indecent or obscene performance

[3.48] The common law also recognises an offence of indecent or obscene performance which was used to prosecute theatrical performances.[82] The decision in *Attorney General v Simpson*[83] arose out of a prosecution in the District Court where the accused was charged with showing 'for gain an indecent and profane performance'.[84] The judgment was given at the preliminary investigation stage in the District Court. The accused was charged on three counts of showing for gain an 'indecent and profane' performance. The District Judge said that, strictly speaking, the charges were more in the nature of indecent exhibition than obscenity, but proceeded to quote from a treatise on criminal law[85] the following passages which equated the two offences:

> The offence described as obscene libel, which in former editions of this work was placed in collocation with blasphemous, seditious and defamatory libel, seems more properly to belong to the law of public mischief. In general all open lewdness, grossly scandalous, and whatever openly outrages decency or is offensive and disgusting, or is injurious to public morals by tending to corrupt the mind and destroy the love of decency, morality and good order, is a misdemeanour indictable at common law. The acts which fall within the general definition may be classified as (i) obscene publications, (ii) obscene or indecent exhibitions; and (iii) indecent exposure of the human body.

> Indecent Exhibitions – Exhibitions of an obscene, indecent or grossly offensive and disgusting character which do not fall within the definition of obscene libel are, nevertheless, regarded as indictable misdemeanours; such as the performance of an obscene and indecent play.

[3.49] The District Judge granted a request that the words 'and obscene' be placed after the word 'indecent' in two of the counts, stating 'it might well be held that profanity and indecency and obscenity are related offences'. The Law Reform Commission disagreed with that view, stating that '[w]hatever about the relation between obscenity and indecency, profanity only occasionally intersects with these two concepts and such intersection is not a logical necessity.'[86]

---

81. Consultation Paper, *Simplification of Criminal Law: Public Nuisance and Outraging Public Decency* (Law Commission, 2010), para 5.51.
82. See *Consultation Paper on the Crime of Libel* (Law Reform Commission, 1991), para 128.
83. *Attorney General v Simpson* (1959) 93 ILTR 33.
84. The Law Reform Commission has noted that at common law the offence was publication of obscene matter *simpliciter*, and it was in legislation only that the 'for gain' aspect was introduced. The performance giving rise to the charge was of a Tennessee Williams play, *The Rose Tattoo*, at the Pike Theatre, Herbert Lane, Dublin; *Consultation Paper on the Crime of Libel* (Law Reform Commission, 1991), para 128.
85. *Russell on Crime* (12 edn, Stevens, 1964), 778.
86. *Consultation Paper on the Crime of Libel* (Law Reform Commission,1991), para 129.

[3.50] The District Judge also seemed to mix the concepts of obscenity and indecency when he referred to Article 40.6.1°(i) and its prohibition on indecency, concluding:

> There we have a clear statement of the concern with the elimination of indecency or obscenity in our various means of communication in order to protect the public interest and foster the general good, the elimination, I should say, of things which violate the natural law and are responsible for serious harm to the community.

The District Judge went on to say that as there was no Irish authority, the appropriate law was the English common law and the decisions concerning obscenity under the Obscene Publications Act 1857. He accepted *Hicklin* as the case laying down the central test of obscenity, but said the law in England was 'extremely vague' and that the authorities were conflicting.[87]

Miscellaneous examples of statutory measures regulating obscenity and indecency

[3.51] There are a large number of statutory provisions creating offences connected with obscene or indecent publications or displays including the Vagrancy Acts 1824–1988, s 4; the Dublin Police Act 1842, s 14; the Towns Improvement (Ireland) Act 1854, s 72; the Customs Consolidation Act 1876, s 42; the Indecent Advertisements Act 1889 (retained by the Statute Law Revision Act 2007); the Post Office Act 1908, s 63 and the Post Office (Amendment) Act 1951, s 13 as amended by the Postal and Telecommunications Services (Amendment) Act 1999, s 7 and the Communications Regulation (Amendment) Act, s 11; the Criminal Justice (Public Order) Act 1994, s 7; the Child Trafficking and Pornography Act 1998, s 5; and the Electoral Act 1992, s 25(6)(b) as substituted by the Electoral (Amendment) Act 2001, s 11.

[3.52] The Criminal Justice (Public Order) Act 1994, s 7 provides that it is an offence for a person 'in a public place to distribute or display any writing, sign or visible representation which is threatening, abusive, insulting or obscene with intent to provoke a breach of the peace or being reckless as to whether a breach of the peace may be occasioned'.

---

87. He stated that his duty was to decide whether there was a prima facie case, asking 'Is the play a filthy play? That is the question.' Then he summarised what the play in his view portrayed and said:

> Does the play as described in the evidence tend to corrupt and deprave? Does it lead to certain lascivious thoughts and lustful desires which will affect character and action? Is the play a cloak for something sinister, and to repeat the words of Mr Justice Stable, 'is it camouflage to render the crudity, the sex of the book sufficiently wrapped up to pass the critical standards of the Director of Public Prosecutions?'

> Later, he said the question was whether the accused 'was exploiting a filthy business and showing a complete disregard of the primary requirements of decency?, and whether the accused intended to deprave and corrupt other persons. The reference to Justice Stable is from the case of *R v Secker and Warburg* [1954] 2 All ER 683.

[3.53] Under s 5 of the Child Trafficking and Pornography Act 1998, it is an offence knowingly to produce, distribute, publish, import, sell or display child pornography. Possession of child pornography is also an offence under s 6.

It is not generally an offence to have indecent or obscene material in one's private possession but customs authorities have the power to seize same under s 46 of the Customs Consolidation Act 1876.

[3.54] Section s 25(6)(b) of the Electoral Act 1992, as substituted by s 11 of the Electoral (Amendment) Act 2001 provides that the Registrar of Political Parties shall not grant a request for the registration of an emblem where it is 'obscene or offensive'.

Censorship of publications

[3.55] Censorship of publications is dealt with under the Censorship of Publications Acts 1929 to 1967. The 1929 Act was substantially repealed and amended by the Censorship of Publications Act 1946[88] (the 1946 Act) which established the Censorship of Publications Board.[89] The 1946 Act provides for a board constituted of five members appointed by the Minister for Justice. Section 3 of the 1946 Act provides for the establishment of the Censorship of Publications Appeal Board. The latter body is also comprised of five members – four ordinary members and a chairman who must be a judge of either the Supreme Court, the High Court or the Circuit Court, or a practising barrister or solicitor of not less than seven years' standing.

[3.56] The Censorship of Publications Board may examine books of its own volition or may have books referred to it by customs and excise officials under s 5.[90] Members of the public may also complain to the Board about books under the Censorship of Publications Regulations 1980.[91] Periodicals can only be examined by the Board where there is a complaint from a member of the public.

[3.57] As Keane CJ explained, describing the role of complainants in the Censorship of Publications Acts:

> [W]hen that code was introduced in Ireland for the first time in 1929, the Oireachtas and the Executive were of the view that it would have been an impractical and time wasting process to employ inspectors for the purpose of monitoring the vast range of books and periodicals on sale in the State. They relied instead on a system of voluntary complaints in the expectation, which was not disappointed, that there would be a significant number of persons or organisations willing to bring to the attention of the Board books and periodicals for examination by them.[92]

---

88. See also the Censorship of Publications Act 1967.
89. Censorship of Publications Act 1946, s 2.
90. Censorship of Publications Act 1946, s 5.
91. SI 292/1980, made by the Minister for Justice in exercise of the powers conferred on him by Censorship of Publications Act 1946, s 20.
92. *Melton Enterprises Ltd v The Censorship of Publications Board Ireland* [2003] 3 IR 628, 638.

Books

[3.58] In its examination of a book referred to it by an officer of customs and excise, or a member of the public, the Board is required to have regard to the following matters: the literary, artistic, scientific or historic merit or importance, and the general tenor of, the book; the language in which it is written; the nature and extent of the circulation which, in their opinion, it is likely to have; the class of reader which, in their opinion, may reasonably be expected to read it; and any other matter relating to the book which appears to them to be relevant.[93] The Board may communicate with the author, editor or publisher of the book and has a discretion to take into account any representation made by him relating to the book.[94]

[3.59] If, after examining a book, the Board is of the opinion that:

> … it is indecent or obscene or

> that it advocates the unnatural prevention of conception or the procurement of abortion or miscarriage or the use of any method, treatment or appliance for the purpose of such prevention or procurement, and that for any of the said reasons its sale and distribution in the State should be prohibited, they shall by order prohibit such sale and distribution.[95]

Books may only be prohibited for a maximum of 12 years.[96]

Periodicals

[3.60] Sections 9 and 10 of the 1946 Act deal with periodicals. Under these provisions, the board shall examine issues recently published of every periodical publication in respect of which it receives a complaint. The Board may prohibit the issues examined by it and future issues of the periodical where it is of the opinion that the issues have usually or frequently been obscene, have advocated the unnatural prevention of conception or the procurement of abortion or miscarriage or the use of any method, treatment or appliance for the purpose of such prevention or procurement, or have devoted an unduly large proportion of space to the publication of matter relating to crime.[97] The Board may prohibit the sale and distribution of the issues actually examined by it and any future issues. Periodicals may only be banned for defined periods of time – three, six or 12 months depending on the frequency of the periodical.[98]

---

93. Censorship of Publications Act 1946, s 6(2).
94. Censorship of Publications Act 1946, s 6(3).
95. Censorship of Publications Act 1946, s 7.
96. Censorship of Publications Act 1967, s 2.
97. Cf *Melton Enterprises Ltd v The Censorship of Publications Board Ireland* [2003] 3 IR 628 where the publishers of two periodicals sought to challenge the procedure by which the Board considered making prohibition orders in respect of those publications.
98. See the Censorship of Publications Act 1946, s 9(3).

Meaning of 'obscene' and 'indecent' under the Censorship of Publications Acts

[3.61] Those parts of the 1929 Act which were retained after 1946 include s 14 which makes it an offence to print or publish in relation to any judicial proceedings:

(a)   any indecent matter the publication of which would be calculated to injure public morals, or

(b)   any indecent medical, surgical or physiological details the publication of which would be calculated to injure public morals.

Bona fide technical publications for the legal professions are not covered by this prohibition.

[3.62] There is no definition given of 'obscene' in the Censorship of Publications Acts. The term 'indecent' is defined in s 1 as 'suggestive of, or inciting to, sexual immorality or unnatural vice or likely in any other similar way to corrupt or deprave'. Prior to the 1946 Act, the 1929 Act had used the phrase 'in its general tendency indecent or obscene' in place of the phrase 'indecent or obscene'. Hogan and Whyte note[99] that the dropping of the words 'general tendency' was understood to be a tightening up of censorship in that it suggested that isolated passages might be viewed as sufficient to justify prohibition. Kenny J, in *Irish Family Planning Association Ltd v Ryan*[100] found that the formulation had the same meaning under the 1946 Act as it had under the 1929 Act.

Censorship of abortion information

[3.63] Under s 16, as amended by s 12(i) of the Health (Family Planning) Act 1979, the printing, publishing, sale or distribution of 'any book or periodical publication ... which advocates or which might reasonably be supposed to advocate the procurement of an abortion or miscarriage or any method, treatment, or appliance to be used for the purpose of such procurement' is prohibited.

[3.64] Section 14 of the Regulation of Information (Services Outside the State for Termination of Pregnancies) Act 1995 qualifies the prohibition by excluding from it any book or periodical:

> ...in so far, but only in so far, as Act information is published in the printed or written matter, book or periodical publication, advertisement or notice or in a book or publication to which the printed or written matter, advertisement or notice relates and the information and the method and manner of its publication are in compliance with this Act.

Books and periodicals that advocated contraception were potentially caught by the legislation and publications which advocated abortion remained subject to censorship.

---

99.   Hogan and Whyte, *Kelly: The Irish Constitution* (4th edn, Bloomsbury Professional, 2003), 1758 (fn 135).

100.   *Irish Family Planning Association Ltd v Ryan* [1979] IR 295.

[3.65] The protection of the right to life of the unborn inserted into the Irish Constitution following the adoption of the Eighth Amendment in 1983 also gave rise to difficulties as it was thought that the advertisement of abortion information was in breach of this provision. In *AG (Society for the Protection of the Unborn Child (Ireland) Ltd) v Open Door Counselling Ltd*,[101] the plaintiff[102] (known as SPUC) sought a declaration that the activities of the applicant companies in counselling pregnant women within the jurisdiction of the court to travel abroad to obtain an abortion were unlawful having regard to Article 40.3.3° of the Constitution which protects the right to life of the unborn and an order restraining the defendants from such counselling or assistance. One of the issues which arose in the course of the litigation was whether there existed a constitutional right to information about the availability of abortion outside the State. Finlay CJ, in the Supreme Court, upheld the High Court decision to grant an injunction restraining the defendants from their activities[103] and went on to consider the application of Article 40.6.1°(i) in the context of the information provided by the defendants. He found that:

> [T]here could not be an implied and unenumerated constitutional right to information about the availability of a service of abortion outside the State which, if availed of, would have the direct consequence of destroying the expressly guaranteed constitutional right to life of the unborn. As part of the submission on this issue it was further suggested that the right to receive and give information which, it was alleged, existed and was material to this case was, though not expressly granted, impliedly referred to or involved in the right of citizens to express freely their convictions and opinions provided by Article 40, s.6, sub-s 1(i) of the Constitution, since, it was claimed, the right to express freely convictions and opinions may, under some circumstances, involve as an ancillary right the right to obtain information. I am satisfied that no right could constitutionally arise to obtain information the purpose of the obtaining of which was to defeat the constitutional right to life of the unborn child.[104]

[3.66] The matter was brought before the European Court of Human Rights by the defendant counselling service providers.[105] A majority of the court (15:8) found that the injunction breached Article 10 of the Convention. It was accepted that the injunction interfered with their right to impart information and the right of other joined individuals to receive information in the event of being pregnant. The court found that the interference was prescribed by law and that it had a legitimate aim – the protection of morals. It went on to find, however, that the interference was not proportionate to the aim. In so holding, it noted that information was available from magazines and other

101.   *AG (Society for the Protection of the Unborn Child (Ireland) Ltd) v Open Door Counselling Ltd* [1988] IR 593.
102.   The action was converted into a relator action brought at the suit of the Attorney General by order of the High Court on 24 September 1986.
103.   The terms of the injunction were altered in the Supreme Court from that ordered in the High Court.
104.   *AG (Society for the Protection of the Unborn Child (Ireland) Ltd) v Open Door Counselling Ltd* [1988] IR 593, 625.
105.   *Open Door and Dublin Well Woman v Ireland* (1993) 15 EHRR 244.

sources, the perpetual nature of the injunction, the fact that it was not a criminal offence to travel to have a termination and the fact that the services were lawful in other Convention countries.

[3.67] In November 1992, shortly after the European Court of Human Rights gave its decision finding Ireland in breach of Article 10 of the Convention, the electorate adopted by referendum two proposals amending Article 40.3.3°. The second of these dealt with the provision of information about termination services. It provides that the protection of the right to life of the unborn 'shall not limit freedom to obtain or make available, in the State, subject to such conditions as may be laid down by law, information relating to services lawfully available in another state.'

[3.68] The Regulation of Information (Services Outside the State for the Termination of Pregnancies) Act 1995 amended the Censorship of Publications Acts so as to exempt publications complying with the new regulations regarding abortion information from censorship.[106]

Constitutional challenges to the Censorship of Publications Acts

[3.69] In *Irish Family Planning Association Ltd v Ryan*,[107] one of the plaintiff's publications had been banned and it challenged the Censorship of Publications Acts on the basis that, among other things, they were contrary to the rights of citizens to express their own opinions and to impart information and ideas without interference by public authority, subject to public order and morality. This constitutional question was not reached as the Board lost the case on a narrower ground that the Board had acted contrary to fair procedures.

[3.70] In *Melton Enterprises Ltd v The Censorship of Publications Board Ireland*,[108] the Supreme Court considered a constitutional challenge to the Censorship of Publications Act 1946 on the basis that the Board created thereunder was exercising judicial functions not of a limited nature, contrary to Article 37.1. Keane CJ gave the judgment of the court in which he rejected that challenge. He held that while there could be criminal consequences for breaching the legislation, the Board itself did not determine criminal liability. He also held that any judicial functions exercised by the Board were limited in their ambit.[109]

Appeals from decisions of the Censorship of Publications Board

[3.71] Appeals against prohibition orders may be brought to the Appeals Board in respect of prohibited books[110] and periodicals[111] – this was a feature absent from the

---

106. Regulation of Information (Services Outside the State for the Termination of Pregnancies) Act 1995, s 14.
107. *Irish Family Planning Association Ltd v Ryan* [1979] IR 295.
108. *Melton Enterprises Ltd v The Censorship of Publications Board Ireland* [2003] 3 IR 628.
109. *Re Solicitors Act 1954* [1960] IR 239 distinguished.
110. Censorship of Publications Act 1946, s 8.
111. Censorship of Publications Act 1946, s 10.

1929 Act and introduced by the creation of an Appeal Board under s 3 of the 1946 Act. While the Act is silent on the matter, an appellant who is unsuccessful before the Appeals Board may take judicial review proceedings in the usual way. Aggrieved members of the public wishing to force the Censorship of Publications Board to prohibit works may face difficulties in establishing the necessary locus standi. [112]

Censorship of publications and the requirements of procedural fairness

[3.72] The Censorship of Publications Board and the Appeals Board are, like all similar bodies, obliged to observe the constitutional requirements of fair procedures in performing their functions. The requirements of fair procedures may vary in different contexts. The courts have considered some aspects of these requirements under the Censorship of Publications Acts.

[3.73] In *Irish Family Planning Association Ltd v Ryan*,[113] their failure to communicate with the plaintiff to allow it to defend the publication rendered the decision to prohibit the publication void. Kenny J pointed out that such an obligation to communicate would not arise in a case of patent pornography as that would frustrate the censorship of anonymous pornography. As the publication in question was in more of a grey area, however, the Board was required to communicate with the publisher.

[3.74] In *Melton Enterprises Ltd*, the appellants were the publishers of a two periodicals. The Board had written to them indicating that it was considering making a prohibition order in respect of one of them. On request, the Board provided the appellant with a copy of the substance of the complaint received by it but it refused to reveal the identities of the complainants. Keane CJ, giving the judgment of the Supreme Court, stated that:

> Undoubtedly, the requirements of fairness and openness demand that the publishers should be furnished with all the material in the complaints and the Board must at least consider whether they should be invited to make representations to the Board in respect of the complaints.

He did not, however, consider that it was necessary for the Board to reveal the identity of any complainant. This was because the role of the complaint was merely to trigger the consideration of publication by the Board which must come to its own view independently. Keane CJ noted that:

> Whether the complainant is a public figure whose particular status might lead to his or her view that a publication should be banned (*sic*) being treated with respect by some members of the public, or is a crusading zealot whose views might only evoke support from those of a similar way of thinking, or is a meddlesome crank

---

112.   An attempt to judicially review an alleged failure by the Censorship of Publications Board to prohibit the *Examiner* newspaper for publishing advertisements for massage services was refused leave on the basis that it was out of time. The judgment also indicates that the applicant did not have locus standi. See *Grimes v Censorship of Publications Board, ex tempore* (22 February 2000, unreported), HC, Smyth J.

113.   *Irish Family Planning Association Ltd v Ryan* [1979] IR 295.

or busybody or is even a business competitor of the publisher are not factors which the Board are entitled to take into account in any way when reaching the purely subjective opinion they are required to form. [114]

Register and list of prohibited publications

[3.75] Section 16 of the 1946 Act provides for the keeping of a register of prohibited publications by the board and provides that that the fact that a publication is at any particular time entered in the register shall be conclusive evidence that a prohibition order has been made in regard to it and that the order is at that time still in force. Customs and excise officers examining baggage of incoming travellers have a duty under s 16(6) to exhibit on demand a list of all prohibited publications.

Censorship of films

[3.76] The censorship of films in Ireland is governed by the Censorship of Films Act 1923–1992. The 1923 Act established the office of the Irish Film Censor and provided for a system of film classification which still operates today. In 2008[115] the name of the body was changed to 'the Irish Film Classification Office' (IFCO) and the title of Film Censor was changed to Director of Film Classification.

Films shown in public must be fit for viewing

[3.77] Under the 1923 Act, no film may be exhibited in public unless the Director of Film Classification certifies that it is suitable and a certificate must be exhibited to that effect.[116] Under s 7(2) of the Act, the Director of Film Classification may refuse to certify a film where it (or some part of it):

> ...is unfit for general exhibition in public by reason of its being indecent, obscene or blasphemous or because the exhibition thereof in public would tend to inculcate principles contrary to public morality or would be otherwise subversive of public morality.'

The Director of Film Classification may prohibit a film or impose conditions or restrictions on its exhibition.

[3.78] Subsequent legislation retained the provisions of the 1923 Act and extended the regime set up thereunder to 'talkies';[117] enabled the re-submission of films for certification following the lapse of a period of seven years[118] and enabled the Minister for Justice to appoint assistant censors to assist the Official Censor of Films to perform

---

114. *Melton Enterprises Ltd v The Censorship of Publications Board Ireland* [2003] 3 IR 628.
115. The Civil Law (Miscellaneous Provisions) Act 2008.
116. For a history of film censorship in the State, see Rockett, *Irish film censorship: a cultural journey from silent cinema to internet pornography* (Four Courts Press, 2004).
117. Censorship of Films (Amendment) Act 1930.
118. Censorship of Films (Amendment) Act 1970.

his functions.[119] Under the Censorship of Films (Amendment) Act 1925, the provisions of the 1923 Act were applied to trailers[120] so that these must be certified as fit for public viewing also.

[3.79] The 1925 Act also censors any pictorial poster, card, handbill, or other pictorial advertisement for a film, providing that the Official Censor may prohibit the display of these where he is of the opinion that such an advertisement is 'unfit for display in public by reason of its being indecent, obscene, or blasphemous, or because the display thereof in public would convey suggestions contrary to public morality or would be otherwise subversive of public morality'.[121]

[3.80] The Censorship of Films (Amendment) Act 1970 provided that new applications for certificates could be made for films which had been refused a certificate prior to January 1965. The Act also builds in the opportunity to make new applications once seven years have elapsed from the date of refusal of a certificate.

Video recordings and DVDs

[3.81] The Video Recordings Acts 1989–1992[122] extended the reach of film censorship to this new medium, described in the Act as a 'video work'. This is defined in s 1 as:

> ...any series of visual images (whether with or without sound) (a) produced, whether electronically or by other means, by the use of information contained on any disc or magnetic tape, and (b) shown as a moving picture.

[3.82] The Director of Film Classification may refuse to certify a video as being fit for viewing under s 3. The meaning of unfitness in this context is fleshed out in s 3(1) which provides that a video is unfit for viewing where: it would be likely to cause persons to commit a crime; it would be likely to stir up hatred against a group of persons on account of their race, colour, nationality, religion, ethnic or national origins, membership of the travelling community or sexual orientation; it would tend to deprave or corrupt because it is obscene or indecent; it depicts acts of gross violence or cruelty (including mutilation and torture) towards humans or animals.

[3.83] He may also make a prohibition order in respect of a video where it is not fit for viewing according to the same test. Once a prohibition order is made in respect of a video, it is an offence to possess it for the purpose of supplying it to another; to supply

---

119. Censorship of Films (Amendment) Act 1992.
120. Censorship of Films (Amendment) Act 1925, s 2.
121. Censorship of Films (Amendment) Act 1925, s 3.
122. The Censorship of Publications (Amendment) Act 1992 provided for the appointment of Assistant Censors. Section 4 of this Act amended the Video Recordings Act 1989, s 10 by providing that where a video was granted a higher classification as a result of an appeal, the fee for the appeal would be refunded to the appellant. By virtue of s 6(2) of the Act, it and those parts of it that referred to the Video Recordings Act 1989 are cited collectively as the Video Recordings Acts 1989–1992.

or offer to supply it; to exhibit it other than in a private dwelling and to import it into the State without a permit.

Refusals of certification

[3.84] Where certification of a film or video is refused by the Director of Film Classification, s 8 of the Censorship of Films Act 1923 provides for a right of appeal to an appeals board. If the appellant is successful before the board, a certificate must be granted. Where an appellant is unsuccessful and wishes to challenge the decision of the appeals board, he may do so by way of judicial review.

The Civil Law (Miscellaneous Provisions) Act 2008

[3.85] The Civil Law (Miscellaneous Provisions) Act 2008 made a number of changes to the Censorship of Film and Video Recordings Acts.[123] It provided for a statutory offence for retailers supplying DVDs to children under the age specified in the film classification.[124] Penalties for breaches of both Acts were also increased.

It also introduced a requirement to consider the 'likely to cause harm to children' provision under s 7(2) of the Censorship of Films Act 1923[125] so that films must pass that test if they are to be certified as fit for viewing.

Video games

[3.86] Video games are exempted from the classification scheme under the Video Recordings Acts 1989–1992,[126] but may be prohibited. A prohibition order has been issued in respect of at least one video game[127] where it was judged to be unfit for viewing under s 7(1)(b) of the Video Recordings Act 1989 which refers to 'acts of gross violence or cruelty (including mutilation and torture)'.

Censorship of films and fair procedures – duty to give reasons

[3.87] In determining whether to certify, classify or prohibit a film, the IFCO is bound by the usual requirements of fair procedures, including a duty to give reasons. In *Byrne v The Official Censor*,[128] the High Court held that the duty to give reasons for the initial refusal of certification was met in that case by the repetition of the words in s 3(1)(a)(iii) of the statute that the video 'would tend, in the opinion of the censors by reason in the inclusion in it of obscene or indecent matter, to deprave or corrupt persons who might view it' and that the failure to give any further statement of reason – for example

123. See the Civil Law (Miscellaneous Provisions) Act 2008, s 69.
124. See the Civil Law (Miscellaneous Provisions) Act 2008, ss 70 and 71.
125. See the Civil Law (Miscellaneous Provisions) Act 2008, s 70(c).
126. IFCO is a member of Pan European Game Information which operates an age rating system for video games primarily aimed at parents. See www.pegi.eu.
127. A prohibition order was made by IFCO in relation to the video game *Manhunt 2* on 18 June 2007.
128. *Byrne v The Official Censor* (21 December 2007, unreported), HC, O'Higgins J.

identifying which particular parts of the video were objectionable – did not render the appeals process unfair.[129]

Obscenity and indecency in the European Court of Human Rights

[3.88] Article 10(2) of the European Convention on Human Rights provides for restrictions on the exercise of freedom of expression for the protection of morals. The court has tended to give the states a wide margin of appreciation in the cases that have come before it which raise issues of morality.

[3.89] In the case of *Handyside v UK*,[130] the court considered whether the seizure of a publication and subsequent prosecution and conviction of the publisher under the Obscene Publications Acts 1959 and 1964 was contrary to Article 10. The publication was designed to be read by 12- to 18-year olds and included chapters on sex, including homosexual sex, drugs and pornography. The book was anti-authoritarian in tone, for example it made no reference to marriage in any of the discussions of sex. The police seized the book and the manuscript and the applicant was convicted and fined under the Obscene Publications Acts 1959 and 1964. The trial judge had taken the view that the book was likely to 'deprave and corrupt' a substantial proportion of its intended readers in its challenges to authority, including parental authority and the teachings of the Church. The court found that the law was sufficiently clear to pass the requirement that an interference with Article 10 rights be 'prescribed by law' and accepted that the law on obscene libel had a legitimate aim – the protection of morals.

[3.90] The applicant argued that the seizure of the book and prosecution and conviction were not necessary in a democratic society, pointing out that the book was on sale in a number of states in Europe. He also pointed out that no prosecution had been brought in the Isle of Man or Northern Ireland. The court emphasised heavily the margin of appreciation enjoyed by states in the field of moral censorship. It noted that a revised edition of the book had been permitted to circulate freely which suggested that the authorities were not disproportionate in their interference with free speech.

[3.91] In a paragraph which summarised the approach taken in a number of subsequent cases concerning restrictions based on morality, the court held that:

> [I]t is not possible to find in the domestic law of the various Contracting States a uniform European conception of morals. The view taken by their respective laws of the requirements of morals varies from time to time and from place to place, especially in our era which is characterised by a rapid and far-reaching evolution of opinions on the subject. By reason of their direct and continuous contact with the vital forces of their countries, State authorities are in principle in a better position than the international judge to give an opinion on the exact content of

---

129.   The applicant was the owner of an adult shop who had sought certification for a video work entitled *Anabolic Initiations '#5'*.

130.   *Handyside v UK* (1976) 1 EHRR 77.

these requirements as well as on the 'necessity' of a 'restriction' or 'penalty' intended to meet them.[131]

Mosley J's dissent was critical of the approach of the majority in assuming that the prosecution had a legitimate aim[132] and in failing to address adequately the proportionality of the State's actions in the case.

[3.92] A similarly deferential approach was taken in *Muller v Switzerland*,[133] where the court considered the confiscation of paintings depicting homosexuality and bestiality in crude forms. It noted in that case that there was no warning to the audience about the content of the exhibition. There was no age limit, nor was there a charge for entry to the exhibition, and it was accessible even to small children.[134]

[3.93] In *Scherer v Switzerland*,[135] the Commission suggested that the conviction of the proprietor of a sex shop for showing explicit video for homosexuals violated Article 10. It pointed out that the audience was self-selecting and that it was unlikely that any person would be confronted with the videos against their will. It also noted that only a limited number of consenting adults who chose to pay the admission fee would see the film and it would not be visible from the street. The case was not considered by the court.[136]

[3.94] The decisions of the court in *Otto Premiger Institut* and *Wingrove*, discussed above,[137] are further examples of a generous approach to State interference with free speech in the interests of protecting morality.

[3.95] In *Perrin v UK*[138] the applicant was convicted under the Obscene Publications Act for publishing web pages with extreme photographs. Having repeated its comments in *Handyside* and *Muller* concerning the lack of consensus between European states in the area of morality, the court emphasised the margin of appreciation enjoyed by the UK.

[3.96] The court was not swayed by the argument that the contested site was operated and published by a US-based company and that the material was lawfully available in other states.

[3.97] The applicant in the case was convicted on three counts of obscene publication. The first related to a preview page for which there was no need to register. The other two

---

131. *Handyside v UK* (1976) 1 EHRR 77, para 48.
132. He pointed out that the prosecution had not been shown to have had any effect in terms of protecting young people.
133. *Muller v Switzerland* (1988) 13 EHRR 212.
134. *Muller v Switzerland* (1988) 13 EHRR 2121, para 36.
135. *Scherer v Switzerland* (1994) 18 EHRR 276.
136. The case was struck out of the list and never came before the court. Compare with the Commission decision on admissibility in *Hoare v UK* (Application No 31211/96) 2 July 1997 where obscene tapes were subject to no further controls once supplied.
137. **[3.14]** and **[3.15]**.
138. *Perrin v UK* (Application No 5446/03) 18 October 2005 (Fourth Section), decision on admissibility.

related to material subsequently accessed by a police officer, having subscribed to the site. The approach of the court draws no distinction between these even though it is arguable that penalising the first alone might have constituted a lesser interference with freedom of expression.

[3.98] The court ignored this aspect of the factual circumstances of the case, noting that:

> [I]t would have been possible for the applicant to have avoided the harm and, consequently, the conviction, while still carrying on his business, by ensuring that none of the photographs were available on the free preview page (where there were no age checks). He chose not to do so, no doubt because he hoped to attract more customers by leaving the photographs on the free preview page.

In the face of suggestions that the Act was ineffective in its purported aim of protecting morals, the court held that 'the fact that the 1959 Act may provide only limited protection to vulnerable people is no reason why a responsible Government should abandon the attempt to protect them'.

[3.99] The court also emphasised that the purpose of the expression was:

> ... purely commercial and there is no suggestion that it contributed to any public debate on a matter of public interest or that it was of any artistic merit: the applicant's conviction cannot therefore be said to engender any obviously detrimental chilling effect.

[3.100] In relation to the 30 months' imprisonment to which the applicant was sentenced, the court refused to find the length or the fact of the imprisonment disproportionate. It noted that:

> [G]iven that the applicant stood to gain financially by putting obscene photographs on his preview page, it was reasonable for the domestic authorities to consider that a purely financial penalty would not have constituted sufficient punishment or deterrent.

It thus found that the complaint by the applicant was manifestly unfounded and refused to refer it to a full hearing.

Advertising

[3.101] Advertisements in the media are subject to the same requirements as other communications as well as some additional requirements, including the Indecent Advertisements Act 1889.

[3.102] Print ads are covered by the Censorship of Publications Act 1929. Section 17 of that Act prohibits advertisements that relate or refer to any sexual disease, complaint or infirmity or to the prevention or removal of irregularities in menstruation or abortifacients. As originally enacted, the Act prohibited advertisements for contraceptives but these were removed by s 12(2) of the Health (Family Planning) Act 1979.

[3.103] Billboards in public places are covered by the Indecent Advertisements Act 1889.[139]

[3.104] Trailers for films are covered by s 2 of the Censorship of Films (Amendment) Act 1925. They are subject to the same rules as films themselves discussed above. The 1925 Act also covers any pictorial poster, card, handbill, or other pictorial advertisement. Under s 3(1), these must be submitted to IFCO along with any film in respect of which an application for a certificate is made. Under s 3(2), where the Director of Film Classification may prohibit such advertisements where he is of the view that they are unfit for public display because they are 'indecent, obscene, or blasphemous, or because the display thereof in public would convey suggestions contrary to public morality or would be otherwise subversive of public morality.

[3.105] By virtue of s 2 thereof, provisions of the Broadcasting Act 2009 which regulate the content of programme material apply to the broadcasting of advertisements. In addition, the Act precludes religious and political advertising and restricts the amount of advertising to a daily maximum of 15% of total broadcasting time and a maximum of 10 minutes in any hour may be given to advertisements.[140]

[3.106] The Broadcasting Authority of Ireland is required to produce and revise codes of conduct relating to advertising. These include a code ensuring that advertising, teleshopping material, sponsorship and other forms of commercial promotion employed in any broadcasting service protect the interests of children and, in the case of advertising which relates to matters likely to be of direct or indirect interest to children, protect the interests of children, with particular regard to their health.[141] The BAI General Communications Code also covers advertising of specific products such as alcohol and medicines.

In addition to the above, the Advertising Standards Authority of Ireland, which is a self-regulatory body, operates a Code of Conduct with which its members are required to comply.[142]

---

139. See also the Misuse of Drugs Act 1984, s 5 which makes it an offence to publish, sell or distribute printed matter including any advertisements for controlled drugs.
140. Broadcasting Act 2009, s 41.
141. Broadcasting Act 2009, s 42(2)(g) and (h). For the current versions of these codes, BAI Rules on Advertising & Teleshopping (Daily and Hourly Limits) 2010, BAI Children's Commercial Communications Code 2010 available from www.bai.ie.
142. Available from www.asai.ie. The ASAI also publishes a bulletin indicating its decisions in respect of complaints received by it on its website. See also the Alcohol, Marketing, Communications and Sponsorship Code of Practice 2008.

Chapter 4

THE MEDIA AND POLITICS

INTRODUCTION

[4.01] The media coverage of political affairs has traditionally been the primary source of information about those matters for most citizens. While the growth of the internet may provide an opportunity for other arenas of political discussion in the form of blogs, chatrooms and other virtual platforms, the role of the traditional mass media is still seen to be crucial. The contribution of the media to political discourse is indispensable. It is, as argued in **Ch 1**, one of the primary rationales for the constitutional guarantee of media freedom of expression. In that chapter, it was noted that there is a school of thought which suggests that the protection of political expression must necessarily involve some form of regulation to safeguard the integrity of the political process itself. This seems to be the justification relied upon for the regulation of broadcasting around elections and referenda – discussed further below. The former s 31 ban,[1] which lapsed in 1994, generated some case law which, while it may seem out of step with modern jurisprudence in its restrictive view of free speech, is nonetheless part of the body of law concerning media freedom of expression and it is also covered in this chapter. The Irish State places a prohibition on the broadcasting of 'political advertising'. That prohibition, while it has been upheld by the Supreme Court, is almost certainly contrary to Article 10 of the European Convention on Human Rights. The House of Lords has recently ruled in favour of retaining the United Kingdom's prohibition on such advertising.[2] These developments are discussed below. Finally, the content-based restrictions discussed in this chapter all target broadcasting while leaving other forms of media alone. The concluding section of this chapter assesses whether this special treatment is justified, particularly given the growing use of the internet as a medium of political discourse. The particular importance of media commentary on political affairs has been recognised under the Irish Constitution and the European Convention on Human Rights and that jurisprudence is dealt with in **Ch 2**.

NEWS AND CURRENT AFFAIRS – THE REQUIREMENT OF IMPARTIALITY

Section 39 of the Broadcasting Act 2009

[4.02] Broadcast coverage of news and current affairs is required to observe a principle of impartiality. This is currently reflected in s 39 of the Broadcasting Act 2009[3] which

---

1. The Broadcasting Act 1960, s 31, discussed below **[4.54]–[4.72]**.
2. See the decision of the House of Lords in *R (Animal Defenders International) v Secretary of State for Culture, Media and Sport* [2008] 2 WLR 781 discussed **[4.119]–[4.127]**.
3. The Radio and Television Act 1988 (s 9) and the Broadcasting Act 1960 (s 18(1) as amended by the Broadcasting (Amendment) Act 1976.) formerly contained these obligations.

provides that broadcasters must ensure that 'all news broadcast by the broadcaster is reported and presented in an objective and impartial manner and without any expression of the broadcaster's own views'[4] and that:

> the broadcast treatment of current affairs, including matters which are either of public controversy or the subject of current public debate, is fair to all interests concerned and that the broadcast matter is presented in an objective and impartial manner and without any expression of his or her own views, except that should it prove impracticable in relation to a single broadcast to apply this paragraph, two or more related broadcasts may be considered as a whole, if the broadcasts are transmitted within a reasonable period of each other.[5]

The role of the Broadcasting Authority and broadcasters

[4.03] The media are under an obligation, under s 39(5) of the Broadcasting Act 2009 to ensure that proposals concerning broadcasting policy are reported and presented in an objective and impartial manner. Under s 42 of the Act, the Broadcasting Authority is required to prepare a broadcasting code setting out these requirements of impartiality and objectivity.

[4.04] The Broadcasting Authority for Ireland is responsible for monitoring compliance with these requirements. It also monitors compliance with various codes of conduct.[6] The Code of Programme Standards[7] includes provisions relating to factual programming which cover current affairs and documentaries. These include a stipulation that references should not emphasise age, colour, gender, national or ethnic origin, disability, race, religion or sexual orientation unless such references are justified in the context of the programme or in the public interest.[8]

---

4. The Broadcasting Act 2009, s 39(1).
5. The Broadcasting Act 2009, s 39(2).
6. The Broadcasting Authority is required to prepare codes relating to various matters by virtue of the Broadcasting Act 2009, s 42. See the General Commercial Communications Code 2010; Children's Commercial Communications Code 2010. Code of Programme Standards (Broadcasting Commission of Ireland) 2007. All available from www.bai.ie.
7. Code of Programme Standards (Broadcasting Commission of Ireland) 2007. The Code was published by the Broadcasting Commission of Ireland in 2007. The functions of that body have since transferred to the Broadcasting Authority of Ireland under the Broadcasting Act 2009. The Code is available from www.bai.ie.
8. Broadcasting Commission of Ireland, Code of Programme Standards, at para 3.5.3. The remaining obligations in relation to factual programming set out in para 3.5 are that such factual programming should not contain material that could be reasonably expected to prejudice respect for human dignity, or cause undue distress or offence unless it is editorially justified and in the public interest. Factual programming is also permitted to emphasise age, colour, gender, national or ethnic origin, disability, race, religion or sexual orientation when such references are justified in the context of the programme or in the public interest. Such programmes must treat the dead with respect and the moment of death may not be shown nor shall the dead be shown in close-up unless, in exceptional circumstances, this may be justified in the public interest.

[4.05] Broadcasters themselves are obliged under s 47 of the Broadcasting Act 2009 to put in place a code of practice to deal with complaints which must be made generally available to the public. In addition, alleged breaches of s 39 or the Code of Programme Standards are dealt with by the Compliance Committee of the Broadcasting Authority of Ireland[9] which publishes its decisions regularly on its website.[10] While the decisions of the Committee do not constitute binding precedents as a matter of law, the vast majority of complaints are processed by the Committee and its approach is significant in practice. The section below sets out some of the principles that emerge from the Committee's published decisions in 2010.

Decisions of the Compliance Committee relating to impartiality

[4.06] One point to note is that the Committee has emphasised the importance of context when assessing whether there has been a breach of the requirements of s 39(2) and has had regard to the style of presentation of programmes with which the regular listener would be familiar when assessing a complaint.[11] In this regard, audience participation which leads to a debate that is 'challenging and robust' has been found to comply with s 39.[12]

[4.07] While there is generally a requirement to present more than one viewpoint in current affairs programmes, not every news item which simply reports on a matter opens up a debate which requires the inclusion of opposing points of view.[13] The fact that a programme may touch on current affairs does not necessarily mean that it is a current affairs programme. Thus where a complaint was made about the content of a programme reviewing a book advocating strong views about climate change, the fact that the three

9. The procedure for complaints is dealt with under the Broadcasting Act 2009, s 48. The Compliance Committee may deal with complaints in relation to objectivity & impartiality in news; fairness, objectivity & impartiality in current affairs; harm & offence under the Code of Programme Standards; law & order; and privacy of an individual. The Broadcasting Act 2009, s 48(1)(a)–(c). Complaints must be made within 30 days of a broadcast. Where a complaint relates to more than one broadcast, it must be made within 30 days of the later of the broadcasts complained of. Under the old legislation, the Broadcasting Complaints Commission had the function of hearing complaints. This function is now allocated to the Complaints Committee of the newly established Broadcasting Authority of Ireland.

10. See www.bai.ie. The names of complainants are generally reported in these decisions but the Authority may consider requests for anonymity in the context of complaints relating to privacy of an individual under s 48(1)(c).

11. Reference 197/10, 198/10 and 199/10, *Comer v RTÉ Radio 1* ('Today with Pat Kenny') Report of the Compliance Committee Meeting, 11 May 2010, 23.

12. Reference 212/10, *O'Brien v RTÉ One* ('The Frontline') Report of the Compliance Committee Meeting, 11 May 2010, 32.

13. Reference 238/10, *IRDA v RTÉ One* ('6.01 News') Report of the Compliance Committee Meeting, 15 June 2010, 57. See also Reference 167 and 169/10, *Connolly v RTÉ Radio 1* ('Liveline') Report of the Compliance Committee, Meeting 11 April 2010, 58.

reviewers all shared a similar viewpoint was found not to contravene the requirement of impartiality.[14]

[4.08] Generally, however, current affairs programmes are expected to put forward competing viewpoints. While the refusal of individuals representing a particular viewpoint on an issue to participate in a programme does not preclude the programme maker from airing it, the Committee has stated that there is a greater onus on the programme maker to ensure those missing viewpoints are represented in that situation.[15] Where a fresh allegation is made during a current affairs programme which has not up until that point been part of the public discourse on the issue, there may be an onus on a presenter to challenge same.[16]

[4.09] As for the role of the presenter, the Committee has upheld a complaint where radio interviewees have complained of inappropriate and unfair questioning.[17] Interruption of panel members during a discussion about current affairs is not, however, necessarily evidence of bias.[18] The Committee has also indicated that presenters may give their views provided they are based on an accurate presentation of the facts.[19] A presenter who works in other media formats and expresses views on an issue therein is not precluded from presenting programmes about the same issue where his position is made clear at the outset of the programme.[20]

[4.10] As noted above, these decisions are not binding legal authorities for the principles identifiable therein but are indicative of the approach of the Committee.

No appeals from decisions of the Compliance Committee

[4.11] It is worth noting that there is no provision in the Broadcasting Act 2009 for appealing from decisions of the Broadcasting Authority Compliance Committee. In

---

14. Reference 208/2010, *Stafford v RTÉ Radio 1* ('Off the Shelf') Report of the Compliance Committee Meeting, 11 May 2010, 30.
15. Reference 240/10, *Griffin v RTÉ One* ('Prime Time') Report of the Compliance Committee Meeting, 15 June 2010, 8. See related complaints: Reference 254/2010, *Kierans v RTÉ One*, Report of the Compliance Committee Meeting, 15 June 2010, 19; Reference 255/2010, *Murphy v RTÉ One*, Report of the Compliance Committee Meeting, 15 June 2010, 28; Reference 257/2010, *Leahy v RTÉ One*, Report of the Compliance Committee Meeting, 15 June 2010, 39; and Reference 265/10, *Jones v RTÉ One*, Report of the Compliance Committee Meeting, 15 June 2010, 48.
16. Reference 181/10, *O'Donoghue v RTÉ Radio 1* ('Drivetime') Report of the Compliance Committee Meeting, 11 April 2010, 32.
17. Reference 7/10, *Casey v Newstalk 106–108* ('The Wide Angle'), Report of the Compliance Committee Meeting, 11 May 2010, 8.
18. Reference 182/10, *O'Donoghue v RTÉ One* ('Prime Time') Report of the Compliance Committee Meeting, 11 April 2010, 68.
19. Reference 214./10, *MacGabhann v RTÉ One* ('6.01 News') Report of the Compliance Committee Meeting, 11 May 2010, 34.
20. Reference 241/10, *Donlon v 4 FM* ('McGurk on 4') Report of the Compliance Committee Meeting 15 June 2010, 62. See the related complaint, Reference 264/10, *Long v 4FM* Report of the Compliance Committee Meeting, 15 June 2010, 64.

many situations, complainants may have an alternative cause of action such as defamation or breach of privacy. Successful actions via those legal proceedings may vindicate the harm done to the complainant by the broadcast but they do not reverse the findings of the Compliance Committee as such. Potential litigants wishing to challenge those decisions specifically are thus left with the option of judicial review.

[4.12] In *R (on the Application of Ford) v Press Complaints Commission*,[21] the English High Court considered an application for leave to issue judicial review proceedings challenging a decision of the UK Press Complaints Commission. The complaint had been brought by a newsreader and related to photographs of her and her partner that had been reproduced in the press. She argued that these violated the provisions relating to privacy under the UK Press Commission's Code of Conduct. The Press Complaints Commission rejected the complaint. In considering her application for leave to challenge the decision of the Press Complaints Commission by way of judicial review, Silber J referred to the limited supervisory jurisdiction the court enjoyed in respect of the Press Commission, given the specialist expertise that body had.[22]

While the refusal of leave was based partly on the fact that the applicant was out of time, the decision suggests a very restrictive view of the potential for judicial review of bodies such as the Press Council.[23]

Referendum coverage

[4.13] The Irish Constitution may be amended by referendum with relative ease and referenda have been a recurring feature of the political life of the State.[24] Media coverage of referenda has an important role to play in educating and informing the public both of the content of referenda proposals and of the merits and consequences of a 'Yes' or 'No' vote. The question of referenda coverage in the media came before the courts in *McKenna v An Taoiseach (No 2)*.[25] In that case, the practice of the government of using public funds to finance its referendum campaigns was challenged. The case

21.   *R (on the Application of Ford) v Press Complaints Commission* [2001] EWHC Admin 683.
22.   *R (on the Application of Ford) v Press Complaints Commission* [2001] EWHC Admin 683, para 28. The judge referred to the previous decisions in *R v Broadcasting Standards Commission, ex parte British Broadcasting Corp* [2000] EMLR 587 and *R v Press Complaints Commission, ex parte Stewart Brady* [1997] EMLR 185; *R v Director of Public Prosecutions, ex parte Kebilene* [2000] 2 AC 326; *R v Secretary of State for the Home Department, ex parte Daly* [2001] 2 WLR 1622; *R v Secretary of State for the Home Department, ex parte Mahmood* [2001] 1 WLR 840.
23.   Compare *Brandon Book Publishing Ltd v RTÉ* [1993] ILRM 606, *O'Toole v RTÉ* [1997] ILRM 458 and *Madigan v RTÉ* [1994] 2 ILRM 472.
24.   A simple majority of the votes cast is sufficient to carry a referendum to amend the Constitution. See the Constitution, Articles 46 and 47 and the Referendum Acts 1994–2001. Referenda have held on 30 occasions since the promulgation of the Constitution, resulting in 22 amendments to the text. See O'Neill, 'The Referendum Process in Ireland' (2000) 35 Irish Jurist 305 for an account and analysis of the referendum procedure in Ireland.
25.   *McKenna v An Taoiseach (No 2)* [1995] 2 IR 10. In an earlier case, *McKenna v An Taoiseach (No 1)* [1995] 2 IR 1, Costello J had ruled that substantially the same complaint was non-justiciable.

arose in the context of the divorce referendum in 1995.[26] The government ran a campaign advocating a 'Yes' vote financed by £500,000 of public funds. Public funding of a government campaign had also been used in earlier referendum campaigns.[27]

[4.14] The Supreme Court upheld the right of the government to express its own position and views and to urge the acceptance of these views. It found, however, that the government was not entitled to use public funds to finance a campaign intended to induce a particular result in the referendum[28] and that this was unconstitutional.[29] The reasoning of the majority was based on the equality guarantee in Article 40.1, with two of the judges referring also to the right to fair procedures.[30] Denham J alone referred to freedom of expression in this context, stating that:

> The freedom to express opinions incorporates the corollary right that in the democratic process of free elections, public funds should not be used to fund one side of an electoral process, whether it be a referendum or a general election, to the detriment of the other side of the argument.[31]

[4.15] After the judgment of the Supreme Court in *McKenna (No 2)*, the Referendum Act 1998 was enacted. This Act established the Referendum Commission, and from that point on the government ceased all expenditure of public funds on referendum campaigns except for funding allocated to the Referendum Commission.

[4.16] The *McKenna (No 2)* decision was criticised for preventing the government from publicly funding constitutional changes that enjoyed popular support and impeding meaningful discussion on constitutional change.[32] The broad interpretation given to the

---

26. The narrow success of this referendum proposal (50.3% to 49.7%) led to the Fifteenth Amendment to the Constitution which removed the constitutional prohibition on divorce in Article 41.3.2°.
27. For prescient early criticism of this practice, see Quinn, 'The Systems-Maintenance Function of Constitutional Rights and the Case of Government Speech' (1989) 7 *Irish Law Times* 8.
28. Egan J dissented on the grounds that there being no specific prohibition on such expenditure, it was a matter for the executive to determine whether to use public funds in this way or not. *McKenna v An Taoiseach (No 2)* [1995] 2 IR 10, 46–47.
29. The judgment in *McKenna (No 2)* was delivered one week prior to the referendum itself. In a subsequent case, *Hanafin v Minister for the Environment* [1996] 2 IR 321, an unsuccessful challenge was brought to the outcome of the referendum on the basis that the government spending prior to *McKenna v An Taoiseach (No 2)* [1995] 2 IR 10 had tainted the referendum process.
30. See Hamilton CJ and Blayney J, *McKenna v An Taoiseach (No 2)* [1995] 2 IR 10, 42 and 50 respectively.
31. *McKenna v An Taoiseach (No 2)* [1995] 2 IR 10, 53.
32. The All-Party Oireachtas Committee on the Constitution, *Sixth Progress Report: Referendums* (Stationery Office, 2001), 16–17. See Barrett: 'Overall, the result of the combination of judicial activism in McKenna (No 2) and subsequent legislative lethargy has been the crippling of the power of democratically-elected governments to intervene in any effective sense in a referendum campaign, whilst private parties with no democratic mandate whatsoever suffer no equivalent such comprehensive disadvantage.' Barrett, 'Building a Swiss Chalet in an Irish Legal Landscape? Referendums on European Union Treaties in Ireland and the Impact of Supreme Court Jurisprudence' (2009) 5 European Constitutional Law Review 32, 58.

judgment by successive governments has also been criticised.[33] The decision also gave support to a subsequent case which had significant consequences for the media coverage of referendum campaigns.

[4.17] The applicant in *Coughlan v Broadcasting Complaints Commission*[34] had complained to the Broadcasting Complaints Commission[35] regarding RTÉ's coverage of the divorce referendum. The complaint related to the fact that RTÉ had permitted a number of political parties, all of whom were committed to a 'Yes' vote, to each have party political broadcasts transmitted during the referendum campaign. It had also allowed two non-party groups in favour of divorce and two non-party groups opposed to divorce to transmit programmes similar in form to party political broadcasts. In total 40[36] minutes of broadcasting time had been accorded to the 'Yes' side of the argument and only 10 minutes to the 'No' side of the argument. The applicant argued that this was contrary to s 18 of the Broadcasting Act 1960 as amended.[37] Section 18(1) required the impartial and objective reporting and presentation of news and current affairs. Section 18(2) stated that nothing in that section was to prevent the transmission of party political broadcasts.[38] The Broadcasting Complaints Commission rejected the complaint and the applicant took judicial review proceedings in the High Court.

[4.18] In the High Court, Carney J referred back to *McKenna (No 2)*, which he found to resolve the issue in favour of the applicant. Noting that RTÉ was bound under the Constitution and s 17(b) of the Broadcasting Act 1960[39] to uphold the democratic values of the Constitution, he found that 'a package of uncontested or partisan broadcasts by the national broadcasting service weighted on one side of the argument is an

---

33. Scott, 'The House that the Supreme Court Built: The Rulings in Coughlan and McKenna, the Lisbon Treaty and the Constitutional Referendum in Ireland' (2010) 10 Hibernian Law Journal 219.

34. *Coughlan v Broadcasting Complaints Commission* [2000] 3 IR 1.

35. The functions of the Broadcasting Complaints Commission have now passed to the Broadcasting Authority of Ireland under the Broadcasting Act 2009.

36. The accidental repeat broadcasting of one of the 'Yes' broadcasts added a further two-and-a-half minutes on to the 40-minute calculation but this was discounted by the High Court and the Supreme Court.

37. The Broadcasting Authority (Amendment) Act 1976, s 3.

38. The Broadcasting Act 1960, s 18, as amended by the Broadcasting Authority (Amendment) Act 1976, s 3, provided in relevant part that: '(1) Subject to subsection (1A) of this section, it shall be the duty of the Authority to ensure that (a) all news broadcast by it is reported and presented in an objective and impartial manner and without any expression of the Authority's own views; (b) the broadcast treatment of current affairs, including matters which are either of public controversy or the subject of current debate, is fair to all interests concerned and that the broadcast matter is presented in an objective and impartial manner and without any expression of the Authority's own views'. (2) 'Nothing in this section shall prevent the Authority from transmitting political party broadcasts.'

39. As amended by the Broadcasting (Amendment) Act 1976, s 13, this required RTÉ to 'uphold the democratic values enshrined in the Constitution, especially those relating to rightful liberty of expression' in its programming.

interference with the referendum process of a kind contemplated by Hamilton CJ as undemocratic and is a constitutionally unfair procedure.'[40]

[4.19] The Broadcasting Complaints Commission appealed the decision to the Supreme Court which upheld the decision of the High Court. Barrington J dissented from the majority decision. His dissent referred to the overall coverage of the referendum by RTÉ:

> It may well be that the second respondent is under a constitutional obligation to observe some kind of proportionality in the amount of time it allots to the private citizens collectively on the one hand and to the political parties on the other. In the present case it allotted approximately 98.5% of the time to monitored broadcasts between private citizens or private associations of citizens and something approximating to 1.5% of the time to the political parties. No one could say that this constituted a disproportionate bias in favour of political parties and no one has.[41]

[4.20] He went on to emphasise the important role politicians play in the referendum process and stated that '[i]n this context to play down, or neutralise, the role of political leaders in favour of committed amateurs would be, to say the least, unwise.'[42] He thus rejected the argument that RTÉ had acted in breach of the guarantee of equality under the Constitution by allowing the party political broadcasts to go ahead, noting:

> When the people are performing the ultimate act of sovereignty it is clearly right and proper that the views of all citizens should, so far as practicable, be heard. But it is also right and proper that the special position of political leaders should be recognised. In my view there is, in principle, no constitutional inequality or unfairness and no breach of democratic values in allowing political leaders access to the airwaves at referendum time on conditions dissimilar to those granted to private citizens but related to their social function as political leaders of the people.[43]

[4.21] The majority took a different view, finding that RTÉ was under an obligation, when permitting party political broadcasts in the context of a referendum, to make sure to 'hold scales equally between those who support and those who oppose the amendment'.[44]

[4.22] The difficulty with this is, of course, that RTÉ cannot control what is expressed in a party political broadcast. If there is a situation where a majority of parties are in favour of a referendum (which is commonly the case), how is RTÉ to respond? Denham J noted that:

> Mathematical equality is not a requirement of constitutional fairness and equality. However, if all the parties are either in favour of or opposed to a referendum then

40. *Coughlan v Broadcasting Complaints Commission* [2000] 3 IR 1, 12.
41. *Coughlan v Broadcasting Complaints Commission* [2000] 3 IR 1, 39.
42. *Coughlan v Broadcasting Complaints Commission* [2000] 3 IR 1, 43.
43. *Coughlan v Broadcasting Complaints Commission* [2000] 3 IR 1, 46.
44. *Coughlan v Broadcasting Complaints Commission* [2000] 3 IR 1, *per* Hamilton CJ at 25.

party political broadcasts become *prima facie*, unfair and unequal and the issue must be approached from the standpoint of the overall obligations imposed by the legislation and the Constitution ...

... It might be necessary to decide to hold no party political broadcasts in a referendum campaign.[45]

[4.23] Keane J also recognised this problem, stating:

It may be that, having regard to those circumstances, the present state of the law leaves the second respondent in the position that it cannot safely transmit party political broadcasts during the course of referendum campaigns as distinct from other campaigns. Whether the difficulties confronting the second respondent in this area can or should be dealt with by legislation and, if so, how, are not matters for this Court.[46]

[4.24] The decision in *Coughlan* was interpreted as requiring a rigidly equal allocation of campaign coverage by broadcasters between 'Yes' and 'No' viewpoints. After the people rejected the Lisbon Treaty in the first referendum on the issue,[47] the Broadcasting Commission of Ireland issued updated guidelines[48] in advance of the second referendum. These new guidelines state that while there is an obligation of fairness, objectivity and impartiality in the coverage of referenda, there is no requirement on broadcasters to allocate airtime between groups who oppose and support a referendum proposal on the basis of absolute equality. The allocation of airtime is required to be fair to all interests and undertaken in a transparent manner by editors.[49] News coverage must be reported and presented in an objective and impartial way and must not express the broadcaster's own views.[50] Current affairs coverage is subject to the guidelines and must also ensure that each side of the debate is presented in the same programme or in related programmes broadcast within a reasonable time of each other. Where programmes involve audience participation, there is an obligation to ensure that each side of the debate is fairly represented in the issues, questions or comments raised in the programme. Care must also be taken to ensure that extracts shown subsequently

---

45. *Coughlan v Broadcasting Complaints Commission* [2000] 3 IR 1, 32.
46. *Coughlan v Broadcasting Complaints Commission* [2000] 3 IR 1, 58.
47. Since the decision of the Supreme Court in *Crotty v An Taoiseach* [1987] IR 713, [1987] ILRM 400 successive governments have held referenda whenever Ireland proposes to sign a new Treaty involving further integration with the European Communities. As with the referendum on the Nice Treaty, the referendum on the Lisbon Treaty was defeated on its first vote in 2008.
48. Broadcasting Commission of Ireland, *Guidelines in Respect of Coverage of the Referendum on the Treaty of Lisbon and Related Constitutional Amendments 2009. Available from:* www.bci.ie/documents.
49. Broadcasting Commission of Ireland, *Guidelines in Respect of Coverage of the Referendum on the Treaty of Lisbon and Related Constitutional Amendments 2009*, para 4.
50. Broadcasting Commission of Ireland, *Guidelines in Respect of Coverage of the Referendum on the Treaty of Lisbon and Related Constitutional Amendments 2009*, para 5.

from such programmes on other programmes also reflect fairness, objectivity and impartiality.[51]

[4.25] With regard to party political broadcasts, the guidelines note that there is no requirement to carry party political broadcasts. They go on to provide, however, that if party political broadcasts are broadcast, equal airtime must be allocated to parties who support the referendum proposals and those who are against it.[52]

[4.26] The current position as regards referendum coverage has been criticised for its restriction of party political broadcasts for the reasons similar to those described by Barrington J in his dissent in *Coughlan*, namely that 'the absolutely equal allocation of broadcasting time for party political broadcasts in the context of referenda does not reflect the representation of the electorate'.[53] In the second Lisbon referendum, only one political party[54] which met the criteria for making a party political broadcast was advocating a 'No' vote and the other four parties[55] were all in favour of adopting the Treaty.

[4.27] After the second referendum on the Lisbon Treaty, the European Commission took a survey of Irish voters which found that 29% of respondents cited political parties as the most important information source about the referendum.[56] Given that *McKenna (No 2)* has impacted on the extent to which the government can campaign for a result, this restriction of party political broadcasts has been characterised as particularly unfortunate as the impact of that case was that politicians and political parties were left to advocate about referenda to the public.[57]

[4.28] Curiously, in neither *McKenna (No 2)* nor in *Coughlan* was any reference made in the judgments to the earlier decision of the High Court in *McCann v An Taoiseach*.[58] In that case, considered below, the Taoiseach was held to be allowed to direct the allocation of broadcasting time under s 31 of the Broadcasting Act 1960 to make a ministerial announcement regarding the forthcoming referendum on the Treaty on European Union.

---

51.   Broadcasting Commission of Ireland, *Guidelines in Respect of Coverage of the Referendum on the Treaty of Lisbon and Related Constitutional Amendments 2009,* para 6.
52.   Broadcasting Commission of Ireland, *Guidelines in Respect of Coverage of the Referendum on the Treaty of Lisbon and Related Constitutional Amendments 2009,* para 7.
53.   See Scott, 'The House that the Supreme Court Built: The Rulings in Coughlan and McKenna, the Lisbon Treaty and the Constitutional Referendum in Ireland' (2010) 10 Hibernian Law Journal 219.
54.   Sinn Féin.
55.   Fianna Fáil, Fine Gael, Labour and the Green Party.
56.   *Lisbon Treaty Post Referendum Survey Ireland 2009* (European Commission, October 2009), http://ec.europa.eu.
57.   Barrett, 'Building a Swiss Chalet in an Irish Legal Landscape? Referendums on European Union Treaties in Ireland and the Impact of Supreme Court Jurisprudence' (2009) 5 European Constitutional Law Review 32, 36.
58.   *McCann v An Taoiseach* [1994] 2 IR 1. The judgment (which was then unreported) was cited to the Supreme Court by counsel for the plaintiff in *McKenna (No 2)* [1995] 2 IR 10, 21 but not referred to in the judgments. In *Coughlan*, it appears not to have been cited at all.

Carney J expressly recognised that this announcement would be partisan but saw no constitutional difficulty with this and further, saw no constitutional necessity for a right of reply. The case is inconsistent with the Supreme Court's decision in *Coughlan* which implicitly overruled it.

The role of the Referendum Commission

[4.29] After the decision in *McKenna (No 2)*, the Referendum Act 1998 was enacted, establishing the Referendum Commission. The Referendum Commission is an independent body which convenes once a referendum is formally proposed.[59] The creation of a referendum commission in advance of each referendum is purely at the discretion of the Minister. As established in 1998, the Referendum Commission had three main functions: to prepare statements that would impartially outline the issues arising in the referendum; to outline arguments for and against the proposal and to endeavour to foster and facilitate debate or discussion in a fair manner.[60] The Referendum Act 2001 altered the function of the Commission and it is now only responsible for making the public aware that a referendum is due to take place, outlining the issues involved in the referendum and encouraging voter turnout.

[4.30] Under s 41(6) of the Broadcasting Act 2009, advertisements broadcast at the request of the Referendum Commission[61] do not fall within the prohibition on political advertising contained in s 41(3).[62] The Compliance Committee of the Broadcasting Authority of Ireland has also indicated that broadcasts by the Referendum Commission do not come within the scope of the General Advertising Code.[63]

Party political broadcasts and ministerial announcements

[4.31] Section 18(2) of the Broadcasting Act 1960 (as amended by the Broadcasting (Amendment) Act 1976) contained the provisions as to impartiality and objectivity discussed above in the context of the Broadcasting Act 2009. Section 18(2)(b) went on to provide that 'Nothing in this section shall prevent the authority from transmitting political party broadcasts.'[64] The content of the old provision in s 18(2) of the

---

59. In practice, this means that the Commission has relatively little time in which to prepare for the referendum. See Scott, 'The House that the Supreme Court Built: The Rulings in *Coughlan* and *McKenna*, the Lisbon Treaty and the Constitutional Referendum in Ireland' (2010) 10 Hibernian Law Journal 219. The Referendum Commission may be comprised of a former judge of the Supreme Court or the High Court (on nomination by the Chief Justice), the Clerk of the Seanad, the Clerk of the Dáil, the Ombudsman and the Comptroller and Auditor General.
60. For criticism of the Referendum Commission, see Mansergh, 'Two referendums and the Referendum Commission: The Irish Experience' (1999) Irish Political Studies 14.
61. See the Referendum Act 1998, s 3.
62. See [4.89].
63. Reference 565 and 566/10, *McKenna v RTÉ Radio 1* ('Referendum Commission Broadcast – Lisbon Treaty') Report of the Compliance Committee Meeting, 11 May 2010, 13.
64. Cf *R (on the application of Prolife Alliance) v British Broadcasting Corporation* [2004] 1 AC 185, where the BBC refused to broadcast a party election broadcast featuring graphic anti-abortion material on grounds of taste and decency.

Broadcasting Act 1960, regarding party political broadcasts has now been amended in the 2009 Act to specifically require fair allocation of time in the context of party political broadcasts.[65] The general provision relating to ministerial announcements has been omitted from the 2009 Act which contains only a more limited provision requiring the co-operation of broadcasters in the event of an emergency.[66]

[4.32] The old provisions on ministerial announcements were considered in *McCann v An Taoiseach*.[67] The Minister for Communications had issued a direction under s 31(2) of the Broadcasting Authority Act 1960. This provided that the Minister could direct RTÉ to allocate broadcasting time for any announcements by or on behalf of any Minister of State in connection with the functions of that Minister of State. In the instant case, the Minister had directed such an allocation of broadcasting time for a ministerial announcement by the Taoiseach in relation to the referendum on the Treaty on European Union. There was no provision made for a replying broadcast. The plaintiff assumed that the intended broadcast would be partisan in favour of the proposed amendment and argued that it could not be characterised as 'an announcement'. He sought an injunction restraining the proposed broadcast or in the alternative an order directing that time for a formal reply be made available by RTÉ for a broadcast to be made either by public figures nominated by the plaintiff or by the plaintiff himself.

[4.33] The government argued that it was the right and duty of the Taoiseach to announce and advocate government policy and such statements could not be restrained by an injunction. RTÉ argued that it was under an obligation to be impartial and balanced in broadcasting current affairs in general matters but there was no such requirement when broadcasting party political broadcasts and ministerial announcements.

[4.34] Carney J, in the High Court, held that a broadcast by the Taoiseach stating and advocating government policy was an announcement within the meaning of s 31 of the Broadcasting Authority Act 1960. He rejected the argument that the term announcement suggested a neutral statement, stating that this would be 'contrary to reason and common sense' and noting that:

> An Taoiseach in the projected broadcast will clearly announce Government policy in relation to the Maastricht Treaty. Having 'announced' or stated Government policy what will he do then? Nobody would expect him to say that as it happens he personally is not particularly enamoured of the policy and he is positively precluded from so doing by Article 28, s 4, sub-s 2 of the Constitution. The middle course is that he announce or state Government policy on the Maastricht

---

65.   The text of s 39(2) (replacing the Broadcasting Act 1960, s 18(2)) provides as follows:
      '(2) Nothing in *subsection (1) (a)* or *(b)* prevents a broadcaster from transmitting party political broadcasts provided that a broadcaster does not, in the allocation of time for such broadcasts, give an unfair preference to any political party...'
66.   Broadcasting Act 2009, s 122.
67.   *McCann v An Taoiseach* [1994] 2 IR 1.

Treaty in a wooden fashion and leave it at that. It can reasonably be expected that what he intends to do is to announce or state the Government position on the Maastricht Treaty and vigorously encourage his audience to vote for that position with every argument and power of eloquence and advocacy which he can muster.[68]

Carney J found that this was the duty of the Taoiseach and that it was permissible within the context of a ministerial announcement.

[4.35] He also found that there was no statutory right of reply to a ministerial announcement and considered whether a right of reply was required under the Constitution. He found that there would be a practical difficulty in identifying the appropriate party to exercise such a right:

> The first difficulty would be the practical one of which opposite view? In a situation such as this there will be a multiplicity of different organisations putting different shades of opposition to Government policy. RTÉ would be put in an impossible, unlawful and unconstitutional position in having to make a choice. It would be similarly inappropriate for the courts to be called upon to make such a choice.[69]

He thus rejected the plaintiff's application. The decision in this case, in so far as it relates to a ministerial announcement advocating votes in a favour of a referendum, is at odds with the decision of the Supreme Court in *Coughlan*, considered above, which considered the constitutionality of allowing for party political broadcasts in favour of a referendum.

[4.36] In *Madigan v RTÉ*,[70] the applicant was an independent candidate running in the European Parliament elections. RTÉ broadcast a number of programmes in relation to the election, some of which included the presence in the studio of certain nominated candidates from the main political parties. The applicant was concerned about the coverage proposed for independent candidates including himself. In response to a letter from the applicant, RTÉ stated that its broad policy was 'to take account of the support gained by the various parties at the last election'. It also said that it did take into consideration independent candidates and referred to the applicant's participation in the audience of the two television programmes.[71]

[4.37] The applicant took judicial review proceedings challenging RTÉ's policy regarding independent candidates. One of the arguments made by him was that RTÉ were wrong to take the results of the last election into account as the statutory requirement of impartiality dealt with the present time.

---

68. *McCann v An Taoiseach* [1994] 2 IR 1, 5.
69. *McCann v An Taoiseach* [1994] 2 IR 1, 6–7.
70. *Madigan v RTÉ* [1994] 2 ILRM 472.
71. The applicant had appeared in the audience in *Prime Time* and in a Dublin constituency profile programme.

[4.38] Kinlen J found in favour of RTÉ. He indicated that if RTÉ was to determine coverage on the basis of the last election alone that would be unacceptable. In the case at hand, however, he found that the policy adopted by RTÉ had also taken into account the personalities, politics and background of independent candidates and the divergence of views on different issues. He accepted the argument canvassed by RTÉ that the requirement was to treat candidates fairly but that this did not require total equality of treatment. He also accepted that RTÉ was entitled to have a fluid policy in this regard.[72]

[4.39] As noted above, the practical impact of *McKenna (No 2)* has been to restrain the broadcasting of party political broadcasts in the run up to referenda.

[4.40] In *Green Party v RTÉ*,[73] the applicant was a political party which sought judicial review of a decision by RTÉ not to provide live coverage of its party political conference. RTÉ justified the decision on the basis of criteria for such coverage which required that the party have at least seven TDs or 5% of the first preference votes at the most recent general election. The Green Party had six TDs, two Members of the European Parliament and 3.8% of the first preference votes in the 2002 general election. It sought a declaration that the decision not to cover its conference was unlawful and an order compelling RTÉ to provide such coverage of its conference as it claimed had previously been provided to comparable political parties' conferences. The Green Party relied in particular on the fact that RTÉ had provided reduced live coverage of the Progressive Democrats' party conference in 1997, at a time when that party had four TDs and 4.7% of the first preference votes in the previous general election.

[4.41] The Green Party claimed that RTÉ's refusal to cover their conference was contrary to the guarantee of equality in Article 40.1 of the Constitution and contrary to the requirements of equality and fairness contained in the Broadcasting Authority Act 1960. It also claimed that the criteria applied by the RTÉ in this context were irrational excessively rigid.

[4.42] The criteria adopted by RTÉ in this case had been developed by it under s 18 of the Broadcasting Authority Act 1960, as amended by s 3 of the Broadcasting Authority (Amendment) Act 1976, which provided in relevant part that:

> (1) Subject to the subsection (1A) of this section, it shall be the duty of the Authority to ensure that –
>
>   (a)   all news broadcast by it is reported and presented in an objective and impartial manner and without any expression of the Authority's own views,
>
>   (b)   the broadcast treatment of current affairs, including matters which are either of public controversy or the subject of current public debate, is fair to all interests concerned and that the broadcast matter is presented in an

---

72.   In reviewing RTÉ, Kinlen J applied the narrowly drawn test of *Wednesbury* reasonableness, referring to *O'Keeffe v An Bord Pleanála* [1993] 1 IR 39 and *State (Keegan) v Stardust Compensation Tribunal* [1986] IR 642.

73.   *Green Party v Radio Telefís Éireann* [2003] 1 IR 558.

objective and impartial manner and without any expression of the Authority's own views…

(2) Nothing in this section shall prevent the Authority from transmitting party political broadcasts.

[4.43] The Green Party relied on *Madigan* and argued that, in coverage of adversarial politics there was an overriding requirement of equivalence of treatment which did not mean mathematical equality; that criteria based on performance in the previous general election should not be the exclusive test for determining equivalence; and that over-rigidity in criteria was not permissible.

[4.44] Carroll J, in the High Court, found that the Green Party was entitled to rely on the constitutional guarantee of equality in Article 40.1,[74] but noted the difficulty in adjudicating on equality in the circumstances of the case where she was being asked to make a factual finding that the Green Party had equivalent political stature with other political parties.[75] While declining to do so, she did accept that:

> … the Progressive Democrats with fewer TDs and 4.7% of the first preference vote were accorded limited live coverage after the 1997 election while the applicant which now has six TDs and two Members of the European Parliament with 3.8% of the first preference votes was refused live coverage for its conference on the 1st and 2nd March.[76]

[4.45] In considering whether this amounted to what the judge described as 'constitutional unfairness', she rejected the arguments based on *Coughlan*, finding that:

> This situation is not comparable to a referendum. It refers to the allocation of time to a live broadcast of a party political conference. In my opinion, I am constrained to apply the principles applicable to judicial review, namely whether the impugned decision is one which plainly and unambiguously flies in the face of fundamental reason and common sense. I cannot honestly say that it does.[77]

[4.46] In applying this standard of review,[78] she found that while RTÉ could have rounded up the Green Party's figures by counting the Members of the European Parliament, the decision not to do so was neither 'illogical nor untenable'. There being no suggestion of bad faith on the part of RTÉ, the Green Party's challenge failed.[79]

---

74. *Coughlan v Broadcasting Complaints Commission* [2000] 3 IR 1, referred to by Carroll J in *Green Party v Radio Telefís Éireann* [2003] 1 IR 558, 565.
75. Carroll J referred to this as 'an impossible task'. *Green Party v Radio Telefís Éireann* [2003] 1 IR 558, 565.
76. *Green Party v Radio Telefís Éireann* [2003] 1 IR 558, 565–566.
77. *Green Party v Radio Telefís Éireann* [2003] 1 IR 558, 566.
78. *O'Keeffe v An Bord Pleanála* [1993] 1 IR 39 and *State (Keegan) v Stardust Compensation Tribunal* [1986] IR 642, as applied to RTÉ in *Brandon Book Publishers Ltd v Radio Telefís Éireann* [1993] ILRM 806 and *Madigan v RTÉ* [1994] 2 ILRM 472.
79. *Green Party v Radio Telefís Éireann* [2003] 1 IR 558, 566.

THE 'AUTHORITY OF THE STATE'

[4.47] Article 40.6.1°(i) refers to the right of the media (organs of public opinion) to criticise government policy but goes on to state that the government shall ensure that the media is not used to 'undermine the authority of the State'. The provision goes on to state that the publication or utterance of seditious matter is an offence.

[4.48] The general reference to the 'authority of the State', while it may seem dangerously broad in scope, has not been relied on by the State to justify general interferences with media expression. The reference has been read, however, as justifying the imposition of a broadcasting restriction inserted into broadcasting legislation in 1976 which was the subject of a number of constitutional challenges. This case law is discussed below, following a separate consideration of the reference in the provision to 'seditious matter'.

Seditious matter[80]

[4.49] Prior to 2009, the common law offence of seditious libel rendered the publication of seditious matter a criminal offence, albeit one in respect of which there had been no recorded prosecutions since the establishment of the Irish State. The Law Reform Commission recommended the abolition of the offence[81] and s 35 of the Defamation Act 2009 has abolished the offence in Irish law. The provision also repealed the common law offence of blasphemous libel which was replaced with a statutory offence aimed at blasphemous publication.[82] The offence of publishing seditious matter was not replaced with a new offence, presumably on the basis that there are already a number of provisions in the Offences Against the State Act 1939 which implement this constitutionally mandated criminal offence.[83]

[4.50] The Offences Against the State Act 1939 provides in s 10(1) that:

> It shall not be lawful to set up in type, print, publish, send through the post, distribute, sell, or offer for sale any document—
>
> (a)   which is or contains or includes an incriminating document, or
>
> (b)   which is or contains or includes a treasonable document, or
>
> (c)   which is or contains or includes a seditious document.

---

80.   For a critique of the justifications for restricting seditious expression, see Sorial, 'Can saying something make it so? The nature of seditious harm' [2010] Law and Philosophy 273.
81.   *Report on the Crime of Libel* (Law Reform Commission, 1991), 10.
82.   See **Ch 3**.
83.   Earlier legislation (since repealed) which precluded seditious publications included the Public Safety Act 1927, s 9. See also the Constitution of the Irish Free, Article 2A(23) inserted by the Constitution (Amendment No 17) Act. See also the Emergency Powers Act 1939, 2(2) which permitted wide-ranging censorship of the media during WWII. (The legislation was temporary and lapsed in 1946).

[4.51] The definitions of incriminating, treasonable and seditious documents are set out in s 2 of the Act. A seditious document is stated to include:

(a)   a document consisting of or containing matter calculated or tending to undermine the public order or the authority of the State, and

(b)   a document which alleges, implies, or suggests or is calculated to suggest that the government functioning under the Constitution is not the lawful government of the State or that there is in existence in the State any body or organisation not functioning under the Constitution which is entitled to be recognised as being the government of the country, and

(c)   a document which alleges, implies, or suggests or is calculated to suggest that the military forces maintained under the Constitution are not the lawful military forces of the State, or that there is in existence in the State a body or organisation not established and maintained by virtue of the Constitution which is entitled to be recognised as a military force, and

(d)   a document in which words, abbreviations, or symbols referable to a military body are used in referring to an unlawful organisation.

[4.52] Section 10(2) provides that it is unlawful to send or contribute to newspapers or other periodical:

... any letter, article or communication which is sent or contributed or purports to be sent or contributed by or on behalf of an unlawful organisation or which is of such nature or character that the printing of it would be a contravention of [the provisions relating to incriminating, treasonable or seditious documents in s 10(1)].'

It is also an offence for 'the proprietor' of any such publication to publish such letters, articles or communications.

[4.53] There is a ban on the importation of newspapers or periodicals which contain seditious matter under s 11. Under s 12 it is an offence merely to be in possession of a treasonable, incriminating or seditious document.

[4.54] Section 13 of the Act provides that, save in the case of periodicals printed by the proprietor thereof on his own premises:

(1) Every person who shall print for reward any document shall do every of the following things, that is to say:

(a)   at the time of or within twenty-four hours after printing such document, print or write on at least one copy of such document the name and address of the person for whom or on whose instructions such document was printed;

(b)   retain, for six months from the date on which such document was printed, a copy of such document on which the said name and address is printed or written as aforesaid;

    (c)   on the request of a member of the Gárda Síochána at any time during the said period of six months, produce for the inspection of such member the said copy of such document so retained as aforesaid.

[4.55] Under s 14, printers must print their names and addresses on documents printed for reward (with some exceptions)[84] and which they know or have reason to believe are intended for sale, distribution or display whether general or limited.

[4.56] The Constitution Review Group questioned whether these provisions were compatible with the Constitution and the European Convention on Human Rights.[85] The Committee to Review the Offences Against the State Acts 1939–1998 recommended the repeal of ss 10, 11, 13 and 14 on the basis that they were 'overbroad, outdated in the modern era of the internet and effectively unenforceable'.[86]

Official secrecy

[4.57] The Official Secrets Act 1963 is a broadly drafted statute which has implications for the media in terms of access to information and in terms of what can be done with information which is caught by the Act. The Act was modelled on pre-existing British legislation which it replaced and it has commented that the Irish Act results in a situation where:

> … a small nation with a written constitution and a neutral standing in international affairs has virtually the same draconic powers of Government Secrecy as a front-line NATO state with no written constitution.[87]

[4.58] Section 4 of the 1963 Act provides that:

> (1) A person shall not communicate any official information to any other person unless he is duly authorised to do so or does so in the course of and in accordance with his duties as the holder of a public office or when it is his duty in the interest of the State to communicate it.

> (2) A person to whom subsection (1) applies shall take reasonable care to avoid any unlawful communication of such information.

> (3) A person shall not obtain official information where he is aware or has reasonable grounds for believing that the communication of such information to him would be a contravention of subsection (1).

---

84.   Under s 14(3), the obligations of printers in that section do not apply to (a) currency notes, bank notes, bills of exchange, promissory notes, cheques, receipts and other financial or commercial documents, (b) writs, orders, summonses, warrants, affidavits, and other documents for the purposes of or for use in any lawful court or tribunal, (c) any document printed by order of the Government, either House of the Oireachtas, a Minister of State, or any officer of the State in the execution of his duties as such officer, (d) any document which the Minister for Justice shall by order declare to be a document to which this section does not apply.

85.   *Report of the Constitution Review Group* (1996), 298.

86.   *Report of the Committee to Review the Offences Against the State Acts 1939–1998* (2002), para 6.123.

87.   Cook, 'Why we need open government in Ireland' Seirbhís Phoiblí, Vol 6, No 3, Mean Fomhair 1985, 23.

(4) In this section 'duly authorised' means authorised by a Minister or State authority or by some person authorised in that behalf by a Minister or State authority.

[4.59] The definition of 'official information' in s 2 is broad and covers:

... any secret official code word or password, and any sketch, plan, model, article, note, document or information which is secret or confidential or is expressed to be either and which is or has been in the possession, custody or control of a holder of a public office, or to which he has or had access, by virtue of his office, and includes information recorded by film or magnetic tape or by any other recording medium;

[4.60] While prosecutions of the media are rare under the Act,[88] it has been pointed out, that the Irish legislation 'makes no attempt to distinguish between sensitive information, disclosure of which ought to be prohibited and information of a trivial nature which does not warrant criminal sanction.'[89]

[4.61] The provision in s 4 of the 1963 Act must now be read subject to the provision under s 48 of the Freedom of Information Act 1997 which amends it so that:

(1) A person who is, or reasonably believes that he or she is, authorised by this Act to communicate official information to another person shall be deemed for the purposes of section 4 of the Official Secrets Act, 1963, to be duly authorised to communicate that information.

(2) In a prosecution for an offence under section 5 or 9 of that Act, it shall be a defence to prove that the act to which the charge of the offence relates is authorised, or is reasonably believed by the person charged to be authorised, by this Act.

[4.62] Section 5 limits the disclosure of confidential information by staff of public bodies about their contracts.[90]

---

88. See the two examples below.
89. McDonagh, 'Access to Official Information in Ireland: Part I: Legal Constraints on Disclosure of Information' (1995) 13 *Irish Law Times* 182. The British Act was amended in 1989 and now prohibits disclosure in six particularly sensitive areas.
90. Section 5 provides as follows:
    (1) A person who is or has been—
    (a) a party to a contract with a Minister or State authority or with any person on behalf of a Minister or State authority, or
    (b) employed by such party,
    shall not communicate to any third party any information relating to the contract and expressed therein to be confidential.
    (2) A person to whom subsection (1) applies shall take reasonable care to avoid any unlawful communication of such information.
    (3) It shall be a good defence to a prosecution for a contravention of this section to prove that the communication was authorised in writing by the Minister or State authority or by the party contracting on behalf of the Minister or State authority.

[4.63] Section 6 preludes the retention of official documents or documents containing official information and provides that persons holding such documentation may be directed to dispose of same by direction of the Minister, a secretary of a government department or a person authorised under seal by the Minister to give such directions.

[4.64] Under s 9 of the Act, persons may not 'in any manner prejudicial to the safety or preservation of the State ... obtain, record, communicate to any other person or publish, or ... have in his possession or under his control any document containing, or other record whatsoever of, information relating to' the Defence Forces, the Gardaí or information which might be prejudicial to the preservation of the State.[91]

[4.65] There is a statutory defence to prosecution for breaching these restrictions where the accused can prove 'that the act in respect of which he is charged was authorised by a Minister or by some person authorised in that behalf by a Minister or was done in the course of and in accordance with his duties as the holder of a public office.'[92]

[4.66] It is an offence to contravene or to attempt to contravene any of the provisions of the Official Secrets Act[93] and prosecutions may only be brought with the consent of the Attorney General.[94]

The Act does not appear to have been used to restrain the media in many cases. One exception is *DPP v Independent Newspapers*,[95] where the *Independent* and its editor were convicted and fined IR£100 under the Official Secrets Act 1963 for publishing two Garda indentikit pictures of suspects in a criminal investigation. They were found guilty of having obtained and communicated to the public official information which they had reproduced from a Garda bulletin.

[4.67] In 1995 the District Court fined a journalist and the *Independent* for publication of a confidential Garda document. The document indicated that the Gardaí had prior knowledge of the commission of a high-profile bank robbery.[96]

[4.68] Arguments in favour of injuncting the publication of a book which may have breached UK official secrecy legislation were rejected in *AG for England and Wales v*

---

91. The categories of information covered by the provision are as follows '(i) the number, description, armament, equipment, disposition, movement or condition of any of the Defence Forces or of any of the vessels or aircraft belonging to the State,

   (ii) any operations or projected operations of any of the Defence Forces or of the Garda Síochána or of any of the vessels or aircraft belonging to the State,

   (iii) any measures for the defence or fortification of any place on behalf of the State

   (iv) munitions of war, or

   (v) any other matter whatsoever information as to which would or might be prejudicial to the safety or preservation of the State.'

92. Official Secrets Act 1963, s 9(2).

93. Official Secrets Act 1963, s 13.

94. Official Secrets Act 1963, s 14.

95. *DPP v Independent Newspapers* (1984) *Irish Times*, 8 February and 20 July.

96. (1995) *Irish Times*, 8 November and 16 December.

Brandon Book Publishers Ltd.[97] There, an application was made to the Irish High Court seeking an injunction to prevent the distribution of a book which contained material relating to the war-time activities of the British Secret Service. The book related to matters that had taken place over 30 years previously but which were covered by UK official secrecy legislation. The book was not covered by the Irish legislation, nor could it have been said to threaten the authority of the State. The argument canvassed in support of the injunction thus focused on whether the author had been bound by confidentiality under her terms of employment. Carroll J refused the injunction, pointing out that any claims to confidentiality had to be balanced against the public interest in publication.

Public order

[4.69] The Constitution also refers to freedom of expression as being subject to public order. Most of the provisions which concern expression and public order are unlikely to be of relevance to the media and are dealt with only briefly here. Relevant measures which might affect expression under the heading of public order include the common law offence of breach of the peace;[98] provoking a breach of the peace through the use of threatening, abusive or insulting words under s 6 of the Criminal Justice (Public Order) Act 1994; engaging in unreasonable behaviour which, having regard to all the circumstances, is likely to cause serious offence or serious annoyance to any person who is or might reasonably be expected to be aware of such behaviour in a public place between 07.00 and midnight or at any other time having been requested by a garda under s 5 of the Criminal Justice (Public Order) Act 1994; threats to damage property under s 3 of the Criminal Damage Act 1991; or threats to kill or seriously injure another person under s 5 of the Non-Fatal Offences Against the Person Act 1997. Section 10 of the latter Act also provides for an offence of harassing another by persistently following, watching, pestering, besetting or communicating with him without lawful authority or reasonable excuse. The common law offence of criminal libel was repealed by the Defamation Act 2009. Section 12 of the Criminal Law Act 1976 creates an offence where a person (a) knowingly makes a false report or statement tending to show that an offence has been committed, whether by himself or another person, or tending to give rise to apprehension for the safety of persons or property, or (b) knowingly makes a false report or statement tending to show that he has information material to any inquiries by the Garda Síochána and thereby causes the time of the Garda Síochána to be wastefully employed. The common law recognises that it is an offence to incite another to commit an offence[99] and there are a number of statutory provisions which also refer to incitement.[100]

---

97. *AG for England and Wales v Brandon Book Publishers Ltd* [1986] IR 587; [1987] ILRM 135.
98. See *Thorpe v DPP* (17 February 2006, unreported), HC, Murphy J.
99. *People (AG) v Capaldi* (1949) 1 Frewen 95.
100. See Charleton, McDermott and Bolger, *Criminal Law* (Bloomsbury Professional, 1999), 327–344.

Section 31 of the Broadcasting Act 1960

[4.70] Section 31 of the Broadcasting Act 1960 as amended by s 16 of the Broadcasting (Amendment) Act 1976[101] gave the Minister for Communications the power to prohibit broadcasting in certain circumstances. It provided that:

> Where the Minister is of the opinion that the broadcasting of a particular matter or any matter of a particular class would be likely to promote, or incite to, crime or would tend to undermine the authority of the State, he may by order direct the Authority to refrain from broadcasting the matters, or any matter of the particular class, and the Authority shall comply with the order.[102]

[4.71] Orders made by the Minister under s 31(1) had to be laid before the Oireachtas which had the power to annul the orders.[103] Orders issued under this provision were to remain in force for the period stated therein, not exceeding 12 months. The period could be extended for up to 12 months at a time by further ministerial order or by a resolution passed by both Houses of the Oireachtas.[104]

[4.72] This power was used to prohibit the making of election broadcasts on behalf of Sinn Féin because of that organisation's association with and support of the Provisional IRA. In *State (Lynch) v Cooney*,[105] a challenge was brought by a candidate in the run up to a general election, seeking to protect its projected party political broadcasts on radio and television. The broadcasting authority had agreed to allow Sinn Féin to deliver addresses. The Minister subsequently made an order under s 31 directing the broadcasting authority to refrain from broadcasting any matter, whether being a political party broadcast or not, made by or on behalf of, or inviting support for, the Sinn Féin organisation and the addresses were not transmitted. The applicant argued that s 31 was in breach of Article 40.6.1°(i). Having obtained a conditional order of certiorari from Barrington J in the High Court, the case came before O'Hanlon J who made the order absolute.

---

101. Prior to its amendment in 1976, the Broadcasting Act 1960, s 31 contained a much broader (and almost certainly unconstitutional) power of prohibition, providing that: 'The Minister may direct the Authority in writing to refrain from broadcasting any particular matter or matter of any particular class, and the Authority shall comply with the direction.' The amendments were added to render the provision constitutional – see comments of O'Hanlon J in *State (Lynch) v Cooney* [1982] IR 337, 343 and 354.
102. For academic critiques of s 31, see Hall, *The Electronic Age: Telecommunications in Ireland* (Dublin, 1993), 233–251; D Morgan, 'Section 31: the broadcasting ban' (1990–2) 25–27 Irish Jurist 117; Kenny, 'Section 31 and the censorship of programmes' (1994) 12 *Irish Law Times* 50; Clarke, 'Section 31 and censorship: a philosophical perspective' (1994) 12 *Irish Law Times* 53; Hogan, 'The Demise of the Irish Broadcasting Ban' (1995) 1 European Public Law 69.
103. The Broadcasting Act 1960, s 31(1B) as inserted by the Broadcasting (Amendment) Act 1976, s 16.
104. The Broadcasting Act 1960, s 31(1A) as inserted by the Broadcasting (Amendment) Act 1976, s 16.
105. *State (Lynch) v Cooney* [1982] IR 337; [1983] ILRM 89.

[4.73] O'Hanlon J, in the High Court, found that the decision of the Minister to make an order was essentially unreviewable unless it could be shown that there was bad faith on his part. He went on to consider whether the allocation of such a discretion rendered s 31 unconstitutional. He referred to the 'delicate balance' required by Article 40.6.1°(i) between freedom of expression and maintaining the authority of the State. Ultimately, he concluded that the power given to the Minister under s 31 failed to reach an appropriate balance:

> That appears to me to contain insufficient safeguards for the constitutionally guaranteed rights of freedom for the expression of convictions and opinions with particular reference to the protection of freedom of the press and the radio, and now of television, from the control of the Executive.[106]

[4.74] The Supreme Court disagreed with the finding by O'Hanlon J that s 31 created an unreviewable power. O'Higgins CJ referred to the double construction rule in *East Donegal Co-Operative* and held that s 31 should be read as creating a reviewable discretion if that was what was required to render it constitutional.[107] Having so decided, he went on to consider the Order itself. He noted that:

> On the basis of the information which he had, it cannot be doubted that the Minister had cogent grounds for believing that Sinn Féin aimed at undermining the authority of the State. Therefore, any broadcast which sought support for such an organisation could properly be regarded by him as being likely to promote or incite to crime or to tend to undermine the State's authority.[108]

The Supreme Court thus overturned O'Hanlon J's decision and found that the Order was not ultra vires the Minister's power under s 31.[109]

[4.75] Apart from banning party political broadcasts by Sinn Féin, s 31 was also used as the basis for banning broadcasting interviews with spokesmen for Sinn Féin, broadcasts made by or on behalf of or inviting support for the organisation and broadcasts by persons representing the organisation. Spokespersons for Sinn Féin had their voices dubbed in any broadcasts in which they featured.

[4.76] In *Purcell v Ireland*,[110] an attempt was made to challenge s 31 under the European Convention on Human Rights. The applicants were a number of journalists and

---

106. *State (Lynch) v Cooney* [1982] IR 337, 356.
107. *State (Lynch) v Cooney* [1982] IR 337, 360.
108. *State (Lynch) v Cooney* [1982] IR 337, 366. See also Walsh J [1982] IR 337, 372.
109. The court rejected the argument that there had been a failure to observe fair procedures in that the applicant had not been given an opportunity to object to the order, noting that the time available was short and the matter urgent.
110. *Purcell v Ireland* (1991) 70 DR 262 (Application No 15404/89). See also *Brind v UK* (1994) 77 DR 42 (Application No 18714/91) where a challenge was brought to the UK broadcasting ban on the voices of persons who were members or supporters of Sinn Féin and certain other organisations. This followed the rejection of a challenge by the House of Lords in *Brind v Secretary of State for Home Department* [1991] AC 696. The European Commission on Human Rights found that the complaint was manifestly unfounded for similar reasons to those set out by it in *Purcell*.

television producers and two trade unions.[111] They argued that the effect of the s 31 order and the RTÉ guidelines issued in relation to it was:

> ... gravely to distort coverage of all news events, current affairs and social developments in Northern Ireland, to deter journalists and/or producers from choosing to put on programmes relating to any issue in Northern Ireland and to prevent journalists and producers from complying with the requirement as to balance and impartiality in its programmes produced.[112]

[4.77] They also argued that s 18 of the Broadcasting Act 1960 was sufficient to protect the interests addressed by the order as it precluded the broadcasting of any matter 'which may reasonably be regarded as being likely to promote, or incite to, crime or as tending to undermine the authority of the State.'

[4.78] The European Commission of Human Rights found that the trade unions could not themselves constitute victims under Article 25 of the European Convention on Human Rights. The government's argument that the individual applicants were not capable of being victims was rejected by the Commission which noted that:

> All the individual applicants are full-time broadcasting journalists or producers of radio and television programmes. As employees of RTÉ they are bound to comply with the Section 31 Order, in accordance with the guidelines issued by their employer. The exercise of their freedom to receive and impart information is directly affected by the terms of the Order, and they face disciplinary action for failure to comply with it.

The Commission accepted that the applicants met the requirement of having exhausted their domestic remedies given the conclusive determination of the Supreme Court in *Lynch*.

[4.79] In considering whether the ban was contrary to Article 10 of the Convention, the Commission accepted that it was sufficiently clear to meet the criterion of being prescribed by law and that it had the legitimate aim of protecting the interest of national security, bearing in mind the evidence accepted by the Irish Supreme Court in *Lynch*. In the Commission's analysis of whether the ban was necessary in a democratic society, it emphasised the margin of appreciation enjoyed by Member States, stating that:

> [T]he Commission's sole task is to examine whether the reasons underlying the Section 31 Order are relevant and sufficient under Article 10 para 2 (article 10–2) (cf Eur Court HR, Müller and Others judgment, loc cit), ie whether the Minister had convincing reasons for assuming the existence of a pressing social need for imposing the impugned restrictions on the applicants.

[4.80] In this regard, the Commission described what it saw as the context of the ban:

> In a situation where politically motivated violence poses a constant threat to the lives and security of the population and where the advocates of this violence seek access to the mass media for publicity purposes, it is particularly difficult to strike

---

111. SIPTU and the NUJ.
112. As summarised by the Commission.

a fair balance between the requirements of protecting freedom of information and the imperatives of protecting the State and the public against armed conspiracies seeking to overthrow the democratic order which guarantees this freedom and other human rights.

[4.81] It noted that the prohibition did not apply so as to restrict the content of television and radio programmes. Its purpose was to ensure that spokesmen for the relevant organisations did not use the opportunity of a live interview or other broadcasts to promote illegal activities. The Commission also identified a second purpose:

... to deny representatives of known terrorist organisations and their political supporters the possibility of using the broadcast media as a platform for advocating their cause, encouraging support for their organisations and conveying the impression of their legitimacy.

[4.82] The Commission accepted that broadcasting was a special case, noting that:

In contemporary society radio and television are media of considerable power and influence. Their impact is more immediate than that of the print media, and the possibilities for the broadcaster to correct, qualify, interpret or comment on any statement made on radio or television are limited in comparison with those available to journalists in the press. Live statements could also involve a special risk of coded messages being conveyed, a risk which even conscientious journalists cannot control within the exercise of their professional judgment.

[4.83] The Commission thus found that the complaint was manifestly unfounded within the meaning of Article 27(2) of the Convention. The consequence of this finding was that the complaint did not proceed to a hearing in the European Court of Human Rights.

[4.84] After the failure of the *Purcell* complaint, an attempt was made to challenge a directive issued by RTÉ implementing the s 31 order. Staff at RTÉ were directed that interviews with members of a number of organisations (including Sinn Féin) were banned regardless of the topic of the interview. In *O'Toole v RTÉ*[113] the applicant was a member of Sinn Féin and also the spokesman for a strike committee which was involved in an industrial dispute. RTÉ refused to broadcast a number of interviews with him concerning the industrial dispute and he took a challenge to the RTÉ direction. Finlay CJ, delivering the judgment of the Supreme Court, found that the RTÉ direction was an amendment of the terms of the ministerial order and that the broadcasts in question in the case did not in fact fall within the scope of the order. RTÉ defended the blanket ban on the basis that it was the only practical way to ensure that all interviews implemented the order consistently. It was also argued that there was a danger that interviewees could use the opportunity of a live interview about an innocuous topic to suddenly make statements about the organizations to which they belonged. The court rejected both these arguments, noting that the issue of consistency could be addressed by monitoring broadcasts and that the latter concern could be addressed by insisting on broadcasting pre-recorded interviews with such persons as opposed to live ones.

---

113. *O'Toole v RTÉ* [1993] ILRM 458.

[4.85] Section 31 arose for consideration again in *Brandon Book Publishers Ltd v RTÉ*.[114] In that case, the applicant was a publisher which had published a book of short stories written by Gerry Adams, President of Sinn Féin. The script of a proposed radio advertisement for the book was sent to RTÉ for clearance. It read as follows:

> This is Gerry Adams speaking. My new book is called *'The Street and Other Stories'* and it's on sale in good bookshops in the 32 Counties. Most of the stories are about ordinary people and everyday events, and there's a fair bit of craic in them too. That's *'The Street and Other Stories'* and this is Gerry Adams. I think you might enjoy it. Slán.

It was rejected by RTÉ on the basis that s 31 of the Broadcasting Act 1960 precluded RTÉ from taking any comments from the author.

[4.86] The applicant took proceedings, essentially arguing that the Supreme Court decision in *O'Toole* meant that he could be broadcast as an author of short stories. RTÉ accepted that ordinary members of Sinn Féin could now be broadcast talking about various topics but argued that Gerry Adams was:

> ... the public face of the organisation to such a degree that to broadcast Mr Adams on any subject, no matter how apparently innocuous, would, in fact, amount to inviting support for Sinn Féin, be in fact a broadcast by a person representing Sinn Féin and tend to undermine the authority of the State.[115]

RTÉ argued that Mr Adams could not be separated in the public mind from advancing the cause of Sinn Féin.

[4.87] Carney J, in the High Court, found that whether this was the case or not was a matter for RTÉ to judge, using its expertise as the national broadcasting authority. He found that such a judgment was not reviewable by the courts, distinguishing *O'Toole* on the basis that it had not involved an exercise of judgment as the ban in that case was a blanket ban.

[4.88] The ministerial order banning the broadcasting of subversive material lapsed in 1994, against the background of the peace process in Northern Ireland and was not renewed. Section 31(1)–(1B) was repealed by s 3 of the Broadcasting Act 2001. That provision also repealed s 12 of the Radio and Television Act 1988 which had applied s 31 to independent broadcasters. Section 18(1A) of the Broadcasting Act 1960 (as inserted by s 3 of the Broadcasting (Amendment) Act 1976) was left intact and has been reproduced in s 39(1)(d) of the Broadcasting Act 2009 which provides in relevant part that every broadcaster must ensure that 'anything which may reasonably be regarded as causing harm or offence, or as being likely to promote, or incite to, crime or as tending to undermine the authority of the State, is not broadcast by the broadcaster'.

---

114. *Brandon Book Publishers Ltd v RTÉ* [1993] ILRM 806. Proceedings were also taken against the IRTC – see (1993) *Irish Times*, 30 October.
115. *Brandon Book Publishers Ltd v RTÉ* [1993] ILRM 806.

POLITICAL ADVERTISING

The prohibition on political advertising in the Broadcasting Act 2009

[4.89] Broadcasts of political and religious advertisements were both prohibited prior to the enactment of the Broadcasting Act 2009. Section 41(3) of the Broadcasting Act 2009 continues the pre-existing ban, providing that 'a broadcaster shall not broadcast an advertisement which is directed towards a political end which has any relation to an industrial dispute'. The pre-existing ban on religious advertising is now contained in s 41(4) which prohibits the broadcast of 'an advertisement which addresses the issue of the merits or otherwise of adhering to any religious faith or belief or of becoming a member of any religion or religious organisation.'[116]

[4.90] The ban on political advertising has been justified on the grounds that it would be impossible for an independent authority to adjudicate on disputes arising from such advertisements.[117] While it has been subject to vehement academic criticism,[118] it seems that there is little consensus among the public about the ban.[119] The Irish courts have refused to hold the ban unconstitutional on free speech grounds – a position which seems to be at odds with the recent case law from the European Court of Human Rights.

Political advertising – the Irish cases

[4.91] The ban came before the High Court in *Colgan v IRTC*.[120] The applicant was a member of 'Youth Defence', an organisation committed to the protection of the right to life of the unborn. The organisation had commissioned a 30-second radio advertisement to raise awareness about abortion. The ad started with the muffled sound of a heartbeat with a subsequent voice-over stating:

> [H]er heart has been beating since she was 18 days old. At eight weeks she's perfectly formed. She sucks her thumb. And she already has 20 milk-teeth buds. [The sound of the heartbeat stopped and the voiceover continued] In another two weeks she would have had fingernails. She might have grown up to be a doctor, scientist, a mother. But now nobody will ever know. Have you any conception what abortion is about?

---

116. This is a change from the original wording of that prohibition. See the discussion of censorship of religious advertising in **Ch 3**.
117. Minister for Communications, Eamonn Ryan stated in respect of the retention of the ban in the Broadcasting Act 2009: 'In regard to the political code restriction, the general direction from the Legislature is that we should not open up political advertising as it would be almost impossible for an authority to judge the political aspect of such advertisements and to make calls in terms of whether it is accurate, inaccurate, acceptable or unacceptable. It is a difficult and grey area.' Oireachtas Debate, 4 June 2009.
118. Knight, 'Monkeying around with Free Speech' [2008] Law Quarterly Review 557.
119. In a 2009 opinion poll, 57% of those polled did not favour the removal of the ban. See K Rafter, *Political Advertising: the Regulatory Position and the Public View* (November 2009). Available from www.bai.ie.
120. *Colgan v IRTC* [2000] 2 IR 490.

The ad was banned by the IRTC on the grounds that it was a political advertisement within the meaning of s 10(3) of the Radio and Television Act 1988 which provided that an independent broadcaster could not broadcast any advertisement 'which is directed towards any religious or political end or which has any relation to an industrial dispute.' The applicant sought to quash the decision of the IRTC and to have s 10(3) declared to be unconstitutional.

[4.92] The applicant submitted that the advertisement was merely providing information concerning abortion and not making an argument against it so that it could not be described as having a 'political end'. It was further argued that as s 10(3) was interfering with constitutional rights it should be construed restrictively so as to produce minimal interference with the applicant's constitutional rights of freedom of communication and expression. According to the applicant, this could be achieved by reading the reference 'political end' as importing the meaning 'party political'. The right to life of the unborn under Article 40.3.3° of the Constitution was also relied upon. The applicant also argued that the IRTC in reaching its decision had had regard to the general background of Youth Defence as an anti-abortion movement and that this should not have been taken into account in making any decision regarding the nature and content of the advertisement.

[4.93] O'Sullivan J refused to find that the provision referred to party politics, noting that the concept of a 'party political broadcast' appeared elsewhere in the Act[121] so that the Oireachtas must have intended a broader meaning when using the words 'political end' in s 10(3). His interpretation of the term 'political end' was broad:

> I consider that an advertisement has a political end within the meaning of s 10(3) if it is directed towards furthering the interests of a particular political party or towards procuring changes in the laws of this country or, I would add, countering suggested changes in those laws, or towards procuring changes in the laws of a foreign country or countering suggested changes in those laws or procuring a reversal of government policy or of particular decisions of governmental authorities in this country or, I would add, countering suggested reversals thereof or procuring a reversal of governmental policy or of particular decisions of governmental authorities in a foreign country or countering suggested reversals thereof.[122]

He found that the IRTC was required to take into account the identity of the advertiser in assessing whether the advertisement was directed at a political end given that the advertisement itself specified that it was sponsored by that organisation.[123] The applicant also argued that the advertisement was aimed at dissuading women from travelling abroad for abortions but that it was not aimed at the political end of changing or retaining the law on abortion in the State. Noting that it was one of the professed objectives of Youth Defence to procure a referendum on abortion, O'Sullivan J rejected

---

121. Broadcasting Act 2009, s 9(2).
122. *Colgan v IRTC* [2000] 2 IR 490, 504.
123. *Colgan v IRTC* [2000] 2 IR 490, 505.

the argument that it was irrelevant in circumstances where no referendum campaign was in being. He noted:

> The issues connected with the several constitutional amendments dealing with abortion have been rightly described as deeply divisive of our people and are capable of stirring up powerfully felt emotions on either side. These emotions and the arguments on either side, not to mention the individuals or entities connected with them, are not easily forgotten and the issue of changing the law or adapting it remains a live issue on the political agenda not least because the Supreme Court has indicated that such a change must be brought about. In this context, a powerful advertisement clearly directed against the evil of abortion and proclaiming itself to be sponsored by a group itself clearly identified with a campaign for a new referendum and a change in the law is itself inextricably bound up with this project of bringing about a change in our law. I have to conclude, therefore, that the first respondent was correct in coming to the view that the advertisement in this case was directed towards a political end within the meaning of the relevant statutory provision as I have defined it.[124]

[4.94] He also rejected the argument that the main purpose of the advertisement was to dissuade young Irish mothers from going abroad for abortions. He stated that this was not the only 'purpose' or 'end' of the advertisement and that 'a listener, who can clearly be other than a young Irish mother, might well be induced by this advertisement to offer support to Project Truth, a Youth Defence project.'[125] In O'Sullivan J's view, the advertisement was 'so closely bound up with the political objectives of Youth Defence that it would be unrealistic and artificial to shut one's eyes to these objectives and construe the advertisement out of context and severed from its background.'[126]

[4.95] Having found that the advertisement came within the scope of the prohibition in s 10(3), O'Sullivan J then proceeded to consider the constitutionality of that provision. He referred back to the decision of the Supreme Court in *Murphy v IRTC*[127] where, in rejecting a challenge to the prohibition on religious advertising, Barrington J had stated that:

> All three kinds of banned advertisement relate to matters which have proved extremely divisive in Irish society in the past. The Oireachtas was entitled to take the view that the citizens would resent having advertisements touching on these topics broadcast into their homes and that such advertisements, if permitted, might lead to unrest. Moreover, the Oireachtas may well have thought that in relation to matters of such sensitivity, rich men should not be able to buy access to the airwaves to the detriment of their poorer rivals.[128]

---

124. *Colgan v IRTC* [2000] 2 IR 490, 507.
125. *Colgan v IRTC* [2000] 2 IR 490, 507.
126. *Colgan v IRTC* [2000] 2 IR 490, 507.
127. *Murphy v IRTC* [1999] 1 IR 12. *Murphy* is considered in detail in **Ch 3**.
128. *Murphy v IRTC* [1999] 1 IR 12, 22.

[4.96] O'Sullivan J stated that he was bound by the Supreme Court's decision in that case that the ban was based on the purpose identified by the Supreme Court in that case.[129] He held that there was:

> ...no rational distinction in this judgment in terms of degrees of sensitivity as between religious and political advertisements. It is clear that the Supreme Court dealt with these two categories of advertisement and those relating to industrial disputes as each of them being concerned with matters which have proved divisive and which were potentially offensive. It made no distinction between these categories in terms of degrees of divisiveness or sensitivity.[130]

He also professed himself to be bound by the Supreme Court's finding in *Murphy* 'that the intrusion in that case was minimalist'[131] and interpreted Barrington J's judgment in the case as proving that:

> [T]he correct approach for this court when considering whether the infringement of a constitutionally protected right impairs that right as little as possible is to refrain from condemning a wider infringement such as a blanket ban notwithstanding that a more selective alternative is admittedly available, if a rational explanation for the wider infringement is available to the Court.[132]

[4.97] O'Sullivan J's reasoning in the case, which treats the ban on religious advertising the same way as the ban on political advertising, is at odds with the position subsequently taken by the European Court of Human Rights. While that court ruled that the ban on religious advertising was compatible with the Convention in *Murphy*,[133] it has held that blanket prohibitions of political advertising are in breach of Article 10 of the European Convention on Human Rights.[134] As discussed below, the English courts have refused to adopt the approach of the Strasbourg court on this issue, despite having incorporated the European Convention on Human Rights into UK law in 2000.

BCI decisions rejecting political advertisements

[4.98] The Broadcasting Commission of Ireland has rejected a number of advertisements on the basis that they were political within the meaning of the legislation.[135]

---

129. *Colgan v IRTC* [2000] 2 IR 490, 508.
130. *Colgan v IRTC* [2000] 2 IR 490, 511.
131. *Colgan v IRTC* [2000] 2 IR 490, 511.
132. *Colgan v IRTC* [2000] 2 IR 490, 512.
133. See paras **[3.23]–[3.27]**.
134. *VgT Verein Gegen Tierfabriken v Switzerland* (2002) 34 EHRR 4; *TV Vest As & Rugaland Persjonistparti v Norway* (2009) 48 EHRR 51
135. See Rafter, *Political Advertising: the Regulatory Position and the Public View* (November 2009), 16–17. Available from www.bai.ie.

[4.99] In 2003 Brandon Books sought to publicise a book written by Gerry Adams, President of Sinn Féin. Adams himself recorded a 20-second radio advertisement for the book to be broadcast on several local radio stations. The radio advertisement stated:

> This is Gerry Adams. My new book is called Hope and History. It's on sale in good bookshops in all 32 counties. It's the story of the effort to bring about a change in this country. It's the story of the difficult and ongoing struggle for peace. That's Hope and History and this is Gerry Adams. Slán agus beannacht.

The BCI banned the ad under the 1988 Act on the basis that it was written by a current politician who was giving his views on events in which he and his party continued to be involved and which were the subject of political debate.

[4.100] In 2004 the Irish Anti-War Movement sought to promote a music concert being held to raise funds and protest at the US invasion of Iraq. The concert was billed as 'When Bush comes to shove: an anti-war gig'. The BCI rejected the ad because the aims of the group and the aims of the concert were political. A separate ad calling on members of the public to attend protests against the Bush visit was also rejected.

[4.101] The National Consumer Agency, which is a publicly funded body, sought to gain support for changes in the Groceries Orders which outlawed below-cost selling. A public consultation process was ongoing and the Agency sought contributions from members of the public on that issue. The Agency planned a radio campaign but was unable to pursue it because the campaign sought to influence a political decision-making process.

[4.102] In 2007 Trocaire, the Catholic development agency, commissioned a number of radio and television ads promoting gender equality. The ads were to coincide with the charity's Lenten campaign which placed emphasis on women in conflict and rallying support for a UN resolution which pledges to protect women and children. Trocaire called on the government to fully implement the resolution. It highlighted the difficulties of female children and encouraged the public to sign a petition calling on the government to enact a specific UN resolution and asking the public to donate online or through a collection box. RTÉ approved the ad on the basis that it was general in nature and concerned an international campaign. The BCI banned the ad and later approved it where it was reworded from 'Support Trocaire's Lenten Campaign to help end gender inequality' to 'Support Trocaire to end gender inequality'.

[4.103] The blanket prohibition on political advertising[136] is not compatible with Article 10 of the European Convention on Human Rights, as interpreted by the European Court of Human Rights in a number of cases.

---

136. The ban on religious advertising was qualified in the Broadcasting Act 2009, s 41 but the provision relating to political advertising was retained in the same form. See discussion of religious advertising in **Ch 3**.

Political advertising in the European Court of Human Rights

[4.104] The European Court of Human Rights has considered the issue of political advertising in a number of decisions.[137] In *VgT Verein Gegen Tierfabriken v Switzerland*[138] (*Tierfabriken I*) the Swiss Commercial Television Company refused to broadcast an advert created by an organisation called Verein gegen Tierfabriken Schweiz (VgT). The advert expressed criticism of battery pig-farming and included a scene showing a noisy hall with pigs in small pens. The advertisement concluded with the words: 'Eat less meat, for the sake of your health, the animals and the environment!' The company's refusal of permission to broadcast the commercial was upheld in the Swiss courts as being consistent with the ban on political advertising contained in s 18(5) of the Swiss Radio and Television Act.

[4.105] When the challenge was brought in the European Court of Human Rights, the Swiss government argued that the ban placed on the advert had the 'legitimate aim' under Article 10(2) of 'enabling the formation of public opinion protected from the pressures of powerful financial groups while at the same time promoting equal opportunities for the different components of society.'[139] The court accepted this as a legitimate aim but nevertheless found that a breach of Article 10 had occurred as there was a lack of proportionality between the measures employed by the Swiss government in order to secure the 'legitimate aim' pursued.

[4.106] The court held that as the advert in question contained 'political speech', the margin of appreciation afforded to them in deciding whether or not there was a necessity to ban the advertisement was more circumscribed than in the context of commercial speech.

[4.107] The court examined whether there was proportionality between the ban on advertising and the aim pursued. The court made a number of points.

[4.108] It accepted that it was legitimate to restrict speech in the interests of maintaining pluralism and that this could be particularly important in the context of broadcasting.[140] The Swiss court of final appeal had emphasised that television had a greater impact on the public because of its dissemination and immediacy. The European Court of Human Rights stated:

> In the Court's opinion, however, while the domestic authorities may have had valid reasons for this differential treatment, a prohibition of political advertising which applies only to certain media, and not to others, does not appear to be of a particularly pressing nature.[141]

---

137. See *Lehideaux and Isorni v France* (2000) 30 EHRR 665. The case concerned an advertisement in Le Monde seeking the rehabilitation of Marshal Pétain. This arguably concerned political advertising but was treated by the Court as a straightforward political expression case.
138. *VgT Verein Gegen Tierfabriken v Switzerland* (2002) 34 EHRR 4.
139. *VgT Verein Gegen Tierfabriken v Switzerland* (2002) 34 EHRR 4, para 60.
140. The court referred back to its decision in *Informationsverein Lentia v Austria (No 1)* (Series A No 276) judgment of 24 November 1993, 16.
141. *VgT Verein Gegen Tierfabriken v Switzerland* (2002) 34 EHRR 4, para 74.

[4.109] The court did not exclude the possibility that prohibitions on political advertising might be compatible with Article 10 in some circumstances but suggested that a blanket ban was not acceptable.[142] In this regard, the court noted that it had not been argued by the Swiss authorities that VgT was a powerful financial group which could exert significant influence on the independence of Swiss broadcasting, nor was it argued that they were abusing a competitive advantage.[143]

[4.110] It also noted that the only means that VGT had at its disposal to reach the Swiss public was to broadcast through the Swiss Radio and Television Company as there was no other television company which broadcast throughout Switzerland.[144]

[4.111] The court accordingly found that the measure at issue was not necessary in a democratic society. In a subsequent ruling (*Tierfabriken II*) following the persistent refusal to broadcast the advertisements, the Grand Chamber held that there was a positive obligation on the Swiss authorities to authorise the broadcasting of the advertisement following the decision of the European Court of Human Rights in the first case and that the failure to do so represented a fresh violation of Article 10.[145]

[4.112] Prior to the ruling of the Grand Chamber in *Tierfabriken II*, the question of political advertising came before the court again in *TV Vest As & Rogaland Pensjonistparti v Norway*.[146] This case concerned a fine imposed on TV Vest for showing adverts for the Pensioners' Party without authorisation prior to local and regional elections held in 2003. The advertisements consisted of a short portrayal of the Pensioners' Party and a call to vote for it in the forthcoming elections. The relevant regulatory body had warned TV Vest that they could be fined for breaching the prohibition on political advertising on television.[147] TV Vest nevertheless continued with the broadcasts, arguing that it was a question of freedom of expression. As a consequence, TV Vest was fined NOK35,000 (approximately €4,351) for breaching the prohibition on political advertising. TV Vest appealed this fine to both the Oslo City Court and the Supreme Court and failed in its arguments regarding its Article 10 rights before both courts. It then challenged the imposition of the fine before the European Court of Human Rights.

---

142. *VgT Verein Gegen Tierfabriken v Switzerland* (2002) 34 EHRR 4, para 75.
143. *VgT Verein Gegen Tierfabriken v Switzerland* (2002) 34 EHRR 4, para 75.
144. *VgT Verein Gegen Tierfabriken v Switzerland* (2002) 34 EHRR 4, para 77.
145. See *VgT Verein gegen Tierfabriken v Switzerland (No 2)* (Application No 32772/02), Grand Chamber, 30 June 2009. For an analysis of the remedial aspect of the case, see unattributed case comment in [2009] European Human Rights Law Review 716.
146. *TV Vest As & Rogaland Pensjonistparti v Norway* (2009) 48 EHRR 51. For commentary on the case, see McCormick, 'Right to freedom of political expression – prohibition on political advertising on television' [2009] Entertainment Law Review 190; unattributed case comment, [2009] European Human Rights Law Review 263.
147. The Norwegian Broadcasting Act 1992, s 10–3 and the Broadcasting Regulation, s 10–2 thereunder.

[4.113] The court[148] noted that it had been fined on the ground that it had broadcast political adverts for the Pensioners' Party in breach of the prohibition on television broadcasting of political advertising laid down in the Broadcasting Act in Norway. That prohibition was permanent and absolute and applied only to political advertising on television. It accepted the Norwegian courts' view that the ban was necessary as political debate could be distorted by financially powerful groups who could buy greater access to the airwaves. However, the European Court of Human Rights also noted that paid advertising on television had been the sole means for the Pensioners' Party to get its message across to the public through that type of medium. Having been denied this possibility under the law, the Pensioners' Party had moreover been put at a disadvantage in comparison to the major political parties. In those circumstances, the court held that the fact that television had a more immediate and powerful effect than other media, could not justify the prohibition and fine imposed on TV Vest. It found that there had not been a reasonable relationship of proportionality between the legitimate aim pursued by the prohibition and the means used to achieve that aim. The prohibition could not therefore be viewed as 'necessary in a democratic society', as *per* the provisions of Article 10 and imposition of such a fine on the applicants was therefore in violation of Article 10.

[4.114] The current case law from the European Court of Human Rights has made it clear that a blanket ban on political advertising is incompatible with Article 10 of the Convention. While the Irish courts have not had an opportunity to revisit the issue since the decision in *Colgan*, the House of Lords considered the approach taken in *Tierfabriken I* in *R (Animal Defenders International) v Secretary of State for Culture, Media and Sport*,[149] discussed below.

UK case law on political advertising

[4.115] Like Ireland, the United Kingdom also prohibits political advertising. The current provisions are contained in ss 319 and 321 of the Communications Act 2003.[150]

---

148. The case was heard by the First Chamber.
149. *R (Animal Defenders International) v Secretary of State for Culture, Media and Sport* [2008] 2 WLR 781. The case was a 'leapfrog' appeal to the House of Lords from the High Court. For commentary on the case, see Knight, 'Monkeying around with Free Speech' [2008] Law Quarterly Review 557; Rowbottom, 'The Ban on Political Advertising and Article 10' (2007) 18 Entertainment Law Review 91; Munro, 'Time Up for the Ban?' [2007] 157 New Law Journal 886; Lewis and Cumper, 'Balancing freedom of political expression against equality of political opportunity: the courts and the UK's broadcasting ban on political advertising' [2009] Public Law 89.
150. The UK provisions are slightly more detailed than their Irish counterparts in that they set out what is meant by 'political' in the context of the ban as follows in the Communications Act 2003, s 321(2):
   ... an advertisement contravenes the prohibition on political advertising if it is
   (a) an advertisement which is inserted by or on behalf of a body whose objects are wholly or mainly of a political nature; (contd \...)

That legislation was introduced after the incorporation of the European Convention on Human Rights into English law. The Act was implemented under s 19(b) of the Human Rights Act 2000, which provides that a Minister may state their intention to introduce a Bill notwithstanding their inability to issue a declaration that the legislation concerned is compatible with the Convention.[151]

[4.116] Ofcom is the body ultimately responsible for ensuring that the prohibition is upheld.[152] In deciding the question of whether a body's objects are 'mainly political' or not, Ofcom follows the approach taken in *R v Radio Authority ex parte Bull*[153] where Lord Woolf found that ancillary objectives that might be viewed as non-political in a different context can be viewed as political in the context of a body's objectives.

[4.117] As with the Broadcasting Authority of Ireland, Ofcom publishes its decisions. In 2005, for example, it held that a 'Make Poverty History' campaign advertisement fell foul of the political advertising ban.[154] A caption on the advert directed viewers to the Make Poverty History website and encouraged viewers to lobby the government to make this issue a high priority on their agenda. Ofcom determined that the main object of the advert was to direct viewers to the website which in turn, encouraged viewers to lobby government on a specific issue – and this was to a political end. Furthermore, it held that Make Poverty History was a 'political group' in that it was focused on lobbying government with a view to changing its policy.

[4.118] The Court of Appeal considered the ban on political advertising on the radio in *R v Radio Authority ex parte Bull*.[155] In that case, Amnesty International wished to advertise and publicise the plight of the people in Rwanda and Burundi during a civil war. The UK Radio Authority rejected the advertisement on the basis that the organisation was barred from advertising as a body whose objects were 'wholly or mainly of a political nature'.[156]

---

150. (contd)
    (b) an advertisement which is directed towards a political end; or
    (c) an advertisement which has a connection with an industrial dispute.
151. *Hansard*, HC, Vol 395, col 789 (3 December 2002).
152. Communications Act 2003, s 319(1). As the BBC does not carry paid advertising under Art 10 of its licence agreement, the prohibition is of no real direct relevance to it.
153. *R v Radio Authority ex parte Bull* [1997] 3 WLR 1094. The relevant legislative provision at the time this case arose was contained in the Broadcasting Act 1990, s 92. For commentary on the case, see Stevens and Feldman, 'Broadcasting advertisements by bodies with political objectives, judicial review and the influence of charities law' [1997] Public Law 615.
154. See Ofcom's Broadcast Bulletin of 12 September 2005, Issue 43 at: http://stakeholders.ofcom.org.uk/binaries/enforcement/broadcast-bulletins/pcb52/issue43a.pdf. See also Byrne, 'Campaigning against poverty is too political for TV watchdog', *The Independent*, 13 September 2005.
155. *R v Radio Authority ex parte Bull* [1997] 3 WLR 1094.
156. Amnesty initiated proceedings in Strasbourg but the Radio Authority reversed its decision before the case was heard – see *Amnesty International (UK) v UK* (Application No 38383/97) 18 January 2000.

[4.119] The House of Lords considered the ban in *R (Animal Defenders International) v Secretary of State for Culture, Media and Sport.*[157] The claimant was a non-profit company whose aims included the suppression, by lawful means, of cruelty to animals. It campaigned against the use of animals in commerce, science and leisure and lobbied for changes in law and public policy to that end. In 2005 it had launched a campaign entitled 'My Mate's a Primate' with the object of directing public attention towards the use of primates by humans and the threat presented by such use to their survival.

[4.120] The Law Lords found that the prohibition passed the tests of being prescribed by law and having a legitimate aim and their judgments focus primarily on the issue of whether the ban was 'necessary in a democratic society'. Lord Bingham's judgment emphasised the crucial role played by free speech in a democracy, stating that:

> [F]ree communication of information, opinions and argument about laws which a state should enact and policies its government ... should pursue [was] an essential condition of truly democratic government.' [158]

[4.121] He went on to add that it was also 'highly desirable that the playing field of debate should as far as possible be level.'[159] He noted the potentially distortive effect of advertising in this context, noting that a 'level playing field':

> ... is not achieved if political parties can, in proportion to their resources, buy unlimited opportunities to advertise in the most effective media, so that elections become little more than an auction. Nor is it achieved if well-endowed interests which are not political parties are able to use the power of the purse to give enhanced prominence to views which may be true or false, attractive to progressive minds or unattractive, beneficial or injurious. The risk is that objects which are essentially political may come to be accepted by the public not because they are shown by public debate to be right but because, by dint of constant repetition, the public has been conditioned to accept them. The rights of others which a restriction on the exercise of the right to free expression may properly be designed to protect must ... include a right to be protected against the potential mischief of partial political advertising.[160]

---

157. *R (Animal Defenders International) v Secretary of State for Culture, Media and Sport* [2008] 2 WLR 781. The case was a 'leapfrog' appeal to the House of Lords from the High Court. For commentary on the case, see Knight, 'Monkeying around with Free Speech' [2008] Law Quarterly Review 557; J Rowbottom, 'The Ban on Political Advertising and Article 10' (2007) 18 Entertainment Law Review 91; C Munro, 'Time Up for the Ban?' [2007] 157 New Law Journal 886; T Lewis and P Cumper, 'Balancing freedom of political expression against equality of political opportunity: the courts and the UK's broadcasting ban on political advertising' [2009] Public Law 89.

158. *R (Animal Defenders International) v Secretary of State for Culture, Media and Sport* [2008] 2 WLR 781, para 27.

159. *R (Animal Defenders International) v Secretary of State for Culture, Media and Sport* [2008] 2 WLR 781, para 28.

160. *R (Animal Defenders International) v Secretary of State for Culture, Media and Sport* [2008] 2 WLR 781, para 28. See also Lord Scott, para 40 and Baroness Hale, para 49 to similar effect.

[4.122] One of the points made by the European Court of Human Rights in *Tierfabriken I*, was that a blanket ban could not be considered proportionate in cases where it caught organisations who were not at a financial advantage. Lord Bingham took the view, however, that it was difficult to see how any system to cap or ration advertising could be devised that would not be circumvented. He also pointed out that any such system would be likely to accord excessive discretion to officials which would give rise to many legal challenges. Lord Bingham also highlighted the duty of impartiality on broadcasters which he felt would be rendered even more difficult to perform if account had to be taken of political advertising. He noted that the government 'had considered that no fair and workable compromise solution could be found which would address the problem – a judgment which Parliament accepted' and which Lord Bingham saw 'no reason to challenge'.[161]

[4.123] Lord Bingham also noted that there was not a total prohibition on political advertising as the ban covered broadcast media only, leaving open the other myriad of outlets for advertisement including newspapers, magazines, direct mailshots, billboards, public meetings and marches.[162]

[4.124] Lord Bingham noted that the differential treatment of the broadcast media was justified and because of the 'greater immediacy and impact of television and radio advertising ... it [was] not really a matter of serious debate but that the broadcast media [was] more pervasive and potent than any other form of media'.[163]

[4.125] Under s 2 of the Human Rights Act 2000, the House of Lords has an obligation which meant that the judgment of the European Court of Human Rights in *Tierfabriken I* had to be 'taken into account ... in so far as, in the opinion of the court ... it [was] relevant to the proceedings'.[164] In considering the decision in *Tierfabriken I*, Lord Bingham stated that the argument that it was necessary to keep the 'playing field of debate ... so far as practicable level' had not been 'deployed' to its 'full strength' in *Tierfabriken I*. He also found the factual situation in that case distinguishable as the applicant in *Tierfabriken I* had been seeking to respond to commercials broadcast by the

---

161. *R (Animal Defenders International) v Secretary of State for Culture, Media and Sport* [2008] 2 WLR 781, para 31.
162. *R (Animal Defenders International) v Secretary of State for Culture, Media and Sport* [2008] 2 WLR 781, para 32.
163. *R (Animal Defenders International) v Secretary of State for Culture, Media and Sport* [2008] 2 WLR 781, para 30 quoting Ouseley J in the Divisional Court *ADI* [2006] EWHC 3069, para 90.
164. The Law Lords differed in their view of this obligation. Lord Bingham (*R (Animal Defenders International) v Secretary of State for Culture, Media and Sport* [2008] 2 WLR 781, para 37) and Baroness Hale ([2008] 2 WLR 781, para 53) found that the domestic courts had to follow, in the absence of special circumstances, the jurisprudence of the European Court which had the ultimate interpretative authority for Convention rights. Lord Scott ([2008] 2 WLR 781, para 44) on the other hand, envisaged two streams of case law – one domestic and one from Strasbourg. See Lewis, 'The European Ceiling on Human Rights' [2007] Public Law 720; Masterman, 'Aspiration or foundation? The status of Strasbourg jurisprudence and the "Convention rights" in domestic law' in Fenwick, Phillipson and Masterman (eds), *Judicial Reasoning under the UK Human Rights Act* (Cambridge University Press, 2007), 57.

meat industry.[165] Lord Scott similarly cautioned against the slavish importation of principles developed by the Strasbourg Court, stating that the judgments in such cases were fact-dependent and thus it was 'perilous to transpose the outcome of one case to another where the facts are different'.[166]

[4.126] Despite the fact that the Strasbourg Court had specifically found in *Tierfabriken I* that the margin of appreciation was narrow when it came to political speech, Lord Bingham noted:

> ... that there was no settled practice among European states on the issue of political advertising, 'a factor tending to widen the margin of appreciation' and it 'may be that each state [was] best fitted to judge the checks and balances necessary to safeguard, consistently with Art.10, the integrity of its own democracy'.[167]

[4.127] The Law Lords in *Animal Defenders* did, however, indicate that they might be willing to find fault with the ban were a different fact situation to come before them. Lord Scott noted that the ban was capable of catching broadcasts by organisations which contained no political content and seemed to suggest that the court might treat that situation differently.[168]

Conclusions re: political advertising

[4.128] The ban on political advertising has been subjected to heavy criticism.[169] It has been argued that it 'encourages campaign groups to disguise their message in the form of news to be delivered onscreen without the inherent subconscious warning that advertisements carry.'[170]

---

165. *R (Animal Defenders International) v Secretary of State for Culture, Media and Sport* [2008] 2 WLR 781, para 28–29.

166. *R (Animal Defenders International) v Secretary of State for Culture, Media and Sport* [2008] 2 WLR 781, para 43.

167. *R (Animal Defenders International) v Secretary of State for Culture, Media and Sport* [2008] 2 WLR 781, para 35.

168. *R (Animal Defenders International) v Secretary of State for Culture, Media and Sport* [2008] 2 WLR 781, para 42.

169. Knight, 'Monkeying around with Free Speech' [2008] Law Quarterly Review 557; Scott, 'A monstrous and unjustifiable infringement'? Political expression and the broadcasting ban on advocacy advertising' (2006) 66 Modern Law Review 224; Lewis and Cumper, 'Balancing freedom of political expression against equality of political opportunity: the courts and the UK's broadcasting ban on political advertising' [2009] Public Law 89; Geddis, 'If Thy Right Eye Offend Thee, Pluck it Out' (2003) 66 Modern Law Review 885. For a less critical view, see Rowbottom, 'The ban on political advertising and Article 10' (2007) 18 Entertainment Law Review 91.

170. Knight, 'Monkeying around with Free Speech' [2008] Law Quarterly Review 557, 559.

[4.129] It can also be seen as a fundamentally conservative measure which maintains the status quo and reduces the potential for transformative social change. Thus, as one critic of the English ban has pointed out:

> A 1950s campaign to decriminalise homosexuality would be caught by the ban. A 1970s campaign to persuade government, national or local, to avoid any dealings with apartheid South Africa would be caught by the ban because of the attempt to influence policy.[171]

A further argument against its retention is that stated in the Strasbourg case law, namely that it is overly broad and thus disproportionate.[172]

[4.130] The main argument canvassed in support of the prohibition of political advertising is that it ensures a level playing field and, more specifically, avoids a situation where those in a position to pay for broadcast advertising can drown out the voices of less financially well off interest groups. This argument is exemplified by the judgment of Lord Bingham in *Animal Defenders*, where he stated as follows:

> The fundamental rationale of the democratic process is that if competing views, opinions and policies are publicly debated and exposed to public scrutiny the good will over time drive out the bad and the true prevail over the false. It must be assumed that, given time, the public will make a sound choice when, in the course of the democratic process, it has the right to choose. But it is highly desirable that the playing field of debate should be so far as practicable level. This is achieved where, in public discussion, differing views are expressed, contradicted, answered and debated. It is the duty of broadcasters to achieve this object in an impartial way by presenting balanced programmes in which all lawful views may be ventilated. It is not achieved if political parties can, in proportion to their resources, buy unlimited opportunities to advertise in the most effective media, so that elections become little more than an auction. Nor is it achieved if well-endowed interests which are not political parties are able to use the power of the purse to give enhanced prominence to views which may be true or false, attractive to progressive minds or unattractive, beneficial or injurious. The risk is that objects which are essentially political may come to be accepted by the public not because they are shown in public debate to be right but because, by dint of constant repetition, the public has been conditioned to accept them.[173]

This does not address the point that the European Court of Human Rights made in *Tierfabriken I* that a more narrow and tailored prohibition would constitute a more proportionate response. The approach of the English and Irish courts in *Animal Defenders* and *Colgan* respectively demonstrates an unwillingness to engage in anything other than a superficial review of legislative policy in this area.

---

171. Knight, 'Monkeying around with Free Speech' [2008] Law Quarterly Review 557, 561.

172. See Knight, 'Monkeying around with Free Speech' [2008] Law Quarterly Review 557: 'The way to deal with one person in an argument shouting too loud is not to cancel the argument altogether. Procedural limits on speech have always been accepted, but a procedural limitation taken to an extreme becomes substantively unfair. A blanket ban is not the proportionate method of dealing with the problem of unfair speech competition' (561).

173. *R (Animal Defenders International) v Secretary of State for Culture, Media and Sport* [2008] 2 WLR 781, para 28.

[4.131] Baroness Hale, in her judgment in *Animal Defenders*, referred to 'an elephant in the committee room' in the context of that case, namely the 'the dominance of advertising, not only in elections but also in the formation of political opinion, in the United States of America.'[174] She saw the case as being about more than 'permissible restrictions on freedom of expression. It is about striking the right balance between the two most important components of a democracy: freedom of expression and voter equality'.[175] One of the reasons for the dominance to which Baroness Hale referred is the insistence of the United States Supreme Court that the First Amendment covers restrictions on the volume of speech so that limitations on expenditure on political advertising are characterised as violating freedom of expression. The Supreme Court started down that road in *Buckley v Valeo*,[176] where it struck down restrictions on expenditure in political campaigns on the basis that such limitations violated the First Amendment by reducing the volume of political speech.[177] While subsequent case law fluctuated between expanding and contracting the protection of 'money-that-pays-for-speech', the most recent decision of the US Supreme Court in *Citizens United v Federal Election Commission*[178] indicates that the approach taken in *Buckley* retains its vitality despite its detractors.[179]

[4.132] One of the key justifications for retaining a prohibition on political advertising is that it is necessary to ensure the wealthy do not drown out the voices of the less

---

174. *R (Animal Defenders International) v Secretary of State for Culture, Media and Sport* [2008] 2 WLR 781, para 47.
175. *R (Animal Defenders International) v Secretary of State for Culture, Media and Sport* [2008] 2 WLR 781, para 49.
176. *Buckley v Valeo* 424 US 1 (1976). Hereafter referred to as *Buckley*. For a brief account of the case law that follows, see Levine, 'The (Un)Informed Electorate: Insights into the Supreme Court's Electoral Speech Cases' (2003) 54 Case W Res L Rev 225, 262–276.
177. The alchemical conversion of money into speech was not without its objectors. Justice White, in particular, was adamant that: The First Amendment protects the right to speak, not the right to spend, and limitations on the amount of money that can be spent are not the same as restrictions on speaking. I agree with the majority that the expenditures in this case 'produce' core First Amendment speech … But that is precisely the point: they produce such speech; they are not speech itself. At least in these circumstances, I cannot accept the identification of speech with its antecedents. Such a house-that-Jack-built approach could equally be used to find a First Amendment right to a job or to a minimum wage to 'produce' the money to 'produce' the speech. *Federal Election Commission v National Conservative Political Action Committee* 470 US 480 (1985), 508, dissenting.
178. *Citizens United v Federal Election Commission* 558 US 50 (2010).
179. Key post-*Buckley* case law includes *First National Bank of Boston v Bellotti* 435 US 765 (1978); *Austin v Michigan Chamber of Commerce* 494 US 652 (1990); *Federal Election Commission v Beaumont (Docket No 02–403) (2003)*; *McConnell v Federal Election Commission* 540 US 93 (2003). For a discussion of the case law on campaign finance see Raskin, 'The Campaign Finance Crucible: Is Laissez Fair?' (2003) 101 Michigan Law Review 1532; Levine, 'The (Un)Informed Electorate: Insights into the Supreme Court's Electoral Speech Cases' (2003) 54 Case Western Res Law Review 225; Grant, 'Election campaign funding reform and judicial review in the United States' [2004] Public Law 501; O'Neill, 'Corporate Freedom of Expression' (2005) 27 Dublin University Law Journal 185.

wealthy. The European Court of Human Rights has not rejected that argument, rather its approach is critical of measures which are insufficiently narrowly drawn to achieve that purpose. The approach taken in the Strasbourg case law indicates that Article 10 requires contracting states which operate a prohibition on political advertising to exempt from it those whose voices may require amplification. Fundamental to that approach is the understanding of Article 10 as a measure which has a particular contribution to make to the functioning of democracy.[180] The main objection to this raised in *Animal Defenders* was the practical difficulty of choosing which advertisements to permit and the concern that allowing any access to broadcasting would inevitably lead to the dominance of the voices of the wealthy.

[4.133] It is interesting to note that the argument was made in *Buckley* that limitations on campaign contributions were required to avoid the drowning out of the voices of the less well resourced. The argument was rejected by the US Supreme Court on the basis that 'the concept that government may restrict the speech of some elements of our society in order to enhance the relative voice of others is wholly foreign to the First Amendment'[181] and that '[t]he First Amendment's protection against governmental abridgment of free expression cannot properly be made to depend on a person's financial ability to engage in public discussion.'[182] The difference in approach illustrates the ideological distance between US and European free speech theory.[183]

WHY IS BROADCASTING SPECIAL?

[4.134] The restrictions of political expression considered above are all confined to broadcasting and leave print media and the internet alone. Statutory regulation of broadcasting is an established policy in a number of jurisdictions and seems to be regarded as less constitutionally offensive than equivalent restrictions on the press.[184] It has been argued that this dichotomy is indefensible as a matter of constitutional principle.[185]

[4.135] A number of rationales have been canvassed for this differential treatment of broadcasting. One justification for singling out broadcasting for special regulation is its capacity to influence millions of viewers.[186] It has also been suggested that the press, at least in the United Kingdom, is seen as openly partisan with popular newspapers being

---

180. See discussion in **Ch 2**.
181. *Buckley v Valeo* 424 US 1 (1976), 48–49.
182. *Buckley v Valeo* 424 US 1 (1976), 49.
183. See discussion in **Ch 2**.
184. Fenwick and Phillipson, *Media Freedom under the Human Rights Act* (Oxford University Press, 2006), 994.
185. Hogan, 'Federal Republic of Germany and Ireland and the United Kingdom: Three European Approaches to Political Campaign Regulation' [1992] 21 *Capital University Law Review* 501, 506.
186. Fenwick and Phillipson, *Media Freedom under the Human Rights Act* (Oxford University Press, 2006), Ch 20.

known for their left or right leanings, whereas broadcasting provides the only apparently impartial source of information to viewers. Thus Barendt notes that:

> [T]he more recent evolution of broadcasting has meant that the public has different expectations of the audiovisual media than it has of newspapers or magazines. While it expects the print media to be biased or to adopt a selective coverage of issues of public interest, it has relied on radio and television to provide objective news …'[187]

[4.136] In *Animal Defenders* Lord Bingham stated that it was 'not really a matter of serious debate but that the broadcast media [was] more pervasive and potent than any other form of media'.[188]

[4.137] While the growing influence of the internet might be thought to undermine the special treatment meted out to broadcasting, it has been commented that:

> Despite the growth of the internet in recent years, the most powerful medium of modern mass communication would appear to remain that of broadcasting. It can be used to communicate messages to millions of people in persuasive, seductive and effective ways.[189]

One area, however, in which the internet's growing influence has arguably circumvented the regulation of broadcasting is in the area of political campaigning and political advertisements. The advertisement at issue in the *Tierfabriken* litigation was eventually released on YouTube. In fact, in *TV Vest* the respondent state argued that the advertisement prohibited in that case could be circulated via the web so that the prohibition on its broadcasting was not a serious interference with freedom of expression. The recognition that alternative channels are open for dissemination of political advertisements arguably undermines the proportionality of restricting their distribution via a total ban in the first place.[190]

While political campaigning and advertising on the internet is an unregulated area of Irish law, the US Federal Election Commission changed its rules in 2006 to include within its regulatory remit paid internet advertisements placed on another person's website.[191]

---

187. Barendt, *Freedom of Speech* (2nd edn, Oxford University Press, 2005), 447.
188. *R (Animal Defenders International) v Secretary of State for Culture, Media and Sport* [2008] 2 WLR 781, para 30 quoting Ouseley J in the Divisional Court *ADI* [2006] EWHC 3069, para 90.
189. Lewis and Cumper, 'Balancing freedom of political expression against equality of political opportunity: the courts and the UK's broadcasting ban on political advertising' [2009] Public Law 89, 90.
190. Lord Bingham referred to the possibility of other mechanisms to circulate political advertising in *Animal Defenders*, para 32. See also Baroness Hale, para 51.
191. See www.fec.gov/law/cfr/ej_compilation/2006/notice_2006-8.pdf.

Chapter 5
THE MEDIA AND THE COURTS

INTRODUCTION

[5.01] The interaction between the media and legal system raises a number of important questions and has given rise to case law concerning the public administration of justice, the law of contempt and journalists' privilege. This chapter explores the extent to which the media may have access to the courts, the legal limitations on reporting of what is observed in court and the important area of the protection of journalists' sources which has seen recent developments under the influence of the case law from the European Court of Human Rights.

[5.02] The importance of public and press access to the courts was recognised at common law[1] and was included in the Irish Constitution under Article 34.1 of the Irish Constitution.[2] This provision requires that justice be administered in public 'save in such special and limited circumstances as may be prescribed by law'. As Walsh J put it in *Re R Ltd*,[3] 'the doors of the court must be open so that members of the general public may come and see for themselves that justice is done'.[4] As the number of individual citizens who actually attend and witness the administration of justice is relatively small, the media has an important role to play in reporting on court proceedings. This important role has been recognised in the context of Article 34.1. Thus, in *Irish Times Ltd v Ireland*,[5] Morris P noted that 'freedom of publication by the media is an integral part of the administration of justice in public'.[6] This view was echoed by Keane J on appeal where he referred back to the judgment of Walsh J in *Re R Ltd* and stated that:

> [T]he very fact that physical and other constraints prevent more than a minuscule section of the entire population from being present in court while justice is being administered makes it all the more imperative that the media should have the widest possible freedom to report what happens in court which is consistent with the proper administration of justice. It is manifest that the right of the public to know what is happening in our courts, a right which is clearly recognised and guaranteed by Article 34, would be eroded almost to vanishing point if the public had to depend on the account that might be transmitted to them by such people as happened to gain admission to the court room for the trial in question. In modern conditions, the media are the eyes and ears of the public and the ordinary citizen is almost entirely dependent on them for his knowledge of what goes on in court.

---

1. See the comments of the Master of the Rolls on the rationale for media access to the courts in *Attorney-General v Guardian Newspapers Ltd (No 2)* [1988] 3 All ER 595, 600.
2. There is no requirement of publicity for proceedings before courts under. Article 38.3 or 38.4 or 28.3.3 according to Art icle38.6.
3. *Re R Ltd* [1989] 1 IR 126.
4. Walsh J, *Re R* [1989] 1 IR 126, 134.
5. *Irish Times Ltd v Ireland* [1998] 1 IR 359; [1997] 2 ILRM 541.
6. *Irish Times Ltd v Ireland* [1998] 1 IR 359, 367, Morris P.

Justice must be administered in public, not in order to satisfy the merely prurient or mindlessly inquisitive, but because, if it were not, an essential feature of a truly democratic society would be missing. Such a society could not tolerate the huge void that would be left if the public had to rely on what might be seen or heard by casual observers, rather than on a detailed daily commentary by press, radio and television. The most benign climate for the growth of corruption and abuse of powers, whether by the judiciary or members of the legal profession, is one of secrecy.[7]

[5.03] There are, however, limitations on the way in which judicial proceedings may be covered by the media. For example, Irish courts do not permit live broadcasting of court proceedings and television cameras are excluded from them.[8] Apart from restrictions on the means of reporting court proceedings, there are also limitations on the extent to which certain proceedings can be covered at all and these exceptions to the principle of open justice are considered below.[9]

[5.04] While the media undoubtedly play an important role in the dissemination of information concerning legal proceedings, their role can be seen as interfering with or disrupting the administration of justice in certain situations.[10] The law of contempt regulates, albeit somewhat archaically, the content of coverage of court proceedings and the parameters of acceptable expression concerning the judiciary. This area is also considered in this chapter.

[5.05] There are other circumstances in which the interests of the media may clash with those of the administration of justice. It is generally accepted that professional ethics require journalists to preserve anonymity of their sources. This is seen by the profession as crucial to the preservation of a flow of information from members of the public to the media. The Irish courts had previously refused to recognise the entitlement of journalists to maintain the confidentiality of their sources. Prompted in no small part by the increasing influence of the case law from Strasbourg in this area, the Supreme Court has recently indicated a more pro-media stance on this issue. This development, together with related case law from the European Court of Human Rights is discussed below.

---

7.   *Irish Times Ltd v Ireland* [1998] 1 IR 359, 409; [1997] 2 ILRM 541. For similar views of the importance of open justice, see the decision of the US Supreme Court in *Richmond Newspapers v Virginia* (1980) 448 US 555 and the Supreme Court of Canada in *Edmonton Journal v AG for Alberta* (1989) 64 DLR (4th) 577.

8.   For a survey of Irish judicial attitudes towards such broadcasting in the wake of the OJ Simpson trial, see Lambert, 'Judicial Questionnaire on Courtroom Broadcasting' (1997) 15 *Irish Law Times* 50. For an arguments in favour of televised court proceedings, see Dockray, 'Courts on Television' (1988) Modern Law Review 593.

9.   For an analysis of some of the practical issues that arise in respect of exceptions to Article 34.1, see Fahy, 'Open Justice? The Practical Operation of Article 34.1 of the Constitution' (2003) 21 *Irish Law Times* 303 (Pt 1) and 316 (Pt 2).

10.   For a discussion of the rights and responsibilities of media coverage of the courts see Lord Irvine, 'Reporting the Courts – the Media's Rights and Responsibilities' (1999) 34 Irish Jurist 1.

THE PRINCIPLE OF OPEN JUSTICE
Article 34.1 of the Irish Constitution

[5.06] The wording of Article 34.1 itself provides for certain exceptions to the general rule that the public must have access to the courtroom. Litigants may wish to have proceedings heard in camera for many reasons. The media, on the other hand, have an interest in being able to report on trials of interest to the public. The contribution such coverage can make is not limited to the mere provision of information. The lack of media access to and exposure of judicial decision-making can adversely affect the quality of justice by failing to expose areas of the law that require reform. The Irish media have been praised for their 'great public service' in the 1980s when a number of newspapers, including the *Irish Times*, published careful reports of criminal prosecutions for incest, despite the fact that such coverage was thought to be in breach of the Punishment of Incest Act 1908.[11]

[5.07] The general rule that the public and the media are excluded from family law proceedings was criticised by the Working Group on a Courts Commission in its Sixth Report, which observed that:

> [T]he operation of the in camera rule has hidden from the public at large the extent of marriage breakdown and consequent family law litigation in our society. This can, for instance, prevent public representatives from evaluating properly the situation, such as the need for the provision of support services to aid couples whose marriages are in difficulty.[12]

By way of response to such criticism, a Family Law Reporting Pilot Project[13] to gather information about family law cases and impart it to the public operated for one year[14] and was followed by a more extensive project run under the auspices of the Courts Service which seeks to produce bulletins on family law matters.[15]

[5.08] The Irish courts have made a number of robust pronouncements in defence of the public nature of court proceedings. Prior to the statements in *Re R Ltd* and *Irish Times,* considered above, in *Beamish & Crawford Limited v Crowley,*[16] Ó'Dálaigh CJ considered the argument that publicity might affect the reputations of litigants in a civil dispute. He responded by stating that:

> [P]ublicity, deserved or otherwise, is inseparable from the administration of justice in public; this is a principle which, as the Constitution declares, may not be

---

11. Editorial, 'Freedom of Information and Reporting the Courts' (1997) 15 *Irish Law Times* 73.
12. Working Group on a Courts Commission, *Sixth Report*, November 1998, at 72. Available from www.courts.ie.
13. Established by the recommendation of the Family Law Development Committee, chaired by Mrs Justice Susan Denham following the recommendation of the Working Group.
14. For a description of the pilot project, see S Flockton, 'The Family Law Reporting Project' (2003) 6 Irish Journal of Family Law 17.
15. Coulter, *Report to the Board of the Courts Service* 2007 and subsequent reports available from www.courts.ie.
16. *Beamish & Crawford Limited v Crowley* [1969] IR 142.

departed from except in such special and limited cases as may be prescribed by law: Article 34, section 1. I cannot accept that the fact that the trial will, for one of the parties, attract more undesirable publicity in one venue than in another is a matter proper to be taken into account in determining the venue.[17]

Non-statutory exceptions

[5.09] As noted by Ó'Dálaigh CJ, the wording of Article 34.1 seems to require that any restrictions on the media's entitlement to report on court proceedings must be 'prescribed by law'. In *Re R Ltd,*[18] Walsh J read this as meaning that 'the Constitution of 1937 removed any judicial discretion to have proceedings heard other than in public save where expressly conferred by statute'.[19] Finlay CJ took a similar view in *Irish Press Plc v Ingersoll.*[20]

[5.10] This position was reiterated in a number of cases. In *Re Greendale Developments (No 1),*[21] Laffoy J noted that it was:

... well settled that the effect of Article 34, s 1 of the Constitution is that justice must be administered in public in the absence of a statutory provision enacted or re-enacted or applied by a law enacted by the Oireachtas subsequent to the coming into force of the Constitution.[22]

[5.11] In *Wright v Board of Management of Gorey Community School,*[23] the plaintiffs had allegedly been involved in the use of illicit substances. One had been suspended and the other expelled. Both complained that the decisions to take this disciplinary action had been reached in breach of fair procedures and that their constitutional right to education had been violated. At the outset of the proceedings, counsel requested that the court place restrictions on the reporting of the proceedings. The plaintiffs were 13 and 15 years of age and counsel asked that the name of their school and the name of any

---

17. *Beamish & Crawford Limited v Crowley* [1969] IR 142, 146.
18. *Re R Ltd* [1989] 1 IR 126.
19. *Re R Ltd* [1989] 1 IR 126, at 135.
20. *Irish Press Plc v Ingersoll* [1993] ILRM 747.
21. *Re Greendale Developments (No 1)* [1997] 3 IR 540. Here, a liquidator sought an order pursuant to the Companies Act 1963, s 231 granting him liberty to pursue two plenary actions which had been commenced by the company prior to the commencement of the winding-up. The liquidator sought to have this application heard in camera and this was dealt with as a preliminary issue by Laffoy J. The focus in the case was on whether the decision to grant the order sought under s 231 would constitute the administration of justice within the meaning of Article 34.1 applying the criteria set out in *McDonald v Bord na gCon* [1965] IR 217.
22. *Re Greendale Developments (No 1)* [1997] 3 IR 540, 549, referring back to *Re R Ltd* [1989] 1 IR 126 and *Irish Press plc v Ingersoll Irish Publications Ltd (No 1)* [1994] 1 IR 176.
23. *Wright v Board of Management of Gorey Community School* (28 March 2000, unreported), HC, O'Sullivan J.

minor referred to in the affidavits be disguised or deleted. O'Sullivan J refused to make any such order, noting that while it was desirable that minors be protected, this was a matter for the Oireachtas to prescribe.[24]

[5.12] A similar approach was taken in two cases which arose in the context of infected blood products. In *The Claimant v Board of Saint James' Hospital*,[25] the plaintiffs were haemophiliacs who alleged that they had contracted HIV as a result of using infected blood products supplied to them. The plaintiffs applied to the President of the High Court for an order giving them liberty to issue a plenary summons and serve a statement of claim on the intended defendants without disclosing the names or addresses of the plaintiffs. Hamilton P refused the application on the basis that Article 34.1 was both 'specific' and 'mandatory'. He noted that there was nothing in the law or rules of court which would justify a departure from the requirement that justice be administered in public.

[5.13] This decision was referred to approvingly in *Roe v Blood Transfusion Service Board*,[26] where the plaintiff (who had used infected blood products and contracted Hepatitis C) sought to sue the defendant board under an assumed name to protect her privacy. The plaintiff argued that she was not seeking to have her case heard otherwise than in public and that she was seeking to keep her identity private. A practice in the United States whereby litigants could use fictitious names was referred to. Laffoy J, having referred back to *Re R Ltd*, noted that the plaintiff's objective was to keep her true identity out of the public domain. She expressed her view that:

> [I]n the context of the underlying rationale of Article 34, s 1, the public disclosure of the true identities of parties to civil litigation is essential if justice is to be administered in public. In a situation in which the true identity of a plaintiff in a civil action is known to the parties to the action and to the court but is concealed from the public, members of the general public cannot see for themselves that justice is done.[27]

Similarly, in *Re Ansbacher (Cayman) Ltd*,[28] McCracken J refused an application to have civil proceedings heard in camera. The applicants were seeking ultimately to challenge their names being published in a report by inspectors appointed to a company which they said would impact adversely on their good names. Given the context of the application, the court agreed to hear that application itself in camera. The judgment by

---

24.   He also noted that in *State (Derek Smullen and Declan Smullen) v Duffy* [1980] ILRM 46, Finlay P had made no such order. In *Student A and Student B v Dublin Secondary School* (25 November 1999, unreported), HC, Kearns J, a different approach was taken in a very similar case where Kearns J granted orders protecting the anonymity of the minor plaintiffs but noted that the issue was not 'entirely free from doubt'.

25.   *The Claimant v Board of Saint James' Hospital* (10 May, 1989, unreported), HC, Hamilton P.

26.   *Roe v Blood Transfusion Service Board* [1996] 3 IR 67.

27.   *Roe v Blood Transfusion Service Board* [1996] 3 IR 67, 71.

28.   *Re Ansbacher (Cayman) Ltd* [2002] 2 IR 517.

McCracken J sets out a robust defence of the principle of open justice. He rejected the application to have further matters dealt with in camera, stating:

> The fact that Article 34.1 requires Courts to administer justice in public by its very nature requires the attendant publicity, including the identification of parties seeking justice. It is a small price to be paid to ensure the integrity and openness of one of the three organs of the State namely the judicial process, in which openness is a vital element. It is often said that justice must not only be done, but must also be seen to be done, and if this involves innocent parties being brought before the Courts in either civil or criminal proceedings, and wrongly accused, that is unfortunate, but is essential for the protection of the entire judicial system. I do not believe I am called upon to consider any hierarchy of rights in the present case, but if I had to do so, I have no hesitation whatever in saying that the right to have justice administered in public far exceeds any right to privacy, confidentiality or a good name.[29]

[5.14] In *Irish Times v Ireland*,[30] a trial judge presiding over a criminal trial in the Circuit Court had concerns over the accuracy of particular reports in the media discussing some preliminary matters surrounding the trial. He expressed his concern that inappropriate media coverage could result in a mistrial, a trial for a similar offence having previously collapsed due to inaccurate reporting. Due to the concern of a potential mistrial in the case before him, he made an order which restrained contemporaneous reporting of the trial, limiting it to the fact that the trial was proceeding in open court; the names and addresses of the accused parties; the nature of the crimes alleged in the indictment; where the trial was taking place; and the fact that a connected party had pleaded guilty to the charge. The media were prohibited from reporting that the accused persons were in custody. The ban was to apply only during the course of the trial.

[5.15] A number of newspapers, together with RTÉ, challenged the ban. Both the High Court and Supreme Court found that this was a trial otherwise than 'in public' within the meaning of Article 34.1. Morris P, in the High Court, pointed out that:

> [I]f one were to hold that proceedings in Court were 'in public' while such a ban on publication by the media was in place then the reasoning which would support that conclusion would equally support the conclusion that a trial held in circumstances in which no member of the public was allowed to communicate to anyone outside of the Court what transpired in Court, would be equally valid. I do not think that any reasonable person could be satisfied that such a trial was being held in public.[31]

[5.16] In the Supreme Court, O'Flaherty J noted that:

> [P]ostponement rather than total prohibition will most always be but poor consolation for the press; the whole point of the speed with which news is reported

---

29.   *Re Ansbacher (Cayman) Ltd* [2002] 2 IR 517.
30.   *Irish Times v Ireland* [1998] 1 IR 359.
31.   *Irish Times v Ireland* [1998] 1 IR 359, 367.

nowadays is that it will often only be relevant for the public if it is reported *immediately*.[32]

[5.17] Both the High Court and Supreme Court also agreed that the situations in which the courts could order a trial to be held otherwise than in public were not limited solely to those exceptions created by statute.[33] While Walsh J's judgment in *Re R Ltd* suggested that only the Oireachtas could create exceptions to the principle set out in Article 34.1, Hamilton CJ considered and rejected the argument that exceptions to the public hearing requirement of Article 34.1 were strictly limited to litigation governed by specific legislative provisions, holding that:

> The effect of such submission, if valid, would be to remove from a trial judge the jurisdiction and discretion which he enjoyed at common law to prohibit reports of proceedings when he considered such reporting would frustrate or render impractical the administration of justice and to vest in the Oireachtas solely the jurisdiction of deciding what aspects of the administration of justice would be conducted in private.[34]

[5.18] While the judgments in *Irish Times v Ireland* suggest a potentially broad approach to judge-made exceptions to Article 34.1, the case itself was concerned with the balancing of the requirement to administer justice in public and the right to a fair trial under Article 38.1 and seems to have been interpreted in later cases (discussed below) as applying only in that situaton.[35]

[5.19] The judgments in *Irish Times v Ireland* referred to the need to postpone reporting of trials where this was necessary to preserve the right of an accused person to a fair trial under Article 38.1; for example, where there was a trial within a trial to consider the admissibility of confession evidence or where two persons were indicted for an offence together but subject to separate trials.

[5.20] The test to be applied when assessing whether a reporting restriction could be imposed was whether there was a real risk of an unfair trial in circumstances where the trial judge could not remedy the prejudice through jury direction or other means. While Morris P had found that the trial judge had justifiable concerns about the trial in the case at hand, the Supreme Court overturned him on this point. The judgments noted that the trial judge had not been entitled to assume that media coverage would be other than fair and accurate. They also pointed out that any issues that did arise could have been dealt with by jury directions and by subjecting the media to the contempt jurisdiction of the court.

---

32. *Irish Times v Ireland* [1998] 1 IR 359, 393.
33. See also *Student A and Student B v Dublin Secondary School* (25 November, 1999, unreported), HC, Kearns J.
34. *Irish Times v Ireland* [1998] 1 IR 359, 384.
35. See *De Gortari v Smithwick J* [1999] 4 IR 223; *Re Ansbacher (Cayman) Ltd* [2002] 2 IR 517.

[5.21] In *De Gortari v Smithwick J*,[36] Denham J reiterated that proceedings concerned with criminal matters might be held otherwise than in public in order to ensure the fairness of a criminal trial. In that case, French prosecuting authorities sought an order pursuant to s 51 of the Criminal Justice Act 1994 that evidence should be obtained by the applicant to assist the French authorities. The applicant refused to answer some of the questions put to him and claimed that he was not required to do so under the 1994 Act. The District Judge ruled against him and the applicant instituted judicial review proceedings. He applied to have the judicial review proceedings heard in camera. That application was refused in the High Court. Denham J, hearing the appeal from that refusal, stated that:

> The right to have justice administered in public is not absolute. An accused's rights may require a hearing to be held otherwise than in public. There is an inherent jurisdiction in the Courts to order that a criminal trial be held otherwise than in public: *Irish Times Limited v Ireland* [1998] 1 IR 359. The right of an accused to a fair trial is one of the most fundamental constitutional rights afforded to persons and on a hierarchy of constitutional rights is a superior right: *D v Director of Public Prosecutions* [1994] 2 IR 465. A Court may limit the publication of proceedings where that is necessary in order to protect the right of an accused person to a fair trial. However, in order to exercise this discretion the trial judge must be satisfied (a) that there is a real risk of an unfair trial if contemporaneous reporting is permitted, and, (b) that the damage which any reporting would cause could not be remedied by the trial judge either by giving appropriate directions to the jury or otherwise.[37]

[5.22] In *Re Ansbacher (Cayman) Ltd*[38] (discussed above), McCracken J considered both *Irish Times v Ireland* and *De Gortari* and the ambit of judge-made exceptions to Article 34.1. In that case, as noted above, the applicants were seeking to preserve their anonymity in order to protect their good names. McCracken J noted that both *Irish Times* and *De Gortari* had been concerned with balancing the right of accused persons with the requirements of Article 34.1. He noted that the applicant in the case before him relied on the right to privacy and the right to one's good name. He considered whether the engagement of these rights gave rise to a special and limited case such that a hearing could be held without disclosing the names of the applicants. He found that this was not such a case, noting the inevitability of some invasion of privacy and the right to one's good name in legal proceedings as follows:

> The fact that Article 34.1 requires Courts to administer justice in public by its very nature requires the attendant publicity, including the identification of parties seeking justice. It is a small price to be paid to ensure the integrity and openness of one of the three organs of the State namely the judicial process, in which openness is a vital element. It is often said that justice must not only be done, but must also be seen to be done, and if this involves innocent parties being brought before the

---

36.   *De Gortari v Smithwick J* [1999] 4 IR 223.
37.   *De Gortari v Smithwick J* [1999] 4 IR 223, 229.
38.   *Re Ansbacher (Cayman) Ltd* [2002] 2 IR 517.

Courts in either civil or criminal proceedings, and wrongly accused, that is unfortunate, but is essential for the protection of the entire judicial system.[39]

[5.23] The importance of the principle of open justice means that the courts have also held that it may outweigh the competing interests of individuals who are not parties to the litigation themselves. In *MCD v Liberty Syndicate Management Ltd*,[40] Kelly J refused an application to allow the evidence of a witness about his health to be taken on oath. The case concerned the cancellation of a concert at Slane Castle by American rapper Eminem. The concert had been cancelled because of the rapper's 'exhaustion'. The concert promoters initiated legal action against three insurance companies in the course of which Eminem was required to give evidence about his personal health. Kelly J rejected the application that this evidence be heard in private because this would violate the constitutional requirement that justice be administered in public.

Statutory exceptions

[5.24] While the Oireachtas may prescribe in statute exceptions to the public administration of justice, the courts have indicated that they will look carefully at the application of statutory exceptions to Article 34.1 and have read them strictly on occasion.

SECTION 205 OF THE COMPANIES ACT 1963

[5.25] In *Re R Ltd*,[41] for example, the petitioner had brought a petition under s 205 of the Companies Act 1963 claiming that the affairs of the company (of which he was a shareholder and chief executive) had been carried on in a manner oppressive to him. Section 205(7) of the Companies Act provided as follows:

> If, in the opinion of the court, the hearing of proceedings under this section would involve the disclosure of information the publication of which would be seriously prejudicial to the legitimate interests of the company, the court may order that the hearing of the proceedings or any part thereof shall be in camera.

An application was made on behalf of the company to have the petition heard in camera on the basis that the petitioner's grounding affidavit contained sensitive business information. The High Court granted the order and this was overturned by the Supreme Court. Walsh J found that the facts of the case did not justify the hearing of the petition otherwise than in public. He went on to indicate that, even if the circumstances did merit an in-camera hearing in respect of some of the matters concerned, Article 34 would require that those aspects of the judgment that did not disclose the sensitive information should be pronounced in public.

---

39.   *Re Ansbacher (Cayman) Ltd* [2002] 2 IR 517. See also *Doe v Revenue Commissioners* [2008] IEHC 5.

40.   *MCD v Liberty Syndicate Management Ltd* (5 March 2007, unreported), HC, Kelly J. See 'Judge seeks evidence from rapper' (2007) *The Irish Times*, 6 March. The case ultimately settled before the star was required to give evidence.

41.   *Re R Ltd* [1989] 1 IR 126.

[5.26] The issue arose again in the context of a s 205 petition in *Irish Press Plc v Ingersoll*.[42] In that case, the parties were joint shareholders in two newspaper publishing companies. The issue was whether a petition brought by one of the shareholders against the other should be heard in camera. The Supreme Court referred to the 'admittedly heavy onus of proof' resting on a litigant seeking a hearing in camera. In this case, it was pointed out, the evidence demonstrated that the nature of the disagreement between the parties was information already in the public domain. Finlay CJ referred to the 'fundamental constitutional right vested in the public, namely, the administration of justice in public' and pointed out that the court could not, 'therefore, make an order under s 205(7) merely on the consent of all the parties concerned in the petition before it'. He went on to state that the provision for in-camera orders in s 205(7) had to be read strictly given that Article 34.1 of the Constitution only permitted the Oireachtas to prescribe by law for the administration of justice other than in public in 'special and limited cases'. In the context of s 205 petitions, he held that the court should only direct an in-camera hearing where the damage which would be caused by publication of evidence concerning the company would outweigh the potential for the court to grant an adequate remedy to the wronged party.

SECTION 8(3) OF THE PROCEEDS OF CRIME ACT 1996 – 2005

[5.27] Similarly, in *CAB v Mac Aviation Ltd*,[43] an application under s 8(3) of the Proceeds of Crime Acts 1996–2005 to have a hearing other than in public was rejected. That statutory provision states that:

> Proceedings under this Act in relation to an interim order shall be heard otherwise than in public and any other proceedings under this Act may, if the respondent or any other party to the proceedings (other than the applicant) so requests and the Court considers it proper, be heard otherwise than in public.

[5.28] Feeney J considered the provision and noted that it:

> ... provides a Court with a discretion as to whether or not proceedings are heard in public and the test which is laid down is whether or not the Court considers it proper that the matter be heard otherwise than in public. In considering the issue of 'what is or is not proper' the Court must consider that matter against the framework of the Constitution but also the Convention on Human Rights in relation to the requirement to administer justice in public. Counsel for the Criminal Assets Bureau urged that such discretion should only be exercised in the most exceptional cases. The Court is satisfied that the correct test does not require an applicant to establish exceptional circumstances, but the Court is satisfied that it must be careful to ensure that it has been established by a party applying under s 8(3) that there are real and discernible reasons to lead the Court to exercise its discretion.[44]

---

42. *Irish Press Plc v Ingersoll* [1993] ILRM 747.
43. *CAB v Mac Aviation Ltd* (22 March 2010, unreported), HC, Feeney J.
44. *CAB v Mac Aviation Ltd* (22 March 2010, unreported), HC, para 5.

The applicant in the case argued that the first respondent was a commercial concern engaged in trade and that it could suffer commercial damage. It also argued that it could impact on a fair trial subsequently, criminal proceedings having commenced in the United States. Feeney J noted that the applicant's business activities had already been the subject of publicity. He also pointed out that there were no criminal proceedings in being in the State and that any such proceedings would involve a time lag. On the basis of the foregoing, he found that the applicant had failed to demonstrate a real risk of an unfair trial. As far as damage to the trading activities of the applicant was concerned, Feeney J noted that the respondents had not identified any business involving trading within the jurisdiction.

[5.29] The court also pointed out that the affidavit evidence in the case revealed that the first named respondent has carried out its business activities using the name of fictitious persons and that this had not been explained. Feeney J found that the use of fictitious names within the first named respondent's business activities was a matter which was relevant in considering whether or not it was proper to hear the application otherwise than in public. He stated that:

> A public hearing of a case provides the potential of a real countermeasure of such inaccurate and erroneous recordkeeping. This Court is faced with a factual situation where it has been averred that the first named respondent's records demonstrate the use of fictitious names and that matter has not been either explained or denied in any affidavits sworn on behalf of the first named respondent. Faced with that situation, this Court must place considerable emphasis on the benefits that a trial in public would have where the use of fictitious names has been identified. A hearing otherwise than in public would have the potential to make the identification of such fictitious persons more difficult and is a matter which this Court must take into account in exercising its discretion.[45]

SECTION 45 OF THE COURTS (SUPPLEMENTAL PROVISIONS) ACT 1961

[5.30] Section 45 of the Courts (Supplemental Provisions) Act 1961 has been judicially considered in a number of cases. This provides for applications of an urgent nature for relief by way of habeas corpus, bail, prohibition or injunction, matrimonial causes and matters, lunacy and matters involving minors, and proceedings involving the disclosure of a secret manufacturing process.

[5.31] In *State (Cremin) v Cork Circuit Judge*,[46] An application for habeas corpus was made by way of an informal letter. The High Court judge told his registrar to respond to the letter refusing the application. In finding that this was the administration of justice other than in public, O'Dalaigh CJ noted that s 45 was confined to cases involving urgency and that habeas corpus applications should generally be dealt with publicly.[47]

---

45.   *CAB v Mac Aviation Ltd* (22 March 2010, unreported), HC, para 13.

46.   *State (Cremin) v Cork Circuit Judge* (8 February 1965, unreported), SC.

47.   See also *Long v Saorstát and Continental Steamship Co (No 2)* (1960) 94 ILTR 134 where an issue paper was treated as a nullity by the Supreme Court – it had been handed to the judge by the foreman of the jury through the registrar after both parties and counsel had left the courtroom believing that the jury had disagreed.

[5.32] In *Attorney General v X*,[48] the case in which the Attorney General sought an injunction to preclude a girl from travelling to the UK to have an abortion, the case was heard in camera. A number of details of the case were published in the newspapers prior to the publication of the judgment. While the Attorney General expressed a view that this might constitute contempt,[49] commentators have doubted whether this correct.[50]

[5.33] Costello J heard the *X case* in camera to protect the interests of the minor involved but indicated that he would circulate the judgment in the usual way, while preserving her anonymity. The Supreme Court approved of his decision to hear the case in camera in the interests of justice and the public interest.[51]

[5.34] In *Z v Director of Public Prosecutions*,[52] the man who had allegedly committed sexual offences against and impregnated the minor in the *X case* sought to prohibit his trial. He argued that it was an application of an urgent nature for relief and sought to have the application heard in camera. Hamilton P refused to hear the application in private noting that the purpose of s 45(1) is to facilitate the hearing of applications of such an urgent nature that they must be made to a judge in his home or some place where the public do not have access.

[5.35] In *Re a Ward of Court (No 1)*,[53] Lynch J heard the application to withdraw treatment from a patient in a near persistent vegetative state to allow her to die naturally in camera, while holding that the judgment would be pronounced publicly. He justified the decision to hold the hearing in private on the basis that it would promote the frankness of the evidence given. When the case was appealed, the Supreme Court refused to hear it in camera. Hamilton CJ stated that the public were entitled to hear the arguments, the circumstances and the basis for the judgment to be given by the court and the appeal should be heard in public.[54]

Other examples of statutory exceptions

[5.36] There are numerous other statutory provisions which provide for the hearing of cases otherwise than in public in specific circumstances. An exhaustive account of same is not intended in what follows but rather an indication of the types of matters which the legislature has exempted from public hearing.

[5.37] There are some examples in which the intimate and private nature of a matter has been seen as justification for in camera hearings. For examples, certain applications to the High Court under s 25 of the Commission to Inquire into Child Abuse Act 2004 as amended by s 17 of the Commission to Inquire into Child Abuse (Amendment) Act

---

48. *Attorney General v X* [1992] 1 IR 1, [1992] ILRM 401.
49. (1992) *The Irish Times*, 14 February.
50. Hogan and Whyte, *Kelly's Irish Constitution* (4th edn, LexisNexis, 2003), 739.
51. *Attorney General v X* [1992] 1 IR 1, 46.
52. *Z v Director of Public Prosecutions* [1994] 2 IR 476.
53. *Re a Ward of Court (No 1)* [1996] 2 IR 73.
54. (1995) *The Irish Times*, 15 June.

2005 may be heard otherwise than in public. Similarly, s 5(17)(a) of the Hepatitis C Compensation Tribunal Act 1997 seeks to protect the privacy of claimants by providing that an appeal under s 5 shall be heard otherwise than in public at the request of the claimant making the appeal.

[5.38] In some situations, the Oireachtas has determined that only certain parties should be able to seek a private hearing. For example, s 8(3) of the Proceeds of Crime Act 1996 provides that proceedings under the Act in relation to an interim order are heard otherwise than in public. In any other proceedings they may be so heard if the respondent or any other party to the proceedings (other than the applicant) requests it and the court considers it proper.

[5.39] Apart from individual privacy, there are also statutory provisions that seek to protect commercial interests through allowing for private hearings. Examples include s 81(5) of the National Asset Management Agency Act 2009 and s 170 of the Credit Union Act 1997. The latter provides that the whole or any part of any proceedings relating to examinership of credit unions may be heard otherwise than in public if the court, in the interests of justice, considers that the interests of the credit union concerned or its creditors or its members as a whole so require.

[5.40] Numerous statutes in the area of criminal law seek to protect the investigative process by allowing for in camera and often ex parte applications. For example, s 26 of the Criminal Justice (Amendment) Act 2009 provides that an application under any enactment to a court, or a judge of a court, for a search warrant shall be heard otherwise than in public. Under s 13 of the Criminal Justice (Mutual Assistance) Act 2008: a member of the Garda Síochána not below the rank of inspector may apply ex parte and otherwise than in public to a judge of the High Court for an account information order or an account monitoring order or for both of those orders. Variations or discharges of such orders may also be heard otherwise than in public under s 20. See also the Criminal Justice (Surveillance) Act 2009 which allows for the private hearing of applications under s 5 for authorisation of surveillance.

[5.41] Matters of family law are generally heard in camera and there are numerous statutory provisions which deal with particular situations. The following is a non-exhaustive sample of provisions in the area: s 20 of the Adoption Act 1952 (questions of law referred by the Adoption Board to the High Court for determination may, subject to the rules of court, be heard in camera.); ss 56(12), 119 and 122 of the Succession Act 1965 (disputes relating to the appropriation of the family home, provision for spouse and children and dispositions for the purpose of disinheriting spouse and children shall be heard in chambers); s 25 of the Family Law (Maintenance of Spouses and Children) Act 1976 (proceedings under that Act shall be heard otherwise than in public); s 34 of the Judicial Separation and Family Law Reform Act 1989 and s 38(5) of the Family Law (Divorce) Act 1996;[55] s 29(1) of the Child Care Act 1991 and s 16(1) of the Domestic Violence Act 1996 (civil proceedings); s 36(4) of the Status of Children Act 1987 (a declaration of parentage application shall be heard otherwise than in public unless the

---

55.   See *RM v DM (Practice; in camera)* [2000] 3 IR 377.

court so directs.); s 33(2)(b) of the Family Law Act 1995 (a court may hear and determine an application to dispense with the age of marriage or notice of marriage requirements otherwise than in public). The Adoption Act 2010 also makes provision for a variety of matters to be dealt with privately. Section 49(4) of that Act provides that the questions of law referred by the Authority to the High Court relating to applications for adoption orders or recognition of an intercountry adoption effected outside the State may be heard in private subject to rules of court. Under s 56(4), orders by the High Court authorising the Authority to make adoption orders for children whose parents fail in their duty to them shall be heard in private. Under s 92(8), if the High Court so determines, directions of the High Court in respect of entry into register of intercountry adoptions shall be heard in private.

[5.42] Section 19 of the Refugee Act 1996 prohibits the broadcast or publication of any matter likely to lead members of the public to identify a person as an applicant under the Act without the consent of that person and the consent of the Minister for Justice, Equality and Law Reform (which shall not be unreasonably withheld). The provision was challenged in *Jonathan v Ireland*.[56] The applicant in that case was in the process of taking judicial review proceedings concerning a refusal to grant her refugee status. She wished to have these proceedings reported freely in the media and argued that the provision in the Act requiring the Minister's consent rendered it unconstitutional on the grounds that it constituted a violation of Article 34.1 as well as an interference with freedom of expression under Article 40.6.1°(i). In particular, the applicant argued that the necessity to obtain the consent of the Minister would have a chilling effect on media coverage of her case. By the time the matter fell to be determined by the High Court, the Minister had sent a letter indicating that he gave his consent under s 19 so that Murphy J found the matter to be moot. The constitutionality of this provision must surely be in question, not least because it makes no provision for a time limit within which the Minister must decide whether to grant or withhold consent. The court noted that the Department of Justice, in its evidence in the case, had indicated that consent had never been withheld by the Minister and that a more prompt procedure was being put in place to deal with requests for consent. This does not address the other main difficulty with the provision which is that it does not indicate the grounds upon which the Minister may withhold consent, subjecting his discretion to an overall requirement of reasonableness.

Non-statutory exceptions

[5.43] The courts have refused to rely on the fact that the Oireachtas has provided a statutory exception in one context to extend it to another proceeding where the same interests are engaged. In *Cahill & Hollingsworth v Minister for Education*,[57] two dyslexic students initiated a claim before the Equality Tribunal concerning the Department of Education's practice of annotating Leaving Certificate results in which an exemption from a core element of the examination had been given. Hearings before

---

56.   *Jonathan v Ireland* [2002] IEHC 59, Murphy J.
57.   *Cahill & Hollingsworth v Minister for Education* (19 October 2007, unreported), Circuit Court, Hunt J.

the Equality Tribunal are conducted in private.[58] The complainants succeeded before the Equality Tribunal but the matter was appealed to the Circuit Court by the Minister. Unlike the situation in the earlier cases, they were not the party driving this stage of the process and thus could not be said to have voluntarily agreed to this risk of disclosure. The complainants made a preliminary application seeking an order that they not be identified. They submitted that the absence of a statutory provision ensuring the privacy of appeals from the Equality Tribunal was a lacuna in the Act. Hunt J rejected their application, holding that the absence of any such statutory exemption reflected a recognition on the part of the Oireachtas of the constitutional imperative of Article 34.1.

The requirement of a public hearing under the European Convention on Human Rights

[5.44] Article 6(1) of the Convention provides that:

> In the determination of his civil rights and obligations or of any criminal charge against him, everyone is entitled to a fair and public hearing within a reasonable time by an independent and impartial tribunal established by law. Judgement shall be pronounced publicly but the press and public may be excluded from all or part of the trial in the interest of morals, public order or national security in a democratic society, where the interests of juveniles or the protection of the private life of the parties so require, to the extent strictly necessary in the opinion of the court in special circumstances where publicity would prejudice the interests of justice.

The European Court of Human Rights has noted that the requirement of a public trial protects litigants from the administration of justice in secret[59] and maintains the public's confidence in the judicial system.[60] The court has held that media coverage of court proceedings 'contributes to their publicity and is thus perfectly consonant with the requirement under Article 6(1) of the Convention that hearings be public'.[61]

[5.45] The court has also noted that while the media have an important role to play in reporting and commenting on court proceedings, the competing interest of the individual right to privacy under Article 8 will still apply to individuals accused of criminal offences:

> [T]he public nature of court proceedings does not function as a *carte blanche* relieving the media of their duty to show due care in communicating information received in the course of those proceedings (see Council of Europe Recommendation No Rec (2003)13 on the provision of information through the media in relation to criminal proceedings.[62]

---

58. Equal Status Act 2000, s 25(2).
59. *Pretto v Italy* (1983) 6 EHRR 182.
60. *Diennet v France* (1995) 21 EHRR 554.
61. *Tuomela v Finland* (Application No 25711/04) 6 April 2010 (Second Section), para 49.
62. *Tuomela v Finland* (Application No 25711/04) 6 April 2010, 49. See also *Flinkkilä v Finland,* (Application No 25576/04) 6 April 2010; *Jokitaipale v Finland* (Application No 43349/05) 6 April 2010; *Iltalehti and Karhuvaara v Finland* (Application No 6372/06) 6 April 2010; *Soila v Finland (*Application No 6806/06) (Fourth Section).

The court has also made reference to the presumption of innocence as a matter to be considered when assessing media expression which refers to criminal proceedings:

> Also of relevance for the balancing of competing interests which the Court must carry out is the fact that under Article 6 § 2 of the Convention a person has a right to be presumed innocent of any criminal offence until proved guilty.[63]

[5.46] The scope of Article 6(1) is wide-ranging and it applies to all criminal proceedings and most civil proceedings such as those arising in tort, contract, family law and employment law. It also applies to the majority of licensing proceedings[64] and proceedings before professional disciplinary tribunals.[65] Ordinarily, prison disciplinary proceedings must be held in public but where public order and security require it, they can be held inside the prison and the media and public excluded.[66] No such exemption applies for ordinary criminal proceedings.[67] The court has held that the matters concerning the residence of children could be heard otherwise than in public to protect the privacy of the parties including the children.[68]

[5.47] The relationship between the principle of open justice and media freedom of expression arose for consideration in *Atkinson, Crook and The Independent v UK*.[69] The European Commission of Human Rights considered an application brought by two journalists seeking to challenge the decision of a trial judge to hold a sentencing hearing in private following a conviction for a serious drugs offence. Following complaints by an association of journalists, the trial judge offered to give the chairperson of the association her reasons for the closure of the court in private on condition that the chairperson would not disclose them. The Commission referred to Article 6(1) and the fact that the decision to hold the hearing in camera had been made following an application by counsel on behalf of the convicted party, an application to which the prosecuting counsel had agreed. The respondent state argued that the decision had been necessary to protect the rights of others including the family of the convicted party due to the sensitive matters that were likely to be raised by way of a plea in mitigation. The Commission ruled the application to be manifestly unfounded and inadmissible.

[5.48] In *P4 Radio Hele Norge ASA*,[70] the court considered a complaint relating to a refusal by a trial court hearing criminal proceedings to grant an application for radio broadcasting directly from the court hearing room. The applicant radio broadcasting company argued that this violated its rights under Article 10 in that it restricted its choices as to the means of imparting information. The court reiterated its holding in an

63. *Tuomela v Finland* (Application No 25711/04) 6 April 2010, 51.
64. *X v Belgium* (1980) 23 DR 237.
65. *Guchez v Belgium* (1984) 40 DR 100 (Application No 10087/82).
66. *Campbell and Fell v UK* (1984) 7 EHRR 165.
67. *Campbell and Fell v UK* (1984) 7 EHRR 165, para 87.
68. *B and P v UK* (2002) 34 EHRR 529.
69. *Atkinson, Crook and The Independent v UK* (Application No 13366/87) Decision on Admissibility, 3 December 1990.
70. *P4 Radio Hele Norge ASA* (Application No 76682/01) Decision on Admissibility, 6 May 2003 (Third Section).

earlier case that Article 10 applies not only to the content of information but also to the means of transmission or reception[71] and accepted that the refusal may have interfered with this 'to a degree'. The court noted:

> [T]here seems to be no common ground between the domestic systems in the Contracting States to the effect that live transmission, be it by radio or television, is regarded as a vital means for the press of imparting information and ideas on judicial proceedings. It is not unusual that hearing rooms of domestic courts in the Contracting States are designed in a particular way so as to take into account, not only the need to secure transparency in the administration of justice, but also the need to avoid that the conduct of the proceedings be disturbed or influenced by the presence of members of the public in the hearing room. Depending on the circumstances, live broadcasting of sound and pictures from a court hearing room may alter its characteristics, generate additional pressure on those involved in the trial and, even, unduly influence the manner in which they behave and hence prejudice the fair administration of justice. Furthermore, whereas live broadcasting represents the advantage of making it possible for the public at large to listen to and observe court hearings, it will normally include an element of journalistic choice and filtering, albeit different from that of reporting by the written media. The national authorities, in particular the courts, after hearing the views of the parties, are better placed than the European Court in assessing whether live broadcasting in a given case may be prejudicial to the fair administration of justice.

The court thus held that the respondent state had a wide margin of appreciation concerning the question of live broadcasting from the courtroom. The restrictions on expression in this case were proportionate in circumstances where the trial was held in open court and members of the public were free to attend and to report outside as to what they had heard. Additional facilities had been made available involving the live transmission of pictures and sound to a nearby press hall where the media could follow the trial. The court thus found that the application was inadmissible as it was manifestly ill-founded.

[5.49] In *Egeland v Norway*,[72] a further Article 10 issue arose out of the same criminal trial as that which formed the background to the *P4* case. In this case, the court indicated that the principle of open justice extends only as far as the courtroom door. The applicants in *Egeland* were editors of two major national newspapers in Norway which had published photographs of a person, B, who had just been convicted of a major crime, outside the court house without B's permission. The photographs showed B holding a handkerchief to her face and were taken shortly after her conviction was announced. The applicants were ultimately convicted and subjected to moderate fines for breaching national laws precluding the taking of photographs of individuals on their way to and from court hearings. The applicants complained that their convictions were in breach of Article 10 of the Convention. The European Court of Human Rights noted

71. *Autronic AG v Switzerland* (1990) 12 EHRR 485.
72. *Egeland v Norway* (Application No 34438/04) 16 April 2009 (First Section).

that the trial concerned 'was probably the most spectacular and media-focused criminal case in Norwegian history'.[73]

[5.50] The court considered that the state should be given a wide margin of appreciation in respect of its laws concerning photographs. The court noted that:

> ... Norway is not in an isolated position with regard to prohibition to photograph charged or convicted persons in connection with court proceedings. According to information available to the Court, similar prohibitions exist in the domestic laws of Cyprus, England and Wales, and legal restrictions apply also in Austria and Denmark. Whilst in a number of countries such matters are left to self-regulation by the press, it cannot be said that there is a European consensus to this effect.[74]

[5.51] In considering whether the convictions were necessary in a democratic society, the court considered the approach that had been taken by the national Supreme Court. That court had emphasised the role of the legislation concerned in protecting due process. The European Court of Human Rights noted that, from a Convention perspective, the right to privacy under Article 8 was 'predominant' but seemed to accept the relevance of Article 6 also.[75] It found that:

> [W]hen considered in the aggregate, both reasons corresponded to a pressing social need and were sufficient. The interests in restricting publication of the photographs outweighed those of the press in informing the public on a matter of public concern.[76]

CONTEMPT

Contempt and freedom of media expression under the Irish Constitution

[5.52] The media, like individuals, are subject to the contempt jurisdiction of the Irish courts.[77] The law of contempt is based on the common law[78] and it gives courts the

---

73. *Egeland v Norway* (Application No 34438/04) 16 April 2009 (First Section), para 6.
74. *Egeland v Norway* (Application No 34438/04) 16 April 2009 (First Section), para 54.
75. *Egeland v Norway* (Application No 34438/04) 16 April 2009 (First Section), para 53.
76. *Egeland v Norway* (Application No 34438/04) 16 April 2009 (First Section), para 63.
77. The Special Criminal Court is given the same jurisdiction in relation to contempt as the High Court by virtue of the Offences Against the State Act 1939, s 43(e). Cf *Murphy v BBC and Daily Mail* (2001) *The Irish Times*, 27 February and 1 August discussed in McGonagle, *Media Law* (2nd edn, Thomson Round Hall 2003), 225.
78. See also the Offences Against the State (Amendment) Act 1972, s 4(1) which renders the making of public statements (oral or written) which interfere with the course of justice a criminal offence. A statement is caught by this section where is 'is intended, or is of such a character as to be likely, directly or indirectly to influence any court, person or authority concerned with the institution, conduct or defence of any civil or criminal proceedings (including a party or a witness) as to whether or how the proceedings should be instituted, conducted, continued or defended, or as to what should be their outcome'. The constitutionality of this provision was doubted by the *Report of the Committee to Review the Offences Against the State Acts 1939–1998* (2002), para 6.181 and it recommended its repeal.

power to impose fines and imprisonment. Such a draconian power has obvious implications for freedom of expression.[79] The courts guard jealously their power to impose sanction for breaches of the rules on contempt which is seen as an important weapon (and perhaps even the only weapon) with which the judicial branch can defend itself while retaining its independence.

[5.53] Technically, there are two forms of contempt – civil contempt and criminal contempt. The punishment for civil contempt may be imprisonment – a measure not usually associated with civil proceedings. The distinction between the two is far from clear cut.[80] Generally stated, civil contempt is taken to be coercive rather than punitive in nature. Its purpose is to compel compliance with a court order rather than to punish for breach of one.[81] In *Keegan v de Burca*[82] O'Dalaigh CJ described the distinction as follows:

> The distinction between civil and criminal contempt is not new law. Criminal contempt consists in behaviour calculated to prejudice the due course of justice, such as contempt *in facie curiae*,[83] words written or spoken or acts calculated to prejudice the due course of justice or disobedience to a writ of *habeas corpus* by the person to whom it is directed at to give but some examples of this class of contempt. Civil contempt usually arises where there is a disobedience to an order of the court by a party to the proceedings and in which the court has generally no interest to interfere unless moved by the party for whose benefit the order was made. Criminal contempt is a common-law misdemeanour and, as such, is punishable by both imprisonment and fine at discretion, that is to say, without statutory limit, its object is punitive: see the judgment of this Court in *In Re Haughey*. Civil contempt, on the other hand, is not punitive in its object but coercive in its purpose of compelling the party committed to comply with the order of the court, and the period of committal would be until such time as the order is complied with or until it is waived by the party for whose benefit the order was made. In the case of civil contempt only the court can order release but the period of committal cannot be commuted or remitted as a sentence for a term definite in a criminal matter can be commuted or remitted pursuant to Article 13, s 6, of the Constitution.[84]

The distinction drawn above has broken down to a certain extent, with the recognition (discussed below) that civil contempt can be punitive in nature also. Most of the case law concerning the media has arisen in the context of criminal contempt and this jurisprudence is also considered in detail below.[85]

---

79. Henchy, 'Contempt of Court and Freedom of Expression' (1982) 33 NILQ 326.
80. See O'Donnell, 'Some Reflections on the Law of Contempt' [2002] Judicial Studies Institute 88.
81. Although see *Lawlor v Flood* [2002] 3 IR 67 and *Shell E&P Ireland Ltd v McGrath* [2007] 1 IR 671, discussed below.
82. *Keegan v de Burca* [1973] IR 223.
83. This translates as 'in the face of the court'.
84. *Keegan v de Burca* [1973] IR 223, 227.
85. The Law Reform Commission reviewed this area of Irish law in the 1990s. See Law Reform Commission Consultation Paper *Contempt of Court* (July 1991) and Law Reform Commission *Report on Contempt of Court*(1994).

Civil contempt

[5.54] Civil contempt generally arises where one party to a civil dispute breaches a court order. This can arise either at the conclusion of proceedings or during the course of them. The primary purpose of civil contempt is to coerce compliance with court orders and to thus ensure the authority of the courts. The contempt jurisdiction includes a power to fine the contemnor or to imprison them until their contempt is purged. For this reason, periods of imprisonment for civil contempt can be imposed without specifying a date for release.[86] The contemnor may be imprisoned until such time as he purges his contempt.

[5.55] Generally speaking, civil contempt will involve one party to proceedings making an application to the court bringing to its attention the fact that the other party has breached a court order.[87] The jurisdiction is thus most often exercised in the context of inter partes litigation.[88] In *Lawlor v Flood*,[89] however, the Supreme Court recognised that the civil contempt powers of the High Court could be used to advance the proper and prompt investigation of matters the subject of a tribunal of inquiry.

[5.56] In that case, the plaintiff was the sole member of a tribunal of inquiry. He ordered the defendant to make discovery of certain categories of documentation. The High Court subsequently made an order compelling the defendant to comply and to attend before the plaintiff to give evidence. The plaintiff did not comply with the order for discovery and refused to answer questions at the tribunal. The plaintiff brought a motion for the attachment and committal of the defendant for contempt of court. The High Court sentenced the defendant to three months' imprisonment with the first seven days to be actually served, with the balance of the sentence to be suspended to enable the defendant to comply with the order of discovery and swear a full and proper affidavit of discovery. The defendant subsequently made discovery in respect of a considerable volume of documentation. The plaintiff was not satisfied with the discovery made and the matter was re-entered for hearing before the High Court. The High Court found that there had been non-compliance by the defendant of a serious nature and ordered, inter alia, that the defendant should serve a further seven days of the sentence, pay a fine of £5,000 and make further and better discovery on oath in the form prescribed by the Rules of the Superior Courts 1986. The defendant appealed to the Supreme Court. Keane CJ considered the judgment of the Court in *Keegan* and noted that:

> In that case, the essential issue for determination was as to whether a refusal to answer a question during the course of civil proceedings constituted contempt in the face of the court which was criminal contempt and accordingly punishable only by a determinate sentence. The majority of the court were of the view that it

86. This is sometimes referred to as imprisonment 'sine die'.
87. See *Davern v Butler* [1927] IR 182; *Little v Cooper* [1937] IR 510; *O'Conghaile v Wallace* [1938] IR 526; *Eastern Health Board v E (No 2)* [2000] 1 IR 451.
88. *Davern v Butler* [1927] IR 182; *Little v Cooper* [1937] IR 510; *O'Conghaile v Wallace* [1938] IR 526; *Ross Co Ltd v Swan* [1981] ILRM 416.
89. *Lawlor v Flood* [2002] 3 IR 67.

was a criminal contempt and hence punishable by a determinate sentence only. McLoughlin J was of the view that, since the primary object of the imposition of the sentence in that case was to ensure that the question was answered, it was appropriate to deal with it by means of an indeterminate sentence until the contemnor had purged her contempt.[90]

[5.57] Keane CJ continued, stating that:

> Accordingly, while the decision suggests that there may be some room for a difference of view as to whether a sentence imposed in respect of civil contempt is exclusively – as distinct from primarily – coercive in its nature in civil proceedings generally, I am satisfied that where, as here, the proceedings are inquisitorial in their nature and the legislature has expressly empowered the High Court to secure compliance with the orders of the tribunal, it cannot be said that a sentence imposed in respect of a contumelious disregard of the orders of the tribunal and the High Court is coercive only in its nature. The machinery available for dealing with contempt of this nature exists not simply to advance the private, although legitimate, interests of a litigant: it is there to advance the public interest in the proper and expeditious investigation of the matters within the remit of the tribunal and so as to ensure that, not merely the defendant in this case, but all persons who are required by law to give evidence, whether by way of oral testimony or in documentary form, to the tribunal comply with their obligations fully and without qualification.

> I am also satisfied that a court has jurisdiction to suspend, in whole or part, a sentence of imprisonment imposed in respect of civil contempt and thereafter, in the event of a further contempt, may at its discretion require the party in default to serve some or all of the balance of the sentence.[91]

[5.58] In *Shell E&P Ireland Ltd v McGrath*,[92] an injunction had been granted against the defendants restraining them from interfering with the entry by the plaintiff onto certain lands. The defendants had breached this injunction and had been attached and committed for contempt of court. On the 94th day of their imprisonment, the plaintiff had sought the discharge of the injunction on the basis that it was not necessary to continue it during the winter months as the plaintiff would not need to access the land for that time period. Finnegan P discharged the injunction. The contemnors, however, refused to purge their contempt or to undertake to comply with further orders of the court. They argued that once the injunction had been lifted, the court enjoyed no further powers of committal. In considering how to proceed in these circumstances, Finnegan P discussed the nature of the civil contempt. He noted that it was primarily coercive but that in cases of serious misconduct the High Court had the power to punish the contemnor in order to vindicate the authority of the court.[93] This could be done by the

---

90. *Lawlor v Flood* [2002] 3 IR 67, 79.
91. *Lawlor v Flood* [2002] 3 IR 67, 79–80.
92. *Shell E&P Ireland Ltd v McGrath* [2007] 1 IR 671.
93. He referred to a number of authorities to reach this conclusion: *Ross Co Ltd v Swan* [1981] ILRM 416, *Yager v Musa* [1961] 2 QB 214, *Danchevsky v Danchevsky* [1975] Fam 17, *Jennison v Baker* [1972] 2 QB 52, *Phonographic Performance Ltd v Amusement Caterers (Peckham) Ltd* [1964] Ch. 195, *Flood v Lawlor* [2002] 3 IR 67 and *State (Commins) v McRann* [1977] IR 78.

court of its own motion and did not require the application of a private party.[94] He found that where the purpose of a imprisonment was punitive, it should be imposed for a definite term.[95] In deciding whether to commit by way of punishment, he considered the consequences of the contemnors' refusal to comply with the court order, the punitive element of the time already spent in prison by the contemnors and the disadvantages that would be suffered by them, as the litigation progressed, as a result of their refusal to purge their contempt. The contemnors in this case were not subject to any further period of imprisonment.

Criminal contempt

[5.59] There are various categories of criminal contempt.[96] Contempt in the face of the court is one such. This is constituted by disruptive behaviour in or immediately outside the court which may constitute criminal contempt. The second category is that of scandalising the court. This is where courts or judges are abused in such a way as to bring the administration of justice into disrepute. Thirdly, there is a category of criminal contempt committed by the use of words or conduct calculated to interfere with the administration of justice. This might involve interference with witnesses, judges or lawyers, breach of the in camera rule or statements prejudicial to a fair trial. To these might be added a fourth category – the obstruction of justice.[97] The latter covers matters such as refusals to answer relevant questions during cross-examination[98] and refusal to obey an order of habeas corpus to produce an infant.[99]

BREACH OF IN CAMERA ORDERS

[5.60] Where a court orders matters to be withheld from the public domain, defiance of such a ruling may constitute criminal contempt. Thus in *Re Kennedy and McCann*,[100] it was held to be criminal contempt to publish details of a family law case in defiance of an order of the High Court directing the proceedings to be held in camera.

---

94.   Relying on *Jennison v Baker* [1972] 2 QB 52 and *Seaward v Paterson* [1897] 1 Ch 545.

95.   He referred to two authorities in which this approach had been taken: *Yager v Musa* [1961] 2 QB 214 and *Danchevsky v Danchevsky* [1975] Fam 17.

96.   O'Donnell, 'Some Reflections on the Law of Contempt' [2002] Judicial Studies Institute 88, 93–94.

97.   See Hogan and Whyte, *Kelly's Irish Constitution* (4th edn, Bloomsbury Professional, 2003), 705–706. In *State (Quinn) v Ryan* [1965] IR 70, the Supreme Court found that there had been 'contempt of the courts' in a case where the British and Irish police forces had been guilty of same in arranging to remove a citizen from the jurisdiction pursuant to a statutory procedure later found to be unconstitutional. The case is generally regarded as standing on its own and has not led to the development of a jurisprudence concerning this category of 'contempt'.

98.   *O'Brennan v Tully* (1935) 69 ILTR 115.

99.   *Re Earle* [1938] IR 485.

100. *Re Kennedy and McCann* [1976] IR 382.

FRUSTRATING AN ORDER DESIGNED TO PROTECT CONFIDENTIALITY

[5.61] In *Council of the Bar of Ireland v Sunday Business Post Ltd*,[101] an injunction had been issued against the defendant newspaper prohibiting the publication of a confidential letter written during the course of a disciplinary investigation. A rival newspaper published it thus nullifying the effect of the injunction. Costello J held that the injunction had been granted so as to preserve the confidentiality of the letter and that its publication was an interference with the administration of justice.

THE SUB JUDICE RULE

[5.62] The courts have acted in the past to prevent the publication of statements which tend to influence the decision to be made on a case pending before the courts. The Supreme Court initially accepted that the rule applied primarily in cases where matters were pending before a jury, before later accepting that the rule applied where matters were pending before the judiciary alone. This aspect of the sub judice rule as it is sometimes called was discussed at length in *Cullen v Toibin*[102] and *Kelly v O'Neill*.[103]

[5.63] In *Cullen v Toibin*, a convicted person had appealed his conviction to the Court of Criminal Appeal. The only evidence against the accused at trial was that of an alleged accomplice. While the appeal was pending, *Magill* entered into an exclusive contract to publish the accomplice's account of her relationship with the plaintiff, including events which were the subject of his trial. In the High Court, Barrington J granted an injunction holding that while the appeal would be heard by professional judges trained to exclude irrelevant material from their minds, it would be unwise to assume they would not be affected by publication of the article. He cautioned against the assumption that judges as opposed to jurors are immune to such material.

[5.64] The Supreme Court overruled the decision. O'Higgins CJ held that:

> The basis for the application for the injunction which Mr Cullen has been granted is that the publication of the article would be prejudicial to the conduct of the appeal in that in one way or another the judges hearing the appeal would be biased in regard to the consideration of that appeal. I can see no basis for this suggestion. The Court of Criminal Appeal will be asked to consider pure questions of law relative to the appeal. It cannot be suggested that in considering such questions, publication of this or any number of articles in any number of periodicals would have the slightest effect on the objective consideration of legal arguments. It seems to me that such an argument is unsustainable.
>
> That is not to say that one approves of the publication of this article. I think that better taste might indicate that articles of this kind should not be published during the currency of legal proceedings involving a citizen. There is, however, the matter of the freedom of the press and of communication which is guaranteed by the Constitution and which cannot be lightly curtailed. Such can only be curtailed or

---

101. *Council of the Bar of Ireland v Sunday Business Post Ltd* (30 March 1993, unreported), HC.
102. *Cullen v Toibin* [1984] ILRM 577.
103. *Kelly v O'Neill* [2000] 1 IR 354.

restricted by the courts in the manner sought in these proceedings where such action is necessary for the administration of justice.

> While I sympathise with the view that anybody reading the article might be affected by the article, that is not the issue. There is not any reason for suggesting prejudice or any form of contempt in relation to the hearing before the Court of Criminal Appeal.[104]

[5.65] In *Kelly v O'Neill*, the applicant had been convicted in the Circuit Court of two drug-related offences. Sentencing was postponed (as is usual) to a later date. Before the sentencing hearing an article appeared in a newspaper under the heading 'Gardaí believe Kelly was involved in other major crimes'. It gave details of the applicant, including that he had previous dealing with a criminal family and that he had been involved in fraudulent trading. The article also reported claims from garda sources that were not adduced in evidence at the trial relating to the applicant's involvement in the drug trade. The applicant was sentenced to a term of 14 years' imprisonment and the same sentence was imposed following a retrial ordered by the Court of Criminal Appeal. An application was made by the applicant seeking the attachment of the editor of the paper and the journalist who had written the article for contempt of court. The trial judge held that the article constituted contempt of court and imposed a fine of £5,000.

[5.66] The respondents appealed to the High Court, which stated a consultative case for the opinion of the Supreme Court asking as follows:

(a)   Can it be a contempt of court to publish an article in the terms of that complained of after a criminal trial has passed from the *seisin* of the jury and where the remainder of the hearing will take place before a judge sitting alone?

(b)   Given the constitutional right to freedom of expression of the press – could the publication of the article complained of ever constitute a contempt of court when published after conviction and before sentencing?

[5.67] The Supreme Court considered that the mere fact that a trial was no longer a matter for a jury did not mean that the sub judice rule ceased to apply. Keane J stated:

> I have not been persuaded by the arguments in this case that the application of due process ceases in this context once the jury have returned their verdict, because of the assumed immunity of the judges from the frailties to which juries are acknowledged to be subject.[105]

[5.68] In considering the second question, he noted as follows:

> The second question, in effect, asks whether that conclusion should be modified in the light of the constitutionally guaranteed right to freedom of expression of the press. I am satisfied that it should not. Freedom of expression is undoubtedly a value of critical importance in a democratic society, but like every other right

---

104.   *Cullen v Toibín* [1984] ILRM 577, 581–582.
105.   *Kelly v O'Neill* [2000] 1 IR 354, 381. For a similar view, see Denham J in *Wong v Minister for Justice* [1994] 1 IR 223.

guaranteed, either expressly or by implication, by the Constitution it is not an absolute right. The limitations on freedom of expression required by the machinery of contempt of court were found not to be of themselves in violation of the right of freedom of expression guaranteed by the European Convention on Human Rights in *Times Newspapers Ltd v United Kingdom* (1979) 2 EHRR 245. I appreciate that deferring publication of an article of this nature until after sentence had been imposed might be commercially unattractive to the newspaper concerned. But the restraint is in a different category from the absolute prohibition on publication required by the 'scandalising the court' doctrine, which suggests that an even greater caution should be exercised by the courts in that area. A temporary restraint on a publication of this nature, lasting sometimes for no more than a day or two and at most a few weeks, seems to me a not disproportionate restriction, when weighed in the balance against the damage which could be done to the administration of justice if the press, television and radio or any one else were to have an unrestricted licence, subject only to the law of defamation, to comment freely and publish material, however untrue and damaging, concerning a trial at a stage when it was still in progress and the accused, although found guilty, was still entitled to the solemn constitutional guarantee of a trial in due course of law.[106]

[5.69] The case law has recognised that one justification for the sub judice rule is to protect the right to a fair trial.[107] This right is also protected under the case law generated by Article 38.1 which recognises that adverse pre-trial publicity may render a trial unfair. This case law also recognises the effect of the 'fade factor' on such publicity, ie that fact that as time passes the jurors are less likely to be prejudiced by same.[108] Given that a lengthy period of time may elapse between initial media coverage and the trial date, the courts have often found that by the time of the latter there is no real risk of an unfair trial. In *Director of Public Prosecutions v Independent Newspapers*,[109] the *Evening Herald* tried to rely on this doctrine to resist an application for criminal contempt.[110]

[5.70] In that case, an individual had been charged with the murder of his sister. He appeared before the District Court on 1 December 2004 and was remanded in custody to St Patrick's Institution. The following day, the *Evening Herald* published a number of articles about the matter, one of which purported to describe in detail the nature of the assault on the deceased and the way in which she died. The other articles in the same edition purported to describe the family of the deceased and accused and included comments about them from members of the local community. One of the articles

---

106. *Kelly v O'Neill* [2000] 1 IR 354, 381–2.

107. See *Re McArthur* [1983] ILRM 355.

108. See *Z v Director of Public Prosecutions* [1994] 2 IR 476; *Zoe Developments v DPP* (3 March 1999, unreported), HC; *Redmond v Director of Public Prosecutions* [2002] 4 IR 133; *People (DPP) v Nevin* [2003] 3 IR 321.

109. *Director of Public Prosecutions v Independent Newspapers* [2005] IEHC 128, High Court, Deane J, 3 May 2005.

110. The respondent in fact brought a motion for a directed acquittal on the basis that there was no case to answer for contempt.

purported to give details arising from the post-mortem examination of the deceased. Dunne J accepted that the applicant in a criminal contempt case had to prove beyond a reasonable doubt that the respondents were guilty of criminal contempt. She also accepted that, as part of this test, the applicant had to demonstrate a risk of prejudice to the trial of the accused and found that this had not been done.

[5.71] This case was appealed to the Supreme Court. As a preliminary issue, the court considered whether an appeal could lie as against an acquittal of contempt in the High Court. It was argued by the respondents that the High Court in hearing criminal matters was sitting as the Central Criminal Court so that an appeal could not lie by virtue of s 11 of the Criminal Procedure Act 1993. This argument was rejected by the Supreme Court which held that an appeal from such a decision did lie.[111] Subsequently, the appeal proper came before the court which considered the approach taken by Dunne J to have been incorrect in that she had considered the likely prejudice to the accused arising from the publication.[112] According to Geoghegan J,[113] the fade factor, ie the extent to which a jury might forget about previous coverage of events, was relevant to whether a trial could proceed but not relevant to a motion for contempt. He pointed out that contempt applications could be made prior to the trial itself and in advance of the date of trial being known. The question of contempt was one to be determined at the time of publication and not by reference to later events.[114]

[5.72] In any event, the purpose of the contempt jurisdiction is as much to protect the authority of the courts and the public perception of the administration of justice as it is the right to a fair trial. This was recognised in *Kelly v O'Neill*, where Denham J referred to the danger that:

> ... the community's concern that justice be done and be seen to be done may be undermined. The concept that articles may be written mid-trial to blacken a convicted person pre-sentence may gain credence as a method of achieving a result – such as shouting at a referee at a match in the hope of affecting his decision! This then raises the risk of prejudicing the administration of justice as a whole, or the perception of the administration of justice.[115]

PUBLIC OBLOQUY

[5.73] As well as covering statements tending to influence a judge or jury, the sub judice rule covers conduct which abuses or pillories a party to litigation or subjects him to public obloquy such as to dissuade him from obtaining the adjudication of a court to

---

111. [2008] 4 IR 88. Hardiman J dissented.
112. *DPP v Independent Newspapers* [2009] 3 IR 589.
113. Referring to his previous decision in *Rattigan v Director of Public Prosecutions* [2008] IESC 34, [2008] 4 IR 639.
114. Referring to Mason CJ and Toohey J in *R v Glennon* (1992) 173 CLR 592. The court also held that on a motion to dismiss an application for criminal contempt, the court should only be concerned as to whether a prima facie case had been made out in respect of the contempt.
115. *Kelly v O'Neill* [2000] 1 IR 354, 370.

which he is entitled. This aspect of the rule was considered in *Desmond v Glackin (No 1)*.[116] In that case, the plaintiff claimed that the then Minister for Industry and Commerce had so pilloried the plaintiff in an interview with RTÉ. O'Hanlon J noted that the plaintiff had himself made serious allegations of bad faith against the defendant Minister in an affidavit and concluded that the Minister should have some entitlement to respond to same. While the comments of the Minister were indiscreet and injudicious, he did not find them to constitute contempt.

[5.74] In *Wong v Minister for Justice*,[117] a newspaper had inaccurately linked the applicant with the Chinese underworld. The applicant had at the time instituted proceedings challenging a decision by the Minister not to allow him to remain in Ireland. Denham J found that this was contempt but did not impose any punishment, considering the apologies to the court to be sufficient. She noted:

> The basis of this ground is wider than solely the concern that the court will be biased as a result of the report. The basis is that the administration of justice suffers as a result of a litigant mid-trial being held up to such public obloquy. If such false reporting were to be the norm then the administration of justice would suffer.[118]

CONTEMPTUOUS BREACH OF THE SUB JUDICE RULE REQUIRES THAT
PROCEEDINGS ARE IN BEING

[5.75] The law of contempt is primarily concerned with protecting the administration of justice and the authority of the court. One consequent restriction on the law of criminal contempt is that it has been held to apply only when proceedings are actually in being. This issue arose in *State (DPP) v Independent Newspapers Ltd*.[119] The case arose out of an article dated 30 March 1984, which stated that the Director of Public Prosecutions intended to bring indecency charges against an unnamed local authority councillor. The local authority was not named but the councillor's political party was. No charges had been brought at the time the article was published, but two days later a charge of indecency was brought against a named person and the affidavit grounding the application linked that charge with the article. The DPP applied for a conditional order of attachment against the publisher and editor of the *Evening Herald* newspaper together with a journalist employed by the paper. O'Hanlon J refused the application. In his comments on the general law of contempt,[120] he doubted whether such an application could be brought prior to charges being preferred.

---

116. *Desmond v Glackin (No 1)* [1993] 3 IR 1; [1992] ILRM 490.
117. *Wong v Minister for Justice* [1994] 1 IR 223.
118. *Wong v Minister for Justice* [1994] 1 IR 223, 237.
119. *State (DPP) v Independent Newspapers Ltd* [1985] ILRM 183.
120. He also referred to the Criminal Procedure Act 1967, s 17 which provided specifically that it was an offence to publish certain details of a preliminary examination in the District Court leading to an indictment.

[5.76] This approach was followed by Kelly J in *DPP v Independent Newspapers*.[121] In that case, two minors had been involved in a motor collision on 11 January 2003 which resulted in the death of the driver of another vehicle. The car in which the minors were driving was believed to have been stolen. They were arrested and detained on 12 January and charged later that day with offences arising out of the incident. They were held in custody overnight and charged in the District Court on 13 January. On 12 and 13 January, a number of newspapers contained reports of the incident. The reports all made reference to the fact that the two minors were on bail on other charges pending before the courts and gave details of their criminal records, published photographs of them and/ or identified them by name. On the morning of 13 January, RTÉ broadcast an interview concerning the fatal collision. In the course of the interview, one of the individuals was named and reference was made to the fact that both of them had numerous previous convictions. It was not stated that they were on bail on other charges at the time of the incident.

[5.77] The DPP applied to the High Court for an order for the attachment of the respondents for contempt of court and for an injunction restraining the respondents from further interfering with the integrity of the trial process between the applicant and the two accused.

[5.78] Kelly J refused the application on the basis that the publication and broadcast complained of had taken place prior to the charges being preferred in court. The DPP argued that contempt proceedings could be brought in respect of publications or broadcasts made at a time when proceedings were imminent. Referring back to O'Hanlon J's judgment discussed above, Kelly J rejected this argument:

> With no legislation in place the applicant invited the court to bridge the gap by adopting his formula so as to extend the court's summary jurisdiction in order to punish publication contempt when proceedings are 'imminent'. The adoption of such a formula by the court would give rise to huge uncertainty. (Would for example proceedings be 'imminent' in circumstances where a person is arrested then released and a file sent to the Director of Public Prosecutions?) It could lead to the possible undue cramping of the media in their coverage of public affairs and newsworthy events thus improperly interfering with the freedom of the press.
>
> If publications of this type are to be treated as contempts of courts where they are made at a time when the persons against whom they are directed have not 'entered the jurisdiction and protection' of the courts, such will have to be provided for by legislation.[122]

SCANDALISING THE COURT

[5.79] The courts have long recognised a form of criminal contempt described as scandalising the court.[123] This covers words or conduct tending to destroy public

---

121. *DPP v Independent Newspapers* [2003] 2 IR 367.
122. *DPP v Independent Newspapers* [2003] 2 IR 367, 394–395.
123. See Walker, 'Scandalising in the Eighties' (1985) 101 LQR 359.

confidence in the court against which it is directed. This area of contempt law, more than any other, creates potential difficulties for freedom of expression. An expansive view of what constitutes 'scandalising' has obvious chilling implications for commentary on the administration of justice. It has been criticised by O'Donnell on the basis that:

> The decisions of the courts would suggest that the line is drawn when criticism becomes scurrilous abuse or wild and baseless allegations. If there is indeed a dividing line at this point, is there any real benefit in maintaining it? Allegations which are clearly wild and baseless may in some cases be less damaging than plausible and restrained criticism.[124]

This form of contempt was described by O'Higgins CJ in *State (DPP) v Walsh*[125] in the following terms:

> This form of contempt is committed where what is said or done is of such a nature as to be calculated to endanger public confidence in the court which is attacked and, thereby, to obstruct and interfere with the administration of justice. It is not committed by mere criticism of judges as judges, or by the expression of disagreement—even emphatic disagreement—with what has been decided by a court. The right of citizens to express freely, subject to public order, convictions and opinions is wide enough to comprehend such criticism or expressed disagreement.

> Such contempt occurs where wild and baseless allegations of corruption or malpractice are made against a court so as to hold the judges '... to the odium of the people as actors *playing a sinister part in a caricature of justice*'—*per Gavan Duffy P in The Attorney General v Connolly* [1947] IR 213 at p 220 of the report.[126]

[5.80] The jurisdiction to punish for scandalising the court has been exercised by the Irish courts in a number of cases. In *Attorney General v O'Kelly*,[127] for example, a newspaper had published an article which accused a High Court judge of 'insolence to jurors'. The article was critical of the way in which the judge spoke to jurors and a successful application to attach the editor of the paper was taken by the Attorney General. In *Attorney General v Connolly*,[128] it was found to be a contempt to insult the Special Criminal Court by suggesting that the outcome of a trial before that court was predictable. In *Attorney General v Ryan and Boyd*,[129] an editor had published a letter

---

124. O'Donnell, 'Some Reflections on the Law of Contempt' [2002] Judicial Studies Institute 88, 110. This seems to have been recognised in the case of *Attorney General v Ryan and Boyd* [1946] IR 70 where the editor of a paper which published a letter containing insults to a Circuit Court judge was said by the President of the High Court to have performed a public service for the administration of justice on the basis that the allegations in the offending letter was so wildly absurd that it destroyed the credibility of the allegations therein. The author of the letter, however, was punished for his contempt. See discussion below.
125. *State (DPP) v Walsh* [1981] IR 412.
126. *State (DPP) v Walsh* [1981] IR 412, 421–422.
127. *Attorney General v O'Kelly* [1928] IR 308.
128. *Attorney General v Connolly* [1947] IR 213.
129. *Attorney General v Ryan and Boyd* [1946] IR 70.

containing statements that insulted a Circuit Court judge. Maguire P noted the importance of preserving free and fair criticism of the judges and indicated a preference for a cautious approach to the exercise of the contempt jurisdiction in this kind of case. Notwithstanding this, the author of the letter was punished for contempt.[130]

[5.81] A further example of scandalising the court is provided by *Re Hibernia National Review Ltd.*[131] In that case, the owner and editor of the respondent publication had published a letter in it describing a murder trial before the Special Criminal Court in inverted commas as a 'trial' and making a number of other insinuations. The Supreme Court granted a conditional order of attachment, finding that the letter suggested that the members of the Special Criminal Court 'conducted a travesty of a trial to procure a false verdict of guilty'. Kenny J stated that it was 'difficult to think of a more serious charge against the Court'.[132] He noted that criticism of the death penalty or the establishment of the Special Criminal Court did not constitute contempt:

> Reasonable criticism of courts or a system of law they operated, or penalties they imposed, was not contempt of court. What is contempt is the publication of a statement which brings a court or a judge of the court into contempt and in each case the distinction has to be drawn by the court between the criticism, be it informed or uninformed, and remarks which have as their purpose the bringing of the court into contempt.[133]

[5.82] In *Re Kennedy and McCann,*[134] an application was made against the editor of the *Sunday World* newspaper and one of its journalists for imputations against the courts in a dispute under the Guardianship of Infants Act 1964. The court had awarded sole custody of two children to their father. The article stated that the courts had disregarded the welfare of children which was the principal criterion to be considered in decisions under the Act. The piece suggested that 'money and the lifestyle it could buy was regarded by the courts as by far the most important consideration'. It referred to Ireland as being a 'sick society', 'hypocritical about motherhood, morality and the family' and indicated that justice could not be obtained from the Irish courts. The editor and the journalist concerned apologised, a matter to which the Supreme Court gave 'considerable weight'. They were nonetheless fined for their contempt, seemingly on the basis that to accept an apology alone might send the wrong message.[135]

[5.83] O'Higgins CJ stated that:

> The right of free speech and the free expression of opinion are valued rights. Their preservation, however, depends on the observance of the acceptable limit that they must not be used to undermine public order or morality or the authority of the State. Contempt of court of this nature carries the exercise of these rights beyond

130. Curiously, the editor was not. See *Attorney General v Connolly* [1947] IR 213 where Gavin Duffy P indicated that there were limits to the judicial reluctance to commit for scandalising the court.
131. *Re Hibernia National Review Ltd* [1976] IR 388.
132. *Re Hibernia National Review Ltd* [1976] IR 388, 390.
133. *Re Hibernia National Review Ltd* [1976] IR 388, 391.
134. *Re Kennedy and McCann* [1976] IR 382.
135. See comments made by O'Higgins CJ, *Re Hibernia National Review Ltd* [1976] IR 388, 388.

this acceptable limit because it tends to bring the administration of justice into disrepute and to undermine the confidence which the people should have in judges appointed under the Constitution to administer justice in our Courts.[136]

He cited the dictum of Lord Russell of Killowen CJ in *R v Gray*,[137] that '[a]ny act done or writing published calculated to bring a Court or a judge of the Court into contempt, or to lower his authority, is contempt of Court'.[138] He went on to note that the article in this case had been in breach of an order prohibiting publication and had contained a distortion of the facts. Further, it:

> ...was calculated to scandalise the members of [the] Court who have dealt with or [were] dealing with this case, for it imputed to them base and unworthy motives which, if substantiated, would render them unfit for their office ...

> ... The offence of contempt by scandalising the court is committed when, as here, a false publication is made which intentionally or recklessly imputes base or improper motives or conduct to the judge or judges in question. Here the publication bears on its face, if not an intent, at least the stamp of recklessness.[139]

[5.84] *Walsh* arose out of an article in the *Irish Times* citing the views of an association opposed to the death penalty on a trial that had been held in the Special Criminal Court. The trial was for capital murder, the two accused having been charged with the unlawful killing of members of the Gardaí. Following the conviction of the accused, the *Irish Times* included statements from the association to the effect that the members of the Special Criminal Court had no judicial independence and that, in trying the accused, they had 'so abused the rules of evidence as to make the court akin to a sentencing tribunal'.

[5.85] Henchy J considered the content of the article:

> The principal impression which this statement was calculated to make on the ordinary reader of the newspaper was that the three judges who constituted the Special Criminal Court were so craven, biased, and incompetent or corrupt, that they had abused the rules of evidence, to the detriment of the accused, so that they (the judges) were little better than a sentencing tribunal. It would be difficult to conceive of an allegation more calculated to undermine the reputation of the Special Criminal Court as a source of justice. If true, this imputation of judicial misbehaviour would render the three judges in question unfit to hold judicial office of any kind and would cause the Special Criminal Court to be held in the opinion of the public at large to be so debased as to be disqualified from dispensing justice. In short, the facts adduced in this application to commit for

---

136. *Re Hibernia National Review Ltd* [1976] IR 388, 386.
137. *R v Gray* [1900] 2 QB 36.
138. *R v Gray* [1900] 2 QB 36, 40. Cited by O'Higgins CJ in *Re Hibernia National Review Ltd* [1976] IR 388, 387.
139. *Re Hibernia National Review Ltd* [1976] IR 388, 387.

contempt (to which facts no rebuttal has been offered) constitute a classical example of the crime of contempt by scandalising a court.[140]

[5.86] In *Weeland v DPP*,[141] the plaintiff sought an interlocutory injunction restraining RTÉ from broadcasting a television programme concerning certain land transactions. The plaintiff was a party to those transactions which were the subject matter of an appeal to the High Court from a decision in the Circuit Court. The plaintiff argued that some of the tone and manner of the references to the Circuit Court decision in the case amounted to contempt because it suggested criticism of the decision. He also argued that the programme was a deliberate interference with the High Court appeal. Carroll J refused to grant the injunction. She stated that the plaintiff was not entitled to an injunction merely because there were legal proceedings pending and emphasised that to obtain such an order, he would have to show that contempt of court. The plaintiff had argued that the programme presumed to instruct the High Court how to dispose of the appeal. Carroll J rejected the idea that a High Court judge would be influenced by a programme broadcast months before the appeal as opposed to the evidence in the case. She also held that the programme was not abusive of the decision of the Circuit Court judge. While it disagreed with it and failed to set out all the reasons given by the judge for the decision, it did not suggest any improper motive on his part. Emphasising that judgments were not immune from criticism, Carroll J indicated that:

> I do not see why a judgment cannot be criticised, provided it is not done in a manner calculated to bring the court or the judge into contempt. If that element is not present there is no reason why judgments should not be criticised. Nor does the criticism have to be confined to scholarly articles in legal journals. The mass media are entitled to have their say as well. The public take a great interest in court cases and it is only natural that discussion should concentrate on the result of cases. So criticism which does not subvert justice should be allowed. Even though this programme was, in my opinion, unbalanced in relation to the judgment of Judge Gleeson it did not pass over the boundary of acceptable limits. I do not believe that any of the criticisms or allegations by the plaintiff concerning contempt of the court or of Judge Gleeson amount to contempt of court.[142]

[5.87] In *Desmond v Glackin (No 1)*,[143] the defendant Minister for Industry and Commerce had given a television interview to RTÉ in which he expressed his amazement that the High Court had granted the plaintiff an injunction restraining an investigation pursuant to Pt II of the Companies Acts 1990 which the Minister had authorised. The Minister stated that the High Court had facilitated the plaintiff in blocking the inquiry. He also criticised the court for accepting an allegation on oath that

---

140. *State (DPP) v Walsh* [1981] IR 412, 441–442.

141. *Weeland v DPP* [1987] IR 662.

142. *Weeland v DPP* [1987] IR 662, 666. Note that Kelly J has indicated that to misrepresent matters expressed by a judge in the course of proceedings could constitute contempt of court. The comment was made in relation to a letter sent by Michael O'Leary to the Minister for Transport which misquoted the judge as being critical of the behaviour of the Minister. See (2010) *Irish Independent*, 27 March.

143. *Desmond v Glackin (No 1)* [1993] 3 IR 1; [1992] ILRM 490.

the Minister had acted illegally. O'Hanlon J did not accept that these statements scandalised the court. The expression of amazement at the High Court order was within the bounds of acceptable criticism. The allegation that the High Court had facilitated the blocking of the inquiry was found by O'Hanlon J to have referred to the promptness with which the order was granted rather than the making of the order itself. The final statement objected to was dismissed as innocuous speculation by the Minister.

Statutory contempt measures

[5.88] There are a number of statutory provisions[144] which expose persons to charges akin to contempt for failure to cooperate with bodies other than courts. As it is not possible to be in contempt of bodies other than courts, the statutory formulation is usually to the effect that transgressions may be dealt with 'in like manner' as if they were contempt of the High Court. Examples include tribunals of inquiry,[145] commissions of investigation[146] and company inspectors.[147] Other provisions make it an offence to do something before a body which if done before a court would constitute contempt – for example the Committees of the Houses of the Oireachtas.[148] The Constitution requires a determination as to whether there has been contempt to be a matter for the High Court[149] which hears these matters and is responsible for punishing this form of 'contempt'.

[5.89] Other statutory provisions create offences which seem very similar to contempt. For example, see s 4 of the Offences Against the State (Amendment) Act 1972 which provides that a 'public statement made orally, in writing or otherwise…that constitutes an interference with the course of justice' or 'is intended, or is of such a character as to be likely, directly or indirectly, to influence any court' is a criminal offence. The provision states that nothing contained in it affects the law of contempt of court so that the provision appears to be intended to extend the reach of the criminal law in this area.[150]

---

144. See the Law Reform Commission Consultation Paper *Contempt of Court* (July 1991) and Law Reform Commission *Report on Contempt of Court* (1994). See also the Private Security Services Act 2004.
145. Tribunals of Inquiry Acts 1921–79.
146. Commission of Investigations Act 2004.
147. Companies Act 1990, Pt II.
148. See the Committee of the Houses of the Oireachtas (Compellability, Privileges and Immunities of Witnesses) Act 1997.
149. *Desmond v Glackin (No 2)* [1993] 3 IR 67, striking down the Companies Act 1990, s 10(5).
150. For concerns about the interference of this provision with freedom of expression see Casey, *Constitutional Law in Ireland* (3rd edn, Round Hall Sweet & Maxwell, 2000), 554 and McGonagle, *Media Law* (2nd edn, Thomson Round Hall, 2003), 225. In fact, the requirements of the double construction rule of constitutional interpretation (as well as the interpretive obligation under the European Convention on Human Rights Act 2003) suggest that a restrictive view would be taken of this provision in a case involving media expression so that it may not actually be any more problematic for the media than the common law of contempt of court.

Contempt and media expression under the ECHR

[5.90] The compatibility of the common law relating to contempt of court and Article 10 arose in *Sunday Times v United Kingdom*.[151] In that case, the House of Lords had granted an injunction to prevent the publication of a newspaper article discussing the responsibility of a drugs company for harm caused by one of its products in circumstances where settlement negotiations had been going on for a number of years.[152] The court referred back to its judgment in *Handyside*, where it had held that freedom of expression extended 'not only to information or ideas that are favourably received or regarded as inoffensive or as a matter of indifference, but also to those that offend, shock or disturb the State or any sector of the population'.[153] The court went on to note that:

> These principles are of particular importance as far as the press is concerned. They are equally applicable to the field of the administration of justice, which serves the interests of the community at large and requires the co-operation of an enlightened public. There is general recognition of the fact that the courts cannot operate in a vacuum. Whilst they are the forum for the settlement of disputes, this does not mean that there can be no prior discussion of disputes elsewhere, be it in specialised journals, in the general press or amongst the public at large. Furthermore, whilst the mass media must not overstep the bounds imposed in the interests of the proper administration of justice, it is incumbent on them to impart information and ideas concerning matters that come before the courts just as in other areas of public interest. Not only do the media have the task of imparting such information and ideas: the public also has a right to receive them.[154]

The court noted that the House of Lords, in granting the injunction, had held that there was an absolute rule that it was impermissible to prejudge issues in pending cases. The Law Lords had taken the view that to strike the balance between expression and the administration of justice in each case would generate too much uncertainty in the law. The European Court of Human Rights found that this blanket rule was incompatible with Article 10.[155]

---

151. *Sunday Times v United Kingdom* (1979) 2 EHRR 245. See also *Nikula v Finland* (Application No 31611/96) 21 March 2002 (Former Fourth Section) where the conviction for defamation of a defence lawyer arising from comments made in court about a public prosecutor was held to violate Art 10.
152. See **[2.58]–[2.62]**.
153. *Sunday Times v United Kingdom* (1979) 2 EHRR 245, para 65.
154. *Sunday Times v United Kingdom* (1979) 2 EHRR 245, para 65.
155. Subsequent to the judgment in *Sunday Times*, the UK enacted the Contempt of Court Act 1981. The Act made a number of significant changes to contempt law, specifying the stage in proceedings from which the sub judice rule would apply so as to impose strict liability for publication. The English courts have decided a number of cases in which the compatibility of that legislation with the Convention protection of media expression has arisen. See *Attorney-General v Times Newspapers Ltd* [1992] 1 AC 191; *Attorney-General v Punch Ltd* [2002] UKHL 50; [2003] 1 AC 1046; *R v Shayler* [2002] UKHL 11, Smith Casenote [2002] Cambridge Law Journal 514. See also Smith and Eady, *Arlidge, Eady and Smith on Contempt* (3rd edn, Sweet & Maxwell, 2009).

[5.91] In *Kyprianou v Cyprus*,[156] a criminal defence lawyer had been punished for contempt in the face of the court due to his response to the court's intervention in his cross-examination. The applicant claimed that, in the particular circumstances of his case, the fact that the same judges of the court in respect of which he had allegedly committed contempt tried, convicted and sentenced him, raised objectively justified doubts as to the impartiality of that court, contrary to Article 6 of the Convention which requires an impartial trial. Ireland, the UK and Malta intervened in the case which had obvious implications for Irish contempt law. The European Court of Human Rights, however, eschewed the opportunity to make general statements about the law of contempt, stating that it did 'not regard it as necessary or desirable to review generally the law on contempt and the practice of summary proceedings in Cyprus and other common-law systems.'[157] Instead, the court explicitly confined its comments to the use of summary proceedings in the specific circumstances of the case before it. Nonetheless, the approach of the court is interesting in that it seems to suggest that in certain cases at least, the practice whereby the contumned court deals with the contempt itself may be contrary to Article 6. The court identified two types of bias that might render contempt proceedings contrary to Article 6 – objective or 'functional' bias and subjective bias. In the case before it, the court found that there was functional bias due to the trial of the contempt issue by the original court itself. There was also subjective bias on the part of the judges in the case which was identifiable by the language used in the contempt decision and their statement that they had been deeply insulted by the applicant. The fact that there was a review of the decision by the Supreme Court did not remedy these defects as it did not involve a full retrial.

[5.92] The court also found that there had been a breach of the applicant's right to freedom of expression under Article 10. This finding was based specifically on the need to avoid a chilling effect on the function of lawyers in defending their clients' interests and is not of direct relevance to media expression.[158]

[5.93] The European Court of Human Rights has also considered contempt of court in the context of journalists' privilege. This case law is considered below.

JOURNALISTIC PRIVILEGE

[5.94] Privilege to refuse to answer questions in court is enjoyed in certain circumstances by solicitors, clergy and members of the Oireachtas. Up until relatively recently, there was no recognition in this jurisdiction of such a privilege for journalists seeking to protect their sources. That position was stated in *Re Kevin O'Kelly*.[159] In that

---

156. *Kyprianou v Cyprus* (Application No 73797/01) 15 December 2005.
157. *Kyprianou v Cyprus* (Application No 73797/01) 15 December 2005, para 125.
158. In addition to the case law on journalists' sources discussed below, see also *Amihalachioaie v Moldova* (Application No 60115/00) 20 April 2004 (Second Section) where it was held that the punishment of the President of the Bar Council for criticism of the Constitutional Court was in violation of Art 10.
159. *Re Kevin O'Kelly* (1974) 108 ILTR 97.

case, the journalist concerned had refused to give evidence of an interview he had conducted with an accused person on the basis that this was contrary to professional ethics. He was held to be in contempt in the face of the court and committed to prison. The Court of Criminal Appeal replaced the prison sentence with a fine but confirmed the conviction. Walsh J stated unequivocally that while confidentiality may be necessary to the gathering of some information by journalists:

> [J]ournalists or reporters are not any more constitutionally or legally immune than other citizens from disclosing information received in confidence. The fact that a communication was made under terms of express confidence or implied confidence does not create a privilege against disclosure. So far as the administration of justice is concerned the public has a right to every man's evidence except for those persons protected by a constitutional or other established or recognised privilege.[160]

[5.95] In *Mahon v Keena*,[161] the Supreme Court departed from the approach in *O'Kelly*. The plaintiffs in *Mahon* were members of the Tribunal of Inquiry into Certain Planning Matters. The appellants were the public affairs correspondent (Colm Keena) and editor (Geraldine Kennedy) of the *Irish Times*. Keena had received anonymously an unsolicited copy of a letter sent by the tribunal to a witness. The letter sent by the tribunal sought information from that individual in relation to certain payments said to have been made to Mr Bertie Ahern TD. The letter contained information concerning payments said to have been made to Mr Ahern (then Taoiseach) at a time when he was Minister for Finance. The envelope which contained the letter was marked 'strictly private and confidential – to be opened by addressee only.' The final paragraph of the letter was as follows: 'This inquiry is being made of you as part of the Tribunal's confidential inquiry in private. The fact of this letter or its content should not be disclosed to any third party save your legal advisor, if you should choose to seek legal advice in respect of this request.'

[5.96] The *Irish Times* published an article on the front page under Keena's name with the headline 'Tribunal examines payments to Taoiseach'. The article quoted from the tribunal letter. The tribunal made an order pursuant to its statutory powers[162] requiring the editor of the newspaper and Mr Keena to produce to it all documents which comprised the communication received by the *Irish Times* which led to the publication of the article. Kennedy replied the same day, stating that the *Irish Times* could not comply with this order as the material sought had been destroyed. Her letter disputed the right of the tribunal to make the order and cited journalistic privilege. She asserted that it was in the public interest that this obligation and right be protected.

[5.97] The tribunal subsequently served summonses on Mr Keena and Ms Kennedy directing them to attend before it and to produce the letter. It also ordered them to

---

160. *Re Kevin O'Kelly* (1974) 108 ILTR 97.
161. *Mahon v Keena* [2009] 2 ILRM 373.
162. The Tribunals of Inquiry (Evidence) Act 1921, s 1(i)(b) as amended by the Tribunals of Inquiry (Evidence) (Amendment) Act 1979, s 3.

answer all questions to which the tribunal might 'require answers in relation to the source and present whereabouts of the documents ... referred to ...' The defendants furnished written statements of their evidence to the tribunal which stated that they were unable to produce the documents sought because they had destroyed them. They declined to answer any questions which in their view would give any assistance in identifying the source of the anonymous communication.

[5.98] The tribunal considered that the behaviour of the defendants amounted to breaches of its orders. It decided to exercise its statutory powers[163] to seek orders from the High Court compelling the defendants to comply with the tribunal's orders and took High Court proceedings essentially to have the editor and the journalist ordered to appear before it to answer questions in relation to the article.

[5.99] The proceedings were successful in the High Court. The court[164] considered the importance of freedom of expression, particularly in light of the incorporation of the European Convention on Human Rights into Irish law by virtue of the 2003 Act. It considered a number of cases emanating from the ECtHR in which that court had discussed the issue of protecting journalists' sources. The High Court itself referred to:

> ... the critical importance of a free press as an essential organ in a democratic society. An essential feature of the operation of a free press is the availability of sources of information. Without sources of information journalists will be unable to keep society informed on matters which are or should be of public interest. Thus there is a very great public interest in the cultivation of and protection of journalistic sources of information as an essential feature of a free and effective press.

It went on to note that the case law from the European Court of Human Rights illustrated:

> ... a stalwart defence of freedom of expression, and a trend of strictly construing potential interferences with that right that might claim justification under the variety of justifiable interferences set out in Article 10(2).

The High Court pointed out that:

> This approach by the European Court of Human Rights is particularly evident in cases involving publications relating to political matters. There was no reported case opened to us in which the European Court of Human Rights has upheld an order of a domestic court ordering the disclosure of a journalistic source.

While emphasising the legitimate interests of journalists in protecting their sources, the court went on to criticise heavily the conduct of the editor in ordering the destruction of the documents. It described this as 'an outstanding and a flagrant disregard of the rule of law' by which 'the defendants cast themselves as the adjudicators of the proper balance to be struck between the rights and interests of all concerned.' According to the court,

---

163. Under the Tribunals of Inquiry (Evidence) (Amendment) Act 1997, s 4.
164. Johnson, Kelly and O'Neill JJ, sitting as a Divisional High Court.

'such a manner of proceeding is anathema to the rule of law and an affront to democratic order. If tolerated it is the surest way to anarchy.'

[5.100] While the case had not been brought before the High Court as a contempt matter, the court indicated that the conduct of the defendants was a relevant matter in its determination whether to make the orders sought by the tribunal.

[5.101] The High Court went on to note that the destruction of the documents made it unlikely that the source of the leak would be found so that the interests of the journalists in preserving the anonymity of that source was not in issue. On the other hand, according to the court, the tribunal had an interest in asking the questions proposed as it might be able to ascertain whether the leak had come from it or not.

[5.102] The case was appealed to the Supreme Court which overturned the High Court decision. In so doing, Fennelly J was critical of the emphasis placed by the High Court on the reprehensible nature of the decision to destroy the letter. He referred at length to the decisions of the European Court of Human Rights in *Fressoz and Roire v France*[165] and *Goodwin v United Kingdom*.[166]

[5.103] The applicants in *Fressoz and Roire* were a publisher and a journalist with the French satirical newspaper, *Le Canard Enchaîné*. During a period of industrial unrest involving the motorcar manufacturer, Peugeot, the applicants published an article which included details of the personal notices of assessment to tax of the chairman and managing director of the company. The journalist said that the documents had been sent anonymously in an envelope addressed to him by name. The applicants were prosecuted and convicted by a French court of a criminal offence consisting of handling documents which had been obtained through a breach of professional confidence by an unidentified tax official. They were fined and ordered to pay the managing director nominal damages and costs.

[5.104] The European Court emphasised the public interest in the subject matter of the article. The court accepted that 'people exercising freedom of expression, including journalists, undertake "duties and responsibilities" the scope of which depends on the situation and technical means they use.'[167] The court went on to state that:

> While recognising the vital role played by the press in a democratic society, the court stresses that journalists cannot, in principle, be released from their duty to obey the ordinary criminal law on the basis that Article 10 affords them protection. Indeed, paragraph 2 of Article 10 defines the boundaries of the exercise of freedom of expression.'

[5.105] The court then noted that it had to determine 'whether the objective of protecting fiscal confidentiality, which in itself is legitimate, constituted a relevant and sufficient justification for the interference.'[168]

---

165. *Fressoz and Roire v France* (1999) 31 EHRR 28.
166. *Goodwin v United Kingdom* (1996) EHRR 123.
167. *Fressoz and Roire v France* (1999) 31 EHRR 28, para 52.
168. *Fressoz and Roire v France* (1999) 31 EHRR 28, para 53.

[5.106] The court then explained the extent to which information about the tax affairs of individuals is, in fact, generally available in France. It noted that while publication of the tax assessments in the present case was prohibited, the information they contained was not confidential so that there was no overriding requirement that the information be protected. The court also noted that there had been no dispute about the accuracy of the article or the good faith of the journalist.

[5.107] On the basis of the foregoing, the court found that there had been a violation of Article 10 as there was not 'a reasonable relationship of proportionality between the legitimate aim pursued by the journalists' conviction and the means deployed to achieve that aim given the interest a democratic society has in ensuring and preserving freedom of the press.'[169]

[5.108] Fennelly J also considered the *Goodwin* case. That case concerned commercial information of a highly confidential character: the plan for the refinancing of an company. Disclosure of this, it was argued, would threaten the business and the livelihood of employees of the company concerned. The information was communicated to a journalist by a person known to him who wished to remain anonymous. The company, having learned of the disclosure, obtained an interim injunction restraining publication. The English courts made orders requiring the journalist to disclose his source. He refused and appealed each time. Eventually, the House of Lords fined him £5000 for contempt of court. In considering whether the applicant demonstrated a breach of Article 10, the European Court discussed the importance of protecting journalists' sources:

> Protection of journalistic sources is one of the basic conditions for press freedom, as is reflected in the laws and the professional codes of conduct in a number of Contracting States and is affirmed in several international instruments on journalistic freedoms. Without such protection, sources may be deterred from assisting the press in informing the public on matters of public interest. As a result the vital public watchdog role of the press may be undermined and the ability of the press to provide accurate and reliable information may be adversely affected. Having regard to the importance of the protection of journalistic sources for press freedom in a democratic society and the potentially chilling effect an order of source disclosure has on the exercise of that freedom, such a measure cannot be compatible with Article 10 of the Convention unless it is justified by an overriding requirement in the public interest.[170]

[5.109] The court noted that the necessity for any restriction on freedom of expression had to be 'convincingly established'. It also pointed out that the 'limitations on the confidentiality of journalistic sources call for the most careful scrutiny by the court.' In so scrutinising the measures taken against the applicant, the court noted that the injunctions granted to the company had effectively prevented further dissemination of the confidential information. While these could not prevent direct communication from the journalist's original source to the company's customers or competitors, the additional

---

169. *Fressoz and Roire v France* (1999) 31 EHRR 28, para 56.
170. *Goodwin v United Kingdom* (1996) EHRR 123.

restriction imposed by the orders to disclose 'was not supported by sufficient reasons for the purposes of Article 10(2) of the Convention.' The balance between identifying the source and thereby precluding further circulation of the confidential information was not such as to outweigh 'the vital public interest in the protection of the applicant journalist's source.'

[5.110] After considering these cases in detail, Fennelly J stated:

> At this point, I raise the question as to whether it can truly be said to be in accord with the interests of a democratic society based on the rule of law that journalists, as a unique class, have the right to decide for themselves to withhold information from any and every public institution or court regardless of the existence of a compelling need, for example, for the production of evidence of the commission of a serious crime. While the present case does not concern information about the commission of serious criminal offences, it cannot be doubted that such a case could arise. Who would decide whether the journalist's source had to be protected? There can be only one answer. In the event of conflict, whether in a civil or criminal context, the courts must adjudicate and decide, while allowing all due respect to the principle of journalistic privilege. No citizen has the right to claim immunity from the processes of the law.[171]

In the case at hand, he found that the balance lay in refusing the order. In so holding, he noted that the order would be of little benefit to the tribunal and that there could not thus be said to be an overriding requirement in the public interest that would justify the interference with journalistic privilege. Unlike the High Court, Fennelly J did not think it was appropriate to emphasise the reprehensible conduct of the defendants in assessing the correct balance.

[5.111] The Supreme Court in *Mahon* referred to the approach taken by the European Court of Human Rights to the question of protecting journalist's sources. The issue has arisen in a number of cases since *Goodwin*. In *Stoll v Switzerland*[172] the applicant journalist had obtained a copy of a confidential document drawn up by the Swiss ambassador to the United States dealing with negotiations that were being conducted between, among others, the World Jewish Congress and Swiss banks concerning compensation due to Holocaust victims for unclaimed assets deposited in Swiss bank accounts.

[5.112] A Zürich Sunday newspaper, *Sonntags-Zeitung*, published two articles by the applicant under the headings 'Carlo Jagmetti [the author of the leaked document] insults the Jews' and 'The ambassador in bathrobe and climbing boots puts his foot in it again', accompanied by extracts from the document in question. The next day, two daily newspapers reproduced extensive extracts from it. The applicant was convicted of breaching the Swiss Criminal Code by publishing secret official deliberations. He was fined 800 francs. The Press Council subsequently upheld a complaint against the

---

171. *Mahon v Keena* [2009] 2 ILRM 373, para 61.
172. *Stoll v Switzerland* (2007) 44 EHRR 53.

applicant on the basis that the articles had represented the ambassador in terms that were sensational and shocking. The applicant argued that his conviction and fine were contrary to Article 10. The Grand Chamber found that the conviction had the legitimate aim of protecting information received in confidence and was prescribed by law. In determining whether the interference was necessary in a democratic society, the court accepted that there was a public interest in the matter and that the articles in question were capable of contributing to debate on the issue. It went on to note that the respondent's actions had been aimed at buttressing the confidentiality of diplomatic communications which was important to ensure the smooth operation of international relations. It cautioned that the confidentiality of diplomatic reports was justified in principle but could not be protected at any price. In balancing the competing interests, the court held that the content of the diplomatic report in question and the potential threat posed by its publication were of greater importance than its nature and form. The court then went on to consider whether the disclosure of the report and/or the impugned articles were, at the time of publication, capable of causing 'considerable damage' to the country's interests. Given the content of the report, the language used by the ambassador, and the timing of publication at a particularly delicate juncture, the court decided that that the articles were liable to cause considerable damage to the interests of the Swiss State and that the conviction (for a minor offence and with a small fine) was justified. The court's judgment was critical of the standard of journalistic ethics of the applicant and the fact that the purpose of the articles was to provoke a scandal rather than promote reasoned debate. The fact that the publishers of the other subsequent articles had not been prosecuted was found to be a matter within the State's discretion although the court noted the higher quality of those articles. Judges Zagrebelsky, Lorenzen, Fura-Sandström, Jaeger and Popovi delivered strong dissents. In their view the interests of the State in smooth diplomatic relations did not outweigh the public interest in the articles. Further, the minority was critical of the emphasis placed by the majority on the quality and form of the articles in question in circumstances where the ambassador had not seen fit to take defamation proceedings.

[5.113] Since the decision in *Mahon*, the question of the protection of journalists' sources has arisen again before the European Court of Human Rights. In *Financial Times Ltd v United Kingdom*,[173] the Fourth Section of the court considered this in the context of the common law *Norwich Pharmacal* principle, whereby if a person through no fault of his own becomes involved in the wrongdoing of others so as to facilitate that wrongdoing, he comes under a duty to assist the person who has been wronged by giving him full information and disclosing the identity of the wrongdoer. The case arose when a journalist working for the *Financial Times* received from an anonymous source a copy of a leaked document relating to a possible takeover bid by Interbrew, a Belgian brewing company, for South African Breweries plc (SAB). The journalist informed Goldman Sachs, the producer of the document, that he had received it. Goldman Sachs relayed the conversation to Interbrew, whose CEO then told the *Financial Times*, on the

---

173. *Financial Times Ltd v United Kingdom* (Application No 821/03) 15 December 2009 (Fourth Section).

record, that Interbrew had carried out research into SAB but had not reached the advanced stages of preparing an offer. The *Financial Times* subsequently published an article stating that Interbrew had been plotting a bid for SAB. *The Times, Reuters,* the *Guardian* and the *Independent* also published articles referring to the leaked document and possible bid.

[5.114] The press coverage had a significant impact on the market in shares of Interbrew and SAB. Interbrew was advised that access to the original leaked document might assist the investigation into the identity of the person responsible for the leak. Interbrew launched proceedings against the applicants in the High Court and sought disclosure of the leaked documents. It applied for and was granted a temporary injunction to prevent the applicants from destroying the leaked documents. The High Court ordered the delivery of the documents on the basis of the principle in *Norwich Pharmacal* described above. The court also found that the person responsible for the leak had deliberately mixed false information with the confidential information, to create a false market in the shares of Interbrew and SAB. The court noted that this was a serious criminal offence and that there was a substantial public interest in identifying the person responsible and taking all necessary steps to prevent any repetition. An appeal by the applicants to the Court of Appeal was rejected and leave to appeal to the House of Lords refused. When the case came before the European Court of Human Rights, the disclosure order had not yet been enforced as against the applicants. The court found that the fact that it was capable of enforcement was sufficient to constitute an interference with freedom of expression under Article 10. The interference was also found to have been 'prescribed by law' within the meaning of Article 10(2), as it was authorised by the common law principle in *Norwich Pharmacal.* In finding that the order met the requirement of having a 'legitimate aim', the court noted that the interference was intended to protect the rights of others (by enabling Interbrew to ascertain the identity of the proper defendant to a breach of a confidence action) and to prevent the disclosure of information received in confidence.

[5.115] The court then considered whether the order was necessary in a democratic society. Referring back to its judgment in *Goodwin,* the court noted that this required it to take into account the importance of the protection of journalistic sources for press freedom in a democratic society and the potentially chilling effect that an order for disclosure of a source has on the exercise of that freedom.

[5.116] The court took the view that ordering disclosure to prevent future leaks would only be justified in exceptional circumstances where no reasonable and less invasive alternative means were available to discover the source and where the risk threatened was sufficiently serious and defined. It found that this was not the case in these proceedings as it was not clear whether other means of identifying the source had been fully considered. Interestingly, the court did not recognise any real distinction between a situation where the disclosure of information would directly result in the identification of the source, and the disclosure of information which might, upon examination, lead to such identification. It noted that a chilling effect arises wherever journalists are seen to assist in the identification of anonymous sources. In the case before it, the court concluded that Interbrew's interests in eliminating, by proceedings against the source, the threat of damage through future dissemination of confidential information and obtaining damages for past breaches of confidence were insufficient to outweigh the public interest in the protection of journalists' sources.[174]

[5.117] The question of the protection of sources also arose in an earlier case, *Sanoma Uitgevers BV v Netherlands*.[175] The applicant was a company which published a motoring magazine. It had in its possession a CD-ROM with pictures of an illegal street car race. The pictures had been taken on the basis that the identities of the persons involved would not be revealed by the magazine in its coverage of the street race. The police intervened to bring the race to an end. Subsequently, the police sought the CD-ROM from the magazine's chief editor in circumstances where they had information that one of the participants was someone that they suspected of a number of robberies. The police ordered the chief editor to hand over the CD-ROM and detained him for three hours when he refused. The investigating judge, while recognising that he had no legal role in respect of the issue, intervened and advised the applicant to release the CD-ROM which it did under protest. It took proceedings for its return. These were successful but the national court refused to grant orders sought by the applicant precluding the use of information gleaned from the CD-ROM. The Third Chamber found that there was no violation of Article 10 on the grounds that, while the order might have a chilling effect on the exercise of journalistic freedom of expression, the interests served by the protection of journalistic sources were outweighed by those served by prosecuting the crimes concerned. It emphasised that the CD-ROM contained information that was relevant and capable of identifying the perpetrators of robberies and the authorities had only used that information for those purposes. The case was appealed to the Grand

---

174. The judgment of the Court in *Financial Times* was the second time that UK law on disclosure of journalist's sources had been found to be contrary to the Convention – see *Goodwin* discussed earlier. The law in this area in the UK is governed by the Contempt of Court Act 1981, s 10. This provides that '[n]o court may require a person to disclose, nor is any person guilty of contempt of court for refusing to disclose, the source of information contained in a publication for which he is responsible, unless it be established to the satisfaction of the court that disclosure is necessary in the interests of justice or national security or for the prevention of disorder or crime.' The UK courts traditionally took the view that the common law privilege against non-disclosure was strictly at the discretion of the court. See *Attorney-General v Mullholland and Foster* [1963] 2 QB 477, *British Steel Corp v Granada Television Ltd* [1981] AC 1096; *Attorney-General v Ludin* [1982] 75 Cr App R 90. For an analysis of some of the case law from the UK courts applying the Contempt of Court Act 1981, s 10 before and after the incorporation of the Convention into domestic law, see R Costigan, 'Protection of Journalists' Sources' [2007] Public Law 464. For a comparative perspective on this area, see Brabin, 'Protection Against Judicially Compelled Disclosure of the Identity of News Gatherers' Confidential Sources in Common Law Jurisdictions' (2006) 69 Modern Law Review 895.

175. *Sanoma Uitgevers BV v Netherlands* (Application No 38224/03) European Court of Human Rights (Third Section): judgment of March 31, 2009. See also *Roemen and Schmit v Luxembourg* (Application No 51772/99) 25 February 2003, *Ernst v Belgium* (Application No 33400/96) 15 July 2003, *Voskuil v the Netherlands* (Application No 64752/01) 22 November 2007, *Tillack v Belgium* (Application No 20477/05) 27 November 2007.

Chamber which stressed the importance of procedural safeguards in this context, noting that:[176]

> Given the vital importance to press freedom of the protection of journalistic sources and of information that could lead to their identification any interference with the right to protection of such sources must be attended with legal procedural safeguards commensurate with the importance of the principle at stake… orders to disclose sources potentially have a detrimental impact, not only on the source, whose identity may be revealed, but also on the newspaper or other publication against which the order is directed, whose reputation may be negatively affected in the eyes of future potential sources by the disclosure, and on members of the public, who have an interest in receiving information imparted through anonymous sources.[177]

[5.118] It considered 'the guarantee of review by a judge or other independent and impartial decision making body' as a crucial safeguard.[178] The involvement of the investigating judge in this case had not provided an adequate safeguard as there was no legal basis for it and he had apparently played an 'advisory role'. The court found that the interference was thus not prescribed by law as:

> [T]he quality of the law was deficient in that there was no procedure attended by adequate legal safeguards for the applicant company in order to enable an independent assessment as to whether the interest of the criminal investigation overrode the public interest in the protection of journalistic sources.[179]

THE TRIAL OF CRIMINAL CONTEMPT

[5.119] One issue which has arisen is the way in which criminal contempt should be dealt with by the courts and its status as a criminal offence. This arose in *State (DPP) v Walsh*.[180] In that case, the facts of which are discussed above, the DPP obtained a conditional order in the High Court attaching the respondents for contempt of court for their part in the preparation and publication of the news item. The conditional order commanded them both to attend the court on a specified day 'to answer the matters alleged' by the DPP. The evidence adduced by the DPP when applying for the conditional order was that Walsh, as chairman of the association, had accepted full responsibility for the statement which had been issued on its behalf. The second respondent, and the respondent as secretary of the association, had issued the statement to the press for publication. The respondents both attended on the day specified in the conditional order but did not adduce any evidence in answer to the matters alleged by the DPP, arguing that the judge lacked jurisdiction to try them without a jury on charges of contempt of court. They made an application for trials with a jury. The judge found

---

176. Application No 38224/03, judgment of the Grand Chamber, 14 September 2010.
177. Application No 38224/03, judgment of the Grand Chamber, 14 September 2010, paras 88–89.
178. Application No 38224/03, judgment of the Grand Chamber, 14 September 2010, para 90.
179. Application No 38224/03, judgment of the Grand Chamber, 14 September 2010, para 100.
180. *State (DPP) v Walsh* [1981] IR 412.

that they were not entitled to a jury trial. The respondents appealed to the Supreme Court.

[5.120] The court held that there was no entitlement to a trial by jury in the case at hand. Three of the judges[181] were of the view that, if the facts alleged to constitute the contempt were in issue, a jury might be required by virtue of Article 38.5 of the Constitution but that the lack of any such dispute in the case at hand obviated the necessity for a jury trial. Two of the judges[182] found that the law of contempt fell outside the ambit of Article 38.5 as it was not an aspect of the substantive criminal law and was historically dealt with summarily.

[5.121] Henchy J, in explaining the limited function a jury could have in a trial for criminal contempt, emphasised the important role of the judiciary in ensuring respect for their office:

> The ultimate responsibility for the setting, and the application, of the standards necessary for the due administration of justice must rest with the judges. They cannot abdicate that responsibility, which is what they would be doing if they allowed juries of laymen to say whether the conduct proved or admitted amounted to criminal contempt. It may be said that it is short of the ideal that a judge may sit in judgment on a matter in which he, or a colleague, may be personally involved. Nevertheless, in such matters judges have to be trusted, for it is they and they alone who are constitutionally qualified to maintain necessary constitutional standards. In upholding the current position, to the extent of saying that it is for a judge and not for a jury to say if the established facts constitute a major criminal contempt, I would stress that, in both the factual and legal aspects of the hearing of the charge, the elementary requirements of justice in the circumstances would have to be observed. There is a presumption that our law in this respect is in conformity with the European Convention on Human Rights, particularly Articles 5 and 10(2) thereof.[183]

[5.122] O'Higgins CJ (joined by Parke J) noted the danger to the independence of the judiciary that might ensue if criminal contempt was treated as an ordinary crime. He noted that if Article 38.5 applied to non-minor contempt, by virtue of Article 30.3 of the Constitution it would be prosecutable only at the suit of the Director of Public Prosecutions.[184] He emphasised the importance of judges being able to deal with criminal contempt without relying on the co-operation of the executive:

> But under the Constitution it is the solemn duty of judges to see that justice is administered in the Courts. Surely the imposition of this duty carries with it both the power and the corresponding duty to act in protection of justice, if its fair or effective administration is endangered or threatened. In my view, the judicial power of government (which, in accordance with Article 6 of the Constitution, is exercisable only by or on the authority of the Courts as the organ of State

---

181. Henchy, Griffin and Kenny JJ.
182. O'Higgins CJ joined by Parke J.
183. *State (DPP) v Walsh* [1981] IR 412, 440.
184. *State (DPP) v Walsh* [1981] IR 4122, 425.

established by the Constitution for that purpose) is sufficiently extensive to authorise the Courts to take any action that is necessary for the due administration of justice. Such action must include, where necessary, the power to try summarily those accused of interfering in any manner with the administration of justice. Such an accusation comprises, in my view, all forms of criminal contempt.[185]

[5.123] Henchy J also referred to this point but was of the view that:

> To the extent that such mode of trial may require the co-operation of the Director of Public Prosecutions, I think that, if such co-operation were not forthcoming, the inherent powers of the Courts would comprehend the capacity to compel such co-operation.[186]

[5.124] The question of whether a person other than the DPP could bring a prosecution for criminal contempt arose directly in *Murphy v British Broadcasting Corporation*.[187] There, the applicant had been charged with offences directly related to the Omagh bombing. Whilst the charges were pending before the Special Criminal Court, the respondent broadcast a special television programme on the bombing. During the programme, it stated that the applicant was a seasoned terrorist with previous convictions and that he had made admissions to Gardaí in relation to the use of his mobile telephone by a named individual 'to move bombs' on the date of the bombing. The applicant claimed that the programme influenced public opinion in a manner prejudicial to him and that he might not receive a fair trial. He initiated contempt proceedings against the respondent.[188] Those proceedings were initially taken in the Special Criminal Court itself. That court, while holding that it had jurisdiction to deal with the matter, held that the High Court would be a more convenient forum for the application and the application was ultimately heard there. The DPP was a notice party to the application before the Special Criminal Court. When the case came before the High Court, McKechnie J noted that the DPP had been invited to take over the prosecution of the proceedings but had declined to do so. The respondent argued that the applicant was not entitled to pursue the application as the matter was one which the DPP alone could prosecute. It was also argued that the matter was one which required a jury trial.

[5.125] In considering both of these issues, McKechnie J referred back to the judgments in *Walsh*. He agreed with the judgments in the case which highlighted the dangers of leaving contempt verdicts to a jury. He disagreed however with the judgment of Henchy J (which he described as obiter) in so far as it suggested that there could be some limited role for a jury under Article 38.5, stating that this would not be workable under the terms of Article 38.5. He preferred the approach of O'Higgins CJ which excluded the

---

185.   *State (DPP) v Walsh* [1981] IR 412, 426.
186.   *State (DPP) v Walsh* [1981] IR 412, 441.
187.   *Murphy v British Broadcasting Corporation* [2005] 3 IR 336.
188.   Proceedings were initiated in the Special Criminal Court. An issue arose as to its jurisdiction to hear the latter. The court decided that it had jurisdiction to hear the matter pursuant to the Offences against the State Act 1939, s 45(1)(e) but that the High Court would be a more convenient venue for the contempt proceedings.

jury from criminal trials for contempt, an approach McKechnie J believed was supported by the earlier case law. Relying to these earlier authorities,[189] he stated that:

> It is, in my view, of the first importance that a court of and by itself can vindicate its own authority and that the competence to so do is inherent from its very creation and from the purpose of its existence. It would be seriously impotent if it was otherwise. It is of crucial significance that its integrity be maintained and that its dignity, from both a principled and operational point of view, is not undermined by groundless words, actions or deeds. Under the separation of powers within our Constitution, courts are not only entrusted but are mandated to deliver justice and for that purpose judges have a constitutional safeguard of independence. Their capacity to achieve this would be seriously inhibited if they could not master their own destiny. Moreover since judges have the responsibility of setting not simply minimum, but due and proper standards for the effective administration of justice (see p 440 of *The State (DPP) v Walsh* [1981] IR 412), it appears to me that as a necessary corollary they must likewise have the power to impose those standards against all. Public respect and public confidence demand and would not accept anything less.[190]

McKechnie J noted that there were a number of precedents for private parties moving criminal contempt proceedings.[191] He also referred back to the different approaches taken by Henchy J and O'Higgins CJ in *Walsh* where the former took the view that the DPP could be compelled to prosecute for criminal contempt whereas the Chief Justice was of the view that this would not be possible. Without expressing a view on whether the DPP could be compelled, McKechnie J stated:

> As this case therefore demonstrates, the allegation of contempt made could not proceed if he was solely in charge of its movement. For several reasons this would create quite an unacceptable position. He is as previously noted the prosecuting agent and thus a party to the criminal proceedings. He, if he so wished could move the motion but if on the question of standing his submissions were correct, the applicant could not. Whilst this court should not speculate on the reasons for the notice party's refusal, it cannot I feel, have been solely based on a view that either on the law or the merits the application was bound to fail. There are, at least *prima facie,* serious matters which justify access to the courts. The courts themselves cannot be expected to act as the initiating mover in all such cases. Despite the enormity of the background atrocity of the bombing, the public at large as well as the applicant have a vested and personal interest in the purity of the administration of justice. It is therefore in my view of fundamental importance to the integrity and preservation of justice, to the upholding of judicial independence and to the administration of constitutional fairness and fair procedures, that the law of

---

189. *Attorney General v O'Kelly* [1928] IR 308; *Attorney General v Connolly* [1947] IR 213, referred to by McKechnie J at *Murphy v British Broadcasting Corporation* [2005] 3 IR 336, 374.
190. *Murphy v British Broadcasting Corporation* [2005] 3 IR 336, 374.
191. *PSS v JAS (orse C)* (19 and 22 May 1995, unreported), IIC, Budd J; *De Rossa v Independent Newspapers Ltd* [1998] 2 ILRM 293 and *Kelly v O'Neill* [2000] 1 IR 354. See also *Re MacArthur* [1983] ILRM 355 where the issue was left open.

contempt should, in the context under discussion, remain in the same state today as it was prior to 1922.[192]

[5.126] The question of a jury trial was referred to by Geoghegan J in *DPP v Independent Newspapers*,[193] where he seemed to prefer the approach taken by Henchy J in *Walsh*, noting that:

> [I]t would seem to me that under the procedure contemplated by Henchy J, the Judge of the High Court, hearing a motion for attachment and committal, could sit with a jury in the case of a non-minor criminal contempt and where there was controversy about actual facts which it would be appropriate to have determined by a jury.[194]

---

192. *Murphy v British Broadcasting Corporation* [2005] 3 IR 336, 376.
193. *DPP v Independent Newspapers* [2009] 3 IR 589.
194. *DPP v Independent Newspapers* [2009] 3 IR 589, 609. See also *De Rossa v Independent Newspapers Ltd* [1998] 2 ILRM 293.

Chapter 6

DEFAMATION

THE RIGHT TO A GOOD NAME AND REPUTATION

[6.01] The tort of defamation has long been controversial, in large part because of the way in which it operates as the primary means of regulating the frequently conflicting relationship between the media's freedom of expression on the one hand, and the individual's right to his or her good name on the other.

[6.02] Bunreacht na hÉireann was, in many ways, ahead of its time in expressly conferring constitutional protection on the individual's good name. Thus, while Article 40.6.1°(i) acknowledges 'th[e] rightful liberty of expression, including criticism of Government policy' of the media, Article 40.3.2° also pledges that the State, as part of its general obligation to defend and vindicate the personal rights of the citizen, will 'in particular, by its laws protect as best it may from unjust attack and, in the case of injustice done, vindicate the ... good name ... of every citizen'.[1]

[6.03] More recently, the individual's right to their reputation and good name has been recognised as an aspect of their Article 8 entitlements under the European Convention on Human Rights. The European Court of Human Rights has similarly acknowledged on several occasions that a right to reputation forms part of Article 8.[2] This position has also been adopted by the United Kingdom Supreme Court, which has recognised that Article 8 confers on an individual an entitlement 'to have her good name and reputation protected'.[3]

[6.04] As the European Court of Human Rights explained in *Pfeifer v Austria*:

> [T]he Court reiterates that 'private life' extends to aspects relating to personal identity, such as a person's name or picture, and furthermore includes a person's physical and psychological integrity; the guarantee afforded by Article 8 of the Convention is primarily intended to ensure the development, without outside interference, of the personality of each individual in his relations with other human beings. There is therefore a zone of interaction of a person with others, even in a public context, which may fall within the scope of 'private life' ...
>
> What is at issue in the present case is a publication affecting the applicant's reputation ...
>
> The Court considers that a person's reputation, even if that person is criticised in the context of a public debate, forms part of his or her personal identity and

---

1. See further, the discussion of the significance of this right in *Barrett v Independent Newspapers* [1986] IR 13.
2. See, for example, *Turek v Slovakia* (2007) 44 EHRR 43; *White v Sweden* (2008) 46 EHRR 3.
3. *R (on the application of L) v Metropolitan Police Commissioner* [2010] 1 All ER 113, 126, [2009] UKSC para 24.

psychological integrity and therefore also falls within the scope of his or her 'private life'.[4]

The consequence of this is that the law of defamation is frequently faced with the challenge of striving to strike a balance between these two important social and constitutional values.

BALANCING REPUTATION WITH FREEDOM OF EXPRESSION

[6.05] The European Court of Human Rights discussed at some length the difficulties involved in striking this balance in its decision in *Chauvy v France*. The case concerned a complaint by a writer and publishing company that a conviction for criminal libel which had been imposed in respect of a book which questioned the account of a hero of the French Resistance and implicitly suggested that he may have betrayed his comrades was a breach of their rights under Article 10. In considering the complaint, the court observed that:

> Freedom of expression constitutes one of the essential foundations of a democratic society and one of the basic conditions for its progress and each individual's self-fulfilment. Subject to para 2 of Article 10, it is applicable not only to 'information' or 'ideas' that are favourably received or regarded as inoffensive or as a matter of indifference, but also to those that offend, shock or disturb. Such are the demands of that pluralism, tolerance and broadmindedness without which there is no 'democratic society'. As set forth in Article 10, this freedom is subject to exceptions, which must, however, be construed strictly, and the need for any restrictions must be established convincingly.
>
> ...
>
> The Court has on many occasions stressed the essential role the press plays in a democratic society. It has, *inter alia*, stated that although the press must not overstep certain bounds, in particular in respect of the rights of others, its duty is nevertheless to impart—in a manner consistent with its obligations and responsibilities—information and ideas on all matters of public interest. Not only does the press have the task of imparting such information and ideas: the public also has a right to receive them. The national margin of appreciation is circumscribed by the interest of democratic society in enabling the press to exercise its vital role of 'public watchdog'.
>
> These principles apply to the publication of books or other written materials such as periodicals that have been or are due to be published, if they concern issues of general interest.
>
> ... However, the Court must balance the public interest in being informed of the circumstances in which Jean Moulin, the main leader of the internal Resistance in France, was arrested by the Nazis on June 21, 1943, and the need to protect the reputation of Mr and Mrs Aubrac, who were themselves important members of the Resistance. More than half a century after the events there was a risk that their

---

4. *Pfeifer v Austria* (2009) 48 EHRR 8, paras 34–36.

honour and reputation would be seriously tarnished by a book that raised the possibility, albeit by way of innuendo, that they had betrayed Jean Moulin and had thereby been responsible for his arrest, suffering and death.

In exercising its supervisory jurisdiction, the Court must look at the impugned interference in the light of the case as a whole, including the content of the remarks held against the applicants and the context in which they made them. In particular, it must determine whether the interference in issue was 'proportionate to the legitimate aims pursued' and whether the reasons adduced by the national authorities to justify it are 'relevant and sufficient'. In so doing, the Court has to satisfy itself that the national authorities applied standards which were in conformity with the principles embodied in Article 10 and, moreover, that they based their decisions on an acceptable assessment of the relevant facts.

In addition, in the exercise of its European supervisory duties, the Court must verify whether the authorities struck a fair balance when protecting two values guaranteed by the Convention which may come into conflict with each other in this type of case, namely, on the one hand, freedom of expression protected by Article 10 and, on the other, the right of the persons attacked by the book to protect their reputation, a right which is protected by Article 8 of the Convention as part of the right to respect for private life.[5]

In striking this balance, however, it was argued for many years that the Irish law of defamation attached insufficient importance to the media's freedom of expression and was weighted too heavily in favour of the individual's right to a good name.[6] Cox has commented that 'it may fairly be said that, certainly prior to recent developments, Irish defamation law was extraordinarily strict and protected the plaintiff's right to a good name far more effectively than it did the defendant's right to free speech'.[7] This was attributable in part to the qualified nature of the constitutional guarantee of media freedom of expression[8] but also, perhaps, to the more conservative nature of some elements of Irish society or of the judiciary.

[6.06] In recent decades, however, there occurred something of a shift in the legal protection provided to the media's freedom of expression under Irish law. This evolution in Irish attitudes to freedom of expression was animated primarily by the increasing influence of the European Court of Human Rights' Article 10 jurisprudence. Even in advance of the incorporation of the Convention by the European Convention on Human Rights Act 2003, the Irish courts had begun to have regard to Article 10 in their treatment of challenges concerning freedom of expression.[9] Denham J, for example,

---

5.   (2005) 41 EHRR 29, paras 63–70.
6.   See, for example, O'Dell, 'Does Defamation Value Free Expression?' (1990) 12 DULJ 50.
7.   Cox, *Defamation Law* (FirstLaw, 2007), 3.
8.   For further discussion of this, see **Ch 2**.
9.   See, for example, Barrington J's discussion of the 'significant similarities' between Art 40.6.1°(i) and Art 10 in *Irish Times v Ireland* [1998] 1 IR 359, at 404. However, the Supreme Court was also careful to reject any 'suggestion that one could by examining the European Convention decide on whether a statute violated the Irish Constitution or not'. *Murphy v IRTC* [1999] 1 IR 12, [1998] 2 ILRM 360.

held in both *De Rossa v Independent Newspapers*[10] and in *O'Brien v Mirror Group Newspapers*[11] that it was appropriate to refer to the Convention when considering fundamental rights under the Irish Constitution. In *Hunter v Duckworth*,[12] O'Caoimh J similarly observed that 'no essential difference exists between the provisions of the Convention and the provisions of Article 40.6.1° of the Constitution'.The result is that the level of protection provided to media freedom of expression is significantly greater than was formerly the case.[13] In fact, it has been argued that, with recent developments in the case law of the European Court of Human Rights, the media's freedom of expression may enjoy a more rigorous level of protection in Ireland than in Strasbourg.[14]

THE ENACTMENT OF THE DEFAMATION ACT 2009

[6.07] However, while the level of constitutional protection enjoyed by the media had improved in recent years, it was arguable that this had had an insufficient impact upon the tort of defamation (or, probably more accurately, that the pace of reform was too slow)[15] and that statutory reform of the area was required. Thus, a Defamation Bill was introduced to the Oireachtas in 2006. After much debate and many amendments, the Bill was eventually enacted as the Defamation Act 2009. This Act repeals the Defamation Act 1961[16] which had, together with the underlying principles of the common law tort, governed Irish defamation law for almost half a century.

[6.08] As such, it represents a significant change in Irish law on this issue. As O'Dowd has observed, 'the Act attempts something not far short of a complete restatement of the law of defamation'.[17] For this reason, this chapter will focus primarily on the new Act rather than on the pre-existing common law principles. The relative novelty means that it has not, at the time of writing, yet been subjected to judicial scrutiny. Thus, the law pre–2009 will be referred to where it may assist in shedding light on how the courts may approach the task of interpreting the 2009 Act. However, as the key source of Irish defamation law in the future, this chapter will concentrate chiefly on the text of the new Act.

[6.09] One final introductory point to note is that the new Act has received a considerable amount of negative criticism. Some have accused the Act of going too far

---

10. *De Rossa v Independent Newspapers* [1999] 4 IR 432. It should be noted that, although she dissented from the majority's view on the appropriate outcome of the appeal in *De Rossa*, the majority agreed with Denham J that regard could be had to Art 10 in this context.
11. *O'Brien v Mirror Group Newspapers* [2001] 1 IR 1.
12. *Hunter v Duckworth* [2003] IEHC 81.
13. See, for example, *Mahon v Post Publications* [2007] 3 IR 338; *Mahon v Keena* [2009] IESC 64.
14. Carolan, 'The Changing Face of Media Freedom under the ECHR' (2008) *The Bar Review.*
15. See, for example, the prolonged uncertainty over whether the so-called Reynolds privilege established by the *House of Lords in Reynolds v Times Newspapers* [2001] 2 AC 127 would be adopted into Irish law. *Hunter v Duckworth* [2003] IEHC 81; *Leech v Independent Newspapers* [2007] IEHC 223.
16. Defamation Act 1961, s 4.
17. O'Dowd, 'Ireland's new Defamation Act' [2009] 2 *Journal of Media Law* 173, 182.

in favour of increasing the media's freedom to publish,[18] some have accused it of not going far enough,[19] while others still have suggested that some of its widely-heralded reforms will have less practical impact than some have predicted.[20]

This undoubtedly reflects, to some degree, the fact, as previously discussed, that the articulation of any rules or principles in this area necessarily requires the decision-maker (be it the Oireachtas or a court) to attach greater or lesser weight to either media freedom of expression or the right to reputation and to a good name. This lack of consensus about how specific provisions will operate in practice may also reflect, to some degree, the significant role which the jury continues to have in defamation actions under the 2009 Act.

[6.10] However, while journalistic and academic commentary in most jurisdictions often tends to come down on the side of media freedom of expression, there is also a sense in which this approach may be influenced by natural self-interest on the part of journalists and, perhaps, a residual generational attachment on the part of others (be they journalists, commentators or academics) to the reforming enthusiasm, idealism and drama of *New York Times v Sullivan*, Watergate, the Pentagon Papers, and other landmark US free speech issues of that era.[21] This overlooks the fact that, for reasons outlined elsewhere, the US's peculiarly aggressive protection of freedom of expression has subsequently been shown to suffer from a number of flaws[22] and has not been followed by any other country in the common law world.

[6.11] In an interesting piece, Mullis and Scott have recently argued with respect to English law that:

> [T]he [conventional] critique of the libel regime is too one-sided and the reforms
> proposed ill thought-out, too sweeping and indiscriminate. We are highly sceptical
> as to whether the substantive law of libel contributes at all directly to the existence
> of the perceived problems. Where once the law could be rightly lambasted as
> comprising 'a surfeit of technicality, complexity and the absurd', the range of

---

18. See, for example, the comments of Paul O'Higgins SC at a Trinity College Dublin conference on the Defamation Act 2009 on 28 November 2009.

19. See, for example, the comments of Dr Eoin O'Dell at a Trinity College Dublin conference on the Defamation Act 2009 on 28 November 2009.

20. See, for example, the comments of Paula Mulooly of Simon McAleese Solicitors and of Eoin McCullough SC on s 24 at a Trinity College Dublin conference on the Defamation Act 2009 on 28 November 2009.

21. Nor are such criticisms necessarily a new phenomenon. In 1967 for example, Barron complained that: 'There is an anomaly in our constitutional law. While we protect expression once it has come to the fore, our law is indifferent to creating opportunities for expression. Our constitutional theory is in the grip of a romantic conception of free expression, a belief that the "marketplace of ideas" is freely accessible. But if ever there were a self-operating marketplace of ideas, it has long ceased to exist.' Barron, 'Access to the Press – A New First Amendment Right' (1967) 80 *Harv L Rev* 1641, at 1641.

22. See, for example, the difficulties caused by the fact that the absolutist nature of First Amendment rights has encouraged the US courts to adopt a categorical approach under which certain forms of ostensibly expressive activity are not treated as 'speech' for constitutional purposes. See Schlag, 'An Attack on Categorical Approaches to Freedom of Speech' (1983) 30 UCLA L Rev 671.

legislative and jurisprudential changes given effect over the last two decades leaves any such critique dated and largely inappropriate.[23]

As their article points out, the tort of defamation's position at the juncture between media freedom of expression and the right to reputation and a good name means that there is a necessity for balance in any debate on this topic, and in the adoption of any reforms. This is the complex and frequently unenviable task which confronts courts in this area and which the Irish courts, in particular, may be asked to undertake in interpreting the various provisions of the new Act.

THE TORT OF DEFAMATION

[6.12] The Defamation Act 2009 replaces the 'irritating, complicated and unnecessary distinction'[24] which existed at common law between the causes of action in libel and slander with a single tort of defamation.[25] The requirement in most cases of alleged slander to prove special damage[26] has been abolished such that all claims of defamation are actionable without proof of special damage.[27]

This unified tort consists of the publication, by any means, of a defamatory statement concerning a person to another person or persons.[28]

The plaintiff

[6.13] A person who has been the subject of a defamatory statement concerning them will normally be entitled to sue. However, an action in defamation may not be brought on behalf of the deceased,[29] although an individual's estate will be allowed to continue with an action commenced before the person's death. General damages, punitive damages or aggravated damages will not be available in any cause of action for defamation which survives for the benefit of the estate of a deceased person.[30]

[6.14] Corporate persons are also entitled to sue in respect of a defamatory statement whether or not the company has incurred or is likely to incur financial loss as a result of the publication of that statement.[31] An action will only lie, however, in relation to damage to the company's reputation.[32]

---

23. Mullins & Scott 'Something rotten in the state of English libel law? A rejoinder to the clamour for reform of defamation' (2009) *Communications Law* 173, 173.
24. Robertson & Nicol, *Media Law* (4th edn, Penguin, 2002), 87.
25. Defamation Act 2009, s 6(1).
26. See, for example, *Lynch v Knight* (1861) 9 HL Cas 592.
27. Defamation Act 2009, s 6(5).
28. Defamation Act 2009, s 6(2).
29. See the litigation in *Hilliard v Penfield Enterprises* [1990] 1 IR 138; *Dennehy v Independent Star* [2009] IEHC 458.
30. Civil Liability Act 1961, s 6, as amended by Defamation Act 2009, s 39(2).
31. Defamation Act 2009, s 12.
32. *McDonalds v Steel & Morris* (31 March 1999, unreported), CA; *Al Rajhi Banking v Wall Street Journal* [2003] EWHC 1358 (QB); *Jameel v Wall Street Journal* [2006] UKHL 44.

[6.15] It is unclear whether public bodies may bring an action for defamation. It was held as a matter of English law that it would be inconsistent with Article 10 and with the common law's commitment to free speech to allow local authorities to sue.[33] The rationale for the court's decision was that criticism of political[34] or public bodies is an essential part of freedom of expression in a democracy. The Constitution acknowledges the right of the press to criticise Government policy but a narrow reading of this Article would confine its application to criticisms of the Cabinet. However, it is submitted that the broader view would be more in keeping with the protection of political expression required by Article 10 and with the Irish courts' strong defence of freedom of expression on democratic grounds.[35] It is arguably also supported by the fact that the text of Article 40.6.1°(i) appears to identify the media's right to criticise Government policy as a specific but non-exhaustive aspect of its general 'rightful liberty of expression'.

The defendant

[6.16] In most situations of alleged defamation, a broad range of individuals may be sued. Any person involved in the publication is a potential defendant. While media organisations are generally named as defendants (not least because they will often be the party with the deepest pockets), all individuals involved in the production and distribution of the publication are potentially liable. This means that individual employees or agents of an organisation may be exposed to an action in defamation in relation to its output.[36] Similarly, a media organisation may be liable for anything it publishes, regardless of whether the material in question was created by an individual for whom it is responsible or over whom it exercises some control.

The introduction of the new defence of 'innocent publication' in s 27 of the 2009 Act is accordingly significant for secondary publishers as it provides them with a statutory defence[37] in certain circumstances where they acted without knowledge and with reasonable care.[38]

For those not covered by s 27, s 40 confirms that they may be protected by an agreement to indemnify provided that they did not know at the time of the publication that the statement was defamatory, and that they did not reasonably believe that there is a defence to any action brought upon it that would succeed.

The jurisdiction of the Circuit Court

[6.17] Section 41 of the 2009 Act amends the Courts (Supplemental Provisions) Act 1961 with the effect that action for defamation where the amount of the claim does not

---

33. *Derbyshire CC v Times Newspapers* [1993] AC 534. See also *British Coal Corporation v NUM* (28 June 1996, unreported).
34. *Goldsmith v Bhoyrul* [1998] 2 WLR 435.
35. See **Ch 2**.
36. *R v Clerk* (1728) 1 Barn 304.
37. Some protection was also previously available at common law. See, for example, *Ross v Eason & Son* (1911) 45 ILTR 89; *Fitzgibbon v Eason & Son* (1911) 45 ILTR 91; *Sun Life Assurance v WH Smith* [1933] All ER 432.
38. See the discussion of Defamation Act 2009, s 27 below.

exceed €50,000 may be brought in the Circuit Court in the Circuit where the defamation is alleged to have been committed, or where the defendant or one of the defendants resides. As matters in the Circuit Court are dealt with by a judge alone, this is a provision which seems designed to encourage more actions to be taken in the Circuit Court where they are likely to be disposed of with greater speed and less expense.

Statute of limitations

[6.18] The 2009 Act reduces the time available to plaintiffs in which to bring defamation proceedings. A defamation action must now be brought within one year of the date on which the cause of action accrued, or within two years where the court so directs.[39] The date of accrual of the action is defined as the date upon which the defamatory statement is first published and, where the statement is published through the medium of the internet, the date on which it is first capable of being viewed or listened to.[40]

[6.19] An application for a direction of the court allowing an action to be brought outside the one-year period may be brought by originating motion ex parte, grounded upon affidavit.[41] Where a defamation action has not been brought before the court, the application for leave should be brought by originating notice of motion, with the intending plaintiff named as applicant and the intended defendant as respondent.[42] The application shall be grounded upon an affidavit sworn by or on behalf of the moving party. The court may not give a direction allowing an action to be brought after the expiry of the one-year period unless it is satisfied that the interests of justice *require* the giving of the direction, and that the prejudice that the plaintiff would suffer if the direction were not given would significantly outweigh the prejudice that the defendant would suffer if the direction were given. The court is also directed to consider the reason for the failure to bring the action within the one-year period and to consider the extent to which any evidence relevant to the matter is no longer capable of being adduced by virtue of the delay.

[6.20] This change reflects the views expressed by the courts that speed is of the essence in defamation actions. In *Ewins v Independent Newspapers (Ireland) Limited*,[43] Keane CJ opined that:

> A plaintiff in defamation proceedings, as opposed to many other forms of proceedings, is under a particular onus to institute his proceedings instantly and without delay and, of course, not simply because he will otherwise be met with the response that it cannot have been of such significance to his reputation if he delayed so long to bring the proceedings but also in his own interests in order, at once, to restore the damage that he sees to have been done to his reputation by the offending publication.[44]

---

39.   Statute of Limitations Act 1957, s 11, as amended by the Defamation Act 2009, s 38.
40.   Defamation Act 2009, s 38(3).
41.   Order 1B, rule 3(1).
42.   Order 1B, rule 3(2).
43.   *Ewins v Independent Newspapers (Ireland) Limited* [2003] 1 IR 583.
44.   *Ewins v Independent Newspapers (Ireland) Limited* [2003] 1 IR 583, 590.

[6.21] Similarly, in *Desmond v MGN*,[45] Macken J observed that 'it is … axiomatic that in the case of a claim to vindicate the reputation of a person, the rule is that proceedings such as those for defamation must be progressed with extra diligence'.[46] These 'trenchant comments' were followed with approval by Dunne J in *Desmond v Times Newspapers*[47] who added that 'it is necessary for a plaintiff to act quickly in the prosecution of defamation proceedings for the longer a defamatory statement remains unchallenged, the greater the potential damage to a person's reputation.' This would tend to indicate that, in keeping with the strict limits placed on the court's exercise of its power under s 38(1)(c)(ii), the grant of an extension of time for the bringing of an action may be the exception rather than the rule.

[6.22] Furthermore, the European Court of Human Rights has suggested that the imposition of shorter time limits in defamation actions may be justified as protecting the Article 10 rights of publishers.

> [W]hile an aggrieved applicant must be afforded a real opportunity to vindicate his right to reputation, libel proceedings brought against a newspaper after a significant lapse of time may well, in the absence of exceptional circumstances, give rise to a disproportionate interference with press freedom under Article 10.[48]

This reflects the problems that may be posed for defendants in seeking to justify material published many years previously. This was a factor in the court's decision in *Budu v BBC*:

> The court is entitled to have regard to the practical problems facing Defendants who have to face the sort of detailed inquiries into the responsibility of their conduct many years ago which such a defence entails. Given the onus is on the BBC to establish the defence, it is inevitable in my view, that it will be prejudiced, and possibly to a significant degree by the passage of many years since the original investigations; and by the loss of contemporaneous documentation, that is the journalist's notes.[49]

Verifying affidavits

[6.23] A new requirement introduced by the 2009 Act is the obligation placed on both sides to swear verifying affidavits in relation to any pleading which contains any assertions or allegations of fact,[50] except where the plaintiff is seeking a declaratory order under s 28.[51] This mirrors the reforms introduced by the Civil Liability and Courts

---

45. *Desmond v MGN* [2009] 1 IR 737. However, where a plea of justification has been entered, a court may be more reluctant to strike out a claim on the grounds of inordinate and inexcusable delay.
46. *Desmond v MGN* [2009] 1 IR 737, 756.
47. *Desmond v Times Newspapers* [2009] IEHC 271.
48. *Times Newspapers Ltd (Nos 1 and 2) v United Kingdom* [2009] ECHR 3002/03, para 48.
49. *Budu v BBC* [2010] EWHC 616 (QB), para 111.
50. Defamation Act 2009, s 8.
51. Defamation Act 2009, s 8(13).

Act 2004, in accordance with which verifying affidavits are now required in personal injuries ligation.

[6.24] Affidavits should take the form specified in RSC, Order 1B[52] and must be sworn and filed in court not later than two months after the service of the pleading, although this time may be extended by agreement amongst the parties or by direction of the court.[53] Where affidavits are endorsed on a pleading, the affidavit should be delivered within the time allowed for that pleading by the Rules of the Superior Courts.[54] Affidavits must also be filed in the Central Office.[55] Parties may be cross-examined on their affidavits unless the court directs otherwise.[56]

[6.25] Knowingly making a false or misleading statement in a verifying affidavit is a criminal offence[57] and affidavits filed under s 8 must contain a statement to the effect that the person swearing the affidavit is aware of that fact.[58] A person found guilty of this offence is liable on summary conviction to a €3000 fine, a six-month sentence of imprisonment, or both, or on conviction on indictment, to a €50,000 fine, a five-year prison sentence, or both.

[6.26] Where either party fails to comply with s 8, a court may make an order it considers just and equitable, up to and including the dismissal of the plaintiff's action or the entering of judgment in favour of the plaintiff.[59]

Identification

Test for identification

[6.27] A statement will be regarded as one which concerns a person within the meaning of s 6(2) if it could reasonably be understood as referring to him or her.[60] This means that it is possible to sue a defendant in defamation in relation to a defamatory statement which does not specifically identify the plaintiff, provided that the reasonable reader of or audience member for the defamatory publication would identify the plaintiff from the publication.[61]

[6.28] The onus is on the plaintiff to establish that they have been so identified. In his decision in *Magee v MGN*,[62] McKechnie J (citing a passage from the decision in

---

52. Form No 4 in Appendix CC.
53. Defamation Act 2009, s 8(5).
54. Order 1B, rule 2(2).
55. Order 1B, rule 2(3).
56. Defamation Act 2009, s 8(9).
57. Defamation Act 2009, s 8(6).
58. Defamation Act 2009, s 8(8).
59. Defamation Act 2009, s 8(10).
60. Defamation Act 2009, s 6(3).
61. See, for example, *Yousouoff v MGM* (1934) 50 *Times Law Reports* 581; *Hayward v Thompson* [1982] QB 47; *Campbell v Irish Press* (1955) 90 ITLR 105; *Marathon Mutual v Waters* [2009] EWHC 1931 (QB).
62. *Magee v MGN* [2003] IEHC 87, HC; *Duffy v News Group Newspapers* [1992] 2 IR 369.

Knupffer v London Express)[63] explained that establishing that identification had occurred was a two-stage process, involving questions of both fact and law.

> The first question is one of law, namely whether the article can be regarded as being capable of referring to the Plaintiff. The second question is one of fact – does the article, in fact, lead reasonable people who know [the Plaintiff], to the conclusion that it does refer to him? Unless the first question can be answered in favour of [the Plaintiff] the second question does not arise.

[6.29] A plaintiff will be generally regarded as having been identified where the publication refers to him or her by name,[64] or by a well-known nickname.[65] Identification may also be found on the basis of a photograph, image,[66] description or any other specific reference to the plaintiff.[67]

Identification may also be present in circumstances where the publication provides details which are known to some individuals and which thereby allows those individuals to identify the plaintiff.[68]

[6.30] Similarly, the development of automated internet search engines and linking has raised the possibility that individuals could be identified from the cross-referencing of search results. In this situation, a plaintiff who could not be identified from a single publication may become identifiable when that publication is presented by a search engine or website alongside other publications that identify him or her.[69] The common law had traditionally held it is not possible to make a defendant responsible for defamatory statements by other persons which are not either expressly or by implication approved, adopted or repeated in the statement by that defendant in respect of which an action is brought. This meant that a plaintiff could not use a reference in one publication to found a cause of action against a third party in relation to a separate publication.[70] However, these cases did concern situations in which a reader would have had to be aware of the other publications to identify the plaintiff. It is a different matter where the publications – or more probably links to, or headlines from, those publications – are presented on a single webpage.[71] This practical difference means that this is an issue which may receive further consideration in Ireland and which may have implications, in

---

63. *Knupffer v London Express* [1944] AC 116.
64. *Berry v Irish Times* [1973] IR 368.
65. *Every Evening Printing v Buller* 144 F 916; *Murphy v Times Newspapers* [2001] 1 IR 522.
66. *Dunlop v Dunlop Rubber* [1920] 1 IR 280.
67. *Channel 7 Sydney Pty v Parras* [2002] NSWCA 202.
68. *Morgan v Odhams Press* [1971] 1 WLR 1239.
69. *Budu v BBC* [2010] EWHC 616 (QB). The court dismissed the claim on the facts of the case but did not address the question of whether, as a matter of law, identification could be held to have occurred in such circumstances.
70. *Astaire v Campling* [1965] 3 All ER 666, [1966] 1 WLR 34.
71. See the brief discussion in *Ali v Associated Newspapers* [2010] EWHC 100 (QB).

particular, for the maintenance of online archives by publishers, or for the way in which website operators organise and oversee the display of links to other sites or stories.[72]

Evidence of identification

[6.31] Evidence that an individual has been so identified may be adduced.[73] It has been held that the identity of such individuals, as well as any extrinsic linking facts which they are said to know, are part of the plaintiff's cause of action, and they must be pleaded by a plaintiff who wishes to rely upon them.[74] A plaintiff need not, however, supply particulars of such individuals or extrinsic facts where it is his contention that those facts were widely known amongst the general community.[75]

However, the fact that some individuals identified the plaintiff is not determinative. The test at common law was whether the reasonable person would have identified the plaintiff. Thus, the fact that certain persons who were well acquainted with the plaintiff may have identified him or her from the publication in question would not necessarily prove that they would also be identified by a reasonable reader or viewer.

The intention of the publisher

[6.32] Intention is not a necessary element of the act of identification. A plaintiff may be identified by a publication where that was not intended by the publisher, or where the individual in question is not known to the publisher, once the publication in question could reasonably be understood to refer to him or her. One consequence of this is that a publication about a fictional character may be regarded as defamatory if it could reasonably be understood to refer to a living person.[76] It also means that an action may be brought by more than one individual provided all can establish that they could have been identified by a reasonable reader or viewer of the offending publication.[77] Furthermore, a publication about a specific individual may give rise to a cause of action on the part of a second individual if the publication in question either refers to the second individual in error, or describes the first individual in sufficiently general terms that it could be taken to refer to the second individual. Thus, in *Newstead v London Express*, an article about an identified bigamist was found to be defamatory of a second individual who shared the same name.[78]

---

72. Search engines have been held not to be liable for the result of such searches. See, for example, *Metropolitan International Schools Ltd v Designtechnica Corporation* [2009] EWHC 1765 (QB).

73. *Sinclair v Gogarty* [1937] IR 377; *Duffy v News Group Newspapers* [1992] 2 IR 369.

74. *Bruce v Odhams Press Ltd* [1936] 1 KB 697; *Fullam v Newcastle Chronicle* [1977] 1 WLR 655; *Mosley v Focus Magazin Verlag Gmbh* (29 June 2001, unreported), CA.

75. *Byrne v RTÉ* [2006] IEHC 71; *Hughes v Mirror Newspapers* [1985] 3 NSWLR.

76. *Hulton v Jones* [1910] AC 20.

77. *Murphy v Times Newspapers* [2001] 1 IR 522, where two brothers were held to be entitled to initiate proceedings as a result of the same publication.

78. *Newstead v London Express* [1940] 1 KB 331.

[6.33] As Lord Shaw explained the law in *Hulton v Jones*:

> In the publication of matter of libellous character, that is matter which would be
> libellous if applying to an actual person, the responsibility is as follows: In the
> first place there is responsibility for the words used being taken to signify that
> which readers would reasonably understand by them; in the second place there is
> responsibility also for the names used being taken to signify those whom the
> readers would reasonably understand by those names and in the third place the
> same principle is applicable to persons unnamed but sufficiently indicated by
> designation or description.[79]

This statement of the law was subsequently endorsed by Scrutton LJ in *Cassidy v Daily
Mirror* where he held that:

> In my view, since *E Hulton & Co v Jones*, it is impossible for the person
> publishing a statement which, to those who know certain facts, is capable of
> defamatory meaning in regard to A., to defend himself by saying: 'I never heard of
> A and did not mean to injure him.' If he publishes words reasonably capable of
> being read as relating directly or indirectly to A and, to those who know the facts
> about A, capable of a defamatory meaning, he must take the consequences of the
> defamatory inferences reasonably drawn from his words.[80]

[6.34] The fact that the publisher's intention is irrelevant to the existence or otherwise of
identification may impose an increased burden on newspapers and broadcasters in a
small jurisdiction like Ireland, where the reasonable reader or viewer could arguably be
assumed to have a greater degree of acquaintance with their fellow citizens and thus be
able to identify a wider category of individuals than might be the case in larger
jurisdictions.[81] This could arise, for example, in a situation where a broadcaster or
publisher had taken steps to conceal the identity of an individual (by, for example,
changing their name or pixelating their face) but where other elements of the publication
(for example, referring to or showing the locality where the individual lives, revealing
the individual's house or car, or permitting the voice or clothing of the individual to be
seen) would allow others acquainted with the individual to identify them.[82]

[6.35] That the taking of steps to obscure the identity of an individual may not
necessarily be sufficient to avoid liability underscores the fact that the absence of a
requirement to establish intention on the part of the publisher may, in effect, operate as a

---

79. *Hulton v Jones* [1910] AC 20, 26.
80. *Cassidy v Daily Mirror Newspapers* [1929] 2 KB 331, at 341.
81. On a separate but similar point, see the comments of the Court of Appeal of Barbados concerning
    the implications for a defamation action of being brought in relation to a small jurisdiction where
    'gossip seems to travel at the speed of light rather than sound'. See *Philips v Boyce* (2006) 71
    WIR 14.
82. See further the discussion of innuendo below.

form of strict liability in allowing a defendant to be sued in circumstances where there was little or no fault or negligence on their part.[83]

[6.36] In this regard, it is instructive to note that Morland J in the English decision of *O'Shea v MGN*[84] relied on Article 10 of the European Convention on Human Rights as justifying a refusal to apply this principle to circumstances where the defendant argued that it would unfair to impose a strict liability standard on them.

[6.37] The case related to the publication of an advertisement for an online pornography service. The advertisement used a photograph of a female who bore a strong resemblance to the plaintiff. Several acquaintances, including friends and family, believed that the plaintiff was the individual pictured in the advertisement. Her defamation action failed, however on the basis of the court's finding that Article 10 precluded the imposition of liability on a publisher in such circumstances.

[6.38] For Morland J, 'it would impose an impossible burden on a publisher if he were required to check if the true picture of someone resembled someone else who because of the context of the picture was defamed'.[85] The court also had regard to the fact that this was the first such case which had been initiated in over 100 years. Furthermore, an action for malicious falsehood would be available where the use of a lookalike was deliberate. This meant, in his view, that the aim of protecting individuals against 'lookalike' defamations was not a sufficiently pressing social need to justify the interference with Article 10 which the application of the strict liability standard would require.

[6.39] Cox has argued that the decision in *O'Shea* is illogical in that there was no rational basis for refusing to apply the decision in *Hulton* to the facts of that case. While the court did attempt to provide such rational reasons for the distinction, Cox's conclusion that the decision indicates a potential Convention infirmity in the Hulton principle seems correct. This reflects the fact that the court's logic seems somewhat unconvincing. Not only does the court assume that decided cases accurately correspond to the level of social occurrence (a particularly questionable assumption in an area such as defamation where many actions are settled), but it places arbitrary happenstance ahead of the logic of legal principle. In reality, the court's decision does appear to have been primarily motivated by a judicial discomfort with the severity of this strict liability principle.

---

83. However, this ostensibly strict liability approach would not necessarily apply equally to all cases of alleged defamation. For example, it is possible that s 26 will be interpreted so as to reflect the principle laid down in *Bonnick v Morris* [2003] 1 AC 300 with the effect that that a defendant could not held liable for an unintentional reference to the plaintiff, where the requirements of s 26 are met in relation to the intended subject of the publication and the defendant acted fairly and reasonably in the manner in which he or she identified the person to whom the article was intended to relate.
84. *O'Shea v MGN* [2001] EMLR 40.
85. *O'Shea v MGN* [2001] EMLR 40, para 45.

[6.40] Such discomfort may also arguably be discerned in the earlier decision in *Morgan v Odhams Press*[86] where Lord Reid remarked that:

> It does not matter whether the publisher intended to refer to the plaintiff or not. It does not even matter whether he knew of the plaintiff's existence. And it does not matter that he did not know or could not have known the facts which caused the readers with special knowledge to connect the statement with the plaintiff. Indeed the damage done to the plaintiff by the publication may be of a kind which the publishers could not have foreseen. That may be out of line with the ordinary rule limiting damage for which a tortfeasor is liable, but that point does not arise in this case.[87]

This indicates that this matter may be the subject of further consideration by courts, whether in Ireland or England, in the future. While the strict liability principle is based on an understandable desire to prevent publishers from undermining a person's reputation or good name by underhand or surreptitious means, it has the potential to leave publishers in the impossible position where they may be liable to an award in damages even after making every effort to avoid identifying an individual, whether known or unknown to them. Other reforms in the 2009 Act, such as the offer of amends[88] or apology[89] procedures, may mitigate the stark nature of what seems to have been traditionally regarded by the courts as a binary choice between unfair alternatives. Nonetheless, if it was to continue to be the case that defendants were faced with significant awards of damages even after acting with all possible care, it would seem legitimate to question whether that situation would strike a fair balance between media freedom of expression and the individual's right to reputation and a good name.

Identification as part of a class

[6.41] Before the 2009 Act, one of the circumstances in which the question of identification was most commonly contested was where the allegedly defamatory comment was made in respect of a class of persons of which the plaintiff is a member.[90] The common law required a context-sensitive assessment of whether the plaintiff could be reasonably identified from the impugned publication. This depended on a variety of factors, most commonly the size of the class and the specificity of the statement.

[6.42] The leading common law authority on the question of whether an individual may sue in defamation for a statement made about a group is the decision of the House of Lords in *Knuppfer v London Express Newspapers*.[91] The case concerned a Russian migrant who was resident in London who alleged that he had been defamed by a newspaper report about pro-Nazi Russian migrants attempting to infiltrate the Soviet

---

86. *Morgan v Odhams Press* [1971] 1 WLR 1239.
87. *Morgan v Odhams Press* [1971] 1 WLR 1239, 1242.
88. Defamation Act 2009, s 22.
89. Defamation Act 2009, s 24.
90. *Duffy v News Group Newspapers* [1992] 2 IR 369.
91. *Knuppfer v London Express Newspapers* [1944] AC 116. See also *Aiken v Police Review Publishing Co* (12 April 1995, unreported), CA.

Union. The House of Lords rejected his suit on the basis that the class in question was far too large to allow a reasonable reader to identify the plaintiff as a member of the group.

[6.43] In setting out the relevant law at some length, Lord Atkin held that:

> The only relevant rule is that for an order to be actionable the defamatory words must be understood to be published of and concerning the plaintiff. It is irrelevant that the words arc published of two or more persons if they are proved to be published of him, and it is irrelevant that the two or more persons are called by some generic or class name. There can be no law that a defamatory statement made of a firm or trustees, or the tenants of a particular building is not actionable, if the words would reasonably be understood as published of each member of the firm or each trustee or each tenant. The reason why a libel published by a large or indeterminate number of persons described by some general name generally fails to be actionable is the difficulty of establishing that the plaintiff was, in fact, included in the defamatory statement, for the habit of making unfounded generalisations is ingrained in ill-educated or vulgar minds, or the words occasionally intended to be a facetious exaggeration ... It would be as well for the future for lawyers to concentrate on the question whether the words were published of the plaintiff, rather than on the question whether they were spoken of a class.[92]

[6.44] Expressing himself in less trenchant terms, Lord Porter outlined a similar approach to this issue:

> The question whether the words refer in fact to the plaintiff or plaintiffs is a matter for the jury or for a judge sitting as a judge of fact, but as a prior question it has always to be ascertained whether there is any evidence on which a conclusion that they do so refer could reasonably be reached. In deciding this question the size of the class, the generality of the charge and the extravagance of the accusation may all be elements to be taken into consideration, but none of them is conclusive. Each case must be considered according to its own circumstances. I can imagine it being said that each member of a body, however large, was defamed when the libel consisted in the assertion that no one of the members of a community was elected as a member unless he had committed a murder.[93]

Thus, identification was found to have occurred where an allegation was made that an unnamed member of a 12-strong group of police officers had committed rape,[94] whereas a publication which referred to specific decisions in support of the allegation that 'a handful of solicitors and judges' were undermining the Constitution and its Catholic ethos was held not to identify the plaintiffs, despite them having been involved in the decisions identified therein.[95]

---

92.   *Knuppfer v London Express Newspapers* [1944] AC 116, 121.
93.   *Knuppfer v London Express Newspapers* [1944] AC 116, 124.
94.   *Riches v Newsgroup* [1986] 1 QB 265.
95.   *Gallagher & Shatter v Independent Newspapers* (1980) *The Irish Times*, 10 May.

[6.45] Section 10 of the 2009 Act provides that:

> Where a person publishes a defamatory statement concerning a class of persons, a member of that class shall have a cause of action under this Act against that person if—
>
> (a)   by reason of the number of persons who are members of that class, or
>
> (b)   by virtue of the circumstances in which the statement is published,
>
> the statement could reasonably be understood to refer, in particular, to the member concerned.

It is unclear precisely what impact, if any, the enactment of this section will have on the way in which the law has traditionally operated in this area.

[6.46] On one view, the section provides a degree of additional clarity by specifying the particular factors which may be taken into account in applying the standard of reasonable understanding laid down by both s 10 and s 6(3). Cox points out, however, that this argument is undermined by the fact that the 'second of th[e] criteria [set out in s 10] is so vague as to cover all situations'.[96]

[6.47] An alternative analysis is that s 10 may arguably make it easier for a plaintiff to succeed in a defamation action by expressly providing that identification may be established on the basis of the number of persons who are members of the class alone. Prior to the enactment of the 2009 Act, this was generally regarded as one factor – albeit frequently a decisive one – in the judge or jury's overall assessment of whether a plaintiff could reasonably be regarded as having been identified by the publication in question. The Act makes clear that the number of persons in the relevant group may of itself provide an adequate basis for a finding that the plaintiff was sufficiently identifiable to sustain an action for defamation.

[6.48] On balance, however, the fact that s 10 goes on to apply the traditional test that, regardless of the size of the group, the statement must also be reasonably understood to refer, in particular, to the member concerned, means that s 10 should not result in the application of a lower threshold for establishing identification in the future.

Publication

[6.49] It is clear from the statutory definition set out by s 6(2) that the act of publication remains the critical stage in establishing a cause of action in defamation. It is the publication of the defamatory statement to another party or parties that gives rise to an action in law. Thus, the person against whom an action may lie may not necessarily be the same individual or entity who created the offending statement at first instance.

[6.50] Section 6(2) provides that publication can occur 'by any means'. This indicates that a wide range of activities may be caught by the tort of defamation. The extent of the activities which can potentially constitute publication is further illustrated by the broad

---

96.   Cox, *Defamation Law* (FirstLaw, 2007), 142.

and non-exhaustive definition of 'statement' contained in s 2 which provides that it includes a statement made orally or in writing, visual images, sounds, gestures and any other method of signifying meaning, a statement broadcast on the radio or television, or published on the internet, and an electronic communication.

[6.51] Section 6(2) also makes clear that publication of a defamatory statement to a single third party is sufficient to give rise to an action in defamation. This reflects the fact that, while the communication of a defamatory statement to a large audience is likely to cause greater injury and will frequently lead to a higher award of damages,[97] publication to a small or limited number of individuals can also, in certain situations, cause serious damage to the individual to whom the statement referred. The Supreme Court rejected the argument in *Crofter Properties v Genport*[98] that an award of damages by the High Court should be reduced on appeal by reference to the fact that the defamation in question was made to a limited number of individuals. The case in question concerned anonymous telephone calls which were made to police in the United Kingdom alleging that particular named individuals were involved in money laundering activities. Denham J explained that:

> While the publication was limited, i.e. in contrast to publication by a newspaper, it was published to an important group – police officers. Further, it could be envisaged, and it did happen, that this information would then proceed to other police forces, including to members of the Garda Síochána. The consequences of publication of such false information to such a group would be serious and disproportionate to the number of people to whom it was published. Indeed, a significant part of the information given to the Garda Síochána was investigated by them and found to be without foundation. I am satisfied that the fact that the publication was to this limited number of people is not a ground to reduce the award of general damages given the influential people to whom it was published and the fact that the publication was made with a view to damaging the defendant.[99]

The burden of proving publication rests with the plaintiff. However, in many cases this will be relatively easy to establish. At common law, it was sufficient for a plaintiff to prove that a statement was communicated to a third party or third parties, and that those parties understood the statement.[100,] Where the third party does not understand the statement – such as where, for example, it is made in a foreign language which they do not speak or understand[101] – no publication has occurred.

---

97. In this context, it should be noted that it has been held in Australia that it cannot be assumed that all visitors to a website have read all pieces on that site. This may be relevant to the question of the damages that are appropriate for an instance of online defamation. See *Buddhist Society of Western Australia v Bristle* [2000] WASCA 210.
98. *Crofter Properties v Genport* [2005] 4 IR 28.
99. *Crofter Properties v Genport* [2005] 4 IR 28, 33.
100. *Sadgrove v Hole* [1901] 2 KB 1; *Tolan v An Bord Pleanála* [2008] IEHC 275.
101. *Jones v Davers* (1596) Cro Eliz 496; *Price v Jenkings* (1601) Cro Eliz 865.

[6.52] There is no requirement that publication be intentional. Accidental publication can give rise to liability in defamation where publication was reasonably foreseeable, or was a natural and probable consequence of the defendant's actions.[102] Thus, in *Theaker v Richardson*,[103] publication was held to have occurred where a letter which was addressed to the plaintiff and delivered to her home was opened and read by her husband.

[6.53] This demonstrates that considerable care should be taken in the communication of potentially defamatory statements. The courts have been willing to hold that publication occurs in respect of relatively open methods of communication, such as postcards or telegrams.[104]

[6.54] Furthermore, in applying the reasonable foreseeability test,[105] the courts have also tended to assume a degree of knowledge on the part of defendants such that, for example, it would seem foreseeable that a communication to a director may be read by his or her secretary or personal assistant. Publication may also occur where the third party is not the intended recipient of the communication but is involved in its creation. Hence, in *Bryanston Finance v de Vries*[106] the dictation of a letter to a secretary and the subsequent copying of that letter by another employee was found to constitute publication.

[6.55] The importance of exercising caution in dealing with potentially defamatory material applies not only to its communication but also to its care. A defendant who loses, mislays or misdirects defamatory material may be liable on the basis that it is reasonably foreseeable that a third party may read such material.[107]

[6.56] It has also been held that a defendant may be liable for the re-publication of his or her statement by third parties where that repetition was a natural and probable consequence of the initial publication.[108] This means, for example, that a defendant will be liable for the re-publication of a statement made to a party who was under a duty to communicate it to a third party.[109] A defendant may also be liable for the re-publication where that re-publication was authorised, be it expressly or by implication.[110]

[6.57] Section 27 of the 2009 Act provides for a new defence of innocent publication. This will assist some defendants who find themselves faced with a defamation claim on the basis of an unintended publication. This defence is considered further below.

---

102. *Pullman v William Hill* [1891] QB 524.
103. *Theaker v Richardson* [1962] 1 All ER 229. See also *Maxwell v Gavin Low* (11 January 1967), HC in Cox, *Defamation Law* (FirstLaw, 2007), 33.
104. *Huth v Huth* [1915] 3 KB 32.
105. Although the 'natural and probable consequence' test has also been frequently used, the Court of Appeal in *McManus v Beckham* [2002] 4 All ER 497 argued persuasively that foreseeability rather than causation was the more relevant concept in this area.
106. *Bryanston Finance v de Vries* [1975] QB 703, [1975] 2 All ER 609.
107. *Weld-Blundell v Stephens* [1920] AC 956.
108. *Ewins v Carlton* [1997] 2 ILRM 223; *Hunter v Duckworth* [2000] 1 IR 510.
109. *Black v Holmes* (1822) 1 Fox & Sm 28.
110. *Slipper v BBC* [1990] All ER 165.

Nonetheless, it is important to note at this point that this s 27 defence is quite narrowly drawn and will not apply to many instances of unintended publication.

[6.58] Section 6(4) of the 2009 Act may also be of some comfort to defendants in cases of unintended publication. It provides that:

> There shall be no publication for the purposes of the tort of defamation if the defamatory statement concerned is published to the person to whom it relates and to a person other than the person to whom it relates in circumstances where –
>
> (a)   it was not intended that the statement would be published to the second-mentioned person, and
>
> (b)   it was not reasonably foreseeable that publication of the statement to the first-mentioned person would result in its being published to the second-mentioned person.

Again, however, this section seems likely to be relevant to only a limited number of cases. A literal reading of s 6(4) indicates that both of the specified criteria set out therein must be satisfied before a communication will be regarded as a non-publication for the purposes of this tort. This appears to mean that s 6(4) will only apply where publication to the second person occurs as a result of the communication with the person to whom the statement relates. This means, for example, that this section seems unlikely to apply to situations such as overheard conversations where the communication to the third party was causally unrelated to that with the person to whom the statement relates.

Multiple publications

[6.59] Whereas a cause of action existed at common law in relation to each instance of publication,[111] s 11 of the 2009 Act introduces a variant of the so-called 'single publication' rule into Irish law. The section provides that:

> (1) Subject to *subsection (2)*, a person has one cause of action only in respect of a multiple publication.
>
> (2) A court may grant leave to a person to bring more than one defamation action in respect of a multiple publication where it considers that the interests of justice so require.
>
> (3) In this section 'multiple publication' means publication by a person of the same defamatory statement to 2 or more persons (other than the person in respect of whom the statement is made) whether contemporaneously or not.

[6.60] The single publication rule was developed in the United States[112] where it provides that each edition of a book, newspaper or broadcast is to be treated as a single publication. This means that publication is held to occur only once, that being at the moment the statement is first published or broadcast. This, in turn, means that the

---

111.   *Duke of Brunswick v Harner* (1849) 14 QB 185; *Berezovsky v Michaels* [2000] 1 WLR 1004.

112.   *Wolfson v Syracuse Newspapers* 279 NY 716 (1938); *Gregoire v GP Putnam & Sons* 298 NY 119 (1948); *Firth v State of New York* NY Int 88 (2002).

statute of limitations for defamation actions begins to run from the date the allegedly defamatory material was first published.

[6.61] By contrast, as the decision in *Duke of Brunswick v Harner*[113] demonstrated, a new cause of action could arise at common law in respect of the re-publication of a statement, even where the cause of action in relation to the initial publication had long been statute-barred. While this decision had been criticised in the English courts,[114] the principles established by it have continued to be applied.[115] The view was expressed by the courts there that '[i]f a publisher publishes in a multiplicity of jurisdictions it should understand, and must accept, that it runs the risk of liability in those jurisdictions in which the publication is not lawful and inflicts damage'.[116] This has been criticised, in particular, for the way in which it affects the operators of online archives.[117] The fact that a new defamatory publication was in principle committed each time a person accessed the site in question meant that potential liability of online publishers was incredibly broad from both a geographical and a temporal point of view. Nonetheless, the European Court of Human Rights refused to hold that the ongoing application of the Harner principle breached the United Kingdom's obligations under Article 10.[118]

[6.62] Section 11 appears to operate somewhat differently to the American 'single publication' rule in that the protection applies to the repetition of the defamatory statement rather than to the reproduction of the publication itself. This allows publishers a certain degree of protection where a statement is published across different media and in different forms. Thus, for example, s 11 would seem to protect a news organisation which published the same allegedly defamatory statement across any or all of its outlets – for example, its paper edition, its website, its RSS feed, or in any sort of reduced-format output for mobile phones or other portable devices. This is arguably preferable to the American approach, in accordance with which morning and afternoon editions of newspapers[119] or paperback and hardback versions of books[120] are treated as separate publications.

[6.63] This does raise the question, however, of whether s 11 will protect the repetition of a defamatory allegation where that allegation is communicated in slightly different terms. The reference to the 'same defamatory statement' suggests that this might not be the case. This may be relevant where a media organisation expresses an allegedly

---

113. *Duke of Brunswick v Harner* (1849) 14 QB 185.
114. *Dow Jones v Jameel* [2005] QB 946.
115. *Berezovsky v Michaels* [2000] 1 WLR 1004; *Loutchansky v Times Newspapers* [2002] 1 All ER 652.
116. *King v Lewis* [2005] EMLR 45.
117. See, for example, the many critical responses received by the Law Commission when compiling its 2002 report on internet defamation. See also B Jordan, 'Existing defamation law needs to be updated so that it is fit for the modern age' – the Government's consultation on the multiple publication rule' (2010) *Entertainment Law Review* 41.
118. *Times Newspapers Ltd v UK* (Applications 3002/03 & 23676/03), 10 March 2009.
119. *Cook v Conners* 215 NY 175 (1915).
120. *Rinaldi v Viking Penguin Inc* 52 NY 2d 422 (1981).

defamatory allegation in different forms as the story develops. Whereas it was previously common for a news organisation to publish only one version of a story, the development of 24-hour and online journalism means that a story may be published online in its initial form as breaking news and then amended and re-written over the course of a news cycle. It may further be amended as further information emerges that requires that the archive version of the story be updated. Although the better view may be that the definition of 'defamatory statement' in s 2 indicates that s 11 should apply to the defamatory 'sting' rather than to its specific mode of expression, the drafting of s 11 allows scope for some uncertainty on this issue.

[6.64] Section 11(2) confers a jurisdiction on a court to grant leave to a person to bring more than one defamation action in respect of multiple publications where it considers that the interests of justice so require. In the absence of any judicial consideration of this section, it cannot be said with certainty in what circumstances it might be held that the interests of justice require that a plaintiff be permitted to initiate proceedings in relation to multiple publications.

[6.65] However, it is submitted that leave might be available, for example, where a defendant has intentionally or maliciously sought to take advantage of the protection provided by s 11 to effectively impugn an individual's reputation after the time limit for the bringing of a defamation action has expired.

[6.66] This could arise, for example, where material is published on the internet with a view to it being brought to the intention of a wider audience once a cause of action in defamation is statute-barred. This could be a particular problem given that s 38 specifies that time runs in relation to an internet publication from the point at which it is first capable of being viewed or listened to. This arguably pays insufficient regard to the reality that, unlike newspapers, films or television programmes, there is no typical relationship between the moment most material is first published on the internet and the level of public attention which it receives. A link from a popular site or search engine can garner significant attention for material long after it was first published online. It is submitted that a strict application of ss 11 and 38 which would allow an individual to re-publish a defamatory allegation online in a much more prominent manner would not provide sufficient protection for the individual's right to a good name.[121] In such a situation, it would seem appropriate for leave to be granted under s 11(2) to bring a fresh cause of action.

[6.67] Similar issues seem likely to arise in the context of material which is made available in archive form on the internet. When taken together with the stricter time limits for the bringing of a defamation action under the 2009 Act, the single publication rule may provide some protection for publishers in relation to internet archives. As publication depends upon when the material is accessed,[122] the posting of material on a

---

121. This also raises a distinct but important question of whether an individual would be held to have published a statement where they simply endeavoured to direct attention to a prior publication without ever repeating the defamatory statement.
122. *Jameel v Dow Jones* [2005] EWCA Civ 75, [2005] QB 946, [2005] 2 WLR 1614.

single occasion would constitute multiple publication where it is accessed on multiple occasions. However, the developing jurisprudence on internet archives has suggested that liability may be imposed on those responsible for internet archives where they are informed that there are errors in the archives and fail to correct them.[123] This is discussed further below. However, there is a strong argument to be made that it is appropriate to vindicate the affected person's right to a good name and reputation that publishers be required to undertake such actions, where reasonable.[124] This is another situation in which it might be regarded as being in the interests of justice for leave under s 11(2) to be granted.

Publication and jurisdiction

[6.68] In today's more globalised world, the question of jurisdiction has become a more complex and controversial[125] matter than was formerly the case. This reflects the fact that the publication of material in one jurisdiction is likely to attract viewers or readers in another. As the damage to a person's reputation is caused by the publication of a defamatory allegation *to a third party*, it seems logical, therefore, that a plaintiff be entitled to sue in the jurisdiction where the third party is based. It has accordingly been held that publication occurs where the statement is received rather than when it is sent.[126] This means that an action in defamation may be available in relation to material published outside Ireland provided it has been distributed, read or otherwise accessed in this jurisdiction.[127]

[6.69] Different principles may apply in relation to defamation actions which involve parties based inside and outside the European Union. While standard rules of private international law will apply to litigation involving non-EU parties,[128] a dispute between a plaintiff and defendant who are both resident in the European Union will be governed by the principles set out by the European Court of Justice in *Shevill v Press Alliance*.[129] These principles were expressly adopted as a statement of Irish law by Barr J in *Ewins v Carlton*.[130]

[6.70] The plaintiff in *Shevill* was an English resident who sought to bring a defamation action in the English courts in relation to an article which had been published in France and which concerned her activities in France. Only 230 copies of the newspaper which

---

123. *Flood v Times Newspapers* [2010] EWCA Civ 804; *Metropolitan International Schools Ltd v Designtechnica Corp* [2010] 3 All ER 548.
124. See, for example, *Times Newspapers Ltd (Nos 1 and 2) v United Kingdom* [2009] ECHR 3002/03.
125. See, in particular, the reaction in the United States of America to the perceived problem of 'libel tourism' in the United Kingdom, leading ultimately to the enactment there of the Securing the Protection of our Enduring and Established Constitutional Heritage (SPEECH) Act.
126. *Berezovsky v Michaels* [2000] 1 WLR 1004; *Gregg v O'Gara*
127. *Ewins v Carlton* [1997] 2 ILRM 223; *Hunter v Duckworth* [2000] 1 IR 510.
128. *Lewis v King* [2004] EWCA Civ 1329; *Berezovsky v RTRB* [2008] EWHC 1918 (QB).
129. *Shevill v Press Alliance* [1995] ECR I–415.
130. *Ewins v Carlton* [1997] 2 ILRM 223.

carried the story had been distributed in England. However, the European Court of Justice held that the plaintiff was entitled to sue in either the jurisdiction where the defendant was domiciled, or in each and every EU jurisdiction where the allegedly defamatory allegation had been published. In coming to this conclusion, the court relied on Art 5(3) of the European Convention on Jurisdiction and Enforcement of Judgments 1968, otherwise known as the Brussels Convention which allows a party to be sued in tort in an EU state other than that in which they are domiciled where the harmful event occurred in that other state. In the court's view, the expression 'the place where the harmful event occurred' in Art 5(3) referred in defamation cases to the place where the statement was accessed. Furthermore, the question of whether there had been a harmful event fell to be determined by reference to national law. As all defamation actions are now, post–2009 Act, actionable without proof of special damage,[131] it would seem that an action will automatically be available in this jurisdiction once material published by an individual based in another EU state is accessed here. However, a plaintiff who sues in Ireland in reliance on Art 5(3) can only seek damages in relation to the harm suffered within Ireland.[132]

[6.71] In its decision in *Jameel v Dow Jones*,[133] the English Court of Appeal appeared, to some degree, to depart from the general approach of allowing a defamation suit to be brought in a jurisdiction where publication has occurred. The court held that an action could not be sustained in respect of a statement made on an American website, where that website had only been accessed in the United Kingdom by two parties other than the plaintiff and his legal team. As an action in defamation may arise in respect of the publication of a statement to a single third party, the fact that two individuals had accessed the material in question was sufficient, in law, to allow a claim to be brought. The court held, however, that it would be an abuse of process to allow the action to proceed as the cost of vindicating the putative plaintiff's reputation through a defamation action would far outweigh the negligible damage done to his reputation in the United Kingdom. Of course, the same could have been said in the past in respect of many defamation actions that have been allowed to proceed unhindered through the courts. It may be more accurate to suggest, that this decision was motivated by a reluctance to allow a plaintiff to engage in such a conspicuous example of forum-shopping. It may also have been influenced by a seemingly greater willingness on the part of the English courts in recent years to consider applications to strike out defamation actions on the grounds of an abuse of process[134] than would formerly have been the case.[135]

---

131. Defamation Act 2009, s 6(5).
132. *Murray v Times Newspapers* [1997] 3 IR 97.
133. *Jameel v Dow Jones* [2005] EWCA Civ 75, [2005] QB 946, [2005] 2 WLR 1614.
134. There are similarities between the English courts' application of the abuse of process jurisdiction in these cases and defence of triviality applied in Australia. See, for example, the Defamation Act 2005, s 33.
135. *Williams v MGN Ltd* [2009] EWHC 3150 (QB); *Kaschke v Osler* [2010] EWHC 1075 (QB).

A similar approach was adopted in the more recent case of *Lonzim Plc & others v Sprague*.[136] That concerned a libel action in relation to an article that appeared on the website of a South African magazine. Evidence suggested that the article had received only four visits from the UK in a two-month period. Tugenhadt J held that the claimants had failed to establish 'substantial publication' within the court's jurisdiction. This supports the suggestion that the English courts have developed their abuse of process jurisdiction as a way of preventing the most obvious and egregious instances of forum-shopping for defamation actions.

Defamatory meaning

Reasonable members of society

[6.72] A statement is defined by the 2009 Act as having a defamatory meaning where it 'tends to injure a person's reputation in the eyes of reasonable members of society'.[137] This reformulates the pre-Act test which was couched in terms of the 'right-thinking' rather than 'reasonable' member of society.

[6.73] It is unclear whether this change will have any significant impact on the Irish law of defamation. The argument might be made that a reasonable person may not apply the same strict standards of traditional morality or propriety that might be associated with a 'right-thinking' man and that this reform could, in certain situations, make it more difficult to establish that a person has been defamed. Walsh J's description of the right-thinking person as a member of 'a considerable and respectable class of the community' would lend some support to the view that the former test may have involved examining an allegation in the light of more traditional or morally paternalistic values than may now be appropriate.[138] It could be argued, for example, that the question of whether an allegation of homosexuality is defamatory might be decided differently under a 'reasonable' rather than a 'right-thinking' person test.[139]

[6.74] Regardless of whether s 2 does bring about such a change in the law, it will undoubtedly remain the case that any assessment of whether a statement has a defamatory meaning will necessarily be contingent upon the norms and values of the society and era in which it is made. What offends the sensibilities of the reasonable or right-thinking at one time may attract little or no condemnation at another. Thus, the suggestion that a person had been a victim of rape[140] or that a woman had been seen sitting at a bar while drinking pints[141] have both previously been found to be

---

136. *Lonzim Plc & others v Sprague* [2009] EWHC 2838 (QB).
137. Defamation Act 2009, s 2.
138. *Quigley v Creation* Ltd [1971] IR 269.
139. *Reynolds v Malocco* [1999] 2 IR 203, [1999] 1 ILRM 289.
140. *Yousouoff v MGM* (1934) 50 *Times Law Reports* 581.
141. *Sodden v Image Magazine* (1983) *The Irish Times*, 5 October.

defamatory.[142] This means, as McMahon and Binchy have observed, that '[p]recedents ... in this area must be looked at more suspiciously than in other areas of tort'.[143]

[6.75] Despite the contextual subjectivity of this standard, however, the courts have consistently reiterated that the test of whether a statement carries a defamatory meaning is an objective one. It is not sufficient that a statement mocks[144] or offends[145] the person to whom it refers. The damage incurred must be such as would tend to injure the person's reputation in the eyes of reasonable members of society.

[6.76] A plaintiff should specify the statement[146] and identify the meanings which the statement is alleged to carry in his or her statement of claim. The plaintiff is not obliged to plead all possible defamatory meanings but can choose to limit their claim to particular defamatory 'stings'.[147] This may be considered where there are matters which the plaintiff would prefer were not the subject of argument or evidence at trial. However, it has been held that there is a limit to the plaintiff's ability to cherry-pick aspects of the defamatory statement. The confined meaning pleaded must be truly severable and distinct.[148] A plaintiff cannot prevent matters being brought to the attention of the court or jury where those matters are part of the material about which he or she complains.[149]

[6.77] The question of whether a statement bears a defamatory meaning involves two distinct considerations: what is the meaning of the statement?; and is the meaning of the statement defamatory? The 'reasonable person' standard applies to both of these questions.

Natural and ordinary meaning of the statement

[6.78] This means that the intention of the publisher in making the statement is irrelevant.[150] The meaning of the statement is instead determined by reference to the natural and ordinary meaning which a reasonable person would give to the words or images under examination.[151] The natural and ordinary meaning of a statement has been described as 'the meaning including inferential meaning which the words would convey to the mind of the ordinary, reasonable and fair-minded reader'.[152] The courts have, in

---

142. See also *Moorhouse v Independent Newspapers*. See Managh 'Traveller term not defamatory – ruling' (2002) *The Irish Independent*, 11 December.
143. McMahon & Binchy, *The Law of Torts* (3rd edn, Bloomsbury Professional, 2000), at para 34.51.
144. *Berkoff v Burchall* [1996] 4 All ER 1008.
145. *Crawford v Vance* [1908] 2 IR 521.
146. *Best v Charter Medical of England Limited* [2001] EWCA Civ 1588.
147. *Polly Peck (Holdings) plc v Trelford* [1986] 1 QB 1000.
148. *Warren v Random House* [2008] EWCA Civ 834.
149. For the development of the law in England on this, see *United States Tobacco Inc v BBC* [1998] EMLR 816; *McKeith v News Group Newspapers Ltd* (2005) EMLR 780; *Warren v Random House* [2008] EWCA Civ 834.
150. *Hulton v Jones* [1910] AC 20.
151. *Chapman v Orion Publishing (No 1)* [2005].
152. *Bailey v Irish Mirror Group Ltd* (19 January 2004, unreported), Circuit Court.

particular, cautioned against an unduly technical or artificial analysis of a defendant's statement. In *McGarth v Independent Newspapers*, the High Court cautioned that:

> In determining whether the words are capable of a defamatory meaning the court is obliged to construe the words according to the fair and natural meaning which would be given to them by reasonable persons of ordinary intelligence and will not consider what person setting themselves to work to deduce some unusual meaning might extract from them. The court should avoid an over elaborate analysis of the article because the ordinary reader would not analyse the article in the same manner as a lawyer or accountant would analyse documents or accounts.[153]

[6.79] The courts have over time credited the reasonable person with certain characteristics. A useful summary of these principles may be found in the decision of Eady J in *Galloway v Telegraph Newspapers*[154] where he held that:

> The test to be applied [in determining the natural and ordinary meaning of a statement] is well established. Evidence is not admissible on the issue of natural and ordinary meaning. It is essentially a matter of impression. The Court should give the articles the natural and ordinary meaning(s) which they would have conveyed to the ordinary reasonable reader, reading them once. Hypothetical reasonable readers should not be treated as either naïve or unduly suspicious. They should be treated as being capable of reading between the lines and engaging in some loose thinking, but not as being avid for scandal.[155]

This means that the context of a publication is critically important in determining its meaning.

[6.80] The courts have also assumed, somewhat contentiously,[156] that the reasonable person will read or view a publication in its entirety.[157]

[6.81] This raises the question of whether it can be assumed that the reasonable person who reads a section of a report on a website will proceed to 'click through' to the full piece. It is submitted that this should not be the case as the interactive and user-specific way in which websites are generally visited and read would not support such an assumption. This matter was briefly considered in *Ali v Associated Newspapers*[158] where Eady J rejected the suggestion that material to which a website links should as a general rule be taken into account in considering the publication as a whole.

> It was said that it is so far undecided in the authorities whether, as a matter of generality, any material to which attention is drawn in a blog by this means should

---

153. *McGarth v Independent Newspapers* [2004] 2 IR 425.
154. *Galloway v Telegraph Newspapers* [2004] EWHC 2786 (QB).
155. *Galloway v Telegraph Newspapers* [2004] EWHC 2786 (QB), para 47. See also *Lewis v Daily Telegraph* [1964] AC 234; *Skuse v Granada Television* [1996] EMLR 278; *Armstrong v Times Newspapers* [2006] EWHC 1614.
156. See Prescott, 'Libel and Pornography' (1995) 58 MLR 752; Cox, *Defamation Law* (FirstLaw, 2007), 93.
157. *Charleston v News Group Newspapers* [1995] 2 AC 65; *Jameel v Times Newspapers* [2004] EWCA Civ 983; *McGarth v Independent Newspapers* [2004] 2 IR 425.
158. *Ali v Associated Newspapers* [2010] EWHC 100 (QB).

be taken to be incorporated as part of the blog itself. I suspect that a general rule of thumb is unlikely to be adopted. Much will depend on the circumstances of the particular case.[159]

In most cases, however, the principle that the reasonable person must be taken to have received the publication in its entirety means that the courts frequently have to consider whether the damaging character of a particular statement or passage was sufficiently alleviated by the remainder of the piece. This meant that the use of a fake pornographic photograph of two well-known soap stars was not defamatory where the text accompanying the picture made clear that the image was a mock-up which was intended to illustrate a story about pornographic computer games.[160] Similarly, the juxtaposition of a photograph of an employee of CIE with a headline about the business affairs of Osama bin Laden was held not to be defamatory when considered in the context of the newspaper page as a whole.[161]

[6.82] There is a limit, however, to the material which a court will assume a reasonable person may take into account in considering a publication. In *Cruise v Express Newspapers*,[162] the defendant was not permitted to rely on material elsewhere in the newspaper to remove the defamatory 'sting' of a particular piece. This indicates, as Cox points out, 'cases like McGarth and Charleston [may] represent the exception rather than the rule'.[163] It should not be assumed that a publication containing potentially defamatory material can be absolved of its tortious character by the simple expedient of including some material that portrays the relevant individual in a less negative light.

[6.83] It is obvious that, even after applying the test of the natural and ordinary understanding of a reasonable person, a publication may be capable of several interpretations. Some may be defamatory, some may not be defamatory and others may be defamatory but also be capable of being defended in law. It is necessary in a defamation action for the court to decide as a matter of fact on a single meaning to be attributed to the publication.[164] As the court explained the rule in *Charleston*:

> [A]lthough a combination of words may in fact convey different meanings to the minds of different readers, the jury in a libel action applying the criterion in which the first principle dictates is required to determine the single meaning which the publication conveyed to the notional, reasonable reader and to place its verdict and any award of damages on the assumption that this was the one sense in which all readers would have understood it.[165]

---

159. *Ali v Associated Newspapers* [2010] EWHC 100 (QB), para 28.
160. *Charleston v News Group Newspapers* [1995] 2 AC 65.
161. *MacGarth v Independent Newspapers* [2004] 2 IR 425.
162. *Cruise v Express Newspapers* (1998) EMLR 780.
163. Cox, *Defamation Law* (FirstLaw, 2007), 96.
164. *Grubb v Bristol United Press* [1963] 1 QB 309.
165. *Charleston v News Group Newspapers* [1995] 2 AC 65, 71. See also *Slim v Daily Telegraph Ltd* [1968] 2 QB 157. This passage was applied by the Circuit Court in *Bailey v Irish Mirror Group Ltd* (19 January 2004, unreported), Circuit Court.

Innuendo

TRUE OR LEGAL INNUENDO

[6.84] The only exception to the above principle applies in cases of so-called 'true' innuendo where it is accepted that a statement may give rise to different meanings. This occurs in circumstances where a statement seems, at face value, to be unobjectionable but has a defamatory meaning when juxtaposed with extrinsic facts about the plaintiff that are known to third parties.[166]

[6.85] At common law, a plaintiff was entitled to bring separate causes of action in respect of the plain meaning and true innuendo but this would now seem to be prohibited by s 9 of the 2009 Act, which provides that a person only has one cause of action in respect of the publication of a defamatory statement concerning the person even if more than one defamatory imputation in respect of that person is borne by that statement.

[6.86] Where a plaintiff seeks to assert the existence of a true innuendo, he or she is obliged to plead this in their statement of claim[167] and must adduce evidence at trial of the extrinsic facts known to third parties which gave the publication its defamatory character.

[6.87] The plaintiff may be obliged in certain circumstances to provide particulars of the individuals who are alleged to have had possession of such extrinsic facts. In *Fullam v Newcastle Chronicle*[168] a former priest sued for defamation in relation to a statement that he had left his position seven years previously. He had actually left much earlier and had subsequently married and fathered a child. He pleaded that the article implied that he had fathered an illegitimate child while still a priest serving in a parish and that he had wrongly continued to serve as a priest after his marriage. The defendant sought particulars of the identity of the readers who knew that he had married and had a child more than seven years before. Denning MR held that the defendants were entitled to such particulars, holding that the plaintiff must specify in his statement of claim the particular person or persons to whom they were published and the special circumstances known to that person or persons. He explained that:

> In such cases as those, the identity of the person (who has knowledge of the special circumstances) is a most material fact in the cause of action. It is the publication to him which is the very foundation of the cause of action. So he should be identified in the pleading itself or in particulars under it.[169]

---

166. *Cassidy v Daily Mirror Newspapers* [1929] KB 331; *Tolley v Fry* [1931] AC 1933; *Hough v London Express* [1940] 2 KB 507; *Winyard v Tatler Publishing* (1991) *The Independent*, 1 July.
167. See *Shanson v Howard* (30 January 1997, unreported), CA (where a lay litigant was not permitted to argue for a 'true' innuendo that had not been pleaded). See also *Thornton v Telegraph Media Group* [2010] EWHC 1414 (QB).
168. *Fullam v Newcastle Chronicle* [1977] 3 All ER 32, [1977] 1 WLR 651.
169. *Fullam v Newcastle Chronicle* [1977] 3 All ER 32, [1977] 1 WLR 651.

However, in *Byrne v RTÉ* McMenamin J distinguished *Fullam* in holding that it was not necessary in all cases of alleged 'true' innuendo to provide particulars of the individuals to whom the defamatory publication was allegedly made. Where the plaintiff's claim was that the extrinsic facts were widely known to the public, evidence of such general knowledge would suffice. In his view:

> An examination of the case as pleaded by the plaintiff demonstrates what arises here is not simply a question of a publication to a particular class of persons. This is essentially a 'mass media' case; thus the plaintiff is entitled in the first instance to rely on the natural and ordinary meaning of the matters complained of as supporting an innuendo. It is not open to the defendants to contend that the plaintiff must elect between the general effect of the imputations and the effect upon a particular class of person when, as here, there is a prima facie mass media case and where publication has taken place to the general public on matters within the general knowledge of the community. This case is distinguishable from *Fullam v Newcastle Chronicle*. There the ordinary readers of the newspaper would not have derived from the words complained of the innuendo alleged. Thus the plaintiff was required to particularise not only the special circumstances alleged to give rise to the innuendo, but also to the identity of the readers of the paper who were alleged to know of those special circumstances, since the identity of those readers was a material fact in which the plaintiff relied in support of his cause of action. But, on the facts, that is not the case here, and one need go no further than considering the nature of the words complained of, the imputations in their context, and the surrounding circumstances, to see that this is so.[170]

FALSE OR POPULAR INNUENDO

[6.88] A false innuendo exists where the defamatory statement is not expressly made but is nonetheless still evident from the publication itself.[171] The defamatory meaning in such a case does not depend on the reader or viewer's knowledge of extrinsic facts but should rather be discernible to the reasonable person in their position.[172] This means that the false innuendo does not give rise to a separate cause of action. Furthermore, while the defamatory meaning of the publication derives from the natural and ordinary meaning of the words or image, a plaintiff should specifically identify in his or her pleadings any additional defamatory meaning which he or she is asserting on the basis on an alleged false innuendo.[173]

The roles of the judge and jury in a defamation trial

[6.89] The jury plays a central role in an action for defamation. 'The place of the jury in our legal system as the decision-maker on the issue as to whether there has been a

---

170. See also *Fannin and Co Ltd v Surgical Distributors Ltd* (27 February 1975, unreported), SC; *Hughes v Mirror Newspapers* [1985] 3 NSWLR.
171. *Loughans v Odhams Press Ltd* [1963] 1 QB 299; *Grubb v Bristol United Press Ltd* [1963] 1 QB 309; *Hill v Cork Examiner* [2001] 4 IR 219.
172. *Monson v Tussauds* [1894] 1 QB 671.
173. *Allsop v Church of England Newspapers Ltd* [1972] 2 QB 161.

defamation or not has been keenly guarded by the common law'.[174] Thus, it is for the jury to determine as a question of fact whether the impugned statement was defamatory of the plaintiff. This means, as detailed above, that the jury must:

(i)   determine the meaning which ought to be attributed to the statement in question, and then

(ii)   decide whether that meaning would tend to injure the reputation of the plaintiff in the eyes of reasonable members of society.

[6.90] As Denham J explained in the Supreme Court's decision in *Cooper-Flynn v RTÉ*:

[T]he role of the jury is critical. The jury makes the decisions on fact, including the kernel issue as to whether the Plaintiff's reputation suffered material injury. Appellate courts have been slow to interfere with decisions of juries. This is so especially in defamation actions where the role of the jury is pivotal. The unique position of the jury in actions such as this was pointed out by Walsh J in *Quigley v Creation Ltd* [1971] IR 269 at p 272:

'Basically, the question of libel or no libel is a matter of opinion and opinions may vary reasonably within very wide limits. When a jury has found that there has been a libel, this court would be more slow to set aside such a verdict than in other types of actions and it would only do so if it was of opinion that the conclusion reached by the jury was one to which reasonable men could not or ought not have come.'[175]

[6.91] The role of the judge in a defamation case is to rule on any questions of law that may arise. In general, these issues will typically concern whether the statement under examination is capable – as a matter of law – of bearing a defamatory meaning. However, as the Irish courts have consistently emphasised,[176] the judge's role is necessarily ancillary to that of the jury in its capacity as the primary trier of fact. In *Barrett v Independent Newspapers*,[177] Henchy J approved the following passage from *Gatley on Libel and Slander* as an accurate statement of the judge's role:

Where the words are capable of a libellous meaning, the judge must always leave it to the jury to decide whether they are or are not a libel, except where the fact is already admitted on the pleadings. The proper course is for the judge to instruct the jury as to what amounts to a libel in point of law, and then leave it to them, as persons of ordinary intelligence, to say whether the words fall within that definition or not. The judge is not bound to, but he may express to the jury his own view of the meaning of the words, provided that he makes it quite clear that the ultimate decision rests with them. In an ordinary case he must not go further than this. If he directs the jury as a matter of law that the words are libellous, or so directs them as to the meaning of the words that there must be a verdict for the plaintiff, he is determining a question which is not within his province but the

---

174. *De Rossa v Independent Newspapers* [1999] 4 IR 432, 477, *per* Denham J.

175. *Cooper-Flynn v RTÉ* [2004] 2 IR 72, 121. See also *Berry v Irish Times Ltd* [1973] IR 368; *Magee v MGN* [2003] IEHC 87.

176. *De Rossa v Independent Newspapers* [1999] 4 IR 432; *Cooper-Flynn v RTÉ* [2004] 2 IR 72. See also the discussion in *John v Mirror Group Newspapers Ltd* [1997] QB 586.

177. *Barrett v Independent Newspapers* [1986] IR 13.

province of the jury to determine, and the court will grant a new trial on the ground of misdirection, unless a verdict contrary to the judge's direction would have been perverse.[178]

[6.92] Whereas the majority in *Barrett* held that a trial judge could not direct a jury that the statement in question was defamatory, the trial judge is entitled, upon application to him or her by counsel,[179] to withdraw the question of defamation from the jury where of the view that the statement in question is not capable of bearing a defamatory meaning. This function was described by the Court of Appeal in the following terms:

> There is of course a variety of possible circumstances in libel cases in which issues of law may arise for decision by the judge. In so far as questions of this kind properly depend on an evaluation of evidence so as to determine material questions of disputed fact, these are matters for the jury. But ... it is open to the judge in a libel case to come to the conclusion that the evidence, taken at its highest, is such that a jury properly directed could not properly reach a necessary factual conclusion. In those circumstances, it is the judge's duty, upon a submission being made to him, to withdraw that issue from the jury.[180]

[6.93] In keeping with the courts' traditional defence of the role of the jury, however, it has been emphasised that this is not a jurisdiction to be lightly exercised by a trial judge.[181] It appears settled law[182] in England that the test to be applied in considering such an application is the high one that 'a meaning should only be ruled out if a jury would be perverse to uphold it'.[183] Furthermore, it seems likely that an appellate court will be more willing to interfere with any exercise of this power by a trial judge than it would be where the decision was taken by the jury itself.[184] The necessity for such restraint on the part of a trial judge was strongly emphasised by the Court of Appeal in *Jameel v Wall Street Europe*:[185]

> [E]very time a meaning is shut out [by a trial judge] (including any holding that the words complained of either are, or are not, capable of bearing a defamatory meaning) it must be remembered that the judge is taking it upon himself to rule in effect that any jury would be perverse to take a different view on the question. It is

---

178. *Barrett v Independent Newspapers* [1986] IR 13, 22. Finlay CJ and McCarthy J dissented from the majority on this point.

179. This can be done at various times, and through different procedures. See the discussion below.

180. *Alexander v Arts Council of Wales* [2001] 4 All ER 205, 217. See also *Kingshott v Associated Kent Newspapers Ltd* [1991] 2 All ER 99.

181. *Jameel v Wall Street Europe* [2003] EWCA Civ 1694.

182. *Tiscali UK Ltd v British Telecommunications plc* [2008] EWHC 2927 (QB); *Wright v Gregson* [2010] EWHC 1629 (QB).

183. *Miller v Associated Newspapers* [2010] EWHC 700 (QB), para 4. See also, for example, *Skuse v Granada Television Ltd* [1996] EMLR 278; *Gillick v BBC* [1996] EMLR 267; *Gillick v Brooke Advisory Centre* [2001] EWCA Civ 1263.

184. *Cruise v Express Newspapers* [1999] QB 931; *Neeson v Belfast Telegraph* [1999] NIJB 200; *Eastwood v Harper Collins* [2002] NICA 46.

185. *Jameel v Wall Street Europe* [2003] EWCA Civ 1694. This case concerned the corporate reputation of the plaintiff. See O'Neill, 'Corporate Reputation in the House of Lords' (2007) Company Lawyer 76.

a high threshold of exclusion. Ever since Fox's Act 1792 the meaning of words in civil as well as criminal libel proceedings has been constitutionally a matter for the jury. The judge's function is no more and no less than to pre-empt perversity ...

...

... [T]he judge's ascertainment of the range of permissible meanings is 'an exercise in generosity, not in parsimony' and, moreover, an exercise in which this court will be readier to intervene if the judge has withdrawn from the jury (rather than left to them) any particular meaning, so too in my opinion the judge should be warier even than usual of withdrawing meanings unless there is sound reason for doing so.[186]

This was described in *Budu v BBC* as establishing a 'high threshold for exclusion' of meanings.[187] As considered in the next section below, it is arguable that the 2009 Act may make it easier for such applications to succeed in Ireland by introducing a lower threshold for removing this issue from the jury than that which applies at common law in England.

Pre-trial applications

Section 14

[6.94] Section 14 of the 2009 Act allows an application to be brought in advance of the trial on this question of whether the statement in question is capable of bearing a defamatory meaning. An application under this section must be brought by notice of motion[188] and may be brought at any time after the bringing of the defamation action concerned including during the course of the trial of the action.[189] Upon such application, the court is entitled to give a ruling as to whether the statement in question is reasonably capable of bearing the imputation pleaded by the plaintiff, and also as to whether that imputation is reasonably capable of bearing a defamatory meaning. If the court rules that the statement in question does not bear the imputation pleaded, or that it does bear the imputation pleaded but that imputation is not of a defamatory character, it will dismiss the plaintiff's action but only in so far as it relates to that imputation.

[6.95] The provisions of the 2009 Act indicate that the test to be applied in adjudicating on an application under s 14 is one of reasonable capability: is the statement 'reasonably capable' of bearing the imputation in question; and is the imputation 'reasonably capable' of bearing a defamatory meaning? This raises the question of whether this is a lower test than that typically applied at common law.

[6.96] On the one hand, a literal reading of the text would suggest that s 14 should operate in this manner. There is no indication that the judge in exercising this power is

---

186. *Jameel v Wall Street Europe* [2003] EWCA Civ 1694, paras 14–16, quoting *Berezovsky v Forbes* [2001] EMLR 45, para 16, *per* Sedley LJ.
187. *Budu v BBC* [2010] EWHC 616 (QB), para 47.
188. Defamation Act 2009, s 14(3). See also Order 1B, rule 3(3).
189. Defamation Act 2009, s 14(4).

required to qualify his or her own assessment of what is reasonably capable by considering the views of a putative jury. This analysis may also derive support from the fact that the English jurisdiction to give a preliminary ruling on meaning (which is, of course, the rule under which the strict test outlined above applies) does not refer to a reasonableness requirement but instead directs the court to consider whether the statement is simply 'capable' of bearing the meaning contended for.[190]

[6.97] On the other hand the Irish courts, like their English counterparts, have traditionally attached considerable importance to the role of the jury in a defamation action as the primary arbiter of fact. From this perspective, it might be argued that a judge who is dealing with an application under s 14 should continue to consider these issues from the point of view of the reasonable jury, rather than from his or her own view of what is reasonable. This approach would seem likely to make it more difficult for a defendant to succeed in a s 14 application.

A further limitation for a defendant who wishes to make use of the s 14 procedure is that it allows an application to be made only in relation to an 'imputation pleaded by the plaintiff'. This seems to confirm that a defendant is not allowed under Irish law to plead a meaning alternative to that pleaded by the plaintiff as a basis for a defence of truth. Rather the defendant is confined to traversing the plaintiff's plea as to the meaning, even if the defendant is capable of establishing the truth of a different meaning.[191]

[6.98] The purpose of s 14 would seem to be to provide for the possibility of avoiding the costs, where appropriate, of a full trial. This was certainly the approach previously adopted by the courts to the similar jurisdiction to have a point of law raised by the pleadings tried by a judge in advance without a jury.[192]

[6.99] From this point of view, it appears peculiar that s 14 has been drafted in a way which appears to make it available only to those defendants who wish to seek a preliminary ruling on both of the questions referred to therein. This is supported by the use of the word 'and' and the phrasing of subparagraph (b) which appears to regard it as a necessary prerequisite to a ruling on the defamatory meaning or otherwise of a statement that the court has already ruled that that statement is reasonably capable of bearing that imputation. This would, for example, prevent an application being brought under s 14 by a defendant who accepts that the meaning contended for would be defamatory but disputes the claim that the statement bears that meaning. It would also oblige a defendant who primarily seeks a ruling on the defamatory character or otherwise of the imputation in question to submit arguments on the separation question of the appropriate meaning of the statement, regardless of whether he or she wishes to do so at this early stage. For a cost-saving measure, this seems surprising.

190. Practice Direction on Defamation, Pt 53, 4.1.
191. This appears to confirm that *Lucas Box v News Group Ltd* [1986] 1 WLR 147 and *Polly Peck (Holdings) plc v Trelford* [1986] 1 QB 1000 are not part of Irish law. The Irish position would appear to be closer to that supported by Brennan CJ and McHugh J in *Chakravarti v Advertiser Newspaper Ltd* (1998) 194 CLR 519; 72 ALJR 1085.
192. RSC 1986, Order 25 and Order 36, rule 7. See *Duffy v News Group Newspapers* [1994] 3 IR 63.

[6.100] For this reason, it is submitted that it may be more appropriate for the courts to adopt a broader and more purposive interpretation of s 14. Support for this view may be derived from s 14(2) which appears to envisage the court as being capable of having ruled on either the meaning of the statement or the defamatory character of that meaning. This would indicate that the Oireachtas did not intend it to be necessary to secure a favourable ruling on the meaning of the statement before being able to seek a ruling on the issue of whether that statement may be defamatory.[193]

No reasonable cause of action

[6.101] A defendant may also apply to have a plaintiff's cause of action struck out for failure to show reasonable cause of action. This application may be made pursuant to Order 19, rule 28 of the Rules of the Superior Courts[194] or on the basis of the inherent jurisdiction[195] of the court.[196]

[6.102] A defendant may also apply under Order 19, rule 27 to have a particular pleading or pleadings struck out. This latter jurisdiction is a more appropriate one to invoke where a defendant seeks a ruling in relation to only some of the meanings contended for by the plaintiff.

[6.103] However, it should be noted that the courts apply a high threshold to such applications and that they will only succeed in circumstances where the plaintiff's claim is, in effect, unsustainable.[197] An example of this approach in England is provided by the decision of the Court of Appeal in *Spencer v Sillitoe* where it was held that:

> Bearing in mind the emphasis placed on the right to jury trial in section 69 [of the Senior Court Act 1981] and the analogy drawn by this court in Alexander with the criminal practice in *Galbraith*, the question in a case such as the present comes down to whether there is an issue of fact on which, on the evidence so far available, the jury could properly, without being perverse, come to a conclusion in favour of the Claimant.

> That question has to be answered against the background of the great respect that is paid to a jury's assessment of witnesses after seeing and hearing them, and hearing them cross-examined. It is unlikely that a judge will be able to find that a witness will necessarily be disbelieved by a jury; or that for a jury to believe him would be perverse; when he has not actually heard that witness give evidence and be cross-examined: unless, of course, there is counter evidence that plainly

---

193. Of course, even if the narrower approach is adopted, it would still be open to a defendant to seek a ruling under RSC 1986, Order 25 and Order 36, rule 7.
194. *Aer Rianta v Ryanair* [2004] 1 IR 406.
195. *Barry v Buckley* [1981] IR 306; *DK v AK* [1994] 1 IR 166.
196. It is common practice for both jurisdictions to be pleaded in the alternative in any such application.
197. *Conlon v Times Newspapers* [1995] 2 ILRM 76; *Magee v MGN* [2003] IEHC 87. More generally, see Delany & McGrath, *Civil Procedure in the Superior Courts* (2nd edn, Thomson Round Hall, 2005), 190–192 and 413–432.

demonstrates the falsity of the witness's evidence, as opposed, in this case, to rendering it, in the judge's view, implausible.[198]

[6.104] The same approach was evident in *Magee v MGN*, where McKechnie J indicated that this was particularly the case in defamation actions given the primary and pivotal role of the jury at trial. His decision is instructive, particularly for the way in which he emphasises at the conclusion of the passage below the high threshold which a defendant seeking to strike out a plaintiff's claim must satisfy:

> [T]his court must consider the application in question on the basis that there undoubtedly exists an inherent jurisdiction to prevent an abuse of process. If a cause of action is frivolous or vexatious, or is clearly unsustainable or is bound to fail, then to permit its continuation would be an abuse of the court's procedures and would therefore not be permitted. However, given the constitutional right of access to the courts, given the desirability of there being a judicial determination on the merits of every case and given the limitations necessarily involved in this manner of procedure, it has been emphasised, in the various cases above mentioned, that before affirmatively exercising this jurisdiction, the court must accept in favour of the Plaintiff all of the facts and allegations as pleaded and all of the assertions as made, and must not dismiss the action, at this infancy stage, unless fully satisfied and completely convinced that the claim is bound to fail. When that claim is grounded in defamation and in particular where the core question is one of defamatory meaning, then in addition to the matters above set forth, the court should be acutely conscious of the uniqueness of the role which a jury plays on that issue.
>
> ...
>
> The question therefore is whether the claim of such a person that he was defamed ... must fail, in that even accepting the falsity of its material parts and the correctness of the implications as pleaded, no jury, being representative of the opinion of right-thinking members of society in general, could conclude that the Plaintiff had any reputation sustainable in law or that if he had such reputation the same had been adversely affected by that publication.
>
> ... [I]t seems to me that I cannot say this stage of the within proceedings that the Plaintiff's claim must fail. In other words, that it cannot possible succeed. In other words, that before a properly representative jury he could not even argue that the imputations as alleged were defamatory of him. I cannot agree that this is necessary so ... I cannot, as previously stated, conclude with certainty that right thinking members of society generally could not, despite the Plaintiff's past, hold in his favour in the present proceedings.

One consequence of this is that a defendant making an application under these jurisdictions faces a more daunting challenge than one bringing an application under s 14. This was confirmed by McKechnie J in *Magee* where, citing Murphy J's ruling in *Conlon* that '[a]t this stage it is sufficient if the Plaintiff can show that there is at least an argument that the words are capable of the meaning for which he

---

198.   *Spencer v Sillitoe* [2003] EMLR 10, 23–24.

contends',[199] he distinguished between an application to strike out proceedings and an application to withdraw the statement from the jury on meaning. In his view, 'the appropriate test [for withdrawing from a jury] was one of 'capability' whereas with the former it was one of 'arguability', that is whether it was arguable that the words were capable of having a defamatory meaning'.

Inordinate and inexcusable delay

[6.105] The particular onus on a plaintiff to deal expeditiously with an action for defamation means that it may be possible for a defendant to bring an application to dismiss the action for inordinate and inexcusable delay or want or prosecution where there has been a conspicuous failure to prosecute the action by the plaintiff. It was held in *Dowd v Kerry County Council*[200] that there is an obligation on both parties to have proceedings dealt with within a reasonable period but that this particularly applies to the plaintiff. The Supreme Court in *Desmond v MGN*[201] recognised that '[t]hat may mean, in a particular case, moving proceedings with even more speed than is required under the Rules of the Superior Courts'. That this may apply to a defamation action was clear, in the court's view, from the fact that:

> The purpose of a libel action is to enable the plaintiff to clear his name of the libel, to vindicate his character. In an action for defamation in which the plaintiff wishes to achieve this end, he will also wish the action to be heard as soon as possible.[202]

[6.106] The court thus held that:

> If a plaintiff in defamation proceedings has decided, even, as here without any suggestion of mala fides, although the appellant suggests it was a wholly tactical decision, and even on the recommendation or advice of his legal advisors, not to progress his proceedings at least within the normal time limits prescribed, the delay thereby caused may not be excusable. It is certainly a telling factor against excusing delay, if a party retains to himself, as the respondent did here, the right unilaterally to take no further steps in the proceedings for an indeterminate period into the future without, as a very minimum, notifying the other party of his intention to do so. That other party has an entitlement to know the stance being adopted, so that he in turn may take all appropriate steps in his interest in relation to the proceedings. In the present case the appellant was entitled to know after a reasonably limited period of time, that the respondent had not abandoned his claim, so that it could, if it wished, bring an application to strike out the proceedings rather than being lured, by inactivity of the respondent, into the natural belief that the claim was abandoned. It does not seem to me that the appellant has to establish at this stage what steps it might have taken, and I do not think it of any value to require its counsel to speculate as to what the attitude would be, it being submitted in the present appeal by counsel on behalf of the

199. *Conlon v Times Newspapers* [1995] 2 ILRM 76, 80.
200. *Dowd v Kerry County Council* [1970] 2 IR 27.
201. *Desmond v MGN* [2009] 1 IR 737.
202. *Grovit v Doctor* (28 October 1993, unreported).

respondent that even if he had notified the appellant, it in turn would or might have done nothing.

However, the court also held that entry of a plea of justification by a defendant had a significant influence on such applications as to strike out the proceedings would be to leave the plea of justification unchallenged, with the consequence that the plaintiff's reputation would remain impugned.

However, Dunne J pointed out in *Desmond v Times Newspaper* that 'it cannot be the case that a plaintiff's case cannot be dismissed for want of prosecution, only by reason of the fact that there is a plea of justification'.[203] In her view, the fact that a plea of justification had been made was an important factor to be taken into account in assessing where the balance of justice might lie. Having reviewed the relevant caselaw, she held that:

> I am satisfied therefore, that the principle to be derived from the decision in *Desmond v MGN* is that in considering where the balance of justice lies, the scope and ambit of the defence filed by a defendant is a factor which in an appropriate case may be taken into account. In defamation proceedings therefore, the fact that a defence includes a plea of justification is a factor which may be taken into account. It is, of course, not the only factor.
>
> ...
>
> There is no doubt that a plea of justification is an important factor to be borne in mind in considering and assessing where the balance of justice lies. The fact that a plea of justification has been made in defamation proceedings is not, however, a licence to a plaintiff to allow proceedings to languish indefinitely without any activity. Reference has been made to a number of decisions in which the importance of proceeding with expedition in defamation proceedings has been emphasised. The essence of defamation proceedings is the vindication of an individual's good name. A person's reputation is at the heart of such proceedings. That is why it is necessary for a plaintiff to act quickly in the prosecution of defamation proceedings for the longer a defamatory statement remains unchallenged, the greater the potential damage to a person's reputation. The taint of wrongdoing implicit in a plea of justification and the fact that that will be allowed to remain on the record is a significant matter in considering where the balance of justice lies.

Abuse of process

[6.107] A defendant is also entitled to bring an application seeking to strike out a defamation action on the grounds that it is an abuse of process. The Irish courts have consistently held that they retain an inherent jurisdiction to strike out or stay proceedings on such grounds.[204] Delany & McGrath have pointed out that 'the concept of an abuse of process is somewhat nebulous and can be invoked in a wide range of circumstances'.[205] Thus, it has been held that proceedings may be struck out as an abuse

---

203. *Desmond v MGN* [2009] IEHC 271.
204. See, for example, *Barry v Buckley* [1981] IR 306.
205. Delany & McGrath, *Civil Procedure in the Superior Courts* (2nd, edn, Thomson, 2005).

of process on the basis that they are frivolous or vexatious,[206] that they have been brought for an improper purpose,[207] that they have been litigated in an improper manner,[208] that they are based on unfounded allegations[209] or that they will not confer any benefit on the plaintiff.[210]

Although this jurisdiction is a general one, there are a number of specific characteristics of defamation proceedings which may affect the way in which the courts deal with applications in this context. In particular, the fact that the mere bringing of proceedings may adversely impact upon the freedom of expression of the defendant means that an argument can be made that the courts should be more willing to consider striking out proceedings as an abuse of process than would otherwise be the case.

[6.108] In general, the Irish courts have emphasised that this jurisdiction should be exercised sparingly and only in very clear cases.[211] Furthermore, the courts have tended not to engage in a detailed assessment of the position of the parties at this preliminary stage, preferring instead to proceed only by reference to admitted facts.[212] This reflects the fact that this jurisdiction to strike out proceedings before they are fully heard represents an interference with the plaintiff's constitutional right of access to the courts.

However, defamation proceedings engage not simply the plaintiff's right to a good name and right of access to the courts but also the defendant's freedom of expression. This creates an argument that it may be appropriate for the courts to modify their approach to this jurisdiction (and indeed, to the complementary jurisdictions under Order 19 of the Rules of the Superior Courts) to reflect the necessary balancing of rights which must occur in this context.

Support for such an approach may be found in several recent decisions of the English courts. Although the courts there continue to emphasise that proceedings should be struck out as an abuse of process only in very limited situations, a number of defamation proceedings have been struck out on such grounds in recent years.[213] In so doing, the English courts have had regard both to the costs of defamation actions and the impact which such proceedings have on freedom of expression.

[6.109] In *Jameel v Dow Jones*[214] the Court of Appeal acknowledged that defamation proceedings raise specific freedom of expression concerns:

> We accept that in the rare case where a Claimant brings an action for defamation
> in circumstances where his reputation has suffered no or minimal actual damage,

---

206. *Fay v Tegral Pipes* [2005] IR 261. Such applications may also be brought pursuant to Order 19, rule 28 of the Rules of the Superior Courts.
207. *Quinn Group v An Bord Pleanála* [2001] 1 IR 505.
208. *Cavern Systems Ltd v Clontarf Residents Association* [1984] ILRM 24.
209. *Doherty v Minister for Justice, Equality and Law Reform* [2009] IEHC 246.
210. *MacSorley v O'Mahony* (6 November 1997, unreported) HC.
211. *Barry v Buckley* [1981] IR 306; *Sun Fat Chan v Osseous Ltd* [1992] 1 IR 425.
212. *Sun Fat Chan v Osseous Ltd* [1992] 1 IR 425; *Doe v Armour Pharmaceutical* (31 July 1997, unreported) HC, 1997; *Ruby Property Co Ltd v Kilty* (1 December 1999, unreported) HC.
213. See, for example, *Lonzim plc v Sprague* [2009] EWHC 2838 (QB); *Williams v MGN* [2009] EWHC 3150 (QB); *Kaschke v Osler* [2010] EWHC 1075 (QB).
214. *Jameel v Dow Jones* [2005] EWCA Civ 75, [2005] QB 946.

this may constitute an interference with freedom of expression that is not necessary for the protection of the Claimant's reputation. In such circumstances the appropriate remedy for the Defendant may well be to ... seek to strike out the action as an abuse of process.[215]

The Court of Appeal stated that the courts were now 'more ready to entertain a submission that pursuit of a libel action is an abuse of process' than would formerly have been the case. This greater willingness to consider such applications was justified in part on procedural reforms that are specific to the English law of defamation. The Court also based this approach on the freedom of expression rights enjoyed by defendants under Article 10:

> Keeping a proper balance between the Article 10 right of freedom of expression and the protection of individual reputation must, so it seems to us, require the court to bring to a stop as an abuse of process defamation proceedings that are not serving the legitimate purpose of protecting the Claimant's reputation, which includes compensating the Claimant only if that reputation has been unlawfully damaged.[216]

The Court thus concluded that the action could be struck out as an abuse of process on the grounds that the benefit to the plaintiff of pursuing the action was outweighed by the impact which the action would have on the rights and interests of the defendants:

> If the Claimant succeeds in this action and is awarded a small amount of damages, it can perhaps be said that he will have achieved vindication for the damage done to his reputation in this country, but both the damage and the vindication will be minimal. The cost of the exercise will have been out of all proportion to what has been achieved. The game will not merely not have been worth the candle, it will not have been worth the wick.[217]

These considerations of cost and of freedom of expression were also cited by Tugenhadt J in *Lonzim plc v Sprague*[218] in striking out the plaintiff's action. In his view:

> 'It is not enough for a Claimant to say that a Defendant to a slander action should raise his defence and the matter go to trial. The fact of being sued at all is a serious interference with freedom of expression ... The prospect for a shareholder at a company meeting of being sued by Claimants such as these, for expressing opinions or views such as those alleged here to be slanders, would inhibit free expression. It would be very much against the public interest. The public interest in relation to company meetings is that there should be a free expression of views, and that differences be resolved by the votes cast.'

These decisions were reviewed by Eady J in *Kaschke v Osler*[219] where the court again found that the action should be struck out as an abuse of process.[220] In his view, those

---

215. *Jameel v Dow Jones* [2005] EWCA Civ 75, 40.
216. *Jameel v Dow Jones* [2005] EWCA Civ 75, 55.
217. *Jameel v Dow Jones* [2005] EWCA Civ 75, 69.
218. *Lonzim plc v Sprague* [2009] EWHC 2838 (QB).
219. *Kaschke v Osler* [2010] EWHC 1075 (QB).
220. The Court of Appeal decline to grant the plaintiff's permission to appeal: *Kaschke v Osler* [2010] EWCA Civ 1066.

cases confirmed that the abuse of process jurisdiction could be used to strike out actions which may have some basis in law on the grounds that the potential benefit for the plaintiff did not justify the expense and interference with freedom of expression which would be created by allowing the action proceed to a full hearing.

> [The courts in previous decisions] applied the test of whether or not a 'real and substantial tort' had been committed and also considered the question of whether any damages recovered might be so small as to be totally disproportionate to the very high costs that any libel action involves. It is an important consideration for the court to have in mind on any abuse application that the fact of being sued at all is a serious interference with freedom of expression. That may be appropriate in the majority of libel actions, where it is necessary to countenance such interference in order to vindicate the rights of another person in respect of whom a real and substantial tort has occurred. But the court must be vigilant to recognise the small minority of cases where the legitimate objective of vindication is not required or, at least, cannot be achieved without a wholly disproportionate interference with the rights of the Defendant(s).

These decisions suggest that the courts in England and Wales have come to the view that freedom of expression justifies allowing proceedings to be struck out where an alleged defamation has caused only negligible damage to the plaintiff's good name. Of course, such a development is of persuasive value only. Furthermore, as noted above, the development of this approach under English law has been partly influenced by procedural considerations that are specific to that jurisdiction. However, the argument that freedom of expression should be a factor in the courts' consideration of such applications is a reasonable one. This is particularly so when it is considered that it has been suggested that defamation proceedings are sometimes issued by unscrupulous plaintiffs whose primary concern is to bring an unwelcome debate or investigation to a close.[221] It remains to be seen, therefore, whether Irish law may evolve in a similar fashion in the future.

Actions where multiple wrongs are alleged

[6.110] It may be the case that a plaintiff issues proceedings against a defendant in relation to a number of alleged wrongs, which wrongs include a claim for defamation. This is increasingly common, especially in circumstances where a plaintiff alleges that he or she has been defamed and that there has been a breach of his or her right to privacy. This raises a practical question in relation to how such proceedings should be dealt with, given the entitlement of a plaintiff in a defamation action to have the matter heard by a judge and jury. It will usually be necessary for the parties to either agree upon the appropriate nature and form of a trial or, in the alternative, have the matter dealt with by way of a contested pre-trial application.

---

221. See, for example, Corbyn, 'Academy's freedoms threatened as libel laws land scholars in dock', (2010) *The Times*, 14 January.

[6.111] The Supreme Court considered this general issue in a non-defamation context in *Sheridan v Kelly*.[222] The Court held that a jury trial could be held where the proceedings included claims for multiple wrongs, only some of which would usually be tried before a jury. It was necessary, however, that the claims be based on the same act or omission. In Sheridan, the Supreme Court found that all of the plaintiff's allegations, being a claim for personal injuries for negligence and for trespass to the person, could be traced back to the core allegation of the plaintiff's claim.

[6.112] This was considered by Dunne J in the context of a defamation claim in *Kerwick v Sunday Newspapers Ltd*.[223] This concerned proceedings in which the plaintiff sought damages from the defendant for, inter alia, defamation, intentional infliction of emotional distress, malicious and injurious falsehood and breach of privacy. The plaintiff sought to have the defamation claim dealt with by way of a hearing before a judge and jury with the remaining issues determined by a judge acting alone. This was opposed by the defendant. Dunne J concluded that s 1 of the Courts Act 1988 prevented this action being heard by a jury. She held that this section abolished the right to trial by jury in relation to personal injuries claims. As this action included a personal injury claim, it was caught by section 1. In her view, this concluded the matter. It would be inappropriate to have different aspects of the same proceedings dealt with in different for a:

> There is no basis for the contention that it is permissible to separate the various causes of action herein and have them tried separately ... Imagine that this case is set down for trial without a jury and that the plaintiff made an application to have the trial of the two causes of action heard at the same time and the trial of the third cause of action held at a later time. Imagine that there would be two separate assessments made in respect of damages. There would be a duplication of evidence, the case would take longer, the costs would be greater and it is arguable that there could be an overlap in respect of the damages that might be awarded. It is difficult to see how such an approach could be permissible in any circumstances.

[6.113] Dunne J's decision appears to suggest that actions where claims of other wrongs are made in conjunction with an allegation of defamation will rarely be heard by a jury. However, in *Bradley v Maher*[224] Clarke J emphasised that the courts retain a discretion to allow such actions to be dealt with before a jury as appropriate:

> In the ordinary way, a plaintiff or defendant is entitled to a jury trial in this Court in defamation proceedings. However, that entitlement is not absolute. Where a single set of proceedings involve more than one cause of action, the court has to exercise a discretion as to the appropriate way in which all issues in the case can be disposed of. That discretion arises even in cases where no question of a right to trial by jury exists. For example, the question of whether all issues in a single case which is to be tried by a judge alone should be determined at a single unitary

---

222.   *Sheridan v Kelly* [2006] 1 IR 314.
223.   *Kerwick v Sunday Newspapers Ltd* (10 July 2009, unreported), HC, ex tempore.
224.   *Bradley v Maher* [2009] IEHC 389.

hearing, or in two or more separate hearings, is a matter over which the court retains a discretion which should be exercised, as should all judicial discretion, on a principled basis.

[6.114] In his view, a court faced with such a pre-trial application has three options:

A. A single unitary trial in which all issues are determined at a single hearing. It seems clear that if that is the option which justice demands then it necessarily follows that such a trial will not be a trial by jury as it would be inappropriate to extend trial by jury to issues which are not properly tried, in civil proceedings, by a judge sitting with a jury. Obviously where one of the claims made is a personal injury claim then the application of s 1(3) of the Courts Act 1988, would need to be considered.

B. Two fully separate trials. In such circumstances, the court has a discretion to direct that there should be a separate trial before a jury of the defamation aspect of the proceedings with a further trial of all other issues before a judge sitting alone. Clearly whether such a course of action is satisfactory will be highly dependent on the inter connection between the issues likely to arise at the respective hearings. Factors such as whether or not there is likely to be a significant waste of court time and parties expense in the duplication of evidence where the facts relevant to both matters are the same or similar will be an important factor. Likewise, the necessity to ensure consistency in relation to all findings of fact must be taken into account and may give rise to difficulties in circumstances where a jury will simply deliver a verdict on the basis of general questions asked of the jury concerned, and without giving detailed reasons or detailed findings of fact. The possibility of a judge being placed in the difficult position of having to assess the same facts as a jury had previously addressed with an obligation to give proper recognition to the findings of the jury, but at the same time being unaware of the precise factual basis on which the jury came to its conclusion needs to be weighed significantly in the balance. In addition, regard should be had to the circumstances in which the dispute between the parties as to whether there should be a jury trial has arisen. For example, note should be taken of the fact that it is normally a plaintiff who decides the causes of action which are to arise in a single set of proceedings (although, of course, as here, a defendant may add to those causes of action by reason of raising issues in a counterclaim). Care should be exercised to ensure that a plaintiff should not be allowed to exclude the possibility of a jury trial simply by adding some form of relief to a claim which is substantially one in defamation. It is, of course, the case that other factors may loom to a greater or lesser extent as important matters to be weighed in the balance on the facts of any individual case.

C. A hybrid trial. Order 36, rule 7 of the Rules of the Superior Courts provides as follows:

> The court may, if it shall appear desirable, direct a trial without a jury of any question or issue of fact, or party of fact and partly of law, arising in any cause or matter which, without any consent of parties, can be tried without a jury, and such trial may, if so ordered by the court, take place at the same time as the trial by a jury of any issues of fact in the same cause or matter.

It is clear from that order that the court has an entitlement to direct that there be a trial of certain issues before a jury with the same trial judge continuing on to deal with other issues (not appropriate for jury trial) after the jury has reached its conclusions. It follows that, in such cases, the evidence heard before a jury will also form part of the evidence which the judge will be entitled to consider when dealing with any other issues which remain for decision by the judge sitting alone. Whether such a form of hearing is satisfactory (and that is the test for the rule speaks of it appearing 'desirable') will again depend on the circumstances of the case. The extent, for example, that it might be necessary to call the same witnesses again will be important. Such witnesses may have to be called again because lines of cross examination that might not have been relevant to the jury trial (and would therefore have been inappropriate to pursue before the jury) might nonetheless be appropriate in respect of issues which the judge had to try. All proper weight would need to be attached to any complications of that variety which might arise. Likewise, dependent on the facts of the case under consideration, the difficulties which the judge might encounter in having to approach the issues which were for the judge to determine on a consistent basis with the findings of the jury, but without knowledge of the precise basis on which the jury came to its conclusions, would arise under this heading as well. Furthermore, there is always the possibility that other individual aspects of any case under consideration might prove important to weigh in the balance under this heading as well.

Ultimately, Clarke J concluded that the matter should be dealt with by way of a jury trial.

[6.115] Clarke J acknowledged that 'it seems almost certain that each case will depend, to a significant extent, on its own facts'. Thus, the fact that the decision reached in Bradley differed to that in Kerwick is not, of itself, indicative of a difference of approach on the part of the Court in those cases. There does, however, appear to be something of a difference of emphasis in these judgments. In particular, Dunne J's decision placed emphasis on the fact that the Oireachtas had removed the right to a jury trial in relation to the non-defamation claims in that case, whereas Clarke J repeatedly referred to the fact that a plaintiff in a defamation action has a statutory right, in the normal course of events, to have their action dealt with by a jury. It is unclear at present, therefore, whether non-jury or hybrid trials of actions where multiple claims are made will be the exception or the rule. As indicated in Bradley, the context-sensitive nature of these considerations means that it may not be possible or appropriate for hard and fast rules to develop on this issue. At present, however, this would seem to be an issue which it is important to take into account in determining how a plaintiff's claim ought to be pleaded.

Defamation and the internet

[6.116] Although many of the principles outlined above are capable of applying to material posted online, the courts have recognised that communication on the internet has several distinct characteristics which mean that, in certain circumstances, the law should adopt a different approach to online publications. As the High Court of Australia observed in *Dow Jones & Co Inc v Gutnick*,[225] many conventional legal principles will have to be re-thought and refined to take account of these differences. The main differences identified by the courts thus far are set out in brief below.[226] It should be noted, however, that this is an area which is still developing rapidly. As Eady J recently observed in *Metropolitan International Schools Ltd*, 'it is surprising how little authority there is within this jurisdiction applying the common law of publication or its modern statutory refinements to internet communications'.[227] It is likely that the law's attitude to defamation on the internet will be subject to further changes as the courts are provided with more opportunities to consider these issues in the future.

Publication

[6.117] Publication occurs on each occasion when the material at issue is seen or heard by a third party. While s 11 has limited the scope of a publisher's liability in relation to multiple publications, it does not appear to have changed the conventional rule that publication occurs in such circumstances. For material posted on the internet, therefore, publication occurs each time the site in question is accessed by a third party.

[6.118] However, in contrast to the approach adopted by the courts to newspapers and television broadcasts, the courts in England have refused to apply a presumption that substantial publication has occurred once material becomes available on the internet.[228] This reflects the fact that there is no guarantee that a website will ever be visited or accessed by a third party.

[6.119] This means that a plaintiff must provide evidence in support of their claim that the website in question was seen by third parties. The English High Court in *Carrie v Tolkien* held that '[t]here must be some evidence on which an inference can be drawn' that publication has occurred. This was particularly so in that case where the relevant period in which the material was available was just over four hours. With such a short period of time, the court was unwilling to assume that the site had been seen by any third party.[229]

[6.120] In the English courts, the issue is one which will be determined by reference to what can be inferred from the evidence adduced. Hence, the court was satisfied in *Gregg v O'Gara* that publication had occurred where the evidence indicated that the material in question was highly ranked in web searches related to the Yorkshire Ripper. Evidence was given by the plaintiff that this was how he had found the site, and that he had been contacted by others about it.

> [T]he defamatory material was immediately accessible to anyone who fed the words 'Yorkshire Ripper' into a standard search engine and, of course, the

---

225. *Dow Jones & Co Inc v Gutnick* (2002) 194 ALR 433, (2002) 210 CLR 575.
226. For a much more detailed treatment of this specific topic, see Collins, *The Law of Defamation and the Internet* (3rd edn, OUP, due December 2010).
227. *Metropolitan International Schools Ltd v Designtechnica Corp* [2010] 3 All ER 548, 556.
228. *Al Amoudi v Brisard* [2006] 3 All ER 294; *Carrie v Tolkien* [2009] EWHC 29 (QB).
229. *Carrie v Tolkien* [2009] EWHC 29 (QB), para 17.

> Yorkshire Ripper is a topic of continuing interest to members of the public in this country. The Claimant himself gives ample evidence of his being contacted by people in different professions across the media, the law and the police, all of whom have become aware of the defamatory allegations in circulation.[230]

Thus, the court was willing to infer that publication had occurred.

[6.121] However, the court in *Budu* held that it was not sufficient for a plaintiff to argue that the defendant had not sought particulars of the third parties to whom publication had allegedly occurred. The onus was on the plaintiff to persuade the court that publication had taken place in order to establish the alleged cause of action.[231]

Liability

THE E-COMMERCE REGULATIONS

[6.122] Many of the companies or persons involved in the process by which material is published online will be protected against liability for defamation under the European Communities (Directive 2000/31/EC) Regulations 2003.[232] These Regulations give effect to Directive 2000/31/EC as a matter of Irish law. This Directive is more commonly known as the E-Commerce Directive. Its purpose has been described as follows:

> The E-Commerce Directive was put in place to remove obstacles to cross-border online services and to provide a legal framework for E-Commerce. The E-Commerce Directive, amongst many other things, defines the circumstances in which internet intermediaries, as defined, can be held accountable for material which is hosted, cached or carried by them but which they did not create. The relevant provisions are not confined to the publication of defamatory material.[233]

The Regulations exclude certain parties, inter alia, from liability in damages for any infringement of another person's legal rights or from being subject to any civil or criminal proceedings in relation to the acts covered by the Regulations.[234] The relevant provisions in this context are regs 16, 17 and 18 which provide as follows:

Liability of intermediary service providers – 'mere conduit.'

16. (1) An intermediary service provider shall not be liable for information transmitted by him or her in a communication network if —

    (a)   the information has been provided to him or her by a recipient of a relevant service provided by him or her (being a service consisting of the transmission in a communication network of that information), or

    (b)   a relevant service provided by him or her consists of the provision of access to a communication network,

---

230. *Gregg v O'Gara* [2008] EWHC 658 (QB).
231. *Budu v BBC* [2010] EWHC 616 (QB).
232. European Communities (Directive 2000/31/EC) Regulations 2003 (SI 68/2003).
233. *Mulvaney v Sporting Exchange Ltd* [2009] IEHC 133.
234. European Communities (Directive 2000/31/EC) Regulations 2003 (SI 68/2003), reg 15.

and, in either case, the following conditions are complied with —

(i)   the intermediary service provider did not initiate the transmission,

(ii) the intermediary service provider did not select the receiver of the transmission, and

(iii) the intermediary service provider did not select or modify the information contained in the transmission.

(2) References in paragraph (1) to an act of transmission and of provision of access include references to the automatic, intermediate and transient storage of the information transmitted in so far as this takes place for the sole purpose of carrying out the transmission in the communications network, and provided that the information is not stored for any period longer than is reasonably necessary for the transmission.

(3) This Regulation shall not affect the power of any court to make an order against an intermediary service provider requiring the provider not to infringe, or to cease to infringe, any legal rights.

Caching.

17. (1) An intermediary service provider shall not be liable for the automatic, intermediate and temporary storage of information which is performed for the sole purpose of making more efficient that information's onward transmission to other users of the service upon their request, if —

(a)   that storage is done in the context of the provision of a relevant service by the relevant service provider consisting of the transmission in a communication network of information provided by a recipient of that service, and

(b)   the following conditions are complied with —

(i)   the intermediary service provider does not modify the information,

(ii)   the intermediary service provider complies with conditions relating to access to the information,

(iii) the intermediary service provider complies with any rules regarding the updating of the information that have been specified in a manner widely recognised and used by industry,

(iv)   the intermediary service provider does not interfere with the lawful use of technology, widely recognised and used by industry to obtain data on the use of the information, and

(v)   the intermediary service provider acts expeditiously to remove or disable access to the information it has stored upon obtaining actual knowledge of the fact that the information at the initial source of the transmission has been removed from the network, or access to it has been disabled, or that a court or an administrative authority has ordered such removal or disablement.

(2) This Regulation shall not affect the power of any court to make an order against an intermediary service provider requiring the provider not to infringe, or to cease to infringe, any legal rights.

Hosting.

18. (1) An intermediary service provider who provides a relevant service consisting of the storage of information provided by a recipient of the service shall not be liable for the information stored at the request of that recipient if —

    (a)   the intermediary service provider does not have actual knowledge of the unlawful activity concerned and, as regards claims for damages, is not aware of facts or circumstances from which that unlawful activity is apparent, or

    (b)   the intermediary service provider, upon obtaining such knowledge or awareness, acts expeditiously to remove or to disable access to the information.

(2) Paragraph (1) shall not apply where the recipient of the service is acting under the authority or the control of the intermediary service provider referred to in that paragraph.

(3) This Regulation shall not affect the power of any court to make an order against an intermediary service provider requiring the provider not to infringe, or to cease to infringe, any legal rights.

These Regulations were considered by Clarke J in *Mulvaney v Sporting Exchange Ltd*.[235] This decision is notable for the relatively broad way in which the Regulations were construed by the court. It was argued by the plaintiff that the defendant company, which hosted a chatroom as part of their wider gambling business, were excluded from the Regulations. In considering the plaintiff's arguments, the court had regard to the recitals of the Directive as part of a broadly purposive interpretation of the scope of the Regulations. Given the rapidly changing nature of electronic communications, this approach seems appropriate.

[6.123] In particular, the court referred to recitals 18 and 20 of the Directive.

Recital 20 states that:

> The definition of 'recipient of a service' covers all types of usage of information society services, both by persons who provide information to open networks such as the Internet and by persons who seek information on the Internet for private of professional reasons.

Recital 18 provides that:

> Information society services span a wide range of economic activities which take place on-line; these activities can, in particular, consist of selling goods on-line; activities such as the delivery of goods as such or the provision of service off-line are not covered; information society services are not solely restricted to services giving rise to on-line contracting but also, in so far as they represent an economic activity, extend to services which are not remunerated by those who receive them, such as those offering on-line information or commercial communications, or those providing tools allowing for search, access and retrieval of data; information society services also include services consisting of the transmission of

---

235.   *Mulvaney v Sporting Exchange Ltd* [2009] IEHC 133.

information via a communication network, in providing access to a communication network or in hosting information provided by a recipient of the service.

The court concluded from this that chatrooms came within the scope of Art 18 and were accordingly exempt from liability for defamation in circumstances where those responsible for the chatroom did not have actual knowledge of the allegedly defamatory comments; were not aware of the allegedly defamatory comments; and/or, on being made aware of the potentially defamatory comments, acted expeditiously to remove or disable access to the comments.

[6.124] A similarly broad approach has also been favoured by the English courts in relation to the E-Commerce Directive. In *Metropolitan International Schools Ltd v Designtechnica Corp*,[236] Eady J referred to the same recitals as Clarke J in support of his view that a search engine might come within the UK's Regulations despite not satisfying the strict terms of the definition of an 'information services provider' as providing a service for remuneration. While he ultimately concluded that it was not necessary to determine this point, he did state that 'it would appear on balance that the provisions of the 2002 Regulations are apt to cover those providing search engine services.'

[6.125] In *EMI v UPC*,[237] Charleton J held that the defendant internet service provider was a mere conduit on the ground that it was not in any way actively involved in unlawful peer-to-peer transmission of copyrighted works. In his view, the mere conduct defence was available as 'there is no modification of information in these transmissions which is affected by UPC'. However, he also emphasised the necessity for passivity for a defendant seeking to rely on this defence, adding that '[t]acking on an advertisement to a transmission or modifying it so that some of it is lost as opposed to being transmitted slowly, would disable the mere conduit defence'.[238]

This issue was also the subject of some consideration in the recent European Court of Justice decision in *Google France v Louis Vuitton Malletier*.[239] Although the decision primarily concerned EU rules on trademarks, the Court also considered whether Google was entitled to rely on the hosting defence in Article 14 in relation to its 'AdWords' service. The Court held that this was a question for national courts to determine on the basis of whether Google's involvement was 'neutral, in the sense that its conduct is merely technical, automatic and passive, pointing to a lack of knowledge or control of the data which it stores'. This indicates that the fact that Google received an economic benefit from the service was not sufficient to deprive it of the benefit of the hosting defence. However, it also suggests that some knowledge on the part of an information services provider of the potentially unlawful or wrongful character of the impugned conduct may be sufficient to place it outside the scope of Article 14 in situations where its conduct can be regarded as non-neutral.

---

236. *Metropolitan International Schools Ltd v Designtechnica Corp* [2010] 3 All ER 548.
237. *EMI v UPC* (11 October 2010, unreported) HC.
238. *EMI v UPC* (11 October 2010, unreported) HC, 108.
239. *Google France v Louis Vuitton Malletier* (Case C-236/08) 23 March 2010.

Liability at common law

[6.126] In addition to the protection provided by the E-Commerce Directive, the courts in England have also considered whether certain parties involved in online publication may be able to avoid liability for defamation at common law. As this case law is concerned with the initial imposition of liability, rather than the availability of a defence, the persuasive value of this jurisprudence should not be affected by the provisions of s 15 of the 2009 Act.

It should also be noted that s 27 of the Defamation Act 2009, which creates a new defence of innocent publication, will provide protection to such parties in many situations.

LIABILITY OF THIRD PARTIES FOR PUBLISHED MATERIAL

[6.127] The technology-dependent nature of the internet means that there are several parties involved in the publication of material online. As previously noted, the common law has traditionally adopted the view that any person involved in the process of publication is potentially liable in defamation. This meant that, as a matter of logic, third parties such as internet service providers, operators of discussion boards and caching services were all potentially liable for the posting of defamatory material online. This was confirmed when, in one of the first decisions in this area in England, Morland J held that an internet service provider was liable in defamation for material posted on a discussion group which was hosted by its servers.[240]

[6.128] The decision in *Godfrey v Demon Internet* has, however, been interpreted and applied in subsequent cases in a way which reduces the scope for liability to be imposed on third party service providers. It has been held in several recent cases that liability for a defamatory publication will only attach where there is a sufficient mental element on the part of the prospective defendant. Eady J held in *Bunt v Tilley* that:

> In determining responsibility for publication in the context of the law of defamation, it seems to me to be important to focus on what the person did, or failed to do, in the chain of communication. It is clear that the state of a defendant's knowledge can be an important factor. If a person knowingly permits another to communicate information which is defamatory, when there would be an opportunity to prevent the publication, there would seem to be no reason in principle why liability should not accrue. So too, if the true position were that the applicants had been (in the claimant's words) responsible for 'corporate sponsorship and approval of their illegal activities'.
>
> I have little doubt, however, that to impose legal responsibility upon anyone under the common law for the publication of words it is essential to demonstrate a degree of awareness or at least an assumption of general responsibility, such as has long been recognised in the context of editorial responsibility.[241]

240.   *Godfrey v Demon Internet Ltd* [1999] 4 All ER 342, [2001] QB 201.
241.   *Bunt v Tilley* [2006] EWHC 407 (QB), [2006] 3 All ER 336, [2007] 1 WLR 1243, paras 21–22.

This approach was applied by the same judge in *Metropolitan International Schools Ltd v Designtechnica Corp*[242] to find that a web search engine would not be liable for the results of searches carried out by its systems, where those searches published allegedly defamatory material. It had been argued in that case that liability should apply on the basis that the search engine had extracted particularly defamatory material from a third party site and presented it out of context in a way which either caused or exacerbated the defamatory impact. Eady J, in rejecting this argument, relied heavily on the fact that the search results were produced automatically by computers with no opportunity for human input. While he accepted that liability could apply where a person amplified or extracted a defamatory statement from another party's work, he felt that it would not be appropriate where that was produced by an automated process. As he explained:

> Here, an analogy may be drawn perhaps with a search carried out in a large conventional library. If a scholar wishes to check for references to his research topic, he may well consult the library catalogue. On doing so, he may find that there are some potentially relevant books in one of the bays and make his way there to see whether he can make use of the content. It is hardly realistic to attribute responsibility for the content of those books to the compiler(s) of the catalogue. On the other hand, if the compilers have made an effort to be more informative, by quoting brief snippets from the book, the position may be different. Suppose the catalogue records that a particular book contains allegations of corruption against a living politician, or perhaps it goes further and spells out a particular activity, such as 'flipping' homes to avoid capital gains tax, then there could be legal liability on the part of the compiler under the 'repetition rule'.

> No doubt it would be said here too, by analogy, that the third defendant should be liable for repeating the 'scam' allegations against the claimant. Yet, whereas a compiler of a conventional library catalogue will consciously at some point have chosen the wording of any 'snippet' or summary included, that is not so in the case of a search engine. There will have been no intervention on the part of any human agent. It has all been done by the web-crawling 'robots'.[243]

[6.129] He distinguished *Godfrey* on these grounds, pointing out that Morland J had relied heavily in that case on the fact that the defendant had failed to take down the impugned material after being informed about it.

> In the circumstances before Morland J, in *Godfrey v Demon Internet Ltd* … the acquisition of knowledge was clearly regarded as critical. That is largely because the law recognises that a person can become liable for the publication of a libel by acquiescence; that is to say, by permitting publication to continue when he or she has the power to prevent it. As I have said, someone hosting a website will generally be able to remove material that is legally objectionable. If this is not done, then there may be liability on the basis of authorisation or acquiescence.

This indicates that liability may not attach to companies or individuals who are involved in assisting with the publication of material online provided that they can demonstrate

---

242. *Metropolitan International Schools Ltd v Designtechnica Corp* [2010] 3 All ER 548.
243. *Metropolitan International Schools Ltd v Designtechnica Corp* [2010] 3 All ER 548, 561–562.

that they were unaware of or had no grounds to suspect the existence of the defamatory material.[244]

[6.130] Eady J's decision in *Metropolitan International Schools* further indicates that practical considerations may be taken into account by a court in assessing the extent to which a third party could be said to have the requisite mental element to found an action in defamation. This is important as there may be grounds to argue in some situations that the company or person in question could have taken additional steps to reduce the danger of defamatory material being posted. For example, it could be argued in the situation in that case that the main defamatory sting could have been avoided or minimised if the defendant search engine did not adopt the practice of providing search results with accompanying extracts from the pages in question. Eady J seemed, however, to take the view that companies should not be held to a standard of perfection but should be judged in what was reasonable. In his view, '[t]here is no doubt room for debate as to what further blocking steps it would be open for it to take, or how effective they might be, but that does not seem to me to affect my overall conclusion on liability'.

[6.131] However, in *Budu v BBC*, Sharp J pointed out that this did not provide an absolute defence to third party service providers and that there may be circumstances in which liability could be imposed on such persons:

> As was contemplated by Eady J in *Metropolitan* a company such as Google might at some point become liable, if the publication of a defamatory search result (or a 'signpost to a conduit' as he described it) continued after notification of the specific URL from which the words complained of originated (though not, as Eady J said, while efforts were made by the operator of the search engine to achieve a 'take down').[245]

This underlines the fact that, while third party service providers are unlikely to be held to be liable in relation to statements of which they were unaware, different principles may apply once they are informed that they are involved in the publication of the statement in question. In such situations, it is advisable for the person or company in question to consider removing or blocking the material in question. Where the material has been published by a third party on several occasions, or where that third party has threatened to publish the material again, it may also be advisable to consider blocking that user's access to the service.

ARCHIVED MATERIAL

[6.132] An issue which has been examined in some detail by the English courts recently is the question of whether a defendant may be liable for defamation in relation to material contained in online archives. As discussed above, it is arguable in Ireland that s 11 will apply such that it will be more difficult for a plaintiff to sue in relation to

---

244. On the issue of how liability may be influenced by the potential for human involvement, see also *Flood v Times Newspapers Ltd* [2009] EWHC 2375 (QB); *Flood v Times Newspapers* [2010] EWCA Civ 804.

245. *Budu v BBC* [2010] EWHC 616 (QB), para 74.

archive material once the time limit for the taking of an action in defamation has expired. However, it has also been held that there are good reasons from a plaintiff's perspective for it to be possible – at least in principle – to take an action in respect of archive material in some situations.[246] This reflects the reality, as recognised by O'Donnell J in *Galway City Council v Samuel Kingston Construction Ltd* that the continued presence of archive material online may have a serious impact on a person's right to reputation and a good name. In that case, O'Donnell J observed (in an obiter comment) that:

> The allegation also has the potential to cause maximum damage both to the decision maker and to the process of decision making, because it has an almost tabloid capacity for immediate impact. It is capable of being grasped immediately by a person who pays even fleeting attention to the issue, and it holds the decision maker up to the prospect of immediate ridicule which, in an internet age will forever attach to his or her name, whatever the outcome of the proceedings. This can be immensely unfair and irretrievably damaging to a reputation, perhaps carefully and painstakingly acquired over many years.[247]

There is therefore a reasonable argument to be made that it may be in the interests of justice in many cases for leave to be granted under s 11(2) in relation to archive material online.

[6.133] It has been held on several occasions in England that a publisher will be liable in defamation for archive material as a result of an omission to correct or remedy a defamatory statement of which he or she was aware.[248] This may apply even where the initial publication of the statement would not have supported the bringing of an action. As was noted in *Flood v Times Newspapers*,[249] a report which was protected by Reynolds privilege when it was initially published might no longer be regarded as responsible journalism in the public interest once it had been confirmed that the allegations made in it were untrue. As the High Court explained:

> The failure to remove the article from the website, or to attach ... a suitable qualification, cannot possibly be described as responsible journalism. It is not in the public interest that there should continue to be recorded on the internet the questions as to [DS Flood's] honesty which were raised in 2006, and it is not fair to him. It is not in the public interest.[250]

[6.134] The Court of Appeal in *Flood* also held that the onus was on the defendant to deal with the offending publication once it became aware of it. It had been argued in that

---

246. See, for example, *Times Newspapers Ltd (Nos 1 and 2) v United Kingdom* [2009] ECHR 3002/03, para 48.

247. *Galway City Council v Samuel Kingston Construction Ltd* [2010] IESC 18.

248. *Godfrey v Demon Internet Ltd* [2001] QB 201; *Loutchansky* [2002] QB 783; *Budu v BBC* [2010] EWHC 616 (QB).

249. *Flood v Times Newspapers* [2010] EWCA Civ 804.

250. *Flood v Times Newspapers* [2009] EWHC 2375 (QB). While the Court of Appeal reversed the decision, it described this statement by the High Court as 'plainly right'.

case that the failure of the plaintiff to agree a form of words to be added to the site in question precluded him from succeeding in his claim. The court instead held that:

> [T]he risk in relation to the Reynolds public interest defence lay on TNL, and not on the Claimant. It is for a defendant to make good his defence. It may well be good practice to seek to agree a form of follow-up publication in a case such as this. But if there is no agreement, then the publisher must take his own course, and then defend it if he can at trial. He cannot offer the claimant a form of words which the claimant refuses to accept, and then rely on that refusal to relieve him of the obligation of acting responsibly and fairly, at least when the claimant's refusal is reasonable, as it was here.

> The only qualification I would make to that analysis relates to the last sentence. The fact that the claimant's refusal is unreasonable will, save perhaps in the most unusual circumstances, not be enough to justify the defendant doing nothing if responsible journalism would otherwise require him to retract or modify a website publication if further relevant information comes to light. The essential point is that it is for a defendant to decide on the appropriate course to take. As well as being contrary to principle, it seems to me to be literally adding insult to injury to enable a defendant to require a claimant, after new evidence has come to light, to agree a form of words to amend a publication, which is defamatory of him but against which he cannot protect himself in law, so as to ensure he still cannot protect himself against it in law.[251]

However, the court also accepted that 'in an appropriate case, a claimant may be held to be unreasonable in his attitude to a defendant's proposal, and this could be reflected in any order for costs a court may make, or even, conceivably, in the measure of damages it awards'.[252]

HUMAN RIGHTS CONSIDERATIONS

[6.135] It should also be noted that recent legislative developments in EU law have provided additional protection for the human rights of end users of electronic communications network. Article 1(3A) of the amended Directive 2002/21/EC on a common regulatory framework for electronic communications networks and services now provides that:[253]

> Measures taken by Member States regarding end-users access' to, or use of, services and applications through electronic communications networks shall respect the fundamental rights and freedoms of natural persons, as guaranteed by the European Convention for the Protection of Human Rights and Fundamental Freedoms and general principles of Community law.

Any of these measures regarding end-users' access to, or use of, services and applications through electronic communications networks liable to restrict those fundamental rights or freedoms may only be imposed if they are appropriate,

---

251. *Flood v Times Newspapers* [2010] EWCA Civ 804, paras 80–81.
252. *Flood v Times Newspapers* [2010] EWCA Civ 804, para 82.
253. As amended by Directive 2009/140/EC.

proportionate and necessary within a democratic society, and their implementation shall be subject to adequate procedural safeguards in conformity with the European Convention for the Protection of Human Rights and Fundamental Freedoms and with general principles of Community law, including effective judicial protection and due process. Accordingly, these measures may only be taken with due respect for the principle of the presumption of innocence and the right to privacy. A prior, fair and impartial procedure shall be guaranteed, including the right to be heard of the person or persons concerned, subject to the need for appropriate conditions and procedural arrangements in duly substantiated cases of urgency in conformity with the European Convention for the Protection of Human Rights and Fundamental Freedoms. The right to effective and timely judicial review shall be guaranteed.

Discovery in relation to online publications – Norwich Pharmacal *orders*

[6.136] It is axiomatic that a person who creates material for publication on the internet will be liable for any defamatory content.[254] The practical issue of identification of anonymous or pseudonymous tortfeasors often thus arises. Where wrongdoing can be established, it is possible to seek discovery to ascertain the identities of wrongdoers to enable the bringing of an action under the principle in *Norwich Pharmacal Co v Customs and Excise Commissioners*.[255]

The availability of *Norwich Pharmacal* orders in this jurisdiction was confirmed by the Supreme Court in *Megaleasing UK Ltd v Barrett*.[256] Finlay CJ in that case held that:

> The remedy should be confined to cases where very clear proof of a wrongdoing exists and possibly, so far as it applies to an action for discovery alone prior to the institution of any other proceedings, to cases where what is really sought is the names and identity of the wrongdoers rather than the factual information concerning the commission of the wrong.[257]

Norwich Pharmacal itself arose in the context of breach of patent and has been applied in the context of an intellectual property action in *EMI Records (Ireland) Limited v Eircom Ltd*.[258] In that case, Kelly J made number of orders compelling Eircom, as an internet service provider to disclose the names of customers illegally downloading

254. See, for example, *Applause Store Inc v Raphael* [2008] EWHC 1781 (QB).
255. *Norwich Pharmacal Co v Customs and Excise Commissioners* [1974] AC 133; [1973] 3 WLR 164, [1973] 2 All ER 943. The House of Lords in that case granted discovery to the plaintiff to compel the defendants to reveal the identities of parties who were breaching the plaintiff's patent. *Norwich Pharmacal* orders allow a party who claims that a civil wrong has been perpetrated to obtain a court order against a party holding information that would enable the identification of the wrongdoer.
256. *Megaleasing UK Ltd v Barrett* [1993] IRLM 497.
257. *Megaleasing UK Ltd v Barrett* [1993] IRLM 497, at 504. See also *Societe Romanaise de la Chaussure S. v British Shoe Corporation Limited* [1991] FSR 1. In *Ryanair v Johnston* (12 July 2006, unreported) HC, Smyth J, an order to disclose the identities of persons posting to an on-line bulletin board was refused in the absence of any clear evidence of wrongdoing. The jurisdiction seems to be strictly confined to situations where the plaintiff can show that he has suffered a wrong and cannot institute proceedings as he does not know the identity of the wrongdoer and the defendant is in a position to establish the identity of the wrongdoer . See also *Doyle v Garda Commissioner* [1999] 1 IR 249; [1998] 2 ILRM 523.
258. *EMI Records (Ireland) Limited v Eircom Ltd* [2005] 4 IR 148.

music from the Internet. The plaintiff recording companies argued that this downloading infringed their copyright and demonstrated a series of IP addresses of the responsible subscriber. Their request was that Eircom be forced to identify the customers whose IP addresses identified them as engaging in breach of copyright. Kelly J found that where a wrongful activity had been committed by unidentified persons, an order could be made requiring a defendant to identify such persons for the purposes of a legal action.[259]

Kelly J noted that any such orders must be proportionate. This suggests that the orders may not be available in situations where the damage to the plaintiff's reputation or good name is so slight that it may not justify the envisaged interference with the other party's rights to privacy or confidentiality. The Court of Appeal in England has held that the scope of the order sought will be a factor to be taken into account in determining whether it is appropriate to require a party to provide the material in question.[260]

Norwich Pharmacal orders have been made in a number of contexts. In addition to breach of copyright[261] and employment disputes,[262] the jurisdiction has been exercised in the context of defamatory postings on a website[263] and breaches of privacy on a website.[264]

Norwich Pharmacal orders have been characterised as a justifiable interference with any rights to privacy or confidentiality owed to individual's accessing the internet. As Kelly J observed in ordering an internet service provider to make discovery in a different context in *EMI Records (Ireland) Ltd v Eircom*:

> I am satisfied that whether the right to confidentiality arises by statute or by contract or at common law, it cannot be relied on by a wrongdoer or a person against whom there is evidence of wrongdoing to protect his or her identity. The right to privacy or confidentiality of identity must give way where there is prima facie evidence of wrongdoing.[265]

---

259. Kelly J referred in his judgment to the decision of the Federal Court of Appeal of Canada in *BMG Canada Inc v Doe* [2005] FCA 193. His application of the *Norwich Pharmacal* principle was endorsed by Charleton J in *EMI Records (Ireland) Ltd & Ors v UPC Communications Ireland Ltd* [2010] IEHC 377, (10 November 2010, unreported) HC, Charleton J.
260. *Smith v ADVFN plc* [2008] EWCA Civ 518.
261. *Societe Romanaise de la Chaussure SA v British Shoe Corporation Limited* [1991] FSR 1.
262. *P v T Ltd* [1997] 1 WLR 1309.
263. *Totalise v Motley Fool Limited* [2001] EMLR 29. See also *Sheffield Wednesday Football Club Ltd v Hargreaves* [2007] EWHC 2375, High Court of England, Parkes QC, 18 October 2007; *Smith v ADVFN Plc* [2008] EWHC 577, High Court of England, Mackay J, 13 March 2008; [2008] EWCA Civ 518, Court of Appeal of England and Wales 15 April 2008. Cf *Maguire v Gill* (5 October 2006, unreported) HC, where Hanna J order an internet service provider to make discovery of material which could identify the person or persons who were responsible for posting allegedly defamatory statements online.
264. *G and G v Wikipedia Foundation Inc* [2009] EWHC 3148, High Court of England, Tugendhat J, 2 December 2009.
265. *EMI Records (Ireland) Ltd v Eircom* [2005] IEHC 233; [2005] 4 IR 148. A Swedish Court has made a reference for preliminary ruling to the European Court of Justice concerning a national rule with similar effect to a *Norwich Pharmacal* order is compatible with the Data Retention Directive (Directive 2006/24/EC). The Swedish law is based on the EU IP Rights Enforcement Directive (2004/48/EC), which provides that an Internet Service Provider in a civil case can be ordered to provide a copyright owner or a rights holder with information on which subscriber holds a specific IP address assigned by the Internet Service Provider, from which address the infringement is alleged to have taken place.

On the other hand, where the disclosure is ordered in respect of a journalist's source, the freedom of expression interests at stake may outweigh the interests of a private party in pursuing litigation, at least as far as the European Court of Human Rights is concerned.[266]

DEFENCES

Abolition of common law defences

[6.137] One of the most significant changes introduced by the 2009 Act was the general[267] abolition by s 15 of the defences which were formerly available to defendants at common law. These are replaced by the new defences set out in Pt 3 of the Act. This is particularly important given the incremental way in which the common law had developed defences to actions for libel and slander. Because defamation is a particularly context-sensitive tort, the law which governs the liability of defendants has tended to evolve over time. The development of so-called Reynolds privilege[268] in the United Kingdom is a notable example of how the flexibility of the common law allowed courts to refine or extend the relevant legal principles to deal with new or unforeseen circumstances[269] or with changes in the general legal or social environment.[270]

[6.138] The abolition of these defences by s 15 has a number of consequences. It means that the courts, in entertaining defamation actions, will no longer have the power to rely on common law principles or authorities to assist them in dealing with any issues that may arise. This in turn means that there may be difficulties with the 2009 Act from a constitutional or Convention perspective if the defences set out therein fail to provide adequate protection for a defendant's freedom of expression or, indeed, the plaintiff's right to reputation and a good name.

[6.139] It also means that there is a notable lack of certainty at the time of publication of this work how many of these defences will operate in the future. In many respects, the 2009 Act does not codify pre-existing legal principles but instead establishes new defences which only loosely resemble those formerly available at common law. This reduces the value of previous Irish authorities as precedents. While previous decisions of the courts may cast some light on how Pt 3 of the 2009 Act will be interpreted, the text of the new provisions must be the starting point for an analysis of any issues that arise. As discussed further below, in many respects the law established by this text appears different to that which preceded it. For that reason, this section of this chapter

---

266. See discussion of *Financial Times Ltd v United Kingdom* (Application No 821/03) 15 December 2009 (Fourth Section), discussed above at **[5.113]**.
267. See Defamation Act 2009, ss 17 and 18 below.
268. *Reynolds v Times Newspapers* [2001] 2 AC 127.
269. See, for example, the way in which qualified privilege was applied to new situations in cases such as *Watts v Times Newspapers* [1996] 1 All ER 152.
270. The development of Reynolds privilege arguably reflected changes in the attitude of English judges to issues of freedom of expression and, in particular, the increased influence in that jurisdiction of the European Convention on Human Rights, Art 10.

will focus primarily on the terms of the 2009 Act rather than on the intricacies of the common law principles which it has supplanted.

Truth

[6.140] Section 16 of the 2009 Act established a new defence of truth. This broadly replaces the previous common law defence of justification.[271] Section 16 provides that:

> (1) It shall be a defence (to be known and in this Act referred to as the 'defence of truth') to a defamation action for the defendant to prove that the statement in respect of which the action was brought is true in all material respects.

> (2) In a defamation action in respect of a statement containing 2 or more distinct allegations against the plaintiff, the defence of truth shall not fail by reason only of the truth of every allegation not being proved, if the words not proved to be true do not materially injure the plaintiff's reputation having regard to the truth of the remaining allegations.

The burden of proof for this defence rests on the defendant. It is necessary for him or her to prove to the satisfaction of the court that the statement under examination was true in all material respects.

[6.141] It should be remembered that it will not be sufficient for the defendant to prove that the statement was true in the way that he or she intended it. The statement may be capable of more than one meaning. Thus, it is necessary for a defendant who wishes to raise this defence to satisfy a court about the truth in all material respects of the defamatory meaning which the statement is capable of bearing. This underlines the importance of the jury's initial determination (or that of a judge if an application is made on this point) of the natural and ordinary meaning which a reasonable person would give to the words or images under examination.[272] It is the truth of this meaning that the defendant must establish to the satisfaction of the court.

[6.142] It will usually be in the defendant's interest when raising the defence of truth to attempt to persuade the jury that any allegedly defamatory meaning represents a general rather than a specific allegation. A defendant might be thought more likely to be able to prove the truth of a general allegation rather than a series of specific allegations, each of which may have to be specifically supported by evidence. Furthermore, the range of evidence which may be admitted as part of an effort to support a general allegation is likely to be broader and may include events which occur after publication.[273]

[6.143] The phrase 'in all material respects' might be thought to emphasise the task faced by a defendant in establishing the defence of truth. It is plain that a defendant will

---

271.   See, for example, *Norbrook Laboratories v Smith Kline Beecham* [1999] 2 IR 192.
272.   *Chapman v Orion Publishing (No 1)* [2005] EWHC.
273.   *Cohen v Daily Telegraph* [1968] 1 WLR 916; *Bennett v News Group Newspapers* [2002] EMLR 860; *Chase v News Group Newspapers* [2003] EMLR 11.

not generally[274] succeed in avoiding liability if they cannot prove the truth of those portions of the statement which have a defamatory meaning.

[6.144] However, the particular way in which this provision is drafted might also be argued to indicate that it is a prerequisite to the establishment of a defence of truth that 'the defendant ... prove that the statement in respect of which the action was brought is true in all material respects'. This reading of s 16 would call into question whether it remains permissible to offer a defence of partial 'truth', in accordance with which a defendant seeks to justify only some element of the statement in question. This was an option open to the defendant at common law.[275] However, as matters were only capable of being severed in this way where they were separate and distinct allegations,[276] it is submitted that this should continue to be the approach adopted under s 16(1) on the basis that any allegations that are distinct in this way are separate defamatory statements.[277]

[6.145] Section 16(2)[278] confirms that the failure of a defendant to prove the truth of all allegations will not necessarily be fatal, provided that the truth of the major defamatory imputations can be established. This section allows a court to consider the allegedly defamatory character of the publication afresh, leaving to one side those allegations that have been proven to be true.[279]

[6.146] This makes it clear that a defendant is not required to establish or address the truth of other allegations which may have been made in the course of the publication. Nor may he or she do so even if they wish to. A claimant is entitled to confine his or her complaint to a published defamatory meaning, and a defendant is not then entitled to enlarge the ambit of the contest by seeking to justify a separate and distinct meaning which the claimant does not complain and which is not embraced within a common sting of the publication complained of.[280] This principle is typically most relevant in circumstances where a defendant seeks to adduce evidence in relation to other matters which may reflect poorly on the plaintiff. As Eady J has commented in England, 'where a plea of justification contains irrelevant and embarrassing material, its inclusion cannot be justified on the rather lame ground that it is 'part of the factual matrix'.[281] In that situation, it is usually advisable to apply in advance to have such pleadings struck out under Order 19, rule 27.

---

274. For the exception to this, see 16(2) and the discussion of this below.
275. *Norbrook Laboratories v Smith Kline Beecham* [1999] 2 IR 192.
276. *S & K Holdings v Throgmorton Publications* [1972] 1 WLR 1036; *United States Tobacco Inc v BBC* [1998] EMLR 816; *McKeith v News Group Newspapers Ltd* (2005) EMLR 780; *Warren v Random House* [2008] EWCA Civ 834.
277. Even if separate actions could not be brought by virtue of Defamation Act 2009, s 9.
278. See also Defamation Act 1961, s 22.
279. *Irving v Penguin* (14 April 2000, unreported), HC; *Bailey v Irish Mirror Group Ltd* (19 January 2004, unreported), Circuit Court.
280. *Polly Peck (Holdings) plc v Trelford* [1986] 1 QB 1000; *Fallon v MGN* [2006] EMLR 19.
281. *Prince Radu of Hohenzollern v Houston* [2009] EWHC 398 (QB), para 4.

[6.147] A defendant was also entitled to raise the defence of justification only where he or she believed the defence to be true, intended to prove that and had reasonable grounds for that belief.[282] The latter requirement begged the obvious question of whether a defendant was required to identify in advance of the hearing what the basis for the defence was. This has led to extensive litigation in England on the issue of whether a defendant is obliged to plead and/or supply particulars of the matters upon which the defence will be based at trial[283] such that the law in that jurisdiction appears now to be that full particulars of the facts, matters[284] and meanings[285] which the defendant will raise as part of this defence must be provided.

[6.148] By contrast, Irish law before the 2009 Act did not seem to require a similar level of detail.[286] In *Doyle v Independent Newspapers (Ireland) Ltd*, for example,[287] Keane CJ declined to require the defendants to provide particulars of the identities of the witnesses who were to be called to support the claim that the coach of the Irish rugby team had been ostracised by 'the decision making core of the team'.

> In the present case, as matters stand, the plaintiff will be informed of the manner in which it is alleged that he was ostracised or shunned by senior players in the team because that has been so ordered by the High Court and not appealed from, and it must be assumed that the defendants will comply, as they must, with that order. Given that this is a relatively specific allegation that is made in the article, confined to what must, on any view, be a relatively small number of people, I would have thought that the pleading could not be described as so general or imprecise that the plaintiff in this case could not know what case he will have to meet in the trial. The defendants have undertaken the burden of establishing and, of course, the onus of proof will be on them, that the plaintiff was, in truth, shunned or ostracised by senior members of the Irish rugby squad, the decision making core of the Irish rugby squad during the course of his tenure of the position of rugby coach, indeed, confined to two particular seasons stretching, one supposes, over three years. That is what they will have to establish and not merely that, they will have to establish the specific incidents which are being relied upon in support of that statement in the article, because that is what they have been directed to furnish. When those particulars are furnished, as they must be, I would find it difficult to see how it could be said that the pleading was now so general or imprecise, that the plaintiff did not know what case he has to meet at the trial.[288]

[6.149] In *McDonagh v Sunday Newspapers Ltd*,[289] Macken J – having described the defence of justification as having been pleaded simpliciter – accepted that a

---

282. *McDonagh v Sunday Newspapers Ltd* [2005] 4 IR 528.
283. See for example *Musa King v Telegraph Corporation* [2004] EMLR 23.
284. [2001] 4 IR 594.
285. *Lucas Box v News Group Newspapers* [1986] 1 WLR 147; *Hewitt v Grunwald* [2004] EWHC 2959 (QB); *McKenna v MGN* [2006] EWHC 1996 (QB).
286. *Cooney v Browne* [1985] IR 185; *McDonell v Sunday Business Post* [2000] IEHC 19.
287. *Doyle v Independent Newspapers (Ireland) Ltd* [2001] 4 IR 594.
288. *Doyle v Independent Newspapers (Ireland) Ltd* [2001] 4 IR 594, 597–598.
289. *McDonagh v Sunday Newspapers Ltd* [2005] 4 IR 528.

defendant was not required to particularise the basis of a justification plea in his or her defence.[290] She referred to the difference of approach between English and Irish law on this matter but felt that this reflected the different statutory and procedural rules which applied in Ireland. However, she also held that a defendant was not entitled to seek discovery in respect of a defence of justification without providing some degree of clarification of the basis upon which that defence was being raised:

> In the earlier case law what appears to have been required before discovery was granted, was actual evidence of the justification plea. I am not satisfied that a defendant must disclose his hand, by presenting actual evidence, in detail, in order to be entitled to discovery and more recent jurisprudence would not support such a constraint on a defendant. It is sufficient, in order to do justice between the parties and maintain the appropriate balances between a defendant's entitlement to plead the truth in substance and in fact of the words used and the plaintiff's right to have his good name adequately vindicated and knowledge of the case he has to meet when there is a plea of justification, that appropriate details of the plea, if material facts have not been pleaded, is available to the court in the affidavit grounding a discovery application.

> Provided, therefore, that a defendant in such a case can 'particularise' his plea of justification … it is not necessary that actual evidence be disclosed to the court.

> Without these [particulars], not only is it impossible to establish that the discovery is sought to advance the defendant's plea of justification, a very important issue in a case such as this, rather than to make a case on that plea, it is also not clear how the question of the relevance and necessity of the discovery sought can be assessed, even if in respect of these, in the ordinary case, one frequently equates with the other.

> … [I]n a libel action in which a defendant pleads justification simpliciter, there must be before the court, at least at the time discovery is sought, sufficient information, particulars or material facts, however phrased, upon which the court can conclude that the application for discovery is firstly, intended to advance the plea of justification and not merely make such a case for the defendant, secondly, to establish that the documents sought are relevant to the issues arising between the parties and thirdly, to establish that they are necessary for the purposes of disposing of the action.[291]

Macken J's decision appears to envisage a more flexible approach to the pleadings and particulars necessary to raise this defence than is the case in England. Her view appears to be that the level of detail required will vary according to the context of the case and the needs of the respective parties.

---

290. Although she notably did not comment on whether this pleading would have been sufficient if pleadings had closed.
291. *McDonagh v Sunday Newspapers Ltd* [2005] 4 IR 528, 550–551.

[6.150] This was confirmed by Dunne J in *Quinn Insurance v Tribune Newspapers*,[292] where she held that:

> It goes without saying that a party is entitled to know the case being made against them. If necessary, particulars may be ordered to clarify the issues or to prevent the party from being taken by surprise at the trial of the action. However, a party is only entitled to know the broad outline of the case that he/she will have to meet. A party is not entitled to know the evidence that will be given against them in advance of the hearing. Further, it is not usual to order the names and addresses of witnesses to be furnished in advance of the hearing of an action.
>
> The absence of particulars in relation to a plea of justification may result in an order to furnish such particulars, although the level of specificity is not as great in this jurisdiction as is required in the jurisdiction of England and Wales. The Rules in England and Wales do require a party pleading justification to set out the particulars of justification in their defence. The Rules of the Superior Courts do not impose a similar requirement on the party pleading justification in this jurisdiction, although it has been noted in a number of decisions that a party pleading justification should not do so lightly or without consideration of the evidence available to support such a plea.
>
> Finally, the names and addresses of potential witnesses may be ordered in circumstances where not to do so would be to the litigious disadvantage of the party pleading justification and to the considerable advantage of a plaintiff in a manner that would be unfair. The overriding principle in deciding whether to order replies to particulars which would have the effect of disclosing the names and addresses of potential witnesses, should be the need to ensure a fair trial for both parties to the litigation.

Applying those principles to the case before her, she held that the plaintiff company was not entitled to the particulars sought in relation to the plea of justification. The relatively specific nature of the allegations made in the original piece – that the company had employed Gardaí to investigate claims, for example – meant that the plaintiffs were not at risk of a trial by ambush.

In the absence of any specific provision addressing this issue in the 2009 Act, there seems no reason to expect the Irish courts to adopt a different approach to the defence of truth under s 16.

Rumour

[6.151] Because liability attaches to the defamatory meaning of a statement (and s 11 would seem to apply only to repetition by the same person), an individual may be liable in defamation for repeating or reporting on third party rumours about the plaintiff. A defendant in such a situation who wishes to rely on s 16 seems likely to have to prove the truth of the rumours themselves as it is the content, rather than the mere existence of the

---

292. *Quinn Insurance v Tribune Newspapers* [2009] IEHC 229.

rumours, which generally carries the defamatory meaning.[293] They cannot rely on the fact that others have reported similar rumours in the past.[294]

[6.152] In addressing this issue, the English courts have developed a somewhat complicated distinction between different levels of allegation. These are commonly referred to as Chase level meanings, after the decision in *Chase v News Group Newspapers*[295] where the Court of Appeal observed that:

> The sting of a libel may be capable of meaning that a claimant has in fact committed some serious act, such as murder. Alternatively it may be suggested that the words mean that there are reasonable grounds to suspect that he/she has committed such an act. A third possibility is that they may mean that there are grounds for investigating whether he/she has been responsible for such an act.[296]

This has been followed in subsequent cases such that claims based on rumour and repetition are frequently described as level 1 (actual commission of the act), level 2 (grounds to suspect) or level 3 (grounds to investigate). Furthermore, these levels have been relied on to allow the application of different principles and approaches to each level.[297] There is a sense that this approach may be overly complex in that it relies on an arguably unduly compartmentalised analysis of such cases. It remains to be seen whether these categories will be adopted by the Irish courts. In general, however, the approach that seems to have been adopted to such cases is that the onus of proof is placed on a defendant to establish on the basis of non-hearsay[298] evidence adduced the truth of the underlying allegation, whether that be that the plaintiff actually committed the actions in question or that there were reasonable grounds for suspicion or investigation. As a matter of general principle, the English and Australian courts have tended to require that any such reasonable grounds for suspicion be based on the plaintiff's proven conduct, except in cases of clear circumstantial evidence.[299]

[6.153] It is self-evident that a defendant may face significant difficulties in raising this defence. While a defendant may have plausible grounds to suspect that an allegation or

---

293. This was the rule at common law where a defendant who has repeated an allegation of a defamatory nature about the claimant can only succeed in justifying it by proving the truth of the underlying allegation – not merely the fact that the allegation has been made. See *Cookson v Harewood* [1932] 2 KB 478; *Lewis v Daily Telegraph* [1964] AC 234; *Bennett v News Group Newspaper* [2002] EMLR 860; *Shah v Standard Chartered* [1999] 2 QB 241; *Miller v Associated Newspapers* [2005] EWHC 557 (QB).

294. *Associated Newspapers Ltd v Dingle* [1964] AC 371, [1962] 2 All ER 737.

295. *Chase v News Group Newspapers* [2002] EWCA Civ 1772.

296. *Chase v News Group Newspapers* [2002] EWCA Civ 1772, para 45.

297. See, for example, the lengthy analysis of the proper approach to cases of 'level 2' meaning in *Musa King v Telegraph Group Ltd* [2004] EMLR 429, para 22. See also *Al Rajhi Banking v Wall Street Journal* [2003] EWHC 1358 (QB), [27]; *Prince Radu of Hohenzollern v Houston* [2009] EWHC 398 (QB), paras 13–14.

298. *Musa King v Telegraph Group Ltd* [2004] EMLR 429.

299. See *Greig vv WIN Television NSW Pty Limited* [2009] NSWSC 632 (10 July 2009).

statement is true, this is an entirely different matter to establishing it as a true proposition to the satisfaction of a court.[300]

[6.154] This difficulty is compounded by the traditional principle that a plea of this sort amounts to an effective restatement of the offending allegation and, if unsuccessful, justifies an award of aggravated damages. Geoghegan J summarised this approach when observing that '[t]he plea of justification in a defamation action has always been considered to be a most serious plea and certainly not one to be made lightly.[301] Given the frequently high level of damages awarded by Irish juries before the enactment of the 2009 Act, this was a particularly important tactical question for defendants and their legal teams to consider.

[6.155] Cox has argued that this approach is 'inherently problematic'[302] on the basis that any injury to the plaintiff's reputation or feelings which may be caused by the examination of such issues in open court is a consequence of the decision to bring an action in defamation in the first place. Strictly speaking, the law's response to this would seem most likely to be that it was the defendant's publication of the alleged defamation which required the plaintiff to initiate proceedings as the appropriate means of vindicating their reputation. However, there is much to be said for the general sentiment expressed by Cox to the effect that it should not automatically follow from an unsuccessful plea of justification (or truth) that aggravated damages will be appropriate.[303] It may be that the changes to the damages regime introduced by the 2009 Act may remove some of the pressure from defendants considering whether to make such a plea. However, even allowing for this potential practical improvement on the former situation, it does seem questionable that a party who honestly mounts a defence where that defence has some reasonable basis but who fails to persuade a jury of their version of events should thereby, and for that reason alone, be penalised in aggravated damages.[304]

Absolute privilege

Constitutional privilege

[6.156] A constitutional immunity from suit applies to certain offices and institutions of the State. This applies in the defamation context in a manner similar to the defence of absolute privilege such that the relevant individuals may not be sued in respect of any publications or communications made by them within the limits of their immunity.

---

300. See, for example, *Liberace v Daily Mirror Newspapers* (1959) *The Times*, 18 June.
301. *Desmond v MGN Ltd* [2009] 1 IR 737, 740.
302. Cox, *Defamation Law* (FirstLaw, 2007), 145.
303. For the European Convention on Human Rights dimension to this argument, see *Miloslavsky v UK* (1995) 20 EHRR 442; *Independent News and Media and Independent Newspapers Ireland Ltd v Ireland* [2005] ECHR 55120/00; *John v Mirror Group Newspapers Ltd* [1997] QB 586; *Mosley v MGN* [2008] EWHC 1777 (QB).
304. See, for example, *De Rossa v Independent Newspapers* [1999] 4 IR 32.

[6.157] Thus, the President, for example, enjoys complete immunity 'for the exercise of the powers and functions of his office or for any act done or purporting to be done by him in the exercise and performance of these powers and functions'.[305] Similarly, members of the Oireachtas enjoy constitutional protection in relation to any utterances made in either House.[306]

[6.158] Members of the executive[307] and the judiciary[308] have also been acknowledged as having a privilege against suit.

Common law

[6.159] At common law, absolute privilege was a complete defence to an action for defamation. Unlike the defence of qualified privilege, it could not be defeated by proof of malice.[309] It applied to publications which were made in the context of a relationship[310] or situation[311] which was regarded by the law as being absolutely privileged. The complete nature of this defence meant that it was confined to a small category of 'exceptional cases'[312] where, for various reasons of public policy, it was felt to be necessary to encourage frank and unfettered communication. As Lord Hoffman explained, '[t]he policy of the immunity is to enable people to speak freely without fear of being sued, whether successfully or not'.[313]

[6.160] Because of the serious implications for the prospective plaintiff of being denied a remedy in relation to a false and defamatory statement, regardless of the circumstances in which it was made,[314] the common law courts have always been reluctant to extend the categories of absolute privilege. The Australian courts have warned, for example, that 'the general rule is that the extension of absolute privilege is 'viewed with the most jealous suspicion, and resisted, unless its necessity is demonstrated'[315] while the New Zealand courts agreed that '[t]he protection should not be given any wider application than is absolutely necessary in the interests of the administration of justice'.[316] However, the courts in other jurisdictions appeared to

---

305. Constitution of Ireland, Article 13.8.
306. Constitution of Ireland, Articless 15.12 and 15.13. See *Maguire v Ardagh* [2002] 1 IR 385; *Howlin v Morris* [2006] 2 IR 321.
307. *Chatterton v Secretary of State for India* [1895] 2 QB 189; *AG v Simpson* [1959] IR 105.
308. *Kemmy v Ireland* [2009] IEHC 178.
309. See *Horrocks v Lowe* [1975] AC 135.
310. *Watson v McEwan* [1905] AC 480.
311. *Fagan v Burgess* [1999] 3 IR 306; *Looney v Bank of Ireland* [1996] 1 IR 157.
312. *Hunter v Duckworth* [2003] IEHC 81.
313. *Taylor v Director of the Serious Fraud Office* [1998] 4 All ER 801, 813–814.
314. A challenge by a plaintiff to the principle of absolute privilege as a breach of Articles 6 and 13 was rejected by the European Court of Human Rights in *A v UK* [2002] ECHR 35373/97. See also *O'Faolain v Ireland* [1996] EHRR 326; *Westcott v Westcott* [2007] EWHC 2501 (QB).
315. *Mann v O'Neill* (1997) 145 ALR 682, 686. This was cited with approval in *Darker v Chief Constable of the West Midlands Police* [2000] 4 All ER 193, [2001] 1 AC 435.
316. *Rees v Sinclair* [1974] 1 NZLR 180.

accept that they were entitled, albeit in rare cases, to extend the categories of absolute privilege. Thus in *Meadow v General Medical Council*,[317] it was notable that Clarke MR, in accepting the Attorney General's submission that it was primarily for Parliament rather than the courts to create new categories of immunity, specifically reserved his position on whether the courts could nonetheless so act where it was necessary to do so. That he immediately added that 'the common law is always capable of development to meet new challenges'[318] would tend to suggest that he recognised a residual jurisdiction on the part of the courts to extend the scope of this common law defence.[319]

[6.161] Section 17 of the 2009 Act, on the other hand, appears to close off the possibility of the categories of absolute privilege being extended in Ireland in the future. Section 17(1) requires a defendant who wishes to raise the defence of absolute privilege to prove that the statement in respect of which the action was brought would, if it had been made immediately before the commencement of this section, have been considered under the law in force immediately before such commencement as having been made on an occasion of absolute privilege.

[6.162] This does, however, raise a question in relation to how this limitation may be interpreted by the courts. In particular, it is not clear how a court should approach a claim that the occasion in question is one which would have been absolutely privileged before the 2009 Act but where the Irish courts had not had an opportunity to confirm that this was the case. This would seem most problematic in circumstances where a common law court in another jurisdiction may have recognised a new category of absolute privilege before 2009. In general, however, by virtue of the fact that the common law has always been developed on the basis that the courts uncover existing principles rather than inventing new ones, this is an argument which would be potentially open to any defendant to make. However, it might be thought doubtful that a court would be willing to engage in such speculative hypothesising about how a case may have been decided in the past.

Section 17

[6.163] It is more likely to be the case, therefore, that a defendant seeking to claim that a publication was absolutely privileged under s 17(1) will have to identify a pre-2009 Act precedent or constitutional provision that applies to their situation if they are to be successful. Alternatively, they will be entitled to claim absolute privilege if they are covered by the provisions of s 17(2), which sets out a lengthy list of situations in respect

---

317. *Meadow v General Medical Council* [2007] 1 All ER 1.

318. *Meadow v General Medical Council* [2007] 1 All ER 1, 16.

319. Clarke MR also referred elsewhere in his decision to 'the principle … that any extension of the existing immunity should be confined as narrowly as reasonably possible', *Meadow v General Medical Council* [2007] 1 All ER 1, 9.

of which the defence of absolute privilege will be available. The list is reproduced in full below:

(2) Subject to section 11(2) of the Committees of the Houses of the Oireachtas (Compellability, Privileges and Immunities of Witnesses) Act 1997, and without prejudice to the generality of subsection (1), it shall be a defence to a defamation action for the defendant to prove that the statement in respect of which the action was brought was—

(a) made in either House of the Oireachtas by a member of either House of the Oireachtas,

(b) contained in a report of a statement, to which paragraph (a) applies, produced by or on the authority of either such House,

(c) made in the European Parliament by a member of that Parliament,

(d) contained in a report of a statement, to which paragraph (c) applies, produced by or on the authority of the European Parliament,

(e) contained in a judgment of a court established by law in the State,

(f) made by a judge, or other person, performing a judicial function,

(g) made by a party, witness, legal representative or juror in the course of proceedings presided over by a judge, or other person, performing a judicial function,

(h) made in the course of proceedings involving the exercise of limited functions and powers of a judicial nature in accordance with Article 37 of the Constitution, where the statement is connected with those proceedings,

(i) a fair and accurate report of proceedings publicly heard before, or decision made public by, any court—

　(i) established by law in the State, or

　(ii) established under the law of Northern Ireland,

(j) a fair and accurate report of proceedings to which a relevant enactment referred to in section 40 of the Civil Liability and Courts Act 2004 applies,

(k) a fair and accurate report of proceedings publicly heard before, or decision made public by, any court or arbitral tribunal established by an international agreement to which the State is a party including the Court of Justice of the European Communities, the Court of First Instance of the European Communities, the European Court of Human Rights and the International Court of Justice,

(l) made in proceedings before a committee appointed by either House of the Oireachtas or jointly by both Houses of the Oireachtas,

(m) made in proceedings before a committee of the European Parliament,

(n) made in the course of proceedings before a tribunal established under the Tribunals of Inquiry (Evidence) Acts 1921 to 2004, where the statement is connected with those proceedings,

(o) contained in a report of any such tribunal,

(p) made in the course of proceedings before a commission of investigation established under the Commissions of Investigation Act 2004, where the statement is connected with those proceedings,

(q) contained in a report of any such commission,

(r) made in the course of an inquest by a coroner or contained in a decision made or verdict given at or during such inquest,

(s)   made in the course of an inquiry conducted on the authority of a Minister of the Government, the Government, the Oireachtas, either House of the Oireachtas or a court established by law in the State,

(t)   made in the course of an inquiry conducted in Northern Ireland on the authority of a person or body corresponding to a person or body referred to in paragraph (s),

(u)   contained in a report of an inquiry referred to in paragraph (s) or (t),

(v)   made in the course of proceedings before an arbitral tribunal where the statement is connected with those proceedings,

(w)   made pursuant to and in accordance with an order of a court established by law in the State.

Qualified privilege

[6.164] The defence of qualified privilege is now governed by the provisions of ss 18 and 19 of the 2009 Act. Section 18(1) confirms that the common law principles which existed immediately before the coming into force of the 2009 Act will continue to apply, such that the defence will be available in respect of a statement which would have been considered at that time to have been made on an occasion of qualified privilege at common law.

[6.165] One of the features of this defence at common law which was repeatedly reiterated by the courts was that the categories of qualified privilege were not closed.[320] This flexibility is largely preserved under s 18. A defendant will be entitled to claim qualified privilege in relation to any statement which is published to a person or persons who had a legal, moral or social duty[321] to receive, or a legal, moral or social interest[322] in receiving the information contained in the statement[323] provided the defendant also had a corresponding duty to communicate, or interest in communicating, the information to such person or persons.[324] Privilege will also apply where the defendant believed upon reasonable grounds[325] that the person or persons in question had such a duty or interest, provided, once again, that the defendant had a corresponding duty to communicate, or interest in communicating, the information to them. However, the defence of qualified privilege shall fail if, in relation to the publication of the statement in respect of which the action was brought, the plaintiff proves that the defendant acted with malice.[326]

[6.166] The provisions of s 18(2) substantially mirror the principles previously applied at common law. At common law, a defendant was regarded as subject to a duty to

---

320.   *Hynes-O'Sullivan v O'Driscoll* [1988] IR 436; *Reynolds v Times Newspapers* [2001] 2 AC 127; *Roberts v Gable* [2008] QB 502.

321.   Defamation Act 2009, s 18(7).

322.   Defamation Act 2009, s 18(7).

323.   Defamation Act 2009, s 18(2)(a).

324.   Defamation Act 2009, s 18(2).

325.   Defamation Act 2009, s 18(2)(b).

326.   Defamation Act 2009, s 19(1).

publish where that duty was set down by statute,[327] established by contract,[328] required by regulatory rules or principles,[329] arose in an existing relationship[330] or where it was necessary to do so (or believed to be necessary to do so) in the interests of another party or in the public interest.[331] A duty would also be generally found to exist where information was requested of the defendant by a party with a legitimate interest in that information.[332] Lindley LJ attempted to provide a definition of what constituted a moral or social duty in *Stuart v Bell*:

> I take moral or social duty to mean a duty recognised by English people of ordinary intelligence and moral principle, but at the same time not a duty enforceable by legal proceedings, whether civil or criminal. My own conviction is that all or, at all events, the great mass of right-minded men in the position of the defendant would have considered it their duty, under the circumstances, [to publish] ...[333]

Nonetheless, the reference to a 'social' or 'moral' duty remains ambiguous and is likely to continue to generate uncertainty in the future about precisely when a duty or interest will be held to exist.

[6.167] The same difficulty arises in relation to situations where a defendant claims he or she had a legal, social or moral interest in the publication in question. The concept of an interest is plainly broader than that of a duty. This has accordingly been held at common law to protect a public rebuttal by an individual[334] or their agent[335] of charges laid against him or her by the plaintiff, provided the rebuttal does not go further than is necessary or proportionate to meet the accusation or allegation made against them.[336] Similarly, a statement made in defence of the defendant's rights or property will be covered by qualified privilege.[337] It would seem reasonable to argue, in Ireland, at least that this would also apply in relation to statements made in defence of the family unit, as protected by the Constitution.[338]

[6.168] For the defence of qualified privilege to be available, the defendant must be able to establish that the duty or interest which existed (or which was reasonably believed to exist) upon them corresponds to a reciprocal interest on the part of the person to whom

---

327. *Little v Pommeroy* (1873) IR 7 CL 79; *Henderson v Hackney LBC* [2010] EWHC 1651 (QB).
328. *Buckley v Kiernan* (1857) 7 ICLR 75; *Lillie v Newcastle CC* [2002] EWHC 1600; *Meade v Pugh* [2004] EWHC 408.
329. *Bray v Deutsche Bank* [2008] EWHC 1263 (QB).
330. *Moffat v Coats* (1906) 44 SLR 20; *Kearns v Bar Council* [2003] EWCA Civ 331.
331. *Stuart v Bell* [1891] 2 QB 341; *Hartery v Welltrade* [1978] ILRM 38.
332. *Meade v Pugh* [2004] EWHC 408.
333. *Stuart v Bell* (1891) 2 QB 341, 350. See also *Watt v Longsdon* [1930] 1 KB 130; *Beach v Freeson* [1972] 1 QB 14; *Loutchansky v Times Newspapers* [2001] EWCA Civ 1805.
334. *Adam v Ward* [1917] AC 309.
335. *Regan v Taylor* [2000] 1 All ER 307.
336. *Adam v Ward* [1917] AC 308; *Nevin v Carty* [1935] IR 397.
337. *Robinson v Jones* (1879) 4 LR Ir 391; *McCormack v Olsthoorn* [2004] IEHC 431. But see *L v L* [1992] 2 IR 77; *H v John Murphy & Sons Ltd* [1987] IR 621.
338. Constitution of Ireland, Articles 41 and 42.

the publication was made. This reciprocity is an essential ingredient of this defence.[339] Thus, the making of allegations by a senior politician and leader of the opposition in Jamaica against a senior police officer during a meeting was not covered by qualified privilege where those allegations were made in the knowledge that the media were present at the meeting. The Privy Council held that the publication of these allegations to the public via the media lacked the necessary reciprocity to found a defence of qualified privilege.[340]

[6.169] However, the simple presence of disinterested parties did not at common law lead automatically to the non-availability of the defence, if their presence was incidental and publication in the circumstances was reasonable. In this regard, it should also be noted that the 2009 Act provides that the defence of qualified privilege will not fail 'only' by reason of the fact that the statement was published to the person because the publisher mistook him or her for a person with a duty or interest in receiving the information contained in the statement.[341]

[6.170] The requirement that the publication must be made by a person with a duty or interest to a person with a reciprocal duty or interest would logically suggest that the privilege will only apply where there was this reciprocity of interest and duty. This means, for example, that a publication may not be privileged if the situation of privilege comes into existence after publication or, in the alternative, if it has ceased to exist prior to publication. This appears to have been the traditional understanding of the law.[342]

[6.171] However, the High Court in England has more recently held that the defence of qualified privilege cannot be defeated on the basis of passage of time alone. Tugenhadt J distinguished between the situation in *Ley v Hamilton* (where the once privileged relationship between the parties had come to an end at the time of publication) and the situation in which a publication is made in the context of a privileged relationship but is accessed (and thus re-published as a matter of law) at a subsequent date when the original occasion of privilege has come to an end. He concluded that it was necessary in an age of online archives for privilege to be capable of continuing to apply even after the original occasion had come to an end:

> The consequences of the proposition [the privilege would in some cases be lost by the passage of time] would make the law unworkable. It is hard to see how the keeper of a library or database can guard against the risk of liability for defamation where there is a publication of a statement written at a time when it was protected by common law privilege (of the reciprocal duty and interest type), but where the same reciprocal duty and interest may not subsist at some subsequent date upon which the document is read by a new reader.[343]

---

339. *Adam v Ward* [1917] AC 308; *Seray-Wurie v Charity Commission of England and Wales* [2008] EWHC 870 (QB).
340. *Seaga v Harper* [2008] UKPC 9, [2009] AC 1.
341. Defamation Act 2009, s 19(2).
342. *Ley v Hamilton* [1935] 153 LTR 384. See also Cox, *Defamation Law* (FirstLaw, 2007), 242.
343. *Bray v Deutsche Bank* [2008] EWHC 1263 (QB).

[6.172] It is submitted that this is a sensible approach to the defence of qualified privilege and that s 18(2) should be applied in a similar manner. Furthermore, the fact that the section uses the past tense to refer to the circumstances in which the 'statement was published' also supports this view.

[6.173] The 2009 Act also identifies an extensive range of situations and circumstances to which qualified privilege will apply. Section 18(3) applies the defence to any statements, determinations, reports, copies, extracts or summaries published in the following circumstances:

1. A fair and accurate report of any matter to which the defence of absolute privilege would apply (other than a fair and accurate report referred to in section 17(2)(i) or (k)).

2. A fair and accurate report of any proceedings publicly heard before, or decision made public by a court (including a court-martial) established under the law of any state or place (other than the State or Northern Ireland).

3. A fair and accurate report of the proceedings (other than court proceedings) presided over by a judge of a court established under the law of Northern Ireland.

4. A fair and accurate report of any proceedings in public of a house of any legislature (including a subordinate or federal legislature) of any state other than the State.

5. A fair and accurate report of proceedings in public of any body duly appointed, in the State, on the authority of a Minister of the Government, the Government, the Oireachtas, either House of the Oireachtas or a court established by law in the State to conduct a public inquiry on a matter of public importance.

6. A fair and accurate report of proceedings in public of any body duly appointed, in Northern Ireland, on the authority of a person or body corresponding to a person or body referred to in paragraph 5 to conduct a public inquiry on a matter of public importance.

7. A fair and accurate report of any proceedings in public of any body—

   (a)   that is part of any legislature (including a subordinate or federal legislature) of any state (other than the State), or

   (b)   duly appointed in a state other than the State, on the authority of a person or body corresponding to a person or body referred to in paragraph 5, to conduct a public inquiry on a matter of public importance.

8. A fair and accurate report of any proceedings in public of an international organisation of which the State or Government is a member or the proceedings which are of interest to the State.

9. A fair and accurate report of any proceedings in public of any international conference to which the Government sends a representative or observer or at which governments of states (other than the State) are represented.

10. A fair and accurate copy or extract from any register kept in pursuance of any law which is open to inspection by the public or of any other document which is required by law to be open to inspection by the public.

11. A fair and accurate report, copy or summary of any notice or advertisement published by or on the authority of any court established by law in the State or under the law of a Member State of the European Union, or any judge or officer of such a court.

12. A fair and accurate report or copy or summary of any notice or other document issued for the information of the public by or on behalf of any Department of State for which a Minister of the Government is responsible, local authority or the Commissioner of the Garda Síochána, or by or on behalf of a corresponding department, authority or officer in a Member State of the European Union.

13. A fair and accurate report or copy or summary of any notice or document issued by or on the authority of a committee appointed by either House of the Oireachtas or jointly by both Houses of the Oireachtas.

14. A determination of the Press Ombudsman referred to in paragraph 9(2) of Schedule 2.

15. A determination of the Press Council referred to in paragraph 9(4) of Schedule 2 or a report of the Press Council relating to the past performance of its functions.

16. Any statement published pursuant to, and in accordance with, a determination of the Press Ombudsman or the Press Council.

17. Any statement made during the investigation or hearing of a complaint by the Press Ombudsman in accordance with Schedule 2.

18. Any statement made during the hearing of an appeal from a determination of the Press Ombudsman in accordance with Schedule 2.

19. Any statement published by a person in accordance with a requirement under an Act of the Oireachtas whether or not that person is the author of the statement.[344]

The most significant requirement here is that a publication will only be protected in many of these situations where the defendant is able to establish that it was a 'fair and accurate' report or copy. This means that a publisher must take care to avoid any suggestion of bias, exaggeration, sensationalism or of a particular agenda[345] in a report and should confine themselves to a fair summary of all known facts if they wish to have the option of relying on s 18(3).

[6.174] Section 18(3) will also not provide protection for the publication of any statement where that publication is prohibited by law, or where the statement in question is not of public concern and the publication is not for the public benefit.[346]

[6.175] Section 18(4) meanwhile provides protection for a similar list of situations in respect of which the defence of qualified privilege may be available:

1. A fair and accurate report of the proceedings, findings or decisions of an association, or a committee or governing body of an association, whether

---

344. Defamation Act 2009, Sch 1, Pt 1.
345. *Henry v BBC* [2005] EWHC 1756.
346. Defamation Act 2009, s 18(5).

incorporated or not in the State or in a Member State of the European Union, relating to a member of the association or to a person subject, by contract or otherwise, to control by the association.

2. A fair and accurate report of the proceedings at any public meeting, held in the State or in a Member State of the European Union, being a meeting held for a lawful purpose and for the discussion of any matter of public concern whether the admission to the meeting is general or restricted.

3. A fair and accurate report of the proceedings at a general meeting, whether in the State or in a Member State of the European Union, of any company or association established by or under statute or incorporated by charter.

4. A fair and accurate report of the proceedings at any meeting or sitting of any local authority or the Health Service Executive, and any corresponding body in a Member State of the European Union.

5. A fair and accurate report of a press conference convened by or on behalf of a body to which this Part applies or the organisers of a public meeting within the meaning of paragraph 2 to give an account to the public of the proceedings or meeting.

6. A fair and accurate report of a report to which the defence of qualified privilege would apply.

7. A copy or fair and accurate report or summary of any ruling, direction, report, investigation, statement (including any advice, admonition or censure given or administered by the Irish Takeover Panel under section 20 of the Irish Takeover Panel Act 1997) or notice made, given, prepared, published or served by the Irish Takeover Panel.

However, the defence will not be open to a defendant who seeks to rely on s 18(4) if the plaintiff is able to prove that he or she requested that the defendant publish in like form a reasonable statement by way of explanation or contradiction and that the defendant refused or failed to do so in a manner that is not adequate or reasonable having regard to all of the circumstances.

[6.176] It should also be noted that the Act's definition of the circumstances in which the defence of qualified privilege will be available is expressed to be 'without prejudice' to the Act's preservation of the defences available at common law prior to the passing of the Act. This raises again the possibility that a defendant who finds themselves outside the parameters of s 18(2), (3) or (4) may seek to argue that their position was protected at common law before the passing of the Act, even in the absence of a judicial authority to that effect. This argument may have somewhat more force in this context given the courts' traditional willingness to recognise new categories of qualified privilege. However, as s 18(2), in particular, largely reflects the principles applied at common law, it is difficult to imagine many circumstances in which this issue would realistically arise.

Malice[347]

[6.177] Although the defence of qualified privilege can be defeated by malice, this is often very difficult for a plaintiff to establish.[348] Section 19(1) makes clear that the onus of proving malice continues to rest on the plaintiff. The English courts have emphasised the high threshold which a plaintiff has to meet in this regard, holding that 'the law requires evidence of at least probability of malice; mere possibility is not enough'.[349] Furthermore, even where a plaintiff succeeds in establishing malice against one of the defendants, the defence will continue to be available to any other defendants who meet the relevant criteria unless those defendants were vicariously liable for the acts or omissions of the first-mentioned defendant which gave rise to the cause of action concerned.[350]

[6.178] For the purposes of qualified privilege, it has been held that 'malice may take the form of either a dominant improper motive or an absence of honest belief in the truth of what was published or both'.[351] Thus, the mere fact that a defendant was 'hasty, prejudiced or foolish in jumping to a conclusion' will not constitute malice.[352] The courts have emphasised that the intention of the defendant is critical in considering whether the privilege has been lost. This is a subjective rather than an objective standard.[353] This reflects the logic, as Lord Diplock explained it in *Horrocks v Lowe*, that:

> [T]o destroy the privilege the desire to injure must be the dominant motive for the defamatory publication; knowledge that it will have that effect is not enough if the defendant is nevertheless acting in accordance with a sense of duty or in bona fide protection of his own legitimate interests.[354]

[6.179] Lord Diplock went on to set out in some detail the principles to be applied in considering whether a plaintiff has established malice on the part of the defendant:

> The motive with which a person published defamatory matter can only be inferred from what he did or said or knew. If it be proved that he did not believe that what he published was true this is generally conclusive evidence of express malice, for no sense of duty or desire to protect his own legitimate interests can justify a man in telling deliberate and injurious falsehoods about another, save in the exceptional case where a person may be under a duty to pass on, without endorsing, defamatory reports made by some other person.

---

347. For further discussion of the amendments made prior to the enactment of this section of the 2009 Act, see O'Dowd 'Ireland's new Defamation Act' [2009] 2 *Journal of Media Law* 173.
348. *Hennessy v K-Tel Ltd* (12 June 1997, unreported), SC.
349. *Ratiu v Conway* [2005] EWCA Civ 1302, para 146. See also *Telnikoff v Matusevitch* [1991] 1 QB 102, [1990] 3 All ER 865.
350. Defamation Act 2009, s 19(3).
351. *Rackham v Sandy* [2005] EWHC 482 (QB).
352. *Doyle v Canty* [2005] IEHC 234.
353. *Loveless v Earl* [1999] EMLR 530; *Ratiu v Conway* [2005] EWCA Civ 1302.
354. *Horrocks v Lowe* [1975] AC 135, 149.

Apart from those exceptional cases, what is required on the part of the defamer to entitle him to the protection of the privilege is positive belief in the truth of what he published or, as it is generally though tortologously termed, 'honest belief'. If he publishes untrue defamatory matter recklessly, without considering or caring whether it be true or not, he is in this, as in other branches of the law, treated as if he knew it to be false. But indifference to the truth of what he publishes is not to be equated with carelessness, impulsiveness or irrationality in arriving at a positive belief that it is true. The freedom of speech protected by the law of qualified privilege may be availed of by all sorts and conditions of men. In affording to them immunity from suit if they have acted in good faith in compliance with a legal or moral duty or in protection of a legitimate interest the law must take them as it finds them. In ordinary life it is rare indeed for people to form their beliefs by a process of logical deduction from facts ascertained by a rigorous search for all available evidence and a judicious assessment of its probative value. In greater or in less degree according to their temperaments, their training, their intelligence, they are swayed by prejudice, rely on intuition instead of reasoning, leap to conclusions on inadequate evidence and fail to recognise the cogency of material which might cast doubt on the validity of the conclusions they reach. But despite the imperfection of the mental process by which the belief is arrived at it may still be 'honest', that is, a positive belief that the conclusions they have reached are true. The law demands no more.

Even a positive belief in the truth of what is published on a privileged occasion – which is presumed unless the contrary is proved – may not be sufficient to negative express malice if it can be proved that the defendant misused the occasion for some purpose other than that for which the privilege is accorded by the law. The commonest case is where the dominant motive which actuates the defendant is not a desire to perform the relevant duty or to protect the relevant interest, but to give vent to his personal spite or ill will towards the person he defames. If this be proved, then even positive belief in the truth of what is published will not enable the defamer to avail himself of the protection of the privilege to which he would otherwise have been entitled. There may be instances of improper motives which destroy the privilege apart from personal spite. A defendant's dominant motive may have been to obtain some private advantage unconnected with the duty or the interest which constitutes the reason for the privilege. If so, he loses the benefit of the privilege despite his positive belief that what he said or wrote was true.

Judges and juries should, however, be very slow to draw the inference that a defendant was so far actuated by improper motives as to deprive him of the protection of the privilege unless they are satisfied that he did not believe that what he said or wrote was true or that he was indifferent to its truth or falsity. The motives with which human beings act are mixed. They find it difficult to have the sin but love the sinner. Qualified privilege would be illusory, and the public interest that it is meant to serve defeated, if the protection which it affords were lost merely because a person, although acting in compliance with a duty or in protection of a legitimate interest, disliked the person whom he defamed or was indignant at what he believed to be that person's conduct and welcomed the opportunity of exposing it. It is only where his desire to comply with the relevant duty or to protect the relevant interest plays no significant part in his motives for publishing what he believes to be true that 'express malice' can properly be found.[355]

[6.180] It is clear from Lord Diplock's discussion, as well as from a purely common sense consideration of the matter, that proof that a defendant was aware of the falsity of the impugned statement (or, indeed, did not believe in or care about the truth of the statement) may sometimes be sufficient – as a matter of practice – to establish malice. That does not mean, however, that lack of belief is the same as malice. Thus, for example, a conscious and erroneous communication about the plaintiff may not be regarded as malice where the defendant acted without any ill intent.[356] This was recognised by Gleeson CJ in the High Court of Australia in *Roberts v Bass*[357] where, following a consideration of Lord Diplock's decision, he explained that:

> If the defendant knew that the statement was untrue when he or she made it, it is almost invariably conclusive evidence of malice. That is because a defendant who knowingly publishes false and defamatory material almost certainly has some improper motive for doing so, despite the inability of the plaintiff to identify the motive. In *Barbaro v Amalgamated Television Services Pty Ltd* (1985) 1 NSWLR 30 at 51, Hunt J said that '[i]n some of the older authorities, an absence of honest belief on the part of the defendant is treated merely as some evidence of an indirect motive which alone is said to constitute express malice, but the better view, in my opinion, is to treat the two as different kinds of malice'. His Honour cited no authority for this novel proposition. Some years later, in *Hanhrahan v Ainsworth* (1990) 22 NSWLR 73 at 102–103, Clarke JA said that, since Horrocks 'it has been accepted that if it is proved that a person has made a defamatory statement without an honest belief in its truth or for a dominant improper purpose … malice will be made out'.

> The knowledge and experience of Justice Hunt in defamation matters is well recognised. But with great respect to his Honour and Clarke JA, they erred in asserting that lack of honest belief defeated a defence of qualified privilege. There is no basis in principle or authority for treating knowledge of falsity or lack of honest belief as a separate head of, or equivalent to, malice. In the law of qualified privilege, the common law has always regarded malice as the publishing of defamatory material with an improper motive. Knowledge of falsity is 'almost conclusive evidence' that the defendant may have some improper motive in publishing the material and that it actuated the publication. That judges have treated knowledge of falsity as almost conclusive evidence of malice is no ground, however, for treating it as a separate head of, or equivalent to, malice. In some circumstances, lack of honest belief in what has been published may also give rise to the inference that the matter was published for a motive or purpose that is foreign to the occasion of qualified privilege. Nothing in Lord Diplock's speech in *Horrocks* supports treating the defendant's knowledge or lack of belief as a separate head of, or equivalent to, malice. Indeed, Lord Diplock expressly said

355. *Horrocks v Lowe* [1975] AC 135, 149.
356. *Berber v Dunnes Stores* [2006] IEHC 327.
357. *Roberts v Bass* [2002] HCA 57, 77–78.

that, if it is proved that the defendant did not believe that what he or she published was true, it was 'generally conclusive evidence' of improper motive.

This analysis is supported by the decision of Hedigan J in *Tolan v An Bord Pleanála*[358] where he held that a defence of qualified privilege was not available to the defendants in relation to their refusal to remove a letter from a publicly accessible record where they were aware that it was false and defamatory. While the court made no finding in relation to malice, it held that the privilege was not available in circumstances where 'the defendants have no belief whatever in the truth of the words and, indeed, acknowledge them as false'.

Excessive or disproportionate publication

[6.181] One issue which is likely to feature in future litigation in this area is the question of whether the defence of qualified privilege may be lost – or, more probably, partly lost – in circumstances where the publication which is the subject of proceedings went beyond what was reasonable or proportionate on the occasion of qualified privilege in question. Historically, the courts tended not to examine the relevance or necessity of a publication once it occurred within the confines of a privileged relationship.[359] The rationale for this rule was set out in *Horrocks v Lowe* as follows:

> Logically it might be said that such irrelevant matter falls outside the privilege altogether. But if this were so it would involve application by the court of an objective test of relevance to every part of the defamatory matter published on the privileged occasion; whereas, as everyone knows, ordinary human beings vary in their ability to distinguish that which is logically relevant from that which is not and few, apart from lawyers, have had any training which qualifies them to do so. So the protection afforded by the privilege would be illusory if it were lost in respect of any defamatory matter which on logical analysis could be shown to be irrelevant to the fulfilment of the duty or the protection of the right upon which the privilege was founded.

> As Lord Dunedin pointed out in *Adam v Ward* [1917] AC 309 at 326, 327, [1916–17] All ER Rep at 167) the proper rule as respects irrelevant defamatory matter incorporated in a statement made on a privileged occasion is to treat it as one of the factors to be taken into consideration in deciding whether, in all the circumstances, an inference that the defendant was actuated by express malice can properly be drawn. As regards irrelevant matter the test is not whether it is logically relevant but whether, in all the circumstances, it can be inferred that the defendant either did not believe it to be true or, though believing it to be true, realised that it had nothing to do with the particular duty or interest on which the privilege was based, but nevertheless seized the opportunity to drag in irrelevant defamatory matter to vent his personal spite, or for some other improper motive. Here, too, judges and juries should be slow to draw this inference.[360]

---

358. *Tolan v An Bord Pleanála* [2008] IEHC 275.
359. *Kearns v Bar Council* [2003] EWCA Civ 331.
360. *Horrocks v Lowe* [1974] 1 All ER 662, 670–671, [1975] AC 135, 151.

However, a different approach was adopted more recently by the English courts in the decision of *Clift v Slough BC*.[361] It was held there that qualified privilege might not apply to protect information which was not necessary for the performance of the particular duty or the protection of the particular interest upon which the privilege is founded, and that a court could review the impugned publication in some detail in order to determine which aspects of publication were relevant and which were not.

[6.182] The reasons for this departure from the traditional approach were two-fold. In the first place, the court had regard to the fact that technological changes had increased the opportunities and likelihood of excessive and irrelevant publication:

> Documents are now normally held and communicated electronically. It is easy and common to circulate by e-mail to very large numbers of people, within (and outside) an organisation, information which, in the past, would have been addressed in a letter or memo to very few. It is therefore much more likely than in the past that information will be communicated to persons to whom no duty is owed, or who do not have a legally sufficient interest in receiving the information.[362]

Secondly, the court also concluded that the traditional approach, which had emphasised the importance of free and frank disclosure, provided inadequate protection for the putative plaintiff's rights under Article 8 of the Convention.

> The common law in the form it had reached up to the mid–1990s had the significant advantage of certainty, at least in those cases where a duty and interest clearly existed … But the important criticism to be made of the common law is more fundamental. There is obvious potential injustice to the person who is the subject of a reference or warning.[363]

[6.183] The court accordingly examined whether the circulation of the information in the e-mail which was the subject of that claim was necessary and proportionate in the circumstances of the case. It concluded that the publication of the e-mail to some employees was justified but that the disclosure of the information in question to others was not. As a result, publication to this latter group of employees was not protected by qualified privilege.

[6.184] It does not appear as if an Irish court has had the opportunity to consider this development. The provisions of the 2009 Act provides little clear guidance as to the way in which this issue should be addressed. On balance, the fact that s 18(2) confines the defence to situations where the corresponding duty and interest pertain to the 'information contained in the statement' would tend to support the approach adopted in *Clift*. The court's reasoning in *Clift* is also persuasive. At the same time, it should also be borne in mind that the *Clift* rule would require persons operating in situations that are generally accepted as being covered by privilege to nonetheless monitor their communications more closely lest a particular portion of it be regarded as going beyond

---

361. *Clift v Slough BC* [2009] 4 All ER 756.
362. *Clift v Slough BC* [2009] 4 All ER 756, 784.
363. *Clift v Slough BC* [2009] 4 All ER 756, 786.

what was necessary or proportionate. It might be thought that this is how such persons should act anyway, given the importance of a person's right to reputation and good name. However, any requirement for greater caution would reduce the scope for the sort of free and frank communication which has traditionally justified the defence of qualified privilege. It may be that the courts, in assessing whether the approach adopted in Clift is required by the Constitution and/or by Article 8 of the Convention, may have to consider whether these notions of necessity and proportionality are sufficiently flexible to allow the law to strike an appropriate balance between these competing values.[364]

Honest opinion

[6.185] Section 20 of the 2009 Act establishes a new defence of 'honest opinion', which effectively replaces the defence of fair comment at common law. This defence will be available to a defendant who can prove that, in the case of a statement consisting of an opinion, the opinion was honestly held.[365]

[6.186] It has been accepted by the courts that the availability of this type of defence reflects the importance from the point of view of freedom of expression of facilitating free expression of opinions. Article 40.6.1°(i), it will be recalled, expressly guarantees 'the right of citizens to express freely their convictions and opinions'. The relationship between the common law defence of fair comment and freedom of expression was explained in more detail by Lord Nicholls in *Tse Wai Chun Paul v Albert Cheng*:[366]

> [T]he purpose for which the defence of fair comment exists is to facilitate freedom of expression by commenting on matters of public interest. This accords with the constitutional guarantee of freedom of expression. And it is in the public interest that everyone should be free to express his own, honestly held, views on such matters, subject always to the safeguards provided by the objective limits mentioned above. These safeguards ensure that defamatory comments can be seen for what they are, namely, comments as distinct from statements of fact. They also ensure that those reading the comments have the material enabling them to make up their own minds on whether they agree or disagree.[367]

This means that an opinion may be expressed in 'pungent and offensive terms' but still enjoy protection on the basis of the principle that 'hard-hitting comments may be made on matters of public interest without the author being hobbled by the constraints of conventional good manners'.[368]

---

364. One option, for example, could be to focus on the necessity for full, frank and uninhibited communication in a particular relationship, such that the law may allow greater latitude for statements made in the course of some relationships rather than others. This might provide greater protection for a plaintiff while continuing to offer some degree of certainty to those acting within those categories about the possible legal consequences of their actions.
365. Defamation Act 2009, s 20(1).
366. *Tse Wai Chun Paul v Albert Cheng* [2001] EMLR 777.
367. *Tse Wai Chun Paul v Albert Cheng* [2001] EMLR 777, para 41.
368. *Keady v Guardian Newspapers* [2003] EWHC 1565, para 21.

[6.187] The circumstances in which an opinion will be regarded as honestly held are relatively narrow. A defendant must be able to prove that either the defendant believed in the truth of the opinion at the time of publication or, where the defendant is not the author of the opinion, believed that the author believed it to be true.[369] In addition, if the opinion is one based on allegations of fact, those facts must have been specified in the statement containing the opinion,[370] be facts which would be covered by privilege,[371] or if referred to in the statement, be facts which were known, or might reasonably be expected to have been known, by the persons to whom the statement was published.[372] Finally, it is also necessary to show that the opinion related to a matter of public interest.[373]

[6.188] The rechristening of this defence as one of honest opinion reflects the way in which the common law has developed in recent decades. At common law, the defence would fail if it could be shown that the comment was not fair. In practice, however, this test of fairness was concerned with issues of honesty. As McMahon & Binchy explained, 'the comment must be fair in the sense that it must be honestly made'.[374] This was recognised by Lord Nicholls in *Reynolds v Times Newspapers Ltd* when he recommended that the traditional terminology of fairness ought to be replaced with an approach which focused more clearly on considerations of honesty.

> Traditionally one of the ingredients of this defence is that the comment must be fair, fairness being judged by the objective standard of whether any fair-minded person could honestly express the opinion in question. Judges have emphasised the latitude to be applied in interpreting this standard. So much so, that the time has come to recognise that in this context the epithet 'fair' is now meaningless and misleading. Comment must be relevant to the facts to which it is addressed. It cannot be used as a cloak for mere invective. But the basis of our public life is that the crank, the enthusiast, may say what he honestly thinks as much as the reasonable person who sits on a jury. The true test is whether the opinion, however exaggerated, obstinate or prejudiced, was honestly held by the person expressing it.[375]

Burden on defendant

[6.189] However, while the creation of a defence of honest opinion may mirror developments at common law, the drafting of s 20 suggests that there may be differences between the new statutory defence and the old common law defence of fair comment. At common law, the test of honest opinion was regarded as a primarily objective standard. They considered whether 'the comment [was] one which could have been made by an

---

369. Defamation Act 2009, s 20(2)(a).
370. Defamation Act 2009, s 20(2)(b)(i)I. See *Oliver v Northumbria CC* [2003] EWHC 2417.
371. Defamation Act 2009, s 20(2)(b)(ii).
372. Defamation Act 2009, s 20(2)(b)(i)II. See, for example, *Kemsely v Foot* [1952] AC 345; *Lowe v Associated Newspapers* [2006] EWHC 320.
373. Defamation Act 2009, s 20(2)(c).
374. *The Law of Torts* (3rd edn, 2000), [34.218].
375. *Reynolds v Times Newspapers Ltd* [1999] 4 All ER 609.

honest person, however prejudiced he might be, and however exaggerated or obstinate his views'.[376] A defendant did not have to produce evidence to demonstrate his own subjective honesty of opinion. The court asked rather 'whether a hypothetical commentator could express the views in question honestly'.[377] A defendant only had to establish that an honest person could have held the opinion in question, not that he would have.[378]

[6.190] The defendant's subjective opinion was relevant only to the extent that the plaintiff was able to prove malice on the part of the publisher. The plaintiff was able to rebut the defence by proving that when he made his comment the defendant was, in the time-hallowed expression, 'actuated by malice'.[379] Unlike the preliminary question of whether the opinion was one which could be honestly held, the question of malice was subjective. 'It looks to the defendant's state of mind'.[380] The defendant's own views would only be capable of defeating the defence in the very limited circumstances where a plaintiff could, first of all, introduce some evidence of lack of honesty and, secondly, provide enough evidence to satisfy the very high standard of malice. In the context of the fair comment defence, malice applied only where a defendant had published the comment 'while not believing in its truth'.[381]

[6.191] By contrast, s 20(2) appears to be drafted in a way which requires a defendant to prove either that he or she believed in the truth of the opinion or, where relevant, that he or she believed that the author believed it to be true. This effectively incorporates the absence of malice (the burden of establishing which formerly rested on the plaintiff)[382] as one of the essential ingredients of the defence of honest opinion. As s 20(1) places the burden of establishing this defence on the defendant, this appears both a more onerous and a more subjective test than that which applied at common law. The fact that the onus appears to rest on the defendant[383] to establish that he honestly believed something to be true may make this defence much more difficult to invoke.[384] There is a crucial distinction between a defence which may be defeated by proof of an absence of honest belief in the truth of an opinion and one which can only be invoked where an honest belief in the truth of an opinion can be positively established in evidence. A belief cannot be proved as true. Opinions, 'operating in the realm of norms rather than facts, are simply incapable of ... [undergoing an] empirical process of validation or refutation'.[385] Given the importance from a constitutional or Convention perspective of

---

376. *Cheng Albert v Tse Wai Chun Paul* (2000) 10 BHRC 525, 529, Lord Nicholls.
377. *Branson v Bower* [2002] QB 737, para 5.
378. *Convery v Irish News* [2008] NICA 14, para 65.
379. *Cheng Albert v Tse Wai Chun Paul* (2000) 10 BHRC 525, 530.
380. *Cheng Albert v Tse Wai Chun Paul* (2000) 10 BHRC 525, 530.
381. Cox, *Defamation Law* (FirstLaw, 2007), 176. See *Blake v Associated Newspapers* [2002] EWHC 677.
382. It is instructive to note that the courts had recognised that this was a difficult burden for a plaintiff to discharge. See, for example, *Telnikoff v Matusevitvh* [1991] 4 All ER 817.
383. Defamation Act 2009, s 20(1).
384. *WIC Radio Ltd v Simpson* [2008] 2 SCR 420.
385. McMahon & Binchy at [34.210].

allowing relatively free expression of opinions and ideas, it might be argued that s 20(2) should be interpreted in a way which does not impose an unduly onerous burden on defendants in seeking to rely on s 20.

[6.192] That an unduly strict approach to the defence of honest opinion may be problematic is illustrated by the Article 10 case law of the European Court of Human Rights. The court has consistently held that it is impossible to prove the truth of an opinion or belief. The imposition of a legal requirement to do so contravenes the guarantee of freedom of expression under Article 10. As the court observed in *Lingens v Austria*:

> [A] careful distinction needs to be made between facts and value-judgments. The existence of facts can be demonstrated, whereas the truth of value-judgments is not susceptible of proof … Under [the relevant Austrian law] … journalists in a case such as this cannot escape conviction for the matters specified in paragraph 1 unless they can prove the truth of their statements … As regards value-judgments this requirement is impossible of fulfilment and it infringes freedom of opinion itself, which is a fundamental part of the right secured by Article 10 of the Convention.[386]

[6.193] The court has nonetheless held that the expression of opinions on matters of public interest may be regulated by the State. In *Jerusalem v Austria*,[387] the court found that the Austrian courts had infringed Article 10 by treating an opinion as a statement of fact which was therefore capable of being proved as true. The court went on, however, to review the legitimacy of the expressed opinion in terms of its basis in fact. The court observed (at para 43) that:

> [E]ven where a statement amounts to a value judgment, the proportionality of an interference may depend on whether there exists a sufficient factual basis for the impugned statement, since even a value judgment without any factual basis to support it may be excessive.

[6.194] The question of what threshold a defendant could be required to meet to establish honest opinion was considered by Eady J in *Branson v Bower*. He expressed the view that:

> A defendant should not be required to justify value judgments or opinions expressed on matters of public interest as though they were matters of objectively verifiable fact. That conclusion is not only in line with established common law principles but is also consonant with the jurisprudence of the European Court of Human Rights.[388]

---

386. *Lingens v Austria* (1986) 8 EHRR 407, para 46. See also *Dalban v Romania* [1999] ECHR 28114/95 (Application No 28114/95) 28 September 1999; *McVicar v United Kingdom* (Application No 46311/99) 7 May 2002; *Pedersen v Denmark* (Application No 49017/99) 19 June 2003; *Dyuldin v Russia* (Application No 25968/02) 31 July 2007; *Kulis v Poland* (Application No 15601/02) 26 February 2008.
387. *Jerusalem v Austria* (2003) 37 EHRR 25. See also *Prager v Austria* (1996) 21 EHRR 1; *De Haes v Belgium* (1998) 25 EHRR 1.
388. *Branson v Bower* [2002] QB 737, para 1.

This reflected the fact that:

> It is clear (as illustrated in a number of European cases) that there is a significant inhibition upon freedom of speech if one is required to prove the unprovable. A commentator may be able to prove facts objectively, but it is neither just nor logical to seek to subject opinion to the same test.[389]

[6.195] Eady J thus held that the imposition of a standard higher than that of honesty was questionable under Article 10.

> It is necessary to acknowledge that if a defendant does indeed have to pass any more restrictive test, going beyond that of honesty, then the consequence would be a significant inhibiting effect on freedom of expression on matters of public interest. There would be an especially chilling effect, at least in theory, upon those who wish to criticise persons in public life or those with sufficient wealth or power to impact upon the way we live our lives.[390]

[6.196] Similarly, in *Hamilton v Clifford* the same judge reiterated his view that a requirement to prove the truth of a published opinion on a matter of public interest would constitute an unacceptable infringement of freedom of expression:

> English law needs to accommodate the strand of Article 10 jurisprudence which is intended to protect libel defendants, and journalists in particular, from having to prove the unprovable. It is consistent with established English principles in drawing a clear distinction between fact and comment. There is nothing inherently inconsistent with Article 10 in a body of law which requires journalists to treat facts as sacred and to be prepared to prove them where necessary. By contrast, there would be an undesirable inhibition on the journalist's role if he were also required to justify matters which are incapable of objective verification.[391]

For this reason, it is submitted that it may be necessary to read the defence of honest opinion in a way which does not oblige the defendant to prove by positive evidence that he subjectively believed in the truth of the statement. Decisions such as *Jerusalem v Austria* confirm that it is permissible to require – as was the case at common law – a statement of opinion to have some minimum basis in fact. It may go too far, however, to require a defendant to adduce positive evidence of an honest belief in the *truth* of a statement. This would mean, for example, that the section arguably would not apply to a situation where a person made a statement of opinion without a determined view of the truth or otherwise of that opinion but in the honest belief that there are reasonable grounds to believe that it *might* be (or even probably is) true. It is submitted that the law should continue to allow the defendant's state of mind to be established on the basis of inferences from the circumstances such that it ought to be sufficient to establish that the opinion was one which a person in his position could have believed to be true. If s 20(2) cannot be read in a way that facilitates this, it may be open to challenge on constitutional or (more probably) Convention grounds.

---

389. *Branson v Bower* [2002] QB 737, para 27.
390. *Branson v Bower* [2002] QB 737, para 23.
391. *Hamilton v Clifford* [2004] EWHC 1542 (QB), para 56.

Level of belief required

[6.197] A further potential difficulty with s 20(2)(a) is the requirement that a defendant who is not the author of a statement must believe the author to believe it to be true. This could pose problems for media organisations by effectively obliging them to form a view as to the honesty of beliefs held by those whom they interview, or on whom they wish to report. For example, it may be the case that a news organisation wishes to report on the fact that one person has made an allegation against another where the making of the allegation is the newsworthy aspect of the report. This would apply also to some newspaper columnists. Where those columnists or opinion writers are known controversialists, can it always be said that they truly believe in the opinions being expressed? The same can be said of thought pieces or publications where the author's opinion or argument is expressed in a deliberately exaggerated or satirical manner.[392] While it is possible that some of these publications may be covered by other defences in some situations,[393] these examples demonstrate how a requirement to form a view as to the beliefs of another person may, in some circumstances, be incompatible with the role of a journalist, columnist or media organisation.

[6.198] Somewhat similar concerns apply in relation to s 20(3) of the Act, which provides that the defence of honest opinion shall fail, if the opinion concerned is based on allegations of fact which were specified in the statement, or were known or might reasonably be expected to be known to the reader or viewer of the statement unless the defendant is able to prove the truth of those allegations. Where a defendant cannot prove the truth of all of the allegations, they may still rely on the defence if, having regard to the allegations of fact that can be proven to be true, the opinion is shown to be honestly held.[394] This latter provision may go some way to address the sort of Convention or constitutional concerns discussed above. However, the drafting of this section is somewhat ambiguous. Section 20(3)(a)(ii) appears to allow a defendant to maintain the defence on the simple basis that the opinion was honestly held, regardless of their ability to prove all of the allegations of fact to be true.[395]

[6.199] The definition of when an opinion is honestly held is contained in s 20(2) but this is expressly stated to be subject to sub-s (3). However, a natural reading of the negative way in which sub-s (3) is expressed would seem to indicate it can only apply after the defence has been provisionally established under sub-s (2). A defendant relying on sub-s (3) will thus already have proven that he or she believed in the truth of their opinion,[396] that it was based on allegations of fact and that it was on a matter of public interest.

---

392. See for example, *Kulis v Poland*, App No 27209/03, 6 October 2009; *Silva v Portugal*, App No 41665/07, 20 October 2009.
393. See, for example, Defamation Act 2009, s 26.
394. Defamation Act 2009, s 20(3)(a)(ii).
395. It is not clear whether this option is available, even as a matter of principle, to a defendant who cannot prove any of the allegations of fact to be true.
396. Or believed that the author believed in the truth of his or her opinion.

In general, it would seem more difficult to positively prove a belief in the truth of a statement than it would be to demonstrate an honestly held belief. This begs the question of what additional consideration, if any, should be taken into account as a result of the reference to an honestly held belief under sub-s (3)?

Or can sub-s (3) operate as a stand-alone assessment of the defendant's honesty of belief, as applied at common law? This would not seem the most obvious reading of sub-s (3) but it may alleviate some of the concerns considered in the previous section. It is arguably also supported by the fact that sub-s (3) specifically refers to s 2(b)(i), which suggests that it might appropriately be read as qualifying s 2(b)(i) only and not the other parts of s 20(2).

[6.200] Section 20(3)(b) further provides that the defence will fail in respect of an opinion based on allegations of fact which would be privileged unless the defendant can prove the truth of those allegations,[397] or, failing that, where the opinion could not reasonably be understood as implying that those allegations were true and at the time of the publication of the opinion the defendant did not know or could not reasonably have been expected to know that those allegations were untrue.[398]

The distinction between fact and opinion

[6.201] As at common law,[399] s 20(1) confirms that the defence is available only in respect of 'a statement consisting of an opinion'. As many publications will consist of a mixture of fact and opinion, any issue will frequently arise in relation to whether a particular publication, or portion of a publication, should be regarded as a statement of fact or of opinion.

[6.202] As the discussion of the ingredients of the tort above indicates, this will often be a question of some significance. Where a statement is one of fact, this defence will not be available.[400] In addition, it appears to be a requirement in s 20(3)(a) of raising the defence of honest opinion that a defendant should have to prove the truth of at least some of the allegations of fact contained in the statement. By contrast, where a statement is categorised as one of opinion, the defendant may rely on this defence provided he or she can meet the presumptively lower requirements of s 20(2). From the defendant's perspective, it is thus plainly preferable to have any statements made that are outlandish, exaggerated or simply more difficult to prove the truth of, classified as statements of opinion.

[6.203] The distinction between facts and opinions is one which may often be difficult to draw[401] and which has 'been the subject of extensive discussion in the authorities' at

---

397.   Defamation Act 2009, s 20(3)(b)(i).
398.   Defamation Act 2009, s 20(3)(b)(ii).
399.   *Eglantine Inn v Smith* [1948] NI 29.
400.   See the comments of Lord Nicholls that '[i]f the imputation is one of fact, a ground of defence must be sought elsewhere, for example, justification or privilege.' *Tse Wai Chun Paul v Albert Cheng* [2001] EMLR 777, para 17.
401.   See the comments of Lord Porter in *Kemsley v Foot* [1952] AC 345, 356.

common law.[402] Where the two cannot be distinguished, it would appear that this defence will not be available.[403] Comment has been defined as 'something which is or can reasonably be inferred to be a deduction, inference, conclusion, criticism, remark, observation, etc'.[404] The courts have consistently emphasised the importance of context in attempting to draw this distinction. Tugenhadt J has warned that '[w]hat might otherwise appear to be a statement or at least an inference of fact may be seen to be a factual inference when account is taken of admissible surrounding circumstances'.[405] As a result, the courts when dealing with cases of alleged 'fair comment' have consistently emphasised the importance of considering the full circumstances in which the impugned statement was made. Robertson J for example, expressed the view that:

> [T]he approach adopted of isolating particular phrases or clauses and considering whether those taken in isolation are expressions of opinion is flawed. It is not necessary for the jury – still less the Judge, who is not the trier of fact – to isolate which passages in the broadcast are expressions of opinion and which are statements of fact. The jury is entitled to look at the entire broadcast in determining whether imputations which it has found to exist were conveyed by the publication as expressions of opinion.[406]

This means that courts have traditionally taken into account factors such as the presentation of the statement, its manner of expression and the context in which it was made. This means, for example, that statements made in a comment[407] or opinion piece or in the review of a restaurant[408] or artistic performance[409] would not be treated in the same way as statements made in the course of a report about a newsworthy occurrence. This was well illustrated by the decision of the Northern Ireland Court of Appeal in *Convery v Irish News* where the court found that the trial judge had erred in directing a jury considering a restaurant review by indicating that many of the statements made in the course of the review – such as, for example, that the Coke served was flat – were statements of fact. The Court of Appeal disagreed, and held that the statement that the Coke was flat represented the reviewer's opinion. The court went on to underline the importance of always considering the context in which statements are made, noting that '[i]f the jury had recognised from the start that most of the article comprised comment, it would have realised that a fairly slender substratum for this was all that was needed'.[410]

---

402. *Thornton v Telegraph Media Group* [2009] EWHC 2863 (QB), para 16.
403. *London Artists v Littler* [1969] 2 QB 375.
404. Gatley (10th edn, *Sweet & Maxwell*, 2003), para 12. 6, citing *Clarke v Norton* [1910] VLR 494. See also *Branson v Bower* [2001] EWCA Civ 791; *Convery v Irish News* [2008] NICA 14.
405. *Thornton v Media Telegraph Group* [2009] EWHC 2863 (QB), para 35.
406. *Television New Zealand Ltd v Haines* [2006] 2 NZLR 433, para 104.
407. *Keady v Guardian Newspapers* [2003] EWHC 1565.
408. *Convery v Irish News* [2008] NICA 14.
409. *Associated Newspapers Ltd v Burstein* [2007] EMLR 21.
410. *Convery v Irish News* [2008] NICA 14, para 35.

[6.204] As the Court of Appeal in England explained, again in the context of a review case:

> [T]he words complained of were contained in a review by a critic, as any reader would appreciate, and which the reader will expect contain a subjective commentary by the critic. The words also embody, quite obviously, powerful elements of value judgments – the word 'heroic' in itself does that . . . such value judgments are not something which a writer should be required to prove are objectively valid, as the Strasbourg Court has pointed out when dealing with the Article 10 right in *Nilsen v Norway* [2000] 30 EHRR 878 at 50.[411]

In this regard, it may be useful to bear in mind the observation made in the recent decision in *British Chiropractor Association v Singh* that it is a 'false dichotomy' to 'trea[t] 'verifiable fact' as antithetical to comment, so that any assertion which ranks as the former cannot qualify as the latter.[412] The fact that a statement in one context may be capable of being verified does not necessarily mean that it cannot constitute a statement of opinion in another.

[6.205] Because of the uncertainty which the task of distinguishing fact from comment has tended to create, it is helpful that the 2009 Act attempts to provide greater clarity on the approach to be adopted by the courts when dealing with the new defence of honest opinion. Section 21 provides that:

> The matters to which the court in a defamation action shall have regard, for the purposes of distinguishing between a statement consisting of allegations of fact and a statement consisting of opinion, shall include the following:
>
> (a) the extent to which the statement is capable of being proved;
>
> (b) the extent to which the statement was made in circumstances in which it was likely to have been reasonably understood as a statement of opinion rather than a statement consisting of an allegation of fact; and
>
> (c) the words used in the statement and the extent to which the statement was subject to a qualification or a disclaimer or was accompanied by cautionary words.

It is clear that this is a non-exhaustive list of factors and that the courts may therefore continue to have regard to other considerations. Furthermore, the factors themselves are reasonably broad. In particular, sub-s (b) effectively gives statutory force to the context-sensitive approach discussed above by directing the court to consider the general circumstances in which the statement was made. It is submitted that this is the most important of the factors identified by s 21 in the sense that, whereas a court is always likely to look to the circumstances of a statement, sub-ss (a) and (c) may not necessarily be determining factors in all situations. For example, as the case law above illustrates, the fact that statements may be capable of being verified should not automatically lead to a finding that they are facts rather than opinion. Similarly, while cautionary words may be a useful indicator of the defendant's intention, they should not necessarily be

411. *Associated Newspapers Ltd v Burstein* [2007] EMLR 21, para 32.
412. *British Chiropractor Association v Singh* [2010] EWCA Civ 350, paras 17–18. But see *Campbell v Safra* [2006] EWHC 819.

decisive in all cases. This would give greater protection to a particular manner of expression which would raise concerns from a freedom of expression perspective. It would also provide the unscrupulous publisher with a means of seeking to avoid potential liability for his actions by simply attaching a cautionary warning to statements made, no matter how outrageous. Thus, while the courts must have regard to these factors, the better view would seem to be that they should not be treated as relevant considerations in all cases.

[6.206] Because of the breadth of these factors, it is likely that parties to a defamation action will still be required to struggle with the difficult distinction between fact and opinion. It would seem advisable, therefore, for defendants to continue to make use of the rolled-up plea. This is a plea to the effect that any statements of fact made were true in substance and in fact, and that any statements of opinion made were honestly held.[413]

Public interest

[6.207] The 2009 Act also maintains the common law requirement that a publication must relate to a matter of public interest if it is to be covered by this defence. This has been relatively broadly interpreted to encompass not only the types of public interest publication covered by Reynolds privilege,[414] but also other matters of legitimate public comment such as reviews[415] or responses to public statements. In *London Artists Ltd v Littler*, Lord Denning MR explained:

> There is no definition in the books as to what is a matter of public interest. All we are given is a list of examples, coupled with the statement that it is for the judge and not for the jury. I would not myself confine it within narrow limits. Whenever a matter is such as to affect people at large, so that they may be legitimately interested in, or concerned at, what is going on; or what may happen to them or to others; then it is a matter of public interest on which everyone is entitled to make fair comment.[416]

[6.208] Lord Nicholls expressed the view that this broad approach to the concept of public interest was justified by the connection between freedom of expression and the protection of the free expression of opinions:

> Nor is it for the courts to choose between 'public' and 'private' purposes, or between purposes they regard as morally or socially or politically desirable and those they regard as undesirable. That would be a highly dangerous course. That way lies censorship. That would defeat the purpose for which the law accords the

---

413. An important point to note is Cox's argument that Hamilton J was incorrect in *Cooney v Browne* [1985] IR 185 to treat the rolled-up plea as a plea of fair and comment and justification. His view is that justification (or presumably now 'truth') must be pleaded as a distinct defence. See Cox, *Defamation Law* (FirstLaw, 2007), 182–183.
414. *Reynolds v Times Newspapers* [2001] 2 AC 127; *Leech v Independent Newspapers* [2007] IEHC 223. This is discussed further below.
415. *Convery v Irish News* [2008] NICA 14; *Associated Newspapers Ltd v Burstein* [2007] EMLR 21.
416. *London Artists Ltd v Littler* [1969] 2 QB 375, 391.

defence of freedom to make comments on matters of public interest. The objective safeguards, coupled with the need to have a genuine belief in what is said, are adequate to keep the ambit of permissible comment within reasonable bounds.[417]

Thus, the public interest has been held to extend to the expression of opinions on sport,[418] art,[419] television,[420] the conduct of music artists,[421] and so on. It is clear that this extends beyond the definition of public interest that applies in other aspects of the law of defamation[422] or, indeed, of privacy.[423]

Fair and reasonable publication on a matter of public interest

Reynolds privilege and s 26

[6.209] The new s 26 defence of fair and reasonable publication on a matter of public interest was one of the most widely discussed reforms introduced by the 2009 Act. One of the most significant changes in the English law of defamation in the last decade was the recognition by the House of Lords of so-called 'Reynolds privilege' in its decision in *Reynolds v Times Newspaper*.[424] While the precise nature of this privilege has been the subject of much debate,[425] it is clear that the defence was developed by the House of Lords as a mechanism to provide greater legal protection for the media in relation to what the Lords described as 'responsible journalism'[426] – in essence, responsible publications on matters of public interest.[427] This decision was based on the view of the House of Lords that freedom of expression, and in particular, Article 10 of the European Convention on Human Rights, required that the law of defamation should not unduly restrict journalists or media organisations engaged in the production of this type of publication. As Lord Nicholls explained, in reliance on multiple decisions of the European Court of Human Rights,[428] '[t]he press discharges vital functions as a

---

417. Tse Wai Chun Paul v Albert Cheng [2001] EMLR 777, para 41.
418. *Campbell v Irish Press* (1955) 90 ILTR 105.
419. *Associated Newspapers Ltd v Burstein* [2007] EMLR 21.
420. *Buffery v Guardian Newspapers* [2004] EWHC 1514.
421. *Spiller v Joseph* [2009] EWCA Civ 1075.
422. *Leech v Independent Newspapers* [2007] IEHC 223.
423. *Cogley v RTÉ* [2005] 4 IR 79.
424. *Reynolds v Times Newspapers* [2001] 2 AC 127.
425. See, for example, Merris, 'Can we speak freely now? Freedom of expression under the Human Rights Act' (2002) 6 EHRLR 750; Loveland, 'The ongoing evolution of Reynolds privilege in domestic libel law (2003) 14 Ent LR 178.
426. *Reynolds v Times Newspapers* [2001] 2 AC 127, 202.
427. The language of responsibility has also featured prominently in the more recent jurisprudence of the European Court of Human Rights. See, for example, the comment that '[w]hen exercising its right to freedom of expression, the press must act in a manner consistent with its duties and responsibilities'. See *Times Newspapers Ltd (Nos 1 and 2) v United Kingdom* (App Nos 3002/03 and 23676/03) [2009] ECHR 3002/0, para 41; *Stoll v Switzerland* (2007) 24 BHRC 258.
428. See, for example, *Lingens v Austria* (1986) 8 EHRR 407; *Oberschlick v Austria* (1991) 19 EHRR 389; *Thorgeirson v Iceland* (1992) 14 EHRR 843; *Bladet Tromso v Norway* (1999) 29 EHRR 125.

bloodhound as well as a watchdog'.[429] It was accordingly appropriate, in his view, that it be protected in the exercise of this important democratic function.

[6.210] As 'Reynolds privilege' developed in the English courts,[430] there was considerable certainty as to whether the defence might be available to Irish defendants. Two decisions of the High Court expressed the view that Reynolds privilege existed under Irish law. In *Hunter v Duckworth*, O'Caoimh J delivered a very lengthy judgment in which he reviewed developments in freedom of expression jurisprudence in several common law countries. He ultimately concluded that 'the flexible approach represented by the decision of the House of Lords in *Reynolds v Times Newspapers Ltd* is the most appropriate way of approaching the problems in the instant case, in the absence of a clear legislative framework'.[431] A similar view was expressed by Charleton J in his ex tempore ruling in *Leech v Independent Newspapers*.[432] However, in the absence of an authoritative Supreme Court decision, it could not be said with certainty that this defence was open to a media defendant.

[6.211] This therefore was the background against which s 26 was enacted. It appears that the section was intended to fulfil a broadly similar purpose to that for which Reynolds privilege was developed by the English courts – namely the protection of responsible publications on matters of public interest as a recognition of the particular value of such publications for democracy and for freedom of expression.

[6.212] However, as discussed in more detail below, there are several notable differences between Reynolds privilege and the defence established by s 26. In particular, it seems reasonable to suggest that a defendant may find it more difficult to invoke this s 26 defence successfully than would have been the case (at least in theory)[433] under Reynolds privilege. O'Dowd, referring to this criticism of s 26, has noted that '[t]he reason for the complaint of "too many hurdles" is fairly plain, given the accumulation of criteria to be assessed when determining what is fair and reasonable under the provision'.[434]

[6.213] This raises a number of issues. One is that, to the extent that *Hunter* and *Leech* represented good law in Ireland, this putatively pro-media enactment may actually restrict rather than expand the media's freedom of expression on matters of public interest.[435] However, O'Dowd has expressed the view that such concerns are influenced

---

429. *Reynolds v Times Newspapers* [2001] 2 AC 127, 205.
430. See, for example, *Loutchansky v Times Newspapers (No 2)* [2002] 1 All ER 652; *Galloway v Telegraph Group* [2004] EWHC 2786 (QB); *Jameel v Wall Street Europe* [2006] 4 All ER 1279; *Flood v Times Newspapers* [2010] EWCA Civ 804.
431. *Hunter v Duckworth* [2003] IEHC 81.
432. *Leech v Independent Newspapers* [2007] IEHC 223.
433. In practice, Reynolds privilege has proved very difficult for defendants to establish successfully. See the discussion of this in *Jameel v Wall Street Journal* [2006] UKHL 44, [2007] 1 AC 359, [2006] 4 All ER 1279.
434. O'Dowd, 'Ireland's new Defamation Act' [2009] 2 *Journal of Media Law* 173, 187.
435. See Cox, *Defamation Law* (FirstLaw, 2007), 337.

by the fact that the original version of the defence in the Defamation Bill 2006 was unduly restrictive. He argues that, while 'it is not surprising that many observers considered s 26, in the form in which it was originally introduced and of which it still bears some traces, to be a highly diluted version of the Reynolds defence and, perhaps, an attempt to curtail the reception of that defence into Irish law', the final version of s 26 'belies many of these concerns'.[436]

[6.214] Secondly, the fact that s 15 abolishes the majority of the defences available before the coming into force of the Act may deprive the courts of the ability to further develop this form of defence in the future, thereby fixing s 26 – with its relatively onerous requirements – as the sole defence available to a media defendant on Reynolds-type grounds of freedom of expression.

[6.215] Thirdly, the enactment of s 26 leaves open, to some extent, the question of whether Reynolds privilege continues to be available under Irish law. It seems likely that the section was intended to replace rather than to complement this defence. Furthermore, it should also be noted that O'Caoimh J's decision in *Hunter* was in part based on the absence of a legislative enactment dealing with this issue. Now that the Oireachtas has acted to fill that void, this rationale for the introduction and/or maintenance of this defence has been removed. For that reason, this section of this chapter will focus primarily on the provisions of s 26. Despite the legally and academically interesting way in which Reynolds privilege continues to develop, it may no longer have much relevance for Irish law. However, as will be discussed further below, it can also be argued that it should continue to apply (assuming that it did) as one of the pre-existing occasions of qualified privilege, which occasions continue to enjoy legal protection under s 18(1). For that reason, a short discussion of Reynolds privilege is included at the end of this section.

Section 26

[6.216] Section 26(1) provides that:

> It shall be a defence (to be known, and in this section referred to, as the 'defence of fair and reasonable publication') to a defamation action for the defendant to prove that—
>
> (a)   the statement in respect of which the action was brought was published—
>
>   (i)   in good faith, and
>
>   (ii) in the course of, or for the purpose of, the discussion of a subject of public interest, the discussion of which was for the public benefit,
>
> (b)   in all of the circumstances of the case, the manner and extent of publication of the statement did not exceed that which was reasonably sufficient, and
>
> (c)   in all of the circumstances of the case, it was fair and reasonable to publish the statement.

---

436.   O'Dowd, 'Ireland's new Defamation Act' [2009] 2 *Journal of Media Law* 173, 190.

There are thus a number of distinct ingredients which a defendant must prove in order to be able to successfully invoke this new defence.

[6.217] Subsection (a) requires that a defendant must prove that:

- the statement was published in good faith;

- the statement was published in the course of, or for the purpose of, the discussion of a subject of public interest; and

- the discussion of the subject in question was for the public benefit.

Good faith

[6.218] There are a number of points to note in relation to these requirements. The first requirement of good faith seems to be directed towards the intentions of the defendant. In particular, it seems most likely that this requirement would not be satisfied where there was malice or recklessness on the part of the defendant. For similar reasons to those discussed above in relation to the defence of honest opinion, it is submitted that it is preferable for the courts to refrain from requiring a defendant to positively establish an absence of malice. While the burden of proof in relation to this a defence, in general, clearly rests on the defendant, it ought to be borne in mind that this a defence which has a particular resonance for the guarantee of media freedom of expression provided by the Constitution and by Article 10 of the Convention. While this may not, in practice, be a significant issue in many cases, it is arguable that the balance would be weighted too far in favour of plaintiffs if it was incumbent on a defendant to positively establish an absence of malice. It should also be noted that s 24(4) of the original Defamation Bill, which would have effectively required the defendant to show that he or she did not act with malice, was ultimately removed from the text before its enactment.

Public interest

[6.219] The second requirement – that the subject matter must be in the public interest – is more likely to feature prominently in future litigation. In this regard, it is particularly relevant to note that the definition of 'public interest' which applied to Reynolds privilege seemed narrower than that which applied to the defence of fair comment. The courts have tended to discuss the relationship between the concept of public interest publications and the media's constitutional right to freedom of expression in terms of political or governmental matters. It was instructive, for example, that the High Court in both *Cogley v RTÉ*[437] and *Leech v Independent Newspapers*[438] explained the public interest in the relevant publications in terms of their connection with statutory or

---

437. *Cogley v RTÉ* [2005] 4 IR 79, 93–94.
438. *Leech v Independent Newspapers* [2007] IEHC 223.

regulatory matters. As Baroness Hale described the notion of 'public interest' under Reynolds privilege:

> [Reynolds privilege] is a defence of publication in the public interest. This does not mean a free-for-all to publish without being damned. The public only have a right to be told if … there [is] a real public interest in communicating and receiving the information. This is, as we all know, very different from saying that it is information which interests the public – the most vapid tittle-tattle about the activities of footballers' wives and girlfriends interests large sections of the public but no-one could claim any real public interest in our being told all about it. It is also different from the test suggested by Mr Robertson, on behalf of the 'Wall Street Journal Europe', of whether the information is 'newsworthy'. That is too subjective a test, based on the target audience, inclinations and interests of the particular publication. There must be some real public interest in having this information in the public domain. But this is less than a test that the public 'need to know', which would be far too limited.[439]

While it might be suggested that this understanding of the public interest in media expression is unduly narrow, it does have a plausible constitutional basis in that it logically corresponds to the democratic conception of the media which the Constitution appears to espouse.[440]

[6.220] In relation to the pleading of this defence, it should be noted that Charleton J expressed the view in *Leech v Independent Newspapers*[441] that it would be appropriate for a defendant to provide particulars of the public interest alleged. In his view:

> I note that it is argued that particulars ought to have been given in relation to the public interest defence as pleaded in this case. It seems to me, insofar as this ruling may establish a precedent, that that is correct. A public interest defence, if pleaded, should be particularised in reference to the overall test, which I have approved, as set out in *Jameel* and, if necessary, with reference to the individual points set out helpfully by Lord Nichols in *Reynolds*.

[6.221] Dunne J's decision in *Quinn Insurance v Tribune Newspapers*[442] suggests that it will not be necessary for a defendant to address all of the factors referred to in s 26(2). Particulars which identify the general category of public interest at issue should be sufficient in most circumstances to adequately inform the plaintiff of the nature of the defence which will be made at trial.

Public benefit

[6.222] The final requirement of sub-s (a) is that the defendant must prove that the discussion in question was for the public benefit. For this limb to be at issue, the discussion will already have to have been shown to concern a matter of public interest. It is unclear, therefore, what significance this requirement may have. Cox argues that 'it is

---

439. *Jameel v Wall Street Europe* [2007] 1 AC 359, 408.
440. See further the discussion of the democratic theory of media expression in **Chs 1 and 2**.
441. *Leech v Independent Newspapers* [2007] IEHC 223.
442. *Quinn Insurance v Tribune Newspapers* [2009] IEHC 229.

difficult to conceive of a situation where discussion of a matter of public importance[443] could not be for the public benefit'. Although the terms of the section have been amended somewhat, the basic logic of this argument still applies. If a subject is in the public interest – particularly if the public interest continues to be interpreted as a concept connected with political or governmental affairs – it is doubtful whether it would be appropriate from either a constitutional or Convention point of view for a court to hold that it was not for the public's benefit for an otherwise fair and reasonable story to be published. This distinction between public interest and public benefit appears to assume that there are some matters of public interest which it would be better for the public to know little or nothing about. From a freedom of expression perspective, this seems unduly paternalistic. It begs the question, for example, whether a government or public body would be entitled to argue that an otherwise fair and reasonable publication on a matter of public interest should not be protected by s 26 because it might have adverse consequences for, for example, national security or economic confidence. By definition, this section seems likely to have most application to governmental matters which would otherwise be secret. Yet, as the Grand Chamber of the European Court of Human Rights has acknowledged, '[p]ress freedom assumes even greater importance in circumstances in which state activities and decisions escape democratic or judicial scrutiny on account of their confidential or secret nature.'[444] If the Act is intended to operate in this manner, this is likely to place courts in the very difficult and questionable position of having to determine what is best for the public in the context of a publication which has already been adjudged to be on a matter of public interest. Once the finding is made that a publication concerns a matter of public interest, the State's entitlement to interfere with the publisher's freedom of expression must be considerably circumscribed. It is submitted therefore that there would be relatively few, if any, circumstances in which considerations of 'public benefit' could possibly meet the high threshold of a 'pressing social need'[445] which would be required to justify an interference with a publication on a matter of public interest.

[6.223] Subsection (b) states that the defendant must show not only that the manner and extent of the publication did not go beyond what was reasonably necessary. This confirms that a defendant is required to defend his or her actions not only by reference to the occasion or subject-matter to which the publication related but also on the basis of the content and presentation of the publication itself. This concern with the content and scope of the publication is broadly similar to that exhibited by the European Court of Human Rights in *Stoll v Switzerland*[446] where it held that a publication on a matter of public interest might enjoy a reduced level of protection under Article 10 where it was expressed in a sensationalist or exaggerated manner. Subsection (b) suggests that a defendant who publishes defamatory material where that material is expressed in a sensationalist or exaggerated fashion, or where that material goes beyond what is

---

443. As the relevant section of the Bill was then expressed.
444. *Stoll v Switzerland* (2007) 44 EHRR 53, para 110.
445. *Times Newspapers Ltd v United Kingdom* (1979) 2 EHRR 245.
446. European Court of Human Rights in *Stoll v Switzerland* (2007) 44 EHRR 53.

reasonably related to the public interest matter under discussion, is unlikely to be able to rely on this defence.

[6.224] An example of this type of approach is provided by the decision of the Court of Appeal in *Flood v Times Newspapers* where it held that Reynolds privilege applied to a report concerning an investigation of a police officer for corruption, but did not extend to protect the reporting of the content of the allegations being investigated. As Moses LJ explained:

> Such allegations merely added credence to the grounds on which the investigation was pursued; they invited the reader to think that, although they had not been investigated let alone substantiated, there might be 'something in them'. The greater the detail, the greater the potential for harm. The details added nothing to the public interest on which the claim to qualified privilege was based.[447]

The terms of sub-s (b) thus suggest that it may be advisable for media organisations to consider whether it can be said that all major elements of a report, as well as the publication as a whole, can be said to be fair and reasonable in the public interest.

Fair and reasonable publication

[6.225] Finally, sub-s (c) requires that the defendant prove that it was fair and reasonable to publish the statement in question. This is a context-sensitive test which will require the courts to consider the circumstances in which the statement was published. In this regard, it is broadly similar to the contextual approach set out by the House of Lords (and Lord Nicholls in particular) in *Reynolds* where it was explained, in assessing the availability of the privilege, that 'the weight to be given to ... relevant factors will vary from case to case'.[448] Furthermore, in an echo of Lord Nicholls' well-known 10 non-exhaustive indicia of responsible journalism,[449] s 26(2) identifies a non-exhaustive list of factors which a court may take into account. However, as Cox has observed, the test of fairness and reasonableness applied under s 26 is different to the approach adopted under *Reynolds*, in accordance with which the court examined whether there was a public duty on the defendant to publish and a public interest in receiving that

---

447. *Flood v Times Newspapers* [2010] EWCA Civ 804, para 116.
448. *Reynolds v Times Newspapers* [2001] 2 AC 127, 205.
449. These are: '1. The seriousness of the allegation. The more serious the charge, the more the public is misinformed and the individual harmed, if the allegation is not true. 2. The nature of the information, and the extent to which the subject matter is a matter of public concern. 3. The source of the information. Some informants have no direct knowledge of the events. Some have their own axes to grind, or are being paid for their stories. 4. The steps taken to verify the information. 5. The status of the information. The allegation may have already been the subject of an investigation which commands respect. 6. The urgency of the matter. News is often a perishable commodity. 7. Whether comment was sought from the plaintiff. He may have information others do not possess or have not disclosed. An approach to the plaintiff will not always be necessary. 8. Whether the article contained the gist of the plaintiff's side of the story. 9. The tone of the article. A newspaper can raise queries or call for an investigation. It need not adopt allegations as statements of fact. 10. The circumstances of the publication, including the timing.' *Reynolds v Times Newspapers* [2001] 2 AC 127, 205.

publication.[450] It is unclear what the difference between these tests might be. However, it may be arguable that there are some important differences between responsible journalism and fair and reasonable journalism. For example, the notion of fairness may require a defendant to demonstrate more balance with regard to the views and position of the plaintiff than would be necessary under a standard of responsibility, in accordance with which a media defendant could possibly claim some greater degree of editorial licence. Thus, while there are certain similarities between these tests, it may be that English authorities on what is regarded as responsible under *Reynolds* may have less direct relevance to Irish law than might be initially thought.

[6.226] The factors which a court shall take into account under s 26(2), where relevant, in considering whether it was fair and reasonable to publish the allegedly defamatory statement are as follows:

(a) the extent to which the statement concerned refers to the performance by the person of his or her public functions;

(b) the seriousness of any allegations made in the statement;

(c) the context and content (including the language used) of the statement;

(d) the extent to which the statement drew a distinction between suspicions, allegations and facts;

(e) the extent to which there were exceptional circumstances that necessitated the publication of the statement on the date of publication;

(f) in the case of a statement published in a periodical by a person who, at the time of publication, was a member of the Press Council, the extent to which the person adhered to the code of standards of the Press Council and abided by determinations of the Press Ombudsman and determinations of the Press Council;

(g) in the case of a statement published in a periodical by a person who, at the time of publication, was not a member of the Press Council, the extent to which the publisher of the periodical adhered to standards equivalent to the standards specified in paragraph (f);

(h) the extent to which the plaintiff's version of events was represented in the publication concerned and given the same or similar prominence as was given to the statement concerned;

(i) if the plaintiff's version of events was not so represented, the extent to which a reasonable attempt was made by the publisher to obtain and publish a response from that person; and

(j) the attempts made, and the means used, by the defendant to verify the assertions and allegations concerning the plaintiff in the statement.

The Act makes clear that this is a non-exhaustive list of guidelines for the decision-maker to consider and that they may therefore have regard to other matters in assessing whether it was fair and reasonable to publish the statement at issue. In the absence of any judicial analysis of this section, it is difficult to predict how important these considerations will be. It may be, for example, that some of these factors will tend to have more influence than others. It could also be that additional factors beyond those

---

450. Cox, *Defamation Law* (FirstLaw, 2007), 335.

identified in sub-s (2) will prove significant in practice. Experience may ultimately show that these considerations were more or less influential in determining the outcome of an action than may have originally been predicted. Allowing for that uncertainty, however, there are a number of specific aspects of sub-s (2) which merit a brief comment at this point.

[6.227] The first is the general observation that it will be important that undue emphasis is not placed on the factors set out in s 26(2). It seems clear that they are intended to have regard to these factors, where relevant. In some situations, they will not be relevant to an assessment of what was fair and reasonable in those circumstances. The experience with Lord Nicholls' 10 factors post-Reynolds was that they tended to be used by lower courts as a fixed checklist for responsible journalism. This was criticised by the House of Lords in *Jameel v Wall Street Europe* where it was stated that:

> [Lord Nicholls' 10 factors] are not tests which the publication has to pass. In the hands of a judge hostile to the spirit of *Reynolds*, they can become ten hurdles at any of which the defence may fail. That is how Eady J treated them. The defence, he said, can be sustained only after 'the closest and most rigorous scrutiny' by the application of what he called 'Lord Nicholls's ten tests'. But that, in my opinion, is not what Lord Nicholls meant ... [T]he standard of conduct required of the newspaper must be applied in a practical and flexible manner. It must have regard to practical realities.[451]

[6.228] This was reiterated by the Privy Council in *Seaga v Harper*:

> [The 10 factors] are not like a statute, nor are they a series of conditions each of which has to be satisfied or tests which the publication has to pass. As Lord Hoffmann said in Jameel's case ... []the standard of conduct required of the publisher of the material must be applied in a practical manner and have regard to practical realities: ibid. The material should ... be looked at as a whole, not dissected or assessed piece by piece, without regard to the whole context.[452]

The non-exhaustive nature of s 26(2) would appear to evince an intention on the part of the Oireachtas that a similar approach be adopted in Ireland.

[6.229] Another point of note is the reference in factor (a) to the connection between the statement in question and the plaintiff's performance of his or her public functions. This seems to indicate an assumption that one of the main types of publications which may be covered by this defence will be those concerning individuals that hold public functions. This seems narrower than the notion of a public figure which has been adopted elsewhere by the courts, which concept has tended to include, for example, celebrities[453] and influential business figures.[454] It also tends to suggest that the defence may be more likely to apply to reports concerning the exercise of public functions by such figures and that it might not, for example, be readily available in relation to statements concerning

---

451. [2007] 1 AC 359, 384.
452. *Seaga v Harper* [2009] AC 1, 9.
453. *Campbell v MGN* [2004] 2 AC 457.
454. *Browne v Associated Newspapers* [2007] EWCA Civ 295.

the private or quasi-private lives of such individuals. It could even indicate that the defence may be more difficult to avail of for a defendant who has published a report concerning a matter of public knowledge or interest about an individual but which does not strictly concern the public functions which that individual holds. While this echoes, to some extent, the European Court of Human Rights' acknowledgment that public figures, including elected officials, are entitled to some degree of protection in respect of the media's coverage of their private matters,[455] it should also be borne in mind that this question will only arise after a court has already found that the matter is one that relates to a matter of public interest, the discussion of which was in the public benefit. This latter consideration will be particularly relevant if the courts, as considered above, ultimately read 'public interest' in this context as pertaining to primarily governmental matters. It is submitted, that – having already found the material to concern a matter of public interest – the courts should be reluctant to use this consideration to further limit the scope of this defence.

[6.230] Factor (c) is also likely to prove important in that a publication which would otherwise be fair and reasonable on a matter of public interest might be expected to lose the protection of s 26 where the presentation, tone or content of the publication is unfair to the plaintiff.[456] That should not mean, of course, that the defence should be available only in respect of one particular style of publication. This would run counter to the principle under Article 10 that journalistic freedom must include some latitude to have 'possible recourse to a degree of exaggeration, or even provocation',[457] and has been specifically rejected by the English courts. As Eady J held in *Houston* 'reliance on this form of privilege does not entail that any special "tone" needs to be adopted'.[458] The courts, where they are required to consider this issue, should be wary of second guessing the decisions of journalists and editors with the benefit of hindsight. Some 'weight must be given to the professional judgment of the journalist'.[459]

[6.231] In a similar vein, factors (i) and (j) would also seem likely to feature prominently in the court's consideration of what was fair in the circumstances. A failure to seek or to publish the plaintiff's account of events has been one of the most common factors upon which attempts to invoke this defence in England have foundered.[460] It has been held at common law that this is not essential and can, for example, be justified where contacting the plaintiff would have made no difference, or where the plaintiff's version of events was widely known.[461] However, the plaintiff does not seem to bear the

---

455. *Tammer v Estonia* (2001) 37 EHRR 857; *Schussel v Austria*, 21 February 2002; *Craxi v Italy (No 2)* (2004) 38 EHRR 47.
456. *Galloway v Telegraph Group* [2004] EWHC 2786 (QB).
457. See, for example, *Dalban v Romania* [1999] ECHR 28114/95 (Application No 28114/95) 28 September 199, para 49.
458. *Prince Radu of Hohenzollern v Houston* [2009] EWHC 398 (QB), para 19.
459. *Charman v Orion Publishing Group* [2008] 1 All ER 750, 773.
460. *Reynolds v Times Newspapers* [2001] 2 AC 127; *Prince Radu of Hohenzollern v Houston* [2009] EWHC 398 (QB).
461. *Jameel v Wall Street Europe* [2007] 1 AC 359.

burden of positively establishing that it would have made a difference to the publication if he or she had been contacted for their version of events in advance.[462]

[6.232] Factor (j) appears to indicate that other attempts at verification may be taken into account, such that a defendant would not appear to be excluded from s 26 by reason only of the fact that they did not contact the plaintiff directly.

[6.233] However, the Act also appears to suggest that a defendant cannot rely on the mere fact that efforts were made to contact a plaintiff as sufficient verification to satisfy the threshold of fair and reasonable publications. Section 26(3) states that the failure or refusal of a plaintiff to respond to attempts by or on behalf of the defendant to elicit the plaintiff's version of events, shall not constitute or imply consent to the publication of the statement or entitle the court to draw any inference therefrom. This would seem to cover a situation where, for example, a plaintiff is contacted very shortly before publication and presented with the prospect of the publication of a particular story as an effective fait accompli. However, the prohibition on the drawing of 'any inference' could be taken to refer to inferences both against the plaintiff and in favour of a defendant. Thus it would seem inadvisable, pending further clarification by the courts, for a media organisation to rely on making contact with a plaintiff as their sole or primary means of verifying a potentially defamatory story, particularly where that plaintiff does not respond.

Reportage

[6.234] While verification is likely to be an important issue in many cases, the English courts have recognised that there are particular types of publication where it is unnecessary or inappropriate for a media defendant to attempt to verify the truth of the subject—matter of the report. To reflect this, Reynolds privilege has been held to apply to a specific category of publication, which is described in English law as 'reportage'. The 'reportage' doctrine applies to publications where a media organisation reports an attributed allegation 'in a fair, neutral and disinterested way'.[463] It has been defined as 'responsible reporting on matters of public interest under the principle in *Reynolds v Times Newspapers Ltd* ... in circumstances in which it does not adopt the allegation, which it reports neutrally'.[464] The privilege for 'reportage' has been held to apply where a media organisation adopts the allegation as its own, embellishes it, elaborates upon it or generally presents it in a way which means that the 'scales are heavily tilted'[465] against one side.[466]

[6.235] Under Reynolds privilege, reportage publications are not subject, therefore, to the same verification requirements as other forms of public interest publication. This reflects a recognition on the part of the English judiciary of the way in which the media

462. *Prince Radu of Hohenzollern v Houston* [2008] EWCA Civ 921.
463. *Roberts v Gable* [2007] All ER (D) 182 (Jul), para 61(5).
464. *Curistan v Times Newspapers* [2008] EWCA Civ 432, para 57.
465. *Prince Radu v Houston* (2007) All ER (D) 365 (Nov), para 40.
466. See, for example, *Charman v Orion Publishing Group Ltd* [2008] 1 All ER 750.

contributes as both 'watchdog' and bloodhound'[467] to the vital democratic value of informed public debate. The media supports the functioning of the democratic state as much by 'report[ing] on matters of public concern' as by 'pursu[ing] ... investigative journalism'.[468] Reportage protects the media in its performance of its role as 'reporter ... [where it] acts, in a very literal sense, as a medium of communication'.[469] It is a 'a special example of Reynolds qualified privilege, a special kind of responsible journalism but with distinctive features of its own'.[470]

[6.236] The development of the reportage doctrine by the English courts reflects a recognition on their part of the inappropriateness of requiring editorial or journalistic verification in all cases. Reynolds privilege will usually only apply where a defendant has made reasonable efforts at verification of an allegation or story before publication. In reportage cases, however, the courts have acknowledged that verification may be unnecessary, or even inappropriate. In *Al-Fagih*, Simon Brown LJ commented that 'in the present context, verification could ... be thought inconsistent with the objective reporting of a dispute'.[471] That was a case which concerned a relatively bitter dispute between prominent members of a particular Saudi political group. The defendant argued that, given the position of these individuals, the fact that they had engaged in this sort of personalised dispute was a matter of public importance. The Court of Appeal agreed. Requiring the newspaper to verify the allegations on either side would have obscured the focus of the story (the fact of the personalised disagreement) and would have resulted in a delay or lack of coverage of a matter which was unquestionably in the public interest.

[6.237] This was cited with approval by Eady J in *Prince Radu of Hohenzollern v Houston*.[472] Verification, in his view, was irrelevant to, and potentially inconsistent with the objective coverage of allegations 'because it is the accuracy (and balance) of the reporting which is important, rather than the accuracy of the underlying allegations'.[473]

[6.238] However, verification will frequently still be required in relation to a piece of reportage.[474] It will be appropriate in some circumstances for some efforts to be made to verify a report, even where the report is intended as a neutral and disinterested account of a particular event. This reflects the reality that the neutral character of reportage does not prevent it from potentially harming a plaintiff's reputation.[475] It is still necessary, at common law, to show that the reporting was responsible in the circumstances.

[6.239] This was underlined by the decision of the Court of Appeal in *Flood v Times Newspapers*. The court there expressed considerable doubt as to whether the defence of

467. *Al-Fagih v HH Saudi Research and Marketing Ltd* [2001] All ER (D) 48 (Nov), para 6.
468. *Al-Fagih v HH Saudi Research and Marketing Ltd* [2001] All ER (D) 48 (Nov), para 6.
469. *McCartan Turkington Breen v Times Newspapers Ltd* [2000] 3 WLR 1670, 1680.
470. *Roberts v Gable* [2007] All ER (D) 182 (Jul), para 60.
471. *Al-Fagih v HH Saudi Research and Marketing Ltd* [2001] All ER (D) 48 (Nov), para 50.
472. *Hohenzollern v Houston* [2007] EWHC 2735 (QB).
473. *Hohenzollern v Houston* [2007] EWHC 2735 (QB), para 50.
474. *Malik v Newspost* [2007] EWHC 3063 (QB).
475. *Mark v Associated Newspapers Ltd* [2002] EMLR 839.

reportage would be available in relation to the publication of an ex parte allegation. The fact that the police were investigating an allegation of corruption did not, in the court's view, remove the burden of verification from the media. In particular, it did not justify the publication of the name of the person being investigated alongside the details of the alleged misconduct. Noting that '[t]he reportage defence needs to be treated restrictively', the court held that Reynolds privilege did not apply:

> Both limbs of Reynolds privilege are based on the public interest: journalists should be relatively free to report matters which it is in the public interest to place in the public domain, and journalists should take reasonable care to verify the accuracy of stories which may damage reputations. It is hard to see why those principles should not apply to publication of ex parte allegations made against an individual, simply because those allegations are being, and are publicly known to be, investigated by the police. The fact that the allegations are being investigated by the police may, depending on all the circumstances, influence the question of what investigations a responsible journalist might make, but I see no reason why it should go any further than that.
>
> ...
>
> The fact that an unidentified insider has given specific information which, if true, may incriminate a claimant, will very rarely be justifiable reportage. Of course, it will add something to the substance and newsworthiness of the story that the police are investigating the claimant, but it seems to me that it would be tipping the scales too far in favour of the media to hold that not only the name of the claimant, but the details of the allegations against him, can normally be published as part of a story free of any right in the claimant to sue for defamation just because the general subject matter of the story is in the public interest.[476]

[6.240] It is not clear to what extent s 26 will apply to protect this type of 'reportage'. It is notable, for example, that Lord Nicholls' 10 factors refer to the question of whether the newspaper adopted the allegations as its own whereas this is not one of the factors specified in s 26(2).[477] The emphasis on verification in s 26(2) could also be seen to cast some doubt on the status of reportage in Ireland although, as *Flood v Times Newspapers* illustrates, the two are not mutually exclusive. Furthermore, factor (d) encourages a court to have regard to the extent to which a distinction is drawn between suspicions, allegations and facts. This could be read either as recognition that a court can take account of the fact that a publication, as a whole, represents a neutral account of allegations or suspicions, or, on the other hand, as an indication that defendants should always take care to specifically identify any questionable statements as allegations or suspicions, even where it is clear that they are not purporting to adopt them as their own.

[6.241] In reality, the ambiguous nature of s 26(2) leaves the courts with a considerable degree of discretion when considering what constitutes fair and reasonable publication. While the section does not provide the sort of specific reference to reportage that might have been desirable, there is little in the section that could plausibly be said to prevent or

---

476. *Flood v Times Newspapers* [2010] EWCA Civ 804, paras 59–63.
477. Although it might arguably be incorporated as part of the reference to 'tone'.

inhibit the application of this s 26 defence to fair and reasonable examples of this type of journalism. Given the democratic and public value of such reports, it is submitted that they should also be entitled, in principle, to the protection of s 26, even where (as appropriate) little or no attempts to verify the truth or falsity of the underlying material were made.

The Press Council and Ombudsman

[6.242] Several of these factors also refer to the Press Council. This body was established in 2007 and was formally recognised by the Minister for Justice[478] in 2010 as a Press Council for the purposes of the 2009 Act, having met the minimum requirements set out in s 44. This is discussed elsewhere in the book.

Non-media defendants

[6.243] It should also be noted that the defence does not appear to be confined to media organisations. This is also the position under Reynolds privilege at common law, where it has been held that it can extend to publications made by any person who publishes material of public interest in any medium, so long as the conditions framed by Lord Nicholls as being applicable to 'responsible journalism' are satisfied.[479]

Pre-trial applications

[6.244] The discussion above illustrates the importance of context in considering whether a defendant can successfully rely on s 26. For that reason, it might be thought that it will be difficult for a plaintiff to persuade a court in advance of a full hearing that a defendant will not be able to make out this defence at trial. The view has been expressed in England that an application for summary judgment is less likely to be appropriate in a case where the defence is to be based solely on the Reynolds criteria on the basis that the defence can rarely be upheld purely as a matter of law on paper. Eady J felt that, given the necessity to examine the background to the publication, evidence would generally have to be given and tested at trial in order to decide whether those criteria have been fulfilled.[480] Thus, it may be more difficult for a plaintiff to succeed in, for example, an application to restrain publication under s 33 or an application for a summary disposal of the action under s 34 once the defendant asserts that the matter would be covered by s 26.

Reynolds privilege after the 2009 Act

[6.245] Finally, there is an argument to be made that Reynolds privilege may continue to apply as a matter of Irish law, even after the passing of s 26. This may become particularly relevant if it proves difficult for defendants to successfully rely on s 26. If

---

478. Defamation Act 2009 (Press Council) Order 2010 (SI 163/2010).
479. *Jameel v Wall Street Europe* [2007] 1 AC 359; *Seage v Harper* [2008] UKPC 9, [2009] AC 1. But see *Kearns v General Council of the Bar* [2003] 1 WLR 1357.
480. *Seray-Wurie v Charity Commission of England and Wales* [2008] EWHC 870 (QB), para 22.

Reynolds privilege continues to develop in a liberalising manner in England, the situation could arise in which a defendant might consider that they may have a greater prospect of avoiding liability under Reynolds privilege than under s 26.

[6.246] On balance, it would seem that this was unlikely to have been intended by the drafters of the 2009 Act. Section 26 seems to be envisaged as a replacement for Reynolds privilege. However, it might be argued that *Reynolds* – as a species of qualified privilege – continues to have legal force in Ireland as a result of s 18(1).This provides that it shall be a defence for a defendant to prove that the statement in respect of which the action was brought would have been considered under the law in force immediately before the commencement of the Act as having been made on an occasion of qualified privilege.

[6.247] One of the main points of academic and judicial dispute in England has been in relation to the question of whether Reynolds privilege is a form of qualified privilege or whether it is an entirely new type of defence.[481] While it seems to be accepted that Reynolds privilege contains some novel elements that mean that it can operate, in some respects, differently to traditional common law privilege,[482] it is still regarded by many as a form of qualified privilege. That this remains unclear was confirmed by the Privy Council recently in *Seaga v Harper* where Lord Carswell noted the continuing levels of judicial disagreement about the nature of this defence:

> Some have described it as 'a different jurisprudential creature from the traditional form of privilege from which it sprang': *Loutchansky v Times Newspapers Ltd (Nos 2–5)* [2002] QB 783, 806, para 35, *per* Lord Phillips of Worth Matravers MR, with whom Lord Hoffmann agreed in *Jameel's* case [2007] 1 AC 359, para 46. Both Lord Phillips in *Loutchansky v Times Newspapers Ltd (Nos 2–5)* [2002] QB 783, at para 33, and Lord Hoffmann in *Jameel's* case [2007] 1 AC 359, para 46, adopted the view that the privilege in such cases attaches to the publication itself rather than, as in traditional privilege cases, to the occasion on which it is published. Others take the view that the Reynolds privilege is built upon the foundation of the duty-interest privilege, an opinion adopted by Lord Bingham of Cornhill, Lord Hope of Craighead and Lord Scott of Foscote in *Jameel's* case.[483]

Lord Carswell himself expressed no view on the matter, deciding that it was immaterial to the case before him. What this indicates, however, is that one school of thought regards *Reynolds* as a form of qualified privilege. After all, even at common law, publication to the world at large could sometimes be protected by qualified privilege.[484] The language of duty and interest continues to feature prominently in the English authorities on *Reynolds*. This supports the argument that, as a form of qualified privilege, *Reynolds* continues to apply by virtue of s 18(1).[485]

---

481. See, for example, the discussion in *Roberts v Gable* [2008] QB 502, para 32.
482. See, for example, the difference with respect to malice: *Seray-Wurie v Charity Commission of England and Wales* [2008] EWHC 870 (QB), para 21.
483. *Seaga v Harper* [2009] AC 1, 8–9.
484. *Cox v Feeney* (1863) 4 F & F 13; *Underhill v Corser* [2010] EWHC 1195 (QB), para 38.
485. See also O'Dowd, 'Ireland's new Defamation Act' [2009] 2 *Journal of Media Law* 173, 188–189.

[6.248] That assumes, of course, that the decisions in *Hunter v Duckworth*[486] and *Leech v Independent Newspapers*[487] were correct and that a responsible publication on a matter of public interest was a recognised occasion of qualified privilege protected under Irish law before the passing of the 2009 Act.

[6.249] It might also be argued that Reynolds privilege does not pertain to an 'occasion' of qualified privilege but is rather focused on the publication itself. This would ignore, however, the repeated references in *Reynolds* itself to the importance of the principle that privilege attaches to the occasion rather than to the communication itself.[488]

[6.250] Thus, the question would appear to be open as to whether a defendant can seek to rely on *Reynolds* after the passing of the 2009 Act. Given the overlap between the common law principle and s 26, it might be thought unnecessary, inappropriate or confusing for the two defences to exist. However, if the fears that have been expressed about the narrowness of s 26 are accurate, it may be preferable from the point of view of media freedom of expression for defendants to continue to have the possibility of seeking to invoke the more flexible *Reynolds* defence.

Consent

[6.251] Section 25 establishes a defence of consent in accordance with which a defendant may prove that the plaintiff consented to the publication of the statement in respect of which the action was brought. The wording of s 25 underlines the fact that the defendant must show consent to the publication of the allegedly defamatory statement itself.[489] It will not be sufficient to demonstrate a more general consent. For example, the agreement of one person to participate in a television documentary would not, of itself, constitute consent to the making of defamatory statements about him or her by other participants in the programme.

[6.252] Cox argues[490] that this section seems broader than s 34(1)(b) of the Civil Liability Act 1961, which the courts had construed as requiring something approximating to express consent.[491] It may now be, therefore, that a defendant can seek to rely on an implied consent as a basis for invoking s 25. Nonetheless, given the fact that defamation in part protects the individual's constitutional right to a good name, it would still seem reasonable to expect that the courts will be unwilling to readily infer consent on the part of a plaintiff in the absence of positive evidence that the plaintiff understood the implications of their actions in purportedly agreeing to publication.[492] A similar view was expressed by Brooke LJ in the *Friend* decision when, having drawn attention to the important role which defamation plays in protecting reputation, he held

---

486. *Hunter v Duckworth* [2003] IEHC 81.
487. *Leech v Independent Newspapers* [2007] IEHC 223.
488. See for example *Reynolds v Times Newspapers* [2001] 2 AC 127, 229.
489. *Mihaka v Wellington Publishing* [1995] 1 NZLR 10; *Spencer v Stilltoe* [2003] EWHC 1651.
490. Cox, *Defamation Law* (FirstLaw, 2007), 340.
491. *O'Hanlon v ESB* [1969] IR 75.
492. See, for example, *G v An Bord Uchtála* [1980] IR 32.

that 'in most ordinary circumstances there would need to be evidence of a special express consent before a person could be held to have consented to the publication or republication of malicious libels on him/herself'.[493]

[6.253] It can also be argued that a plaintiff consented to publication as a matter of contract.[494] This is most likely to apply where the disclosure in question was allegedly justified by the terms of the plaintiff's contract of employment or membership of a club. However, even if that is the case, it has been held that publication will only be protected where fair procedures have been applied.[495]

[6.254] Although it is not covered elsewhere in the Act, it may be arguable that acquiescence on the part of a plaintiff could be taken to represent implied consent. Eady J held in *Carrie v Tolkien*[496] that the plaintiff's failure to remove material for several months when it was in his power to do so represented sufficient acquiescence to preclude him from subsequently suing for defamation.

Innocent publication

[6.255] Section 27 is intended to address one of the major criticisms of the law as it previously existed in Ireland – namely the way in which individuals who were involved in the publication of a statement but who bore little or no responsibility for its production or content could be named as defendants. Thus, printers, distributors, shopkeepers, and so on were all potentially at risk of a libel action in relation to a book or periodical which they innocently supplied. Similarly, those involved in the publication of material on the internet were potentially at risk of being found liable for the publication online of defamatory statements by third parties.[497]

[6.256] Section 27 accordingly provides that the defence of innocent publication will be available to a defendant who can prove that he or she was not the author, editor or publisher of the statement to which the action relates, that he or she took reasonable care in relation to its publication, that he or she did not know, and had no reason to believe, that what he or she did caused or contributed to the publication of a statement that would give rise to a cause of action in defamation. This, in principle, is a relatively broad defence as it appears likely to generally apply once a defendant can show that they acted with reasonable care and without notice of the defamatory nature of the publication.

[6.257] Section 27(2) provides some guidance as to who will be regarded as an 'author, editor or publisher' and thus be denied the possibility of pleading innocent publication.

---

493. *Friend v Civil Aviation Authority* (29 January 1998, unreported), CA.
494. *Cookson v Harewood* [1932] 2 KB 478; *Friend v Civil Aviation Authority* (29 January 1998, unreported), CA.
495. *Green v Blake* [1948] IR 42.
496. *Carrie v Tolkien* [2009] EWHC 29 (QB).
497. *Godfrey v Demon Internet Ltd* [2001] QB 201. But see *Budu v BBC* [2010] EWHC 616 (QB).

It states that a person shall not be considered to be the author, editor or publisher of a statement if—

(a)   in relation to printed material containing the statement, he or she was responsible for the printing, production, distribution or selling only of the printed material,

(b)   in relation to a film or sound recording containing the statement, he or she was responsible for the processing, copying, distribution, exhibition or selling only of the film or sound recording,

(c)   in relation to any electronic medium on which the statement is recorded or stored, he or she was responsible for the processing, copying, distribution or selling only of the electronic medium or was responsible for the operation or provision only of any equipment, system or service by means of which the statement would be capable of being retrieved, copied, distributed or made available.

This section is non-exhaustive however such that it will still be open to other potential defendants to argue that they too do not come within the definition of an 'author, editor or publisher'.

[6.258] Section 27(3) again supplies some guidance to the courts in considering this defence by providing that:

(3) The court shall, for the purposes of determining whether a person took reasonable care, or had reason to believe that what he or she did caused or contributed to the publication of a defamatory statement, have regard to—

(a)   the extent of the person's responsibility for the content of the statement or the decision to publish it,

(b)   the nature or circumstances of the publication, and

(c)   the previous conduct or character of the person.[498]

One point to note here is that, to the extent that factor (c) might be taken to suggest that some publishers will enjoy less protection under s 27 simply because of their past conduct or character, this seems somewhat questionable. While this may be intended to operate as an incentive to potential defendants to introduce appropriate systems to guard against the publication of potentially defamatory statements, it does seem potentially unfair to suggest that an individual who has exercised all reasonable care could be denied a defence available to all others in his or her situation, by reference to past incidents.

Apology

[6.259] Although this is not, strictly speaking, a defence, it is appropriate to point out at this point that a defendant faced with a defamation action also has the possibility of making an apology to the plaintiff. Section 24 of the 2009 Act provides that a defendant can give evidence in mitigation of damages that he or she made or offered an apology to the plaintiff in respect of the statement to which the action relates, and published the

---

498.   See *Ross v Eason & Son* (1911) 45 ILTR 89; *Fitzgibbon v Eason & Son* (1911) 45 ILTR 91.

apology in such manner as ensured that the apology was given the same or similar prominence as was given to that statement, or offered to publish an apology in such a manner, as soon as practicable after it became aware of the plaintiff's complaint or action. Notice of an intention to adduce such evidence may be included in the defence.[499]

[6.260] The way in which s 24(1) is drafted appears to suggest that a defendant will only be entitled to tender such evidence where they have complied with both the requirement to offer an apology and the requirement to publish it in a prominent manner. The defendant must also give notice in writing to the plaintiff of his or her intention to adduce such evidence at the same time as the defence is filed.[500]

[6.261] Crucially, s 24 also states that any apology cannot be treated as an admission of liability[501] and is not admissible as an admission in any other civil proceedings against the defendant.[502] This is a significant change which reflects the general policy of the 2009 Act to discourage parties from defensively resorting to legal action and encourage them instead to engage in a constructive and positive fashion at an early stage.

Offer of amends

[6.262] Section 22 introduces a new offer of amends procedure which replaces that established by s 21 of the Defamation Act 1961. Where its counterpart was underused and largely irrelevant, it is expected that this radically new procedure may bring about a significant change to the way in which the law of defamation operates in Ireland. Cox has suggested that this 'represents (at least potentially) one of the most important reforms proposed' by the new Act.[503]

[6.263] Section 22 provides that a defendant who has published an allegedly defamatory statement may make an offer of amends. This is a novel and important tactical matter for a defendant and their legal advisers to consider. If a defendant can prove that they made an offer of amends which was rejected by the plaintiff, it will generally provide a defence to the plaintiff's action.[504] However, if it is pleaded as a defence,[505] the defendant is thereby precluded from raising any other defence in relation to the statement, or parts of a statement, to which the offer related.[506]

---

499. Order 1B, rule 9.
500. Defamation Act 2009, s 24(2).
501. Defamation Act 2009, s 24(3).
502. Defamation Act 2009, s 24(4).
503. Cox, *Defamation Law* (FirstLaw, 2007), 350.
504. Defamation Act 2009, s 23(2).
505. It is not necessary to plead this. Defamation Act 2009, s 23(4).
506. Defamation Act 2009, s 23(5).

[6.264] Section 22 sets out in considerable detail the various steps which a defendant must take in order to make a valid offer of amends. The offer must be made before the delivery of a defence,[507] it must be in writing,[508] it must state that it is an offer to make amends for the purposes of s 22,[509] and it must state whether the offer is a full offer in respect of the entire statement[510] or a 'qualified offer' in respect of either a part of the statement or one of the particular defamatory meanings therein.[511] The offer must also offer to make a suitable correction of the statement concerned and a sufficient apology to the person to whom the statement refers or is alleged to refer,[512] to publish that correction and apology in such manner as is reasonable and practicable in the circumstances,[513] and to pay to the person such sum in compensation or damages (if any), and such costs, as may be agreed by them or as may be determined to be payable.[514]

[6.265] These latter considerations will probably provoke the most controversy as plaintiffs and defendants might be thought unlikely to agree as to what constitutes a 'suitable correction' and 'sufficient apology'. Given the potentially damaging implications for plaintiffs of rejecting an offer of amends, however, it would seem imprudent (at least in advance of any judicial consideration of these terms) for a plaintiff to be unduly inflexible in considering whether an offer is sufficient to address their complaint.

[6.266] Once an offer of amends is made, there are a number of possible outcomes to the process. The offer may be withdrawn before being accepted and, if the defendant so wishes, a new offer may be made in its place.[515]

[6.267] If the parties agree to particular terms, those terms may be enforced by direction of the court upon an application being made to it by the party to whom the offer was made.[516] This will also have the effect of precluding an action from being brought against any other person in relation to the offending statement unless the court considers that in all the circumstances of the case it is just and proper to do so.[517]

[6.268] If the parties do not agree, the defendant may, with the leave of the court, make a correction and apology by means of a statement before the court in such terms as may be approved by the court and give an undertaking as to the manner of their publication.[518]

---

507. Defamation Act 2009, s 22(3).
508. Defamation Act 2009, s 22(2)(a).
509. Defamation Act 2009, s 22(2)(b).
510. Defamation Act 2009, s 22(2)(c)(i).
511. Defamation Act 2009, s 22(2)(c)(ii).
512. Defamation Act 2009, s 22(5)(a).
513. Defamation Act 2009, s 22(5)(b).
514. Defamation Act 2009, s 22(5)(c).
515. Defamation Act 2009, s 22(4).
516. Defamation Act 2009, s 23(1)(a).
517. Defamation Act 2009, s 23(1)(d).
518. Defamation Act 2009, s 23(1)(b).

If the parties cannot agree on costs or damages, this will be determined by the High Court or the court in which the action has been brought. In dealing with that matter, the court has all powers which it would have if it were determining damages or costs in a defamation action. Furthermore, in considering the level of damages or costs to be awarded, it must also take into account the adequacy of any measures already taken to ensure compliance with the terms of the offer by the person who made the offer.[519]

[6.269] The various applications which may be made to the court as a result of the making of an offer of amends are governed by Order 1B, rules 4–8.

[6.270] Critically, however, s 23(2) provides that it will be a defence to prove that a defendant made an offer of amends and that it was not accepted. If the defendant can establish this, the defence will succeed unless the plaintiff can prove that the defendant knew or ought reasonably to have known at the time of the publication of the statement to which the offer relates that it referred to the plaintiff or was likely to be understood as referring to the plaintiff, and that it was false and defamatory of the plaintiff.

[6.271] This defence is particularly useful for a defendant as, unlike many of the other defences available to him or her under the 2009 Act, he or she bears a relatively light burden of proof. Once it is proved that an offer of amends was made and not accepted, a plaintiff then is required to bear the heavier burden of establishing knowledge or negligence on the part of the defendant. For that reason, it might be expected that the offer of amends procedure may provide a genuine opportunity for defendants to deal, where appropriate, with some potential defamation actions in a more expeditious and cost-effective manner than has previously been possible.

REMEDIES

[6.272] In keeping with its general aim of reducing the cost and time of defamation proceedings, the 2009 Act introduced a suite of new remedies as well as making several important changes to those which had previously been available at common law and under the 1961 Act. Perhaps the most significant changes were those made to the rules concerning the awarding of damages in defamation actions. The high level of damages awarded by Irish juries in some prominent cases had been a source of major concern for media organisations in Ireland. This phenomenon also raised a more general concern about the chilling effect which such awards of damages could have on freedom of expression in Ireland.[520] The 2009 Act attempts to deal with this concern by both amending the rules governing the awarding of damages and by creating a number of alternative remedies for a person who feels that they have been the subject of a defamatory statement. These are considered below.

---

519. Defamation Act 2009, s 23(1)(c).
520. See, for example, *Tolstoy Miloslavsky v UK* (1995) 20 EHRR 442; *De Rossa v Independent Newspapers* [1999] 4 IR 432 *per* Denham J, dissenting.

Summary disposal

[6.273] One of the major changes introduced to the English law of defamation by the Defamation Act 1996 was the creation of a procedure under which various matters could be dealt with summarily in advance of a trial.[521] The experience in practice in England appears to have been that parties make frequent use of this procedure with the result that, in many situations, there is considerable narrowing of the issues that are ultimately litigated in front of a jury at trial.

[6.274] Section 34 introduces a similar procedure into Irish law, under which either party may apply to the court for the summary trial of certain issues. These applications should be brought by way of notice of motion and grounding affidavit,[522] and are dealt with by the court acting alone and without a jury.[523]

[6.275] A plaintiff may obtain summary relief if he or she can satisfy the court that the statement in respect of which the action was brought is defamatory, and the defendant has no defence to the action that is reasonably likely to succeed. As noted previously, this may be a difficult threshold for a plaintiff to meet where the defendant raises a defence – such as s 26 – which can only be properly adjudicated upon once the parties have tendered their evidence.[524] An added difficulty from a plaintiff's perspective is that he or she may only obtain a correction order or an order prohibiting further publication as part of an application under s 34. When taken together with the relatively high threshold of proof required to secure summary relief, this may act as a significant disincentive for plaintiffs who are considering making use of this procedure.

[6.276] A defendant may apply to dismiss the plaintiff's action if it is satisfied that the statement in respect of which the action was brought is not reasonably capable of being found to have a defamatory meaning. This procedure is similar to the role exercised by a judge before the passing of the 2009 Act in determining whether a statement was, in law, capable of having a defamatory meaning and thus could be considered by a jury. Nonetheless, as the focus of the court's enquiry on such an application is a relatively abstract question of interpretation that can be dealt with while requiring little or no evidence from each side, there may be greater scope, as a matter of practice, for defendants than plaintiffs to make use of s 34.

Declaratory order

[6.277] One of the new remedies introduced by the 2009 Act is the declaratory order. Section 28 provides that a person who claims to be the subject of an allegedly defamatory statement may apply to the Circuit Court for an order declaring that the statement is false and defamatory of him or her. This will provide an expeditious and (given that it must be dealt with in the Circuit Court)) comparatively inexpensive way

---

521. Defamation Act 1996, s 8.
522. Defamation Act 2009, s 34(3). See also Order 1B, rule 3(3).
523. Defamation Act 2009, s 34(4).
524. *Seray-Wurie v Charity Commission of England and Wales* [2008] EWHC 870 (QB).

for a plaintiff to restore his or her reputation. However, if a plaintiff makes an application under s 28, they will not be entitled to be awarded damages[525] and will be precluded from bringing any other proceedings in respect of the statement in question.[526] This means that the procedure is likely to be of interest only to those plaintiffs who wish to vindicate their reputation and are not interested in financial recompense. It may also offer an attractive alternative for litigants who – for whatever reason – may already have a damaged reputation in the eyes of the public with the consequence that they might be thought unlikely to obtain damages at trial. This is an option that may, for example, be attractive to public figures, especially politicians, who may wish to have a defamatory report corrected without being accused of excessive greed. However, it is most likely that this remedy will be sought in only a small number of cases.

[6.278] An application under s 28 must be brought by way of a motion on notice to the respondent and a grounding affidavit.[527] The application must be made to the Circuit Court where the defendant resides or where the statement was published.[528]

[6.279] Where an application is made, the court is directed by s 28(2) to make a declaratory order once it is satisfied that the statement is defamatory of the applicant; that the respondent has no defence to the application; that the applicant requested the respondent to make and publish an apology, correction or retraction in relation to that statement; and that the respondent either did not accede to that request or acceded to the request but did not give the apology, correction or retraction the same or similar prominence as was given by the respondent to the statement concerned. Cox argues that the reference to 'that request' may create an incentive for a plaintiff to make unreasonable demands of the defendant on the basis that the court will be obliged to make the order once the request is made and not acceded to.[529] However, an alternative reading of the section is available in accordance with which the defendant must only consider the plaintiff's request for '*an* apology, correction or retraction' and is not bound to accede to or reject any additional demands made by the plaintiff in terms of particular content or prominence. It is submitted that this would be a better approach to s 28. Furthermore, this interpretation also derives some support from the fact that s 28(2)(c) specifies certain standards of prominence for the apology, correction or retraction which, if met, will allow a respondent to avoid a declaratory order. This would tend to suggest that there are limits to the demands, if any, which a prospective plaintiff may make of a defendant/respondent in respect of the apology, correction or retraction.

Although an applicant under s 28 may not receive damages, they are entitled to apply to the court for a correction order[530] or for an order prohibiting publication of the defamatory statement.[531]

---

525. Defamation Act 2009, s 28(8).
526. Defamation Act 2009, s 28(4).
527. Defamation Act 2009, s 28(5). A court may also give further directions with regard to the pleadings and hearing of any issues under Defamation Act 2009, s 28(7).
528. Defamation Act 2009, s 28(9).
529. Cox, *Defamation Law* (FirstLaw, 2007), 442.
530. Defamation Act 2009, ss 28(6) and 30.
531. Defamation Act 2009, ss 28(6) and 33.

Correction order

[6.280] Section 30 of the 2009 Act allows a court to make a correction order, under which a defendant is directed to publish a correction. This again appears designed to provide a plaintiff with a remedy which should, in theory, restore or vindicate his or her reputation without necessarily having to have recourse to financial compensation for the damage incurred.

[6.281] While the court enjoys a general discretion in relation to the manner and form of a correction order, s 30(2) specifies that they should usually specify the date and time upon which, or the period not later than the expiration of which, the correction order shall be published, as well as specifying the form, content, extent and manner of publication of the correction. This is a significant power as it allows the court to effectively dictate the manner and content of publication. Section 30(2) also indicates that the court unless the plaintiff otherwise requests, requires the correction to be published in such manner as will ensure that it is communicated to all or substantially all of those persons to whom the defamatory statement was published.

[6.282] This remedy will only be available after it has been found that the statement is defamatory and that the defendant has no defence. An application may be made by or on behalf of the plaintiff at any time during the trial of the action.[532] However, if a plaintiff wishes to apply for a correction order at trial, they must inform the defendant in writing no later than seven days before the trial of the action,[533] and must also inform the court of that fact at the trial of the action.[534] In the alternative, the court or trial judge is also entitled to direct that an application may be made.

Lodgment

[6.283] Under s 29, a defendant may, upon giving notice in writing to the plaintiff, make a lodgement in court. Any such lodgement will be governed by the rules currently in force on lodgement. At present, the relevant rules are Order 22, rule 1 of the Rules of the Superior Courts, as amended by the Rules of the Superior Courts (Defamation) 2009 (SI 511/2009); and Order 15, rule 9 of the Circuit Court Rules, as amended by the Circuit Court Rules (Defamation) 2009 (SI 486/2009). In contrast to the position before the passing of the 2009 Act,[535] the making of a lodgement will not constitute an admission of liability on the part of a defendant.[536]

Orders restraining publication

[6.284] From a plaintiff's perspective, one of the most obvious means of avoiding reputational damage or of minimising any damage already incurred is to prevent any

---

532. Defamation Act 2009, s 30(4).
533. Defamation Act 2009, s 30(3)(a).
534. Defamation Act 2009, s 30(3)(b).
535. See *Norbrook Laboratories Limited v Smithkline Beecham (Ireland) Limited* [1999] 2 IR 192.
536. Defamation Act 2009, s 29(4).

future publications of the defamatory statement at issue. Success at trial would typically have this effect by making it clear to a defendant that he or she will be liable in tort for any re-publication of the statement. The courts also tended to grant permanent injunctions as a matter of course[537] where there was any demonstrable risk of repetition[538] and it was just and equitable to do so.[539] Section 33 of the 2009 Act maintains the courts' jurisdiction to grant permanent injunctions. There seems no reason to anticipate that this section will bring about any significant change in the courts' previous approach to this issue.

[6.285] However, there are many situations in which a plaintiff might wish to be able to prevent such publications in advance of the full hearing of the issue. This is particularly the case where the material in question has not been published so the potential plaintiff's reputation is, at that point, unharmed. However, as the discussion below demonstrates, the courts have traditionally been very reluctant to issue orders proscribing publication where such orders would have the effect of imposing a prior restraint on as-yet-unexpressed speech. In this regard, the provisions of s 33 may represent a change to Irish law on this issue. Section 33 of the 2009 Act provides that a court may, upon the application of a plaintiff or applicant,[540] make an order prohibiting the publication or further publication of the statement in question. The threshold for the grant of such an order seems lower than that which applied before the passing of the 2009 Act. However, it is arguable, based on the pre–2009 Act jurisprudence, that the application of a lower threshold could contravene the guarantees of freedom of expression laid down by the Constitution and by Article 10 of the European Convention on Human Rights. For that reason, it may be useful in considering how s 33 may operate to examine in some detail the principles which were previously applied to applications for this type of remedy. It seems probable that it will be argued in future litigation that these principles should continue to inform the courts' interpretation of the terms of s 33.

Prior restraints

[6.286] It has been consistently held by both the Irish[541] courts and the European Court of Human Rights that the imposition of prior restraints on expression is a matter of particular concern. The European Court of Human Rights has warned on several occasions that prior restraints on publication entail such dangers that they call for the most careful scrutiny.[542] This is particularly so where an injunction is sought in relation

---

537. *Grobbelaar v News Group Newspapers* [2002] 1 WLR 3049.
538. *Proctor v Baylet* (1889) 42 Ch D 390.
539. *Dunlop v Dunlop* [1920] 1 IR 280.
540. Defamation Act 2009, s 28(6).
541. See, for example, *Garraghy v Bord na gCon* [2002] 3 IR 566; *Foley v Sunday Newspapers* [2005] 1 IR 88; *Cogley v RTÉ* [2005] 4 IR 79; *Mahon v Post Publications* [2007] 3 IR 338; *Evans v Carlyle* [2008] IEHC 143.
542. See, for example, *Sunday Times v UK (No 2)* [1991] ECHR 13166/87, para 51; *Dammann v Switzerland* [2006] ECHR 77551/01, para 52; *(VgT) v Switzerland (No 2)* (App No 32772/02 [2009] ECHR 32772/02.

to political or electoral matters.[543] This view has also been echoed by the English,[544] Australian[545] and New Zealand[546] courts. That does not mean, however, that such restraints are always impermissible. It requires rather, that any such interference with freedom of expression must have a clear legal basis,[547] must correspond to a pressing social need[548] and must be subjected to a very careful and searching degree of scrutiny by the court. Because of the importance of media expression, the Contracting State will enjoy only a limited margin of appreciation in such cases considering whether the interference meets a pressing social need and was therefore necessary in a democratic society.[549] As the court summarised the principle in *Observer & Guardian v United Kingdom*:

> Article 10 of the Convention does not in terms prohibit the imposition of prior restraints on publication, as such. ... On the other hand, the dangers inherent in prior restraints are such that they call for the most careful scrutiny by the Court. This is especially so as far as the press is concerned, for news is a perishable commodity and to delay its publication, even for a short period, may well deprive it of all its value and interest.[550]

This means that the courts have applied a very rigorous level of analysis to the arguments and the evidence adduced in applications for orders restraining media expression. As Munby J explained in *Kelly v British Broadcasting Corporation*:

> If those who seek to bring themselves within para 2 of Article 10 are to establish 'convincingly' that they are – and that is what they have to establish – they cannot do so by mere assertion, however eminent the person making the assertion, nor by simply inviting the court to make assumptions; what is required ... is proper evidence.[551]

The rule in Bonnard v Perryman

[6.287] As a result, the English courts have taken the view that freedom of expression requires that a very onerous burden be placed on the party seeking an interlocutory order restraining publication of an allegedly defamatory statement pending trial. In

---

543. *Quinlivan v O'Dea* [2009] IEHC 187.
544. *R (Laporte) v Chief Constable of Gloucestershire Constabulary* [2007] 2 AC 105; *Hall v Mayor of London* [2010] EWCA Civ 817.
545. *Australian Broadcasting Corporation v O'Neill* [2006] HCA 46, (2006) 22 BHRC 305.
546. *Hosking v Runting* [2005] 1 NZLR 1.
547. *Nikula v Finland* [2002] ECHR 31611/96; *Financial Times Ltd v United Kingdom* (2009) 28 BHRC 616 (App No 821/03).
548. *Bladet Tromso v Norway* (1999) 29 EHRR 125; *Kulis v Poland* (ApplicationKohl No 27209/03) [2009] ECHR 27209/03.
549. *Bladet Tromso v Norway* (1999) 29 EHRR 125, para 59; *Editions Plon v France* [2004] ECHR 58148/00, para 44; *Obukhova v Russia* (App No 34736/03) [2009] ECHR 34736/03; *Gül v Turkey* (App No 4870/02) [2010] ECHR 4870/02.
550. *Observer & Guardian v United Kingdom* (1992) 14 EHRR 153.
551. *Kelly v British Broadcasting Corporation* [2001] Fam 59.

general, applications for interlocutory injunctions are governed by the principles laid down by Lord Diplock in *American Cyanamid Co v Ethicon Limited*.[552] In short, these guidelines require a plaintiff who seeks an interlocutory order to demonstrate:

- the existence of a serious question to be tried;

- the inadequacy of damages; and

- that the balance of convenience lies in favour of the grant of the injunction.

However, while these principles are applicable to the majority of applications, the courts have also accepted that there are certain specific contexts in which different principles should apply. One such category is applications made in relation to allegedly defamatory statements. These cases are governed in England by what is known as the rule in *Bonnard v Perryman*.[553] It was held by the court in *Bonnard* that the courts retained a jurisdiction to grant interlocutory injunctive relief but that this should only be exercised to restrain the publication of an alleged libel in exceptional cases. In particular the court indicated that, in circumstances where a defendant pleaded justification, the order could only be granted where it was clear that the defence would fail. Lord Coleridge CJ explained the rationale for this rule as follows:

> The subject matter of an action for defamation is so special as to require exceptional caution in exercising the jurisdiction to interfere by injunction before the trial of an action to prevent an anticipated wrong. The right of free speech is one which it is for the public interest that individuals should possess, and, indeed, that they should exercise without impediment, so long as no wrongful act is done; and, unless an alleged libel is untrue, there is no wrong committed; but, on the contrary, often a very wholesome act is performed in the publication and repetition of an alleged libel. Until it is clear that an alleged libel is untrue, it is not clear that any right at all has been infringed; and the importance of leaving free speech unfettered is a strong reason in cases of libel for dealing most cautiously and warily with the granting of interim injunctions.[554]

[6.288] The English courts have continued to adopt this approach to application for interlocutory orders in defamation actions. A robust restatement of the principle was provided in the decision in *Greene v Associated Newspapers*, where the courts rejected the suggestion that the introduction of the Human Rights Act 1998, with its increased protection of the plaintiff's Article 8 rights, required that the rule in *Bonnard v Perryman* be re-evaluated and relaxed. In response, the court vigorously defended the underlying rationale for the rule:

> [I]n an action for defamation a court will not impose a prior restraint on publication unless it is clear that no defence will succeed at the trial. This is partly due to the importance the court attaches to freedom of speech. It is partly because a judge must not usurp the constitutional function of the jury unless he is satisfied

---

552. *American Cyanamid Co v Ethicon Limited* [1975] AC 396.
553. *Bonnard v Perryman* [1891] 2 Ch 269.
554. *Bonnard v Perryman* [1891] 2 Ch 269.

that there is no case to go to a jury. The rule is also partly founded on the pragmatic grounds that until there has been disclosure of documents and cross-examination at the trial a court cannot safely proceed on the basis that what the defendants wish to say is not true. And if it is or might be true the court has no business to stop them saying it. This is another way of putting the point … that a court cannot know whether the plaintiff has a right to his/her reputation until the trial process has shown where the truth lies. And if the defence fails, the defendants will have to pay damages (which in an appropriate case may include aggravated and/or exemplary damages as well).[555]

[6.289] It was thus held in *Greene* that the rule continued to apply such that, where a defendant pleaded justification, a claimant would not be able to obtain an interim injunction unless it were plain that the plea of justification was bound to fail. The Court of Appeal also pointed out that if a claimant were able to restrain a defendant in the exercise of his or her freedom of expression by arguing on paper-based evidence that it was more likely than not that the defendant could not show that what it wished to say about the claimant was true, that would seriously weaken the defendant's freedom of expression under Article 10. Thus the court warned that:

> [I]n a defamation action, on the other hand, while some damage may be done by permitting the publication of what may later turn out to be false, everyone knows that it is at the trial that truth or falsehood will be tested and the claimant vindicated if the defendant cannot prove that the sting of the libel is justified or that he has some other defence the law will recognise. The damage that may on occasion be done by refusing an injunction where a less strict rule would facilitate its grant pales into insignificance compared with the damage which would be done to freedom of expression and the freedom of the press if the rule in *Bonnard v Perryman* was relaxed.[556]

[6.290] The strictness of the rule in *Bonnard v Perryman* has had a number of implications for the litigation of defamation actions in England. One obvious consequence of placing this considerably heavier burden on plaintiffs in defamation actions is that individuals whose primary concern is to prevent or minimise damage to their reputation by preventing future publication have a significant incentive to base their claims on another cause of action. The English courts have thus been required to be alert to ensure that the rule is not circumvented by such tactical pleadings. While the rule in *Bonnard v Perryman* will not apply to claims based on other causes of action where a claim in defamation might also have been brought, the overriding need to protect freedom of speech means that the courts will apply the rule in *Bonnard v Perryman* if they take the view that a claim based on some other course of action was in reality a claim brought to protect the claimant's reputation.[557] Thus, it was decided in

---

555. [2005] QB 972, 990, [2005] 1 All ER 30.
556. *Greene v Associated Newspapers* [2005] QB 972, 994.
557. *Microdata Information Services v Riverdale* [1991] FSR 681; *Service Corporation International plc v Channel Four Television Corp* [1999] EMLR 83; *Boehringer Ingelheim Ltd v Vetplus Ltd* [2007] EWCA Civ 583.

LNS v Persons Unknown[558] that the plaintiff (then England football captain John Terry), while couching his claim in terms of a right to privacy, was primarily seeking to protect the commercial value of his reputation and that the rule in *Bonnard v Perryman* would accordingly apply. Tugenhadt J held that '[h]aving decided that the nub of this application is a desire to protect what is in substance reputation, it follows that in accordance with *Bonnard v Perryman* no injunction should be granted'.

[6.291] Another consequence of the strict application of this rule in England has been that it is very difficult, if not impossible, for plaintiffs to obtain injunctive relief once a defence of justification has been raised. This may be unfair in some situations where a defendant's case is very weak. This was evident, for example, in *Mosley v News Group Newspapers*[559] where the defendant's plea of justification in relation to the claim that the plaintiff had been involved in group sexual activity with a Nazi theme was a significant factor in the court refusing the plaintiff's application for interlocutory injunctive relief. This was so despite the fact that the allegation of a Nazi theme appeared primarily based on the fact that German was spoken during sexual activities which had a prison theme. Eady J accepted that the justification offered 'certainly appears very weak' but felt bound by the rule in *Bonnard v Perryman* to treat the mere fact of the plea, however weak, as a strong factor in his refusal to grant an order. That this can be unfair and damaging for a plaintiff is evident from Eady J's concluding addendum to his decision in which having received a copy of the newspaper's coverage after finishing the writing of his judgment, he observes that 'the newspaper has taken full advantage of the opportunity to criticise Mr Mosley yet again, including by reasserting its case that the sexual activities represented Nazi role-play'.[560]

The rule in Bonnard v Perryman *in Ireland*

[6.292] While the view has been expressed at various times that there was some uncertainty about the precise status of the rule in *Bonnard v Perryman* under Irish law,[561] it is submitted that a number of recent decisions of the courts had clarified that the rule – or at least some very similar variant of it – applied to interlocutory applications for injunctive relief in respect of allegedly defamatory statements prior to the passing of the 2009 Act.

[6.293] Much of the confusion derived from the decision of Carroll J in *Connolly v RTÉ*,[562] in which she appeared to hold that an application for an interlocutory injunction in a defamation action could be dealt with on the basis of the conventional principles laid down by the court in *Campus Oil v Minister for Industry & Energy (No 2)*,[563] which

---

558. *LNS v Persons Unknown* [2010] EWHC 119 (QB).
559. *Mosley v News Group Newspapers* [2008] EWHC 687 (QB).
560. *Mosley v News Group Newspapers* [2008] EWHC 687 (QB), para 39.
561. See, for example, Cox, *Defamation Law* (FirstLaw, 2007), 413.
562. *Connolly v RTÉ* [1991] 2 IR 446.
563. *Campus Oil v Minister for Industry & Energy (No 2)* [1983] IR 88.

principles broadly correspond to those set out in *American Cyanamid*.[564] In more recent decisions, however, the view has consistently been expressed that freedom of expression requires that such applications be dealt with on the basis of a higher threshold for the grant of the relief sought.[565] It is submitted, therefore, that any uncertainty that may have been created by the decision in Connolly had been removed by the time the 2009 Act was enacted.

[6.294] The rule in *Bonnard v Perryman* was first approved in Ireland by the Supreme Court in its decision in *Sinclair v Gogarty*.[566] O'Sullivan CJ held that:

> I realise that in granting an interlocutory injunction to restrain the publication of a libel the Court is exercising a jurisdiction which has been described as a jurisdiction of a delicate nature. The principle upon which the Court should act in considering such applications was stated by Lord Esher MR in *Coulson v Coulson* and his statement of the principle was approved of and adopted by the Court of Appeal in *Bonnard v Perryman*. The principle is this, that an interlocutory injunction should only be granted in the clearest cases where any jury would say that the matter complained of was libellous, and where if the jury did not so find the Court would set aside the verdict as unreasonable.[567]

[6.295] This principle has been reiterated by the courts in a number of relatively recent decisions. Kelly J, for example, expressed his support for the rule in *Bonnard v Perryman* in his decisions in *Reynolds v Malocco*,[568] *Gama v Minister for Enterprise, Trade and Employment*[569] and *Foley v Sunday Newspapers*.[570] In *Foley*, for example, he expressed the view that:

> If the present case were an action in defamation it is clear that having regard to what is being said on oath by the defendant to the effect that it stands over the allegations which it has made concerning the plaintiff, an injunction would not be granted.[571]

This reflected his view that:

> In this country we have a free press. The right to freedom of expression is provided for in Article 40 of the Constitution and Article 10 of the European Convention on Human Rights. It is an important right and one which the courts

---

564. *American Cyanamid* [1975] AC 396.
565. *Foley v Sunday Newspapers* [2005] 1 IR 88; *Cogley v RTÉ* [2005] 4 IR 79; *Gama Endustri Tesisleri Imalat Montaj AS v Minister for Enterprise, Trade and Employment* [2005] IEHC 119; *Mahon v Post Publications* [2007] 3 IR 338; *Evans v Carlyle* [2008] IEHC 143.
566. *Sinclair v Gogarty* [1937] IR 377. This view has been disputed by Casey in Casey, 'Injunction and freedom of expression' in Breen, Casey and Kerr (eds), Liber Memoralis – Professor James C Brady (Round Hall, 2001), but the conventional view has been accepted by the Irish courts in, for example, *Foley v Sunday Newspapers* [2005] 1 IR 88.
567. *Sinclair v Gogarty* [1937] IR 377, 383.
568. *Reynolds v Malocco* [1999] 2 IR 203.
569. *Gama v Minister for Enterprise, Trade and Employment* [2005] IEHC 119.
570. *Foley v Sunday Newspapers* [2005] 1 IR 88.
571. *Foley v Sunday Newspapers* [2005] 1 IR 88, 99.

must be extremely circumspect about curtailing particularly at the interlocutory stage of a proceeding.[572]

Thus, the court was satisfied that:

> [B]efore an injunction of this type should be granted the plaintiff would have to demonstrate by proper evidence a convincing case to bring about a curtailment of the freedom of expression of the press.

> This is particularly so having regard to the strongly expressed guarantees in the Constitution in favour of freedom of expression. The Irish (and indeed the English courts in the absence of a written constitution) have always shown a marked reluctance to exercise their injunction jurisdiction in a manner which would entrench on the freedom of expression enjoyed by the press and the media generally. A good example of this is to be found in the judgment of O'Hanlon J in *MM v Drury & Ors* [1994] 2 IR 8.

> This approach is also justified having regard to the provisions of Article 10 of the European Convention on Human Rights and the jurisprudence which has built up on foot of it.[573]

Although the court proceeded in *Foley* to consider the matter on the basis of conventional Campus Oil grounds, that approach was premised on the fact that the application there was grounded not on an alleged defamation but rather on an alleged threat to the applicant's constitutional right to life. The first passage cited above makes clear that the court would have applied the rule in *Bonnard v Perryman* if the case was one which had been framed in defamation.[574]

[6.296] Kelly J's decision in *Reynolds v Malocco* was discussed by Clarke J in *Cogley v RTÉ*[575] where it was described as 'the high water mark' for those seeking interlocutory relief. In Clarke J's view, *Reynolds* indicated that a plaintiff must not only show that he or she 'has raised a serious issue concerning the words complained of' but that it must also be shown 'that there is no doubt that they are defamatory'.

[6.297] It has been suggested, in large part on the basis of the fact that Clarke J referred to the decision in *Campus Oil* in determining this issue, that the decision in Cogley may represents a resilement from the rule in *Bonnard v Perryman*.[576] However, it should also

---

572. *Foley v Sunday Newspapers* [2005] 1 IR 88, 101.
573. *Foley v Sunday Newspapers* [2005] 1 IR 88, 102. It should be noted that Kelly J here was making a statement of general principle and was expressly not considering the specific requirements laid down by the rule in *Bonnard v Perryman*.
574. This leaves open, to some extent, the question of the extent to which the Irish courts would be willing to look behind the form of the pleadings to consider the reality of the plaintiff's claim. However, the decision not to rely on defamation as a cause of action in *Foley* was ostensibly based on the applicant's lack of a reputation which could be damaged. In the circumstances of that case, that seemed appropriate such that it would be inadvisable to read too much into Kelly J's willingness to accept the applicant's choice of cause of action.
575. *Cogley v RTÉ* [2005] 4 IR 79.
576. Cox, *Defamation Law* (FirstLaw, 2007), 414.

be noted that Clarke J cited *Sinclair v Gogarty* as representative of a 'a long line of authority' on the question of the availability of injunctive relief. It is submitted that, on a close reading of the relevant passages of Clarke J's decision, it is clear that his decision continues to impose an onerous burden on plaintiffs seeking an interlocutory injunction in respect of allegedly defamatory comments. Clarke J's view that a plaintiff must establish that a defendant does not have '*any* reasonable basis' for a defence, especially when taken together with his specific identification of various possible defences and his view that the court will not weigh the likelihood of any of these defences succeeding at trial, indicates that, for him, a plaintiff will only obtain relief where it is clear from a relatively cursory examination of the case that the defendant has no prospect of succeeding at trial. In substance, if not in citation, this is analogous to the rule in *Bonnard v Perryman*:

> It seems clear, therefore, that the first question that needs to be addressed in any interlocutory application in which a plaintiff seeks prior restraint on the publication or broadcast of material, on the grounds that it is defamatory is whether, on the evidence available at the interlocutory stage, it is clear that the plaintiff will ultimately succeed at a trial. For reasons which have been fully explored in the content of interlocutory injunctions generally, from the decision of the Supreme Court in *Campus Oil v Minister for Industry (No 2)* [1983] IR 88 onwards, it does not seem to me to be appropriate to ask this court at an interlocutory stage and where it will, necessarily, have available to it only a limited opportunity to consider the merits of a case, to attempt to weigh the likelihood of a plaintiff succeeding or failing. Similarly, it does not seem to be appropriate to invite the court to weigh the likelihood of the defendant succeeding in maintaining any defence in defamation proceedings. Thus the plaintiff will fail to cross the first hurdle if, on the basis of the argument and materials before the court, it appears that there is any reasonable basis for contending that the defendant may succeed at the trial of the action. The defendant may succeed in defending the action for any one of a number of reasons. For example, the words or materials intended to be broadcast or published may not be found to be defamatory in the first place. Though defamatory, the words may be shown, to the extent that they are defamatory, to be justified. There may on the facts of appropriate cases be possible defences of qualified privilege or, possibly, a public interest defence, although the availability and parameters of such a defence in this jurisdiction have yet to be clearly established. I am satisfied that the reference in the authorities to a clear case means a case where it is clear that the plaintiff will succeed and where, therefore, it is equally clear that none of the possible lines of defence which may be open to a defendant could reasonably succeed. [577]

Although the case did not concern the rule in *Bonnard v Perryman* directly, further support for the principle can be derived from the decision of the Supreme Court in *Mahon v Post Publications*[578] where Fennelly J, in particular, expressed his strong

---

577. *Cogley v RTÉ* [2005] 4 IR 79, 86.

578. *Mahon v Post Publications* [2007] 3 IR 338.

support for maintaining a strict approach to the availability of prior restraints under Irish law. He held that:

> It would represent a substantial departure from the existing law if courts were to make general orders of prior restraint in protection of the good name of individuals, even in applications at the suit of those individuals themselves. In the exceptional cases where that is done, the person moving the court must place before it cogent material to demonstrate that his or her name will be irreparably and seriously damaged if an impending publication was to take place.[579]

[6.298] Finally, in *Evans v Carlyle*, Hedigan J again referred to the rule in *Bonnard v Perryman* in his discussion of the relevant Irish law. He emphasised that a court should always 'bear in mind the importance and centrality of freedom of expression in the democratic process', and should only consider issuing an interlocutory order restraining publication 'warily and cautiously'.[580] Hedigan J's careful and commendably clear consideration of the previous authorities is worth setting out in full:

> The court's jurisdiction to grant interlocutory relief in the form of an injunction may be exercised where it is just and convenient to do so under Order 50, Rule 6 of the Rules of the Superior Courts. As has been decided in *Campus Oil v Minister for Industry (No 2)* [1983] IR 88, the court before exercising this jurisdiction must consider whether the plaintiff has raised a fair or serious issue to be determined at the trial of the action. If it considers that such a question has been raised, it must then consider whether damages would be adequate to compensate the plaintiff in respect of any wrong or damage suffered. If not, then it must further consider whether on the balance of convenience an interim injunction should be granted.
>
> In defamation cases, special rules apply. The jurisdiction of the court in this area has been described as 'of a delicate nature' which 'ought only to be exercised in the clearest cases'. (See Lord Esher MR in *Coulson v Coulson* (1887) 3 TLR stated at p 846.)
>
> This description of the jurisdiction was approved by the Supreme Court in *Sinclair v Gogarty* [1937] IR 377. Sullivan CJ delivering the judgment of the court stated (at p 384):
>
> > 'The principle upon which the court should act in considering such applications was stated by Lord Esher MR in *Coulson v Coulson*, and his statement of the principle was approved of and adopted by the Court of Appeal in *Bonnard v Perryman*. The principle is this, that an interlocutory injunction should only be granted in the clearest cases where any jury would say that the matter complained of was libellous, and where if the jury did not so find the court would set aside the verdict as unreasonable.'
>
> I have been referred to the recent judgement of Clarke J in *Cogley v Radio Telefís Éireann* [2005] 4 IR 79 at p 535.

---

579. *Mahon v Post Publications* [2007] 3 IR 338, 370.
580. *Evans v Carlyle* [2008] 2 ILRM 359, (2009) 27 ILT 200. See also the decision of Cooke J in *Quinlivan v O'Dea* [2009] IEHC 187.

Dealing with the granting of injunctions in defamation cases and reviewing the decisions to date, he observed (at p 86):

> 'It seems clear, therefore, that the first question that needs to be addressed in any interlocutory application in which a plaintiff seeks prior restraint on the publication or broadcast of material, on the grounds that it is defamatory is whether, on the evidence available at the interlocutory stage, it is clear that the plaintiff will ultimately succeed at a trial.
>
> For reasons which have been fully explored in the context of interlocutory injunctions generally, from the decision of the Supreme Court in *Campus Oil v Minister for Industry (No 2)* [1983] IR 88 onwards, it does not seem to me to be appropriate to ask this court at an interlocutory stage and where it will, necessarily, have available to it only a limited opportunity to consider the merits of a case, to attempt to weigh the likelihood of a plaintiff succeeding or failing. Similarly, it does not seem to be appropriate to invite the court to weigh the likelihood of the defendant succeeding in maintaining any defence in defamation proceedings. Thus the plaintiff will fail to cross the first hurdle if, on the basis of the argument and materials before the court, it appears that there is any reasonable basis for contending that the defendant may succeed at the trial of the action.'

Referring to the decision of Kelly J in *Reynolds v Malocco* [1999] 2 IR 203 Clarke J continued (at p 86):

> 'I am satisfied that the reference in the authorities to a clear case means a case where it is clear that the plaintiff will succeed and where, therefore, it is equally clear that none of the possible lines of defence which may be open to a defendant could reasonably succeed. Kelly J in *Reynolds v Malocco* did not depart from that principle. He rejected the proposition that a mere assertion of an intention to justify was, of itself, sufficient.'

Kelly J in *Reynolds v Malocco* indicated that the defendant should set out the grounds upon which he might succeed in successfully defending the case.

Applying these principles to cases of prior restraint it would seem clear that where the defendant in such an application can satisfy the court that there is at least a reasonable basis for contending that he may successfully defend the case at the hearing of the action, the court ought not to prohibit the publication.

[6.299] On the facts of the case before him, Hedigan J went on to find that an interlocutory order could be granted, primarily on the basis that this was a case of continuing rather than prior restraint in which the statement in question had plainly been made with malice. However, his decision seems to represent a general endorsement of the principle that, as a matter of common law authority and constitutional principle, interlocutory injunctions should only be granted to restrain publication in advance of a trial of an alleged defamation in those limited cases where a defendant cannot show any reasonable basis for a successful defence of the action.

[6.300] It is submitted that these decisions show that, prior to the passing of the 2009 Act, there was very little difference, if any, between the approach adopted by the Irish and English courts to applications for interlocutory orders in defamation case. The major point of potential difference between the two is the fact that the Irish courts had begun to refer to a requirement of reasonableness in considering whether a defendant might ultimately succeed at trial. Whereas the decision in *Greene* required a plaintiff to show that 'it is clear that no defence will succeed at the trial', the decisions in *Cogley* and *Evans* refer to a defendant having to show 'any' or 'at least' some 'reasonable basis' for a successful defence at trial. As noted above, however, it should also be borne in mind that these decisions also emphasised that the courts ought not to engage in an analysis of the defendant's likely prospects of success at trial. For that reason, it is submitted that there is no real difference in practice between the two tests.[581]

[6.301] On the contrary, it is arguable that the references to reasonableness in the Irish cases are concerned with the specific and relatively narrow question of whether a defendant can resist an application for injunction by the simple expedient of including a bare plea of, for example, justification or Reynolds privilege. The Irish courts, following Kelly J's view in *Reynolds v Malocco*, appear to be of the view that they are entitled in appropriate cases to engage in a prima facie review of the defendant's case so as to avoid the danger – adverted to above in the discussion of Mosley – that 'a rigid rule without an ability on the part of the court to ascertain whether the plea of justification had any substance or not would provide a happy hunting ground for unscrupulous defamers'.[582] This approach appears also to have been adopted in several cases in England.[583] This would tend to suggest that any perceived difference between the Irish and English approaches pre-2009 Act was a matter of semantics rather than reality.

[6.302] In this regard, it may be useful to note the way in which the Australian courts apply the rule in *Bonnard v Perryman* as this tends to support the view that, regardless of the language used, the test appears to be applied in the same way in practice in each jurisdiction:

> [T]he power [to grant an interlocutory injunction in defamation cases] is exercised with great caution, and only in very clear cases. If there is any real room for debate as to whether the statements complained of are defamatory, the injunction will be refused. Indeed, it is only where on this point, the position is so clear that, in the judge's view a subsequent finding by a jury to the contrary would be set aside as unreasonable, that the injunction will go. If, on the evidence before the judge, there is any real ground for supposing that the defendant may succeed upon any such ground as privilege, or of truth and public benefit, or even that the plaintiff if successful, will recover nominal damages only, the injunction will be refused.[584]

---

581. Support for this analysis can be found in the decision of the Australian High Court in *Australian Broadcasting Corporation v O'Neill* [2006] HCA 46, (2006) 22 BHRC 305.
582. *Reynolds v Malocco* [1999] 2 IR 203, 209.
583. *Holey v Smith* [1998] EMLR 133; *Greene v Associated Newspapers* [2005] 1 All ER 30.
584. *Stocker v McElhinney (No 2)* [1961] NSWR 1043, 1048, cited with approval in *Australian Broadcasting Corporation v O'Neill* (2006) 22 BHRC 305, 317.

Section 33

[6.303] This is the background against which s 33 of the 2009 Act was enacted. Section 33(1) provides that:

> The High Court, or where a defamation action has been brought, the court in which it was brought, may, upon the application of the plaintiff, make an order prohibiting the publication or further publication of the statement in respect of which the application was made if in its opinion—
>
> (a)   the statement is defamatory, and
>
> (b)   the defendant has no defence to the action that is reasonably likely to succeed.

Applications under s 33 are to be brought by way of a motion on notice to the opposing party, grounded upon an affidavit.[585] Where no defamation action has yet been brought, an application for an interim order shall, unless the court otherwise directs, be made by originating motion ex parte. The title of such an application should be 'In the matter of s 33' with the prospective plaintiff named as applicant and prospective defendant named as respondent.[586] Where the application is brought for an interlocutory or permanent injunction, it may be brought by way of originating notice of motion.

[6.304] Perhaps the most important question raised by the enactment of s 33(1) is whether it provides for a lower threshold to be applied to applications for interlocutory injunctions. Cox points out that one of the criteria for the granting of an order under this section – that of a defendant having no defence that is 'reasonably likely to succeed' – seems to represent a relaxation of the strict approach previously adopted to such applications in Ireland.[587] Certainly, to the extent that the reference to reasonable *likelihood* of success tends to suggest that the courts should engage in some analysis of the merits of the defendant's case at the interlocutory stage, this analysis seems correct. Such an interpretation of s 33 would represent a radical change in Irish law. In particular, as Cox again points out,[588] it would also raise question marks about the constitutionality and Convention-compatibility of this section. As the discussion above demonstrates, the courts – both in Ireland and elsewhere – have consistently held that freedom of expression requires that prior restraint orders be granted only in the rarest and clearest of cases. If s 33 is designed to make it easier for plaintiffs to secure such orders in advance of a full hearing of the action, this would undoubtedly raise real constitutional and Convention concerns.

[6.305] Nonetheless, it is arguable that s 33 may be capable of operating in a manner which accords with the Constitution's guarantee of freedom of expression and is compatible with Ireland's obligations under Article 10 of the Convention. In this regard,

---

585.   Order 1B, rule, 3(3).
586.   Order 1B, rule 3(4)(i).
587.   Cox, *Defamation Law* (FirstLaw, 2007), 437.
588.   Cox, *Defamation Law* (FirstLaw, 2007), 437.

the double-construction rule[589] of statutory interpretation and the interpretative obligation set out in the European Convention on Human Rights Act 2003[590] may both be relevant. In particular, it is submitted that the continued application by the courts of the principles set out in decisions such as *Reynolds*, *Cogley* and *Evans* to applications for interlocutory relief might alleviate some of the concerns raised by s 33(1)(b). It will be recalled that the courts in those cases held that it was inappropriate for the courts to engage in an assessment of the defendant's prospects of success at the interlocutory stage. It was stated that an application for relief would be rejected once the defendant could demonstrate any reasonable basis for a successful defence at trial. Arguably, this test is not inconsistent with that laid down by s 33(1)(b). This is especially so given the negative formulation of s 33(1)(b) in terms of a defendant having 'no defence'.

[6.306] The key factor in determining whether these applications are dealt with in a way that raises freedom of expression concerns is arguably the extent to which the court engages in an assessment of the prima facie merits of the defendant's case. The courts could, in applying s 33(1)(b), continue to refrain from weighing the defendant's prospects of success in light of the evidence available at that point and instead consider only whether the defendant's case discloses any reasonable basis upon which he or she has any prospect (or to use the language of the section, likelihood) of success. If the test of there being no defence with any reasonable likelihood of success is dealt with on the basis of a judicial assessment of what is possible rather than what is probable, this would seem less likely to give rise to serious constitutional or Convention concerns.

Prior publication

[6.307] It is arguable that it may be easier to obtain an interlocutory injunction where the order would operate not as a prior restraint but as a restriction on the continuation of existing speech. In *Evans v Carlyle*,[591] this was a factor which was taken into account by Hedigan J in coming to the conclusion that the injunction could be granted. Hedigan J, although emphasising that this was an exceptional case and that the courts should continue to be reluctant to grant such orders, did appear to accept that this was a lesser interference with the defendant's freedom of expression:

> In this case there has already been publication. The defendant has had his say. This is significant in the sense that there is a strong public interest in ensuring that a citizen can have his say and call attention to the possibility of corruption in the planning process. There are also his Constitutional and Convention rights to freedom of expression. He has had the opportunity to exercise these rights and has taken it in the most dramatic manner. His freedom of expression, therefore, has already been exercised in an immediate sense.

As against that, it has been held in a number of other cases that prior publication may make it more difficult to obtain an injunction, on the basis that the damage to the plaintiff has already been caused, such that an interlocutory injunction would be of little

---

589. *McDonald v Bord na gCon (No 2)* [1965] IR 217.
590. European Convention on Human Rights Act 2003, s 2.
591. *Evans v Carlyle* [2008] IEHC 143.

benefit.[592] The relevance of this factor may depend on the extent of the prior publication and on whether the defendant was involved in the initial publication.[593]

Quia timet injunctions

[6.308] A plaintiff or applicant may face additional difficulties when seeking to obtain a quia timet injunction restraining the threatened publication of allegedly defamatory material. This is based, in part, on the logic of Hedigan J's position in *Evans v Carlyle*[594] that an order preventing publication where none has previously occurred represents an even greater restriction of the addressee's freedom of expression. It also reflects, however, the fact that a plaintiff will find it difficult to demonstrate that the threat exists and, in particular, that any statement made would be defamatory, in circumstances where there has been no previous publication.

[6.309] As MacDermott LJ observed in the *Northern Irish courts in Finucane v Yorkshire Television*:

> The court has jurisdiction to grant an injunction quia timet before any publication of the defamatory matter takes place. In most cases, however, where the plaintiff is aware that defamatory matter is to be published about him he will not know the actual words which will be used and in these circumstances no injunction is likely to be granted. It is to be remembered that 'no one can obtain a quia timet order by merely saying 'Timeo'; he must aver and prove that what is going on is calculated to infringe his rights'.[595]

However, it was held in *British Data Management plc v Boxer Commercial Removals plc*[596] that this did not require a plaintiff to identify the precise words alleged to be defamatory as a prerequisite to the granting of a quia timet order. However, Hirst LJ indicated that the pleadings must identify the threatened conduct with sufficient precision to meet a threshold of reasonable certainty. In his view:

> [T]here must in all cases be reasonable certainty as to the words complained of, or in the case of a quia timet injunction what words are threatened, and normally this will require the pleading of the actual words or words to the same effect. Only on this basis can the case proceed properly through the interlocutory and pleading stages to trial, and then to the formulation of the questions to be put to the jury and to a proper answer to them.[597]

In this regard, it may be relevant to note that Order 1B requires that an affidavit sworn in an application under s 31 identify with sufficient precision or exhibit a copy or transcript of the statement in respect of which the application is made.[598]

---

592. *M v Drury* [1994] 2 IR 8.
593. *Barclays Bank v Guardian* [2009] EWHC 591 (QB).
594. *Evans v Carlyle* [2008] IEHC 143.
595. *Northern Irish courts in Finucane v Yorkshire Television* (11 July 1996, unreported), HC.
596. *British Data Management plc v Boxer Commercial Removals plc* [1996] 3 All ER 707.
597. *British Data Management plc v Boxer Commercial Removals plc* [1996] 3 All ER 707, 717.
598. Order 1B, rule 3(5).

Ex parte applications

[6.310] It appears as if the courts will be especially reluctant to grant interlocutory applications for injunctions concerning allegedly defamatory statements where those applications have been made on an ex parte basis. In *Cogley v RTÉ*, Clarke J expressed the view that:

> Given that obligation [to grant prior restraint orders only after careful scrutiny] it seems to me that a court should be reluctant to grant interim orders which would have the effect of restraining, in advance, publication in circumstances where the intended publisher has not had an opportunity to be heard. For those reasons it seems to me that where it is at all possible, the court should attempt to afford the defendant at least some opportunity to put before the court its case prior to making any form of restraint order. There will, of course, be cases where, for one reason or another, that is simply not possible. The time between the initial application to the court and the intended publication or broadcast may, in practice, be too short. In such circumstances the court may still have to consider granting an interim order but apart from the general considerations, which are dealt with in more detail later in the course of this judgment, which the court must keep in mind in granting any order of prior restraint, this court should, in my view, in addition at an interim stage have regard to the question of whether the fact, if it be so, that there is no time to put the defendant on notice can, in any way, be attributed to a default or delay on the part of a plaintiff. Thus, if a plaintiff delays in applying to the court in a manner which effectively precludes the court from ensuring that the defendant is given an opportunity to be heard prior to any order being made, that fact of itself must be taken into account by the court as a significant factor which would lean against the grant of an interim order. Furthermore, any delay on the part of a plaintiff which, while not so severe as to preclude the court from affording the defendant an opportunity to be heard prior to the consideration of the making of an order, nonetheless places the defendant in a position where he may be prejudiced in the presentation of his case at a hearing designed to determine whether there should be prior restraint, is also a factor that will have to be taken into account in appropriate cases.[599]

[6.311] This view was echoed by Eady J in *X and Y v The Person or Persons who have Offered and/or Provided to the Publishers of The Mail on Sunday, Mirror and Sun Newspapers Information about the Status of the Claimants' Marriage*[600] to the effect that:

> [A] proper consideration for the Article 10 Convention rights of media publishers, and indeed their rights under Article 6 as well, would require that where a litigant intends to serve a prohibitory injunction upon one or more of them, in reliance on the Spycatcher principle, those individual publishers should be given a realistic opportunity to be heard on the appropriateness or otherwise of granting the injunction, and upon the scope of its terms. As is well known, it is relatively easy

599. *Cogley v RTÉ* [2005] 4 IR 79, 82–83.
600. *X and Y v The Person or Persons who have Offered and/or Provided to the Publishers of The Mail on Sunday, Mirror and Sun Newspapers Information about the Status of the Claimants' Marriage* [2007] 1 FLR 1567.

for the media in such circumstances to instruct their lawyers to come to court at short notice and, if they are content to do so and no conflict arises, to arrange for common representation.[601]

Addressees of order

[6.312] Although an application for an injunction will usually be concerned with a particular defendant, there may be circumstances in which a plaintiff would wish to obtain an order in terms capable of binding other potential publishers. This is particularly relevant in circumstances where the person in question is concerned about publication by unknown or multiple parties, such as might arise in situations where a story or allegation may be covered by a number of media organisations or on the internet.

[6.313] In this regard, it was held by Butler-Sloss P in *Venables v New Groups Newspapers*[602] that the court had a power to issue an injunction contra mundum, particularly where that was necessary to protect an individual's rights under the Convention. However, the view has subsequently been expressed that such orders should only be available in extreme cases.[603]

[6.314] The English courts have also held that injunctions can be granted against persons where the identity of those persons is unknown. It was held in *Bloomsbury Publishing Group Ltd v News Group Newspapers Ltd* that an order can in principle be made against 'persons unknown', provided that they are adequately described.[604] Such orders have also been granted in a number of other cases in England.[605]

[6.315] It has been argued that such so-called 'John Doe' injunctions may not be available in Ireland as a result of the requirement in the Rules of the Superior Courts that a writ be served on a person in personam.[606] However, the High Court was prepared in *Maguire v Gill*[607] to issue an order covering 'all persons having notice of the making of this Order' in circumstances where the identities of some of the persons who had engaged in the publication of allegedly defamatory statements were unknown. It is also arguable that the Rules of the Superior Courts should not take precedence in circumstances where it would be otherwise necessary and appropriate to grant a 'John Doe' injunction to protect the individual's constitutional right to their good name.

---

601. *X and Y v The Person or Persons who have Offered and/or Provided to the Publishers of The Mail on Sunday, Mirror and Sun Newspapers Information about the Status of the Claimants' Marriage* [2007] 1 FLR 1567, 1573–1574.
602. *Venables v New Groups Newspapers* [2001] 1 All ER 90, [2001] 2 WLR 1038.
603. *Mills v News Group Newspapers* [2001] EMLR 957.
604. *Bloomsbury Publishing Group Ltd v News Group Newspapers Ltd* [2003] EWHC 1205 (Ch).
605. *Hampshire Waste Services Ltd v Persons unknown* [2003] EWHC 1738 (Ch); *South Cambridgeshire DC v Persons unknown* [2004] 4 PLR 88; *X & Y v Person unknown* [2007] 1 FLR 1567.
606. Kirwan, *Injunctions: Law and Practice* (Thomson Round Hall, 2008), based on RSC 1986, Order 9, rule 1.
607. *Maguire v Gill* (13 September 2006, unreported), HC.

Damages

General damages

[6.316] Prior to the passing of the 2009 Act, the primary remedy for a successful plaintiff in an action for libel or slander was an award of damages. Damages were regarded as a suitable mechanism to vindicate the plaintiff's right to his or her good name. It has been held by the English courts that:

> An award of general damages for libel serves three functions: first, to act as a consolation to the Claimant for the stress and embarrassment which she has suffered from the publication of defamatory words; secondly, to compensate for the injury to her reputation; and thirdly, to act as vindication for her reputation.[608]

However, the Irish system had long been criticised by defendants (in particular media organisations) for the high level of damages awarded to successful plaintiffs. The description of the English system as '[a] road to untaxed riches ... [the] legal process fail[ing] to command the respect of lawyer and layman alike,'[609] was one which would have been echoed by many defendants in Ireland as well. Cox has observed that such awards can have a deterrent effect on media organisations in particular.[610] However, the very fact that such awards can have such a deterrent effect illustrates the main difficulty with the former system – that by discouraging media organisations from engaging in conduct which might ultimately be found to be defamatory, such awards could have a chilling effect on freedom of expression.[611] The fear was that this chilling effect could apply with as much force to valid hard-hitting journalism as to less defensible forms of media excess.

Thus, the Irish courts and the European Court of Human Rights had been called upon to examine this controversial aspect of Irish defamation law on a number of occasions in recent years. A brief review of these decisions is appropriate in order to consider the significance of the changes introduced by the 2009 Act.

ARTICLE 10 OF THE EUROPEAN CONVENTION ON HUMAN RIGHTS

[6.317] In *Tolstoy Miloslavsky v UK*, the European Court of Human Rights held that an award of damages of £1.5m in a libel action contravened Article 10 as a disproportionate breach of the defendant's Article 10 rights. The court was particularly concerned with the latitude allowed to the jury under English law at the time. While it accepted that the jury should enjoy a wide discretion, the court also had regard to the fact that an award of this sort could not be set aside on appeal simply on the grounds that it was excessive, but only if the award was so unreasonable that it could not have been made by sensible people and must have been arrived at capriciously, unconscionably or

---

608. *Coad v Cruze* [2009] EWHC 3782 (QB), para 39.
609. *John v Mirror Group Newspapers* [1997] QB 586, 611,
610. Cox, *Defamation Law* (FirstLaw, 2007), 362.
611. *Tolstoy Miloslavsky v UK* (1995) 20 EHRR 442.

irrationally. Given the chilling effect which a large award of damages could have on freedom of expression, the court regarded this as insufficient to meet the United Kingdom's obligation under Article 10. In the court's view, 'the scope of judicial control, at the trial and on appeal, at the time of the applicant's case did not offer adequate and effective safeguards against a disproportionately large award'.[612]

[6.318] Prompted in part[613] by the decision in *Tolstoy Miloslavsky*, the English courts sought to develop additional safeguards against the award of excessively high damages by juries. This was done in two ways. One was by the provision of guidelines to juries as to the level of damages which might be considered appropriate. This derived from the decisions in *Rantzen v Mirror Group Newspapers*[614] and *John v Mirror Group Newspapers*.[615] The court in *John* set out in some detail how it hoped such a system might work:

> We can for our part see no reason why the parties' respective counsel in a libel action should not indicate to the jury the level of award which they respectively contend to be appropriate, nor why the judge in directing the jury should not give a similar indication. The plaintiff will not wish the jury to think that his main object is to make money rather than clear his name. The defendant will not wish to add insult to injury by underrating the seriousness of the libel. So we think the figures suggested by responsible counsel are likely to reflect the upper and lower bounds of a realistic bracket. The jury must of course make up their own mind and must be directed to do so. They will not be bound by the submission of counsel or the indication of the judge. If the jury make an award outside the upper or lower bounds of any bracket indicated and such award is the subject of appeal, real weight must be given to the possibility that their judgment is to be preferred to that of the judge. The modest but important changes of practice described above would not in our view undermine the enduring constitutional position of the libel jury. Historically, the significance of the libel jury has lain not in their role of assessing damages but in their role of deciding whether the publication complained of is a libel or no. The changes which we favour will, in our opinion, buttress the constitutional role of the libel jury by rendering their proceedings more rational and so more acceptable to public opinion.

[6.319] It is thus permissible under English law for parties and for a judge to suggest appropriate levels of damage to a jury. Juries may also be directed to consider the damages typically awarded in personal injuries actions. However, some doubts have been expressed that the giving of guidelines to juries may have adverse consequences.

---

612. *Tolstoy Miloslavsky v UK* (1995) 20 EHRR 442, para 50.
613. It should be noted that the decision in *Rantzen v Mirror Group Newspapers* [1994] QB 670 pre-dated the European Court of Human Rights' decision and was, indeed, referred to by the Court in that case.
614. *Rantzen v Mirror Group Newspapers* [1994] QB 670.
615. *John v Mirror Group Newspapers* [1997] QB 586.

Pill LJ, for example, warned in *Kiam v Neil (No 2)*[616] that trial judges may have to be alert to some of the risks inherent in this process. He said, at 516–517:

> I agree that awards which in the words of the Master of the Rolls in John are 'in sums wildly disproportionate to any damage conceivably suffered by the plaintiff' constitute a mischief and there is need to seek means, as the courts have been doing, by which to eliminate that mischief and also to ensure that the Court of Appeal can be, as Lord Lester described it, a safety net. The danger I foresee in inviting juries to make comparisons with other cases, comparisons which would inevitably become elaborate as each party emphasises particular but different features of those other cases, is that the jury will be distracted from their central duty to consider the circumstances of the case in hand and make an award based on their conscientious assessment of what is involved. I agree with the Master of the Rolls' call for discretion in citing awards. In this context, a 'battle of comparable' in front of a jury may produce its own injustice, as well as being time consuming and costly.[617]

[6.320] The second change introduced by the English courts was to allow appellate courts to subject jury award to a higher level of scrutiny than had previously been the case.[618] However, the traditionally pre-eminent position of the jury means that the courts in England remain reluctant to interfere with such awards. In fact, the provision of guidelines to juries has arguably removed some of the justification for allowing appellate courts to interfere with jury awards by reducing the prospect (at least in theory) of a jury reaching a poorly-reasoned conclusion. In *Kiam v Neil (No 2)* for example, Evans LJ insisted that the jury should remain the primary decision-maker on the issue of damages:

> ... I cannot accept [the submission that that the court has to assess what it regards as a 'reasonable' figure without regard to the jury's award]. If correct, it would mean that the measure of compensation and liability would depend upon the views of three (or five) judges rather than of the jury. This would be to usurp the traditional and statutory function of the jury, and whether it would lead to greater certainty in predicting the amount of the eventual award (a factor which has been regarded as important under the European Convention) must be a matter for debate. If on the other hand the appellants' submission is that the court should consider whether the figure is one which 'a reasonable jury' (see the conclusion in *Rantzen* quoted above) could properly award then it seems to me that this is entirely in line not only with Rantzen but also with the common law authorities to which Lord Donaldson MR referred in *Sutcliffe* ... The significance of the judgments in *Rantzen* and *John*, in my view, is that the legal requirements of a valid award have been redefined in the light of recent developments in the law, including recognition as part of the common law of the principles expressed in the European Convention. In considering whether the jury's figure is excessive, or inadequate, therefore, the court has to define the legal limits and decide whether the award is outside them, or not. The limits include the court's own assessment of

---

616. *Kiam v Neil (No 2)* [1996] EMLR 493.
617. *Kiam v Neil (No 2)* [1996] EMLR 493, 516–17.
618. *Rantzen v Mirror Group Newspapers* [1994] QB 670.

what a reasonable jury could properly decide, because that is the only way in which the court can combine the requirements of the law with the jury's freedom of decision. But this does not mean, in my judgment, that within those limits the court is permitted to give effect to its own view as to the reasonableness or otherwise of the jury's award.[619]

[6.321] This reflected, in part, Evans LJ's point that the legislature had not intervened to alter the situation and that therefore the courts should be wary of unduly or inappropriately displacing the position of the jury. Beldam LJ also laid some stress on this consideration:

> It is, I think, necessary to bear in mind that Parliament has repeatedly declined to attenuate the right of a plaintiff who claims trial by jury in a libel action ... Whilst it is tempting to think that the greater the guidance given by judges, the more rational the jury's conclusion is likely to be, it seems to me that if the failure of the jury to keep its award within bounds indicated by a judge gives rise merely to the possibility that their judgment is to be preferred to that of the judge, the court may appear to preserve only the semblance of a right which Parliament has repeatedly affirmed.[620]

It has thus been held as a matter of English law that an appellate court should not interfere with the jury's award unless it regards it as substantially exceeding the most that any jury could reasonably have thought appropriate.[621]

DEVELOPMENTS IN IRELAND

[6.322] During this period, the Irish courts were asked to consider whether Irish law should be amended in light of these developments in England and in Strasbourg. The first major case in which this matter was considered was that of *De Rossa v Independent Newspapers*.[622] This case concerned an appeal to the Supreme Court against an award of £300,000 to the plaintiff for libel. The court refused to follow the English approach of providing guidelines to juries. Hamilton CJ, for the majority, emphasised the unique nature of each individual defamation case and accordingly concluded that figures awarded in other cases based on different facts were not matters which a jury should be entitled to take into account. He also held that the provision of suggested guidelines to a jury by a judge or by the parties would be liable to lead to confusion and would inappropriately trespass on the function of the jury.

[6.323] As regards the ability of the courts to consider setting aside an award of damages on appeal, Hamilton CJ drew a distinction between English and Irish law on this issue. He pointed out that:

> [T]he damages awarded by a jury must be fair and reasonable having regard to all the relevant circumstances and must not be disproportionate to the injury suffered

---

619. *Kiam v Neil (No 2)* [1996] EMLR 493, 513.
620. *Kiam v Neil (No 2)* [1996] EMLR 493, 507–508.
621. *Kiam v MGN Ltd* [2002] EWCA Civ 43, para 48.
622. *De Rossa v Independent Newspapers* [1999] 4 IR 432

by the injured party and the necessity to vindicate such party in the eyes of the public. Awards made by a jury are subject to a right of appeal and on the hearing of such appeal, the award made by a jury is scrutinised to ensure that the award complies with these principles.[623]

Awards made by jury could be set aside by an appellate court if it was satisfied that in all the circumstances, the award is so disproportionate to the injury suffered and wrong done that no reasonable jury would have made such an award.

[6.324] Another attempt was made to re-litigate this issue shortly afterwards in *O'Brien v Mirror Group Newspapers*. Coming so soon after the decision in *De Rossa*, it was not surprising that the Supreme Court confirmed the principles set out by Hamilton CJ in that case. However, unlike *De Rossa*, the court concluded in the circumstances of that case that the award of £250,000 was disproportionate and should be set aside.

[6.325] While these decisions were subject to considerable criticism, it should be noted that the European Court of Human Rights, when presented with the opportunity to consider the *De Rossa* litigation in *Independent Newspapers v Ireland*,[624] held that there had been no breach of Article 10. Their decision was based primarily on the fact that the Irish appellate courts retained the power to consider the proportionality of an award (as had been done in *De Rossa*) and set aside any considered to be disproportionate.

[6.326] However, the practical limitations of relying on the appellate jurisdiction alone as a means of ensuring the proportionality of awards were starkly illustrated by the coda to the *O'Brien v Mirror Group* Newspapers litigation when the plaintiff, having had an award of £250,000 set aside by the Supreme Court as disproportionate, was awarded £750,000 by a second jury when the matter was remitted to the High Court.[625] That jury did not of course have the benefit of information or guidelines about the Supreme Court's decision.

THE 2009 ACT

[6.327] Section 31 of the 2009 Act is designed to deal with a number of the criticisms which had been made in relation to the previous Irish approach to damages. It provides that the parties in a defamation action may make submissions to the court (which means the jury in a High Court action)[626] in relation to the matter of damages,[627] and that a judge in a High Court defamation action *shall* give directions to the jury in relation to the matter of damages.[628] Section 31 goes on to identify a number of non-exhaustive[629] factors to which the court must have regard in making an award of general damages.

---

623. *De Rossa v Independent Newspapers* [1999] 4 IR 432, 462.
624. *Independent Newspapers v Ireland* [2005] ECHR 55120/00.
625. See, for example, 'Bizarre libel law trebles damages to O'Brien', (2006) *The Irish Independent*, 24 November.
626. Defamation Act 2009, s 31(8).
627. Defamation Act 2009, s 31(1).
628. Defamation Act 2009, s 31(2).
629. Defamation Act 2009, s 31(3).

These factors, which are similar to those discussed by Henchy J in *Barrett v Independent Newspapers*,[630] are as follows:[631]

(a) the nature and gravity of any allegation in the defamatory statement concerned,

(b) the means of publication of the defamatory statement including the enduring nature of those means,

(c) the extent to which the defamatory statement was circulated,

(d) the offering or making of any apology, correction or retraction by the defendant to the plaintiff in respect of the defamatory statement,

(e) the making of any offer to make amends under section 22 by the defendant, whether or not the making of that offer was pleaded as a defence,

(f) the importance to the plaintiff of his or her reputation in the eyes of particular or all recipients of the defamatory statement,

(g) the extent (if at all) to which the plaintiff caused or contributed to, or acquiesced in, the publication of the defamatory statement,

(h) evidence given concerning the reputation of the plaintiff,

(i) if the defence of truth is pleaded and the defendant proves the truth of part but not the whole of the defamatory statement, the extent to which that defence is successfully pleaded in relation to the statement.

(j) if the defence of qualified privilege is pleaded, the extent to which the defendant has acceded to the request of the plaintiff to publish a reasonable statement by way of explanation or contradiction, and

(k) any order made under section 33, or any order under that section or correction order that the court proposes to make or, where the action is tried by the High Court sitting with a jury, would propose to make in the event of there being a finding of defamation.

[6.328] Order 1B, rule 10 also appears to suggest that evidence of the circumstances in which the statement was published may be adduced, provided particulars of that evidence are supplied to the plaintiff at least seven days before trial.

[6.329] Furthermore, evidence that a broadcaster granted or offered to grant a right of reply to the plaintiff under s 49 of the Broadcasting Act 2009 in respect of the statement to which the action relates either before the bringing of the action or as soon as practicable thereafter, is admissible in mitigation of damages.[632] However, a defendant who intends to give evidence of this must, at the time of the filing or delivery of the defence to the action, notify the plaintiff in writing of his or her intention to give such evidence.[633]

[6.330] It is reasonably obvious how these individual factors could affect a judge or jury's decision in relation to an award of damages. Thus, the more serious the

---

630. *Barrett v Independent Newspapers* [1986] IR 13.
631. Defamation Act 2009, s 31(4).
632. Broadcasting Act 2009, s 49(14).
633. Broadcasting Act 2009, s 49(15).

defamation, the higher the award of damages may be.[634] Similarly, the greater the circulation of the statement, the higher the award of damages may be.[635]

[6.331] Perhaps the most interesting provision in sub-s (4) is the statement that a defendant is entitled to give evidence concerning the reputation of the plaintiff. While a defendant was always entitled to argue that a plaintiff had no reputation to defame,[636] the common law had been reluctant to entertain arguments that the plaintiff enjoyed an undeserved reputation.[637] Thus, a defendant was only entitled to admit evidence of bad reputation in mitigation of damages and could not provide evidence of instances of specific misconduct which would go to reputation.

[6.332] This so-called rule in *Scott v Sampson* was subject to a number of exceptions at common law. For example, evidence of convictions was admissible in the consideration of damages,[638] as was evidence of misconduct which was submitted as part of a plea of justification.[639]

[6.333] However, in more recent authorities, the courts have tended to demonstrate an increasing willingness to dispense with the strictures of the 'unsatisfactory'[640] rule in *Scott v Sampson*. This has been justified by the English courts on the basis that the rule was introduced as a primarily procedural mechanism to avoid unduly complicating the trial of the action. As the Court of Appeal explained in *Turner v Associated Newspapers*,[641] such considerations carry much less force today:

> [T]he principle in *Scott v Sampson* and its indorsement in the *Plato Films* case were in large part based upon concern about the risks of 'trials within a trial', a concern which as May LJ observed in *Burstein's* case the court is now better equipped to deal with than in the past because of its case management powers; that the principle has never been absolute;

The court held therefore that evidence which qualified as evidence of directly relevant background context had to be evidence which was so clearly relevant to the subject-matter of the libel or to the claimant's reputation or sensitivity in that part of his life that there would be a real risk of the jury assessing damages on a false basis if they were kept in ignorance of the facts to which the evidence related. A defendant who sought to adduce such evidence might ultimately face a penalty in damages but this was a tactical matter for the defendant to judge. This reflected the court's view that '[f]airness requires

634. *De Rossa v Independent Newspapers* [1999] 4 IR 432.
635. *De Rossa v Independent Newspapers* [1999] 4 IR 432; *Crofter Properties Ltd v Genport* [2002] 4 IR 73.
636. *Magee v MGN* [2003] IEHC 87; *Foley v Sunday Newspapers* [2005] 1 IR 88.
637. *Scott v Sampson* (1882) 8 QBD 491.
638. *Hill v Cork Examiner* [2001] 4 IR 219.
639. *Chalmers v Shackell* (1834) 6 C & P 475; *Sutter v Brown* (1926) AD 155; *Pamplin v Express Newspapers Ltd (No 2)* [1988] 1 All ER 282; *Kavanagh v The Leader* [2001] 1 IR 538.
640. *Berezovsky v RTBC* [2010] EWHC 476 (QB).
641. *Turner v Associated Newspapers* [2006] 4 All ER 613.

that a defendant should not be called upon to pay compensation which is unmerited or to vindicate a claimant on a false basis'.[642]

[6.334] The Irish courts too had doubted the applicability of this rule as a matter of Irish law. In *Browne v Tribune Newspapers*, Keane CJ described the law as not being settled beyond doubt, before observing that 'the plaintiff should not be allowed to recover damages for injury to reputation that is not his'.[643] Similarly, in *Cooper-Flynn v RTÉ*,[644] Keane CJ held that evidence of specific acts of misconduct which were relevant to the plaintiff's reputation and which were before the jury could be relied on by the defendant in mitigation of damages.

[6.335] In this regard, it is instructive to note that s 31(6) confirms that a defendant in a defamation action may give evidence for the purpose of mitigating damages of any matter that would have a bearing upon the reputation of the plaintiff, provided that it relates to matters connected with the defamatory statement,[645] or that the plaintiff has already in another defamation action been awarded damages in respect of a defamatory statement that contained substantially the same allegations as are contained in the defamatory statement to which the first-mentioned defamation action relates.[646] This evidence may only be admitted with the leave of the court, a requirement which was inserted into the Act during its passage through the Oireachtas. No guidance is given as to the criteria to be applied in considering an application for leave, although Order 1B, rule 10 requires that, in cases where truth has not been raised as a defence, the plaintiff must be furnished with particulars of any matters going to the character of the plaintiff on which the defendant intends to give evidence in mitigation of damages. If this is not done, such evidence may only be admitted with the leave of the court.

Special damages

[6.336] The court in a defamation action may award special damages to a plaintiff in respect of financial loss suffered by him or her as a result of the injury to his or her reputation caused by the defamatory statement in question.[647]

Punitive damages

[6.337] An award of punitive damages may be made where it has been proved (presumably by the plaintiff) that the defendant intended to publish the defamatory statement to a third party,[648] knew that the defamatory statement would be understood by

---

642.   *Turner v Associated Newspapers* [2006] 4 All ER 613, para 58.
643.   *Browne v Tribune Newspapers* [2001] 1 IR 521, 533.
644.   *Cooper-Flynn v RTÉ* [2004] 2 IR 73.
645.   Defamation Act 2009, s 31(6)(a).
646.   Defamation Act 2009, s 31(6)(b).
647.   Defamation Act 2009, s 31(7).
648.   Defamation Act 2009, s 32(2)(a).

that third party to refer to the plaintiff,[649] and either knew that the statement was untrue or in publishing it was reckless as to whether it was true or untrue.[650]

Punitive damages were previously awarded 'to punish the wrongdoer for his outrageous conduct, to deter him and others from such conduct in the future and to mark the court's detestation and disapproval of that conduct'.[651] In defamation actions, this had been held to apply where there was malice[652] or where 'there was an intention to publish defamatory matter which was intended to refer to the plaintiff and which was known to be false'.[653] In that respect, the emphasis on the knowledge and/or recklessness of the defendant in s 32(2) fulfils a broadly similar role.

Aggravated damages

[6.338] Aggravated damages may be awarded under s 32(1) where an unsuccessful defendant is regarded by the court as having conducted his or her defence in a manner that aggravated the injury caused to the plaintiff's reputation by the defamatory statement. In that situation compensation may be awarded for the aggravation caused. This underlines the fact that the main purpose of any damages awarded is to compensate the plaintiff for the additional damage to their feelings, not to punish the defendant for his or her conduct, and that this is the relevant factor in assessing quantum. For that reason, it has also been held that aggravated damages are not available to a corporate plaintiff.[654]

The most common aggravating factor in defamation cases has traditionally been a plea of justification, but these damages have also been awarded in respect of a refusal to apologise,[655] publication of other statements,[656] republication of the statement[657] or the conduct of the case in court.[658]

---

649. Defamation Act 2009, s 32(2)(b).
650. Defamation Act 2009, s 32(2)(c).
651. *Conway v INTO* [1991] 2 IR 305, 323.
652. *Crofter Properties v Genport* [2002] 4 IR 73.
653. *O'Brien v MGN* [2001] 4 IR 4, 22.
654. *Lewis v Daily Telegraph* [1964] AC 234, 262, Lord Reid; *Collins Stewart Ltd v The Financial Times Ltd* [2005] EWHC 262 (QB).
655. *Shortt v Commissioner of An Garda Síochána* [2007] 4 IR 587.
656. *Collins Stewart Ltd v The Financial Times Ltd* [2005] EWHC 262 (QB).
657. See the discussion of this in *Mosley v MGN* [2008] EWHC 1777 (QB), where the court declined to award aggravated damages.
658. *Campbell v Irish Press* (1955) 90 ILTR 105. *De Rossa v Independent Newspapers* [1999] 4 IR 432.

Chapter 7

PRIVACY

[7.01] From the point of view of the media, one of the most potentially significant legal developments of recent decades has been the recognition of a right to privacy under both Irish and European law. This trend towards the legal or constitutional protection of privacy has particular consequences for media organisations because of the frequency with which an individual's assertion of his or her right to privacy will come into conflict with the media's exercise of its freedom of expression. In the last 10 years in particular, the question of how to strike an appropriate balance between individual privacy and media expression has attracted a great deal of attention and comment across various jurisdictions, including – notably – the European Court of Human Rights and the English courts. The Irish courts too have been called upon to examine this area on a number of occasions. However, the Irish courts have had fewer opportunities than their counterparts in London and Strasbourg to examine these issues in detail. This is at least in part as a result of the tendency for many of the Irish actions in which a breach of the plaintiff's right to privacy is alleged to be settled out of court. The consequence of this is that there is still significant uncertainty about the precise parameters of the action for breach of privacy under Irish law. This is reflected in the extent to which reference is made in this chapter to decisions from other jurisdictions. Such decisions are, of course, of mere persuasive value and are provided only as indications of how an Irish court might deal with the matter in question. Pending further clarification of Irish law in this area, this is an important caveat for prospective plaintiffs and defendants to bear in mind when contemplating whether to take or defend a claim for breach of privacy.

THE NATURE OF THE RIGHT TO PRIVACY

[7.02] To protect and vindicate a constitutional or legal right, it is a prerequisite that courts are able to identify it. While this seems self-evident, the task of defining and explaining the right to privacy has proved a difficult one for legislators, courts and academics to accomplish. Post summarised this difficulty well when he observed that:

> Privacy is a value so complex, so entangled in competing and contradictory dimensions, so engorged with various and distinct meanings, that I sometimes despair whether it can be usefully addressed at all.[1]

This was echoed by Charleton J in *EMI v UPC*[2] where he expressed the view that:

> [P]rivacy as a right is difficult to define adequately ... Privacy in the modern panoptic society must be flexible enough to address new technologies and developments and their privacy implications while at the same time certain enough as to offer guidance and clarity as a matter of law. Keeping this tension in

---

1. Post, 'Three concepts of privacy' (2001) Geo LJ 2087, 2087.
2. *EMI v UPC* (11 October 2010, unreported) HC.

mind, it is extremely difficult to arrive at an appropriate definition. Description is therefore preferable.[3]

As a result, it is a particular necessity for any law of privacy to first define and identify what it aims to protect. It is also useful to develop a clear conception of the principles which justify and underpin the protection of the right, so that the courts are better equipped to accurately identify when a person's right to privacy is engaged and when, on the other hand, that person is simply asserting a 'vacuous'[4] freedom to do as he or she pleases.

[7.03] Craig has identified six reasons for the protection of privacy:[5]

(i)   Refuge: It allows the individual to retreat from the pressures of public scrutiny and social norms.[6]

(ii)   Freedom: Privacy prevents interference in a person's acts.[7]

(iii) Autonomy: It promotes autonomy by encouraging the individual to make his own choices.[8]

(iv) Creativity: By protecting the individual against conformist pressures, it fosters creative experimentation, which leads to social diversity.[9]

(v)   Mental health: Privacy has been linked to individual mental health.[10]

(vi) Intimacy: Privacy is a necessary condition for the creation of relationships of trust and confidence.[11]

While these reasons have been criticised on various grounds, they do provide a broad flavour of the sort of interests with which a right to privacy is concerned. They also individually highlight aspects of the debate about privacy that have led to the articulation at different times of different definitions of the right itself. Privacy has variously been defined as 'the right to be let alone',[12] as a guarantee of inaccessibility,[13] or as a right

---

3.   *EMI v UPC* (11 October 2010, unreported) HC, at para 66.
4.   Barendt, 'Privacy as a Constitutional Right and Value' in Birks (ed), *Privacy and Loyalty* (Clarendon, 1997).
5.   Craig, 'Invasion of Privacy and Charter Values' (1997) 42 McGill LJ 355.
6.   Warren & Brandeis, 'The Right to Privacy' (1890) 4 Harv L Rev 193
7.   *Griswold v Connecticut* 381 US 479 (1965); *Roe v Wade* 410 US 113 (1973); *McGee v AG* [1974] IR 284.
8.   Rössler, *The Value of Privacy* (Polity, 2005); Feldman, 'Privacy-related rights: their social value' in Birks ed, *Privacy and Loyalty* (Clarendon, 1997).
9.   Gavison, 'Privacy and the limits of law' (1980) 83 Yale LJ 421.
10.   Jourard, 'Some Psychological Aspects of Privacy' (1966) 31 *Law and Contemporary Problems* 307.
11.   Rachels, 'Why Privacy is Important' (1975) 4 Phil & Pub Aff 323; Reiman, 'Privacy, Intimacy, and Personhood' (1976) 6 Phil & Pub Aff 26; Westin, Privacy and Freedom (Atheneum, 1967).
12.   Cooley, *A Treatise on the Law of Torts* (2nd edn, 1888); Warren & Brandeis, 'The Right to Privacy' (1890) 4 Harv L Rev 193; *McGee v AG* [1974] IR 284; *Norris v AG* [1984] IR 36.
13.   Gavison, 'Privacy and the limits of law' (1980) 83 Yale LJ 421; Allen, *Uneasy Access: Privacy for Women in a Free Society* (Rowan &Littlefield, 1988); Moreham, 'Privacy in the Common Law: A Doctrinal and Theoretical Analysis' (2005) 121 LQR 628.

that applies only within particular zones such as the home. For reasons discussed in more detail elsewhere, there are problems with all of these understandings of privacy.[14]

[7.04] It has accordingly been argued – and accepted by courts in Ireland,[15] England[16] and in Strasbourg[17] – that the right to privacy is a more flexible concept which is, at its heart, concerned with securing the autonomy of the individual as a social citizen. Furthermore, it has been held that it is for the benefit of society as well as the individual that privacy be protected:

> [Protecting privacy] is necessary if an individual is to lead an autonomous, independent life, enjoy mental happiness, develop a variety of diverse interpersonal relationships, formulate unique ideas, opinions, beliefs and ways-of-living, and participate in a democratic, pluralistic society. The importance of privacy to the individual and society certainly justifies the conclusion that it is a fundamental social value, and should be vigorously protected in law. Each intrusion upon private life is demeaning not only to the dignity and spirit of the individual, but also to the integrity of the society of which the individual is part.[18]

[7.05] The relationship between privacy and autonomy is one which has been discussed at length in the academic literature in this area. Feldman has argued that privacy is a primarily social right which 'derives its weight and importance from its capacity to foster the conditions for a wide range of other aspects of human flourishing'.[19] This reflects the fact, as Rossler explains, that the law's protection of privacy establishes a secure framework within which an individual can truly be autonomous:

> [T]he concept of privacy demarcates for the individual realms or dimensions that he needs in order to be able to enjoy the individual freedom exacted and legally safeguarded in modern societies ... [S]uch realms or dimensions of privacy substantialize the liberties that are secured because the mere securing of freedom ... does not in itself necessarily entail that the conditions are secured for us to be able to enjoy these liberties as we really want to.[20]

[7.06] Where an individual's privacy is not protected, their autonomy is also severely undermined:

> The man who is compelled to live every minute of his life among others and whose every need, thought, desire, fancy or gratification is subject to public scrutiny has been deprived of his individuality and human dignity. Such an individual merges with the mass. His opinions, being public, tend never to be

---

14. Delany & Carolan, *The Right to Privacy* (Thomson Round Hall, 2008), 6–11.

15. See, for example, *Norris v AG* [1974] IR 284, 322; *Caldwell v Mahon* [2006] IEHC 86.

16. See, for example, *Campbell v MGN* [2004] 2 AC 457, para 50. See also '[T]he law [of privacy] is concerned to protect such matters as personal dignity, autonomy and integrity'; *Mosley v Newsgroup Newspapers* [2008] EWHC 1777 (QB), para 214 *per* Eady J.

17. *Von Hannover v Germany* (2005) 40 EHRR 1.

18. Craig, 'Invasion of Privacy and Charter Values' (1997) 42 McGill LJ 355, 361.

19. Feldman, 'Privacy-related rights: their social value' in Birks ed, *Privacy and Loyalty* (Clarendon, 1997), 21.

20. Rossler, *The Value of Privacy* (Polity, 2005), 72.

different; his aspirations, being known, tend always to be conventionally accepted ones; his feelings, being openly exhibited tend to lose their quality of unique personal warmth and to become the feelings of every man. Such a being, although sentient, is fungible; he is not an individual.[21]

This means that a law of privacy must be concerned with more than mere secrets. Privacy is fundamentally about protecting the autonomy of the individual as a social actor. It is about allowing the individual to make their own autonomous choices about how they wish to live their lives, rather than having those choices influenced or directed by the intrusion of government, media or the pressures of public opinion. It is not about solitude. It is about the individual's relationship with society. As Feldman has acknowledged, 'privacy can usefully be considered to have more to do with social ... action and interaction than with the behaviour of hermetically isolated individuals'.[22] 'Without society, there would be no need for privacy':[23]

> Recognising an inviolable sphere of personhood ... must take into account that society to a great extent defines its individual members ... Public dissemination about private matters directly affects how society views an individual, and may affect that individual's role in society. It shapes the individual's social identity and thus affects the individual's actual identity.[24]

[7.07] A right to privacy must accordingly create space for the individual to exercise their own social choices. That does not mean, however, that the individual is entitled to dictate who and what information or access others may receive. There should be no protection, for example, against the consequences of poor judgment or for unrealistic expectations. There may be good reasons of public interest or policy why others may be entitled to access particular information about a person. A right to privacy does not confer an entitlement to exercise complete control. The case law suggests that it is instead a right not to have reasonable expectations about how a person's social identity may be affected by a particular decision, course of conduct or piece of information frustrated or disrupted by the unwarranted and unjustified actions of others. It is, in essence, a recognition that our interactions with others – and, specifically, our autonomous decisions about how we interact with others – take place within a framework of social norms and expectations and that, in some circumstances, it may be appropriate for the law to intervene to protect those expectations from conduct which departs from, or breaches, the rules of this social game.

[7.08] It is important to bear in mind that this understanding of the right represents something of a departure from the way in which rights have traditionally been conceived by common law courts. Hohfeld's insight that what we call constitutional rights are in fact often immunities, is well known and illustrates the primarily negative character of

---

21. Bloustein, 'Privacy as an aspect of human dignity' (1964) 39 NYUL Rev 962, 1003.
22. Feldman, 'Privacy-related rights: their social value' in Birks ed, *Privacy and Loyalty* (Clarendon, 1997), 49.
23. Delany & Carolan, *The Right to Privacy*, (Thomson Round Hall, 2008), 9.
24. Chlapowski, 'The Constitutional Protection of Informational Privacy' (1991) 71 Boston University Law Review 133, 153–154.

many of the entitlements conferred by the Constitution and Convention. As the Article 8 case law of the European Court of Human Rights confirms, privacy, by contrast, is a positive entitlement that requires the active protection of the law if it is to be fully vindicated:

> [P]rivacy is a necessary condition for human flourishing because of the way in which it supports the individual's social existence. '[T]he most important aspects of privacy are those which facilitate constructive social action and intercourse'.[25] It is a right which, when conceived of in this way, does not properly belong to the Anglo-American tradition of negative civil liberties. It is not an immunity which guarantees freedom of action in a limited sphere. Autonomy, on this view, is not secured by the absence of government or external intervention. It is instead supported by the state's active involvement in the protection of privacy. This creates the conditions for autonomy. In its emphasis on state action, this understanding of privacy owes more to traditional European conceptions of rights.

This [European] vision of governance generally regards the state as the necessary player to frame the social community in which individuals develop ... Citizen autonomy, in this view, effectively depends on a backdrop of legal rights.[26]

Privacy and confidentiality

[7.09] One of the most important things to bear in mind in considering a right to privacy is that privacy is fundamentally different to confidentiality or secrecy. There are many matters, such as state or commercial secrets, which may be confidential but which could not plausibly be said to be private. Similarly, there matters which are legally private, such as the situations in *Peck*[27] or *von Hannover*,[28] but which would not be covered by laws relating to confidentiality. Confidentiality is a species of property interest whereas privacy, it has been argued, is concerned with autonomy and personhood. Similarly, confidentiality may be destroyed by the disclosure of the material in question to a third party or third parties whereas a right to privacy may remain in such circumstances. In many situations, of course, the two will overlap but they should always remain conceptually distinct.

PRIVACY AND FREEDOM OF EXPRESSION

[7.10] The adoption by the courts of an autonomy-based understanding of privacy has logical consequences for the relationship between the right to privacy and freedom of expression. It has frequently been observed in the legal context that claims based on

---

25. Feldman, 'Privacy-related rights: their social value' in Birks ed, *Privacy and Loyalty* (Clarendon, 1997), 40.

26. Delany & Carolan, *The Right to Privacy* (Thomson Round Hall, 2008), 18, citing Reidenberg, 'Resolving conflicting international data privacy rules in cyberspace' (2000) 52 Stanford L Rev 1315, 1347.

27. *Peck v United Kingdom* (2003) 36 EHRR 41.

28. *Von Hannover v Germany* (2005) 40 EHRR 1 (recognising a right to privacy in relation to the relatively trivial actions of a public figure in a public place).

these rights often come into conflict. However, recognising that there is a close relationship between privacy and autonomy also suggests that there is a closer relationship between privacy and freedom of expression than is sometimes realised.

[7.11] The connection between freedom of expression and autonomy has been discussed in more detail elsewhere in this book. Richards' seminal article on this topic illustrated the correlation between the two values:

> Freedom of expression permits and encourages the exercise of [the individual's] capacities: it supports a mature individual's sovereign autonomy in deciding how to communicate with others; it disfavours restrictions on communication imposed for the sake of the distorting rigidities of the orthodox and the established. In so doing, it nurtures and sustains the self-respect of the mature person.[29]

This means that privacy and freedom of expression share a common interest in protecting and promoting individual autonomy. The result of this mutual commitment to autonomy is that, in many situations, privacy and freedom of expression may represent complementary rather than conflicting values.

[7.12] This has been acknowledged by courts in the United States of America and in England. In *Bartnicki v Vopper*, the Supreme Court was asked to consider whether individuals whose telephone conversation was intercepted and broadcast on a radio station were entitled to sue for damages. A majority held that the actions of the radio station (which had not intercepted the call) were protected by the First Amendment. However, both the majority and the minority accepted that protecting the right to privacy could have a positive rather than a negative impact on the freedom of expression rights of individuals. Stevens J endorsed the view that:

> In a democratic society, privacy of communication is essential if citizens are to think and act creatively and constructively. Fear or suspicion that one's speech is being monitored by a stranger, even without the reality of such activity, can have a seriously inhibiting effect upon the willingness to voice critical and constructive ideas.[30]

[7.13] Breyer J's concurring opinion (with which O'Connor J agreed) advanced a similar view. He held that the federal prohibition on wire-tapping aimed to protect personal privacy:

> That assurance of privacy helps to overcome our natural reluctance to discuss private matters when we fear that our private conversations may become public.

---

29.   Richards, 'Free Speech and Obscenity Laws: Towards a Moral Theory of the First Amendment' (1974) 123 U Pa L Rev 45 at 62. See also Dworkin, *A Matter of Principle* (Harvard University Press, 1985); Redish, *Freedom of Expression: A Critical Analysis* (Michie, 1984). Strauss, 'Persuasion, Autonomy and Freedom of Expression' (1991) 91 Columbia L Rev 334; Nagel, 'Persona Rights and Public Space' (1995) 24 Philosophy and Public Affairs 83.
30.   President's Commission on Law Enforcement and Administration of Justice, The Challenge of Crime in a Free Society (1967), 533.

And the statutory restrictions consequently encourage conversations that might not otherwise take place.[31]

[7.14] Similarly, Tugenhadt J observed in *LNS v Persons Unknown* that:

> It is of course one of the essential features of the protection of private life, and Article 8 in particular, that it enables people to live freely according to their own choices. Article 8 even promotes freedom of speech, as well as of conduct, since much speech can only be conducted freely if the parties are in private.[32]

A useful example of this was provided by the decision of Eady J in *Author of a Blog v Times Newspapers*.[33] That concerned an application by the author of an anonymous blog which provided the views of a serving police officer on matters connected with the police force for an injunction to prevent him being identified by a national newspaper. Eady J declined to order the injunction, with the result that the individual officer was named and the blog was taken offline. Whatever the legal merits of the decision, it provides a clear demonstration of the way in which a person's privacy can facilitate their freedom of expression, and how the loss of that privacy or anonymity can have a chilling effect on their speech.

[7.15] These decisions underlined the fact that the true distinction between the two in law is typically based not on the inherent nature of the rights themselves but rather on the identities of the parties asserting them. Specifically, the contest is often between the individual's right to privacy and the media's freedom of expression, rather than between individual privacy and individual freedom of expression. As discussed in more detail elsewhere in the book, it is necessary in many situations to distinguish between individual freedom of expression, on the one hand, and media freedom of expression on the other. Barendt has criticised what he regards as the frequent failure to do so, commenting that '[i]n an age when communication has been dominated by the press and broadcasting media, we have lost sight of the free speech interest of individuals, or at least paid them less attention'.[34] The acknowledgment by the courts of this distinction in a number of cases means that this criticism may carry less force than previously. It nonetheless remains conceptually and analytically important that this distinction is consistently applied in appropriate cases. It is necessary to bear in mind 'the most significant distinction between individual and media defendants':

> ... that the law's protection of their interest in expression is premised on the protection of very different values. This means that different interests are engaged in a privacy claim. Conducting a balancing exercise between the right to privacy of an individual and another individual's freedom of expression is an analytically different matter to that involved in weighing an individual's privacy rights against a media outlet's freedom of expression.

---

31. *Bartnicki v Vopper* (2001) 532 US 514, 537.
32. *LNS v Persons Unknown* [2010] EWHC 119 (QB), para 98.
33. *Blog v Times Newspapers* [2009] EWHC 1358 (QB).
34. Barendt, 'Privacy and Freedom of Speech' in Kenyon & Richardson (eds), *New Dimensions In Privacy Law: International and Comparative Perspectives* (2006, Cambridge University Press), 30.

PRIVACY AND THE IRISH CONSTITUTION

The development of a right to privacy

[7.16] The right to privacy in Ireland derives from the unenumerated personal rights guarantee found in Article 40.3.1° of the Constitution. The right was first adverted to in the Supreme Court decision in *McGee v Attorney General*.[35] Budd J, for example, expressed the view (which was echoed by Henchy and Griffin JJ) that the right must be regarded as one of the fundamental personal rights protected by the Constitution:

> Whilst the 'personal rights' are not described specifically, it is scarcely to be doubted in our society that the right to privacy is universally recognised and accepted with possibly the rarest of exceptions, and that the matter of marital relationship must rank as one of the most important of matters in the realm of privacy.[36]

This was reiterated by Henchy and McCarthy JJ in their dissenting judgments in *Norris v Attorney General*[37]. Henchy J maintained that:

> [A] right of privacy inheres in each citizen by virtue of his human personality, and that such right is constitutionally guaranteed as one of the unspecified personal rights comprehended by Article 40, s 3, are propositions that are well attested by previous decisions of this Court.[38]

It was finally confirmed that the right to privacy under the Constitution extended beyond marital privacy to include a right to individual privacy in *Kennedy v Ireland*.[39] Hamilton P held that the unauthorised tapping of the plaintiff's telephones was a breach of his right of privacy. In his view, the right was 'one of the fundamental personal rights of the citizen which flow from the Christian and democratic nature of the State', which was necessary' to ensure the dignity and freedom of an individual in the type of society envisaged by the Constitution, namely, a sovereign, independent and democratic society.'[40] This secured the status of a right to privacy as one of the unenumerated personal rights guaranteed by Article 40.3.1° of the Constitution.

[7.17] The Irish courts have consistently described the right to privacy in a way which emphasises its relationship with dignity and autonomy. In *Kennedy*, for example, Hamilton P spoke of the importance of the 'dignity and freedom of the individual',[41] while Denham J similarly discussed privacy in dignitary terms in *Re Ward of Court (No 2)*.[42] The most notable example of this understanding of privacy is Henchy J's

35.   *McGee v Attorney General* [1974] IR 284.
36.   *McGee v Attorney General* [1974] IR 284, 322.
37.   *Norris v Attorney General* [1984] IR 36.
38.   *Norris v Attorney General* [1984] IR 36, 71.
39.   *Kennedy v Ireland* [1987] IR 587.
40.   *Kennedy v Ireland* [1987] IR 587, 593.
41.   *Kennedy v Ireland* [1987] IR 587, 593.
42.   *Re Ward of Court (No 2)* [1996] 2 IR 79.

judgment in *Norris*.[43] He argued that the protection of privacy was 'necessary for the expression of an individual personality' and held, accordingly, that the right 'inhere[d] in the individual personality of the citizen in his capacity as a vital human component of the social, political and moral order posited by the Constitution.' The right, for him, was a flexible and contextual one:

> '... a complex of rights which vary in nature, purpose and range (each necessarily being a facet of the citizen's core of individuality within the constitutional order) and which may be compendiously referred to as the right of privacy.'[44]

[7.18] It has been argued that this judgment is particularly significant because of the sophisticated nature of Henchy J's analysis:

> Henchy J's analysis is notable for two reasons. First, the judgment's emphasis on individuality indicates a clear commitment to autonomy as a constitutional value. Autonomy is secured where the citizen is free to express their own personality. Henchy J's decision thus justifies the protection of privacy as promoting autonomy. Secondly, Henchy J did not confine the protection of privacy to a narrow sphere. He instead appeared to envisage privacy as an aspect of the individual's social existence. This is reflected in his recognition of the fact that the individual exists as a component of a social and constitutional system. Privacy does not remove the citizen from society. It is instead protected as an acknowledgment of the importance of securing space for 'individuation' within these social and constitutional spheres.[45]

This echoes the analysis set out above in relation to the way in which the right is currently understood by the courts in Ireland and elsewhere. As Hanna J explained in *Caldwell v Mahon*:[46]

> This inviolable core [of privacy] is left behind once an individual enters into relationships with persons outside this closest intimate sphere; the individual's activities then acquire a social dimension and the right to privacy in this context becomes subject to limitation.

Scope of the right

[7.19] This flexible understanding of privacy raises questions in relation to the scope of the right. The circumstances in which the right to privacy will be engaged are considered in more detail below. However, it has been held that the right applies to matters such as marital relationships,[47] medical treatment,[48] business affairs[49] and bodily privacy;[50]

---

43. See, for example, *Foy v An t-Ard Chláraitheoir* [2002] IEHC 116; *Re a Ward of Court (No 2)* [1996] 2 IR 79; *Desmond v Glackin (No 2)* [1993] IR 67.
44. *Norris v Attorney General* [1984] IR 36, 71.
45. Delany & Carolan, *The Right to Privacy* (Thomson Round Hall, 2008), 37.
46. *Caldwell v Mahon* [2006] IEHC 86.
47. *McGee v Attorney General* [1974] IR 284.
48. *Re Ward of Court (No 2)* [1996] 2 IR 79.
49. *Caldwell v Mahon* [2006] IEHC 86; *Cogley v RTÉ* [2005] 4 IR 79.
50. *Sinnott v Nationalist & Leinster Times* (June 2006, unreported), Circuit Court.

places such as the home[51] or workplace;[52] and information concerning relationship issues, such as adoption[53] or other family members.[54] It has also been held that the right may be relied on by corporate persons.[55] It does not, however, appear to apply to persons who are deceased.[56]

[7.20] However, the right is not absolute. The courts have accepted on several occasions that the right can be restricted where that is necessary for reasons of the common good[57] or public interest,[58] or where it comes into conflict with other constitutional values such as freedom of expression[59] or the public administration of justice.[60] In her decision in *Herrity v Associated Newspapers*,[61] Dunne J reviewed the previous authorities in some detail before providing a useful summary of the basic principles which regulate the constitutional right to privacy in Ireland:

(1) There is a constitutional right to privacy.

(2) The right to privacy is not an unqualified right.

(3) The right to privacy may have to be balanced against other competing rights or interests.

(4) The right to privacy may be derived from the nature of the information at issue, that is, matters which are entirely private to an individual and of which it may be validly contended that there is no proper basis for their disclosure either to third parties or to the public generally.

(5) There may be circumstances in which an individual may not be able to maintain that the information concerned must always be kept private, having regard to the competing interests which may be involved, but may make complaint in relation to the manner in which the information was obtained.

(6) The right to sue for damages for breach of the constitutional right to privacy is not confined to actions against the State or state bodies or institutions.

51. *Simple Imports v Revenue Commissioners* [2000] 2 IR 243.
52. *Hanahoe v Hussey* [1998] 3 IR 69.
53. *I O'T v B* [1998] 2 IR 321.
54. *Gray v Minister for Justice* [2007] IEHC 52.
55. *Digital Rights Ireland Ltd v Minister for Communications, Marine and Natural Resources* [2010] IEHC 221. For an alternative view, see O'Neill, *The Constitutional Rights of Companies* (Thomson Round Hall, 2007), 280; Carolan, 'The problems of corporate privacy' (2010) DULJ (forthcoming).
56. *Governors and Guardians of the Hospital for the Relief of Poor Lying-In Women, Dublin v Information Commissioner* [2009] IEHC 315.
57. *Norris v AG* [1984] IR 86.
58. *Cogley v RTÉ* [2005] 4 IR 79; *Murray v Newsgroup Newspapers* [2010] IEHC 248.
59. *M v Drury* [1994] 2 IR 8; *Murray v Newsgroup Newspapers* [2010] IEHC 248.
60. *Roe v Board of St. James Hospital* [1996] 3 IR 67; *Re Ansbacher Ltd* [2002] 2 IR 517; *Doe v Revenue Commissioners* [2008] IEHC 5.
61. *Herrity v Associated Newspapers* [2008] IEHC 249. See also *Dominican v Axa Insurance* [2007] IEHC 14.

These principles have subsequently been cited with approval by Hedigan J in *LK (A Minor) v Independent Star Ltd.*[62] How these principles apply (or might be applied) to specific factual situations is considered in more detail below.

Relationship with freedom of expression

[7.21] A number of recent decisions of the High Court suggest that the right to privacy will rarely prevail over the constitutional guarantee of freedom of expression. This view was expressed by Dunne J in *Herrity*, and has been cited with approval by Kearns P in *Hickey v Sunday Newspapers Ltd*[63] and by Hedigan J in *LK (A Minor) v Independent Star Ltd.*[64] These decisions also indicate, however, that the precise balance between these interests will depend upon the facts of the case.

Furthermore, the courts were not required in these cases to consider the potential implications of the distinction drawn by the Supreme Court in *Murphy v IRTC*[65] between the different forms of freedom of expression protected under Arts 40.3.1° and 40.6.1°(i). This could, in an appropriate case, affect the particular balancing exercise required. Nonetheless, the recent caselaw on this issue seems to suggest that freedom of expression enjoys a type of presumptive primacy in any clash between the two rights.

As the section below indicates, this situation appears to differ from that which presently pertains under English law and under the European Convention on Human Rights.

THE EUROPEAN CONVENTION ON HUMAN RIGHTS

'Private life'

[7.22] Article 8 of the European Convention on Human Rights guarantees a right to respect for private life. The Art provides that:

> Everyone has the right to respect for his private and family life, his home and his correspondence.

> There shall be no interference by a public authority with the exercise of this right except such as is in accordance with the law and is necessary in a democratic society in the interests of national security, public safety or the economic well-being of the country, for the prevention of disorder or crime, for the protection of health or morals, or for the protection of the rights and freedoms of others.

The concept of 'private life' has been given a very broad interpretation by the European Court of Human Rights. The court has refrained from providing an exhaustive definition[66] of what constitutes 'private life' but has held it to include a person's name,[67]

62. *LK (A Minor) v Independent Star Ltd* (3 November 2010, unreported) HC.
63. *Hickey v Sunday Newspapers Ltd* [2010] IEHC 349.
64. *LK (A Minor) v Independent Star Ltd* (3 November 2010, unreported) HC.
65. *Murphy v IRTC* [19991] 1 IR 12. See Ch 2.
66. *Pretty v United Kingdom* (2002) 35 EHRR 1; *Peck v United Kingdom* (2003) 36 EHRR 41.
67. *Burghartz v Switzerland* (1994) 18 EHRR 101.

photograph,[68] personal history,[69] personal information[70] and genetic material.[71] It has also been held to extend to encompass a person's reputation[72] and honour,[73] although one chamber of the court appeared to express some reservations in relation to these latter elements when it observed that 'reputation has only been deemed to be an independent right sporadically and mostly when the factual allegations were of such a seriously offensive nature that their publication had an inevitable direct effect on the applicant's private life'.[74]

[7.23] More generally, the court has explained the notion of a right to respect for private life as 'cover[ing] the physical and psychological or moral integrity of a person[75] and ... sometimes embrac[ing] aspects of an individual's physical and social identity'.[76] The right has been repeatedly described by the court in Strasbourg as including a 'right to establish and develop relationships with other human beings'.[77] Thus, it has been held to include more social dimensions of private life, including a person's social ties to their community.[78] For the same reason, Article 8 is also capable in principle of applying to conduct which occurs in the workplace[79] or in public,[80] even where that conduct is undertaken by public figures.[81] This emphasises again the connection between the right to privacy and the dignity and autonomy of the individual. It has been stated on several occasions that 'the notion of personal autonomy is an important principle underlying the interpretation of [the Article 8] guarantees'.[82] This has been a recurring theme in the case law of the European Court of Human Rights as it has developed its 'broad

---

68. *Schussel v Austria*, 21 February 2002; *Von Hannover v Germany* (2005) 40 EHRR 1; *Egeland v Norway* [2009] ECHR 34438/04.
69. *Odievre v France* (2004) 38 EHRR 43.
70. *Rotaru v Romania* [2000] 8 BHRC 449.
71. *S and Marper v United Kingdom* (30562/04) [2008] ECHR 1581.
72. *Radio France v France* (2004) 40 EHRR 29; *Cumpana v Romania* (2004) 41 EHRR 200; *Chauvy v France* (2005) 41 EHRR 29; *Pfeifer v Austria* [2007] ECHR 12566/03; *Petrina v Romania* [2008] ECHR 78060/01; *Armoniene v Lithuania* [2008] ECHR 36919/0; *Petrenco v Moldova*, (Application No 20928/05).
73. *Sidabras and Dziautas v Lithuania* [2004] ECHR 55480/00 and 59330/00.
74. *Karako v Hungary* [2009] ECHR 39311/05. The question of whether Art 8 encompasses a right to reputation is expected to be argued before the Grand Chamber in the upcoming *Von Hannover (No 2)* case.
75. *X and Y v Netherlands* [1985] ECHR 8978/80; (1986) 8 EHRR 235, *Runinen v Finland* [1997] ECHR 20972/92.
76. *A v Norway* [2009] ECHR 28070/06, para 63. See also *Mikulic v Croatia* [2002] ECHR 53176/99.
77. *Niemitz v Germany* (1992) 16 EHRR 97; *Pretty v United Kingdom* (2002) 35 EHRR 1; *Von Hannover v Germany* (2005) 40 EHRR 1.
78. *Kuric v Slovenia* [2010] ECHR 26828/06.
79. *Copland v United Kingdom* [2007] ECHR 253.
80. *Peck v United Kingdom* (2003) 36 EHRR 41.
81. *Von Hannover v Germany* (2005) 40 EHRR 1.
82. *Pretty v United Kingdom* (2002) 35 EHRR 1; *Gillan & Quinton v United Kingdom* [2009] ECHR 28.

interpretation of Article 8 to encompass notions of personal integrity and the free development of the personality'.[83]

Obligation on the State

[7.24] Article 8 has been held to impose a positive obligation upon Contracting States. The court held in *X & Y v Netherlands* that:

> [A]lthough the object of Article 8 is essentially that of protecting the individual against arbitrary interference by the public authorities, it does not merely compel the State to abstain from such interference: in addition to this primarily negative undertaking, there may be positive obligations inherent in an effective respect for private or family life. These obligations may involve the adoption of measures designed to secure respect for private life even in the sphere of the relations of individuals between themselves.[84]

This does not mean, however, that states are obliged to vindicate all privacy claims made by their citizens. Thus, it was held in *Karako v Hungary*[85] that the Hungarian authorities' failure to prosecute an individual for libel was not a breach of the Article 8 rights of the alleged victim in circumstances where it was open to the victim to bring private law proceedings for defamation. Although the court held that the requirements of Article 8 varied in accordance with the context in which a claim arose, it confirmed that states were required, at a minimum, to provide an effective domestic means of vindicating Article 8 rights. As the court explained:

> [T]he nature of the State's obligation depends on the aspect of private life concerned, and the choice of measures designed to secure compliance with that obligation falls within the Contracting States' margin of appreciation. The Court considers, as a minimum requirement, that an effective legal system must be in place and operating for the protection of the rights falling within the notion of 'private life', and it is satisfied that such a system was indeed available to the applicant in the presen case.[86]

Interference with Article 8

[7.25] Where Article 8 rights are engaged by a domestic measure or omission, the European Court of Human Rights will require the respondent state to demonstrate that the interference in question is in accordance with law and necessary in a democratic society. These are familiar tests from the case law of the court in other areas.

[7.26] In short, the requirement that an interference be in accordance with law dictates that any interference must be prescribed by law. Furthermore, for the domestic measure to constitute a valid 'law', it must satisfy certain minimum standards of legality,

---

83. *Karako v Hungary* [2009] ECHR 39311/05, para 21.
84. *X and Y v Netherlands* [1985] ECHR 8978/80; (1986) 8 EHRR 235, para 23.
85. *Karako v Hungary* [2009] ECHR 39311/05.
86. *Karako v Hungary* [2009] ECHR 39311/05, para 19.

including accessibility and foreseeability.[87] This does not mean, however, that an individual is entitled to full information about state procedures in circumstances where that would defeat the purpose of the law. Thus, in *Malone v UK*[88] it was held that it did not breach Article 8 for the individual in question not to have access to rules regulating surveillance methods. What was necessary was that the system had sufficient precision and internal checks to adequately protect the individual against arbitrary interference with his or her rights.[89] That this is the key test was confirmed in *Gillan & Quinton v UK* where it was held that stop and search powers given to police officers under anti-terrorism legislation were in breach of Article 8. The court considered that the absence of effective supervision, when coupled with the fact that the power could be exercised on the basis of what was 'expedient' rather than 'necessary', meant that the interference was not one which was prescribed by law:

> In matters affecting fundamental rights it would be contrary to the rule of law, one of the basic principles of a democratic society enshrined in the Convention, for a legal discretion granted to the executive to be expressed in terms of an unfettered power. Consequently, the law must indicate with sufficient clarity the scope of any such discretion conferred on the competent authorities and the manner of its exercise ... the safeguards provided by domestic law have not been demonstrated to constitute a real curb on the wide powers afforded to the executive so as to offer the individual adequate protection against arbitrary interference.[90]

An interference will be adjudged to be necessary in a democratic society where the aim of the interference corresponds to a pressing social need, and the means used to achieve it are proportionate to the end pursued. 'Necessary' in this context does not mean indispensable or reasonable or desirable[91] but has rather been held to require the application of a proportionality test. The margin of appreciation enjoyed by Contracting States in making such an assessment will depend upon the context of the case. Thus, whereas states will enjoy a wide margin of appreciation in matters of national morality,[92] the margin of appreciation for purported interferences with political expression is considerably circumscribed.[93]

Balancing Article 8 and Article 10

[7.27] One of the key issues in the recent case law of the European Court of Human Rights has been the relationship between Article 8 rights and the media's freedom of

---

87.   *Sunday Times v UK* (1979) 2 EHRR 245; *Amann v Switzerland* (2000) 30 EHRR 843; *PG & JH v UK* (25 September 2001, unreported); *Maestri v Italy* (Application No 39148/98); *Al-Nashif v Bulgaria* (Application No 50963/99); *Ramazanova v Azerbaijan* (Application No 44363/02); *Glas Nadezhda v Bulgaria* (Application No 14134/02).
88.   *Malone v UK* (1985) 7 EHRR 14.
89.   See also *Kopp v Switzerland* (1999) 27 EHRR 91. *Taylor-Sabori v UK* (2003) 36 EHRR 17; *Copland v United Kingdom* [2007] ECHR 253; *Gillan & Quinton v United Kingdom* [2009] ECHR 28.
90.   *Gillan & Quinton v United Kingdom* [2009] ECHR 28, paras 77–79.
91.   *Handyside v UK* (1979) 1 EHRR 737; *Silver v UK* (1983) 5 EHRR 347.
92.   *Muller v Switzerland* (1991) 13 EHRR 212.
93.   *Lingens v Austria* (1986) 8 EHRR 407.

expression under Article 10. This matter is expected to be the subject of substantial argument before the Grand Chamber of the court in the forthcoming *Von Hannover (No 2) & Springer* litigation. Pending the decision of the court in that case, however, the current approach of the Strasbourg court has been to seek to strike a fair balance between the Article 8 rights of the individual and the Article 10 rights of the media. The jurisprudence has tended to involve a detailed assessment of the specific circumstances of each case. Thus, the more intimate[94] or distressing[95] the material in question, the more difficult it will be to justify an interference with the claimant's Article 8 rights. Similarly, the more closely associated the expression is with the role of the media as watchdog and bloodhound of a democratic society, the more likely it will be that the court will conclude that the media's Article 10 rights outweigh the Article 8 entitlements asserted by the claimant.[96] By contrast, where the expression in question is more difficult to connect with the media's democratic role, it is more likely that a court will find the Article 10 rights to be outweighed by a more serious interference with Article 8.[97] It is important to reiterate, however, that each case depends to a large extent on its facts and that hard and fast rules are impossible to apply at present.

[7.28] The English courts have also given extensive consideration to the correct approach to the enforcement of Article 8 rights in recent years. In particular, the courts there have had cause to examine the way in which the rights protected by Article 8 and Article 10 of the Convention can be reconciled where they come into conflict.

[7.29] The early decisions of the English courts treated Article 10 as having an inherent precedence over Article 8. This encouraged them to approach a claim for a breach of privacy (or, more accurately breach of confidence) by focusing on the justification offered for the threatened infringement of the media's expression interests rather than by considering the extent to which it was legitimate for the media to interfere with the competing Article 8 right. In *Theakston v MGN Ltd*,[98] for example, Eady J held that the onus of proof lay on a plaintiff to establish that it was permissible to restrain media publication, even where the claimant was relying on his established Article 8 right to privacy.

[7.30] By contrast, in *Douglas v Hello! Ltd*,[99] on the other hand, Sedley LJ criticised such preferential treatment of Article 10, arguing instead that the two Convention rights ought to be treated equally: The European Court of Human Rights has always recognised the high importance of free media of communication in a democracy, but its jurisprudence does not – and could not consistently with the Convention itself – give Article 10(1) the presumptive priority which is given, for example, to the First Amendment in the jurisprudence of the United States' courts. Everything will ultimately

---

94. *Peck v United Kingdom* (2003) 36 EHRR 41.
95. *Egeland v Norway* [2009] ECHR 34438/04.
96. *Cumpana v Romania* (2005) 41 EHRR 14; *Karhuvaara v Finland* (2005) 41 EHRR 51.
97. *Prisma Press v France* (Application No 66910/01); *Campmany y Diez de Revenga v Spain* [2000] ECHR 696.
98. *Theakston v MGN Ltd* [2002] EWHC 137.
99. *Douglas v Hello! Ltd* [2001] QB 967.

depend on the proper balance between privacy and publicity in the situation facing the court.'[100]

[7.31] Lord Hope echoed this in *Campbell v MGN Ltd*:[101]

> Any restriction of the right to freedom of expression must be subjected to very close scrutiny. But so too must any restriction of the right to respect for private life. Neither Article 8 nor Article 10 has any pre-eminence over the other in the conduct of this exercise ... [T]hey are neither absolute not in any hierarchical order, since they are of equal value in a democratic society.[102]

As Baroness Hale pointed out in *Campbell*, this is especially true of cases in which the interests of two private parties are involved. Cases before the European Court of Human Rights concern the capacity of the State to allegedly interfere with the rights of a private party. There is therefore usually less need for the ECtHR to consider a balance between individual rights. Domestic courts, however, may be required to conduct a more difficult and acute balancing exercise in cases where two private parties invoke competing fundamental rights.

[7.32] In those circumstances, the English courts currently favour what has been called the 'parallel analysis' approach. Potter P explained it in *A Local Authority v W*[103] as follows:

> The exercise to be performed is one of parallel analysis in which the starting point is presumptive parity in that neither Article has precedence over or 'trumps' the other. The exercise of parallel analysis requires the court to examine the justification for interfering with each right and the issue of proportionality is to be considered in respect of each. It is not a mechanical exercise upon the basis of rival generalities. An intense focus upon the comparative importance of the specific rights being claimed in the individual case is necessary before the ultimate balancing test in terms of proportionality is carried out.

[7.33] Lord Steyn in *Re S (A Child)*[104] described this approach as one involving four key principles:

> First, neither Article has as such precedence over the other. Secondly, where the values under the two Articles are in conflict, an intense focus on the comparative importance of the specific rights being claimed in the individual case is necessary. Thirdly, the justifications for interfering with or restricting each right must be taken into account. Finally, the proportionality test must be applied to each.

---

100. *Douglas v Hello! Ltd* [2001] QB 967, 1004.
101. *Campbell v MGN Ltd* [2004] 2 AC 457.
102. *Campbell v MGN Ltd* [2004] 2 AC 457, 489.
103. *A Local Authority v W* [2005] EWHC 1564 (Fam), para 53.
104. *Re S (A Child)* [2005] 1 AC 593, 603.

[7.34] The law has accordingly 'changed' in England such that 'neither freedom of expression nor reputation has any presumptive priority'.[105] As Eady J concluded in *Mosley*:

> It has to be accepted that any rights of free expression, as protected by Article 10, whether on the part of Woman E or the journalists working for the News of the World, must no longer be regarded as simply 'trumping' any privacy rights that may be established on the part of the Claimant. Language of that kind is no longer used. Nor can it be said, without qualification, that there is a 'public interest that the truth should out'.[106]

The correct approach is instead to balance the two rights by reference to the specific circumstances of the case:

> In order to determine which should take precedence, in the particular circumstances, it is necessary to examine the facts closely as revealed in the evidence at trial and to decide whether (assuming a reasonable expectation of privacy to have been established) some countervailing consideration of public interest may be said to justify any intrusion which has taken place. This is integral to what has been called 'the new methodology'.[107]

Stevens J agreed in *Callaghan v Independent News & Media*:

> The balancing exercise is essentially a question of fact with the weight to be attached to the various considerations being of degree and essentially a matter for the trial judge. In carrying out the balancing exercise of weighing the competing Convention rights no one Convention right takes automatic precedence over another.[108]

THE ACTION FOR BREACH OF PRIVACY

The existence of an action

[7.35] There can be no doubt that an action for breach of privacy is available to plaintiffs as a matter of Irish law. The Constitution's protection of privacy is supplemented by Article 8 of the European Convention of Human Rights which imposes a positive obligation on the State to ensure that the individual's private life is properly respected.[109] While relatively few matters may have come before the courts in recent decades, it has been notable that there has been an increase in very recent years in the number of cases coming before the courts and that plaintiffs have, on several occasions, successfully

---

105. *Flood v Times Newspapers* [2009] EWHC 2375 (QB), para 148.
106. *Mosley v Newsgroup Newspapers* [2008] EWHC 1777 (QB), para 10.
107. *Mosley v Newsgroup Newspapers* [2008] EWHC 1777 (QB), para 11.
108. *Callaghan v Independent News & Media* [2009] NIQB 1, para 24.
109. *Marckx v Belgium* (1979–80) 2 EHRR 330; *Peck v United Kingdom* (2003) 36 EHRR 41; *Von Hannover v Germany* (2005) 40 EHRR 1.

obtained damages for their claimed breach of privacy.[110] In particular, Dunne J confirmed in her decision in *Herrity v Associated Newspapers* that an action in damages could lie against a private party for an invasion of a plaintiff's right to privacy. While *Herrity* restates the principles that have always been applied in relation to breaches of constitutional rights in Ireland,[111] this clear statement from the High Court helpfully removes most[112] of whatever lingering uncertainty may still have existed before her decision.

[7.36] The specific character of the action for breach of privacy remains, however, somewhat ambiguous. It is unclear whether the action is a tort or a direct remedy for breach of constitutional rights. The better view is probably that it is protected in Ireland as a form of constitutional tort. The Irish courts have consistently held that damages may be available for the breach of a constitutional right where that right is not protected by any other cause of action.[113] In *McDonnell v Ireland*,[114] for example, Keane J referred to an action for breach of privacy as a form of tort. Although his views were obiter, they do indicate that the action for breach of privacy may be a constitutional tort under Irish law:

> I take by way of example the unenumerated constitutional right of privacy upheld in *Kennedy v Ireland* [1987] IR 587. It is true that the courts in England have been hesitant in recognising that such a tort exists; see *R v Khan* [1996] 3 DPP 162. But even in the absence of a written constitution, such a novel growth might, for all one knows, have flourished sturdily in this jurisdiction. The fact that it did so in the form of an action for infringement of a constitutional right does not prevent it, in my view, from being classified as a civil wrong. Indeed, I do not know of any other category to which it could be assigned.[115]

It is instructive in this regard that Dunne J's decision in *Herrity* was almost entirely couched in the language of constitutional rights. She also adverted to the fact that she had been referred by the defendants in that case to the decision in *Wainright v Home Office*[116] which decided that there was no common law tort for invasion of privacy. That she did not discuss that decision any further could be taken to indicate a view on the part

---

110. *Kennedy v Ireland* [1987] IR 587; *Hanahoe v Hussey* [1998] 3 IR 69; *Gray v Minister for Justice, Equality and Law Reform* [2007] IEHC 52; *Sinnott v Nationalist & Leinster Times* (2007) *The Irish Times*, 20 January; *Herrity v Associated Newspapers* [2008] IEHC 249.
111. *Meskell v CIE* [1973] IR 121; *Conway v INTO* [1991] 2 IR 305.
112. As a High Court decision, it is obviously possible that the Supreme Court may take a different view. However, as it seems likely that this would require the Supreme Court to depart from (or at least distinguish) previous decisions in respect of other constitutional rights, there is reason to expect that Dunne J's approach would be upheld.
113. *Meskell v CIE* [1973] IR 121; *Kennedy v Ireland* [1987] IR 587; *W v Ireland (No 2)* [1997] 2 IR 141.
114. *McDonnell v Ireland* [1998] 1 IR 134.
115. *McDonnell v Ireland* [1998] 1 IR 134, 157–158.
116. *Wainright v Home Office* [2004] 2 AC 406.

of the court that it was unnecessary to address the question of the existence of the tort at common law, given its clear status in the Constitution.

[7.37] Furthermore, it has been argued that the flexible nature of the law of torts may mean that a constitutional tort is a more appropriate way to deal with the contextual character of the right to privacy than, for example, statutory regulation:

> Privacy actions also have much in common with other torts. Litigants claiming a breach of privacy generally seek damages or injunctive relief against another party who they allege has committed a wrong against them. The diverse nature of the privacy right means that infringements can occur in a wide variety of social situations. Parties to a privacy action will often be private individuals rather than public bodies. That is not the case with all constitutional rights. Many constitutional rights, such as freedom of expression or of assembly, or the right to education, will usually be invoked against the actions of public authorities. In many jurisdictions, constitutional rights may only be invoked against state agencies. The right to privacy is concerned not simply with the relationship between the citizen and the State but with the wider issue of the individual's social existence. Privacy laws thus necessarily involve the regulation of social relationships and inter-personal interactions. As the caselaw on negligence, for example, demonstrates, these are matters with which the law of torts is typically concerned ... The right to privacy is an unusually context-sensitive interest. It can arise in a broad range of circumstances and affect an extensive array of social relationships. Furthermore, because these social relationships may take many different forms, the nature of the privacy interest or the extent to which it is engaged may vary from situation to situation. Hard and fast rules in relation to the right to privacy are difficult to devise and potentially dangerous to apply, given the multiplicity of countervailing public or individual interests that may arise. This concern led the New Zealand Law Reform Commission to warn that the right to privacy 'ought not to be seen as a right in its most stringent form or a 'trump'.[117] This accords with the Irish courts' consistent recognition that it is not an absolute constitutional entitlement.[118] Privacy laws should instead be flexible, adaptable and capable of developing on a case-by-case basis. This is the way in which the law of torts traditionally operates. For that reason, it is arguably most appropriate to regard the Irish action for breach of privacy as a type of constitutional tort.[119]

Defining the action in privacy

[7.38] One of the problems with the sometimes vague character of the right to privacy is that its ambiguity, while relatively unproblematic at an academic level, can make the legal enforcement of a right to privacy very difficult. This was the reason for Prosser's efforts in the United States to sub-divide the right to privacy into four more manageable

---

117. New Zealand Law Reform Commission, *A Conceptual Approach to Privacy* (Law Commission, 2007), para 178.

118. *Norris v Attorney General* [1984] IR 36; *Kennedy v Ireland* [1987] IR 587.

119. Delany & Carolan, 290–291.

and narrowly defined actions.[120] This approach has the benefit of encouraging greater precision in the way in which parties articulate their claim which, as a result, allows the court to engage in a more focused analysis of the interests at stake.

[7.39] This issue has received some attention in an Irish context. In *Cogley v RTÉ*[121] Clarke J drew a distinction between two different types of privacy claim:

> A useful starting point ... seems to me to be to distinguish between a right of privacy in the underlying information whose disclosure it is sought to prevent, on the one hand, and on the other hand, a situation where a right to privacy does not extend to that underlying information but it is contended that the methods by which the information has been obtained amount to a breach of privacy.'

This distinction has also been expressly referred to by Dunne J in *Herrity*[122] and by Irvine J in *Murray v Newsgroup Newspapers*.[123] It suggests that Irish law may recognise the existence of two distinct causes of action under the broad heading of a breach of the right to privacy. The actions might loosely be described as:

•   Disclosure of private information.

•   Invasion of a private space.

[7.40] It has been argued elsewhere that the distinction drawn in *Cogley* represents a conceptually coherent and practically useful approach which ought to be adopted as a useful framework for the articulation and development of the Irish law of privacy:

> ... Clarke J's distinction is a sensible and perceptive approach to privacy actions. It is important to distinguish between the privacy interests involved in a case because this allows the courts to accurately identify the nature of the interference and the extent of the harm caused. Under the disclosure action, a claimant alleges that he has been harmed by the release of information which ought not to have been disclosed because of its private nature. It is the character of the information which causes the harm. With an action for intrusion, the wrong relates to the conduct of the intruder. Information may be obtained by the intruder but the cause of action is not based on that information, even where it is something which the claimant would have preferred the defendant did not have access to. The harm is the act of intrusion, not the material obtained as a result.[124]

Test for identifying a breach of privacy

[7.41] As cases like *R (Countryside Alliance) v AG*[125] demonstrate, one of the dangers of a legal right to privacy is that it is capable in principle of applying to a very broad range

---

120.   Prosser, 'Privacy' (1960) 48 Calif L Rev 383. The four are: Intrusion upon seclusion or solitude, or into private affairs; Public disclosure of embarrassing private facts; Publicity which places a person in a false light in the public eye; and Appropriation of name or likeness.
121.   *Cogley v RTÉ* [2005] 4 IR 79, 90.
122.   *Herrity v Associated Newspapers* [2008] IEHC 249.
123.   *Murray v Newsgroup Newspapers* [2010] IEHC 248.
124.   Delany & Carolan, *The Right to Privacy* (Thomson Round Hall, 2008), 292.
125.   *R (Countryside Alliance) v AG* [2007] UKHL 52.

of activities and spheres. After all, if the protection of a right to privacy is intended to facilitate the individual in the exercise of their autonomy, it could be invoked in almost any situation where a disgruntled plaintiff feels that there has been an interference with their 'autonomy'. To conceive of the right to privacy or value of autonomy in this way – as what Baroness Hale described as a 'freedom to do as one pleases' or 'right to be left alone to do as one likes' – is not supportable as a matter of academic theory or practical logic. Nonetheless, eliding the right to privacy with this type of broader claim has obvious attractions for plaintiffs. As the New Zealand Law Reform Commission observed in its report on privacy:

> The thematic concern coursing through this entire report has been the possibility of a 'legal right to privacy' outrunning the genuinely motivated and honourable intentions of those who conceive of it and having a chilling effect on cherished aspects of human interaction in areas where one would not wish people to be subject to legal actions but to exhibit qualities of transparency and openness in a community setting.[126]

In light of this concern, the test used by the courts to identify when a plaintiff's privacy claim will be legally enforceable acquires particular significance. It is necessary that parties and the court be able to identify the threshold at which a plaintiff's sense that there has been an interference with their 'physical and psychological or moral integrity'[127] crystallises into a valid legal claim.

[7.42] The Supreme Court has not had the opportunity to provide a definitive ruling on this issue.

Highly offensive to a reasonable person of ordinary sensibilities

[7.43] A test of 'highly offensive to a reasonable person of ordinary sensibilities' is used in the Second Restatement of Torts in the United States, and has been employed by some judges in the New Zealand courts. [128] It has also been cited on occasions by the English courts[129] although it appears to have been supplanted in that context by the 'reasonable expectation of privacy' test.[130]

Although he did not specifically adopt this test, Kearns P's recent endorsement of the approach of the New Zealand courts in *Hosking v Runting* may provide some support for the application of this test under Irish law. This is particularly so given his consideration in the course of that decision of the extent to which the material which was the subject of

---

126. New Zealand Law Reform Commission, *A Conceptual Approach to Privacy* (Law Commission, 2007), para 182.
127. *X and Y v Netherlands* [1985] ECHR 8978/80; (1986) 8 EHRR 235.
128. For example, a test of 'highly offensive to a reasonable person of ordinary sensibilities' is used in the Second Restatement of Torts in the United States, and has been employed by some judges in the New Zealand courts. See, for example, *P v D* [2000] 2 NZLR 591 and *Hosking v Runting* [2005] 1 NZLR 1.
129. *Campbell v MGN* [2004] 2 AC 457.
130. See, for example, the doubts expressed by Lords Carswell and Nicholls about this test in *Campbell v MGN* [2004] 2 AC 457.

those proceedings was highly offensive. This suggests that 'offensiveness' may be at least one element of the test for a breach of privacy under Irish law.

However, it should also be noted that this test has been subject to some degree of criticism in both England and Wales, and in New Zealand courts[131] on the grounds that there is no necessary conceptual link between the offensive nature of the material in question and the breach of privacy which its release may entail. This reflects the fact that:

> Privacy is not confined to preventing the disclosure of discreditable facts. The fact that a person has a particular disease is usually not offensive but it is certainly a matter in respect of which he has a right to privacy.[132]

Reasonable expectation of privacy

[7.44] The 'reasonable expectation of privacy' threshold has been consistently applied in recent years in the Article 8 jurisprudence of the European Court of Human Rights[133] and the English courts.[134] As such, this is another candidate test for the evolving Irish law in this area.

The test has the advantage that it reflects the contextual nature of the right to privacy. The focus of the test on expectations rather than entitlements also underlines the fact that a legal right to privacy should not allow an individual to exercise complete control over access to personal information or space. As noted above, the extent to which privacy concerns necessarily engage the rights of others and the interests of society as a whole mean that an individual's desire to regulate the access of others to particular material could never be absolute.

In this regard, it may be instructive to note that Dunne J in Herrity – while not required to address this issue given the plain breach of statute which had occurred in that case – did discuss the plaintiff's right to privacy in terms of her expectations, observing that:

> One must bear in mind that the provisions of s 98 of the Act are there to protect the privacy of an individual's telephone conversations. No one expects to see their private telephone conversations printed in a newspaper to excite the prurient curiosity or to provide amusement for the paper's readers.

[7.45] The test of a 'reasonable expectation of privacy' has been applied in different ways by the European Court of Human Rights and by the English courts. The court in Strasbourg has tended to apply this test as a global assessment of the merits of the

131. See *Rogers v TV New Zealand Inc* [2007] NZSC 91, *per* Elias CJ. See also Moreham, 'Why is Privacy Important? Privacy, Dignity and Development of the New Zealand Breach of Privacy Tort' in Finn and Todd (eds) *Law, Libety and Legislation* (Lexis Nexis, 2008).
132. Delany & Carolan, at 295.
133. *Halford v United Kingdom* (1997) 24 EHRR 523; *PG & JH v United Kingdom* (Application No 42409/98), 25 September 2001; *Von Hannover v Germany* (2005) 40 EHRR 1.
134. *Campbell v MGN* [2004] 2 AC 457; *McKennitt v Ash* [2006] EMLR 10; *Browne v Associated Newspapers* [2007] EMLR 19; *Mosley v Newsgroup Newspapers* [2008] EWHC 1777 (QB); *LNS v Persons Unknown* [2010] EWHC 119 (QB).

plaintiff's case in the round. The court's determination on the question of whether the claimant had a reasonable expectation of privacy concludes the case. The balance between the privacy rights asserted by a claimant and the public interest considerations pleaded by the defendant forms part of the court's assessment of whether the expectation was reasonable or not.[135]

[7.46] By contrast, the English courts have considered the 'reasonable expectation of privacy' test as an initial threshold which a plaintiff must overcome to be able to invoke the protection of Article 8. The reasonableness of the expectation determines whether there is a legal interest capable of being enforced against the defendant. If that test is satisfied, the courts then move on to balance the plaintiff's right against any competing considerations. As Eady J explained the approach in Mosley:

> If the first hurdle can be overcome, by demonstrating a reasonable expectation of privacy, it is now clear that the court is required to carry out the next step of weighing the relevant competing Convention rights.[136]

It is submitted that, to the extent that this distinction exists, the English courts' approach is preferable. It reflects the roots of the right to privacy in social norms and expectations. More importantly, however, it also provides a more precise analytical framework for the courts in considering these cases. By separating out the stages at which the court determines whether there is a right to privacy capable of being enforced and whether that right is, in the circumstances, outweighed by other interests, this approach allows a court to balance any competing rights in a clearer and more rigorous manner.

[7.47] In applying the test, the English courts consider the reasonableness of an expectation considered from the point of view of the plaintiff. The test is a mixed subjective-objective one, in accordance with which the court asks what the expectations of a reasonable person in the plaintiff's position would be. As Lord Hope explained the test in *Campbell v MGN*:

> The mind that has to be examined is that, not of the reader in general, but of the person who is affected by the publicity. The question is what a reasonable person of ordinary sensibilities would feel if she was placed in the same position as the claimant and faced with the same publicity.[137]

This has been cited with approval on a number of subsequent occasions. In *Murray v Express Newspapers*, Clarke MR held that:

> The first question is whether there is a reasonable expectation of privacy. This is of course an objective question. The nature of the question was discussed in

---

135. See, for example, *Peck v United Kingdom* (2003) 36 EHRR 41; *Perry v United Kingdom* (2004) 39 EHRR 3; (2005) 40 EHRR 1.
136. *Mosley v Newsgroup Newspapers* [2008] EWHC 1777 (QB), para 10. See also *Douglas v Hello! Ltd (No 2)* [2006] QB 125; *McKennitt v Ash* [2006] E.MLR 10; *Murray v Express Newspapers Ltd* [2007] EMLR 22; *Browne v Associated Newspapers Ltd* [2007] EMLR 19; *LNS v Persons Unknown* [2010] EWHC 119 (QB).
137. *Campbell v MGN* [2004] 2 AC 457, 484.

Campbell v MGN Limited. Lord Hope emphasised that the reasonable expectation was that of the person who is affected by the publicity. He said, at paragraph 99:

> 'The question is what a reasonable person of ordinary sensibilities would feel if she was placed in the same position as the claimant and faced with the same publicity.'[138]

[7.48] Clarke MR explained that 'the 'reasonable expectation of privacy' is the threshold test which brings the balancing exercise into play'.[139] Tugenhadt J agreed in *LNS v Persons Unknown*:[140]

> At a trial of a claim for misuse of private information a Claimant must first establish that he has a reasonable expectation of privacy in relation to the information of which disclosure is threatened. That is 'whether a reasonable person of ordinary sensibilities would feel if he or she was placed in the same position as the Claimant and faced the same publicity' in all the circumstances. These include:
>
> > 'the attributes of the Claimant, the nature of the activity in which the Claimant was engaged, the place at which it was happening, the nature and purpose of the intrusion, the absence of consent and whether it was known or could be inferred, the effect on the Claimant and the circumstances in which and the purposes for which the information came into the hands of the publisher'.[141]

This seems sensible. It would be undesirable to protect a person's own subjective expectation of privacy where it was unrealistic or out of step with general social norms.

[7.49] However, there is a danger in applying the objective element of the test that the protection provided for privacy at law may be undermined by a decline in the protection actually enjoyed by individuals in practice. This is a particular issue at present given the extent to which technological advances have led to a creeping erosion of people's expectations of privacy in recent years. Of course, one response to this is that people's acceptance of these gradual intrusions indicates that the social norms upon which the protection of privacy is premised have changed. Facebook founder Mark Zuckerberg, for example, has been reported as saying that privacy is no longer a social norm. By contrast, Anderson has argued that an approach based on an empirical assessment of what constitutes a reasonable expectation of privacy is inadequate:

> Instead of deciding how much the individual ought to be protected from public curiosity, the courts ask how much protection we are accustomed to receiving … In determining what information is private, the law is more interested in what is than what ought to be. The law protects privacy to the extent that it is customarily respected … [T]his empirical approach is … self-defeating, or at least self-eroding … [T]he more privacy is invaded the less privacy is respected.

---

138. *Murray v Big Pictures* [2008] 3 WLR 1360; [2008] EWCA Civ 446, para 35.
139. *Murray v Big Pictures* [2008] EWCA Civ 446, para 35.
140. *LNS v Persons Unknown* [2010] EWHC 119 (QB), para 28.
141. *LNS v Persons Unknown* [2010] EWHC 119 (QB), para 55.

In essence, his view is that a focus on what currently happens makes the mistake of confusing an 'is' with an 'ought'.

Deliberate, conscious and unjustified violation of privacy

[7.50] In *LK (A Minor) v Independent Star Ltd*,[142] Hedigan J accepted counsel for the defendant's suggestion that an action for damages for breach of privacy could only be successful if the following four pre-requisites had been established:

(a) the information must be private;

(b) the violation must be deliberate;

(c) the violation must be conscious;

(d) the violation must be justified.[143]

This test appears to have been derived from the decision of Hamilton P in *Kennedy v Ireland*[144] where he described the infringement as one which had been 'carried out deliberately, consciously and without justification' by the relevant State actors.[145]

There are a number of points to note in relation to these pre-requisites. The first is that the Court in *LK* was not considering in this passage whether there had been a breach of the plaintiff's right to privacy. Rather, the test was set out in relation to the narrower question of whether damages could be recovered for an alleged breach of the constitutional right to privacy. These criteria do not therefore seem, strictly speaking, to have been presented as a general test for identifying whether a breach of privacy has occurred.

However, even on this narrower view, there are a number of potential problems with these pre-requisites. The first is that the decision in Kennedy itself does not support the suggestion that these criteria are pre-requisites to the recovery of damages for breach of a person's constitutional right to privacy. The relevant section of the decision in that case seems to indicate that the Court's reference to the deliberate, conscious and unjustified character of the defendants' action was intended simply to describe their conduct rather than to establish a threshold for an action in damages. This is confirmed by the fact that Hamilton P held in *Kennedy* that the third plaintiff was entitled to £10,000 damages for breach of her constitutional rights despite the fact that he also held that the interference with her right to privacy was 'not done consciously or deliberately but incidentally'.[146]

Secondly, these criteria seem to suggest that it will be more difficult to recover damages for breach of the right to privacy than for a breach of other constitutional rights. In *Conway v INTO*,[147] Finlay CJ discussed the circumstances in which damages could be available for a breach of constitutional rights in some detail. He expressed the

---

142. *LK (A Minor) v Independent Star Ltd* (3 November 2010, unreported) HC.
143. *LK (A Minor) v Independent Star Ltd* (3 November 2010, unreported) HC, at para 93.
144. *Kennedy v Ireland* [1987] 1 IR 587.
145. *Kennedy v Ireland* [1987] 1 IR 587, at 594.
146. *Kennedy v Ireland* [1987] 1 IR 587, at 595.
147. *Conway v INTO* [1991] 2 IR 305.

view, inter alia, that damages for breach of a constitutional right could be awarded on the basis of the ordinary approach of compensating a plaintiff for the 'harmful effects of a wrongful act'. The conduct of the defendant, in his view, was more relevant to the availability of aggravated or exemplary damages. To the extent that LK may suggest that ordinary damages may be awarded for a breach of privacy only where the defendant's conduct is not simply wrongful but also deliberate, conscious and unjustified, this seems to diverge from the decision in Conway.

It is not clear why the rights of plaintiffs to recover damaged for a breach of their constitutional right to privacy should be subject to such additional restrictions. This is an issue which may require further judicial development in future cases.

Determining whether there has been a breach of the right to privacy

[7.51] As described above, privacy is a context-sensitive right. Whether there has been a breach of privacy will depend on the specific circumstances of an individual case. This is usefully illustrated by Kearns P's decision in *Hickey v Sunday Newspapers Ltd*[148] where the Court specifically identified a number of relevant factors as part of its overall assessment of the plaintiff's claim. As Phillips MR observed in *HRH Prince of Wales v Associated Newspapers Ltd*,[149] the existence of a reasonable expectation cannot usually be determined on the basis of any one consideration. Regardless of the test used, a court faced with a privacy claim will typically have to examine the specifics of the case at hand, having regard to considerations like the nature of the material, the form it took, the relationship in question, the effect of the invasion or disclosure on the plaintiff, and so on. The merits of the plaintiff's privacy claim are based on an overall assessment of this 'interdependent amalgam of circumstances'.[150] For that reason, this section of the chapter will review a variety of factors which the courts have taken account of in different cases. Obviously, however, the importance of these factors will vary from case to case.

Private information

[7.52] There are certain categories of information that the courts tend to regard as inherently private. These usually involve a very intimate or personal matter. Medical information, for example, has been described as having a 'highly private character',[151] while the courts have also acknowledged that there is 'a powerful argument that the conduct of an intimate or sexual relationship is a matter in respect of which there is "a reasonable or legitimate expectation of privacy"'.[152]

However, it is unwise to adopt a rigidly categorical approach to the question of what constitutes private information. While issues such as medical or sexual matters will

---

148. *Hickey v Sunday Newspapers Ltd* [2010] IEHC 349.
149. *HRH Prince of Wales v Associated Newspapers Ltd* [2007] 3 WLR 222.
150. *HRH Prince of Wales v Associated Newspapers Ltd* [2007] 3 WLR 222, 276.
151. *Campbell v MGN* [2004] 2 AC 457, 467, *per* Lord Nicholls.
152. *CC v AB* [2007] EMLR 11, para 8. See also *Stephens v Avery* [1988] 1 Ch 449; *Theakston v MGN Ltd* [2002] EMLR 22; *A v B plc* [2003] QB 195.

frequently be private, the courts have also pointed out that that will not always be the case. It depends, as with so much of the law of privacy, on the context. In *Theakston v MGN*[153] for example, the court rejected Jack J's statement in *A v B plc*[154] that a reasonable expectation of privacy attached to all forms of sexual relationship. Ouseley J rejected such a hard and fast rule:

> Sexual relations within marriage at home would be at one end of the range or matrix of circumstances to be protected from most forms of disclosure; a one night stand with a recent acquaintance in a hotel bedroom might very well be protected from press publicity. A transitory engagement in a brothel is yet further away.[155]

A similar example of the context-sensitive nature of this action can be found in the discussion by various courts of whether the medical affairs of public figures such as senior politicians will be regarded as private. Whereas Gummow and Hayne JJ expressed doubts in *Australian Broadcasting Corporation v Lenah Game Meats Pty*[156] about whether such information should be private, Dunne J expressed the contrary view in *Herrity* that 'the circumstances which could justify a publication of such private information would seldom arise and only if there was some clear, demonstrable public interest'.

[7.53] A broad summary of the concept of private information in English law may be found in the decision of Phillips MR in *Douglas v Hello! Ltd (No 3)*.[157] For him, private information is information which is personal to the individual who possesses it and that he does not intend shall be shared with the general public. He added that '[t]he nature of the information, or the form in which it is kept, may suffice to make it plain that the information satisfies these criteria'.[158] He reiterated this statement of the law in *HRH Prince of Wales v Associated Newspapers Ltd*,[159] where he held that matters recorded in the Prince of Wales's private journal was private information, public disclosure of which constituted an interference with the claimant's Article 8 rights. However, Lord Phillips MR also emphasised that his decision was not solely based on the fact that the matters in question were in a private journal or diary. On the contrary, he explained that that it was not easy, when concluding that the information was private, to identify the extent to which this was because of the nature of the material, the form in which it was conveyed and the fact that the personal disclosing it was in a confidential relationship with the person to whom it related. Rather, 'these factors form an interdependent amalgam of circumstances'.

[7.54] This is an important reminder of the limitations of a categorical approach to this issue. While it is true that certain types of material will usually be found by a court as

153. *Theakston v MGN* [2002] EMLR 22.
154. *A v B plc* [2001] 1 WLR 2341.
155. *Theakston v MGN* [2002] EMLR 22, para 60.
156. *Australian Broadcasting Corporation v Lenah Game Meats Pty* [2001] 185 ALR 1.
157. *Douglas v Hello! Ltd (No3)* [2006] QB 125, 157.
158. *Douglas v Hello! Ltd (No3)* [2006] QB 125.
159. *HRH Prince of Wales v Associated Newspapers Ltd* [2007] 3 WLR 222, 276.

private, it would seem inadvisable to treat any category of information as automatically entitled to protection. Nonetheless, some of the more reliable categories are considered below.

MEDICAL INFORMATION

[7.55] The European Court of Human Rights has held that Article 8 applies with particular force to information concerning medical records or treatment:

> Respecting the confidentiality of health data is a vital principle in the legal systems of all the Contracting Parties to the Convention. It is crucial not only to respect the sense of privacy of a patient but also to preserve his or her confidence in the medical profession and in the health services in general. Without such protection those in need of medical assistance may be deterred from revealing such information of a personal and intimate nature as may be necessary in order to receive appropriate treatment and, even, from seeking such assistance, thereby endangering their own health and, in the case of transmissible diseases, that of the community.[160]

This was endorsed by McCarthy J in *Governors and Guardians of the Hospital for the Relief of Poor Lying-In Women, Dublin v Information Commissioner*.[161] This illustrates the fact that, in addition to the personal interest of a patient in their own medical history, there is also a public interest in maintaining the confidentiality of medical records. The Court of Appeal in *Ashworth Hospital v MGN Ltd* described the unauthorised disclosure of medical information as 'an attack on an area of confidentiality which should be safeguarded in any democratic society'. Dunne J's discussion in *Herrity* of the limited scope (if any) for the legitimate disclosure of medical information reinforces the fact that medical matters are at the core of what will usually be regarded as private information.

[7.56] However, Baroness Hale also pointed out in *Campbell v MGN* that the fact that information is medical in character will not always support a finding that there is a reasonable expectation that it should not be disclosed. She argued that there would be no or little protection for information that a public figure had a cold or a broken leg.

[7.57] The protection which the law of privacy provides for medical matters may accordingly vary according to how serious or personal the information in question might be. Mental health issues, for example, would appear to receive a very high level of protection,[162] as would information relating to an alleged sexual assault.[163] Where there may be a social stigma attached to a health issue, similar considerations may apply.[164]

---

160. *Z v Finland* (1998) 25 EHRR 371.
161. *Hospital for the Relief of Poor Lying-In Women, Dublin v Information Commissioner* [2009] IEHC 315.
162. *Ashworth Hospital v MGN Ltd* [2002] 1 WLR 2033.
163. *R (TB) v Stafford Combined Court* [2006] EWHC 645.
164. *X v Y* [1988] 2 All ER 648.

[7.58] However, it has also been held that a person's interest in the privacy of their medical records may be outweighed by the public interest in certain situations. Thus, it was held that it was permissible to interfere with this privacy where that was necessary to prevent crime or to protect the public against violent[165] or dangerous[166] individuals. It has also been held to be permissible to require disclosure of medical records where a claim is being made from public funds on the basis of an alleged medical condition.[167]

SEXUAL MATTERS

[7.59] It was held in *A v B plc*[168] that the right to privacy did not apply to all forms of sexual relationship:

> Sexual relations within marriage at home would be at one end of the range or matrix of circumstances to be protected from most forms of disclosure; a one night stand with a recent acquaintance in a hotel bedroom might very well be protected from press publicity. A transitory engagement in a brothel is yet further away.[169]

However, sexual activities or matters relating to sexual orientation will usually be regarded as private. This is, in part, because it has been recognised that sexual activity 'concerns a most intimate aspect of private life'.[170] The courts have also referred to the fact that '[i]n the ordinary way, those who participate in sexual or personal relationships may be expected not to reveal private conversations or activities'.[171] This is capable of applying even where the couple in question are in an adulterous relationship.[172] The strength of this social norm indicates that a person will normally have a reasonable expectation of privacy in respect of their sexual conduct and that this will be sufficient to meet the initial threshold to establish a legally protected interest. As Eady J summarised the position in *Mosley*:

> There is now a considerable body of jurisprudence in Strasbourg and elsewhere which recognises that sexual activity engages the rights protected by Article 8 ... [A]rticle 8 rights protect in this respect 'an essentially private materialisation of the human personality'. There are many statements to similar effect, the more lofty of which do not necessarily withstand rigorous analysis. The precise meaning is not always apparent. Nevertheless, the underlying sentiments are readily understood in everyday language; namely, that people's sex lives are to be regarded as essentially their own business – provided at least that the participants are genuinely consenting adults and there is no question of exploiting the young or vulnerable.[173]

---

165. *W v Egdell* [1990] Ch 359.
166. *Z v Finland* (1998) 25 EHRR 371.
167. *MS v Sweden* (1999) 28 EHRR 313.
168. *A v B plc* [2001] 1 WLR 2341.
169. *Theakston v MGN* [2002] EMLR 22, para 60.
170. *Dudgeon v UK* (1981) 4 EHRR 149.
171. *Mosley v Newsgroup Newspapers* [2008] EWHC 1777 (QB).
172. *CC v AB* [2007] EMLR 11.
173. *Mosley v Newsgroup Newspapers* [2008] EWHC 1777 (QB), paras 98–99.

This does not mean, however, that the right to privacy in relation to sexual matters will always prevail. Lord Hoffman pointed out in *Campbell v MGN*[174] that there could be a genuine public interest in the disclosure of the existence of a sexual relationship, such as where it could be argued that it was connected with favouritism or corruption.

INFORMATION RELATING TO CHILDREN OR VULNERABLE ADULTS

[7.60] It is arguable that children or vulnerable adults may enjoy a greater level of privacy protection, such that information concerning them will often be regarded as private. Clarke MR's decision in *Murray v Associated Newspapers* held that it was significant in that case that the complaint was made on behalf of a child rather than an adult:

> The fact that he is a child is in our view of greater significance than the judge thought. The courts have recognised the importance of the rights of children in many different contexts and so too has the international community: see eg *R v Central Independent Television plc* [1994] Fam 192 *per* Hoffmann LJ at 204–5 and the United Nations Convention on the Rights of the Child, to which the United Kingdom is a party. More specifically, cl 6 of the Press Complaints Commission Editors' Code of Practice contains this sentence under the heading Children 'v) Editors must not use the fame, notoriety or position of the parent or guardian as sole justification for publishing details of a child's private life.' There is also a publication called The Editors' Codebook, which refers to the Code and to the above statement. Although it is true that the Codebook states (at p 51) in a section headed 'Intrusion' that the Press Complaints Commission has ruled that the mere publication of a child's image cannot breach the Code when it is taken in a public place and is unaccompanied by any private details or materials which might embarrass or inconvenience the child, which is particularly unlikely in the case of babies or very young children, it seems to us that everything must depend on the circumstances.

> So, for example, in Tugendhat and Christie on The Law of Privacy and the Media the authors note at para 13.128 (in connection with a complaint made by Mr and Mrs Blair) that the PCC has stated that:

>> 'the acid test to be applied by newspapers in writing about the children of public figures who are not famous in their own right (unlike the Royal Princes) is whether a newspaper would write such a story if it was about an ordinary person.'

As against that, however, it should also be borne in mind that the privacy entitlements of children and vulnerable adults may be affected by their reduced capacity to make autonomous decisions for themselves. This was acknowledged by the Court of Appeal in *A v Independent News & Media*.[175]

[7.61] It may be more accurate therefore to conclude that, while the privacy rights of children and vulnerable adults may not entitle them to the same level of decision-making

---

174. *Campbell v MGN* [2004] 2 AC 459, para 60.
175. *A v Independent News & Media* [2010] EWCA Civ 343.

autonomy as others, their vulnerability may justify a higher level of protection against any intrusions upon their privacy than might otherwise be the case.

TRIVIAL OR ANODYNE INFORMATION

[7.62] The English courts and the European Court of Human Rights have held that an individual may not be entitled to claim a reasonable expectation of privacy in relation to material which is trivial or anodyne. In *Von Hannover v Germany*,[176] it was held that the claimant's Article 8 rights were engaged by the publication of anodyne photographs of her going about her business in public. While the original complaint included photographs which revealed information about her personal relationships, these had been excluded from the litigation by the time the ECtHR delivered its decision. The judgment concerned only relatively trivial photographs of her shopping, skiing, on horseback, with her bodyguard and so on. The court nonetheless concluded that there had been a breach of her Article 8 rights.

[7.63] A different approach was originally adopted by the English courts. In *John v Associated Newspapers*,[177] Eady J held that Elton John did not have a reasonable expectation of privacy in relation to photographs of him in a tracksuit and baseball cap outside his house. They did not reveal any particular information or relate to a specific activity or occurrence. Eady J held that there could be no expectation of privacy for what he described as a 'popping out for a pint of milk' type of case.

[7.64] This approach was also followed at first instance in *Murray v Express Newspapers*[178] where Patten J held that 'routine acts such as the visit to the shop or the ride on the bus should not attract any reasonable expectation of privacy'. His decision was reversed on appeal. The Court of Appeal held that *Von Hannover* required a greater degree of protection for individuals engaged in relatively mundane matters than Patten J had provided for. In its view:

> We recognise that there may well be circumstances in which there will be no reasonable expectation of privacy, even after Von Hannover. However, as we see it all will (as ever) depend upon the facts of the particular case. The judge suggests that a distinction can be drawn between a child (or an adult) engaged in family and sporting activities and something as simple as a walk down a street or a visit to the grocers to buy the milk. This is on the basis that the first type of activity is clearly part of a person's private recreation time intended to be enjoyed in the company of family and friends and that, on the test deployed in Von Hannover, publicity of such activities is intrusive and can adversely affect the exercise of such social activities. We agree with the judge that that is indeed the basis of the ECtHR's approach but we do not agree that it is possible to draw a clear distinction in principle between the two kinds of activity. Thus, an expedition to a café of the kind which occurred here seems to us to be at least arguably part of each member of the family's recreation time intended to be enjoyed by them and such that

---

176. *Von Hannover v Germany* (2005) 40 EHRR 1.
177. *John v Associated Newspapers* [2006] EMLR 27.
178. *Murray v Express Newspapers* [2007] EMLR 22.

publicity of it is intrusive and such as adversely to affect such activities in the future ... We do not share the predisposition identified by [Patten J] that routine acts such as a visit to a shop or a ride on a bus should not attract any reasonable expectation of privacy. All depends upon the circumstances.[179]

It should be noted that it is anticipated that it will be argued before the European Court of Human Rights in the upcoming *Von Hannover (No 2)* litigation that there should be a threshold of seriousness in relation to the information or matters in question, below which Article 8 would not be engaged.

[7.65] Some of the English authorities seem to distinguish situations where the information in question relates to trivial matters from those where the information relates to private matters but is trivial in nature. In *McKennitt v Ash*[180] Eady J issued an injunction preventing further publication of particular passages of a book about the claimant. He refused, however, to grant relief in relation to passages which he found to be anodyne. He held, however, that this triviality was not relevant to the initial establishment of a reasonable expectation of privacy on the part of the claimant:

> [T]he mere fact that information concerning an individual is 'anodyne' or 'trivial' will not necessarily mean that Article 8 is not engaged. For the purpose of determining that initial question, it seems that the subject matter must be carefully assessed. If it is such as to give rise to a 'reasonable expectation of privacy', then questions such as triviality or banality may well need to be considered at the later stage of bringing to bear an 'intense focus' upon the comparative importance of the specific rights being claimed in the individual case. They will be relevant to proportionality.[181]

His decision was upheld by the Court of Appeal.[182] This indicates that the relative triviality of the information impugned may be relevant in some cases to the proportionality of the alleged infringement rather than to the initial threshold issue of determining whether an expectation of privacy has been established. This would typically arise in cases where the expectation of privacy was based on factors other than the content of the information. For example, if information was concerned with medical matters, it would seem that a person would have a prima facie right to privacy in respect of it. In reconciling that right with other interests, however, the fact that the medical is – to use Baroness Hale's example – only a cold or a broken leg may be taken into account in striking a balance with any countervailing interests.

Location of the infringement

[7.66] The place where an alleged invasion of privacy occurred can often have a significant influence on the outcome of the case. This reflects the fact that there are

---

179. *Murray v Big Pictures* [2008] EMLR 399; [2008] EWCA Civ 446, paras 55–56.
180. *McKennitt v Ash* [2006] EMLR 10.
181. *McKennitt v Ash* [2006] EMLR 10, para 21.
182. *McKennitt v Ash* [2007] 3 WLR 194.

certain specific spaces – most notably the home[183] – which are usually regarded as having a particularly strong association with the privacy rights of the individual.

[7.67] This is sensible given the relationship between a legal right to privacy and the reasonable social expectations of the individual. The place where an incident occurs can be a strong indicator of what a person may have expected, or have been entitled to expect. Thus, in *Holden v Express Newspapers*[184] Eady J granted an injunction preventing the publication of topless photographs which had been taken while the claimant was in a private hotel garden. Sara Cox similarly received a reportedly large award of damages in a settlement with the People newspaper after nude photographs were taken of her on honeymoon on a private beach.[185]

[7.68] On the other hand, action which takes place in a public or quasi-public place may be more likely to be regarded as outside the scope of a reasonable expectation of privacy. It was held in *Theakston v MGN Ltd*,[186] for example, that the fact that the applicant could have been seen by any member of the public on the street on his way into the brothel or in the brothel itself undermined his privacy claim. In *X v Y*[187] the court relied in part in coming to its decision on the fact that the activities at issue took place in a public toilet to which anyone had access. Similarly, in *R (Ford) v Press Complaints Commission*[188] Silber J held that the PCC had been entitled to find that the publication of photographs taken on a public beach did not breach the applicant's right to privacy, even where it was claimed that she had deliberately sought out the most secluded parts of the beach. In addition, activities which attract a large public crowd for the purpose of engaging in such activities are obviously unlikely to be private.[189]

[7.69] However, this again is likely to be only one factor to be taken into account by the courts. This is especially so since the European Court of Human Rights' confirmation of the fact that Article 8 may apply to conduct or action that take place in a public or quasi-public place. The European Court of Human Rights held in *Peck v United Kingdom*[190] that a claimant could successfully claim that his Article 8 rights had been infringed when video footage of his attempt to commit suicide in a public place was broadcast.[191] It was thought that this case may have been influenced by the personal nature of the incident in question but this was rejected by the court in *Von Hannover v Germany*[192]

---

183. *Simple Imports v Revenue Commissioners* [2000] 2 IR 243.
184. *Holden v Express Newspapers* (7 June 2001, unreported), HC.
185. 'Sara Cox wins privacy case' (2003) *The Guardian*, 7 June.
186. *Theakston v MGN Ltd* [2002] EMLR 22.
187. [2004] EWCA Civ 662.
188. *R (Ford) v Press Complaints Commission* [2001] EWHC 683 (Admin).
189. *R (Countryside Alliance) v AG* [2007] UKHL 52.
190. *Peck v United Kingdom* (2003) 36 EHRR 41.
191. The circumstances in *Peck* were clearly different to those in a case like *Friedl v Austria* (1996) 21 EHRR 83 where photographs had been taken of a public demonstration which related to a public event in which the applicant was participating voluntarily.
192. *Von Hannover v Germany* (2005) 40 EHRR 1.

where it upheld the claimant's complaint in relation to the publication of photographs taken in a public place.

[7.70] The English courts have followed a similar line. The House of Lords in *Campbell v MGN Ltd*[193] recognised the plaintiff's right to privacy in relation to photographs taken of her on a public street. Eady J summarised the law *McKennitt v Ash*[194] that '[i]t is no longer possible to draw a rigid distinction between that which takes place in private and that which is capable of being witnessed in a public place by other persons'.[195]

[7.71] A somewhat different approach has been adopted in Ireland. In *Atherton v Director of Public Prosecutions*[196] Peart J held that an individual did not have an expectation of privacy in relation to conduct which occurred in the vicinity of his house. The basis for this finding was the fact that the place in question could be seen from the public street. The judge was satisfied that a privacy claim was not sustainable in relation to a place which could be seen by another person. It is submitted, however, that this type of 'bright-line' approach to this issue is out of step with the jurisprudence of the Strasbourg court and it is insufficiently flexible to take account of the context-sensitive nature of the right to privacy.[197]

The more recent decision of Kearns P in *Hickey v Sunday Newspapers Ltd*[198] appears to confirm that there is no strict distinction between public and private places under Irish law. The Court in Hickey was influenced by the fact that the alleged interference in that case occurred in a public place. Kearns P expressed the view that:

> One intuitively feels that a right of privacy is less easily established in public places where a person, in the words of TS Eliot, has had time 'to prepare a face to meet the faces that you meet'. That is particularly the case when one is performing a function of a public nature which I am satisfied the plaintiff and Mr Agnew were performing on this occasion. This was not a private celebration or event in the plaintiff's own home or at some other location to which a legitimate expectancy of privacy attached.

However, the Court went on to add that '[t]hat is not to say, however, that there will never be occasions where a person photographed in a public place can successfully invoke privacy rights'. This suggests that, while an individual is likely to enjoy a lesser right or expectation of privacy in a public place, there may be some circumstances in which a privacy claim may be sustained in relation to events that occur in a public or quasi-public space.

---

193. *Campbell v MGN Ltd* [2004] 2 AC 457.
194. *McKennitt v Ash* [2006] EMLR 10, para 50.
195. *McKennitt v Ash* [2006] EMLR 10, para 50. See also the comment of Eady J at para 57 that 'the European Court [is] not prepared to acknowledge a bright line boundary between private (or secluded) locations and public places'.
196. *Atherton v Director of Public Prosecutions* [2006] 1 IR 245.
197. See further Carolan, 'Stars of Citizen CCTV: Video Surveillance and the Right to Privacy in Public Places' (2006) 28 DULJ 326.
198. *Hickey v Sunday Newspapers Ltd* [2010] IEHC 349.

Photographs or visual footage

[7.72] The European Court of Human Rights has held that the pictures and photographs may constitute a greater interference with a person's privacy than the mere publication of information alone. It was held in *PG & JH v United Kingdom*[199] that the creation of a permanent audio recording of the claimants raised additional Article 8 issues:

> The person who walks down the street will inevitably be visible to any member of the public who is also present. Monitoring by technological means of the same public scene (eg a security guard viewing through close circuit television) is a similar character. Private life considerations may arise however once any systematical permanent record comes into existence of such material from the public domain.[200]

This was discussed further by the court in *Peck v United Kingdom*.[201] The court explained that a permanent record facilitated a much greater degree of interference with a person's privacy. It pointed out that the existence of CCTV footage of the attempted suicide meant that 'the relevant moment was viewed to an extent which far exceeded any exposure to a passer-by or to security observation and to a degree surpassing that which the Applicant could possibly have foreseen when he walked in Brentwood on August 20, 1995'.

[7.73] This was cited with approval by Lord Hoffman in *Campbell v MGN*,[202] where he added that 'the fact that we cannot avoid being photographed does not mean that anyone who takes or obtains such photographs can publish them to the world at large.' Baroness Hale agreed that '[a] picture is "worth a thousand words" because it adds to the impact of what the words convey; but it also adds to the information given in those words.'[203]

[7.74] This logic has been adopted and applied by the English courts in a significant number of decisions. In *Douglas v Hello! Ltd*[204] Keene LJ held that the photographs at issue 'conveyed to the public information not otherwise truly obtainable, that is to say, what the event and its participants looked like'. In *Theakston*, Ouseley J observed that the courts 'have consistently recognised that photographs can be particularly intrusive and have showed a high degree of willingness to prevent the publication of photographs, taken without the consent of the person photographed but which the photographer or someone else sought to exploit and publish.'[205] Lord Phillips MR in *Douglas v Hello! Ltd (No3)*[206] stated that:

> Special considerations attach to photographs in the field of privacy. They are not merely a method of conveying information that is an alternative to verbal

---

199. *PG & JH v United Kingdom* (Application No 42409/98), 25 September 2001.
200. *PG & JH v United Kingdom* (Application No 42409/98), 25 September 2001, para 57.
201. *Peck v United Kingdom* (2003) 36 EHRR 41.
202. *Campbell v MGN* [2004] 2 AC 459.
203. *Campbell v MGN* [2004] 2 AC 459, 501.
204. *Douglas v Hello! Ltd* [2001] QB 967, 1011.
205. *Theakston v MGN Ltd* [2002] EMLR 22, para 78.
206. *Douglas v Hello! Ltd (No3)* [2006] QB 125, 158.

description. They enable the person viewing the photograph to act as a spectator, in some circumstances voyeur would be the more appropriate noun, of whatever it is that the photograph depicts. As a means of invading privacy, a photograph is particularly intrusive. This is quite apart from the fact that the camera, and the telephoto lens, can give access to the viewer of the photograph to scenes where those photographed could reasonably expect that their appearances or actions would not be brought to the notice of the public.'[207]

Tugenhadt J agreed that '[p]hotographs attract special protection because they can be much more intrusive and informative than words'.[208] This meant, in Eady J's view in *Mosley*, that '[t]here can be little doubt that [the publication of] intimate photographs or recording of private sexual activity, however unconventional, would be extremely difficult to justify at all by Strasbourg standards'.[209]

[7.75] The significance of a photograph or picture is also underlined by the fact that the English courts have in several situations drawn a distinction between the disclosure of information and the release of a photograph or video. As Eady J explained in *Mosley*, 'it should not be assumed that, even if the subject-matter of [a report] … was of public interest, the showing of the film or the pictures was a reasonable method of conveying that information'. This is usefully illustrated by the decisions such as *Theakston v MGN Ltd* and *Campbell v MGN Ltd*, where the courts allowed the publication of information about the claimant's conduct but refused to allow the publication of photographs of it.[210]

[7.76] In *Atherton v Director of Public Prosecutions*,[211] Peart J did refer to the fact that recordings of the applicant had been created as raising any additional privacy concerns. It should also be noted that the argument is expected to be made to the European Court of Human Rights in *Von Hannover (No 2)* that there should be no distinction between the disclosure of information and the dissemination of photographs.

[7.77] However, it has been argued that photographs may disrupt a person's expectations to a greater degree and that they therefore may, in certain situations, be subject to greater restrictions than the release of the information to which they may relate:

> [T]he creation of … a permanent record can distort a person's reasonable expectations. When an individual participates in a particular course of conduct in a public or quasi-public place, he undertakes the risk that he will be seen by other people in that place. So, for example, if an actress appears topless in a private hotel pool or on a secluded and isolated breach, she may be argued to have accepted that other people in that place may see her in that state of semi-nudity. When she is surreptitiously filmed or photographed, however, that enables people who were not there – potentially thousands or hundreds of thousands of them – to

---

207. *Douglas v Hello! Ltd (No3)* [2006] QB 125, 157.
208. *LNS v Persons unknown* [2010] EWHC 119 (QB), para 55.
209. *Mosley v Newsgroup Newspapers* [2008] EWHC 1777 (QB), para 132.
210. See also *M v Drury* [1994] 2 IR 8 where the High Court, in refusing to grant an injunction to restrain the publication of material, referred to the fact that the photographs taken of the children in question would not be used.
211. *Atherton v Director of Public Prosecutions* [2006] 1 IR 245.

see her. Furthermore, it enables people to view her in a different way. They may spend a long period of time viewing her in a way that would not have been possible at the time where she would have become aware of such scrutiny. To hold that this does not interfere with her privacy any more than the presence of others in that place did undermines the actress's autonomy in deciding how to conduct her social affairs. It fails to vindicate her initial expectation of privacy and deprives her of the opportunity of making a decision in relation to this new greater degree of exposure. It does not adequately take account of the fact that 'people quite reasonably adapt their self-presentation efforts according to their assessment of who can observe them and will usually have fewer inhibitions and make fewer self-presentation efforts when fewer people are around'[212]...

If it is accepted that a person may be entitled to a reasonable expectation of privacy in relation to public places, it would seem logical to assess the extent of that entitlement by reference to what that person could reasonably have expected. Where a person appears in a place where others might be present but where it is not reasonable to expect photographs to be taken, it seems appropriate that the law should be capable of taking account of such nuances of expectation ... [P]rivacy is not an all-or-nothing concept. An individual exposes differing degrees of himself to others in his interactions with them. Preserving these differing degrees of privacy would protect and vindicate the person's autonomy in constructing his own social identity.[213]

Means of interference

[7.78] The decision of Dunne J in *Herrity v Associated Newspapers* illustrates the potential significance of this factor. In that case, the court's decision was primarily based on the fact that the material at issue had been unlawfully obtained by the tapping of the plaintiff's telephone. It was argued by the defendants in *Herrity* that there was a strong public interest in the publication material in question and that this, together with the media's freedom of expression, should be balanced against the plaintiff's privacy claim. Dunne J rejected the need for a balancing exercise in these circumstances, holding that 'such considerations do not arise where the material comes from a source which is prohibited by law as in this case, namely, telephone tapping'.

Herrity, of course, was a case where the means used to obtain the information was specifically prohibited by statute. The fact that unlawful or surreptitious means are used to obtain material will not necessarily result in all cases in the court upholding the plaintiff's claim. In *Cogley v RTÉ*[214] Clarke J accepted that concealed recording of the claimant's property and conduct was a prima facie trespass and breach of privacy. However, he concluded that it was justified by the public interest in that case.[215]

---

212. Moreham, 'Privacy in Public Places' (2006) 65 CLJ 606, 622.
213. Delany & Carolan, 321–322.
214. *Cogley v RTÉ* [2005] 4 IR 79.
215. See also *TV3 Network Services v Fahey* [1999] 2 NZLR 129.

INVASION OF PRIVACY

[7.79] There may be a difference (or overlap) between cases where the plaintiff's complaint relates to the disclosure of private information obtained by particular means, and situations where it is the means of access that is the main focus of the plaintiff's action. In the latter cases, the complaint specifically concerns the defendant's conduct rather than the information obtained *per se.* To use Clarke J's distinction in *Cogley,* these would seem to be actions for invasion of a private space rather than disclosure of private information. The means the defendant used to achieve this will clearly therefore be a primary consideration for the court. Damages have been awarded in Ireland for this sort of invasion of privacy in cases such as *Kennedy v Ireland*[216] and *O'Connor v McKenna.*[217] In these cases, however, the means used must be sufficiently invasive to themselves justify a finding in favour of the plaintiff.

[7.80] It has been suggested in England that surreptitious recording may, of itself, constitute an actionable wrong. In *Hellewell v Chief Constable of Derbyshire*[218] Laws J argued that:

> If someone with a telephoto lens were to have taken from a distance and with no authority a picture of another engaged in some private act, his subsequent disclosure of the photograph would ... as surely amount to a breach of confidence as if he had found or stolen a letter or diary in which the act was recounted and proceeded to publish it.

[7.81] Laws J confined his statement to circumstances where the individual was engaged in a private act. However, in *Campbell v MGN,*[219] Lord Hoffmann cited Hellewell in support of the broader view that:

> [T]he publication of a photograph taken by intrusion into a private place (for example, by a long distance lens) may in itself be such an infringement, even if there is nothing embarrassing about the picture itself.'

None of the other judges expressed a similar view, although Baroness Hale could be taken to have indicated that English law might in the future develop in that direction by commenting that:

> We have not so far held that the mere fact of covert photography is sufficient to make the information contained in the photograph confidential. The activity photographed must be private.[220]

DISCLOSURE OF PRIVATE INFORMATION

[7.82] By contrast, where the action is concerned with the disclosure of private information, the means used is a factor which may be weighed in the balance but need

---

216. *Kennedy v Ireland* [1987] IR 587.
217. *O'Connor v McKenna* (13 November 2007, unreported), Circuit Court, Griffin J.
218. *Hellewell v Chief Constable of Derbyshire* [1995] 1 WLR 804, 807.
219. *Campbell v MGN* [2004] 2 AC 457, 478.
220. *Campbell v MGN* [2004] 2 AC 457, 501. Emphasis added.

not, of itself, be decisive. The means used will make it more difficult to defend the defendant's conduct in situations where they depart from what the plaintiffs could reasonably have expected. This will be particularly the case with technology such as long-range lenses, concealed cameras or other secret surveillance techniques. As discussed in the previous section, this undermines the plaintiff's ability to make his or her own decisions about how they interact with others.

[7.83] This was explained by Woolf MR in *R v Broadcasting Standards Commission, ex parte BBC*[221] in the following terms:

> The fact that it is clandestine can add an additional ingredient. Both the code and the BBC's own guidance recognise that clandestine filming is regarded as objectionable. The fact that it is secret prevents those who are being filmed from taking any action to avoid the filming of what they are doing.[222]

Silber J agreed in *R (Ford) v Press Complaints Commission.*[223] There, the use of a telephoto lens 'deprived [the applicant] of not only the opportunity of refusing to consent to be photographed but also of the opportunity of moving out of sight of the camera or of taking steps to ensure that no newsworthy photographs were taken of them.'[224]

[7.84] This matter has also been taken into account as a relevant factor in other jurisdictions. In *Shulman v Group W Productions Inc*[225] the Californian courts relied heavily on the fact that a small (but not deliberately concealed) microphone was used to record the plaintiff's comments in finding that her right to privacy had been infringed. Similarly the secret recording of people in their homes[226] or in their workplaces[227] has been found to justify the imposition of liability on defendants. However, the US courts have allowed the use of material which was secretly obtained in circumstances where the claimant was aware that the defendant was a journalist.[228]

Public figures

[7.85] The European Court of Human Rights has confirmed on several occasions that public figures retain an entitlement to a residual level of protection under Article 8.[229]

---

221. *R v Broadcasting Standards Commission, ex parte BBC* [2001] QB 885.
222. *R v Broadcasting Standards Commission, ex parte BBC* [2001] QB 885 at 898.
223. *R (Ford) v Press Complaints Commission* [2001] EWHC 683 (Admin), para 30.
224. See also *Holden v Express Newspapers* (7 June 2001, unreported), HC.
225. *Shulman v Group W Productions Inc* 18 Cal 4th 200 (1998).
226. *Dietemann v Time Inc* 449 2d 245 (1971). The court in Dietemann held that the use of 'hidden mechanical contrivances' constituted an intrusion. In *Desnick v American Broadcasting Co Inc* 44 F 3d 1345 (1995), it was suggested that *Dietemann* could be confined by the fact that the recording took place in the home. This may be doubtful, however, in light of the decision in Sanders.
227. *Sanders v American Broadcasting Corporation* 20 Cal 4th 907 (1999). See also the trespass action in *Food Lion Inc v Capital Cities* 194 F 3d 505 (1999).
228. *Deteresa v American Broadcasting Co Inc* 121 F 3d 460 (1997).
229. See, for example, *Tammer v Estonia* (2001) 37 EHRR 857; *Editions Plons v France* (2006) 42 EHRR 36; *Von Hannover v Germany* (2005) 40 EHRR 1.

Despite earlier indications to the contrary,[230] this was also confirmed to be the position under English law in *Campbell v MGN*.[231] It was held there that the plaintiff, who was an internationally famous model and celebrity, nonetheless retained an entitlement to a reasonable expectation of privacy in relation to her medical affairs. However, the House of Lords also accepted that the scope of the protection enjoyed by a public figure could be lower than that of an ordinary citizen. This was particularly true in relation to celebrities who had courted publicity. Lord Hoffmann explained this point as follows:

> Naomi Campbell is a famous fashion model who lives by publicity. What she has to sell is herself: her personal appearance and her personality. She employs public relations agents to present her personal life to the media in the best possible light just as she employs professionals to advise her on dress and make-up. That is no criticism of her. It is a trade like any other. But it does mean that her relationship with the media is different from that of people who expose less of their private life to the public.[232]

This does not mean, however, that a celebrity who allows access to one aspect of their private life thereby renounces all rights in relation to their private life generally. An argument to this effect was rejected by Eady J in *McKennitt v Ash*.[233] Eady J held that the plaintiff had not courted publicity in relation to many aspects of her private life and that, accordingly, she retained a right of privacy in respect of such matters. This was in spite of the fact that she had done some public charity work which involved her discussing the death of her fiancé in an accident. Eady J observed that:

> [T]here is in this context a significant difference between choosing to reveal aspects of private life with which one feels 'comfortable' and yielding up to public scrutiny every detail of personal life, feelings, thoughts and foibles of character.[234]

The law has thus acknowledged that public figures may be entitled to different levels of privacy protection. This will depend on individual circumstances. Once again, it is a question of context. At one end of the spectrum are people who were previously not known to the public in any way. At the other end of the spectrum are public figures who occupy important social positions and in whom the public have a legitimate interest as well as celebrities who may have courted publicity about their private lives and profited from it.[235] In between the two extremes may be individuals who are known to the public but who do not seek publicity. Their public status means their expectations of privacy may be lower than those of ordinary persons but *McKennitt* shows that they are unlikely to be subject to the same levels of scrutiny as politicians or publicity-seekers.

---

230. *A v B plc* [2003] QB 195.
231. *Campbell v MGN* [2004] 2 AC 457.
232. *Campbell v MGN* [2004] 2 AC 457, 470.
233. *McKennitt v Ash* [2006] EMLR 10; [2007] 3 WLR 194.
234. *McKennitt v Ash* [2006] EMLR 10, para 79. This was upheld on appeal.
235. See the comments of Lord Hoffmann in *Campbell v MGN* [2004] 2 AC 457, 473.

POLITICAL FIGURES

[7.86] The case law of the European Court of Human Rights confirms that politicians may particularly be required to display a greater degree of tolerance towards media interest in their lives.[236] In *Von Hannover v Germany*,[237] the court distinguished between individuals who exercise political functions and those who have no such position:

> [A] fundamental distinction needs to be made between reporting facts-even controversial ones-capable of contributing to a debate in a democratic society relating to politicians in the exercise of their functions, for example, and reporting details of the private life of an individual who, moreover, as in this case, does not exercise official functions. While in the former case the press exercises its vital role of 'watchdog' in a democracy by contributing to imparting information and ideas on matters of public interest it does not do so in the latter case.[238]

This confirms that public figures who occupy political or governmental positions enjoy a greatly reduced right to privacy. The court in *Von Hannover* held that 'the public has a right to be informed, which is an essential right in a democratic society that, in certain special circumstances, can even extend to aspects of the private life of public figures, particularly where politicians are concerned.'[239] However, in *Schussel v Austria*[240] the European Court of Human Rights accepted that political figures may be protected to some degree against intrusions into their privacy. The decisions in *Campmany Y Diez de Revenga v Spain*,[241] *Prisma Presse v France*[242] and *Craxi v Italy (No2)*[243] demonstrate that where the material in question is of a purely private nature and has no relevance to the individual's professional life, politicians may be able to invoke the protection of Article 8.

PUBLICITY SEEKERS

[7.87] The position of public figures who have courted publicity was considered by Lord Hoffmann in *Campbell v MGN Ltd*,[244] where he expressed the view that there was a sufficient public interest in correcting the impression which the claimant had previously given that she did not take drugs. In his view, correcting the misleading impression which the claimant had given was clearly decisive. This issue seems to be based, however, on the public interest in correcting falsity. It is discussed further therefore in the section below on the public interest defence to a privacy action.

---

236. *Radio Twist AS v Slovakia* (Application No 62202/00), 19 December 2006, para 52.
237. *Von Hannover v Germany* (2005) 40 EHRR 1. See also *McKennitt v Ash* [2006] EMLR 10, para 55; *McKennitt v Ash* [2007] 3 WLR 194, 213–214.
238. *Von Hannover v Germany* (2005) 40 EHRR 1. See also *McKennitt v Ash* [2006] EMLR 10, para 63.
239. *Von Hannover v Germany* (2005) 40 EHRR 1, para 64.
240. *Schussel v Austria* (Application 42409/98), 21 February 2002.
241. *Campmany Y Diez de Revenga v Spain (*Application No 54224/00) 12 December 2000.
242. *Prisma Presse v France* (Applications Nos 66910/01 and 71612/02) 1 July 2003.
243. *Craxi v Italy (No2)* (2004) 38 EHRR 47. See also the decision of the German Federal Supreme Court in *Kohl* 29 BGHZ 73, 120, NJW 1979, 647 to similar effect.
244. *Campbell v MGN* [2004] 2 AC 457.

In *Hickey v Independent Star Ltd*,[245] Kearns P appeared to suggest that a person's allegation that their right to privacy had been breached could be affected by their previous conduct in seeking publicity. One of the matters to which the Court referred in dismissing the plaintiff's claim was the fact that she had 'actively sought publicity from the press and media' in relation to her family.

INVOLUNTARY PUBLIC FIGURES

[7.88] *Von Hannover* is an example of another category of case – the involuntary public figure. This may be someone in whom the public is interested not because of what they do but because of who they are. Royalty or the families of those who may be in the public eye are examples of this type of person. Ordinary people may also become involuntarily public figures where they are involved in newsworthy events.[246] It is arguable that such persons enjoy a level of protection for their right to privacy which may be lower than that of a purely 'private' individual but is more than that of a person who deliberately places himself in the public eye. Gault and Blanchard JJ endorsed this view in *Hosking v Runting* when they stated that '[i]nvoluntary public figures may also experience a lessening of expectations of privacy, but not ordinarily to the extent of those who willingly put themselves in the spotlight.'[247]

CONTEXT

[7.89] The above analysis shows that there are a number of considerations which may impact on the extent to which a public figure can claim a reasonable expectation of privacy. These may include the nature of the person's position as a public figure, the extent to which the person has sought or benefited from publicity in the past, and whether the 'information value' of the material in question is concerned with purely private matters. All these factors are matters of degree. As Gault and Blanchard JJ concluded in *Hosking v Runting*:[248]

> The right to privacy is not automatically lost when a person is a public figure, but his or her reasonable expectation of privacy in relation to many areas of his life will be correspondingly reduced as public status increases.

This was echoed more recently by Eady J in *Mosley* where he observed that:

> This modern approach [to privacy claims] is thus obviously incompatible with making broad generalisations of the kind to which the media often resorted in the

---

245. *Hickey v Independent Star Ltd* [2010] IEHC 349.
246. The American courts have consistently held that members of the public who are involved in newsworthy events, even involuntarily, have a reduced expectation of privacy. See, for example, *Macon Telegraph Publishing Co v Tatum* 263 Ga 678 (1993); *Time v Hill* 385 US 374 (1967); *Cape Publications v Bridges* 423 So 2d 426 (1982). This has been found to be even in circumstances where the information revealed was not relevant to the incident for which an individual had come to public attention. *Sipple v Chronicle Publishing* 154 Cal App 3d 1040 (1984).
247. *Hosking v Runting* [2005] 1 NZLR 1, 33.
248. *Hosking v Runting* [2005] 1 NZLR 1, 33.

past such as, for example, 'Public figures must expect to have less privacy' or 'People in positions of responsibility must be seen as 'role models' and set us all an example of how to live upstanding lives'. Sometimes factors of this kind may have a legitimate role to play when the 'ultimate balancing exercise' comes to be carried out, but generalisations can never be determinative. In every case 'it all depends'.[249]

Relationship between the parties

[7.90] This formerly featured as a central element of an action for breach of confidence.[250] As the English courts developed the present more privacy-oriented action of misuse of private information from their breach of confidence jurisprudence, it is unsurprising that this featured prominently in the early case law. However, as Lord Nicholls explained in *Campbell v MGN Ltd*,[251] a claimant is no longer required to establish a pre-existing relationship of confidence between the parties. Where there is no relationship of confidence, the action can be based on the nature of the information in question.[252]

[7.91] However, that does not mean that the relationship between the parties will no longer be relevant. It can still be taken into account as part of the court's assessment of whether the plaintiff's expectation was reasonable in the circumstances. The relationship will frequently be an important factor in this assessment. As Eady J observed in *Mosley*, '[i]n the ordinary way, those who participate in sexual or personal relationships may be expected not to reveal private conversations or activities'. This means that a passing relationship with a prostitute in *Theakston*[253] attracted a lower level of protection than the established relationship in *CC v AB*.[254]

[7.92] This logic applies to non-sexual relationships as well. In *McKennitt v Ash*,[255] significant reliance was placed by the Court of Appeal on the fact that the plaintiff and defendant had enjoyed a close relationship, and that information had been disclosed in the course of that relationship. Buxton LJ expressed the view that:

> [I]n the vast majority of cases the duty of confidence will arise from a transaction or relationship between the parties. And that is our case, which accordingly reverts to a more elemental enquiry into breach of confidence in the traditional understanding of that expression. That does not of course exempt the court from considering whether the material obtained during such a relationship is indeed confidential; but to enquire into that latter question without paying any regard to the nature of the pre-existing relationship between the parties, as the argument for

---

249. *Mosley v Newsgroup Newspapers* [2008] EWHC 1777 (QB), para 12.
250. *Prince Albert v Strange* (1849) 1 H & TW 1; *Campbell v Frisbee* [2002] EWCA Civ 1374; *Argyll v Argyll* [1967] 1 Ch 302; *Stephens v Avery* [1988] 1 Ch 449.
251. *Campbell v MGN* [2004] 2 AC 457, 464. See also *A v B (a company)* [2002] EWCA Civ 337.
252. *McKennitt v Ash* [2007] 3 WLR 194.
253. *Theakston v MGN Ltd* [2002] EMLR 22.
254. *CC v AB* [2006] EWHC 3083 (QB).
255. *McKennitt v Ash* [2007] 3 WLR 194.

the first defendant in this court largely did, is unlikely to produce anything but a distorted outcome.[256]

However, the simple fact that a relationship exists will not automatically indicate that all information disclosed by one party to another will be regarded as private. Clarke MR explained in *Browne v Associated Newspapers*[257] that:

> [T]he mere fact that the information was imparted in the course of a relationship of confidence does not satisfy Lord Nicholls' test of 'expectation of privacy'. An example would be a husband telling his wife that Oxford or Cambridge won the boat race in a particular year. However, the relationship may be of considerable importance in answering the question whether there was an expectation of privacy.[258]

However, the fact that a relationship exists may bring the right to privacy or freedom of expression interests of the other party into play.[259] This is discussed further below. However, it should be noted that Tugenhadt J held in *LNS v Persons Unknown*[260] that it would be inconsistent with the value of autonomy which underpins the right to privacy to allow one party to a relationship to make arguments on the other's behalf.

Form of the material

[7.93] This factor refers to the form in which the material in respect of which a right to privacy is claimed originally existed. It will usually be relevant where the form was such that it indicated the existence of a reasonable expectation of privacy in relation to the material therein.

[7.94] This has been applied, for example, in relation to a personal journal or diary. Lord Goff accepted this proposition in *Attorney-General v Guardian Newspapers Ltd (No 2)*[261] when he provided the example of 'where an obviously confidential document is wafted by an electric fan out of a window into a crowded street, or where an obviously confidential document, such as a private diary, is dropped in a public place, and is then picked up by a passer-by'.[262] It was also relied on by the Court of Appeal in *HRH Prince of Wales v Associated Newspapers*[263] where material contained in a private journal was disclosed. That this was significant was indicated by the observation of Lord Phillips

256. *McKennitt v Ash* [2007] 3 WLR 194, 203. The relationship of employment was also found to be an important factor in *HRH Prince of Wales v Associated Newspapers* [2007] 3 WLR 222. However, the Court of Appeal also held that the circumstances were such that there would have been a reasonable expectation of privacy in the circumstances of the case even in the absence of a relationship of confidence.
257. *Browne v Associated Newspapers* [2007] 3 WLR 289.
258. *Browne v Associated Newspapers* [2007] 3 WLR 289, 300.
259. *McKennitt v Ash* [2006] EWHC 3083 (QB); *CC v AB* [2007] 3 WLR 194.
260. *LNS v Persons Unknown* [2010] EWHC 119 (QB).
261. *Attorney General v Guardian Newspapers Ltd (No 2)* [1990] 1 AC 109.
262. *Attorney General v Guardian Newspapers Ltd (No 2)* [1990] 1 AC 109, 281.
263. *HRH Prince of Wales v Associated Newspapers* [2007] 3 WLR 222.

MR in the Court of Appeal that an expectation of privacy would have been found on the facts of this case even in the absence of an employment relationship:

> If ... one strips out the fact of breach of a confidential relationship, and assumes that a copy of the journal had been brought to the newspaper by someone who had found it dropped in the street, we consider that its form and content would clearly have constituted it private information entitled to the protection of Article 8(1) as qualified by Article 8(2).[264]

This principle may also be applied to electronic material. Tugenhadt J held in *L v L*[265] that a husband had a real prospect of establishing that his wife had unlawfully acted in breach of his rights to privacy and confidentiality by removing a password-protected laptop from the family home.

[7.95] Further, the form of the material may be taken into account in relation to allegedly unlawful access to an event. In those circumstances, the court will examine the surrounding circumstances to assess the existence of a reasonable expectation. In *Creation Records v Newsgroup Newspapers Ltd*[266] Lloyd J held that photographing a band's photo shoot could constitute a breach of confidence where it had clearly been indicated that photography was not allowed. He found that the photographer 'must have been aware of the efforts to prevent people taking photographs of the shoot and can only have succeeded in doing so by being surreptitious and far from being as open as he himself deposes'.[267] Similarly, in *Douglas v Hello! Ltd*[268] the court had regard to the very extensive security precautions taken to prevent photography to justify their finding that the photographer in question must have been aware of these restrictions (not least as that was the only way to explain how he or she had avoided them). In those circumstances, the form in which the event was organised was such that it was evidently expected to remain private.

Government or public records

[7.96] Principle 5 of the Press Council's Code of Conduct states that 'the right to privacy should not prevent publication of matters of public record'. Although this may appear self-evident, it is arguable that there may, in certain cases, be circumstances in which the right to privacy may apply to matters of public records.

[7.97] This issue has been considered in greatest detail in the United States. Most of the cases have concerned court records containing details of criminal trials and convictions.[269] The American authorities have consistently held that material in a

---

264. *HRH Prince of Wales v Associated Newspapers* [2007] 3 WLR 222, 277.
265. *L v L* [2007] EWHC 140 (QB).
266. *Creation Records v Newsgroup Newspapers Ltd* [1997] EMLR 444.
267. *Creation Records v Newsgroup Newspapers Ltd* [1997] EMLR 444, 453
268. *Douglas v Hello! Ltd* [2001] QB 967; [2006] QB 125.
269. See, for example, *Richmond Newspapers Inc v Virginia* 448 US 555 (1980); *Howard v Des Moines Register* 283 N W 2d 289 (1979); *Cox Broadcasting Corporation v Cohn* 420 US 469 (1975); *Florida Star v BJF* 491 US 524 (1989).

publicly available document is presumptively public and cannot therefore support a claim of privacy. This is further supported by the importance of ensuring the open character of judicial proceedings.[270]

[7.98] Thus, in *Florida Star v BJF*,[271] the Supreme Court held that it was permissible for the media to publish the name of a rape victim where it had been included in error in a police incident report, even though such information could not usually be published. Similarly, in *Gates v Discovery Communications*,[272] the defendants were not liable for publishing details of the claimant's conviction 10 years earlier. However, the context of these cases is important:

> It is arguable that this line of authority has been heavily influenced by the constitutional pre-eminence of media speech under the First Amendment. These cases have generally involved situations in which the media has already obtained the material from a public record. The court is therefore generally asked to restrict the media's freedom of action, either by restraining publication or by imposing liability where publication has already occurred. Given the absolutist nature of the US Constitution's First Amendment guarantee, this will rarely be done.[273]

However, the US courts have adopted a more nuanced approach in situations where the media is seeking access to information in public documents. In that context, the courts have held that the disclosure of government records can interfere with an individual's right to privacy. In *Department of Justice v Reporters Committee for Freedom of the Press*[274] the Supreme Court drew a distinction between information which was technically available in a public record and the situation in which that information is widely published in the press. The court acknowledged the 'practical obscurity'[275] of many public records in holding that publication of such matters in the press could raise additional privacy concerns. This is a principle which should be borne in mind given the increasing practice of public bodies to make public records available on the internet. This makes such records much more accessible to the public, which means that there is much greater scope for an individual to have personal information disseminated than would previously have been the case. This view has also recently been endorsed by the ECJ. In *Volken v Land Hessen*,[276] the ECJ found that it breached the privacy rights of farmers receiving agricultural aid for details of the payment received by individuals to be published on the internet. Although the Court accepted the inportance of transparency and of the right of tax payers to be informed about the use of funds, it held that it was disproportionate to these objectives to make individual's details available in this form.

270. *Shepherd v Maxwell* 384 US 333 (1966); *Gannet Co v Pasquale* 443 US 368 (1979); *Globe Newspapers Co v Superior Court* 457 US 596 (1982).
271. *Florida Star v BJF* 491 US 524 (1989).
272. *Gates v Discovery Communications* 101 P 3d 552 (2004). This reversed an earlier decision in *Briscoe v Reader's Digest Association* 483 P 2d 34 (1971).
273. Delany & Carolan, *The Right to Privacy* (Thomson Round Hall, 2008), 332–333.
274. *Department of Justice v Reporters Committee for Freedom of the Press* 489 US 749 (1989).
275. *Department of Justice v Reporters Committee for Freedom of the Press* 489 US 749 (1989), 780.
276. *Volken v Land Hessen* (Case C92/09, 2010).

[7.99] This decision is also relevant to situations where disclosure is sought of a government document which may contain matters of which other people may be aware. Here the question is not one of matters of public record (in the sense that they are publicly available) but rather of matters contained within public (or governmental) records. In *Reporters Committee for Freedom of the Press*, the Supreme Court recognised that the individual may retain privacy rights in relation to such documents. The court held that there is a difference between different people knowing different things about a person and, on the other hand, all of that information being collected together into a single record. In the latter situation, the court concluded, there would be a much greater potential for undue interferences with privacy.

[7.100] A similar decision was made by European Court of Human Rights in *Rotaru v Romania*.[277] There, an individual objected to the disclosure of information contained in a secret Romanian intelligence file. It was argued that the information was not private because it concerned his political activities which were, by definition, matters of which other people and the public were aware. The court held, however, that the creation of a comprehensive record engaged the complainant's Article 8 rights, even where the information contained within it was public. It felt that:

> [P]ublic information can fall within the scope of private life where it is systematically collected and stored in files held by the authorities. That is all the truer where such information concerns a person's distant past.[278]

[7.101] A somewhat similar view was expressed by Quirke J in *National Maternity Hospital v Information Commissioner*[279] when he acknowledged that privacy could apply in relation to matters held in public records:

> The State itself has a general obligation to respect the right to privacy of its citizens. Public bodies and other State agencies entrusted with private sensitive information affecting the rights and interests of individual members of the public are, in general, required to keep that information confidential. Circumstances may arise where the disclosure of sensitive information, which is held by a public body and which concerns and affects the interests of individual citizens, may be required in the public interest.

This was applied in *South Western Health Board v Information Commissioner*,[280] where the High Court held the right to privacy of a mother who had placed her child for adoption justified, overturning a decision to release records relating to the adoption to the adopted daughter. However, in *Hickey v Sunday Newspapers Ltd*,[281] the Court had regard to the fact that information relating to the child in question was a matter of public record as part of its decision to reject the plaintiff's claim.

---

277. *Rotaru v Romania* (Application No 28341/95) 4 May 2000.
278. *Rotaru v Romania* (Application No 28341/95) 4 May 2000, para 43.
279. *National Maternity Hospital v Information Commissioner* [2007] IEHC 113.
280. *South Western Health Board v Information Commissioner* [2005] 2 IR 547.
281. *Hickey v Sunday Newspapers Ltd* [2010] IEHC 349.

Nature of Activity

INTIMATE OR PERSONAL ACTIVITIES

[7.102] In assessing the existence or otherwise of a reasonable expectation of privacy, the English courts and the European Court of Human Rights have often had regard to the nature of the activity in question. In particular, as discussed in more detail above, very personal[282] or intimate activities have tended to attract a significant level of protection. The courts have held that '[p]ersonal sexuality ... is an extremely intimate aspect of a person's private life'[283] and that there will usually, as a result, be a reasonable expectation of privacy in respect of sexual activities even where they occur in a public place[284] or in the context of an adulterous relationship.[285]

ACTIVITIES CONNECTED WITH PERSONAL OR SOCIAL DEVELOPMENT

[7.103] The European Court of Human Rights has strongly emphasised the connection between Article 8 and the individual's ability to develop social relationship with other human beings. The court explained in *Niemitz v Germany*[286] that:

> [I]t would be too restrictive to limit the notion [of private life] to an 'inner circle' in which the individual may live his own personal life as he chooses and to exclude therefrom entirely the outside world not encompassed within that circle. Respect for private life must also comprise to a certain degree the right to establish and develop relationships with other human beings.[287]

However, the concept of social or personal development is an ambiguous one. In *R (Razgar) v Secretary of State for the Home Department*[288] Lord Bingham expressed the opinion that the concept of 'private life' covered 'those features which are integral to a person's identity or ability to function socially as a person'. But the idea of what is 'integral' to a person's identity is an inherently subjective one. For example, in *Von Hannover v Germany*,[289] the right to respect for private life was held to be engaged by the publication of photographs showing, for example, the claimant shopping. This indicates that the idea of 'personal development' may be so broad as to include the ordinary business of every life.

[7.104] The breadth of this understanding of Article 8 was examined by the House of Lords in *R (Countryside Alliance) v Attorney-General*.[290] That involved a challenge to the prohibition of fox-hunting on the grounds that it interfered with an activity which

---

282. *Peck v UK* (2003) 36 EHRR 41.
283. *Douglas v Hello! Ltd* [2001] QB 967, 1012 *per* Keene LJ
284. *Jagger v Darling* [2005] EWHC 683 (QB). See 'Jagger seeks to protect her Best bits' (2005) *The Guardian*, 10 March.
285. *CC v AB* [2007] EMLR 11.
286. *Niemitz v Germany* (1992) 16 EHRR 97.
287. *Niemitz v Germany* (1992) 16 EHRR 97, para 29.
288. *R (Razgar) v Secretary of State for the Home Department* [2004] 2 AC 368.
289. *Von Hannover v Germany* (2005) 40 EHRR 1.
290. *R (Countryside Alliance) v Attorney-General* [2007] UKHL 52.

was integral to their personal life under Article 8. The House of Lords unanimously rejected this argument by reference to the fact that fox-hunting was a public event. However, several of the Law Lords also considered the potential application of Article 8 to other forms of social conduct. Baroness Hale criticised the attempt to transform Article 8 into a 'freedom to do as one pleases' or 'right to be left alone to do as one likes'.[291] While she accepted that the right to private life covered the 'inviolability of ... the personal and psychological space within which each individual develops his or her own sense of self and relationships with other people', this could not protect every possible activity in which a person might engage.[292]

[7.105] Lords Rodger and Brown, however, favoured just such a broad conception of private life. They favoured a primarily subjective view in accordance with which an activity would be integral to the person's identity where it was important to them personally:

> Why should people not be free to engage in whatever pursuits they wish – pursuits, that is, central to their wellbeing ... unless there is good and sufficient reason ... to forbid it? Article 8's protection is recognised to extend to a right to identity and to personal development and ... the notion of personal autonomy. It encompasses almost any aspect of a person's sexuality and a good deal else that is clearly personal. But why should respect for private life not encompass also wider concepts of self-fulfilment? ... Many people in a real sense live for some particular activity, whether their profession or their recreation. In a real sense it defines them. Often it provides them with their feelings of identity, self-esteem and position in the community ... Some perhaps may be regarded as more personal than others, carried out in circumstances of greater intimacy. But why should that be critical? All of them are activities to which people may choose to devote much of their lives and which for some are all-important.[293]

Lord Rodger concurred:

> The activities which I have mentioned are simply examples of 'features which are integral to a person's identity', of ways in which people give expression to their individuality – in which you can see what really makes them tick. For many people the right to express themselves in these ways may be of far more practical importance than, for instance, the right to express some aspect of their sexual identity. It would be strange indeed if such activities were not regarded as part of an individual's private life and worthy of respect in terms of Article 8(1), when they are central to the individuals' lives and often determine how they relate to their families, their friends and the outside world.[294]

This view has been criticised as impractical:

> [This] concept of decisional privacy is potentially over-broad in its application. It is capable of applying to all actions and all activities without offering a way of

---

291. *R (Countryside Alliance) v Attorney-General* [2007] UKHL 52, para 111.
292. *R (Countryside Alliance) v Attorney-General* [2007] UKHL 52, para 116.
293. *R (Countryside Alliance) v Attorney-General* [2007] UKHL 52, paras 139–140.
294. *R (Countryside Alliance) v Attorney-General* [2007] UKHL 52, para 98.

distinguishing those that should be regulated from those which should not. In light of the fact that the claim in the Countryside Alliance case was one of decisional privacy, Baroness Hale's misgivings about the potential scope of Article 8 are well-founded. However the position of Lords Rodger and Brown may be more tenable in context of the distinct concepts of spatial and informational privacy. Certainly their approach would seem to better accord with the view of the European Court of Human Rights in *Von Hannover* that even mundane activities can form an aspect of an individual's protected personal development.[295]

CRIMINAL OR IMMORAL CONDUCT

[7.106] A claimant may not have an expectation of privacy in respect of criminal or immoral conduct which would otherwise be of a private nature. Charleton J stated in *EMI v UPC*[296] that he found it impossible to accept that the right to privacy could ever extend to protect communications which were designed to further a criminal enterprise. A broadly analogous approach is evident in decision of the English Court of Appeal in *X v Y*[297] where the criminal nature of the activity undermined any expectation of privacy in relation to it. This reflects the courts' determination that the right to privacy should not be used as a cover for unlawful actions.

[7.107] However, the fact that a person has previously engaged in criminal conduct does not necessarily mean that they forfeit all rights in relation to their private life. Eady J in Mosley commented that '[i]t is worth remembering that even those who have committed serious crimes do not thereby become 'outlaws' so far as their own rights, including rights of personal privacy, are concerned'.[298] Similarly, in *Callaghan v Independent News & Media*, Stevens J held that 'there is a residuum of privacy afforded to convicted criminals'.[299] The European Court of Human Rights thus has held, for example, that it was an interference with a convicted criminal's Article 8 rights to publish photographs of her in a state of distress after the imposition of a verdict of three life sentences.[300] However, the decision of Irvine J in *Murray v Newsgroup Newspapers*[301] tends to demonstrate that a criminal conviction may have an impact on the extent to which a person may assert a reasonable expectation of privacy in relation to matters associated with that conviction.

[7.108] The courts in England have also considered whether the immoral or morally questionable nature of conduct may affect an individual's expectation or privacy in

295. Delany & Carolan, *The Right to Privacy* (Thomson Round Hall, 2008), 338.
296. *EMI v UPC* (11 October 2010, unreported) HC.
297. *X v Y* [2004] EWCA Civ 662.
298. *Mosley v Newsgroup Newspapers* [2008] EWHC 1777 (QB), para 118, citing *Silver v UK* (1983) 5 EHRR 347; *Polanski v Condé Nast Publications Ltd* [2005] UKHL 10; [2005] 1 All ER 945; [2005] 1 WLR 637.
299. *Callaghan v Independent News & Media* [2009] NIQB 1, para 78.
300. *Egeland v Norway* [2009] ECHR 34438/04.
301. *Murray v Newsgroup Newspapers* [2010] IEHC 248.

relation to it. While this was referred to by the court in *Jagger v Darling*,[302] the court have more recently warned against taking account of morality in assessing a person's expectation of privacy. Given the fact that one of the purposes of protecting privacy is to allow people to make autonomous choices in relation to their conduct, it seems sensible that a person's privacy entitlements should not be reduced by reference to the fact that they depart from conventional norms. Thus, in *CC v AB*,[303] Eady J warned that:

> Judges need to be wary about giving the impression that they are ventilating, while affording or refusing legal redress, some personal moral or social views, and especially at a time when society is far less homogeneous than in the past. At one time, when there was, or was perceived to be, a commonly accepted standard in such matters as sexual morality, it may have been acceptable for the courts to give effect to that standard in exercising discretion or in interpreting legal rights and obligations. Now, however, there is a strong argument for not holding forth about adultery, or attaching greater inherent worth to a relationship which has been formalised by marriage than to any other relationship. A judge, like anyone else, is obviously entitled to hold personal moral views about the issues of the day, but it is important not to let them intrude when interpreting and applying the law ... With such a wide range of differing views in society, perhaps more than for many generations, one must guard against allowing legal judgments to be coloured by personal attitudes. Even among judges, there is no doubt a wide range of opinion. It is all the more important, therefore, that the outcome of a particular case should not be determined by the judge's personal views or, as it used to be said, by 'the length of Chancellor's foot' ... It is not for judges when applying the Convention, which is a secular code applying to those of all religions and none, to give an appearance of sanctimony by damning adulterers.[304]

Although this decision was criticised, Eady J repeated his view in *Mosley* that:

> [I]t is not for the state or for the media to expose sexual conduct which does not involve any significant breach of the criminal law. That is so whether the motive for such intrusion is merely prurience or a moral crusade. It is not for journalists to undermine human rights, or for judges to refuse to enforce them, merely on grounds of taste or moral disapproval. Everyone is naturally entitled to espouse moral or religious beliefs to the effect that certain types of sexual behaviour are wrong or demeaning to those participating. That does not mean that they are entitled to hound those who practise them or to detract from their right to live life as they choose.
>
> It is important, in this new rights-based jurisprudence, to ensure that where breaches occur remedies are not refused because an individual journalist or judge finds the conduct distasteful or contrary to moral or religious teaching. Where the law is not breached, as I said earlier, the private conduct of adults is essentially no-one else's business. The fact that a particular relationship happens to be

---

302. *Jagger v Darling* [2005] EWHC 683 (QB). See 'Jagger seeks to protect her Best bits' (2006) *The Guardian*, 10 March.
303. *CC v AB* [2007] EMLR 11.
304. *CC v AB* [2007] EMLR 11, paras 25–28.

adulterous, or that someone's tastes are unconventional or 'perverted', does not give the media carte blanche.

...

In deciding whether a right has been infringed, and in assessing the relative worth of competing rights, it is not for judges to make individual moral judgments or to be swayed by personal distaste. It is not simply a matter of personal privacy versus the public interest. The modern perception is that there is a public interest in respecting personal privacy. It is thus a question of taking account of conflicting public interest considerations and evaluating them according to increasingly well recognised criteria.

This suggests that the moral nature of conduct may be relevant to a court's analysis where it relates to a recognised legal or public interest. Where it falls short of this, however, it would seem that it should not be taken into account.

Previous publicity

[7.109] Previous publicity may be most relevant to the question of whether an individual has waived his entitlement to privacy. However, there may also be an issue in relation to a matter which was formerly public knowledge but which has receded from the public consciousness. Can it be argued in those circumstances that a claimant has regained a reasonable expectation of privacy?

[7.110] Different views have been expressed on this issue in other jurisdictions. In *Briscoe v Reader's Digest Assocation*,[305] a former hijacker was allowed to maintain an action in relation to the publication of a story about his crime where 11 years had passed.

[7.111] In general, however, the American courts have favoured the view that material which was previously published remains public. Briscoe, for example, was overruled in *Gates v Discovery Communications Inc*.[306] Similarly, in *Sidis v F-R Publishing Corporation*[307] the defendant publication ran a story about a former child prodigy who had since tried to avoid all public attention His action for damages failed on the grounds that the information was not private. Similarly, in *Klein v McGraw-Hill* a former child inventor was not entitled to sue for the publication of his photograph many years later.[308]

[7.112] By contrast, the claimant in the Quebec case of *Ouellet v Pigeon*[309] obtained an order preventing the defendant from broadcasting a retrospective piece about a mother's suicide and murder of her four children 10 years earlier. The court felt that the claimant

---

305. *Briscoe v Reader's Digest Assocation* 483 P 2d 34 (1971).

306. *Gates v Discovery Communications Inc* 101 P 3d 552 (2004).

307. *Sidis v F-R Publishing Corporation* 113 F 2d 806 (1940).

308. *Klein v McGraw-Hill* 263 F Supp 919 (1966).

309. *Ouellet v Pigeon* (1997) RRA 1168.

had an enforceable expectation of privacy, especially in circumstances where he had successfully rebuilt his life after the tragedy.

Truth of the allegations

[7.113] One issue which has received very little detailed attention thus far is whether the right to privacy is capable of applying to prevent the disclosure of false information. It might be thought that there should be no cause of action in privacy in relation to false allegations on the basis that such incidents may be dealt with by way of an action in defamation.

[7.114] However, on balance, there are good arguments in favour of permitting privacy claims to be made in relation to false allegations in particular circumstances. It must be remembered that one of the justifications for protecting a right to privacy is that it allows individuals to exercise their autonomous right to develop and maintain relationships with others. An important element of this right is the ability of a person to make his or her own decisions in relation to the information they share, and who they share it with. The publication of false allegations can interfere with the person's autonomy in this area by requiring them to either ignore the allegation or to deny it. This means that they either have to allow the false impression created about them to persist (thereby undermining the social identity they have created) or to discuss an aspect of their life when they would otherwise have chosen not to do so (thereby undermining their autonomy in relation to their social interactions). By being forced to rebut allegations against his or her will, a person's privacy is arguably engaged.

[7.115] Furthermore, it should also be remembered that the publication of false allegations may interfere with an individual's autonomy or even cause them distress but might not found an action in defamation. For example, the publication of false stories about a celebrity's 'new relationship' or their dealings with a former relationship may be intrusive without being defamatory.[310]

[7.116] The courts in England appear to have taken the view that an action for misuse of private information is available in principle in relation to the disclosure of false information. Thus, in *McKennitt v Ash*[311] the Court of Appeal permitted the plaintiff's privacy claim to succeed in relation to allegations which were false. The High Court was also prepared to uphold the plaintiff's claim in privacy in *Applause Store Productions v Raphael*[312] without enquiring into the truth of the material published in that case.

[7.117] Somewhat similarly, the plaintiff's action in Ireland in *Maguire v Gill*[313] was allowed to proceed as an action in both defamation and privacy, despite the plaintiff's case being that the material in question was untrue.

---

310. For an example of a more detailed discussion of this phenomenon, see 'The Brangelina industry' (2009) *The Guardian*, 24 June.
311. *McKennitt v Ash* [2007] 3 WLR 194.
312. *Applause Store Productions v Raphael* [2008] EWHC 1781 (QB).
313. *Maguire v Gill* (13 September 2006, unreported), HC.

[7.118] However, the Court of Appeal in *McKennitt* did point out that the courts should not permit an applicant to bring a claim in privacy where the primary purpose of the action was to avoid the limitations placed on the remedies available for defamation:

> If it could be shown that a claim in breach of confidence was brought where the nub of the case was a complaint of the falsity of the allegations, and that that was done in order to avoid the rules of the tort of defamation, then objections could be raised in terms of abuse of process. That might be so at the interlocutory stage in an attempt to avoid the rule in *Bonnard v Perryman*: a matter, it will be recalled, that exercised this court in *Woodward v Hutchins*.[314]

This issue arose in the decision of Gray J in *WER v REW*[315] where the applicant sought to obtain an interlocutory injunction preventing the publication of allegations that he had had an extra-marital affair without indicating any position to the court as to the truth or falsity of the claim. Counsel for the applicant explained that his client was concerned that any statement in relation to the truth or falsity of the allegations would be used by the media organisations upon whom notice of the injunction would be served as the basis for further investigation into the matter with a view to discovering material not covered by the injunction. Gray J accepted that a privacy claim could be brought regardless of the truth or falsity of an allegation but expressed himself 'unhappy about the invidious position in which the judge is placed in having to decide whether to grant an injunction when he is, in effect, blindfolded as regards the facts of the case before him'.[316]

Publication on the internet

[7.119] While there have been relatively few decisions on this issue, it seems likely that the publication of material on the internet will be regarded by the courts in most circumstances as undermining a plaintiff's claim to have a reasonable expectation of privacy. This was the conclusion reached by Eady J in *Author of a Blog v Times Newspapers*[317] where he held that an anonymous blogger did not have a reasonable expectation of privacy in relation to his activity online. This decision has been criticised on the grounds that it lead to the closure of the blog in question and deprived the public of information and debate on a matter of public interest. However, the general logic that material posted online thereby loses much of its privacy seems likely to be followed in future cases.

[7.120] One possible caveat to this principle relates to the use made of material which was published online for a limited audience. This issue may most obviously arise in relation to websites such as Facebook which facilitate the publication of material to particular groups only. In many ways, the limited disclosure of material to a select group of individuals is the archetypal example of the sort of autonomous development of a social identity which features prominently in the academic literature discussed at the

---

314. See also *LNS v Persons Unknown* [2010] EWHC 119 (QB).
315. *WER v REW* [2009] EWHC 1029 (QB); [2009] EMLR 304.
316. *WER v REW* [2009] EWHC 1029 (QB); [2009] EMLR 304, para 14.
317. *Blog v Times Newspapers* [2009] EWHC 1358 (QB).

start of this chapter. There is a strong argument that material published to a small number of people does not lose its privacy by virtue of that limited publication.

[7.121] However, more difficult intermediate cases may arise where. The individuals in question may themselves publish the material more widely. As has occurred in the past with particular websites, the privacy policy may be changed so that material originally made available to a small group becomes publicly available by default. Furthermore, given the increasing tendency of media organisations to take material from individuals' personal sites where those individuals become caught up in major events, it might be argued by individuals that there is a difference in expectation between publication online and publication on the front page of a national newspaper. It might be thought, however, that the most likely approach to be adopted will be one under which the courts will be reluctant to uphold a privacy claim where material is made available to all the world by a person, either intentionally or in circumstances where global disclosure was reasonably foreseeable.

McGregor letter

[7.122] A further matter which may be taken into account by a court when assessing whether a person has a reasonable expectation of privacy is whether the person in question has previously issued a 'McGregor letter'. This is a letter which requests media organisations not to take photographs of an individual or named individuals. It is named after the actor Ewan McGregor who asked media organisations not to take photographs of his family. When a photograph of his family was published, he successfully sought an injunction restraining further publication and obtained an agreed award of damages.[318]

However, the plaintiff in *Hickey v Sunday Newspapers Ltd* failed in her action for breach of privacy in relation to the publication of photographs of her family despite contacting the defendant in advance of publication to assert that the material in question was private and requesting that it not be published.

This demonstrates that prior communication of a privacy claim is not, of itself, determinative of the issue but is simply a factor to be taken into account as part of the court's overall assessment of a case. It also reflects the fact that the right to privacy does not confer a right on an individual to exercise absolute control over the access of others to particular material.

DEFENCES

Consent

Express consent

[7.123] Clarke J confirmed in *Cogley v RTÉ*[319] that consent could operate as a valid defence to an action alleging a breach of privacy. The judge held that the privacy rights of residents of the nursing home in question would not be breached in circumstances

---

318. 'McGregor wins damages over Sun story' (2004) *The Guardian*, 6 July.
319. *Cogley v RTÉ* [2005] 4 IR 79.

where the defendants had undertaken to obtain the consent of the patients or of their relatives to the use of the material in question.

[7.124] Consent will only be available as a defence if it can be shown that the claimant actually consented to the conduct about which he is now complaining.[320] It will also only apply where the court is satisfied that the consent in question was voluntarily given. It can accordingly be vitiated by evidence of coercion, duress,[321] undue influence,[322] misrepresentation[323] or fraud.[324] This means that it would be advisable for broadcasters and other media organisations to obtain the clear written consent of any individuals who they intend to feature in a future publication or broadcast.[325]

[7.125] Furthermore, consent may only operate as a defence where the claimant consented to the actual conduct in question. Thus, in *A v B & C (No 1)*[326] McKay J granted an injunction to restrain the publication of pornographic photographs which had been taken of the claimant before she was famous. The claimant had given her consent to the taking of the photographs at the time but now objected to their publication. The court found that her original consent could not be extended to avoid liability for publication in a different context.

[7.126] A similar decision was reached by the Quebec courts in *Thériault v Rousseau*.[327] The plaintiff was a male model who was photographed as part of a fashion event. The photographs were subsequently disseminated by the photographer without his knowledge and ultimately in two gay magazines. The court upheld Theriault's action for breach of privacy.

[7.127] By contrast, the British Columbian courts rejected a claim in *Milton v Savinkoff*[328] concerning the dissemination of topless photographs of the plaintiff which she had mistakenly left in a coat pocket. Cooper J held she had consented to the photograph being taken and to it being seen by others, including the person who originally developed the photograph. This decision has, however, been criticised for its

320. *Bell v Alfred Franks & Bartlett Co Ltd* [1980] 1 WLR 340.
321. *G v An Bord Uchtála* [1980] IR 32; *DB (otherwise O'R) v O'R* [1991] 1 IR 289.
322. *Bank of Nova Scotia v Hogan* [1996] 3 IR 239.
323. *R v Flattery* (1887) 2 QBD 410; *MJ v CJ* (12 February 1991, unreported), HC, MacKenzie J.
324. *Moss v Moss* [1897] P 263. Also discussed in *Walsh v Family Planning Services* [1992] 1 IR 505.
325. It is important to note that, in terms of the plaintiff's establishment of a case, the absence of consent does not appear to constitute a prima facie infringement of privacy. The Canadian Supreme Court held in *Aubry v Les Editions Vice Versa Inc* (1998) 157 DLR 577 that the publication of a photograph of an individual without their consent was actionable as a breach of privacy. The English and New Zealand courts, however, have refused to recognise so broad a right to privacy, finding that the absence of consent, without more, is insufficient to establish a privacy breach. See *Murray v Express Newspapers* [2007] EMLR 22 and *Hosking v Runting* [2005] 1 NZLR 1.
326. *A v B & C (No 1)* (2 March 2001, unreported), HC, cited in *Theakston v MGN Ltd* [2002] EMLR 22.
327. *Thériault v Rousseau* (3 March 1993, unreported) cited in R Morisette, 211.
328. *Milton v Savinkoff* (1993) 18 CCLT (2d) 288.

restrictive conception of the plaintiff's privacy as an all-or-nothing concept.[329] The judgment also fails to distinguish between the distinct privacy interests engaged by the taking of a photograph and by its dissemination to others. It is arguable that the degree of intrusion differs between these two situations.

[7.128] This was also considered by the Court of Appeal in *Wainwright v Home Office*.[330] The Home Office argued that the signing of a consent form to visit the prison extended to cover consent to a strip search while there. Buxton LJ disagreed with the suggestion that, by signing the consent forms, they had effectively 'forfeited their right to complain about anything that was done as part of an activity that could be so described'.[331] He also held that a failure to complain did not constitute consent.

[7.129] Another issue referred to in passing by the Court of Appeal in *Wainwright* was whether consent given in circumstances in which there was an element of coercion or duress can constitute consent in law. Buxton LJ noted that the plaintiffs had been told that they had to consent to the search in order to be allowed access to the prison to visit their relative. He felt that this could have raised the 'question of the distinction between consent and submission, and of the concepts of "social" or "forced" consent'. This was a matter which, in his view, was 'a subject of considerable difficulty'.[332] However, he held that the court did not have to consider this question given its finding that there had been no consent. This underlines the fact that even the obtaining of written consent may not be sufficient to make out a defence to a privacy action where there may be scope for the plaintiff to argue that the consent was not freely and voluntarily given.

[7.130] The principles which have been applied by the courts in other contexts to require that a consent be an informed one may also have some application here.[333] In *East Sussex CC v Newsgroup Newspapers*, for example, the court referred to the fact that the children in question had submitted willingly to having their photographs taken for publication but had not appreciated that the publication of their story would lead to public ridicule and verbal abuse.[334] While it was not relevant in that case, it would seem in an appropriate case that this could be a relevant factor for a court to take into account in considering whether the consent given was valid in law.

Shared information

[7.131] The question of how consent can be applied to shared information arises where one party agrees to disclosure but the other party or parties object. This was examined by the Court of Appeal in *A v B plc*.[335] In that case, a footballer who had had adulterous

---

329. Osborne, 'Case Comment on Milton v Savinkoff' (1993) 18 CCLT 292.
330. *Wainwright v Home Office* [2002] 1 QB 1334. The House of Lords decision in this case is available at [2004] 2 AC 406.
331. *Wainwright v Home Office* [2002] 1 QB 1334, 1366–1367.
332. *Wainwright v Home Office* [2002] 1 QB 1334, 1366.
333. *Walsh v Family Planning Services* [1992] 1 IR 505.
334. *East Sussex CC v Newsgroup Newspapers* [2009] EWHC 935 (Fam).
335. *A v B plc* [2002] 2 All ER 545.

affairs with two women applied for an injunction to prevent the women from selling their stories to the tabloid press. Woolf LCJ felt that the consent of one party to the disclosure of shared information could be sufficient to justify publication. He referred in particular to the fact that the party seeking to disclose was entitled to invoke their own freedom of expression, and added that the balancing exercise between the two would depend on the circumstances of the relationship in question:

> In situations where the parties are not married (when they are, special considerations may arise) the fact that the confidence was a shared confidence which only one of the parties wishes to preserve does not extinguish the other party's right to have the confidence respected, but it does undermine that right. While recognising the special status of a lawful marriage under our law, the courts, for present purposes, have to recognise and give appropriate weight to the extensive range of relationships which now exist. Obviously, the more stable the relationship the greater will be the significance which is attached to it.[336]

This was applied in *CC v AB*[337] where Eady J found that a man who had been carrying on an affair with another man's wife was entitled to restrain the husband from disseminating this information via the media or internet. He struck this balance by concluding that the husband retained his right to freedom of expression but that limits could be placed on the way in which it was exercised. Similarly, in *McKennitt v Ash*,[338] it was held that the fact that an experience was a shared one did not remove one party's right of privacy in relation to it where it had been disclosed in the context of a close relationship.

This issue was also somewhat relevant to the proceedings in *Hickey v Sunday Newspapers Ltd*.[339] The plaintiffs' relationship had been the subject of extensive adverse comment by an interested third party, which comment had been given widespread publicity. The plaintiffs accepted that the third party had a right to express her views but contended that the expression in question had been 'to an excessive level and ... did not need to be repeated in the newspapers for everyone to read'. The Court referred to this publicity as 'a feature of this case which paces it in a somewhat different context from other cases on this topic'. However, the Court also indicated that the exercise by the third party of her freedom of expression would not necessarily have defeated the plaintiff's entitlement to assert a right to privacy if the plaintiff herself had maintained her silence on the topic. This suggests that the expression rights of third parties may be a relevant factor but that they will not, necessarily, defeat a privacy claim in all cases.

Implied consent

[7.132] It is also possible that a defendant may seek to establish that a person impliedly consented to the conduct impugned. This may apply where the defendant's actions in accessing or disclosing the information were reasonably foreseeable. Thus, for example,

---

336. *A v B plc* [2002] 2 All ER 545, 554.
337. *CC v AB* [2007] EMLR 11.
338. *McKennitt v Ash* [2006] EMLR 10; [2007] 3 WLR 194.
339. *Hickey v Sunday Newspapers Ltd* [2010] IEHC 349.

it might be presumed that persons appearing at a press conference consent to the taking and publication of photographs of them at that event.

[7.133] This may become more complicated, however, where a defendant seeks to establish implied consent on the basis of a previous course of action. This was considered by Ouseley J in *Theakston v MGN* where he held that the plaintiff's voluntary disclosure of aspects of his personal life in the past could be relevant to the question of implied consent. His prior conduct:

> ... reflect[ed] in part a consent by the Claimant to this sort of material being published ... I consider that the Claimant has pleaded aspects of his private life, whom he has intimate relations with and his general attitude towards sexual relations and personal relationships into the public domain, discussing them willingly so as to create and project an image calculated to enhance his appeal to those who do or would employ him, through enhancing his fame, popularity and reputation as a man physically and sexually attractive to many women. He has not objected either to those with whom he has had sexual relations discussing those relations both in general and in more explicit and in more intimate detail. These references have been both flattering and to some extent less so. He has courted publicity of that sort and not complained of it when, hitherto, it has been very largely favourable to him ... The Claimant cannot complain if the publicity given to his sexual activities is less favourable in this instance.[340]

Tugendhat and Christie have argued that Ouseley J's approach is misguided, and that prior conduct should go to the question of whether the plaintiff has a reasonable expectation of privacy rather than to the later issue of whether there is a defence to publication. In their view, it was 'unorthodox to regard [the circumstances in *Theakston*] as an application of the doctrine of consent'.[341]

Estoppel

[7.134] Estoppel might be available as a defence where a media organisation has relied to their detriment on a representation or promise made by the plaintiff from which the plaintiff subsequently seeks to resile.[342] The law on estoppel was summarised by Griffin J in *Doran v Thompson Ltd* as follows:

> Where one party has, by his words or conduct, made to the other a clear and unambiguous promise or assurance which was intended to affect the legal relations between them and to be acted on accordingly, and the other party has acted on it by altering his position to his detriment, it is well settled that the one who gave the promise or assurance cannot afterwards be allowed to revert to their previous legal relations as if no promise or assurance had been made by him, and

---

340. *Theakston v MGN Ltd* [2002] EMLR 22, para 68.
341. Tugendhat & Christie, *The Law of Privacy and the Media* (OUP, 2003) 336.
342. See, for example, the decisions in *Revenue Commissioners v Mooney* [1972] IR 372; *Cullen v Cullen* [1962] IR 268; *Re Wyvern Developments Ltd* [1974] 1 WLR 1097.

that he may be restrained in equity from acting inconsistently with such promise or assurance.[343]

This means that, for example, a party who consents to participate in a programme but then seeks to withdraw that consent after the defendant has made the programme could be argued to be estopped from withdrawing that consent. For an estoppel claim to succeed, it would seem necessary for there to be a clear and unambiguous representation made.[344] This should usually be made directly between the parties although it has been held that general representations to a particular group may suffice in particular cases.[345] There should also be knowledge on the part of the plaintiff that the defendant would rely on his actions[346] and evidence also that the defendant did actually rely[347] to his detriment[348] on the conduct of the plaintiff.

[7.135] This type of situation arose in *Dalton v RTÉ*.[349] In that case, the plaintiff had voluntarily participated in the making of a television programme about a family dispute over the inheritance of a farm. The claimant saw an preview of the programme and objected to its content. He threatened to take legal action if the programme as broadcast contained any defamatory material. The programme makers re-edited the film to take account of Mr Dalton's concerns. A year later, Mr Dalton sought an injunction to prevent the broadcast of the show on the day upon which it was due to be shown. Clarke J rejected his application in part because of the fact that the plaintiff had been on notice of RTÉ's intention to broadcast the programme and had let the matter lie for over a year. Although the judge did not refer to the issue of estoppel in his ruling, this is arguably the sort of situation in which it might be appropriate for estoppel to apply.

Waiver

[7.136] The English courts have held that Article 8 incorporates both a right to protect privacy and a right to waive it as part of the development of a circle of social acquaintances.[350] A party may waive their right expressly or by implication. One situation in which a waiver will be held to have occurred is where the individual embarks upon a course of conduct which necessarily involves an interference with his

---

343. *Doran v Thompson Ltd* [1978] IR 223, 230. This passage was recently re-approved by Laffoy J in *Courtney v McCarthy* [2006] IEHC 417.
344. *William Bennett Construction v Greene Ltd* [2004] IESC 15; *Murphy v Grealish* [2006] IEHC 22.
345. *Power & Ors v Minister for Social Welfare* [2006] IEHC 170.
346. *Re Wyvern Developments Ltd* [1974] 1 WLR 1097.
347. *Industrial Yarns v Greene* [1984] ILRM 15; *Wayling v Jones* (1993) 69 P & CR 170; *Daly v Minister for the Marine* [2001] 3 IR 513; *Dunleavy v Dun Laoghaire Rathdown CC* [2005] IEHC 381.
348. *McGuinness v McGuinness* [2002] IEHC 145; *Owens v Duggan* (2 April 2004, unreported), HC, Hardiman J.
349. *Dalton v RTÉ* (ex tempore) (23 October 2006, unreported), HC, Clarke J.
350. *Brown v Executors of the Estate of Her Majesty Queen Elizabeth the Queen Mother* [2007] EWHC 1607 (Fam); *Re Angela Roddy* [2004] EMLR 8.

right to privacy. In *McGrory v ESB*,[351] the Supreme Court held that a plaintiff who sues for alleged personal injuries waives any right to privacy in relation to his medical condition.

[7.137] This issue arises most frequently in circumstances in which it is alleged that the plaintiff has waived his entitlement to privacy as a result of the previous public disclosure of similar material. The pre-Human Rights Act case law in England suggests that a plaintiff may waive their right to privacy or confidentiality as a result of their previous attempts to secure beneficial media publicity. In *Woodward v Hutchins*,[352] the Court of Appeal held that the plaintiff pop group could not maintain an action for breach of confidence. Bridge LJ remarked that 'those who seek and welcome publicity of every kind bearing upon their private lives so long as it shows them in a favourable light are in no position to complain of an invasion of their privacy by publicity which shows them in an unfavourable light'.[353] The same logic was applied in *Lennon v News Group*[354] to deny the couple's application to restrain the publication of material about their relationship in circumstances where that subject had previously been publicly discussed by them.

[7.138] The English courts appear, however, to have resiled from this robust approach to the doctrine of waiver. The Court of Appeal in *Douglas v Hello! Ltd* doubted the decision in *Woodward* as one which 'preceded modern developments ... in relation to breach of confidence claims'.[355] Buxton LJ in *McKennitt v Ash* adopted a similar view, describing the case as one which 'dates back to an era when the Convention had not invaded the consciousness of English lawyers'.[356]

[7.139] As a result, '[t]he better view under English law now appears to be that the plaintiff's behaviour in seeking publicity will be relevant to the issue of waiver only where the previous publicity and impugned publication share the same subject-matter'.[357] In *Douglas v Hello! Ltd*,[358] the court had regard only to the couple's conduct in consenting to the publication of photographs when considering whether they had waived their rights to privacy or confidentiality in relation to that event. Similarly, in *Campbell v MGN*,[359] the plaintiff's entitlement to claim a right to privacy in relation to her drug habit was judged by reference to her previous discussion of drug use. The House of Lords was unanimous in finding that she could potentially retain privacy rights in respect of other aspects of her private life. That applied despite her more general

351. *McGrory v ESB* [2003] 3 IR 407. This was cited with approval in *JF v DPP* [2005] IESC 24.
352. *Woodward v Hutchins* [1977] 1 WLR 760.
353. *Woodward v Hutchins* [1977] 1 WLR 760, 765.
354. *Lennon v News Group* [1978] FSR 573.
355. *Douglas v Hello! Ltd* [2001] QB 967, 995. Doubts were also expressed by Lightman J in *Campbell v Frisbee* [2002] EMLR 10.
356. *McKennitt v Ash* [2007] 3 WLR 194, 207.
357. Delany & Carolan, *The Right to Privacy* (Thomson Round Hall, 2008), 222.
358. *Douglas v Hello! Ltd* [2001] QB 967.
359. *Campbell v MGN* [2004] 2 AC 457.

status as 'a famous fashion model who lives by publicity'.[360] As Lord Hoffman explained, '[a] person may attract or even seek publicity about some aspects of his or her life without creating any public interest in the publication of personal information about other matters'.[361]

[7.140] This suggests that the courts will focus on the subject-matter of any previous disclosure in considering whether an individual has waived their right to privacy. This approach is based on an acceptance that '[t]here is ... a significant difference between choosing to reveal aspects of private life with which one feels 'comfortable' and yielding up to public scrutiny every detail of personal life, feelings, thoughts and foibles of character'.[362]

[7.141] This question was considered at great length by Eady J in the High Court decision of *X & Y v The Person or Persons who have Offered and/or Provided to the Publishers of The Mail on Sunday, Mirror and Sun Newspapers Information about the Status of the Claimants' Marriage*.[363] The court distinguished between persons who sought publicity and others who appear in the press as a result of the public's interest in their behaviour. Waiver would only potentially apply to those in the first category who voluntarily courted publicity:

> It is necessary to distinguish in this context between the concept of being in the public eye and that of being a publicity seeker – although inevitably the two will sometimes overlap. In the present context, that distinction can be of some importance. It by no means follows that an individual who is photographed and described in print, and about whom information or speculation is published regarding his or her private life, must have so behaved as to forfeit or waive the entitlement to privacy with regard to (say) intimate personal relationships or the conduct of a private life generally. Close attention may need to be paid as to how such information came into the public domain and as to its limits. Some well-known people are prepared to go along with 'lifestyle' pieces which reveal, for example, their likes and dislikes, and how they spend their spare time, without wishing to cross boundaries into personal relationships. Others, on the other hand, will be less fastidious and take the view that any publicity is good publicity, being prepared to reveal any titbit to attract attention to themselves or to make money. There is no hard and fast rule, since the general proposition has to be recognised that even well-known people are entitled to some private life ... The court will in every case have to examine the specific evidence and make an evaluation (on which, inevitably, there may be room for differing opinions).[364]

[7.142] Eady J also cautioned against the court being influenced by the common practice of defendants to adduce evidence of prior media coverage of a person's affairs. It was necessary, in his view, to take account of the circumstances in which these reports

---

360. *Campbell v MGN* [2004] 2 AC 457, 470.
361. *Campbell v MGN* [2004] 2 AC 457, 474.
362. *McKennitt v Ash* [2006] EMLR 10, para 79.
363. *X & Y v The Person or Persons* [2006] EWHC 2783 (QB).
364. *X & Y v The Person or Persons* [2006] EWHC 2783 (QB), paras 27–28.

were obtained in order to determine whether there had been a genuine waiver of privacy on the part of the individual. Interaction with the press, or a failure to object to prior publications, would not necessarily constitute a waiver:

> People often give bland answers in response to inquiries as to how things are going in their lives, which do not constitute a 'waiver' of Convention rights. To take an obvious example, if a journalist asks how a celebrity is and she replies, 'Very well, thank you', that can be hardly said to open up her health to journalistic probing or exposure when she subsequently develops a serious illness ... Similarly, if someone asks, 'How's married life treating you?' and the response is 'Fine', that does not mean that the public is entitled to a ringside seat when stresses and strains emerge (as happens in most relationships from time to time). It is disingenuous to pretend otherwise. Ordinary polite 'chit chat' of this kind is qualitatively different from volunteering to release private information for public consumption. To give bland responses when things are going well is very different from having to be subjected to an intrusive investigation of the individual pathology of marital breakdown – still less of every tiff, disagreement or quarrel.[365]

> In Ireland, the constitutional basis of the right to privacy suggests that the doctrine of waiver of constitutional rights might apply. In *G v An Bord Uchtála*,[366] Walsh J held that constitutional rights could be waived only in the clearest of circumstances: [T]he consent, if given, must be such as to amount to a fully-informed, free and willing surrender or an abandonment of these rights. However, I am also of opinion that such a surrender or abandonment may be established by her conduct when it is such as to warrant the clear and unambiguous inference that such was her fully-informed, free and willing intention. In my view, a consent motivated by fear, stress or anxiety, or a consent or conduct which is dictated by poverty or other deprivations does not constitute a valid consent.[367]

This was applied by the court in *AG v Hamilton (No 2)* where it was held that there was a 'necessity for a very clear, unambiguous and unequivocal waiver' in order for a court to conclude that a constitutional privilege had been forfeited.[368]

[7.143] It has been doubted whether it would be appropriate to apply the case law on waiver of constitutional rights to an action for breach of privacy:

> It is questionable if a similarly high standard ought to apply to the waiver of all constitutional rights. In the adoption context, the court's concern to require a high threshold before finding a waiver is justifiable, given the serious and irrevocable nature of the order sought. Of course, it may be said that any infringement of privacy is also irrevocable in the sense that the information disclosed or space invaded can never be restored to its prior pristinely private state. However, unlike the necessarily absolute right to custody of a child, the right to privacy is a flexible and contextualised interest. The extent to which it is protected may vary from situation to situation and from person to person. The necessary connection between the individual's right to privacy and their participation in social life means

---

365. *X & Y v The Person or Persons* [2006] EWHC 2783 (QB), paras 35–37.
366. *G v An Bord Uchtála* [1980] IR 32.
367. *G v An Bord Uchtála* [1980] IR 32, 74.
368. *AG v Hamilton (No 2)* [1993] 3 IR 227, 262.

that an elevated waiver threshold could inappropriately inhibit valuable social intercourse. It is submitted, therefore, that the Supreme Court's willingness in *McGrory*[369] to find that the plaintiff had, through his actions, impliedly waived his right to privacy in respect of his medical affairs is a suitably less stringent approach. If, however, this is not the approach adopted in this area, the considerations outlined above are, as discussed, then likely to be relevant to the determination of the existence, or otherwise, of a reasonable expectation.[370]

The public interest

Introduction

[7.144] By far the most common form of defence invoked by media organisations in response to allegations that they have interfered with an individual's right to privacy is that the interference in question was in the public interest. The way in which this 'public interest' defence operates is crucial to the development of a suitable and effective privacy regime. '[T]he public interest should always be taken into account in defining the scope of the sphere of privacy and in making decisions within that sphere'[371] so as to 'ensure that an individual cannot use the privacy action to hide his or her wrongdoing'.[372]

[7.145] It is accepted by all that the right to privacy may be outweighed by countervailing considerations of the public interest. However, it has also been recognised that the public interest can, in this context, have a wide range of meanings. In particular, the courts have continually emphasised the distinction between the legal notion of the public interest and matters in which the public are interested. As Baroness Hale colourfully put it in *Jameel*:

> [T]he most vapid tittle-tattle about the activities of footballers' wives and girlfriends interests large sections of the public but no-one could claim any real public interest in our being told all about it.[373]

[7.146] Where a publication falls within a class of publications in which there is a public interest, this defence will be available. Where there is no public interest in its publication, the court will be more willing to consider allowing a competing legal or public interest to prevail. As Lord Hoffman explained in *Campbell*:

> Take the example I have just given of the ordinary citizen whose attendance at NA is publicised in his local newspaper. The violation of the citizen's autonomy, dignity and self-esteem is plain and obvious. Do the civil and political values which underlie press freedom make it necessary to deny the citizen the right to

---

369. *McGrory* v ESB [2003] 3 IR 407.
370. Delany & Carolan, *The Right to Privacy* (Thomson Round Hall, 2008), 225–226.
371. Feldman, 'Privacy-related rights: their social value' in Birks ed, *Privacy and Loyalty* (Clarendon, 1997), 16.
372. Moreham, 'Privacy in the Common Law: A Doctrinal and Theoretical Analysis' (2005) 121 LQR 628, 644.
373. *Jameel v Wall Street Europe* [2007] 1 AC 359, 408.

protect such personal information? Not at all. While there is no contrary public interest recognised and protected by the law, the press is free to publish anything it likes ... But when press freedom comes into conflict with another interest protected by the law, the question is whether there is a sufficient public interest in that particular publication to justify curtailment of the conflicting right. In the example I have given, there is no public interest whatever in publishing to the world the fact that the citizen has a drug dependency. The freedom to make such a statement weighs little in the balance against the privacy of personal information.[374]

[7.147] While the courts will allow media organisations some latitude, any assertions that a publication was in the public interest will be subject to scrutiny:

Editors know how to attract the attention and interest of their readers and the courts must defer to their judgement of how best to achieve that result. But it is non sequitur that it can be left to them to judge whether publication of the impugned details is of public interest.[375]

This underlines the importance for a defendant of being able to identify the specific public interest which the publication purports to serve. As Eady J observed in *Mosley*:

One of the more striking developments over the last few years of judicial analysis, both here and in Strasbourg, is the acknowledgment that the balancing process which has to be carried out by individual judges on the facts before them necessarily involves an evaluation of the use to which the relevant Defendant has put, or intends to put, his or her right to freedom of expression. That is inevitable when one is weighing up the relative worth of one person's rights against those of another. It has been accepted, for example, in the House of Lords that generally speaking 'political speech' would be accorded greater value than gossip or 'tittle tattle'.[376]

The section below considers some of the main varieties of public interest that have been held to apply to actions for breach of privacy.

Matters of governmental or public importance

[7.148] One of the most obvious examples of a situation in which the public interest may outweigh the individual's right to privacy is where the information in question relates to a matter of public importance. This has been interpreted to apply with particular force to political and governmental matters. Clarke J's description of the public interest in the RTÉ programme in *Cogley v RTÉ*[377] is one example of this approach. Similarly, Charleton J's identification of the public interest in *Leech v Independent Newspapers (Ireland) Ltd*[378] as 'matters which affect the public in terms of the governance of the country, their safety, their security, and the right to judge their public representatives

---

374. *Campbell v MGN* [2004] 2 AC 457, 474.
375. *Flood v Times Newspapers* [2010] EWCA Civ 804, para 118.
376. *Mosley v Newsgroup Newspapers* [2008] EWHC 1777 (QB), para 15.
377. *Cogley v RTÉ* [2005] 4 IR 79.
378. *Leech v Independent Newspapers (Ireland) Ltd* [2007] IEHC 223.

fairly on the basis of real information' rather than 'matters which are merely titillating or salacious or gossipy' emphasises the connection between politics and the public interest.

[7.149] That does not indicate that the concept of public interest is limited to political or governmental issues only. However, '[t]he further a publication moves away from issues of national governance, the less likely a defendant will be able to claim that its publication is in the public interest'.[379] This approach has been criticised as based on a middle-class mindset which is 'inflected by non-explicit judgments of taste or class'.[380] Robertson & Nicol have argued that:

> [J]udicial attitudes reflect the conditioning of a class or professional life ... Only a lawyer, for example, could so highly value the process of discovery as to accord its confidentiality a status that outweighed the revelation of reasons for the thalidomide tragedy...'[381]

[7.150] However, this emphasis on political or governmental matters does echo the instrumentalist conception of media freedom discussed elsewhere in this book. It also corresponds with the decisions of the courts in England, Canada[382] and Strasbourg which have underlined the relationship between the public interest in media expression and the education of the public on issues of national importance. In *Von Hannover v Germany*,[383] for example, the European Court of Human Rights held that coverage of the private life of a royal celebrity was not connected with the media's performance of its public interest functions. This was repeated in *Campany Y Diez de Revenga v Spain* where the court held that Article 10 did protect the publication of a report about an affair between two well-known figures who had no official or political role: [T]he Court considers that as [the publications] concentrated on the purely private aspects of the life of those concerned and even though those persons were known to the public, the reports in issue cannot be regarded as having contributed to a debate on a matter of general interest to society.[384]

[7.151] Similarly, in *Browne v Associated Newspapers*, Eady J held that stories about the personal affairs of public figures were not necessarily in the public interest:

> Discussions at private dinner parties about the plans or personal affairs of fellow guests, such as Peter Mandelson and Tony Blair, are ... entitled to protection. .... People are entitled to speak freely on such social occasions, within reason, without expecting to have the conversations regurgitated in the press. [T]here is no

---

379. Delany & Carolan, *The Right to Privacy* (Thomson Round Hall, 2008), 227.
380. Kenyon & Richardson, 'New Dimensions in privacy: Communications technologies, media practices and law' in Kenyon & Richardson, *New Dimensions in Privacy Law: International and Comparative Perspectives* (Cambridge University Press, 2006), 1, 9.
381. Robertson & Nicol, *Media Law* (4th edn, Sweet & Maxwell, 2002), 242, citing the example of *Distillers (Biochemicals) Ltd v Times Newspapers* [1975] QB 613.
382. In *Hill v Church of Scientology* [1995] 2 SCR 1130, the Supreme Court of Canada held that untrue stories about public figures were not protected by media freedom of expression because there was no public interest in the public being misinformed or misled.
383. *Von Hannover v Germany* (2005) 40 EHRR 1.
384. *Campany y Diez de Revenga v Spain* (Application No 54224/00) 12 December 2000.

counteravailing public interest in any of the dinner party 'chit chat' described. It certainly could not be characterised as 'contributing to a debate in a democratic society relating to politicians in the exercise of their functions' … It is more akin to what has recently been described in *Jameel v Wall Street Journal* … 'vapid tittle-tattle'. Thus it would fall outside the 'vital role of watchdog' which the European Court at Strasbourg so frequently attributes to the media.[385]

Illegality or wrongdoing

[7.152] There is a clear public interest in ensuring that the right to privacy is not used as a cover for 'hole-in-corner-activities' where individuals 'indulge in anti-social activities in an unaccountable way'.[386] The Irish courts have consistently held that privacy may legitimately be required to yield to the public interest in investigating alleged misconduct.[387] In *Haughey v Moriarty*[388] Hamilton CJ explained that:

> The exigencies of the common good require that matters considered by both Houses of the Oireachtas to be of urgent public importance be inquired into, particularly when such inquiries are necessary to preserve the purity and integrity of our public life without which a successful democracy is impossible.[389]

This principle also applies to the alleged illegality or wrongdoing of private individuals. In *Cogley v RTÉ*,[390] Clarke J recognised that there was a public interest in investigating and exposing the alleged misconduct of the individuals in charge of a nursing home. Similarly, in *Kane v Governor of Mountjoy Prison*,[391] the Supreme Court accepted that surveillance interfered with the individual's right to privacy but held that it was permissible when part of the Gardaí's discharge of their duties to detect and prevent unlawful conduct.

[7.153] The English courts have also held that it is not in the public interest to conceal wrongful conduct from public view.[392] Disclosure of illegal actions will be justified. The courts have further taken the view that there may be a public interest in exposing matters which are not unlawful but which may constitute misconduct. Thus it was legitimate to disclose the questionable conduct of a pop group on an aeroplane[393] or an alleged breach of sporting rules.[394]

---

385. *Browne v Associated Newspapers* [2007] EMLR 515, para 59.
386. Feldman, 'Privacy-related rights: their social value' in Birks ed, *Privacy and Loyalty* (Clarendon, 1997), 19.
387. See, for example, *Redmond v Flood* [1999] 3 IR 79; *Desmond v Moriarty* [2004] 1 IR 334.
388. *Haughey v Moriarty* [1999] 3 IR 1.
389. *Haughey v Moriarty* [1999] 3 IR 1, 59. See also *Redmond v Flood* [1999] 3 IR 79, 88.
390. *Cogley v RTÉ* [2005] 4 IR 79.
391. *Kane v Governor of Mountjoy Prison* [1988] IR 757.
392. See the discussion of this in the decision of the Court of Appeal in *McKennitt v Ash* [2007] 3 WLR 289.
393. *Woodward v Hutchins* [1977] 1 WLR 760.
394. *Francome v MGN* [1984] 1 WLR 892.

[7.154] There may, however, be a minimum threshold of seriousness for there to be a public interest in alleged misconduct. In *McKennitt v Ash*, Eady J held that there was no public interest in revealing misconduct which fell short of a serious standard:

> [F]or a Claimant's conduct to 'trigger the public interest defence' a very high degree of misbehaviour must be demonstrated. Relatively trivial matters, even though falling short of the highest standards people might set for themselves, will not suffice. All of us try to behave well, no doubt, for most of the time but hardly anyone succeeds in achieving that ideal. The mere fact that a 'celebrity' falls short from time to time, like everyone else, could not possibly justify exposure, in the supposed public interest, of every peccadillo or foible cropping up in day-to-day life.[395]

He repeated this view in *Mosley* where he held that there must be proportionality between the conduct in question and the invasion of privacy which is sought to be justified. This applied, in his view, even where the conduct in question was criminal, or potentially criminal in character. It would not, in his view, be sufficient to justify an egregious invasion of privacy to refer to the fact that the individual or individuals in question were engaged in a minor misdemeanour:

> The question has to be asked whether it will always be an automatic defence to intrusive journalism that a crime was being committed on private property, however technical or trivial. Would it justify installing a camera in someone's home, for example, in order to catch him or her smoking a spliff? Surely not. There must be some limits and, even in more serious cases, any such intrusion should be no more than is proportionate.[396]

[7.155] The English courts have also more recently questioned whether the public interest in exposing misconduct can be extended to justify the publication of material concerning allegedly immoral behaviour. That this approach may represent a significant interference with an individual's privacy and autonomy is well illustrated by the decision of the majority in *Norris v AG* where it was held that the State had an 'interest in the general moral wellbeing of the community and [was] entitled ... to discourage conduct which is morally wrong and harmful to a way of life and to values which the State wishes to protect'.[397] By contrast, it has been held in England that the fact that conduct represents a departure from conventional moral standards would not necessarily establish a public interest in revealing information about adulterous[398] or lesbian relationships.[399]

---

395. *McKennitt v Ash* [2006] EMLR 10, para 97.

396. *Mosley v Newsgroup Newspapers* [2008] EWHC 1777 (QB), para 111.

397. *Norris v Attorney General* [1984] IR 36, 64.

398. *CC v AB* [2007] EMLR 11.

399. *Stephens v Avery* [1988] 1 Ch 449.

[7.156] This was discussed in more detail by Eady J in Mosley where he appeared to strongly reject the suggestion that there was an automatic public interest in exposing immoral conduct:

> [I]t is not for the state or for the media to expose sexual conduct which does not involve any significant breach of the criminal law. That is so whether the motive for such intrusion is merely prurience or a moral crusade. It is not for journalists to undermine human rights, or for judges to refuse to enforce them, merely on grounds of taste or moral disapproval. Everyone is naturally entitled to espouse moral or religious beliefs to the effect that certain types of sexual behaviour are wrong or demeaning to those participating. That does not mean that they are entitled to hound those who practise them or to detract from their right to live life as they choose.
>
> It is important, in this new rights-based jurisprudence, to ensure that where breaches occur remedies are not refused because an individual journalist or judge finds the conduct distasteful or contrary to moral or religious teaching. Where the law is not breached, as I said earlier, the private conduct of adults is essentially no-one else's business. The fact that a particular relationship happens to be adulterous, or that someone's tastes are unconventional or 'perverted', does not give the media carte blanche.
>
> …
>
> It is not simply a matter of personal privacy versus the public interest. The modern perception is that there is a public interest in respecting personal privacy. It is thus a question of taking account of conflicting public interest considerations and evaluating them according to increasingly well recognised criteria.
>
> When the courts identify an infringement of a person's Article 8 rights, and in particular in the context of his freedom to conduct his sex life and personal relationships as he wishes, it is right to afford a remedy and to vindicate that right. The only permitted exception is where there is a countervailing public interest which in the particular circumstances is strong enough to outweigh it; that is to say, because one at least of the established 'limiting principles' comes into play. Was it necessary and proportionate for the intrusion to take place, for example, in order to expose illegal activity or to prevent the public from being significantly misled by public claims hitherto made by the individual concerned (as with Naomi Campbell's public denials of drug-taking)? Or was it necessary because the information … would make a contribution to 'a debate of general interest'?

Dangers to public safety

[7.157] The English courts have held that there is a public interest in identifying dangers to public health or safety. In *Beloff v Pressdram*, Ungoed-Thomas J stated that the public interest would justify disclosure of 'matters medically dangerous to the public'.[400] This was the basis for the decision in *Hubbard v Vosper*[401] to find it permissible for details about the practices of Scientologists to be disclosed. However, a balancing must still be

---

400. *Beloff v Pressdram* [1973] 1 All ER 241, 260.
401. *Hubbard v Vosper* [1972] 2 QB 84.

carried out such that there may be circumstances in which a risk to public safety would not outweigh a person's right to privacy. In *X v Y*,[402] the privacy rights of doctors who had contracted AIDS but continued to practise with the permission of the NHS justified the court's refusal to allow the disclosure of their identities.

Correcting false or misleading information

[7.158] This has been one of the public interest grounds which has been most frequently cited in the recent case law in England. In part, this seems to have been a consequence of the emphasis attached to it by the House of Lords in their seminal judgment in *Campbell v MGN*.[403] Lord Nicholls explained that 'where a public figure chooses to present a false image and make untrue pronouncements about his or her life, the press will normally be entitled to put the record straight'.

[7.159] However, it has also previously been endorsed in some of the earlier decisions in this area. In *Woodward v Hutchins*,[404] Denning MR expressed the view that:

> If a group of this kind seek publicity which is to their advantage, it seems to me that they cannot complain if a servant or employee of theirs afterwards discloses the truth about them. If the image which they fostered was not a true image, it is in the public interest that it should be corrected. In these cases of confidential information it is a question of balancing the public interest in maintaining the confidence against the public interest in knowing the truth.[405]

[7.160] More recent confirmation of the public interest in correcting false information was provided by the decision of Eady J in *McKennitt v Ash* where he observed that:

> I have little doubt that, more generally, where a Claimant has deliberately sought to mislead the public on a significant issue, that would be regarded as a sufficient reason for putting the record straight, even if it involved a breach of confidence or an infringement of privacy.[406]

Similarly, King J in *East Sussex CC v Newsgroup Newspapers*[407] recognised that there was a public interest in 'correcting the record' in relation to inaccurate reports that a 13-year-old boy was the father of a child.

[7.161] The court in *McKennitt* did, however, emphasise that are limits to this principle. The defendant had argued in McKennitt that the plaintiff's previous references in public interviews to her 'compass points' – a set of principles by which she claimed to try to live her life – meant that there was a public interest in showing that she herself had not always adhered to these standards, thereby correcting any false impression that had been created. Eady J dismissed this argument. He noted that the plaintiff had never claimed

402. *X v Y* [1988] 2 All ER 648.
403. *Campbell v MGN* [2004] 2 AC 459.
404. *Woodward v Hutchins* [1977] 1 WLR 760.
405. *Woodward v Hutchins* [1977] 1 WLR 760, 763.
406. *McKennitt v Ash* [2006] EMLR 10, para 96.
407. *East Sussex CC v Newsgroup Newspapers* [2009] EWHC 935 (Fam).

that she had at all times adhered to these aspirational standards with the result that there was no misleading impression to correct:

> She recommends them as goals to which she and others can aspire. It thus becomes clear that they represent a fragile peg on which to hang a public interest defence … [If [the defendant's] argument is correct, any person in the public eye who chose to share his or her aspirations with fans, followers, admirers or the general public, would immediately become vulnerable to having every trivial detail in their private lives exposed to public scrutiny. That simply cannot be right.[408]

This indicates that this principle may only apply to situations in which a person has deliberately or intentionally misled the public by taking positive steps to generate an image which is untrue, or where they ought to have been aware that information provided to the public would give rise to a false or misleading impression. This raises a question as to whether the public interest may be limited to correcting information which was false at the time at which it was published. It could be argued that material which is private should not retrospectively have that privacy removed by subsequent conduct which contradicts earlier statements made to the public. As against that, it might be responded that this is a consequence of having sought to create a particular public image in the first place. While there may be situations in which this argument may have merit, the statements of the courts in decisions like *Campbell* would tend to suggest that, in general, the public interest applies to the correction of an image which is currently misleading, rather than one which was misleading at the time of its creation only.

Role models

[7.162] A ground which was cited relatively frequently in the earlier English authorities was the public interest in exposing the failings of individuals who were role models for the public. This was significant as it potentially applied to individuals in the public eye who, in contrast to the cases considered in the previous section, have not themselves undertaken any positive actions to mislead the public.

[7.163] In *Theakston v MGN*, Ouseley J relied in part on this 'role model' principle in finding that there was a public interest in the disclosure of information concerning the visit of a BBC children's television presenter to a brothel. Ouseley J stated that:

> [T]here is a real element of public interest in the publication … of the proposed article … The BBC employs [the claimant] and projects him through his role on 'Top of the Pops' to younger viewers, and also to listeners on his programmes as a suitable person, for them to respect and to receive via the television into their homes. Whilst he may not be presented as a role model, nonetheless the very nature of his job as a TV presenter of programmes for the younger viewer means that he will be seen as somebody whose lifestyle, publicised as it is, is one which does not attract moral opprobrium and would at least be generally harmless if

---

408. *McKennitt v Ash* [2006] EMLR 10, para 100.

followed ... The activity in question here may make viewers or the parents of viewers react differently.[409]

This was approved by Woolf LCJ in *A v B plc*.[410] That case involved allegations of infidelity made against a professional footballer who was also captain of his club. At first instance, Jack J found that the claimant was a public figure only as a footballer and that there was little public interest in material relating to his activities outside that role. In particular, he noted that he had not courted publicity. On appeal, Woolf LCJ rejected Jack J's view that disclosure was not permissible. He accepted that the claimant had not courted publicity in relation to his private life but held that there was a public interest in the material because of his position as a role model for others. In Woolf LCJ's view, this was sufficient to generate a 'legitimate' public interest: The public figure may hold a position where higher standards of conduct can be rightly expected by the public. The public figure may be a role model whose conduct could well be emulated by others. He may set the fashion. The higher the profile of the individual concerned the more likely that this will be the position. Whether you have courted publicity or not you may be a legitimate subject of public attention.[411]

[7.164] A broadly analogous view was endorsed by the German Constitutional Court in *Von Hannover*:

> [C]elebrities embody certain moral values and lifestyles. Many people base their choice of lifestyle on their example. They become points of crystallisation for adoption or rejection and act as examples or counter-examples. This is what explains the public interest in the various ups and downs occurring in their lives.[412]

The approach adopted in *A v B plc* has, however, been doubted in more recent cases. In *Campbell v MGN*, Phillips MR questioned Woolf LCJ's decision:

> When Lord Woolf spoke of the public having 'an understandable and so a legitimate interest in being told' information, even including trivial facts, about a public figure, he was not speaking of private facts that a fair-minded person would consider it offensive to disclose ... For our part we would observe that the fact that an individual has achieved prominence on the public stage does not mean that his private life can be laid bare by the media. We do not see why it should necessarily be in the public interest that an individual who has been adopted as a role model, without seeking this distinction, should be demonstrated to have feet of clay.[413]

[7.165] In *McKennitt v Ash*, Buxton LJ also queried whether the decision in *A v B plc* could be reconciled with the decision of the European Court of Human Rights in *Von Hannover v Germany*[414] that there was no public interest in the private life of a public figure sufficient to outweigh the rights to privacy engaged in that case. Buxton LJ also

---

409. *Theakston v MGN Ltd* [2002] EMLR 22, para 69.
410. *A v B plc* [2002] 2 All ER 545.
411. *A v B plc* [2002] 2 All ER 545, 554–555.
412. Quoted in *Von Hannover v Germany* (2005) 40 EHRR 1, para 25.
413. *Campbell v MGN* [2003] QB 633.
414. *Von Hannover v Germany* (2005) 40 EHRR 1.

endorsed the position of Phillips MR in *Campbell* and drew a distinction between 'involuntary role models' and those whose 'life is an open book'.[415] In *Mosley*, Eady J also referred to the 'broad generalisation' that '[p]eople in positions of responsibility must be seen as 'role models' and set us all an example of how to live upstanding lives' as an example of the sort of attitude which was no longer applicable to the modern Article 8 caselaw.[416]

[7.166] A more nuanced approach might be to acknowledge that there may be a public interest in disclosing the misconduct of a individuals who occupy positions where high standards of conduct are expected. Buxton LJ expressed support for this sort of approach, arguing that such positions would include 'headmasters and clergymen, who according to taste may be joined by politicians, senior civil servants, surgeons and journalists'.[417] The decision in *Theakston* could be justified on this approach, although *A v B plc* would still seem to go too far in expecting high standards of conduct of professional footballers qua professional footballers. However, it might also be reasonably argued that this is simply an extension of the principle that there is a public interest in correcting false impressions.

[7.167] A version of this argument was endorsed by Dunne J in *Herrity v Associated Newspapers*. There, she was referred by counsel for the defendants to the decision in *A v B plc* where it was stated, inter alia, that 'the public figure may hold a position where higher standards of conduct can be rightly expected by the public' and that '[t]he public figure may be a role model whose conduct could well be emulated by others'. This was cited in support of the argument that there was a public interest in exposing alleged conduct by a Catholic priest which was contrary to the teachings of the Catholic Church. Dunne J accepted that 'there is such a public interest of the kind contended for by the defendant'. However, as the individual in question held a position in which it could reasonably be expected that certain standards of behaviour would be followed, it is not clear whether this should be regarded as supporting the broader position adopted by Woolf LCJ in *A v B plc* or the narrower view endorsed by Buxton LJ in *McKennitt*.

Profitability of the press

[7.168] A more general rationale which has been referred to on occasions is the public interest in allowing the media to make a profit, which allows them to discharge their important social and constitutional functions. Woolf LCJ stated in *A v B plc* that:

> The courts must not ignore the fact that if newspapers do not publish information that the public are interested in, there will be fewer newspapers published, which will not be in the public interest. The same is true in relation to other parts of the media.[418]

---

415. *McKennitt v Ash* [2007] 3 WLR 194, 216.
416. *Mosley v Newsgroup Newspapers* [2008] EWHC 1777 (QB), para 12.
417. *Mosley v Newsgroup Newspapers* [2008] EWHC 1777 (QB), para 12
418. [2002] 2 All ER 545, 555.

[7.169] Baroness Hale referred to this argument in *Campbell v MGN* when she observed that:

> [A] newspaper ... wants to keep its readers informed of the activities of celebrity figures, and to expose their weaknesses, lies, evasions and hypocrisies. This sort of story, especially if it has photographs attached, is just the sort of thing that fills, sells and enhances the reputation of the newspaper which gets it first. One reason why press freedom is so important is that we need newspapers to sell in order to ensure that we still have newspapers at all. It may be said that newspapers should be allowed considerable latitude in their intrusions into private grief so that they can maintain circulation and the rest of us can then continue to enjoy the variety of newspapers and other mass media which are available in this country.[419]

[7.170] In *McKennitt v Ash*,[420] however, Buxton LJ expressed doubts about the extent to which weight could be given to the commercial interest of newspapers in publishing private matters which were of interest to the public. He felt that Woolf LCJ's view was 'difficult to reconcile with the long-standing view that what interests the public is not necessarily in the public interest'.[421]

[7.171] This may be an increasingly relevant consideration as the traditional media finds itself under pressure from newer forms of online publication. There is a danger that holding the traditional media to certain standards of objectivity, fairness and restraint may ultimately weaken those values by making it more likely that the public will seek out more prurient or salacious material on the internet. However, Woolf LCJ's argument is capable of applying to all forms of media publication in which the public is interested. As the courts have repeatedly stated, the fact that the public is interested in something does not make it, in law, a matter of public interest. A broad application of Woolf LCJ's position would undermine that principle. It may be preferable, therefore, to treat this not as a public interest defence in its own right but rather as a factor in the court's consideration of the scope for editorial discretion. This is considered in more detail below.

Expressing minority views

[7.172] In *Cogley v RTÉ*, Clarke J commented that:

> It should also be taken into account in assessing the importance of the public interest issues involved that those whom it may be said would suffer should the contentions of the programme be borne out are an extremely vulnerable section of the community who have a limited (or in many cases no) voice of their own.[422]

This suggests that a court may have regard to the extent to which the disclosure in question advocates the views or rights of vulnerable or minority groups in determining the extent to which it can be said to constitute a 'public interest' publication. On one

---

419.   *Campbell v MGN* [2004] 2 AC 457, 498.
420.   *McKennitt v Ash* [2007] 3 WLR 194.
421.   Referring to *Jameel v Wall Street Journal* [2006] 2 AC 465.
422.   *Cogley v RTÉ* [2005] 4 IR 79, 94.

analysis, this could be argued to represent an inegalitarian treatment of the speech rights of different groups. However, the better view is probably that this may be justified by reference to the acknowledged constitutional commitment to fostering public debate on issues of importance. Where a group is habitually under-represented in terms of public or political profile, a plausible argument may be made that there is a public interest in bringing their issues or their opinions to the attention of the general populace. Certainly, as Clarke J seemed to suggest, it could constitute a contributory factor in the court's determination of the overall public interest value of a publication.

'Infotainment'

[7.173] It has been argued that a concentration on the 'public interest' of the specific subject-matter of a report is too narrow and that it should also be recognised that reports which are primarily concerned with entertainment may nonetheless have the effect of educating or informing the public about matters of legitimate concern. This would apply both to fictional material which addresses real world issues or, more pertinently in this context, material relating to the private lives of individuals which serves to educate and inform about the issues which they face. This argument was accepted by the German Constitutional Court in the *Von Hannover* litigation:

> Nor can mere entertainment be denied any role in the formation of opinions. That would amount to unilaterally presuming that entertainment merely satisfies a desire for amusement, relaxation, escapism or diversion. Entertainment can also convey images of reality and propose subjects for debate that spark a process of discussion and assimilation relating to philosophies of life, values and behaviour models. In that respect, it fulfils important social functions ... The same is true about people. Personalization is an important journalistic means of attracting attention. Very often it is this which first arouses interest in a problem and stimulates a desire for factual information. Similarly, interest in a particular event or situation is usually stimulated by personalised accounts.[423]

The German court's decision was overturned by the European Court of Human Rights. However, Phillipson has argued in favour of the German Court's 'subtle and sophisticated view of the legitimate role of the media in a democracy'.[424] It has been argued, however, that there are limits to this argument:

> Programmes or reports which are ostensibly classified as entertainment do sometimes prompt broader national debates about the issues featured in them. Similarly, the media often rely on personalised accounts of individuals' experiences to generate interest in or debate about more abstract social or political policies. It is difficult to see, however, how photographs of the claimant in Von Hannover cycling or shopping could really be regarded as capable of educating the public or of initiating a wider public debate. It may be that this argument will justify the publication of particular examples of so-called 'infotainment' but will

---

423. Quoted in *Von Hannover v Germany* (2005) 40 EHRR 1, para 25.
424. Phillipson, 'Privacy in England and Strasbourg Compared' in Kenyon & Richardson, 184 at 220.

not extend to confer protection upon all aspects of entertainment or celebrity programming.[425]

Degree of disclosure in the public interest

DISCLOSURE TO THE PUBLIC

[7.174] A number of older English authorities suggest that the public interest value of material may only justify disclosure to a limited class. In *AG v Guardian Newspapers (No 2)*, Lord Griffiths felt that evidence of misconduct on the part of the security services could justifiably be disclosed to the relevant authorities but that this would not necessarily apply to publication to all the world.[426] Similarly, in *Francome v MGN*,[427] the public interest in revealing alleged breaches of horse-racing rules was held to only justify the disclosure of material to the police or to the Jockey Club. In *Imutran v Uncaged Campaigns Ltd*,[428] this principle was applied to complex or technical matter which the public would not understand. It was held there that information about animal experiments ought to be disclosed only to the regulatory body responsible for supervising the system.

By contrast, the English courts had also held that disclosure to the public would be necessary in some cases. In *Lions Laboratories Ltd v Evans*,[429] it was found that there was a public interest in informing the public about the risk of unsafe convictions involved in the use of potentially faulty breathalysers. Disclosure to the Home Office would not have sufficed in that case given the public's perception that the government was committed to the use of the machine in all circumstances.

LIMITED OR PROPORTIONATE DISCLOSURE

[7.175] The issue of proportional disclosure has been raised with increasing frequency in recent cases. This is the argument that, as part of the balancing exercise carried out by the courts, it may be appropriate to find that the public interest justifies the disclosure of the material in a partial or particular form. Thus, in *London Regional Transport v Mayor of London*,[430] it was held that the public interest justified the disclosure of a report in breach of a duty of confidence but that this extended only to the disclosure of a redacted version of the report. Similarly, as discussed further above, the courts have distinguished between permitting disclosure of information and permitting the disclosure of photographs or footage on the grounds that that constitutes a greater invasion of privacy. As Eady J summarised this in *Mosley*:

> Sometimes there may be a good case for revealing the fact of wrongdoing to the general public; it will not necessarily follow that photographs of 'every gory

425. Delany & Carolan, 238.
426. *AG v Guardian Newspapers (No 2)* [1988] 3 All ER 545, 657.
427. *Francome v MGN* [1984] 1 WLR 892.
428. *Imutran v Uncaged Campaigns Ltd* [2001] 2 All ER 385.
429. *Lions Laboratories Ltd v Evans* [1985] QB 526.
430. *London Regional Transport v Mayor of London* [2003] EMLR 88.

detail' also need to be published to achieve the public interest objective. Nor will it automatically justify clandestine recording, whether visual or audio.[431]

[7.176] The courts in England have also distinguished between the public interest in revealing information about an issue and the public interest in identifying a person associated with that issue. In *East Sussex CC v Newsgroup Newspapers*, King J accepted that teenage pregnancy was a topic of public importance but went on to find that this did not necessarily justify the publication of any material concerning a particular teenage pregnancy:

> I do not believe there remains any real public interest on the issue of teenage pregnancy in relation to these children. It did indeed lead to public debate but, so far as these children are concerned, what more public interest is there in their sad story? I do not feel such a public interest argument adds significantly to *NGN Ltd's* case.[432]

[7.177] A similar distinction was drawn by the courts in Northern Ireland in *Callaghan v Independent News and Media*. There, Stevens J held that:

> There is ... a recognised legitimate public interest in relation to the debate as to whether it is right to publish detailed information about sex offenders when they are to be released into the community and if so the extent of that information. I will term that 'the wider debate'. On the other hand there is a narrower and particular debate in this case as to whether it is in the public interest to publish unpixelated photographs of a particular individual that is the first plaintiff. I will term that 'the narrower debate'. There are various observations that can be made about the public interest in the wider and narrower debates. It is not necessary to publish photographs of the first plaintiff to participate in the wider debate. A public interest in the wider debate does not establish a public interest in the publication of unpixelated photographs of the first plaintiff.[433]

This logic was not, however, applied by Irvine J in *Murray v Newsgroup Newsapers*.[434] In *Herrity v Associated Newspapers*, Dunne J appeared to address this issue when she accepted the possibility, in principle, that a distinction could be drawn in principle between the public interest in disclosing the allegation that a priest had been having an affair and the public interest in disclosing the identity of the person with whom the affair had allegedly occurred. Given the obvious nature of the interference with the plaintiff's privacy here, Dunne J was not required to consider this issue in detail. However, she did appear to indicate that the public interest claim of defendants in such cases might have to be parsed in more detail in a future case:

> [T]he public interest in this particular case, such as it may be, is asserted to be a public interest in the behaviour of Fr McMahon, who is of course, not the plaintiff herein. Much of the material that appeared in the course of these three articles

431. *Mosley v Newsgroup Newspapers* [2008] EWHC 1777 (QB), para 10.
432. *East Sussex CC v Newsgroup Newspapers* [2009] EWHC 935 (Fam), para 73.
433. *Callaghan v Independent News and Media* [2009] NIQB 1, para 25.
434. *Murray v Newsgroup Newspapers* [2010] IEHC 248.

concerned the plaintiff. Given the nature of the role of a Catholic priest in Irish society, Fr McMahon could well be said to be a person whose conduct may be subject to public scrutiny as outlined in the case of *A v B* referred to above. It is inevitable that if information is disclosed about a public figure such as a priest, that could expose others in the position of the plaintiff herein to unwelcome intrusion into their lives. In such circumstances I think that as a general proposition the right to freedom of expression would outweigh the right to privacy of the individual in the position of the plaintiff herein. However, in considering that aspect of the matter one would also have to have regard to the extent of the information in relation to the individual concerned and once again, one would have to have regard to the means by which the information was obtained and the type of disclosure that occurred. Accepting as I do that there is such a public interest of the kind contended for by the defendant, nonetheless, that public interest remains subject to the caveat that the limits on the right to freedom of expression cannot be ignored simply by recourse to the public interest.

Editorial discretion

[7.178] This raises a related question about the extent to which the courts will defer to the editorial discretion of editors and journalists when considering whether a public interest publication disclosed more material than was necessary on the facts of a case. This was a key issue in *Campbell v MGN*. The majority and minority disagreed about whether the publication of photographs of the model attending a Narcotics Anonymous meeting went beyond what was justified by the public interest. Lord Hoffman (dissenting) argued that the media ought not to be held to unduly strict standards when publishing material in which there was some public interest:

> Where the main substance of the story is conceded to have been justified, should the newspaper be held liable whenever the judge considers that it was not necessary to have published some of the personal information? Or should the newspaper be allowed some margin of choice in the way it chooses to present the story? In my opinion, it would be inconsistent with the approach which has been taken by the courts in a number of recent landmark cases for a newspaper to be held strictly liable for exceeding what a judge considers to have been necessary. The practical exigencies of journalism demand that some latitude must be given. Editorial decisions have to be made quickly and with less information than is available to a court which afterwards reviews the matter at leisure ... It is unreasonable to expect that in matters of judgment any more than accuracy of reporting, newspapers will always get it absolutely right. To require them to do so would tend to inhibit the publication of facts which should in the public interest be made known. That was the basis of the decision of this House in *Reynolds v Times Newspaper* [2001] 2 AC 127 and I think that it is equally applicable to the publication of private personal information in the cases in which the essential part of that information can legitimately be published.'[435]

---

435. *Campbell v MGN* [2004] 2 AC 457, 475.

[7.179] Lord Hoffman relied in particular on the judgment of the European Court of Human Rights in *Fressoz & Roire v France*[436] in which the chief executive of Peugeot claimed that the publication of photographs of his tax assessment infringed his right to privacy. It was accepted that the details of his salary was public information which it was permissible to publish. His claim was therefore, like Naomi Campbell's, one which related not to the information revealed but to the greater degree of disclosure involved in the impugned publication. In the ECtHR's view, Article 10 'leaves it for journalists to decide whether or not it is necessary to reproduce such documents to ensure credibility'.[437]

[7.180] Lord Nicholls agreed with Lord Hoffman's approach to the issue of editorial discretion. He felt that, in striking a balance between the claimant's right to privacy and the media's right to publish information in the public interest, the courts should not apply an overly rigorous test. However, he did also base his decision on his view that the publication of brief details of the claimant's treatment at the group therapy sessions did not go very far beyond what would have been permissible. He appeared to be of the view that it could, in principle, be permissible to find that a public interest publication went beyond what was necessary or proportionate where the balance was differently weighted:

> [P]ublication of this information in the unusual circumstances of this case represents, at most, an intrusion into Miss Campbell's private life to a comparatively minor degree. On the other hand, non-publication of this information would have robbed a legitimate and sympathetic newspaper story of attendant detail which added colour and conviction. This information was published in order to demonstrate Miss Campbell's commitment to tackling her drug problem. The balance ought not to be held at a point which would preclude, in this case, a degree of journalistic latitude in respect of information published for this purpose.[438]

The majority disagreed. Lord Hope, for example, held that:

> The choice of language used to convey information and ideas, and decisions as to whether or not to accompany the printed word by the use of photographs, are pre-eminently editorial matters with which the court will not interfere. The respondents are also entitled to claim that they should be accorded a reasonable margin of appreciation in taking decisions as to what details needed to be included in the article to give it credibility. This is an essential part of the journalistic exercise.[439]

[7.181] Where countervailing privacy rights were at issue, it was his view that the degree of disclosure ought to be considered as part of the court's assessment of the proportionality of a purported infringement. The Law Lords in *Campbell* seemed to disagree primarily on the applications of the proportionality doctrine to the facts of the

436. *Fressoz & Roire v France* (1999) 31 EHRR 28.
437. *Campbell v MGN* [2004] 2 AC 457, 476.
438. *Campbell v MGN* [2004] 2 AC 457, 468.
439. *Campbell v MGN* [2004] 2 AC 457, 489.

case. All seemed to accept that there was scope for editorial licence and all seemed to accept that this could go too far, such that disclosure in a particular form or to a particular degree could be impermissible.

[7.182] This was discussed in some detail by Eady J in his decision in *Mosley*. There he considered whether the courts' approach to Reynolds privilege, under which the actions and conduct of journalists and editors are examined as part of the court's overall assessment of whether the publication in question is protected as responsible journalism in the public interest, had any relevance to the law of privacy:

> I have decided that the only possible element of public interest here, in the different context of privacy, would be if the Nazi role-play and mockery of Holocaust victims were true. I have held that they were not. Does any weight need to 'be given to the professional judgment of [the] editor or journalist' to the contrary? Do I need to consider whether such judgments were 'made in a casual, cavalier, slipshod or careless manner'?
>
> In the defamation context, it seems clear that it is for the court alone to decide 'whether the story as a whole was a matter of public interest', but there is scope for editorial judgment as to what details should be included within the story and as to how it is expressed (see eg also Lord Hoffmann at 51). That distinction seems to be clear, although in individual cases the line may be difficult to draw. Here the situation is that the journalists' perception was, or may have been, that the story was about Nazi role-play. Even though I concluded that this was not the case, should some allowance be made for a different view on the matter? The answer is probably in the negative, because it is only the court's decision which counts on the central issue of public interest.
>
> It might seem reasonable to allow in this context for some difference of opinion. I cannot believe that a journalist's sincere view on public interest, however irrationally arrived at, should be a complete answer. A decision on public interest must be capable of being tested by objectively recognised criteria. But it could be argued as a matter of policy that allowance should be made for a decision reached which falls within a range of reasonably possible conclusions. Little was said in submissions on this aspect of the case.
>
> It would seem odd if the only determining factor was the decision reached by a judge after leisurely debate and careful legal submission – luxuries not available to a hard-pressed journalist as a story is breaking with deadlines to meet. Obviously, on the other hand, the courts could not possibly abdicate the responsibility for deciding issues of public interest and simply leave them to whatever decision the journalist happens to take. As Sir John Donaldson MR observed in *Francome v Mirror Group Newspapers Ltd* [1984] 2 All ER 408, [1984] 1 WLR 892, 898, 'The media ... are peculiarly vulnerable to the error of confusing the public interest with their own interest.'
>
> Against this background, it would seem that there may yet be scope for paying regard to the concept of 'responsible journalism', which has been referred to over recent years in the context of public interest privilege in libel. There is an obvious analogy. This rather vague term has been illuminated and defined in such a way that it could now be regarded as approaching a legal term of art. It has to be

assessed in the round, but there are certain guidelines which have been listed to assist in making a judgment: see eg Lord Nicholls' ten non-exhaustive 'factors' in *Reynolds v Times Newspapers Ltd* [2001] 2 AC 127, 205, [1999] 4 All ER 609, [1999] 3 WLR 1010.

There may be a case for saying, when 'public interest' has to be considered in the field of privacy, that a judge should enquire whether the relevant journalist's decision prior to publication was reached as a result of carrying out enquiries and checks consistent with 'responsible journalism'. In making a judgment about that, with the benefit of hindsight, a judge could no doubt have regard to considerations of that kind, as well as to the broad principles set out in the PCC Code as reflecting acceptable practice. Yet I must not disregard the remarks of Lord Phillips MR in *Campbell* [2003] QB at 61 to the effect that the same test of public interest should not be applied in the 'two very different torts'.

It is submitted that there is considerable merit in Eady J's analysis. He correctly identifies that there is a danger in a court acting with the benefit of hindsight to second-guess the decisions of media professionals taken under pressure. However, his observation that the bona fides of media professionals cannot be the only test against which the public interest in a publication can be judged also has some force. In striking a balance between the necessity to defer to the media's exercise of its freedom of expression and the person's right to have their privacy protected against undue interference, it does seem logical for a court to take into account whether the decisions and conduct in question went beyond what was reasonable or proportionate in the circumstances.

PHOTOGRAPHS

[7.183] The question of editorial discretion is particularly relevant where the plaintiff complains that the defendant's publication of photographs to illustrate or support a publication which was itself in the public interest went beyond what is necessary or proportionate in the circumstances of the case. The authorities indicate that such complaints may be well founded in some circumstances. In *Theakston v MGN*,[440] it was not permissible to publish photographs of the claimant engaged in sexual acts with prostitutes whereas publishing the fact of his visit to the brothel was justified as in the public interest. Similarly, in *Campbell v MGN*, the majority held that the publication of the photographs of the plaintiff attending a drug rehabilitation session went beyond the parameters of proportionate disclosure. Baroness Hale felt that the balancing exercise was different for photographs than for mere text:

A picture is 'worth a thousand words' because it adds to the impact of what the words convey; but it also adds to the information given in those words. If nothing else, it tells the reader what everyone looked like; in this case it also told the reader what the place looked like. In context, it also added to the potential harm, by making her think that she was being followed or betrayed, and deterring her from going back to the same place again.[441]

---

440. *Theakston v MGN Ltd* [2002] EMLR 22.
441. *Campbell v MGN* [2004] 2 AC 457, 501.

[7.184] Baroness Hale accordingly found that the publication of the photographs went beyond what was justified by the public interest in this case. In a classic proportionality-style analysis, she based her decision that the photographs went beyond what was permissible in part on the fact that the material could have been published without photographs, or with stock photographs which had been taken of the model in other less invasive circumstances. Lords Hope and Carswell agreed that this 'additional element in the publication' was sufficient to attract liability. The inclusion of surreptitiously taken photographs 'add[ed] greatly overall to the intrusion which the article as a whole made into her private life'.[442]

[7.185] Lord Hoffman, on the other hand, criticised the majority's judgment for failing to take adequate account of the importance of photographs for the modern media. He agreed that the article could have been published without any accompanying pictures. However, that, in his opinion, would:

> [I]gnore the realities of this kind of journalism ... We value the freedom of the press but the press is a commercial enterprise and can flourish only by selling newspapers. From a journalistic point of view, photographs are an essential part of the story. The picture carried the message, more strongly than anything in the text alone, that the Mirror's story was true. So the decision to publish the pictures was in my opinion within the margin of editorial judgment and something for which appropriate latitude should be allowed.[443]

An exception to this has been recognised by the Irish and English courts in circumstances where the photographs are included to verify the claims made in the impugned publication. Lord Hoffman based his conclusions in *Campbell* in part on his finding that the photographs were justified as adding credibility to the defendant's story.

[7.186] Clarke J in *Cogley v RTÉ* supports this approach. Although he accepted that the secretly filmed footage had a dramatic value which the broadcaster would have valued, he also felt that the material was also intended to verify the allegations made in course of the programme:

> [H]aving regard to the very serious accusations made in respect of the management of the nursing home concerned, it would be likely that a programme which contained those accusations but was not supported by the surreptitious film, would be challenged. In those circumstances, it seems to me that it would be appropriate ... to ... describe the inclusion of surreptitious film in the Leas Cross programme as 'an understandable pre-emptive course of action'.[444]

Establishing a public interest

[7.187] In his decision in *Cogley v RTÉ*, Clarke J emphasised that the courts will not accept a bald claim of public interest as justification for an impugned course of

---

442. *Campbell v MGN* [2004] 2 AC 457, 491.
443. *Campbell v MGN* [2004] 2 AC 457, 478.
444. *Cogley v RTÉ* [2005] 4 IR 79, 96, quoting *TV3 Network Services Ltd v Fahey* [1999] 2 NZLR 129.

action: [A]ny claim to an entitlement to broadcast or publish material which has, arguably, been unlawfully obtained on the basis of a legitimate public interest will necessarily result in the court exercising significant scrutiny over the public interest asserted.[445]

There does not appear to be any reason why the same principle will not apply to cases of disclosure as well as of intrusion. The courts, Clarke J felt, must be 'mindful of the fact that it is all too easy to dress up very many issues with an exaggerated or unreal public dimension'.[446]

Remedy would serve no useful purpose

[7.188] The courts have declined to act on several occasions where they have been of the view that the making of an order would serve no useful purpose. While this is not, strictly speaking, a defence, it is considered here because of the way in which this principle will apply to deny a plaintiff a remedy after he or she has established a prima facie breach of privacy.

[7.189] One of the earliest examples of this principle in operation was the decision of the House of Lords in *AG v Guardian Newspapers (No 2)*.[447] There Lord Goff, having held that the publication of the book in question was a breach of confidence, nonetheless declined to grant the injunction sought on the ground that the book was already widely available. He explained that:

> [I]n the present case ... to prevent the publication of the book in this country would, in the present circumstances, not be in the public interest. It seems to me to be an absurd state of affairs that copies of the book, all of course originating from Peter Wright – imported perhaps from the United States – should now be widely circulating in this country, and that at the same time other sales of the book should be restrained. To me, this simply does not make sense. I do not see why those who succeed in obtaining a copy of the book in the present circumstances should be able to read it, while others should not be able to do so simply by obtaining a copy from their local bookshop or library. In my opinion, artificially to restrict the readership of a widely accessible book in this way is unacceptable: if the information in the book is in the public domain and many people in this country are already able to read it, I do not see why anybody else in this country who wants to read it should be prevented from doing so.[448]

In *Hickey v Sunday Newspapers Ltd*,[449] the Court appeared to place considerable reliance on this factor in dismissing the plaintiff's claim. Kearns P observed that:

> [T]here is an inherent illogicality in asserting rights of privacy over material which is already in public circulation and which was, I would add in this case, notoriously so.

---

445. *Cogley v RTÉ* [2005] 4 IR 79, 98.
446. *Cogley v RTÉ* [2005] 4 IR 79.
447. *AG v Guardian Newspapers (No 2)* [1990] 1 AC 109.
448. *AG v Guardian Newspapers (No 2)* [1990] 1 AC 109, 289.
449. *Hickey v Sunday Newspapers Ltd* [2010] IEHC 349.

A similar approach has been adopted by the English courts in the privacy context. In *Mosley v News Group Newspapers Ltd* Eady J accepted that a person's entitlement to an injunction to restrain a threatened breach of privacy could be undermined by prior publicity about that matter. He held that 'a point may be reached where the information sought to be restricted, by an order of the Court, is so widely and generally accessible "in the public domain" that such an injunction would make no practical difference'.

[7.190] This was endorsed by King J in *East Sussex CC v Newsgroup Newspapers* where the court took particular account of the fact that material relating to the young teenagers in question was widely available on the internet. Although she was obviously dissatisfied with the prospect of further publicity about the children in question, this was a decisive factor in her decision to refuse to grant the orders sought:

> As Mr Millar has pointed out, if someone wishes to search on the Internet for the content of the edited footage, there are various ways to access it notwithstanding any order the Court may choose to make imposing limits on the content of the News of the World website. The Court should guard against slipping into playing the role of King Canute. Even though an order may be desirable for the protection of privacy, and may be made in accordance with the principles currently being applied by the courts, there may come a point where it would simply serve no useful purpose and would merely be characterised, in the traditional terminology, as a brutum fulmen*brutum fulmen*. It is inappropriate for the Court to make vain gestures.

> In the circumstances now prevailing, as disclosed in the evidence before me, I have come to the conclusion that the material is so widely accessible that an order in the terms sought would make very little practical difference. One may express this conclusion either by saying that Mr Mosley no longer has any reasonable expectation of privacy in respect of this now widely familiar material or that, even if he has, it has entered the public domain to the extent that there is, in practical terms, no longer anything which the law can protect. The dam has effectively burst. I have, with some reluctance, come to the conclusion that although this material is intrusive and demeaning, and despite the fact that there is no legitimate public interest in its further publication, the granting of an order against this Respondent at the present juncture would merely be a futile gesture. Anyone who wishes to access the footage can easily do so, and there is no point in barring the News of the World from showing what is already available.[450]

Furthermore, Tugendhadt J referred to the fact that information had been widely circulated amongst the professional football community in *LNS v Persons Unknown*[451] as part of his decision to refuse to grant an injunction. This suggests that disclosure of the information short of full public disclosure may be taken into account in some cases as part of an assessment of whether it is appropriate to grant relief.

One question which does arise in relation to this issue is how material came to be in the public in the first place. The argument might be made that a defendant should not be entitled to benefit from their own wrongdoing – or indeed from the unlawful acts of

---

450. *East Sussex CC v Newsgroup Newspapers* [2009] EWHC 935 (Fam), paras 34–36.
451. *LNS v Persons Unknown* [2010] EWHC 119 (QB).

third parties – to undermine an individual's right to privacy. This could have the effect of creating an incentive for an individual who wishes to interfere with another's privacy to ensure that the initial interference is as wide-ranging and intrusive as possible. However, it is equally unrealistic to expect the courts to take no account of the extent to which material has become public knowledge. These competing considerations may be dealt with differently in different cases. Thus, the fact that material is widely available may be more relevant to the courts' consideration of an application for injunctive relief to restrain publication than it would be to an action for damages for breach of privacy.

REMEDIES

Injunctions

[7.191] In many situations, the primary remedy sought in an action for breach of privacy will be an interim or interlocutory injunction. This reflects the fact that, unlike with defamation cases, damages will usually not be an adequate remedy for any disclosure of private information. While damages may have some utility in an action for invasion of privacy, the chief objective for a person faced with the potential disclosure of private information is to prevent any publication or dissemination of the material in question. Once the matter enters the public domain, the interest which the right to privacy is intended to protect is effectively destroyed. This was acknowledged by Woolf LCJ in *A v B plc* when he observed that 'if the injunction is not granted, the claimant may be deprived of the only remedy which is of any value'.[452] Eady J has agreed that 'it has to be accepted that an infringement of privacy cannot ever be effectively compensated by a monetary award. Judges cannot achieve what is, in the nature of things, impossible.'[453]

[7.192] The difficulty for a litigant in this context is that the courts have traditionally been very reluctant to consider granting an injunction to restrain the publication of material by the media. This is especially so for the archetypal privacy plaintiff in respect of whom no material has yet been published. It has always been accepted that the imposition of this type of prior restraint on publication is a particularly serious interference with the freedom of expression of the media.

[7.193] The classic statement of this principle can be found in the decision of the European Court of Human Rights in *Observer & Guardian v United Kingdom*:

> Article 10 of the Convention does not in terms prohibit the imposition of prior restraints on publication, as such ... On the other hand, the dangers inherent in prior restraints are such that they call for the most careful scrutiny by the Court. This is especially so as far as the press is concerned, for news is a perishable commodity and to delay its publication, even for a short period, may well deprive it of all its value and interest.[454]

---

452. *A v B plc* [2003] QB 195, 204.
453. *Mosley v Newsgroup Newspapers* [2008] EWHC 1777 (QB), para 231.
454. *Observer & Guardian v United Kingdom* (1992) 14 EHRR 153. See also *AG v BBC* [1981] AC 303.

This has been followed and applied by the courts in Ireland. It was recently endorsed in strong terms by the Supreme Court in *Mahon v Post Publications* where, having cited the decision in the *Observer* case, Fennelly J held that 'the court must scrutinise the present application for an injunction seeking prior restraint on publication with particular care.'

[7.194] In the context of actions for defamation, this approach finds expression in the so-called rule in *Bonnard v Perryman*. This is discussed in detail elsewhere in this book. However, in short, the rule holds that a plaintiff seeking to restrain publication of defamatory material in advance of trial bears a heavier burden than usually applies to persons seeking injunctive relief from the courts. Under normal *Campus Oil* principles, a person seeking an injunction must demonstrate the existence of a serious question to be tried, the inadequacy of damages, and that the balance of convenience lies in favour of the grant of the injunction.[455] In a defamation case, however, a plaintiff will usually be unable to obtain an injunction once there is any prospect of a defence being made out at trial. As the court summarised the situation in *Sinclair v Gogarty,* the principle is that an interlocutory injunction should only be granted in the clearest cases where any jury would say that the matter complained of was libellous, and where if the jury did not so find the court would set aside the verdict as unreasonable.[456]

[7.195] Furthermore, this strong resistance to the granting of prior restraint orders has been applied in non-defamation cases in Ireland. *Mahon v Post Publications* was a case concerning an attempt to restrain publication on the grounds of confidentiality. In *Foley v Sunday Newspapers*,[457] meanwhile, Kelly J again emphasised the importance of preserving media expression when dealing with application for an injunction on the grounds of an alleged threat to the applicant's life. The court observed that:

> In this country we have a free press. The right to freedom of expression is provided for in Article 40 of the Constitution and Article 10 of the European Convention on Human Rights. It is an important right and one which the courts must be extremely circumspect about curtailing particularly at the interlocutory stage of a proceeding.[458]

This meant that:

> [B]efore an injunction of this type should be granted the plaintiff would have to demonstrate by proper evidence a convincing case to bring about a curtailment of the freedom of expression of the press.

> This is particularly so having regard to the strongly expressed guarantees in the Constitution in favour of freedom of expression. The Irish (and indeed the English courts in the absence of a written constitution) have always shown a marked reluctance to exercise their injunction jurisdiction in a manner which would

---

455. *Campus Oil v Minister for Industry & Energy (No 2)* [1983] IR 88.
456. *Sinclair v Gogarty* [1937] IR 377, 383.
457. *Foley v Sunday Newspapers* [2005] 1 IR 88.
458. *Foley v Sunday Newspapers* [2005] 1 IR 88, 101.

entrench on the freedom of expression enjoyed by the press and the media generally. A good example of this is to be found in the judgment of O'Hanlon J in *MM v Drury & Ors* [1994] 2 IR 8.

This approach is also justified having regard to the provisions of Article 10 of the European Convention on Human Rights and the jurisprudence which has built up on foot of it.[459]

[7.196] However, for the reasons outlined above, it has been argued that different considerations apply in relation to an action for breach of privacy where the focus of the application is material which has not yet been disclosed and in respect of which publication is allegedly imminent. This was discussed in some detail by Clarke J in his decision in *Cogley v RTÉ*:[460]

> It should be noted that one of the underlying reasons for the reluctance of the courts in this jurisdiction to grant injunctions at an interlocutory stage in relation to defamation stems from the fact that if the traditional basis for the grant of an interlocutory injunction (ie that the plaintiff had established a fair issue to be tried) was sufficient for the grant of an injunction in defamation proceedings, public debate on very many issues would be largely stifled. In a great number of publications or broadcasts which deal with important public issues, persons or bodies will necessarily be criticised. There will frequently be some basis for some such persons or bodies to at least suggest that what is said of them is unfair to the point of being defamatory. If it were necessary only to establish the possibility of such an outcome in order that the publication or broadcast would be restrained, then a disproportionate effect on the conduct of public debate on issues of importance would occur. In that regard it is important to note that both the Constitution itself and the law generally recognises the need for a vigorous and informed public debate on issues of importance. Thus the Constitution confers absolute privilege on the debates of Dáil and Seanad Éireann. The form of parliamentary democracy enshrined in the Constitution requires that there be a vigorous and informed public debate on issues of importance. Any measures which would impose an excessive or unreasonable interference with the conditions necessary for such debate would require very substantial justification. Thus the reluctance of the courts in this jurisdiction (and also the European Court of Human Rights) to justify prior restraint save in unusual circumstances and after careful scrutiny. Similar considerations also apply to a situation where a party may contend that there has been a breach of his right to privacy but where there are competing and significant public interest values at stake. It is for that reason that I have distinguished between a right to privacy which subsists in the underlying information which it is sought to disclose on the one hand and information which might legitimately be the subject of public debate on an issue of public importance (albeit private to some extent) but where there may be a question as to the methods used to obtain that information on the other hand.

---

459. *Foley v Sunday Newspapers* [2005] 1 IR 88, 102. It should be noted that Kelly J here was making a statement of general principle and was expressly not considering the specific requirements laid down by the rule in *Bonnard v Perryman*.

460. *Cogley v RTÉ* [2005] 4 IR 79.

> I would wish to emphasise that the balancing exercise which I have found that the court must engage in is not one which would arise at all in circumstances where the underlying information sought to be disclosed was of a significantly private nature and where there was no, or no significant, legitimate public interest in its disclosure. In such a case (for example where the information intended to be disclosed concerned the private life of a public individual in circumstances where there was no significant public interest of a legitimate variety in the material involved), it would seem to me that the normal criteria for the grant of an interlocutory injunction should be applied. In such cases it is likely that the balance of convenience would favour the grant of an interlocutory injunction on the basis that the information, once published, cannot be unpublished. It is also likely, in such cases, that damages would not be an adequate means of vindicating the right to privacy of the individual.[461]

This is an important and, it is submitted, well-reasoned analysis of the situation.

[7.197] First of all, Clarke J seems correct to distinguish between an action for invasion of privacy and one concerning the disclosure of private information. It is only in the latter situation that the specific privacy-based concerns which may justify the adoption of a different approach to prior restraint could apply.

[7.198] Secondly, and more significantly, Clarke J's decision appears to indicate that, in his view, the principles that usually govern applications for a prior restraint order should not apply with the same force where the claim is concerned with a threatened disclosure of private information. That is not to say, of course, that the strong public interest in protecting freedom of expression against prior restraint should not be taken into account. However, Clarke J's approach suggests that, rather than weighting such applications so heavily in favour of a defendant, it may be necessary to carry out a balancing exercise between these competing interests.

[7.199] By contrast, Irvine J's more recent decision in *Murray v Newsgroup Newspapers* provides a strong restatement of the traditional approach to an application for a prior restraint orders. Relying in particular on Kelly J's decision in *Foley v Sunday Newspaper* and Fennelly J's judgment in *Mahon v Post Publications*, she held that:

> In cases where freedom of expression is sought to be restricted by an interlocutory order I am satisfied that the plaintiff is required, as Kelly J said in *Foley v Sunday Newspapers Ltd* [2005] 1 IR 88, 'to demonstrate, by proper evidence, a convincing case to bring about a curtailment of the freedom of expression of the press'. In my view this is the same as saying that the plaintiff must demonstrate at an interlocutory application that he is likely to establish at the trial of the action that the publication complained of should not be allowed. I agree with what Lord Nicholls said in *Cream Holdings Ltd. v Banerjee* [2005] 1 AC 253 that this requirement should operate in a flexible manner. However, in most cases, at a minimum the plaintiff should be required to adduce 'proper evidence' to support his claim that the publication complained of should be prohibited at the trial of the action. In order to demonstrate a 'convincing case', or that such prohibition is

---

461. *Cogley v RTÉ* [2005] 4 IR 79, 95–96.

'likely' to be ordered, the applicant must show that the interference with freedom of expression sought is justified by one of the recognised exceptions to that right and that the proposed restriction will be proportionate to the aim to be achieved. Furthermore, as Fennelly J said in *Mahon v Post Publications Ltd* [2007] 3 IR 338 the court must scrutinise an application for an injunction seeking prior restraint of a publication 'with particular care'.

Whilst I accept that the plaintiff has demonstrated a prima facie case that his right to life and his right privacy are engaged, and the protection of 'the rights of others' is one of the exceptions to freedom of expression, I am not satisfied that the plaintiff has adduced sufficient evidence at the interlocutory application to demonstrate that he is likely to succeed at the trial of the action in restricting the further publication of photographs identifying him and/or the publication of details of his address. Of course it is not for me to prejudge what evidence may be available and advanced by the plaintiff at the trial of the substantive proceedings and the court at that time will be in a position to consider with much greater precision the entirety of the evidence made available prior to finally resolving the conflicting interests of the parties. The plaintiff may well be able to procure the type of evidence that will convince the court that he should succeed in his action as happened in *Callaghan v Independent News and Media Limited*. However, at this time I have not been furnished with what can be described as proper or cogent evidence to demonstrate he is likely to prove that any potential infringement of his right to life or that any interference with his rights to privacy cannot be justified in the public interest.

[7.200] Although Irvine J accepts the possibility that an interlocutory injunction may be granted to protect a person's right to privacy, her decision is notable both for her description of the test which a person applying for such an injunction must meet and for her application of that test to the case before her. The judge examined the evidence adduced and assertions made by the applicant in some detail, pointing out, for example, that he had not provided any evidence in relation to his rehabilitation and that there was therefore 'little from the plaintiff in terms of cogent or proper evidence to suggest that he is unlikely to offend again'.

[7.201] However, it should also be borne in mind that there was an important difference between the situations being examined by Irvine J in Murray and that discussed by Clarke J in his obiter comments in Cogley. Clarke J was speaking primarily about a situation where an individual seeks to restrain the disclosure of material which is private. By contrast, Irvine J placed considerable emphasis on her view that 'much of the information which the applicant wishes to prohibit being further published is already in the public domain'.

[7.202] The Irish courts also appear to have taken the view that, given the concerns raised by prior restraint orders, they will only be contemplated in circumstances where the court is as fully apprised of the surrounding circumstances as possible. Given the emphasis in the European Court of Human Rights jurisprudence on the necessity for any balancing exercise between Article 8 and Article 10 to be conducted on the basis of a detailed focus on the facts, this seems sensible. Thus, in *Murray*, Irvine J subjected the arguments offered on behalf of the applicant to very detailed scrutiny, arguably above that which would usually apply at the interlocutory stage.

[7.203] Similarly, Clarke J expressed the view in *Cogley* that an application for a prior restraint order should normally be made on notice to the intended publisher. In his view, 'where it is at all possible, the court should attempt to afford the defendant at least some opportunity to put before the court its case prior to making any form of restraint order'. The circumstance-specific nature of the balancing exercise required in this case supports that view.[462]

[7.204] A similar approach was suggested by Eady J in England in *X v Persons Unknown* where he commented that:

> It is not for me to lay down practice directions, but what I can say is that a proper consideration for the Article 10 rights of media publishers, and indeed their rights under Article 6 as well, would require that where a litigant intends to serve a prohibitory injunction upon one or more of them, in reliance on the Spycatcher principle, those individual publishers should be given a realistic opportunity to be heard on the appropriateness or otherwise of granting the injunction, and upon the scope of its terms. As is well known, it is relatively easy for the media in such circumstances to instruct their lawyers to come to court at short notice and, if they are content to do so and no conflict arises, to arrange for common representation.[463]

Gray J held in *WER v REW*[464] that this obligation extended only to media organisations who were believed to have an interest in publishing the material in question. It was not necessary, in his view, to contact all media organisations.

English law

[7.205] The law in England on the granting of interlocutory injunctions is of limited persuasive value for an Irish court given the provisions of s 12 of the Human Rights Act 1998. This section was included to assuage fears that the incorporation of the Convention into English law could have an adverse effect on the freedom of expression enjoyed by citizens, including media organisations, at common law. The European Convention on Human Rights Act 2003 contains no equivalent provision. This means that Irish courts are faced with a different legal framework within which to consider such applications. It might also be argued that, given the similarities between the UK and Irish legislation on other issues, the failure of the Oireachtas to include this type of provision may have represented a deliberate omission. This would obviously further undermine the relevance of the English authorities.

---

462. *Cogley v RTÉ* [2005] 4 IR 79, 82.
463. *X v Persons Unknown* [2006] EWHC 2783 (QB), para 18.
464. *WER v REW* [2009] EWHC 1029 (QB), [2009] EMLR 304.

[7.206] Section 12 provides that:

> (1) This section applies if a court is considering whether to grant any relief which, if granted, might affect the exercise of the Convention right to freedom of expression.
>
> (2) If the person against whom the application for relief is made ('the respondent') is neither present nor represented, no such relief is to be granted unless the court is satisfied—
>
> > (a) that the applicant has taken all practicable steps to notify the respondent; or
> >
> > (b) that there are compelling reasons why the respondent should not be notified.
>
> (3) No such relief is to be granted so as to restrain publication before trial unless the court is satisfied that the applicant is likely to establish that publication should not be allowed.
>
> (4) The court must have particular regard to the importance of the Convention right to freedom of expression and, where the proceedings relate to material which the respondent claims, or which appears to the court, to be journalistic, literary or artistic material (or to conduct connected with such material), to—
>
> > (a) the extent to which—
> >
> > > (i) the material has, or is about to, become available to the public; or
> > >
> > > (ii) it is, or would be, in the public interest for the material to be published;
> >
> > (b) any relevant privacy code.

[7.207] Despite the clear terms of s 12(3), the English courts have held that this provision must be interpreted in light of the obligation to protect other Convention rights as well. The House of Lords accordingly held in *Cream Holdings v Banerjee*[465] that s 12(3) ought to be interpreted in a somewhat flexible manner. In particular, the Lords were of the view that the obligation placed on an applicant to demonstrate that it is likely that publication would not be allowed should not be interpreted to require the applicant in all cases to show that it was 'more likely than not' that he or she would succeed at trial. Lord Nichols explained that:

> There can be no single, rigid standard governing all applications for interim restraint orders. Rather, on its proper construction the effect of section 12(3) is that the court is not to make an interim restraint order unless satisfied the Applicant's prospects of success at the trial are sufficiently favourable to justify such an order being made in the particular circumstances of the case. As to what degree of likelihood makes the prospects of success 'sufficiently favourable', the general approach should be that courts will be exceedingly slow to make interim restraint orders where the Applicant has not satisfied the court he will probably ('more likely than not') succeed at the trial. In general, that should be the threshold an Applicant must cross before the court embarks on exercising its discretion, duly taking into account the relevant jurisprudence on Article 10 and

---

465. *Cream Holdings v Banerjee* [2004] UKHL 44, [2005] 1 AC 253, [2004] 4 All ER 617.

any countervailing Convention rights. But there will be cases where it is necessary for a court to depart from this general approach and a lesser degree of likelihood will suffice as a prerequisite. Circumstances where this may be so include those mentioned above: where the potential adverse consequences of disclosure are particularly grave, or where a short-lived injunction is needed to enable the court to hear and give proper consideration to an application for interim relief pending the trial or any relevant appeal.

[7.208] Lord Nicholls' statement makes it clear that there are no hard and fast rules on this issue and that a court will have to decide to grant or refuse an application on the basis of a close examination of the circumstances of the case before it. His speech appears to suggest that there is no automatic priority for a defendant's freedom of expression and that a balancing exercise between Article 8 and Article 10 rights may be appropriate in some cases. However, that balancing exercise will only arise where the applicant has met the appropriate threshold. In practice, what this has meant is that the courts have relied on Lord Nicholls' indication that they should be 'exceedingly slow' to make interim restraint orders to justify placing a relatively onerous evidential burden on an applicant to demonstrate the seriousness of their case. The result is that prior restraint orders appear to be more readily available in the privacy context than in other areas – but that an applicant will still face a daunting evidential task in persuading a court to grant one. The requirement to satisfy the initial threshold is the main challenge for a privacy applicant seeking a prior restraint order from an English court.[466]

[7.209] This has meant that it is incumbent on an applicant in England to exercise considerable care in presenting their case. This was evident, for example, in *Callaghan v Independent News and Media* where an extensive range of detailed and specific evidence was adduced in support of his application. It has also meant that the courts have been reluctant to grant orders where the applicant has not provided the defendant or prospective defendants with an opportunity to meet the case against them. Thus, in *LNS v Persons Unknown*, Tugenhadt J referred to the fact that the defendants were not before the court to hold that he could not attempt to strike a balance between their Article 10 entitlements and the Article 8 rights of the applicant. As they were not present to meet the applicant's criticisms of the case which they might wish to make, he could not subject their potential arguments to any degree of scrutiny:

> By not giving notice, the Applicant has deprived me of the opportunity to hear the case for the other side, including as to the social utility of whatever it is that the media might be threatening to say about the Applicant. In *Francome v Mirror Group Newspapers Ltd* [1984] 2 All ER 408, [1984] 1 WLR 892, at p 989 Sir John Donaldson MR (as he then was) said:
>
> > 'The 'media', to use a term which comprises not only the newspapers, but also television and radio, are an essential foundation of any democracy. In exposing crime, anti-social behaviour and hypocrisy and in campaigning

---

466. See, for example *John v Associated Newspapers* [2006] EWHC 1611 (QB); *CC v AB* [2006] EWHC 3083 (QB).

> for reform and propagating the view of minorities, they perform an
> invaluable function.'

This expresses part of the reason why I am not able to form a view on the material
before me as to the social utility of the speech that might be in question here, and
why that must be left to argument, if the application for an injunction to restrain
the threatened speech is opposed.

This meant that:

> I cannot decide that s 12(3) is satisfied ('likely to establish that publication should
> not be allowed'), having regard to the potential defence of public interest. It
> follows from that that no injunction should be granted.

This echoes the approach adopted by the Irish courts in *Cogley* and *Murray*.

Damages

[7.210] The other primary remedy that will arise in relation to an action for breach of
privacy is an award in damages. Damages are available under Irish law for breach of a
constitutional right[467] although there is some uncertainty as to whether an infringement
of a constitutional right is actionable *per se*.[468] However, as an action for breach of
privacy will usually involve a claim for mental anguish and distress, this issue seems
unlikely to arise in a significant way.

[7.211] It should also be noted that damages are available under s 3(2) of the European
Convention on Human Rights Act in relation to any injury, loss or damage as a result of
a the failure of an organ of the State to perform its functions in a manner compatible
with the Convention. A breach of Article 8 could therefore give rise to an action in
damages under s 3. This will only apply, however, where no other remedy in damages is
available.

[7.212] Damages have been awarded to successful plaintiffs in several cases in recent
years. It is notable that these damages have typically been lower than those awarded in
defamation cases (although that may change following the recent reforms introduced by
the Defamation Act 2009).

[7.213] Damages for more than mere compensation were awarded to the plaintiffs in
Kennedy v Ireland, although Hamilton P did not specify whether there were aggravated
or exemplary damages. In *Herrity v Associated Newspapers*,[469] the plaintiff was awarded
compensatory, aggravated and punitive damages. This suggests that there is no limit, in
principle, to the categories of damages available to a plaintiff alleging a breach of
privacy under Irish law.

---

467. *Meskell v CIÉ* [1978] IR 121.
468. See further McMahon & Binchy, *The Law of Torts* (3rd ed, Bloomsbury Professional, 2000),
   Ch 1; Delany and Carolan, 247–49.
469. *Herrity v Associated Newspapers* [2008] IEHC 249.

[7.214] By contrast, the view has been expressed in England that exemplary damages are not available in actions for privacy or breach of confidence. Eady J held in *Mosley* that compensatory damages and/or injunctive relief were sufficient to provide an adequate remedy for a plaintiff's Article 8 rights. While Lindsay J expressed the opinion in *Douglas v Hello! Ltd*[470] that exemplary damages could be available, that statement was obiter given the failure to award any in that case. However, Eady J held in *Mosley* that exemplary damages could not be awarded for a breach of privacy. He based this decision on two main factors. The first was that the action for misuse of private information in England had evolved from breach of confidence and that it was therefore uncertain whether it was a tort (in which case exemplary damages might be available) or an equitable action (in which case they would not). Secondly, he referred to the fact that the punitive nature of exemplary damages could have an adverse impact on the defendant's Article 10 rights. In particular, he felt that it would be inappropriate to apply a common law principle of punishment which was unknown in Strasbourg jurisprudence to an action which had been developed from Article 8 of the Convention. While the first limb of his reasoning would not seem applicable to Ireland, the second could be applied by an Irish court. In this regard, it should be noted that this is one of the grounds on which Mr Mosley has lodged a complaint with the European Court of Human Rights so that this issue may be considered by the court there in the near future.

Account for profits

[7.215] In the alternative, a plaintiff may seek an order requiring a plaintiff to account for profits made as a result of the breach of privacy. This was sought, for example, in the *Douglas v Hello* litigation.[471] As this is limited to situations of deliberate deception,[472] it will, however, rarely apply.

Delivery of material

[7.216] This was granted by the High Court of New Zealand in *Rogers v Television New Zealand*[473] and would seem an appropriate order to make in circumstances where there is an apprehension of a future breach.

Other forms of action

[7.217] As the decision in *Wainwright v Home Office*[474] confirmed, no action for breach of privacy existed at common law. However, an invasion of privacy could come under a number of different actions at common law. Because these actions were typically intended to secure separate non-privacy interests, they offered only piecemeal protection to an individual's right to privacy. Nonetheless, they did provide prospective litigants

---

470. *Douglas v Hello! Ltd* [2003] EWHC 786 (Ch).
471. *Douglas v Hello* [2005] EWCA Civ 295.
472. *Conran v Mean Fiddler Holdings* [1997] FSR 856.
473. *Rogers v Television New Zealand* [2005] NZHC 476.
474. *Wainwright v Home Office* [2004] 2 AC 406.

with a possible remedy in limited circumstances, and may continue to have some relevance to privacy actions today.

Breach of confidence

[7.218] This action has the most obvious relevance for a plaintiff who feels that their privacy may have been infringed. Although privacy and confidentiality are different interests, there may often be a substantial overlap between them. This is illustrated by the way in which the action for misuse of private information in England evolved from the common law action for breach of confidence. As the right to privacy had a constitutional basis in Ireland, it was not necessary for the Irish courts to rely on the action for breach of confidence in this way. Nonetheless, there may be certain situations – particularly for corporate plaintiffs – where it may be an appropriate ground of complaint.

[7.219] The traditional rules concerning the action for breach of confidence were laid down by Megarry J in *Coco v AN Clarke (Engineers) Ltd*.[475] He held that three elements were essential:

1. The information was of a confidential nature.
2. The information was communicated in circumstances importing an obligation of confidence.
3. There was an unauthorised use of the information with detriment.

[7.220] This was applied in Ireland in *House of Spring Gardens Ltd v Point Blank*.[476] Costello J held that:

> The court ... is being asked to enforce what is essentially a moral obligation. It must firstly decide whether there exists from the relationship between the parties obligation of confidence regarding the information which has been imparted and it must then decide whether the information which was communicated can properly be regarded as confidential information. In considering both (i) a relationship and (ii) the nature of the information, it is relevant to take into account the degree of skill, time and labour involved in compiling the information. As to (i) if the informant himself has expended skill, time and labour on compiling the information, then he can reasonably regard it as of value and he can reasonably consider that he is conferring on its recipient a benefit. If this benefit is conferred for a specific purpose then an obligation may be imposed to use it for that purpose and for no other purpose. As to the (ii) if the information has been compiled by the expenditure of skill, time and labour by the informant then, although he has obtained it from sources which are public, (in the sense that any member of the public with the same skills could obtain it had he acted like the compiler of the information) the information may still, because of its value, be regarded as 'confidential' information and subject to an obligation of confidence. Furthermore, the court will readily decide that the informant correctly regarded the information he was imparting as confidential information if, although based on material which is accessible to the public, it is of a unique nature which has

---

475. *Coco v AN Clarke (Engineers) Ltd* [1968] FSR 415, [1969] RPC 41.
476. *House of Spring Gardens Ltd v Point Blank* [1984] IR 611.

resulted from the skill and labour of the informant. Once it is established that an obligation in confidence exists and that the information is confidential, then the person to whom it is given has a duty to act in good faith, and this means he must use the information for the purpose for which it has been imparted, and he cannot use it to the detriment of the informant.

This means that information which is public knowledge cannot be the subject of an action for breach of confidence.[477]

Trespass to land

[7.221] Liability for trespass to land may arise where an individual intentionally or negligently[478] enters onto another's land without permission[479] or lawful justification.[480] Permission may be express or implied.[481] It appears that implied permission may however be vitiated by the defendant's conduct in concealing the true purpose of their entry onto, or remaining upon, the premises.[482] It may also be committed by remaining on a person's land without permission or lawful justification,[483] or by directly causing anything to come into contact with it.

[7.222] Like the constitutional guarantee of the inviolability of the dwelling, this action may protect the privacy of the person when they are on their own property. However, the action is premised on the protection of the person's property rather than their privacy. A remedy is usually only available to the person in exclusive possession of the land.[484] It also only applies where a person enters or touches the land. Thus, the taking of photographs with a long lens or from an aeroplane will not constitute a trespass.[485]

[7.223] Trespass to land is actionable *per se*. However, the proprietary basis of the trespass action also means that the quantum of damages will be determined by reference to the amount of damage which has been caused to the property rather than to the person. In the absence of any damage to the property, or any factors which might justify the award of exemplary or aggravated damages, a plaintiff is unlikely to obtain significant compensation. In the privacy context, the trespass action's greatest utility may be as the basis for an application for injunctive relief. This was sought by the plaintiffs in *Cogley v RTÉ*. Although Clarke J did not injunct the broadcast of the programme in question, he did order the defendants to refrain from engaging in any

---

477. See also *Governors and Guardians of the Hospital for the Relief of Poor Lying-In Women, Dublin v Information Commissioner* [2009] IEHC 315.
478. *RDS v Yates* (31 July 1999, unreported), HC, Shanley J.
479. *Representative Church Body v Crawford* (1939) 74 ILTR 49.
480. *DPP v Gaffney* [1987] IR 173; *DPP v Laide & Ryan* [2005] 1 IR 209; *Morris v Beardmore* [1981] AC 446.
481. *DPP v McCreesh* [1992] 2 IR 239; *DPP v Forbes* [1994] 2 IR 542; *DPP v Owens* [1999] 2 IR 16.
482. *Cogley v RTÉ* [2005] 4 IR 79. This decision only dealt with this question at the interlocutory stage however.
483. *Wood v Leadbitter* (1845) 13 M & W 838; *Irish Shell v John Costello Ltd* [1984] 511.
484. *Hegan v Carolan* [1916] 2 IR 27.
485. *Bernstein of Leigh v Skyviews Ltd* [1978] QB 479.

further trespass upon the plaintiff's property. The judge accepted that the defendant's conduct had been motivated by the investigation of issues of public importance. However, no issue of prior restraint arose under the trespass limb of the application. In his view, therefore, the balance of convenience at the interlocutory stage favoured the grant of an injunction.

Nuisance

[7.224] A nuisance action may arise where there has been an unlawful or unreasonable interference,[486] by act or omission,[487] with a person's use or enjoyment of their land,[488] or of some right connected with it. Nuisance is not actionable *per se*. Actual damage must be proved and may consist of damage to land, interference with a person's rights over the land, or a substantial[489] interference with the enjoyment of the land.

[7.225] McMahon & Binchy argue that in determining whether a substantial interference has occurred, the courts will have regard to the utility of the defendant's conduct and the gravity of the harm resulting or likely to result from it.[490] This first limb could potentially allow the courts to incorporate *Cogley*-style public interest considerations into their analysis. Given the proprietary basis of this action, it would seem necessary for a plaintiff to demonstrate that the harm suffered was more than mere subjective discomfort but actually pertained to their ability to enjoy their property. This would arguably be satisfied in a situation where a history of persistent surveillance or photography had the effect of discouraging a plaintiff from enjoying their private property.

[7.226] This sort of expansive interpretation of the nuisance action was evident in the Court of Appeal decision in *Khorasandijan v Bush*.[491] There, the court found that a campaign of telephone harassment by a disgruntled friend could constitute an actionable nuisance. This was, however, subsequently criticised by the House of Lords as an attempt 'to create by the back door a tort of harassment'.[492] Some sympathy for this approach may be discerned, however, from the obiter comments of Clarke J in *Dominican v Axa Insurance*[493] where he reserved for consideration the question of whether a nuisance would arise in respect of 'communication [which] was such as might interfere, to a material extent, with the reasonable enjoyment by a person of their home, place of business, or life'.[494] However, there may be scope to argue that this tort could

---

486. *Hanrahan v Merck, Sharp & Dohme* [1988] ILRM 629; *O'Kane v Campbell* [1985] IR 115; *Christie v Davey* [1893] 1 Ch 316.
487. *Connolly v South of Ireland Asphalt* [1977] IR 99.
488. *RDS v Yates* (31 July 1997, unreported), HC, Shanley J.
489. *Mullin v Hynes* (13 November 1972, unreported), SC.
490. McMahon & Binchy, *The Law of Torts* (3rd edn, Bloomsbury Professional, 2000), 690.
491. *Khorasandijan v Bush* [1993] 3 WLR 476.
492. *Hunter v Canary Wharf* [1997] AC 655.
493. *Dominican v Axa Insurance* [2007] IEHC 14.
494. *Dominican v Axa Insurance* [2007] 2 IR 682.

apply in relation to the actions of journalists or photographers in staking out a person's home.

Injurious falsehood

[7.227] This action will lie in respect of a false statement which is maliciously published and which is calculated to cause, and which causes or is likely to cause damage to the plaintiff. It appears that recklessness will suffice to meet the threshold of malicious publication.[495] Section 20(1) of the Defamation Act 1961 removed the traditional requirement to prove special damage in situations where the words are calculated to cause pecuniary damage in relation to an office, profession, calling, trade or business carried on by the plaintiff, or are published in permanent form.

[7.228] The action will rarely apply in a privacy context. However, it was successfully relied upon by the plaintiff in *Kaye v Robertson*.[496] The Court of Appeal found that the defendants in that case, who had entered the plaintiff's hospital room and interviewed and photographed him while he was in a confused and distressed state, were liable for the publication of an injurious falsehood – namely, that the actor had consented to give the interview and had accordingly lost his entitlement to secure an economic benefit from the sale of photographs and/or an interview about his accident.

Intentional infliction of emotional harm

[7.229] The so-called rule in *Wilkinson v Downton*[497] allows a plaintiff to recover damages in respect of emotional suffering which was caused by the intentional or reckless actions of a defendant. The act impugned must be calculated to cause harm in the sense that the harm must be an objectively likely result of the defendant's conduct.

[7.230] This tort has also traditionally required a plaintiff to show that a degree of physical injury was also caused by the acts in question. Mere distress will not suffice. This was questioned somewhat by Lord Hoffman in *Wainwright v Home Office*[498] when he accepted the possibility that the tort could develop to allow recovery in respect of mental anguish alone. However, he felt that this could only be considered if the law continued to require a very high level of knowledge or recklessness on the part of the defendant.

[7.231] These comments must be considered in light of the general opinion of the House of Lords in *Wainwright* that this action had little or no relevance to the modern law of tort. The Lords indicated that the decision in *Wilkinson v Downton* had been influenced by the refusal of the law to allow recovery for mental damage or 'nervous shock' at that

---

495. *Malone v McQuaid* (28 May 1998, unreported), HC.
496. *Kaye v Robertson* [1991] FSR 62.
497. *Wilkinson v Downton* [1897] 2 QB 57.
498. *Wainwright v Home Office* [2004] 2 AC 406.

time. They accordingly suggested that there was no real need for the action in contemporary times.

[7.232] At the same time, the action has obvious attractions for a prospective privacy plaintiff. Its focus on emotional or mental harm accurately reflects the sort of injury which may be suffered by a person who feels that their privacy has been infringed. The high thresholds of proof required would limit the general utility of this tort but it would also allow the possibility of a remedy in the most egregious cases of privacy infringement, where the defendant shows no regard for the rights of the plaintiff. It could, for example, apply to circumstances in which a person is persistently followed or harassed by members of the paparazzi, or where very sensitive personal information is widely disseminated in a reckless manner. The flexibility of the action has encouraged some authors in other jurisdictions to suggest that it offers the best possibility for the future development of a form of privacy tort. These views are supported by the decision of the New Zealand courts in *Tucker v News Media Ownership Ltd*.[499] There, McGeechan J held at the interlocutory stage that this tort could potentially develop in such a way that it would apply to cases of alleged privacy intrusions. That was particularly so in a case such as *Tucker* where there was evidence that disclosure of the information in question could have a severe, and possibly fatal, impact upon the plaintiff's medical condition.

Passing off

[7.233] This tort may provide a remedy in a very small number of instances of alleged privacy invasion. Its utility is limited, however, by the fact that it is concerned with the protection of commercial interests. It will not, therefore, have any relevance to the vast majority of prospective privacy complaints.

[7.234] Liability will arise for passing off where one commercial actor represents its goods or services as those of another commercial entity, where that representation is likely to mislead the public and to risk causing damage to the plaintiff's business. The ingredients of liability are as follows:

> The first [is] that the Plaintiff must establish a good will or reputation attached to the goods or services which he supplies in the mind of the purchasing public by association with the identifying get-up, such that they are recognised as distinctive specifically to the Plaintiff. Secondly, the Plaintiff must demonstrate a misrepresentation by the Defendant to the public, whether or not intentionally leading or likely to lead the public to believe that the goods or services offered by him are the goods or services of the Plaintiff. Thirdly, the Plaintiff must demonstrate that he suffers, or is likely to suffer, damages by reason of that erroneous belief engendered by the Defendants' belief of misrepresentation.[500]

499. *Tucker v News Media Ownership Ltd* [1986] 2 NZLR 716.
500. *Contech Building Products Ltd v Walsh* [2006] IEHC 45, citing the speech of Lord Oliver in *Reckitt & Coleman Products Limited v Borden Inc* [1990] 1 WLR 491.

[7.235] There is no necessity to prove an intention to deceive on the part of the defendant.[501] Isolated instances of confusion will not establish liability. This is determined on the basis of a test as to whether the representation would deceive the casual and unwary customer.[502]

[7.236] The tort requires that the plaintiff have goodwill or a commercial reputation and that the misrepresentations of the defendant threaten that goodwill or reputation. The tort accordingly protects the plaintiff's 'right to property in his business'[503] rather than any personal entitlement not to have his name, reputation or image appropriated by another for his own use. For this reason, it will rarely be available to the average plaintiff who does not possess a commercial reputation that is put at risk of damage by the defendant.

Negligence

[7.237] Negligence is a sufficiently broad action to provide a remedy for a breach of privacy where the conduct in question can be shown to have breached a duty of care which was owed to the plaintiff by the defendant. The most difficult aspect of this test for a privacy claimant will be to establish the existence of a duty of care. This was successfully done in respect of state agencies in the cases of *Hanahoe v Hussey*[504] and *Gray v Minister for Justice, Equality and Law Reform*.[505] In both cases, the courts found that the Gardaí had been negligent in disclosing information about the plaintiffs or their business to the press. Quirke J found in the latter case that:

> The negligent disclosure of sensitive and confidential information by Garda to journalists or other members of the media will give rise to a cause of action for damages for negligence if the disclosure results in reasonably foreseeable loss, damage or injury to a person affected by the disclosure.

However, he based his finding that there was a duty of care on the fact that the Gardaí, as agents of the State, owed duties to the public in the exercise of their duties. He held that:

> The proximate relationship between the State and those of its citizens who may be affected by the State's procurement of sensitive and confidential information is undeniable. That relationship can give rise to a duty of care owed by the State to persons who may be adversely affected by the disclosure or publication of such information.

This leaves open the question, therefore, of whether a duty of care might be found to exist in circumstances where information is disclosed to the media by a non-State actor. Where damage may reasonably foreseeably result from a disclosure, however, there does

---

501. *Grange Marketing v M & Q Plastic Products* (17 June 1976, unreported), HC, McWilliam J.
502. *Singer Manufacturing Co v Loog* (1882) 8 AC 15.
503. *Polycell Products v O'Carroll* [1959] Ir Jur Rep 34, 36.
504. *Hanahoe v Hussey* [1998] 3 IR 69.
505. *Gray v Minister for Justice, Equality and Law Reform* [2007] IEHC 52.

not seem to be any strong jurisprudential reason why a duty of care could not be found to exist in the circumstances of a particular case.

Data protection

[7.238] The Data Protection Acts 1988 and 2003 may also, in certain circumstances, provide a remedy to an individual who feels that the conduct of the media has interfered with their privacy. The Act provides protection for individuals in relation to the way in which their personal data is handled by others.[506]

[7.239] Restrictions are imposed in relation to the access, usage or disclosure of personal data or sensitive personal data. Personal data is defined as data relating to a living individual who is or can be identified either from the data or from the data in conjunction with other information that is in, or is likely to come into, the possession of the data controller, while sensitive personal data is data which relates to the individual's racial or ethnic origin, political opinions, or religious or philosophical beliefs; membership of a trade union; physical or mental health; sexual life; commission or alleged commission of an offence, or; proceedings for an offence committed or alleged to have been committed.[507]

[7.240] It is clear that the majority of the material that is published or broadcast by the media could be regarded as personal data or, in appropriate situations, as sensitive personal data. This is reinforced by the fact that the definitions contained in the Act do not limit data to written information but would also appear to include, where appropriate, photographs or audio-visual images.[508]

[7.241] The Act thus provides an exemption for journalistic activities. Section 22A[509] provides that:

> Personal data that are processed only for journalistic, artistic or literary purposes shall be exempt from compliance with any provision of this Act specified in subsection (2) of the section if–
>
> (a) the processing is undertaken solely with a view to the publication of any journalistic, literary or artistic material,
>
> (b) the data controller reasonably believes that, having regard in particular to the special importance of the public interest in freedom of expression, such publication would be in the public interest, and
>
> (c) the data controller reasonably believes that, in all the circumstances, compliance with that provision would be incompatible with journalistic, artistic or literary purposes.

---

506. Data protection is, itself, a legal area of considerable complexity. For any detailed questions on this topic, readers are advised to consult a specialist text on data protection such as, for example, Kelleher, *Privacy and Data Protection Law in Ireland* (Bloomsbury Professional, 2006).
507. Data Protection Act 1988, s 1, as amended by the Data Protection (Amendment) Act 2003, s 2.
508. See, for example, Case Study 3 of 2007; Case Study 10 of 2008.
509. As inserted by Data Protection (Amendment) Act 2003, s 21.

The provisions from which journalistic activities are exempt include those relating to the collection, processing, keeping, use and disclosure of personal data;[510] those which confer a right on data subjects to establish the existence of personal data;[511] those relating to the rights of data subjects to access, rectification or erasure;[512] and those which confer a right on data subjects to object to processing which is likely to cause damage or distress.[513]

[7.242] In applying this exemption, however, the Data Protection Commissioner has demonstrated a willingness to consider the public interest of an impugned publication. He does so by reference to any approved code of practice.[514] In 2006, for example, the Commissioner upheld a complaint against the News of the World.[515] The complaint concerned the publication of a photograph of a well-known individual shopping with their child, together with related text expressly identifying the child by name and age, and referring to a third party's perception as to how parent and child were getting along. The photograph was taken without consent. The Commissioner referred to the decision of the European Court of Human Rights in *Von Hannover v Germany*[516] and to the provisions of the relevant newspaper Code of Practice on stories about minors in concluding that the publication in question was not justified by the public interest. As the Commissioner explained his decision:

> This case demonstrates that data protection applies even in relation to the publication of material in the media. However, in such cases, the issue to be considered in the first instance is whether a general public interest could be deemed to apply to the publication of the material. If it does then the general requirements of data protection are set aside. However, if no public interest could legitimately be claimed, then the media must have due regard to their data protection obligations.

In the absence of the journalistic exemption, media organisations may be obliged, *inter alia*, to get and use any information fairly;[517] to make use of the data in a way which is adequate, relevant and not excessive in relation to the purpose or purposes for which they were collected or processed;[518] to use and make known this information only in ways that are in keeping with these purposes; and to make sure that the information is factually correct, complete and up to date.[519] A requirement to adhere to these obligations would obviously have a significant impact on the steps which a media organisation would be entitled to take in obtaining material or in making use of that material for publication.

---

510. Data Protection Act 1988, ss 2, 2A, 2B and 2D.
511. Data Protection Act 1988, s 3.
512. Data Protection Act 1988, ss 4 and 6.
513. Data Protection Act 1988, s 6B.
514. Data Protection Act 1988, s 22A(3).
515. See Case Study 6 of 2006.
516. *Von Hannover v Germany* (2005) 40 EHRR 1.
517. Data Protection Act 1988, s 2(1)(a).
518. Data Protection Act 1988, s 2(1)(c).
519. Data Protection Act 1988, s 2(1)(b).

[7.243] For that reason, the Data Protection Commissioner's willingness to examine the merits of a media organisation's assertion that a particular publication is in the public interest is significant in that it suggests that media organisation may be required to exercise greater care or caution in relation to material in relation to which there is little or no obvious public interest. This obviously also raises the question of whether the approach adopted by the Data Protection Commissioner may have to be refined in light of the dicta of Fennelly J in *Mahon v Post Publications*.[520]

---

520.   *Mahon v Post Publications* [2007] 3 IR 338.

Chapter 8

BROADCASTING REGULATION IN IRELAND

[8.01] It is axiomatic that broadcast media organisations occupy an important and influential position in modern society. Although the emergence of new distribution methods and multiple providers, together with the rise of widely available user-generated content, has adversely affected the audience penetration and impact of traditional broadcasters, they nonetheless remain a powerful social force. As **Ch 2** has discussed, the Constitution and European Convention on Human Rights envisage a particular role for media organisations as the 'bloodhounds' and 'watchdogs' of a democratic society.[1] That broadcast organisations have a significant contribution to make to the media's performance of this function is confirmed by the express references to broadcasting found in both Article 40.6.1°(i) of the Constitution and Article 10 of the European Convention on Human Rights.

IS BROADCASTING DIFFERENT?

[8.02] It has been suggested that it may be justifiable to subject broadcasters to a greater degree of regulation than other media outlets. This view was endorsed by the United States Supreme Court in its decisions in *Red Lion Broad Co v FCC*[2] and *FCC v Pacifica*.[3] In the latter case, the court rejected the broadcaster's complaint that the imposition of a sanction in relation to its broadcast of offensive words was a breach of the broadcaster's freedom of expression. The court based its decision in part on its recognition that 'of all forms of communication, it is broadcasting that has received the most limited First Amendment protection'.[4]

[8.03] The US courts have identified a number of potential rationales for such differential treatment of broadcasters:

1. Frequency limitations mean that there may only be a limited number of broadcasters, which justifies the state's intervention to regulate the allocation of this scarce resource (the 'spectrum scarcity' rationale).[5]

2. The barriers to entry in broadcasting are such that it is difficult for new entrants to establish themselves or attract an audience, which means it is justifiable for the state to impose particular duties or obligations on the few who occupy a successful and influential position in the broadcast market (the 'economic scarcity' rationale).

---

1. *Lingens v Austria* (1986) 8 EHRR 407; *Oberschlick v Austria* (1991) 19 EHRR 389; *Thorgeirson v Iceland* (1992) 14 EHRR 843; *Bladet Tromso v Norway* (1999) 29 EHRR 125; *Roberts v Gable* [2008] QB 502.
2. *Red Lion Broad Co v FCC* 395 US 367 (1969).
3. See, for example, Teeter, *Law of Mass Communications* (9th edn, 1998).
4. *FCC v Pacifica* 438 US 726, 748 (1978).
5. *NBC v US* 319 US 190 (1943).

3. The immediate and accessible nature of broadcast services means that users may access broadcasts at any time, with the result that warnings about the nature of unexpected content are ineffective.

4. Broadcasting is uniquely accessible to children, which justifies additional regulation to protect their interests.

[8.04] The reasoning of the Supreme Court has been subject to serious criticism on a number of grounds.[6] In particular, it has been suggested that technological developments have undermined the spectrum scarcity and economic scarcity rationales. The court itself appeared to accept the validity of this point by holding in *Turner Broad Systems v FCC*[7] that the approach followed in *Red Lion* should not be applied to cable television, given the comparative lack of scarcity in that medium. It has also been argued that there is a notable contradiction between the relatively laissez-faire approach adopted by the federal government to the internet, which shares many of the same characteristics as broadcasting.[8]

[8.05] Nonetheless, the court has continued to apply an approach which appears to provide greater First Amendment protection for traditional media, particularly print newspapers,[9] than broadcasters. This reflects an apparent view that 'differences in the characteristics of new media justify differences in the First Amendment standards applied to them'.[10] As the next section shows, a similar attitude can be discerned in some of the decisions of the European Court of Human Rights. This is a question which has not received detailed attention from the Irish courts. However, this American and European jurisprudence indicates that – despite the questionable nature of at least some of these rationales – it may be arguable that the freedom of expression of the broadcast media may, in certain circumstances, be subject to greater interferences than might be permissible in relation to other forms of media outlet.

BROADCASTERS UNDER THE CONSTITUTION AND CONVENTION

[8.06] As is the case with other media organisations, the Constitution and Convention confirm that broadcasters do not enjoy an unfettered freedom of expression. Both documents acknowledge the necessity for a degree of government regulation of this area. The text of Article 40.6.1°(i), for example, firmly reserves to the State the power to

---

6. See, for example, Logan Jr, 'Getting beyond scarcity: a new paradigm for assessing the constitutionality of broadcast regulation' (1997) 85 California Law Review 1687.
7. *Turner Broad Systems v FCC* 520 US 180 (1997).
8. Shapiro, 'One and the Same: How internet non-regulation undermines the rationales used to support broadcast regulation' (1999) 8 Media Law and Policy 1. This, of course, is an argument which would justify either less regulation of broadcasting or, where practicable, more regulation of the internet.
9. See, for example, *Miami Herald Publishing Co v Tornillo* 418 US 241 (1974).
10. *Red Lion Broad Co v FCC* 395 US 367, 387 (1969).

regulate the content produced by all forms of media organisations, including the forms of broadcaster referred to therein:

> The education of public opinion being, however, a matter of such grave import to the common good, the State shall endeavour to ensure that organs of public opinion, such as the radio, the press, the cinema, while preserving their rightful liberty of expression, including criticism of Government policy, shall not be used to undermine public order or morality or the authority of the State.

Thus, in addition to identifying specific grounds of public order, public morality and the authority of the State upon which State intervention in the actions of media organisations may be justified, this Article also indicates the constitutional guarantee of media freedom of expression as primarily instrumental in nature. Media organisations, including broadcasters, are 'the organs of public opinion' whose constitutional role is connected with the State's interest in the 'education of public opinion'. As discussed in Ch 2, this would tend to suggest that the media's freedom of expression is of a different character to that of the individual citizen and that the State may, in certain circumstances, accordingly find it easier to justify an interference with media expression than with the expression of individuals. It may also mean, as hinted at in *O'Toole v RTÉ*, that media organisations may themselves operate under a constitutional obligation to supervise and monitor their own output, regardless of the statutory regime in place at any particular time.[11]

[8.07] Furthermore, the view has been expressed by the European Court of Human Rights that the audiovisual character of broadcast communications raises separate and distinct issues which may, in certain cases, entitle the State to subject broadcast media to greater regulation than would be appropriate for forms of media expression. The court has held that audiovisual media may have a more powerful impact than print media and that the State may, as a result, have a wider margin of appreciation in regulating this type of expression.[12] As the court explained, in rejecting the applicant's claim that there had been a breach of his Article 10 rights in *Murphy v Ireland*:

> The prohibition concerned only the audio-visual media. The State was, in the Court's view, entitled to be particularly wary of the potential for offence in the broadcasting context, such media being accepted by this Court (see para 69) and acknowledged by the applicant, as having a more immediate, invasive and powerful impact including, as the Government and the High Court noted, on the passive recipient. He was consequently free to advertise the same matter in any of the print media (including local and national newspapers) and during public meetings and other assemblies.[13]

That is not to say that broadcast organisations do not enjoy considerable protection under the Convention. The European Court of Human Rights has held that Article 10 protects not only the content and substance of information but also the means of dissemination since any restriction on the means necessarily interferes with the right to

---

11.   *O'Toole v RTÉ* [1993] ILRM 458.
12.   *Jersild v Denmark* (1995) 19 EHRR 1.
13.   *Murphy v Ireland* (2004) 38 EHRR 13, para 74.

receive and impart information.[14] The express recognition by Article 10(1) of a power on the part of Contracting States to license broadcasting has been held to mean that States are permitted to regulate by means of a licensing system the way in which broadcasting is organised in their territories, particularly with regard to technical issues.[15] In the past, this was justified in part on the basis of both the various limiting factors referred to in Article 10(2) as well as the limited spectrum available for television and radio broadcasts.[16] Technological developments mean that the latter is less relevant today with the result that it has featured less prominently in the court's case law in recent times.

[8.08] In terms of the scope of the state's licensing power, the court has held that a contracting state is entitled to make the grant or refusal of a licence conditional on other considerations of public policy. These have been stated to include such matters as the nature and objectives of a proposed station, its potential audience at national, regional or local level, the rights and needs of a specific audience and the obligations deriving from international legal instruments.[17] Such matters need not be based directly on the considerations referred to in Article 10(2).[18] However, because of the potential for such considerations to be based on unlawful or illegitimate grounds, or to operate in a manner which could contravene other Convention rights, it has also been emphasised that the Article's express recognition of a power to regulate does not operate as a carte blanche for Contracting States. Rather, any measures are capable of being reviewed on the familiar grounds of legitimacy, necessity and proportionality.[19] This means, for example, that any rules regulating broadcast organisations must be sufficiently accessible and precise to comply with the Convention requirement of lawfulness,[20] and that any decisions taken in respect of regulatory issues such as the grant of licences must be sufficiently reasoned and transparent to satisfy the same requirements.[21]

[8.09] It is clear, therefore, that broadcasters may be subject to legitimate regulation on matters of delivery and content under both the Constitution and Convention. Indeed, it is arguable by reference to the dicta of the Supreme Court in *O'Toole* that some degree of regulation, even if only self-organised, may be required as a matter of Irish constitutional law. In any event, the broadcasting sector has been subject to statutory regulation in Ireland for decades.[22] The most recent intervention by the Oireachtas in the field of

---

14. *Ozturk v Turkey* [1999] ECHR 224/9/93.
15. *Groppera Radio AG* [1990] ECHR 10890/84.
16. *United Christian Broadcasting v UK* ECHR 44802/98.
17. *Radio ABC v Austria* [1997] ECHR 19736/92.
18. *Demuth v Switzerland* [2002] ECHR 38743/97 (Application No 38743/97) .
19. *Tele 1 Privatfernsehgesellschaft mbH v Austria* [2000] ECHR 32240/96; *Informations-verein Lentia v Austria* [1993] ECHR 13914/88.
20. *Groppera Radio AG v Switzerland* [1990] ECHR 10890/84.
21. *Glas Nadezhda EOOD v Bulgaria* (2007) 24 BHRC 239.
22. See, for example, the Broadcasting Authority Act 1960; the Broadcasting Authority (Amendment) Act 1966; the Broadcasting Authority (Amendment) Act 1976; the Broadcasting and Wireless Telegraphy Act 1988, the Broadcasting Act 1990; the Broadcasting Authority (Amendment) Act 1993; the Broadcasting Act 2001; and the Broadcasting (Amendment) Act 2007.

broadcasting was the Broadcasting Act 2009. This Act repealed[23] the majority of previous Acts which applied to this area so that it is now the centrepiece of government regulation of broadcasting in Ireland. The Act is a comprehensive and significant piece of legislation which is intended to bring about a significant overhaul of the legal and regulatory regime for Irish broadcasting. As such, it will feature prominently throughout the remainder of this chapter.

[8.10] However, it is also important to bear in mind that there is also a significant supranational dimension to broadcasting laws or regulations. Indeed, with the increasingly international – or, perhaps more accurately, transnational – nature of broadcasting, the European Union legal instruments which impact upon different aspects of European broadcasting are becoming more relevant to the regulation of broadcasting in Ireland. This is illustrated by the fact that, for example, several of the provisions of the 2009 Act of necessity make reference to, or require various public bodies to take account of, relevant European Union measures.[24] Thus, although the focus of this book is Irish media law and regulation, it will be necessary in several places in this chapter to refer to the law of the European Union, where appropriate. However, it should also be borne in mind that the relatively small nature of the Irish broadcasting market and of the organisations operating within it means that activities within the Irish market have rarely (at least up to this point) had the necessary cross-border dimension or potential Union-wide impact to trigger the direct involvement of the various European institutions with responsibility in this field. For Irish media organisations and their advisers, domestic Irish measures remain by far the primary source for the regulation or determination of any legal issues that arise. As a result, the coverage in this chapter is weighted towards domestic law.[25]

THE BROADCASTING AUTHORITY OF IRELAND

[8.11] Part 2 of the 2009 Act provides for the establishment of a new body, to be known as the Broadcasting Authority of Ireland (BAI).[26] Section 6(b) also establishes two sub-groups of the BAI, a Contract Awards Committee and a Compliance Committee, both of which are subject to specific regulation elsewhere in the Act. This body effectively replaces the Broadcasting Commission of Ireland (BCI) and the Broadcasting

---

23. Broadcasting Act 2009, s 3. See also Broadcasting Act 2009, Sch 1.
24. Council Directive 89/552/EEC of 3 October 1989 on the co-ordination of certain provisions laid down by law, regulation or administrative action in Member States concerning the pursuit of television broadcasting activities as amended by Directive 97/36/EC of the European Parliament and of the Council of 30 June 1997 and by Directive 2007/65/EC of the European Parliament and of the Council of 11 December 2007 (the Audiovisual Media Services Directive).
25. For coverage of some of the more complicated or esoteric aspects of EU broadcasting, readers are advised to consult a specialist text on EU broadcasting law. See, for example, Garzaniti, *Telecommunications, Broadcasting and the Internet: EU Competition Law and Regulation* (3rd edn, Sweet & Maxwell, 2010); Nikolinakos, *EU Competition Law and Regulation in the Converging Telecommunications, Media and IT Sectors* (Kluwer, 2006).
26. Broadcasting Act 2009, s 6(a).

Complaints Commission (BCC) which, between them, previously exercised many of the functions now vested in the BAI.

The BAI was established on 1 October 2009 by order of the Minister for Energy, Communications and the Marine.[27] The 2009 Act vests a significant number of powers and functions in the new body, relating to such diverse matters as content, complaints about broadcaster conduct, licensing, funding, technological standards and media plurality. These various functions are considered individually below.

Composition of the BAI

[8.12] The Act specifies that there shall be nine members of the BAI.[28] The function of members is specified to be to represent the public interest in respect of matters of broadcasting.[29] Individuals may not be appointed to the BAI, or to either of its statutory committees, unless they have experience or have demonstrated capacity in one or more of the following areas:

(a)   media affairs;

(b)   public service broadcasting, commercial broadcasting or community broadcasting;

(c)   broadcast content production;

(d)   digital media technologies;

(e)   trade union affairs;

(f)   business or commercial affairs;

(g)   matters pertaining to the development of the Irish language;

(h)   matters pertaining to disability;

(i)   arts, music, sport or culture;

(j)   science, technology or environmental matters;

(k)   legal or regulatory affairs; or

(l)   social, educational or community affairs or Gaeltacht affairs.[30]

A statement in writing specifying the expertise or experience of the members must be set before the Oireachtas by the Minister and published in *Iris Oifigúil*.[31]

---

27.   Broadcasting Authority of Ireland (Establishment Day) Order 2009 (SI 389/2009).
28.   Broadcasting Act 2009, s 8(1).
29.   Broadcasting Act 2009, s 9(2).
30.   Broadcasting Act 2009, s 9(1).
31.   Broadcasting Act 2009, s 10(4).

Appointment of members

[8.13] Five members are appointed by the Government on the nomination of the Minister.[32] The other four are appointed by the Government on the nomination of the Minister after a process of consultation with the Joint Oireachtas Committee with responsibility for broadcasting matters.[33] Under this process, the Minister must inform the Joint Oireachtas Committee of the proposed appointment to the BAI.[34] Within 90 days of the Minister's communication, that Committee must propose a person or persons to the Minister for appointment to the position or positions available.[35] The Committee must also giving reasons for their proposed candidate.[36] The Committee is also entitled to maintain a panel of experienced persons for the purposes of exercising their functions under this section.[37] The Minister must have regard to the Committee's advice on the appointment or appointments although he or she is also entitled to appoint an alternative person if he or she sees fit.[38] The 2009 Act represents the first time that this type of mechanism for involving a Joint Oireachtas Committee in the process of appointing individuals to public bodies has been used and is designed to address concerns about executive dominance over the legislature in this area.

[8.14] The Contracts Committee meanwhile will be comprised of eight members,[39] four of whom shall be appointed by the Government on the nomination of the Minister,[40] and four of whom shall be appointed by the Authority.[41] The latter four will be made up of two members of the BAI and two staff of the BAI. The same rules also apply to the composition of the Compliance Committee.[42] Members of the Contracts Committee cannot simultaneously be members of the Compliance Committee,[43] and vice versa.[44] The Government is also obliged to endeavour to ensure gender balance in these appointments.[45]

[8.15] A person who holds employment or an interest in a broadcasting undertaking, including but not limited to a public service broadcaster, or an undertaking holding a contract under the 2009 Act,[46] or who holds an interest in an undertaking which publishes a newspaper in Ireland,[47] cannot be appointed as a member of the BAI or of a

---

32.   Broadcasting Act 2009, s 8(1)(a).
33.   Broadcasting Act 2009, s 8(1)(b).
34.   Broadcasting Act 2009, s 8(2)(a).
35.   Broadcasting Act 2009, s 8(2)(c).
36.   Broadcasting Act 2009, s 8(2)(c).
37.   Broadcasting Act 2009, s 8(8).
38.   Broadcasting Act 2009, s 8(2)(d).
39.   Broadcasting Act 2009, s 8(4).
40.   Broadcasting Act 2009, s 8(4)(a).
41.   Broadcasting Act 2009, s 8(4)(b).
42.   Broadcasting Act 2009, s 8(6).
43.   Broadcasting Act 2009, s 12(8).
44.   Broadcasting Act 2009, s 12(9).
45.   Broadcasting Act 2009, ss 8(5) and 8(7).
46.   Broadcasting Act 2009, s 12(6).
47.   Broadcasting Act 2009, s 12(7).

statutory committee. Persons entitled to sit in either House of the Oireachtas or who are members of the European Parliament are also prohibited from becoming part of the BAI or relevant committees.[48]

[8.16] Members may be appointed for no more than five years.[49] They are eligible for re-appointment at the end of their initial term[50] but cannot serve more than two consecutive terms of office.[51] A member of the BAI may at any time resign his or her office by letter addressed to the Government with the resignation taking effect on the date specified therein or upon receipt of the letter by the Government, whichever is the later.[52] Members of the BAI who are appointed by it to serve on one of the statutory committees resign their position by letter to the chairman of the Authority.[53]

[8.17] If a member of the BAI or of one of the statutory committees who was appointed by the Minister dies, resigns, is disqualified from office or is otherwise removed, the Government on the nomination of the Minister may appoint a replacement to fill this vacancy for the unexpired period of the previous member's term.[54] Where the relevant Joint Oireachtas Committee was involved in the original appointment of the member who is being replaced, the Minister must have regard to the advice of that Committee in appointing his or her replacement.[55]

Removal of members

[8.18] Under the terms of the 2009 Act, members may be removed by a decision of the Government or by operation of law.

Under s 10(5) a member of either the BAI or of a statutory committee may be removed from his or her position by the Government at any time if, in the Government's opinion, the member has become incapable through ill-health of performing his or her functions, has committed stated misbehaviour, or his or her removal appears to the Government to be necessary for the effective performance by the relevant body of its functions. Although the latter ground in particular gives the Government a relatively broad power to remove members, this power is constrained by a further requirement that he or she may only be removed where both Houses of the Oireachtas have passed resolutions calling for that removal. The requirements of constitutional justice and fair procedures should also apply to the removal process.[56]

[8.19] Members may also be removed by the Minister with the consent of the Government where the member fails to make a declaration in accordance with the

---

48.   Broadcasting Act 2009, s 12(3).
49.   Broadcasting Act 2009, s 9(2).
50.   Broadcasting Act 2009, s 9(4).
51.   Broadcasting Act 2009, s 9(5).
52.   Broadcasting Act 2009, s 9(6).
53.   Broadcasting Act 2009, s 9(7).
54.   Broadcasting Act 2009, s 10(10).
55.   Broadcasting Act 2009, s 10(11).
56.   See, for example, *Garvey v Ireland* [1981] IR 75.

requirements of s 17 of the Ethics in Public Office Act 1995. This requires the member to furnish the Standards in Public Office Commission[57] with a statement in writing of the member's interests and the interests of his or her spouse or child of which the member has actual knowledge.[58] The difference between removal on this ground and removal on the grounds identified in the previous paragraph is that the positive approval of the Oireachtas is not required to remove a member. Rather the Minister must lay the order before each House of the Oireachtas,[59] whereupon it may be annulled within 21 days by a vote of either House.[60] This procedure may also be used by the Minister to remove a member where the member fails to comply with the disclosure requirements laid down by s 21,[61] or where a member fails to attend a meeting of the BAI or relevant committee for a consecutive six-month period.[62] In the latter situation, the Minister may not exercise his or her power of removal if the member can demonstrate to the Minister's satisfaction that the failure to attend was due to illness.

[8.20] A member of either the BAI or a statutory committee shall automatically cease to be a member and be disqualified from further membership in a number of defined situations. This will occur where the member:

(a)   is adjudicated a bankrupt;

(b)   makes a composition or arrangement with creditors;

(c)   on conviction on indictment by a court of competent jurisdiction is sentenced to a term of imprisonment;

(d)   is convicted of an offence involving fraud or dishonesty; or

(e)   is disqualified or restricted from being a director of any company.[63]

Members of either of the statutory committees who are staff of the BAI and are appointed to the committees on that basis will cease to be a member of the committee once their contract of service with the BAI comes to an end.

[8.21] Membership will also be suspended in the event that a member of either the BAI or committee is nominated as a candidate for election to the European Parliament or to either House of the Oireachtas.[64] For BAI staff members, their position is similar in that they are regarded as being seconded for the period between nomination and election or otherwise.[65] This means the member may not participate in meetings of the BAI or statutory committee or receive any remuneration or allowances from the BAI for the

---

57.   Standards of Public Office Act, 2001, s 2.
58.   Broadcasting Act 2009, s 10(8)(c).
59.   Broadcasting Act 2009, s 10(9)(a).
60.   Broadcasting Act 2009, s 10(9)(b).
61.   Broadcasting Act 2009, s 10(8)(b).
62.   Broadcasting Act 2009, s 10(8)(a).
63.   Broadcasting Act 2009, s 10(6).
64.   Broadcasting Act 2009, s 12(1).
65.   Broadcasting Act 2009, s 12(3).

period of suspension.[66] This period will end when the person is regarded as having been not elected. Where a person is elected, they automatically cease to be a member.[67]

[8.22] In addition, members will cease to hold their position automatically where they obtain employment or acquire an interest in a broadcasting undertaking, including but not limited to a public service broadcaster, or an undertaking holding a contract under the 2009 Act,[68] or if they acquire an interest in an undertaking which publishes a newspaper in Ireland.[69]

Chairperson

[8.23] The Government, on the nomination of the Minister, will also appoint a chairperson of the BAI, as well as the chairpersons of the two statutory committees. A chairperson shall, unless he or she dies, resigns the office of chairperson or ceases to be chairperson under the subsection, hold office until the expiration of his or her period of office as a member of the BAI or relevant committee. The chair will cease to hold the position when their term of membership of the BAI or committee is at an end.[70]

[8.24] A chairperson may also resign at any time by sending a letter to the Government, which resignation will take effect (unless withdrawn) at the start of the first meeting of the BAI or committee held after the body has been informed by the Government of the resignation.[71] This would seem to suggest that a chairperson can withdraw his or her letter of resignation after the Government has received the letter and begun to consider replacements but before the next meeting is held. This raises awkward hypothetical questions of sequencing, especially in the event that the Government moves to appoint a new chairperson before the meeting in question. This would suggest that it would be more appropriate that a new chair not be appointed until after the meeting in question and that the meeting proceed with a temporary chairperson, appointed by attendees at the meeting itself from amongst their own number.[72]

Chief executive

[8.25] The BAI also has a chief executive whose primary function is to ensure the efficient and effective management of the administration of the BAI and of its statutory committees.[73] The chief executive is appointed by the Authority with the consent of the Minister after the holding of a public competition.[74] This requirement did not apply in relation to the appointment of the first chief executive of the BAI, as provision was made

---

66.   Broadcasting Act 2009, s 12(1).
67.   Broadcasting Act 2009, s 12(2).
68.   Broadcasting Act 2009, s 12(6).
69.   Broadcasting Act 2009, s 12(7).
70.   Broadcasting Act 2009, s 11(3).
71.   Broadcasting Act 2009, s 11(2).
72.   Broadcasting Act 2009, s 13(5)(b).
73.   Broadcasting Act 2009, s 14(2).
74.   Broadcasting Act 2009, s 14(6).

in the Act for the then chief executive of the BCI to be appointed to the position without the necessity for a public competition.[75] The chief executive may be removed from office by the Authority with the consent of the Minister for stated reasons.[76]

[8.26] The chief executive is accountable to the Dáil Public Accounts Committee and is obliged, where so requested, to attend at meetings of that Committee and give evidence[77] in relation to the regularity and propriety of the transactions recorded or required to be recorded in any records subject to audit by the comptroller and auditor general; the economy and efficiency of the BAI in its use of its resources; the systems, procedures and practices employed by the BAI for the purpose of evaluating the effectiveness of its operations; any matter affecting the BAI referred to in a special report of the comptroller and auditor general;[78] and all matters pertaining to the expenditure by the BAI of monies received by it from the exchequer for the performance of a function of an exceptional nature.[79]

[8.27] Provision is also made for the chief executive (as well as the chairperson) to appear before other committees of the Houses of the Oireachtas.[80]

Meetings

[8.28] Various rules and procedures are laid down by s 13 of the Act governing the holding of meetings of the BAI or of the two statutory committees. The Act specifies that a quorum for the holding of a meeting of ether the BAI[81] or one of the committees will be five members.[82] In the case of the two committees, two of these five must be members appointed by the Government.[83] It also indicates that matters may, as required, be determined by a vote of the members present with the chairperson having the casting vote.[84]

[8.29] Section 13(11) also confirms that meetings may be held be electronic means once all members of the Authority or the relevant statutory committee can hear and be heard. The choice of language here appears slightly unfortunate in that it could be taken to suggest that members of the committee who are, for example, deaf could not validly participate in a meeting by electronic means. This may not arise as an issue in practice but, in the event that it does, it is submitted that a purposive interpretation of this section in accordance with which a meeting will be valid once all persons can participate in it may be more appropriate. Such an interpretation would also be more likely to conform

---

75. Broadcasting Act 2009, s 14(12).
76. Broadcasting Act 2009, s 14(16).
77. Broadcasting Act 2009, s 19(1).
78. See the Comptroller and Auditor General (Amendment) Act 1993, s 11(2).
79. Broadcasting Act 2009, s 34.
80. Broadcasting Act 2009, s 20.
81. Broadcasting Act 2009, s 13(7).
82. Broadcasting Act 2009, s 13(8) and (9).
83. Broadcasting Act 2009, s 13(8) and (9).
84. Broadcasting Act 2009, s 13(6).

to the requirements of the Constitution[85] and the interpretative obligation under s 2 of the European Convention on Human Rights Act 2003.

Advisers

[8.30] The Act makes provision for the establishment by the BAI of advisory committees to advise and assist it or a statutory committee in the performance of its functions.[86] The Act also permits the BAI may to engage such consultants or advisers as it or a statutory committee may consider necessary for the performance of the functions of that body.[87] The BAI, the statutory committees and the chief executive must, where relevant, have regard to the advice of any persons or committees so appointed but are not bound by it.[88]

Disclosure of member interest

[8.31] The 2009 Act makes extensive provision for the disclosure of members' interests, as well as setting out the procedures to be followed in circumstances where a member may have an actual or perceived interest in a matter under discussion. This is significant as the courts have held that the commercial value of some of the decision-making functions vested in the BAI reinforce the necessity as a matter of legal and constitutional principle for it to act, and be seen to act, in a fair and impartial manner. In *Radio Limerick One v IRTC*, Keane J (as he then was) observed that:

> The huge commercial implications of the granting of franchises to private interests for the provision of radio and television services and the profound influence of the media in modern conditions made it obviously of great importance that the process should take place in a scrupulously fair, public and impartial manner.

Furthermore, these rules are important for the BAI as the experience of previous broadcasting regulatory bodies in Ireland was that their decisions were sometimes subject to challenge by unsuccessful applicants on the grounds of objective bias.[89] This reflected the practical difficulty for previous authorities that the relatively small nature of the media and broadcasting market in Ireland made it highly probable that some members of those bodies would have had prior dealings with some of the individuals or entities who were subject to the decisions of those authorities. This difficulty was acknowledged by Keane J in *Radio One Limerick*:

> In the present case, the statutory provisions already referred to clearly envisage that the membership of the commission may consist, in part at least, of persons engaged in the media who may be assumed to have a special knowledge of the matters with which the commission has to deal. The fact that its membership is so

---

85. See, for example, *Clarke v Courts Service & Ors* (14 July 2010, unreported), HC.
86. Broadcasting Act 2009, s 17(1).
87. Broadcasting Act 2009, s 18(1).
88. Broadcasting Act 2009, s 17(4) and 18(2).
89. See, for example, *Radio Limerick One Limited v The Independent Radio and Television Commission* [1997] 2 IR 291; [1997] 2 ILRM 1; *Carlow Kilkenny Radio Ltd, Kildare Radio Ltd and Carlow Kildare Radio Ltd v Broadcasting Commission of Ireland* [2003] 3 IR 528.

composed may mean that, in specific instances, when it comes to deal with matters as crucial as the entering into of a contract or its suspension or termination, its decisions, although undoubtedly quasi-judicial in nature and necessitating the observance of natural justice and fair procedures, may also not have the appearance of impartiality which would be required of a court of justice. That, of itself, would not vitiate its conclusions, provided it reached them in good faith and having given the persons affected the protection of natural justice and fair procedures.[90]

Thus, the court concluded that these bodies could not necessarily be required to demonstrate the same appearance of complete impartiality as might be expected of a court. However, Keane J emphasised that they were obliged to take all reasonable steps to minimise or reduce any potential impression of bias:

> Because of the factors to which I have already referred, a body such as the commission may not, in given circumstances, present the appearance of strict impartiality required of a court administering justice. That, however, does not relieve the commission of the obligation to take every step reasonably open to it to ensure that its conclusions are reached in a manner, not merely free from bias, but also of the apprehension of bias in the minds of reasonable people. But where, as here, a body is obliged to carry out certain statutory functions and no issue arises as to the constitutionality of the relevant provisions, a court cannot by the strict application of the legal principles already referred to it prevent the body from exercising those functions, where all practical steps have been taken by it to free itself, not merely from actual bias but the apprehension of bias in the minds of reasonable people.[91]

[8.32] The 2009 Act accordingly lays down procedures which are designed to meet these concerns. However, Keane J's decision would indicate that the simple fact that the BAI has adhered to these statutory requirements, while generally indicative of a fair and impartial process, will not necessarily mean that the decision-making process of the BAI is thereby immune from challenge. It would appear prudent, therefore, for the BAI to consider in certain situations whether the circumstances of an individual case or process or such measures above those set out by the 2009 Act may be appropriate.

[8.33] Section 21(1) specifies that a member of the BAI or statutory committee who has any interest in any body or concern with which the BAI has made a contract or proposes to make a contract or any interest in any contract which the BAI has made or proposes to make must disclose the fact of such interest and the nature of it to the BAI or committee in question. The member also may not be present at any deliberation or decision relating to that contract. The fact that the Act applies to 'any interest' is a strong indication that the member should err on the side of caution in considering whether they may be covered by the requirements of this section.

---

90. *Radio Limerick One Limited v The Independent Radio and Television Commission* [1997] 2 IR 291, 316. Note, however, that Smyth J expressed a somewhat contrary view at an earlier stage of these proceedings. See *Radio One Limerick v IRTC* [1997] 2 IR 291, [1997] 2 ILRM 1.

91. *Radio Limerick One Limited v The Independent Radio and Television Commission* [1997] 2 IR 291, 316.

[8.34] Similarly, where matters relating to an arrangement or contract with the BAI or its statutory committees (or any proposed arrangement or contract) arise during a meeting, any member present who has an interest[92] in the matter must disclose the fact and nature of the interest. The member must then absent himself or herself from the meeting or part of the meeting where that matter is discussed, must neither influence nor seek to influence a decision to be made in relation to the matter, must take no part in any deliberation of the Authority or the committee relating to the matter, and may not vote on a decision relating to the matter.[93] Any such disclosure must also be recorded in the minutes of the meeting.[94]

[8.35] The section is drafted in a sufficiently broad way that the threshold for the creation of these obligations on members – 'an interest' – is reasonably low. As noted above, however, it is likely that members will frequently have had some prior knowledge or dealing with some of the individuals or organisations with whom the BAI or its committees will deal, or consider dealing. Section 21(5) seeks to balance these considerations by providing a de minimis standard in relation to member's interest. It states that a member will not be regarded as having an interest in any matter by reason only of an interest of that person, or of any company in which he or she has an interest, where that interest is so remote or insignificant that it cannot reasonably be regarded as likely to influence a person in considering, discussing or in voting on, any question relating to the matter, or in performing any function in relation to that matter.

[8.36] Where there is uncertainty over whether an interest is above this threshold and thus whether a member's actions may breach the requirements of sub-ss 1 and 2, the Act provides that this can be discussed at the meeting in question and that the decision of that meeting shall be recorded in the minutes and shall be final.[95] This provision would not, of course, oust the jurisdiction of the courts to entertain a judicial review or any other application in relation to the conduct of the BAI.

[8.37] The BAI is also required to draw up and adopt a code of conduct in respect of controls on interests and ethical behaviour to apply to each member of the Authority, a statutory committee, an advisory committee and each member of the staff.

Objectives of the BAI

[8.38] Section 25(1) identifies the objectives of the BAI, and of its statutory committees. It provides that they, in performing their functions, 'shall endeavour to ensure':

    (a)   that the number and categories of broadcasting services made available in the State by virtue of this Act best serve the needs of the people of the island of Ireland, bearing in mind their languages and traditions and their religious, ethical and cultural diversity,

---

92.   Except where the interest arises in the person's capacity as a member.
93.   Broadcasting Act 2009, s 21(2).
94.   Broadcasting Act 2009, s 21(3).
95.   Broadcasting Act 2009, s 21(5).

    (b)   that the democratic values enshrined in the Constitution, especially those relating to rightful liberty of expression, are upheld, and

    (c)   the provision of open and pluralistic broadcasting services.

[8.39] There are a number of points to note in relation to these objectives. The first is that sub-s (a) may require the BAI to take account of the importance of both Irish cultural traditions and contemporary cultural diversity. The reference to the 'people of the island of Ireland' is ambiguous in the sense that it does not indicate whether it is intended to refer to people currently resident on the island of Ireland or if it is instead intended to require some consideration of the traditions of those who might be termed to have been historically present on the island of Ireland.

[8.40] Subsection (b) is clearly intended to underline the importance of media freedom of expression. However, the reference to 'democratic values' again connects the protection of that media expression with the democratic process which – as discussed in **Ch 2** and elsewhere in this book – suggests an instrumental conception of media expression. It should also be borne in mind that these democratic values would include countervailing constitutional values such as the right to a good name.

[8.41] Subsection (c) is noteworthy as it imposes a statutory obligation on the BAI, and its constituent committees, to have regard to the importance of providing open and pluralistic broadcasting services in performing its functions. This is discussed in more detail elsewhere in this book. However, this would appear to provide the BAI with a statutory mandate to protect and facilitate plurality in Irish broadcasting, both in terms of ownership and in terms of content. Given the criticisms that have been made of the relatively homogenous nature of ownership and content in the Irish media market,[96] and the Advisory Group on Media Mergers' recognition of a potential further 'trend towards the concentration of ownership',[97] this may be a significant provision for the future.

[8.42] Section 25 goes on to identify a number of specific sub-objectives which the BAI and its statutory committees are directed to pursue. These are to:

    (a)   stimulate the provision of high quality, diverse and innovative programming by commercial, community and public service broadcasters and independent producers;

    (b)   facilitate public service broadcasters in the fulfilment of their public service objects as set out in this Act;

    (c)   promote diversity in control of the more influential commercial and community broadcasting services;

    (d)   provide a regulatory environment that will sustain independent and impartial journalism;

    (e)   provide a regulatory environment that will sustain compliance with applicable employment law;

---

96.   See, for example, Browne, 'Ireland's media has never been less diverse than now' (2009) *The Sunday Business Post*, 22 March.
97.   Report of the Advisory Group on Media Mergers (2008), 8.

(f)   protect the interests of children taking into account the vulnerability of children and childhood to undue commercial exploitation;

(g)   provide a regulatory environment that will facilitate the development of a broadcasting sector in Ireland that is responsive to audience needs and in particular is accessible to people with disabilities; and

(h)   promote and stimulate the development of Irish language programming and broadcasting services.[98]

Measures taken in pursuit of any of the stated objectives or sub-objectives must be proportionate, must ensure stable and predictable regulation, must accommodate and encourage technological development and must take account of the spread of broadcast services in the State.[99]

Functions of the BAI

[8.43] Section 26 provides for the vesting of various functions in the BAI. Section 26(1) identifies the principal functions of the BAI. Many are connected with the exercise of its powers under various provisions of the 2009 Act. These are discussed in more detail in the relevant sections of this chapter below. In general, however, the main overarching functions of the BAI are to:

•   prepare a strategy for the provision of broadcasting services in the State additional to those provided by RTÉ, TG4, the Houses of the Oireachtas Channel and the Irish Film Channel;

•   prepare a strategy statement in accordance with the requirements of s 29(1);

•   liaise and consult with the Communications Regulator in the preparation of the allocation plan for the frequency range dedicated to sound and television broadcasting;

•   make a levy order for the funding of the BAI's expenses under s 33(1);

•   prepare or make broadcasting codes and rules;

•   prepare a scheme for the exercise of the right of reply;

•   direct the Contract Awards Committee to make arrangements, in accordance with Pts 6 and 8, to invite, consider and recommend to the BAI proposals for the provision of: broadcasting services additional to any broadcasting services provided by RTÉ, TG4, the Houses of the Oireachtas Channel and the Irish Film Channel under Pt 7, and multiplex services additional to any multiplex services provided by RTÉ under Pts 7 and 8 of the Act;

•   prepare rules and enter into contracts in respect of electronic programme guides;

•   make a report to the Minister under s 139(1) in respect of preparedness for analogue switch-off;

---

98.   Broadcasting Act 2009, s 25(2).
99.   Broadcasting Act 2009, s 25(3).

- provide information to the public on the availability of services by means of television multiplexes; and

- prepare and implement schemes for the granting of funds under the new Broadcasting Fund.

[8.44] The BAI also has a number of ancillary functions under s 26(2). These are to:

(a) to collect and disseminate information on the broadcasting sector in the State;

(b) to monitor developments in broadcasting internationally;

(c) to initiate, organise, facilitate and promote research relating to broadcasting matters;

(d) to collect and disseminate information in relation to the skills requirements of the broadcasting sector;

(e) to co-operate with other bodies, including representative bodies within the broadcasting sector, to promote training activities in areas of skill shortages in the broadcasting sector;

(f) to co-operate with other bodies outside the State which perform similar functions to the Authority; and

(g) to undertake, encourage and foster research, measures and activities which are directed towards the promotion of media literacy, including co-operation with broadcasters, educationalists and other relevant persons.

Contract Awards Committee

[8.45] The functions of the Contract Awards Committee are outlined in s 27 of the Act. The principal functions of the Committee are to make arrangements to invite, consider and recommend proposals to the BAI for new broadcasting services additional to any broadcasting services provided by RTÉ, TG4, the Houses of the Oireachtas Channel and the Irish Film Channel, as well as for new digital multiplex services additional to any multiplex services provided by RTÉ.

Compliance Committee

[8.46] Whereas the Contracts Award Committee, as the name suggests, is concerned with the distribution and awarding of broadcasting contracts, the Compliance Committee is charged with overseeing the performance of bodies who are awarded such contracts. Thus, the principal functions of the Compliance Committee are to monitor compliance by contractors with the terms and conditions of any contract entered into by the BAI under the Act, to enforce the terms and conditions of any such contract as well as to monitor and enforce compliance by broadcasters with specific statutory provisions which apply to them and with any broadcasting code or rule.[100] As part of these functions, the Committee is also responsible for investigating and deciding upon a

---

100. Broadcasting Act 2009, s 28(1).

complaint or requests made under the relevant provisions of the Act.[101] Unlike the Contract Awards Committee, provision is made in the Act for the Compliance Committee to delegate the performance of its functions to BAI staff[102] or to a sub-committee.[103]

Strategy and policy

[8.47] As part of its performance of its statutory functions, the BAI is required to draw up a strategy statement[104] every three years.[105] The statement must be presented to the Minister and relevant Oireachtas committees[106] and must be based on a public consultation process.[107] It must comprise the key objectives, outputs and related strategies, including use of resources, follow any relevant ministerial directions, have regard to the need to ensure the most beneficial, effective and efficient use of resources, include a review of the efficiency and effectiveness of the statement during the preceding three-year period and include the Authority's plans as to the number, nature and scope of contracts that it proposes to enter into during the period covered by the statement.[108]

[8.48] The BAI's policies may also be influenced by policy communications issued to it by the Minister. The BAI must have regard to any such communications.[109] The power of the Minster to issue policy communications is stated by the Act to be provided 'in the interests of the proper and effective regulation of the broadcasting sector and the formulation of policy applicable to such proper and effective regulation'.[110] Although this is a very broad statement, it does provide certain limits to the Minister's power to influence BAI policy. The Minister's power is further restricted by the fact that any communication must first be published in draft form. This draft must allow at least 21 days for interested parties (including, presumably, the BAI) to make representations in relation to it.[111]

[8.49] The Minister may not issue a communication dealing with the performance of the functions of the BAI in respect of individual undertakings or persons.[112] He or she is also not entitled to issue a communication under the subsection in respect of the performance of the functions of the Contract Awards Committee or the Compliance Committee.[113]

---

101. Broadcasting Act 2009, ss 47 and 48.
102. Broadcasting Act 2009, s 28(3).
103. Broadcasting Act 2009, s 28(4).
104. Broadcasting Act 2009, s 29(1).
105. Broadcasting Act 2009, s 29(2)(e).
106. Broadcasting Act 2009, s 29(3).
107. Broadcasting Act 2009, s 29(5).
108. Broadcasting Act 2009, s 29(2).
109. Broadcasting Act 2009, s 30(1).
110. Broadcasting Act 2009, s 30(1).
111. Broadcasting Act 2009, s 30(2).
112. Broadcasting Act 2009, s 30(5).
113. Broadcasting Act 2009, s 30(6).

Broadcasting levy

[8.50] The expenses and operating costs of the BAI and of its committees are funded by means of a levy imposed on broadcasters. There is also provision for exchequer funding to be provided by the Minister but is only permitted in relation to expenses of an exceptional nature which are incurred by the BAI in the performance of its functions.[114] The broadcasting levy is, as a result, the BAI's primary source of funding.

[8.51] The levy is calculated by reference to a levy order which is made by the BAI.[115] The levy order should indicate the method of calculation of the levy and the times and form of payment which is required. It may also provide for the keeping, inspection and provision of records relating to the levy, as well as any exemptions, deferrals or refunds which may be permitted.[116]

[8.52] The Act permits the BAI to make separate levy orders for different categories of broadcaster. Separate levies can be imposed on public service, commercial or community broadcasters and on particular classes of broadcasting contractors.[117]

[8.53] The provision for the imposition of different levies on different broadcasters highlights a potential difficulty for the BAI in the operation of this system. It is axiomatic that any public system for the collection of rates or levies has the potential to impact on persons' property rights and accordingly must operate in a fair and proportionate manner. However, it must also be borne in mind that the imposition of burdens on broadcasters by a statutory body may also engage the freedom of expression rights of those broadcasters. After all, a system which favoured one broadcaster, or one category of broadcaster, could, depending on the circumstances, be regarded as discriminating between different forms of expression. This is significant because, while the courts tend to be reluctant to entertain challenges to taxes or levies on property rights grounds except in the most egregious cases,[118] a more searching standard of scrutiny would seem appropriate in relation to allegations that one form of expression or category of speaker was being treated more favourably or less favourably than another. Thus, it is important that any levy be calculated and applied in an objectively justifiable and proportionate manner.[119]

[8.54] A levy order must be laid before each House of the Oireachtas by the BAI as soon as may be after it is made. Either House of the Oireachtas may, by resolution passed

---

114. Broadcasting Act 2009, s 34(1).
115. Broadcasting Act 2009, s 33(1).
116. Broadcasting Act 2009, s 33(4).
117. Broadcasting Act 2009, s 33(2).
118. See, for example, O'Hanlon J's comments in *Madigan v Attorney General* [1986] ILRM 136, 151 that 'it has been recognized, both in our own jurisdiction and in the United States, where the constitutional guarantees are closely analogous to those provided by the Irish Constitution, that tax laws are in a category of their own, and that very considerable latitude must be allowed to the legislature in the enormously complex task of organising and directing the financial affairs of the State'.
119. See the detailed provisions of the Broadcasting Act 2009 (S 33) Levy Order 2010 (SI 7/2010).

within 21 sitting days after the day on which a levy order was laid before it, pass a resolution annulling the order. Any such annulment of a levy order takes effect immediately on the passing of the resolution concerned but does not affect anything that was done under the order before the passing of the resolution.[120]

Broadcasting codes and rules

[8.55] The Act requires the BAI to create and to periodically revise rules[121] and codes of conduct[122] with which broadcasters must comply.[123] These instruments are drawn up by the BAI following a consultation process during which a draft of the proposed document is made available for inspection[124] before being presented to the Minister[125] and laid before the Oireachtas.[126] Either House of the Oireachtas may pass a resolution annulling the proposed code within 21 days.[127]

[8.56] Broadcasting rules must concern the matters identified in s 43 of the Act. These include rules relating to the daily and hourly limits on advertising[128] and maximum advertising periods,[129] rules concerning the promotion of the understanding and enjoyment of content by the visual or hearing impaired,[130] rules concerning exclusive rights and short news reports in television broadcasting,[131] and the rules governing all media services and all on-demand audiovisual media services laid down by Chapters IIA and IV of the Audiovisual Media Services Directive, respectively.[132]

[8.57] The BAI appears to enjoy a wider discretion in relation to the content and focus of broadcasting codes. Although the Act identifies a number of specific areas such as, for example, the broadcast coverage of news and current affairs, the BAI's basic power to create codes is expressed in more general terms as concerned with 'governing standards and practice to be observed by broadcasters'.[133] In preparing a code, the BAI must have regard to the degree of harm or offence likely to be caused by the inclusion of any particular sort of material in programmes generally, or in programmes of a

---

120. It should be noted that this power has already provoked controversy with the Joint Oireachtas Committee on Communications, Energy and Natural Resources voting unanimously to annul a levy order put laid down by the BAI. See, for example, 'Ryan to face committee as broadcasting levy rejected' (2010) *The Irish Times*, 4 March.
121. Broadcasting Act 2009, s 43(1).
122. Broadcasting Act 2009, s 42(2).
123. Broadcasting Act 2009, ss 42(6) and 43(5).
124. Broadcasting Act 2009, s 44.
125. Broadcasting Act 2009, s 45(1).
126. Broadcasting Act 2009, s 45(2)(a).
127. Broadcasting Act 2009, s 45(2)(b).
128. Broadcasting Act 2009, s 43(1)(a).
129. Broadcasting Act 2009, s 43(1)(b).
130. Broadcasting Act 2009, s 43(1)(c).
131. Broadcasting Act 2009, s 43(4); Directive 97/36/EC (Audiovisual Media Services Directive), Ch V.
132. Broadcasting Act 2009, s 43(4).
133. Broadcasting Act 2009, s 42(1).

particular description;[134] the likely size and composition of the potential audience for programmes of a particular description;[135] the likely expectation of the audience as to the nature of a programme's content and the extent to which the nature of a programme's content can be brought to the attention of potential members of the audience;[136] the likelihood of persons who are unaware of the nature of a programme's content being unintentionally exposed, by their own actions, to that content;[137] the desirability of securing that the content of a broadcasting service identifies when there is a change affecting the nature of the service that is being watched or listened to and, in particular, a change that is relevant to the application of the codes set under this section;[138] and the desirability of maintaining the independence of editorial control over programme content.[139]

Broadcasters' duties and rights

[8.58] Section 39 imposes specific statutory obligation on broadcasters in relation to the manner and content of their coverage. This plainly represents an interference with their freedom of expression. It could also be argued to interfere with the more general freedom of expression of citizens on the basis that it prevents broadcasters from, for example, advocating a particular viewpoint which a citizen or citizens may share, presenting an individual's expression in a particular format where that could be adjudged to be partial, or from providing a platform for individual expression where that individual's speech, however honestly held or well intentioned, does not meet the Act's or the BAI's standards of fairness. These restrictions, while primarily affecting the format or structure of a broadcaster's output, do have the potential to influence editorial decisions concerning the content of what is or is not broadcast. Thus, while the United States Supreme Court has accepted that broadcasting regulations of this type may be justified on the basis of 'the public's First Amendment interest in receiving a balanced presentation of views on diverse matters of public concern',[140] it has nonetheless struck down federal restrictions on partisan editorial comment by broadcasters on the basis, in part, that such comment is a 'form of speech ... that lies at the heart of First Amendment protection'.[141]

[8.59] However, the obligations set out by s 39 appear to reflect the understanding of media expression as an instrumental rather than a deontological value.[142] The majority of the requirements laid down by s 39 appear capable of being justified, at least in theory, as directed towards ensuring that the contribution of broadcasters to the public's

---

134.   Broadcasting Act 2009, s 42(3)(a).
135.   Broadcasting Act 2009, s 42(3)(b).
136.   Broadcasting Act 2009, s 42(3)(c).
137.   Broadcasting Act 2009, s 42(3)(d).
138.   Broadcasting Act 2009, s 42(3)(e).
139.   Broadcasting Act 2009, s 42(3)(f).
140.   *FCC v League of Women Voters Of California* (1984) 468 US 364, 380.
141.   *FCC v League of Women Voters Of California* (1984) 468 US 364, 381 .
142.   See **[1.29]**.

understanding of, and discussion of, matters of public importance meets certain minimum standards of fairness and objectivity. As discussed in **Ch 2** and elsewhere in the book, this would seem to accord with the text of Article 40.6.1°(i) and with the Article 10 jurisprudence of the European Court of Human Rights, which emphasises the importance of the media's contribution to democratic society. Broadcasters enjoy the protection of the Constitution and European Convention on Human Rights not because of what they are but because of what they do. It thus seems justifiable in theory for the Oireachtas to provide for some degree of regulation of the way in which the broadcasters perform this socially useful function.[143] This view might also be thought to derive some support from the way in which the comparative lack of regulation of this area in the United States seems not to have produced the elevated standards of discussion and knowledge on matters of public importance which the efficient free marketplace of ideas was supposed to create.

[8.60] In this regard, it may be relevant to note that the obligation to be objective and impartial does not require a broadcaster to treat different views with absolute equality.[144] Furthermore, in so far as the argument is made that such regulation restricts the freedom of expression of individuals, it should be borne in mind that the Irish Supreme Court has held that individuals do not have a right to require broadcasters to facilitate the dissemination of their views[145] (although it is also impermissible for them to be denied access on arbitrary or unreasonable grounds).[146] In general, broadcasters enjoy a relatively broad discretion in complying with the statutory duties in this area, with which the courts will not interfere once it can be shown that the duty to act impartially has been discharged by the broadcaster.[147]

[8.61] Thus, it would seem that, despite their impact on freedom of expression, the obligations imposed on broadcasters by s 39 are not – in principle – problematic from a constitutional or Convention perspective.

[8.62] Section 39(1) states that:

> Every broadcaster shall ensure that—
>
> (a) all news broadcast by the broadcaster is reported and presented in an objective and impartial manner and without any expression of the broadcaster's own views,

---

143. Although, of course, the content of such regulations and the way in which they operate could give rise to challenge were they to operate in an arbitrary, unfair, disproportionate or over broad manner.

144. *Green Party v RTÉ* [2003] 1 IR 558.

145. *State (Lynch) v Cooney* [1982] IR 337, 361. This does not mean that an individual, however, could not bring a challenge where they had been denied access in breach of their constitutional rights. See, for example, *O'Toole v RTÉ* [1993] ILRM 458.

146. *State (Lynch) v Cooney* [1982] IR 337. See similar decisions of other courts in *Benjamin v Minister for Information* [2001] 1 WLR 1040; *Fernando v Sri Lanka Broadcasting Corporation* (1996) 1 BHRC 104.

147. *Green Party v RTÉ* [2003] 1 IR 558.

(b)   the broadcast treatment of current affairs, including matters which are either of public controversy or the subject of current public debate, is fair to all interests concerned and that the broadcast matter is presented in an objective and impartial manner and without any expression of his or her own views, except that should it prove impracticable in relation to a single broadcast to apply this paragraph, two or more related broadcasts may be considered as a whole, if the broadcasts are transmitted within a reasonable period of each other,

(c)   in the case of sound broadcasters a minimum of—

  (i)   not less than 20 per cent of the broadcasting time, and

  (ii)   if the broadcasting service is provided for more than 12 hours in any one day, two hours of broadcasting time between 07.00 hours and 19.00 hours, is devoted to the broadcasting of news and current affairs programmes, unless a derogation from this requirement is authorised by the Authority under subsection (3),

(d)   anything which may reasonably be regarded as causing harm or offence, or as being likely to promote, or incite to, crime or as tending to undermine the authority of the State, is not broadcast by the broadcaster, and

(e)   in programmes broadcast by the broadcaster, and in the means employed to make such programmes, the privacy of any individual is not unreasonably encroached upon.

[8.63] Subsection (5) also provides a specific obligation in relation to coverage of matters of interest to broadcasters. It requires a broadcaster to ensure that the broadcast treatment of any proposal on broadcasting policy which is of public controversy or the subject of current public debate and which is being considered by the Government or the Minister shall be reported and presented in an objective and impartial manner. However, broadcasters are permitted to express their own views in relation to such proposals.[148]

[8.64] To assist in ensuring that broadcasters comply with these statutory requirements, the BAI is required to prepare, and from time to time, revise, in accordance with this a broadcasting code of standards. This code must include requirements that all news broadcast by a broadcaster is reported and presented in an objective and impartial manner and without any expression of the broadcaster's own views;[149] that the broadcast treatment of current affairs is fair to all interests concerned and is presented in an objective and impartial manner and without any expression of the broadcaster's own views;[150] that anything being likely to promote, or incite to, crime, or undermine the authority of the State,[151] is not broadcast by a broadcaster; and that a broadcaster does not, in the allocation of time for transmitting party political broadcasts, give an unfair preference to any political party.[152]

---

148.   Broadcasting Act 2009, s 39(6).
149.   Broadcasting Act 2009, s 42(2)(a).
150.   Broadcasting Act 2009, s 42(2)(b).
151.   Broadcasting Act 2009, s 42(2)(c).
152.   Broadcasting Act 2009, s 42(2)(e).

[8.65] To assist the Compliance Committee with monitoring compliance with these duties and investigating any complaints made to it, broadcasters are also obliged to record every broadcast made by the broadcaster and every item of programme material supplied by him or her under a broadcasting contract or a content provision contract.[153] A persistent failure to do so may constitute a serious breach of contract sufficient to justify the termination of a contract.[154]

Objectivity and impartiality

[8.66] Compliance by broadcasters with the Code of Programme Standards is dealt with by the Compliance Committee of the BAI. The Committee publishes its decisions and examples of decisions applying the provisions regarding impartiality are considered elsewhere in the book as well the possibility of appeals from such decisions.

Privacy

[8.67] Section 39(1)(e) imposes a statutory obligation on the broadcaster to ensure that the privacy of any individual is not unreasonably encroached upon, either in terms of the content of a broadcast or the way in which it is made. In addition, s 42(2)(d) specifies that the broadcasting codes which the BAI is obliged to create and keep under revision must contain provisions to similar effect.

[8.68] Clarke J held in *Cogley v RTÉ* that this gave rise to 'an arguable entitlement to ensure that the Broadcasting Authority does not unreasonably interfere with their privacy in the course of making and broadcasting programmes',[155] although the court presumably had in mind an entitlement to ensure the Authority in question ensures that broadcasters do not unreasonably interfere with individual's privacy. As Clarke J also pointed out in *Cogley v RTÉ*,[156] which Dunne J echoed in *Herrity v Associated Newspapers*,[157] this obligation is not absolute but requires broadcasters only to refrain from unreasonable encroachment. Given the fact that the language of reasonableness used in this section broadly compares to that applied to the constitutional right to privacy which vests in all citizens, this section may be regarded as a statutory recognition of this constitutional entitlement with which, accordingly, it is likely to have a substantial overlap. In particular, as the constitutional right is directly enforceable against private persons or organisations, there seem unlikely to be many, if any, situations in which it would be necessary or advisable for a person to take action against the BAI for an alleged breach of privacy rather than against the offending broadcaster in question. Nonetheless, this section may usefully supplement a plaintiff's case in any such action against a broadcaster for an alleged breach of privacy. The law applying to such actions is covered in detail elsewhere in this book.

---

153. Broadcasting Act 2009, s 40(1).
154. *Radio One Limerick v IRTC* [1997] 2 IR 291.
155. *Cogley v RTÉ* [2005] 4 IR 79, 90.
156. *Cogley v RTÉ* [2005] 4 IR 79, 90.
157. *Herrity v Associated Newspapers* [2008] IEHC 249.

Offensive material

[8.69] One of the obligations imposed by s 39 is to ensure that broadcasters do not broadcast 'anything which may reasonably be regarded as causing harm or offence'. The imposition of restrictions based on the objective of avoiding offence is controversial as a matter of free speech theory, as it suggests that the expression of one party may be limited by the sensitivity of another.[158] For theories that favour the promotion of 'uninhibited, robust and wide-open debate',[159] this is a problematic proposition. Nonetheless the courts have upheld the imposition of similar restrictions on broadcasters in various other jurisdictions.[160] The most recent example of such a decision is that of Blair J in *Gaunt v Ofcom*[161] where a radio presenter claimed that a determination that he had breached the provisions of the UK code governing offensive and harmful broadcasts contravened his Article 10 rights. The court accepted that the definition of harmful or offensive material was 'elusive' and that 'the concept of harmful and/or offensive material needs to be moderated in the light of Article 10 and the domestic and Strasbourg case law'. However, it concluded that the presenter's rights had not been breached in this case on the grounds that his behaviour was gratuitous and beyond what was contextually justified:

> His freedom of expression may not however extend to gratuitous offensive insult or abuse, nor, we think, to repeated abusive shouting which serves to express no real content. We take gratuitously offensive insult or abuse to comprise offensive insult or abuse which has no contextual content or justification.

This does, however, suggest that there may be scope for a broadcaster to challenge an adverse determination under this section where the standards applied by the regulatory body are vague, imprecise or show insufficient regard for the broadcaster's freedom of expression.

Authority of the State

[8.70] This obligation on broadcasters derives in part from the Constitution[162] and is discussed in more detail elsewhere.

Advertising

[8.71] The 2009 Act regulates a number of aspects of broadcast advertising. Many of its provisions reflect the terms of Arts 9, 10, 11, 19–25 of the Audiovisual Media Services Directive which both places restrictions on domestic regulation of advertising and sets out certain minimum requirements for advertisers to comply with. This is an area of particular interest to broadcasters as such regulations necessarily restrict their ability to generate income. As with its predecessor legislation, the Act represents an attempt to

---

158. See, for example, Feinberg, *Offense to Others* (OUP, 1988).
159. *New York Times v Sullivan* 376 US 254 (1964).
160. *R (Pro-Life Alliance) v BBC* [2004] 1 AC 185; *FCC v Pacifica Foundation* 438 US 726 (1978).
161. *Gaunt v Ofcom* [2010] EWHC 1756 (QB).
162. See *O'Toole v RTÉ* [1993] ILRM 458.

strike a balance between the different interests described by Keane J in *Radio One Limerick*:

> While advertising, of its nature, doubtless has beneficial aspects from the consumer's point of view, as well as providing an essential source of revenue for the operator, the policy of the legislation is clearly to ensure that, in the interests of listeners and viewers, a reasonable balance is struck between such advertising and the provision of news, entertainment and other programmes.[163]

[8.72] Section 41(2) provides that the total daily time for broadcasting advertisements in a sound broadcasting service must not exceed a maximum of 15 per cent of the total daily broadcasting time and the maximum time to be given to advertisements in any hour shall not exceed a maximum of 10 minutes. However, the BAI is also vested with a power under s 43(1), subject to the requirements of s 41(2), to revise the rules regulating the total daily time that shall be allowed for the transmission of advertisements and teleshopping material on a broadcasting service, as well as those that determine the maximum period that shall be allowed in any given hour for the transmission of advertisements and teleshopping material. The BAI can develop different rules for different categories of broadcaster.

[8.73] Advertising is not defined in this Part of the Act but the courts have applied an 'ordinary common sense' approach in situations where a dispute has arisen as to whether particular material constituted advertising. Thus, conducting outside broadcasts from particular commercial premises where those premises were selected on the basis of their expenditure on advertisements was held to constitute advertising in *Radio One Limerick*.[164]

[8.74] The BAI is also entitled to provide guidelines on what constitutes advertising and commercial communications in its rules and codes.

[8.75] This area is also subject to regulation under Audiovisual Media Services Directive. As the purpose of the Directive is to ensure the effective operation of the internal market for television broadcasting services by ensuring the free movement of broadcasting services throughout the EU, there is an obvious reason for the Directive to provide for harmonised standards in relation to advertising.[165] Thus Art 23(1) of the Directive provides that the proportion of television advertising spots and teleshopping spots within a given clock hour shall not exceed 20 per cent.

[8.76] This 12-minute ceiling was given effect to by the BAI after a consultation process[166] when, in purported exercise of its powers under s 43, it introduced new Rules

---

163. *Radio One Limerick v IRTC* [1997] 2 IR 291, 317.
164. *Radio One Limerick v IRTC* [1997] 2 IR 291.
165. Directive 2010/13/EU of the European Parliament and of the Council of 10 March 2010 on the coordination of certain provisions laid down by law, regulation or administrative action in Member States concerning the provision of audiovisual media services (Audiovisual Media Services Directive)
166. Broadcasting Act 2009, s 44.

on Advertising and Teleshopping (Daily and Hourly Limits). Rule 4.1 provides that the total daily time for broadcasting advertising and teleshopping spots on television shall not exceed a maximum of 18 per cent of the total broadcast day and that the time to be given to advertising and teleshopping spots in any clock hour shall not exceed a maximum of 12 minutes. However, the transmission of films made for television or cinema, or television news and current affairs programmes may only be interrupted by advertising and teleshopping segments once for each scheduled period of at least 30 minutes.[167]

[8.77] Rule 4.4 provides for a lower period in relation to commercial radio broadcasters with the total daily time for broadcasting advertising and teleshopping spots being limited to a maximum of 15 per cent of the total broadcast day and the time to be given to advertising in any clock hour confined to a maximum of 10 minutes. Advertising on community radio, meanwhile, is limited to six minutes in any hour.[168]

[8.78] Any broadcasting code prepared or revised by the BAI under s 42 must also provide that advertising, teleshopping material, sponsorship and other forms of commercial promotion employed in any broadcasting service, in particular advertising and other such activities which relate to matters likely to be of direct or indirect interest to children, protect the interests of children having particular regard to the general public health interests of children;[169] and that advertising, teleshopping material, sponsorship and other forms of commercial promotion employed in any broadcasting service protect the interests of the audience.[170]

[8.79] The current code is the General Commercial Communications Code which has been effective since 10 June 2010. This states that one of its primary objectives is to ensure that the public can be confident that commercial communications are legal, honest, truthful and decent. Many of its provisions are accordingly directed to ensuring the accuracy of advertisements, and to preventing the use of advertising techniques which might tend to mislead or confuse members of the public. All commercial communications shall be prepared with a sense of responsibility both to the individual and to society and shall not prejudice the interests of either. All commercial communications shall be legal, honest, decent, truthful and protect the interests of the audience. Thus, for example, surreptitious, subliminal and misleading commercial communications are prohibited.[171] Product placement is subject to strict controls.[172] Furthermore, all pertinent details of an offer contained in a commercial communication shall be stated in a clear and understandable manner. Disclaimers and asterisked or footnoted information which is included or required to be included in commercial communications cannot contradict more prominent aspects of the message and must be

---

167. Rule 4.4 of the BAI's General Commerical Communications Code (June 2010).
168. Rule 4.5.
169. Broadcasting Act 2009, s 42(2)(g).
170. Broadcasting Act 2009, s 42(2)(h).
171. Rule 3.3.
172. Rule 7.

located and presented in such a manner as to be clearly visible or audible.[173] Broadcasters are also directed to be mindful of the potential for sound effects in commercial communications to distract and/or alarm viewers and listeners. Particular care shall be taken when including sound effects such as sirens, horns, ringing phones and screeching tyres. They shall not be included at the beginning of a commercial communication.[174]

[8.80] However, the code also clarifies that certain common advertising techniques are permissible. For example, comparative commercial communications which contain direct or implied comparisons with other products or services may be broadcast provided they objectively compare products or services meeting the same needs or intended for the same purpose, and that they are not compared in a way that confers an unfair advantage on the advertised product. Points of comparison must be based on facts that can be substantiated.[175]

[8.81] Regulation 8 of the European Communities (Audiovisual Media Services) Regulations 2010[176] allows for product placement in particular circumstances. It may be used by broadcasters in relation to on-demand services that are cinematographic works, films and series made for audiovisual media services, sports programmes or light entertainment programmes (but not children's programmes); or where there is no payment for the placement of the product but only the provision of certain goods or services free of charge with a view to their inclusion in a programme. Any such placement must be appropriately identified and cannot influence the content of a programme in such a way as to affect the responsibility and editorial independence of the media service provider. Placements may not give undue prominence to the product in question and may not directly encourage the purchase or rental of goods or services.

Non-commercial advertising

[8.82] Section 41 also imposes a prohibition on the broadcast of particular forms of non-commercial advertising. Section 41(3) provides that a broadcaster shall not broadcast an advertisement which is directed towards a political end[177] or which has any relation to an industrial dispute, while s 41(4) prohibits the broadcasting of an advertisement which addresses the issue of the merits or otherwise of adhering to any religious faith or belief or of becoming a member of any religion or religious organisation.

[8.83] These sections replace (and substantially restate) the prohibition on advertisements relating to political, religious or industrial relations disputes which was previously provided for by s 10(3) of the Radio and Television Act 1988. As discussed in more detail elsewhere in this book, the religious aspect of this prohibition was

---

173. Rule 3.4.
174. Rule 3.6.
175. Rule 3.5.
176. SI 258/2010.
177. This does not prevent the broadcast of party political broadcasts or broadcasts at the request of the Referendum Commission. See Broadcasting Act 2009, s 41(5) and (6).

challenged before both the Irish courts and the European Court of Human Rights on the grounds, inter alia, that it contravened the claimant's freedom of expression. This claim was rejected by the Irish courts[178] and the court in Strasbourg[179] on the basis that there were legitimate grounds for regulating religious advertising. The European Court of Human Rights was particularly concerned with the 'country-specific religious sensitivities'[180] that applied in Ireland, but all courts agreed that it was legitimate for the Oireachtas to restrict religious advertising so as to avoid the dangers that religious advertising might tend to inflame and offence public opinion, and lead to a situation in which wealthy religious groups would be able to exert a pervasive influence on broadcast content.

[8.84] However, the fact that the religious aspect of the prohibition was held to be in accordance with the Constitution and Convention does not necessarily mean that the prohibitions on advertising relating to political ends or industrial relations disputes would survive a similar challenge. This is particularly the case when it is borne in mind that the European Court of Human Rights in *Murphy* specifically noted that the State enjoyed a wider margin of appreciation in relation to the regulation of religious speech than it would where the subject-matter of the regulation in question was political expression.[181] The argument that the prohibition on political advertising may be suspect also derives additional support from the recent decisions of the European Court of Human Rights in cases like *Vgt v Switzerland (No 2)*[182] and *TV Vest v Norway*[183] where it held that a total ban on political advertising was incompatible with the obligations of contracting states under Article 10. As against that, the House of Lords warned against the democratic dangers of allowing removing restrictions on political advertising in *R (Animal Defenders International) v Secretary of State for Culture, Media and Sport*:[184]

> The fundamental rationale of the democratic process is that if competing views, opinions and policies are publicly debated and exposed to public scrutiny the good will over time drive out the bad and the true prevail over the false. It must be assumed that, given time, the public will make a sound choice when, in the course of the democratic process, it has the right to choose. But it is highly desirable that the playing field of debate should be so far as practicable level. This is achieved where, in public discussion, differing views are expressed, contradicted, answered and debated. It is the duty of broadcasters to achieve this object in an impartial way by presenting balanced programmes in which all lawful views may be ventilated. It is not achieved if political parties can, in proportion to their resources, buy unlimited opportunities to advertise in the most effective media, so that elections become little more than an auction. Nor is it achieved if well endowed interests which are not political parties are able to use the power of the

---

178. *Murphy v IRTC* [1998] 2 ILRM 321; [1999] 1 IR 12.
179. *Murphy v Ireland* (2004) 38 EHRR 13.
180. *Murphy v Ireland* (2004) 38 EHRR 13, para 73.
181. *Murphy v Ireland* (2004) 38 EHRR 13, para 67.
182. *Vgt v Switzerland (No 2)* [2009] ECHR 1025.
183. *TV Vest v Norway* (2009) 48 EHRR 51.
184. *R (Animal Defenders International) v Secretary of State for Culture, Media and Sport* [2008] UKHL 15.

purse to give enhanced prominence to views which may be true or false, attractive to progressive minds or unattractive, beneficial or injurious. The risk is that objects which are essentially political may come to be accepted by the public not because they are shown in public debate to be right but because, by dint of constant repetition, the public has been conditioned to accept them. The rights of others which a restriction on the exercise of the right to free expression may properly be designed to protect must, in my judgment, include a right to be protected against the potential mischief of partial political advertising.[185]

Lord Bingham indicated a level of disagreement with the court in Strasbourg, noting that he 'd[id] not think the full strength of this argument was deployed in VgT'. This matter is discussed in further detail elsewhere in the book. However, it is noteworthy that media organisations have begun to criticise this prohibition with greater force in recent times.[186] While this is almost certainly due to the obvious attractions in the current economic climate of securing additional sources of potential revenue by having this ban removed, this is an area where the prospects of a challenge being brought in the future seem reasonably high.

Advertising of specific products

[8.85] The BAI General Communications Code sets out a number of rules and regulations that apply only to particular products which are regarded as giving rise to specific issues of public interest or concern.

ALCOHOL

[8.86] Rule 8.1 of the Code applies to the advertising of alcohol. It states that advertisements for alcoholic drinks may not encourage immoderate consumption of alcohol or present abstinence or moderation in a negative light. These advertisements also may not claim that alcohol has therapeutic qualities, that it is a stimulant, a sedative, tranquilizer or a means of resolving personal conflicts or create the impression that consumption of alcohol contributes to sexual attraction, success or social success. Alcohol also cannot be linked to enhanced physical performance or to driving. Emphasis may not be placed on high alcohol content as being a positive quality of the beverages.

MEDICAL MATTERS

[8.87] Advertisements relating to medical matters such as products or services are subject to very strict regulation by the BAI.[187] They may not contain recommendations

---

185. *R (Animal Defenders International) v Secretary of State for Culture, Media and Sport* [2008] UKHL 15, para 28.
186. See, for example, 'Independent Broadcasters may consider legal challenge to ban on political advertising' (press release from the Independent Broadcasters of Ireland), available at www.ibireland.ie.
187. Rule 8.2.

by health professionals or celebrities which could encourage the use of medicines, medical treatments, products and services, or cosmetic treatments and services. They also cannot contain statements which give the impression of professional advice, or recommendations made by persons who are presented, whether actually or by implication, as being qualified to give such advice or recommendation. Advertisements may not advertise any products intended to treat serious conditions which should receive the attention of a registered medical practitioner, and cannot contain offers to diagnose, or treat by correspondence, any serious complaint, condition, symptom or disease.

[8.88] Such advertisements must not contain the unwarranted and indiscriminate use of such words as 'safe', 'without risk', 'harmless', or similar terms. False claims cannot be made that a product or treatment is in the form in which it occurs in nature or falsely claim that its value lies in its being 'natural'. Exaggerated claims are also impermissible, as are references to fictional medical establishments or bodies.

[8.89] Advertisements may not be calculated to induce fear on the part of the viewer or listener that he or she may, without treatment, suffer, or suffer more severely, from any serious complaint, condition, symptom, or disease. They also cannot directly or indirectly encourage the unnecessary, indiscriminate, irrational or excessive use of medicines, medical treatments, products and services or cosmetic treatments and services.

[8.90] Advertisements for surgical cosmetic treatments and services may contain the address of the service provider and factual descriptions of services available but shall not contain anything which could be deemed an encouragement to use the treatment or service. Information detailing special offers, discounts, references to credit facilities available or any other promotional offers intended to encourage the use of cosmetic treatments or services of this nature are not permitted. Similar restrictions apply to advertisements for hypnosis, hypnotherapy, psychology, psychoanalysis or psychiatry.

[8.91] Advertisements for products or services to assist people to quit smoking must clearly indicate that the product or service is only effective in conjunction with the positive application of the consumer's will power.[188]

SLIMMING PRODUCTS[189]

[8.92] Advertisements cannot contain any offer of a treatment, product or service for slimming which is in itself likely to lead to harmful effects, and is not directly associated with the following of a properly designed diet, and does not clearly state the manner in which slimming will be achieved.

---

188. Rule 8.3.
189. Rule 8.6.

FINANCIAL SERVICES AND PRODUCTS[190]

[8.93] Advertising for financial services and products shall be presented in terms which do not mislead, whether by exaggeration, omission or in any other way. They must also comply with relevant Irish and European legislation and with the rules, regulations and codes of practice issued from time to time by the competent authorities responsible for the implementation of such legislation, notably the Financial Regulator.

BETTING SERVICES[191]

[8.94] The Code confirms that advertising for betting services is permissible. However, such advertisements can contain the address of the service provider and factual descriptions of services available but may not contain anything which could be deemed to be an encouragement to bet. Information detailing special offers, discounts, inducements to visit a bookmakers (including online), references to betting odds available or any promotional offer intended to encourage the use of betting services are impermissible.

PREMIUM-RATE TELECOMMUNICATION SERVICES[192]

[8.95] Advertisements for premium-rate telecommunication services shall clearly state all charges for accessing these services in terms which do not mislead, whether by exaggeration, omission or in any other way.

FORTUNE TELLERS AND OTHER PSYCHIC SERVICES[193]

[8.96] Advertising for fortune tellers or psychic services are only permitted where the service is evidently for entertainment purposes only and this is made clear in the communication. Claims that future events may be predicted, other than as a matter of opinion, are prohibited. Claims to make contact with the dead or claims pertaining to matters of health, cures, curing or healing are also not permitted.

FOODS FOR CHILDREN

[8.97] Section 42(4) specifically permits the BAI to create a broadcasting code which prohibits the advertising of a particular class or classes of foods and beverages considered by the BAI to be the subject of public concern in respect of the general public health interests of children, in particular those which contain fat, trans-fatty acids, salts or sugars. This power has not, at present been exercised by the BAI although Ireland is obliged by Art 9.2 of the Audiovisual Media Services Directive to 'encourage media service providers to develop codes of conduct' on this issue.

---

190.   Rule 8.7.
191.   Rule 8.8.
192.   Rule 8.9.
193.   Rule 8.10.

[8.98] However, the current Children's Commercial Communications Code, which took effect on 1 June 2010, imposes a number of specific restrictions on the way in which food products can be advertised to children.[194] The use of celebrities is heavily restricted. Advertising aimed at children must be responsible in the manner in which food and drink are portrayed and should not encourage an unhealthy lifestyle or unhealthy eating or drinking habits such as immoderate consumption, excessive or compulsive eating. Advertisements must not contain any misleading or incorrect information about the nutritional value of a product or make misleading or incorrect comparisons between foods. They also must not imply that particular foods are a substitute or replacement for fruit or vegetables. Advertisements for confectionary products – defined by the Code to include sugar, honey, preserves, chocolate-covered bars (excluding biscuits), non-chocolate confectionary such as cereal bars, artificial sweeteners, and carbonated drinks (both diet and non-diet) – must display an acoustic or visual message stating that 'snacking on sugary foods and drinks can damage teeth.'

[8.99] Furthermore, all children's advertisements for fast food products, outlets or brands must display an acoustic or visual message stating 'should be eaten in moderation and as part of a balanced diet'. 'Fast food' is defined as 'food coming under the recognised character of fast food and/or inexpensive cooked food which is prepared and served quickly and is readily accessible for purchase by children'. It is not the intention of the definition to include prepared and convenience foods or food which is purchased for preparation and cooking in the home. The term 'fast food' is defined by the BAI to refer to the speed and ease with which the food can be procured and consumed rather than the time taken to eat it.

Right of reply

[8.100] Part 4 of the Act establishes a statutory right of reply in relation to contentious material published by a broadcaster. This was an obligation under Art 28 of the Audiovisual Media Services Directive which further requires Member States to ensure that 'the actual exercise of the right of reply or equivalent remedies is not hindered by the imposition of unreasonable terms or conditions'. This may be relevant where an applicant feels that their right is being frustrated by the actions or omissions of the broadcaster in question, or the BAI.

[8.101] The 2009 Act thus requires broadcasters to establish codes and procedures for dealing with complaints, and provides for complaints to be made to and investigated by the Compliance Committee of the BAI, where appropriate. The intention of the Oireachtas in requiring the establishment of this type of relatively complicated complaints system would seem to be in part to encourage and facilitate the resolution of disputes without recourse to the legal process. It would also appear to be intended to promote balance and accuracy in a broadcaster's treatment of an issue by providing a right for a person or persons whose honour or reputation has been impugned by an assertion of incorrect facts or information to respond to such assertions.

---

194.   Rule 11.

[8.102] While it might be argued that the requirement to provide a right of reply (or, more accurately in an Irish context, to provide a reply, or statement of correction) represents an interference with a broadcaster's freedom of expression and, in particular, editorial control, it seems likely that the imposition of this statutory obligation would be regarded by a court as justifiable in principle as a mechanism for protecting the right to a good name of the affected individual, as well as a means of ensuring the accuracy, balance and responsible journalism expected under the democratic conception of media freedom. This is particularly the case where the right is limited, as here, to those whose reputation or honour has been impugned. It is also instructive to note that the United States Supreme Court has previously upheld a similar form of statutory interference with broadcasters' freedom on the basis that, even under the free market of ideas theory, it is legitimate for the state to take steps to ensure access to the marketplace for all.[195]

[8.103] Section 49 provides for the statutory right of reply. The right applies to any person whose honour or reputation has been impugned by an assertion of incorrect facts or information in a broadcast.[196] The BAI is required to prepare a scheme for the exercise of this right of reply.[197] This scheme must ensure that a right of reply is broadcast within a reasonable time period subsequent to the request for a right of reply being made,[198] and at a time and in a manner appropriate to the broadcast to which the request refers.[199] It must also state to what extent the information contained in the original broadcast was incorrect or misleading.[200] However, the reply will be limited to factual assertions that are necessary to rectify what would otherwise be an incomplete or distorting assertion.[201]

[8.104] Any scheme shall be laid before each House of the Oireachtas by the Minister as soon as may be after it is prepared. Either House of the Oireachtas may pass a resolution to annul the scheme within 21 days.[202]

[8.105] The scheme must be published on the BAI website. The BAI must also review and report to the Minister on the operation, effectiveness and impact of a scheme not later than three years from the date on which it comes into operation and every five years thereafter or at such time as may be requested by the Minister.[203] A copy of a report under the subsection shall be laid by the Minister before each House of the Oireachtas as soon as may be after it has been made to him or her.[204]

---

195. *Red Lion Broadcasting Co v FCC* 395 US 367 (1969).
196. Broadcasting Act 2009, s 49(2).
197. Broadcasting Act 2009, s 49(3).
198. Broadcasting Act 2009, s 49(5)(a)(i).
199. Broadcasting Act 2009, s 49(5)(a)(ii).
200. Broadcasting Act 2009, s 49(5)(b)(i).
201. Broadcasting Act 2009, s 49(5)(b)(ii).
202. Broadcasting Act 2009, s 49(26).
203. Broadcasting Act 2009, s 49(27).
204. Broadcasting Act 2009, s 49(28).

[8.106] The first stage for a person who wishes to exercise a right of reply is to make a request in writing addressed to the broadcaster concerned. This request must state that it is being made under s 49,[205] and must contain sufficient particulars to enable the broadcaster to identify, by the taking of reasonable steps, which asserted incorrect facts impugned the honour or reputation of the requester.[206] If the person making the request requires the right of reply to be given in a particular form or manner, that must also be specified in the written request.[207]

[8.107] A request for a right of reply must be made within 21 days of the making of the broadcast, although this time limit can be extended with the agreement of both parties.[208] Where a request is, in the opinion of the broadcaster, made in good faith and is not of a frivolous or vexatious nature, by a member of the public, the broadcaster is obliged to give due and adequate consideration to it.[209] Where a request is made, the relevant broadcaster must decide whether to grant or refuse the request within 10 days,[210] and notify the requester in writing of that decision.[211] Where notice of a decision is not given to the requester within 10 days, a decision refusing to grant the request is deemed to have been made by the broadcaster.[212]

[8.108] A decision by the broadcaster to grant a request for a right of reply does not constitute an express or implied admission of liability by that broadcaster in any defamation action concerning the material in question, and is not relevant to the determination of liability in the action.[213] Evidence that a broadcaster granted or offered to grant a right of reply to the plaintiff under s 49 in respect of the statement to which the action relates either before the bringing of the action or as soon as practicable thereafter, is admissible in mitigation of damages.[214] However, a defendant who intends to give evidence of this must, at the time of the filing or delivery of the defence to the action, notify the plaintiff in writing of his or her intention to give such evidence.[215]

[8.109] Where a broadcaster refuses to grant the request for a reply, the person who made the original request may make a request in writing to the Compliance Committee of the BAI within 21 days of the decision to refuse,[216] or expiry of the time for a decision, to review the broadcaster's decision.[217] The Committee is directed by s 49(17) to 'endeavour to within 21 days after the receipt of such an application' either affirm the

---

205. Broadcasting Act 2009, s 49(6)(a).
206. Broadcasting Act 2009, s 49(6)(b).
207. Broadcasting Act 2009, s 49(6)(c).
208. Broadcasting Act 2009, s 49(7).
209. Broadcasting Act 2009, s 49(10).
210. Broadcasting Act 2009, s 49(8)(a).
211. Broadcasting Act 2009, s 49(8)(b).
212. Broadcasting Act 2009, s 49(9).
213. Broadcasting Act 2009, s 49(13).
214. Broadcasting Act 2009, s 49(14).
215. Broadcasting Act 2009, s 49(15).
216. Broadcasting Act 2009, s 49(18).
217. Broadcasting Act 2009, s 49(17).

decision, or annul the decision and require the broadcaster concerned to broadcast the Compliance Committee's decision including any correction of inaccurate facts or information relating to the individual concerned within seven days of such decision being communicated to the broadcaster and at a time and in a manner corresponding to that in which the broadcast to which the request relates took place.

[8.110] The Compliance Committee may reject any request for a right of reply. Section 49(21) sets out a non-exhaustive set of grounds upon which the Committee may decline to comply with the request. These are that:

(a) the request is of a frivolous or vexatious nature or was not made in good faith;

(b) a right of reply is manifestly unnecessary owing to the minor significance of the error in the broadcast complained of;

(c) the proposed right of reply cites untrue information or assertions;

(d) the proposed right of reply is a personal opinion;

(e) the proposed right of reply is an assessment or warning against the future conduct of a person;

(f) satisfaction of the proposed right of reply would involve a punishable act;

(g) satisfaction of the proposed right of reply would be harmful or offensive;

(h) satisfaction of the proposed right of reply would render the broadcaster liable to civil law proceedings;

(i) satisfaction of the proposed right of reply would breach a broadcaster's statutory obligation;

(j) satisfaction of the proposed right of reply would breach the terms of a broadcaster's contract with the BAI;

(k) the person who was injured by the contested information has no legally justifiable actual interest in the publication of a right of reply;

(l) the original broadcast also contained a statement from the person affected and such contents are equivalent to a right of reply;

(m) an equivalent editorial correction has been made and the person affected informed;

(n) the content of the proposed right of reply would violate the rights of a third party;

(o) the matter concerned relates to reports on public sessions of the Houses of the Oireachtas or the Courts;

(p) the matter concerned relates to a party political broadcast;

(q) the matter concerned relates to a broadcast by the Referendum Commission under section 3 of the Referendum Act 1998;

(r) the broadcast of a right of reply is not in the public interest; or

(s) the application was not made within the 21 day period specified.

[8.111] Where the Committee decides to investigate the request, it must provide the broadcaster concerned with an opportunity to comment.[218] The broadcaster must, if directed by the Compliance Committee, make available for inspection by the Compliance Committee all records kept by him or her.[219]

[8.112] As soon as may be after they decide on an application to it for a review, the Compliance Committee must send a statement in writing of their decision, and the reasons for it, to the person who made the application, and to the broadcaster concerned.[220]

[8.113] Where the Compliance Committee finds that the broadcaster has failed to comply with a decision under sub-s (17), the Compliance Committee will notify the broadcaster of those findings and give the broadcaster an opportunity to make representations within 10 days, or any longer period agreed, in relation to the notification or remedy for any non-compliance.[221] Where, at the end of that period, the Compliance Committee is of the opinion that the broadcaster concerned has not remedied its non-compliance, the Compliance Committee may make a binding recommendation to the BAI, that it apply to the High Court for such order as may be appropriate in order to ensure compliance.[222] The High Court may, as it thinks fit, on the hearing of the application make an order compelling compliance with the Committee's decision, varying a requirement, or refuse the application.[223]

Complaints

[8.114] Part 4 also provides for a broader complaint system under which complaints may be made by parties who were not directly referred to or implicated by the broadcast in question. Section 48(1) provides a power to the Compliance Committee of the BAI to investigate and decide complaints on the following grounds:

(a)   a complaint that in broadcasting news given by it and specified in the complaint, a broadcaster did not comply with the statutory requirements of objectivity, impartiality and balance, contrary to sections 39(1)(a) and (b);

(b)   a complaint that in broadcasting a programme specified in the complaint, a broadcaster could reasonably be regarded as causing harm or offence, or as being likely to promote, or incite to, crime or as tending to undermine the authority of the State, contrary to in section 39(1)(d);

(c)   a complaint that on an occasion specified in the complaint, there was an unreasonable encroachment on an individual's privacy, contrary to section 39(1)(e);

---

218.   Broadcasting Act 2009, s 49(19).
219.   Broadcasting Act 2009, s 49(11).
220.   Broadcasting Act 2009, s 49(20).
221.   Broadcasting Act 2009, s 49(22).
222.   Broadcasting Act 2009, s 49(23).
223.   Broadcasting Act 2009, s 49(24).

(d)   a complaint that on an occasion specified in the complaint, a broadcaster failed to comply with a provision of a broadcasting code.

A complaint must be made in writing and be made to the Compliance Committee not more than 30 days after the date of the broadcast. Where the complaint relates to two or more unrelated broadcasts, the 30-day period runs from the date of the earlier or earliest, as the case may be, of those broadcasts, whereas it will run from the later or latest broadcast where a complaint relates to two or more related broadcasts.[224]

[8.115] The Compliance Committee may, at their discretion, refer the complaint in the first instance to the broadcaster, for consideration in accordance with a code of practice prepared under s 47(3).[225] The Compliance Committee does not have to investigate a complaint which, in the Committee's opinion, is not made in good faith or is frivolous or vexatious. The Compliance Committee should also not investigate a withdrawn complaint unless it considers that there are special and stated reasons for investigating it.[226]

Broadcaster

[8.116] Where a complaint is made or referred to a broadcaster, s 47 provides that a broadcaster must give due and adequate consideration to it, provided, in the opinion of the broadcaster, the complaint has been made in good faith and is not of a frivolous or vexatious nature. A complaint must be made to the broadcaster not more than 30 days after the date of the broadcast or, in the case of two or more unrelated broadcasts, the date of the earlier or earliest. Where the complaint relates to two or more related broadcasts of which at least two are made on different dates, the later or latest of those dates is the relevant date for the calculation of the 30-day period.[227]

[8.117] Broadcasters must prepare and implement a code of practice for the handling of complaints.[228] The code of practice must make provision for an initial point of contact for complainants, including an email address; a time period within which the broadcaster shall respond to complaints; and the procedures which will be followed by the broadcaster in the resolution of complaints. A copy of this code of practice should be made available on the broadcaster's website.[229] A broadcaster must also keep a record of all complaints made and any replies made to those complaints for a period of two years from the date of receipt of each complaint.[230]

---

224. Broadcasting Act 2009, s 48(2).
225. Broadcasting Act 2009, s 48(3).
226. Broadcasting Act 2009, s 48(13).
227. Broadcasting Act 2009, s 47(2).
228. Broadcasting Act 2009, s 47(3).
229. Broadcasting Act 2009, s 47(4).
230. Broadcasting Act 2009, s 47(7).

Compliance Committee

[8.118] Where the Compliance Committee proposes to investigate a complaint, the Committee must afford to the broadcaster to whom the complaint relates seven days, or a longer specified period, to comment on the complaint.[231] Where the complaint concerns a person employed by the broadcaster or a person commissioned to make that programme, that person may request, for reasons specified by him or her, that the Compliance Committee give him or her a similar opportunity to comment on the complaint. The Compliance Committee must, having considered the reasons so specified, give the person a similar period to comment on the complaint if they are satisfied that the interests of the employee or the prospects of the programme maker obtaining further commissions from the broadcaster concerned, might be adversely affected as a result of the complaint.[232]

[8.119] When the Compliance Committee proposes to consider a complaint that a broadcaster failed to comply with the provision of a broadcasting code concerning advertising, the Compliance Committee shall afford the relevant advertiser seven days or such further period as the Committee allows to comment on the relevant advertisement.[233]

[8.120] Complaints may be considered by the Committee in private.[234] An oral hearing may be held where appropriate.[235] As soon as may be after it decides on a complaint made under this section, the Compliance Committee must send a statement in writing of their decision, including the reasons for it, to the person who made the complaint, and the broadcaster concerned.[236] Unless they consider it inappropriate to do so, the Compliance Committee should also, as soon as may be after the making of the decision, publish particulars of their decision on a complaint in such manner as they consider suitable. Furthermore, where the Committee considers that publication should be by the broadcaster concerned, or should include publication by the broadcaster concerned, the particulars must be published by the broadcaster in the manner agreed between him or her and the Compliance Committee.[237] In general, the broadcaster concerned must, unless the Compliance Committee considers it inappropriate for the broadcaster to do so, broadcast the Compliance Committee's decision on every complaint considered by the Compliance Committee in which the Compliance Committee found in favour, in whole or in part, of the person who made the complaint, within 21 days of such decision and at a time and in a manner corresponding to that in which the broadcast to which the complaint relates took place.[238]

---

231.   Broadcasting Act 2009, s 48(4).
232.   Broadcasting Act 2009, s 48(5).
233.   Broadcasting Act 2009, s 48(6).
234.   Broadcasting Act 2009, s 48(9).
235.   Broadcasting Act 2009, s 48(16).
236.   Broadcasting Act 2009, s 48(7).
237.   Broadcasting Act 2009, s 48(10).
238.   Broadcasting Act 2009, s 48(11).

Contracts and licences

[8.121] Part 6 of the Act regulates the way in which the BAI awards broadcasting licences and enters into broadcasting contracts. It also makes provision for the licensing of programme guides[239] and MMD services.[240] It lays down procedures in relation to the grant or award of different forms of licence and contract. The BAI must, like its predecessors, ensure that natural and constitutional justice is applied during any process to award, remove or suspend a licence or contract.[241] As previously noted, this is an area which has given rise to a considerable amount of litigation in the past. Unsuccessful applicants will frequently have both the incentive and the financial means to consider bringing a challenge to any decision which they regard as unlawful or unfair. This is, as a result, an area where the BAI must – as a matter of prudence as well as principle – seek to ensure that there is a scrupulous adherence on its part to statutory requirements and appropriate standards of fair procedures. However, it should also be remembered that decisions concerning the allocation of broadcasting licences have been described by the Supreme Court as 'quintessentially a matter for [a] specialist body' with the consequence that any applicant seeking to impugn a decision on the basis of the way in which the body exercised its specialist knowledge will bear 'a heavy burden'.[242]

Broadcasting licence

[8.122] Broadcasting licences are granted by the Communications Regulator, pursuant to s 5 of the Wireless Telegraphy Act 1926. These licences are issued in respect of particular sound and television transmitters, which are then subject to a broadcasting contract concluded by the BAI with the contracting broadcaster. Licences are accordingly issued by the Communications Regulator to the BAI, which issuing is a statutory prerequisite to the conclusion of a broadcasting contract.[243] These contracts must contain a condition requiring the broadcasting contractor concerned to establish, maintain and operate the broadcasting transmitter concerned in accordance with such terms and conditions as the Communications Regulator attaches to the broadcasting licence to which the contract relates. The Regulator is also entitled to vary the terms of the licence if it appears to it to be necessary so to do in the interest of good radio frequency management; for the purpose of giving effect to any international agreement to which the State is a party and which has been ratified by the State and which relates to broadcasting; if it appears to it to be in the public interest so to do; if it appears to it to be necessary for the safety or security of persons or property so to do; on request from the Authority after consultation with any affected broadcasting contractor; or on request from the Authority on behalf of a broadcasting contractor.[244]

239. Broadcasting Act 2009, s 75.
240. Broadcasting Act 2009, s 76.
241. See, for example, *TV3 v IRTC* [1994] 2 IR 457; Radio One Limerick v IRTC [1997] 2 IR 291.
242. *Scrollside Ltd (trading as Zed FM) v BCI* [2007] 1 IR 166, 176, *per* Denham J.
243. Broadcasting Act 2009, s 59(1).
244. Broadcasting Act 2009, s 60(1).

[8.123] The Act also makes provision for the suspension or use of broadcast licences by the Government in situations of national emergency. During a national emergency, the Minister may suspend any broadcasting licence or multiplex licence and operate the service directly during the period of the suspension.[245] The BAI is also vested with a power to require broadcasting contractors and network providers to co-operate with the relevant public bodies in the dissemination of relevant information to the public in the event of a major emergency. This specifically includes a power to direct, at the request of the Minister, a broadcasting contractor[246] or network provider[247] to allocate broadcasting time for announcements by any Minister of the Government in the event of a major emergency.

Broadcasting contracts

[8.124] One of the key functions of the BAI is to enter into contracts under which contractors are given the right and duty to establish, maintain and operate sound broadcasting transmitters and to provide a sound broadcasting (radio) service,[248] or to operate a television programme service contract.[249] The power to award these contracts for radio or television broadcasts is to be exercised by the BAI on the basis of the recommendation of the Contracts Awards Committee.

Community sound broadcasting contracts

[8.125] Section 64 of the Act makes provision for community radio services to be operated on a not-for-profit basis. The BAI may, on the recommendation of the Contract Awards Committee, enter into a community sound broadcasting contract with two or more members of a local community or of a community of interest if it is satisfied that those members are representative of, and accountable to, the community concerned, and that the programme material supplied will have the sole objective of specifically addressing the interests of, and seeking to provide a social benefit to the community concerned. In financial terms, the purpose of such a contract must only be to achieve enough income as is reasonably necessary to defray the expenses incurred.

Sound broadcasting contracts

[8.126] The BAI must liaise and consult with the Communications Regulator in relation to the Regulator's preparation of a plan for the allocation of frequencies for radio broadcasts. The purpose of the BAI's involvement is specified to be to secure the orderly development of broadcasting services and to allow for the establishment of a diversity of services in an area catering for a wide range of tastes including those of minority interests. This again illustrates the commitment in the 2009 Act to promoting diversity of media content.

---

245. Broadcasting Act 2009, s 61(2).
246. Broadcasting Act 2009, s 62(5).
247. Broadcasting Act 2009, s 62(6).
248. Broadcasting Act 2009, s 63.
249. Broadcasting Act 2009, s 71.

[8.127] The BAI may then, taking account of any allocation plan and having consulted with the Communications Regulator, invite applications for sound broadcasting contracts in a specific area.[250] In considering the area to specify, the BAI may conduct a study to ascertain the interests and wishes of the relevant area or community in relation to sound broadcasting services, or a study as to the sectoral impact of an additional sound broadcasting contract in that area.[251] The results of any study conducted must be published on the BAI website.[252]

[8.128] It may also direct the Contract Awards Committee to consider the results in its exercise of its functions. Where directed by the BAI, the Contract Awards Committee may by public notice invite expressions of interest in the securing of contracts for sound broadcasting services under this Act. Any expressions of interest must be made within 60 days of the date of such notice and must indicate in general terms the type of service that would be provided. They will not be regarded as an application for a sound broadcasting contract.[253]

Television contracts

[8.129] The BAI is also responsible for entering into contracts for the provision of television broadcasting services. This power is again exercised on the basis of the recommendation of the Contract Awards Committee. Section 70(2) imposes additional obligations on the BAI in relation to the nature of the content provided as part of any television service. It must ensure that any service shall in its programming be responsive to the interests and concerns of the whole community, be mindful of the need for understanding and peace within the whole island of Ireland, ensure that the programmes reflect the varied elements which make up the culture of the people of the whole island of Ireland, and have special regard for the elements which distinguish that culture and in particular for the Irish language. It must also ensure that the programming provided upholds the democratic values enshrined in the Constitution, especially those relating to rightful liberty of expression, has regard to the need for the formation of public awareness and understanding of the values and traditions of other states, and includes a reasonable proportion of news and current affairs programmes.

[8.130] The BAI must also ensure that a reasonable proportion of the television programme service provided is produced in the State or in another Member State of the European Union, and that it is devoted to original programme material produced therein by persons other than the contractor, its subsidiary, its parent or existing broadcasting organisations.[254]

---

250. Broadcasting Act 2009, s 65(2).
251. Broadcasting Act 2009, s 65(3).
252. Broadcasting Act 2009, s 65(4).
253. Broadcasting Act 2009, s 65(6).
254. Broadcasting Act 2009, s 70(4).

Determination of applications

[8.131] Section 66 governs the manner in which the Contracts Award Committee is required to determine applications for both sound broadcasting and television service contracts. The overriding criterion against which applications should be assessed is the obligation imposed on the Committee by s 66(1) to determine 'the most suitable applicant, if any, to be awarded a broadcasting contract'.

[8.132] Section 66(2) identifies a range of criteria to which the Committee must have regard in determining the most suitable applicant. These are as follows:

(a) the character,[255] expertise and experience of the applicant or, if the applicant is a body corporate, the character, expertise and experience of the body and its directors, manager, secretary or other similar officer and its members and the persons entitled to the beneficial ownership of its shares;

(b) the adequacy of the financial resources that will be available to each applicant and the extent to which the application accords with good business and economic principles;

(c) the quality, range and type of the programmes proposed to be provided by each applicant or, if there is only one applicant, by that applicant;

(d) the quantity, quality, range and type of programmes in the Irish language and the extent of programmes relating to Irish culture proposed to be provided;

(e) the extent to which the applicant will create within the proposed broadcasting service new opportunities for talent in music, drama and entertainment and in particular in respect of Irish culture;

(f) the desirability of having a diversity of services in the area specified in the notice catering for a wide range of tastes including those of minority interests;

(g) the desirability of allowing any person, or group of persons, to have control of, or substantial interests in, an undue number of sound broadcasting services in respect of which a sound broadcasting contract has been awarded under this Part;

(h) the desirability of allowing any person, or group of persons, to have control of, or substantial interests in, an undue number of sound broadcasting services in the area specified in the notice;

(i) the desirability of allowing any person, or group of persons, to have control of, or substantial interests in, an undue amount of the communications media in the area specified in the notice;

---

255. It was held by the High Court and by a majority of the Supreme Court in *Scrollside Ltd (trading as Zed FM) v BCI* that this should be interpreted broadly, such that it was not confined to a consideration of the applicant's 'moral fibre' [2007] 1 IR 166.

(j)   the extent to which the service proposed—

    (i)   serves recognisably local communities and is supported by the various interests in the community, or

    (ii)   serves communities of interest;

(k)   any other matters which the Contract Awards Committee considers to be necessary to secure the orderly development of broadcasting services; and

(l)   where directed by the Authority, any of—

    (i)   the amount of a single cash sum payment, as specified by the applicant during the course of his or her application, which the applicant is willing to pay to the Authority in respect of the award of the broadcasting contract,

    (ii)   the amount of a periodic cash sum payment, as specified by the applicant during the course of his or her application, which the applicant is willing to pay to the Authority in respect of the award of the broadcasting contract, and

    (iii)   the amount of a periodic cash sum payment determined by reference to a variable, as specified by the applicant during the course of his or her application, which the applicant is willing to pay to the Authority in respect of the award of the broadcasting contract.

The Committee must also have regard to the overall quality of the performance of the applicant with respect to the provision by him or her of a broadcasting service under any broadcasting contract held by him or her at, or before, the date of the making of the application, as well as any relevant reports of the Compliance Committee.[256]

[8.133] The fact that an applicant meets the criteria advertised or set out in statute, or reaches a particular standard, does not thereby acquire any entitlement to a particular form of decision from the Committee.[257]

[8.134] It is fair to say that the factors to which the Committee must have regard to under s 66(2) are directed at a variety of different ends. The significance, in particular, of the factors concerning media pluralism is discussed elsewhere in this book. The factors as a whole reflect, to a large extent, the varying and occasionally conflicting nature of the public policy objectives which underlie the broadcasting regulation system. Thus the Committee must have regard to the experience, expertise and past performance of applicants at the same time as it is directed to consider the desirability of having any person or group of persons exercising control over or interests in an undue amount of broadcast media organisations. This illustrates the balance which the Committee must strike between, for example, encouraging new entrants or a diversity of ownership and content and, on the other hand, ensuring that any contract awarded will be operated in a viable manner. While this will not necessarily be contradictory, there will be some situations in which these factors favour different applicants. As the body entrusted with

---

256.   Broadcasting Act 2009, s 66(4).
257.   *Magueside Communications Ltd v IRTC* (10 June 1997, unreported), SC.

this statutory function, it is for the Committee rather than the courts to determine the weight to be attached to different factors.[258] As Denham J held in relation to the BAI's predecessor in *Scrollside Ltd v BCI*:

> The courts approach with caution the review of a specialist body. Such a body has particular expertise to apply to decision-making in their arena. That specialist knowledge is not held by the courts.[259]

This means that the Committee may often have a considerable degree of discretion in determining the most suitable applicant, and that it may be difficult to successfully challenge the validity of any such determination before a court. This was acknowledged in *NWR FM v BCI*, where the High Court rejected the argument that the decision to award a licence to a particular applicant was flawed as a result of the fact that the board placed particular weight on some factors over others. Peart J observed that:

> It is inevitable that there may be several factors weighing cumulatively in favour or against a particular application and provided that those reasons are communicated in a way which enables a disappointed applicant to understand the reasons for refusal, there is nothing wrong in my view with having regard to some factors which are more minor than 'key reasons'.[260]

However, he also held that the board would be obliged to indicate to all applicants in advance if it was intended that particular matters would carry greater weight than others in determining the most suitable candidate.[261]

[8.135] Where the Contract Awards Committee decides to refuse to recommend the award of a broadcasting contract to an applicant, the Contract Awards Committee shall notify the applicant of the reasons for the decision; the score of the applicant; and the score of any successful applicant.[262] This requirement arguably gives effect to the view expressed by Keane J in *Radio Limerick One*[263] that the significance of a broadcasting contract makes it particularly important that any award process be conducted in a transparent and objective manner.

[8.136] Where the Contract Awards Committee determines the most suitable applicant, it makes its recommendation to the BAI which is then responsible for entering into a contract with that applicant. Under s 69, the BAI may determine the terms and conditions of the contact which it feels are appropriate. This creates the possibility that an applicant who is determined by the Committee to be the most suitable may ultimately fail to conclude a contract with the BAI. However, it was previously held by the courts that the making of a determination under the former system that a particular applicant is

---

258. *Scrollside Ltd (trading as Zed FM) v BCI* [2005] IEHC 355.
259. *Scrollside Ltd (trading as Zed FM) v BCI* [2007] 1 IR 166, 175. See also, for example, *Ashford Castle v SIPTU* [2007] 4 IR 70; *Calor Teoranta v McCarthy* [2009] IEHC 139.
260. *NWR FM v BCI* [2004] 4 IR 50, 73.
261. *NWR FM v BCI* [2004] 4 IR 50, 83.
262. See the obligation to score applicants under Broadcasting Act 2009, s 65(10).
263. *Radio One Limerick v IRTC* [1997] 2 IR 291.

the most suitable confers certain entitlements on an applicant. Blayney J explained in *TV3 v IRTC* that:

> [I]t is not easy to categorise the relationship which existed between the Commission and the applicants in the period between the determination by the Commission that a particular applicant should be awarded the franchise and the actual finalising of a contract. One thing is clear, however, and it is my conclusion that the Commission were obliged to negotiate with the applicants with a view to entering into a satisfactory contract.[264]

This meant, in his view, that the Commission could not withdraw the offer of a contract during this process without a clear warning and explanation of the circumstances in which such a withdrawal might occur.

INCUMBENT BROADCASTERS

[8.137] In *NWR FM v BCI*, the court was asked to consider the position of incumbent broadcasters who re-applied for a licence in respect of the service which they had previously been operating. Peart J held that, in general, incumbent broadcasters could not claim any entitlement or expectation to a renewal of the licence (or, presumably, contract), regardless of the level of expenditure made by them. The court held that:

> [T]here has in any event been no breach of any property right, since under terms of the applicant's contract it was specifically provided that no right to a renewal of the contract existed. In other words, the applicant was at all times aware that no matter what level of financial or other investment it put into its operation during the currency of its licence, it had no automatic right to a renewal of the licence and that it would have to reapply for a new licence at the appropriate time. Accordingly, there could be no question of any legitimate expectation arising.
>
> ... The applicant was granted a licence for a fixed period. It was well aware of the fact that this was the case and made its commercial decisions from time to time in the knowledge that at the end of the licence period there was no guarantee that it would be granted a new licence. What it is entitled to at the time of making its application for a new licence is a process of decision-making which is both fair and in accordance with the statutory framework, with a right of seeking relief by way of judicial review in the event of there being a breach of fair procedures or a breach of the statutory provisions. The applicant cannot claim a breach of a property right when under the terms of the contract itself, the applicant has acknowledged that it has no such right (to a new contract). I can see that in some circumstances, perhaps where a contract was open ended, or where there was no clear acknowledgement by a licence holder that there would be no automatic right of renewal, there might be arguments to be made, such as suggested by Hogan and Morgan in the passage quoted above, but the present case is not such a case.[265]

---

264. *TV3 v IRTC* [1994] 2 IR 457.
265. *NWR FM v BCI* [2004] 4 IR 50, 88–89.

Although this was based in large part on the clear term in the licence that there was no right to renewal, it might be expected that similar terms will be included in future contracts, such that the same principles would be likely to apply.

Fast track application process

[8.138] The Act also provides for a fast-track procedure in accordance with which the incumbent provider of radio services may have their contract renewed where they are the only bona fide applicant to supply the service in question.[266] This use of this procedure is at the discretion of the Contract Awards Committee. Where the Committee proposes to make use of it, it must publish a notice to that effect on the BAI website and, where appropriate, in a newspaper circulated in the relevant area. If another person expresses in writing a desire to apply for the contract and deposits the amount specified in the notice, the Committee may either proceed to invite applications for the award of the contract for the area under the standard s 65 procedure, or may refer the matter to the Authority for direction. If this material is not received, the Committee may request the Compliance Committee to prepare a report on the incumbent's compliance with its contract, may invite the incumbent to make a proposal to amend the terms of his or her sound broadcasting contract, or may suggest possible amendments itself. Where amendments are proposed, the Committee may reject the contractual changes proposed by the incumbent and invite applications under s 65(8) from other persons for the area concerned; refer the matter to the Authority for direction; or may recommend to the BAI that it agree the amended contract terms.

Any contract extension agreed under this fast-track procedure cannot exceed 10 years.

Must-carry obligations

[8.139] The 2009 Act continues to require the holders of broadcast licences to carry programme content which is regarded as serving a particular public policy interest. This material is primarily that provided by the public service broadcasters operating in Ireland. The obligation applies to 'appropriate network providers', which is defined by s 77(1) to include most providers of broadcast services but to exempt some, such as MMD transmitters,[267] where the cost of re-transmission may be a particular issue.

[8.140] Section 77 obliges an appropriate network provider to ensure the re-transmission of each free-to-air television service provided by RTÉ, TG4 or by the holder of a s 70 television contract for free-to-air services,[268] or any national sound broadcasting service provided by RTÉ.[269] Digital providers are also obliged to carry the Houses of the Oireachtas Channel and the Irish Film Channel.[270] Any disputes relating to this

266. Broadcasting Act 2009, s 67.
267. Broadcasting Act 2009, s 77(1)(c).
268. Broadcasting Act 2009, s 77(4).
269. Broadcasting Act 2009, s 77(6).
270. Broadcasting Act 2009, s 77(3).

obligation must be referred to the BAI for its determination. Any determination is final. The provider may also be obliged by the BAI to transmit material supplied by one of the community content service providers.[271] The appropriate network provider is not entitled to charge for the provision of these services. RTÉ, TG4 and the other relevant television service programme contractor are, however, obliged to ensure that their must-offer services are at all times offered for re-transmission to any appropriate network available in the State, subject to agreement as to fair, reasonable and non-discriminatory terms of use.[272]

[8.141] Similar types of provision were challenged as an interference with freedom of expression in the US courts in *Turner Broad Systems v FCC*,[273] but these were upheld by the Supreme Court as giving effect to a legitimate government interest in ensuring that programming of local origin and interest was provided to the audience.[274] More recently, however, a similar provision was struck down by the Court of Appeals for the District of Columbia Circuit in *Comcast v FCC*.[275] This suggests that this is a matter that may receive further consideration from the Supreme Court in the future.

Enforcement

[8.142] Part 5 of the Act sets out the powers of the BAI and Compliance Committee to enforce the terms of the contracts under which broadcasters operate, and to impose sanctions, where appropriate, in relation to any breaches of those contracts. The courts have acknowledged the importance of broadcasters adhering to the terms of the contracts upon which their entitlement to broadcast is based. In *Radio One Limerick*, Smyth J criticised the broadcaster for its failure to meet its obligations in notably strident terms:

> [T]he Applicant failed to have any proper appreciation of the fact that the Contract once entered into had to be honoured in spirit as well as in letter. In many instances the Applicant adopted a cavalier or laissez faire attitude to contractual obligations. The rights conferred by the contract had a corresponding range of duties – which the evidence makes clear were not honoured – the Contract conferred certain economic advantages on the Applicant which it ought to have been assiduous to protect. The Contract had in-built a certain self monitoring requirement. This in effect placed an obligation of contractual honour on the Applicant which it wholly failed to meet.[276]

One of the first steps in the taking of enforcement proceedings against a broadcaster is the initiation by the Compliance Committee of an investigation into the broadcaster's contractual performance where the Committee has reasonable grounds for believing that a contractor is not providing a service in accordance with the terms of the contractor's

---

271. Broadcasting Act 2009, s 77(8).
272. Broadcasting Act 2009, s 77(11) and (12).
273. *Turner Broad Systems v FCC (Turner I)* 512 US 622 (1994).
274. *Turner Broad Systems v FCC (Turner II)* 520 US 180 (1997).
275. *Comcast Corp v FCC* 579 F 3d 1 (2009).
276. *Radio One Limerick v IRTC* [1997] 2 IR 291, [1997] 2 ILRM 1.

contract.[277] The investigation can examine any or all of the operational, programming, financial, technical or other affairs of the contractor.[278] An investigation may be conducted by a member of the BAI's staff or another person who the Committee considers to be suitably qualified to carry it out.

[8.143] The Compliance Committee must notify the contractor concerned of the matter under investigation and afford the contractor an opportunity to respond, within seven days of the date of the notification, or such further period as the Committee allows, to the matter under investigation.[279]

[8.144] The contractor is under a statutory duty to co-operate in the investigation.[280] The investigator also has specific powers of compulsion to assist, where necessary, with obtaining the contractor's co-operation. Thus, an investigator may require the contractor concerned to produce to the investigator such information or records in the contractor's possession or control relevant to the investigation; to allow the investigator to enter the premises of the contractor to conduct such inspections and make such examinations of broadcasting equipment found there; and, where appropriate, to attend before the investigator for the purposes of the investigation.[281]

[8.145] Where an investigator forms a view that a contractor is not providing the service in accordance with the terms of the contractor's contract, he or she must notify the finding to the contractor and afford that contractor an opportunity to make submissions at a hearing into the investigation which will be held before the Compliance Committee.[282] The Committee must set down rules for the conduct of such a hearing in advance, which rules should cover matters such as the period in which submissions may be made.[283] The contractor must supply the Compliance Committee with any information and records which the Committee considers necessary for the purposes of a hearing.[284] After consideration of any submissions made by the contractor, the Compliance Committee may make a finding that the contractor is not providing the service referred to, or make any such other finding as it considers appropriate in the circumstances.[285]

Termination or suspension of a contract

[8.146] One of the most significant powers the Compliance Committee has in this area is the power to recommend the termination or suspension of the contract in question.[286]

---

277. Broadcasting Act 2009, s 50(2).
278. Broadcasting Act 2009, s 50(1).
279. Broadcasting Act 2009, s 50(3).
280. Broadcasting Act 2009, s 50(3).
281. Broadcasting Act 2009, s 50(4).
282. Broadcasting Act 2009, s 50(5).
283. Broadcasting Act 2009, s 50(8).
284. Broadcasting Act 2009, s 50(6).
285. Broadcasting Act 2009, s 50(7).
286. Broadcasting Act 2009, s 51(1).

This may be done if any false or misleading information of a material nature was given to the Contract Awards Committee by or on behalf of the holder of the contract before the contract was entered into;[287] or if the holder of the contract has been found by the Compliance Committee after an investigation to have failed on one or more occasions to comply with a term or condition of the contract and the nature of that failure is of such seriousness as, in the opinion of the Compliance Committee, warrants the termination or suspension of the contract.[288] It would appear that minor or technical breaches of the contract will not be sufficient to justify such sanction, although they may be taken into account as part of a consideration of more serious matters.[289] Keane J also expressed the view in *Radio One Limerick* that a serious breach may not justify termination of a contract where it is remedied.[290] In those circumstances, the BAI must suspend the contract for the period recommended by the Committee, unless it considers a shorter period appropriate, or terminate the contract as recommended, unless it considers a suspension to be more appropriate. The BAI does not appear to have the power to impose no sanction on a contractor once a recommendation to terminate or suspend has been made by the Committee. The BAI can take further submissions from the contractor in question. It is also provided that the member of the Committee who makes the recommendation may not participate in the decision-making of the BAI on this matter.[291]

[8.147] Where the Compliance Committee proposes to make a recommendation for a suspension or termination, it must notify the holder of the contract concerned and provide an opportunity to make submissions at a hearing before the Committee.[292] This should be done in accordance with the rules laid down by the Committee which may or may not provide, as appropriate, for an oral hearing.[293]

[8.148] The holder of a contract may appeal any decision to terminate or suspend a contract to the High Court. The use of the term decision rather than recommendation indicates that this refers to an appeal from the decision of the BAI rather than the Committee. The fact that there is a provision for a statutory appeal means that it may be more difficult for a broadcaster to secure leave to apply for judicial review in relation to a recommendation by the Committee to terminate or suspend.[294] However, it should be borne in mind that, given the BAI seems required to either terminate or suspend the contract once that recommendation is made by the Committee, there may be some basis for an argument that, in appropriate cases, the damage which would be caused to a broadcaster as the result of even a temporary suspension of the contract would be

---

287. Broadcasting Act 2009, s 51(1)(a).
288. Broadcasting Act 2009, s 51(1)(b).
289. *Radio One Limerick v IRTC* [1997] 2 IR 291; [1997] 2 ILRM 1.
290. *Radio One Limerick v IRTC* [1997] 2 IR 291, 294.
291. Broadcasting Act 2009, s 51(5).
292. Broadcasting Act 2009, s 51(2).
293. Broadcasting Act 2009, s 51(3).
294. See, for example, *State (Glover) v McCarthy* [1981] ILRM 46; *Memorex v Employment Appeals Tribunal* [1992] IR 184; *McGoldrick v An Bord Pleanála* [1997] 1 IR 497; *Stefan v Minister for Justice, Equality and Law Reform* [2002] 2 ILRM 134.

sufficiently serious to justify the taking of a judicial review action on the grounds that the available remedy is not adequate to protect the contractor's interest.

Financial sanctions

[8.149] The Compliance Committee may appoint an investigator where it is of the opinion that there are circumstances suggesting that it is appropriate to investigate and report on any apparent breach by a broadcaster of:

- the duty of objectivity and impartiality imposed on broadcasters under s 39(1);
- the requirement in s 40 to take, preserve and provide recordings of broadcast material to assist with the investigation by the Committee of a complaint;
- the maximum daily and hourly advertising limits in s 41(2);
- the restrictions imposed on religious, political or industrial relations advertising under ss 41(3) and (4);
- the advertising limits fixed under s 106(3);
- the maximum advertising limits for the Irish Film Channel under s 127(6);
- any other broadcasting code or rule.[295]

Where an investigating officer is appointed, he or she must notify the broadcaster concerned of the matter under investigation; supply the broadcaster with copies of any documents relevant to the investigation, and afford to the broadcaster an opportunity to respond within seven days of the date of the notification. Alternatively, the Committee may allow for a longer period up to a maximum of 21 days.[296]

[8.150] Where the investigation concerns a person employed by the broadcaster or a person commissioned to make that programme, those persons may request, for reasons specified by him or her, that the Committee require the investigator to give him or her a similar opportunity to comment on the complaint. The Compliance Committee must, having considered the reasons so specified, give the person a similar period to comment on the complaint if they are satisfied that the interests of the employee or the prospects of the programme maker obtaining further commissions from the broadcaster concerned, might be adversely affected as a result of the complaint, or that it is in the interests of fairness to do so having regard to the good name of the person.[297]

[8.151] The broadcaster has a duty to co-operate in the investigation and provide the investigating officer with such information as he or she considers necessary for the purposes of the investigation.[298] The investigating officer has specific statutory powers to require the broadcaster to provide to the investigating officer such information or

---

295. Broadcasting Act 2009, s 53(1).
296. Broadcasting Act 2009, s 53(3).
297. Broadcasting Act 2009, s 53(5).
298. Broadcasting Act 2009, s 53(4).

records in the broadcaster's possession or control relevant to the investigation;[299] and where appropriate, attend before the investigating officer for the purposes of the investigation.[300]

[8.152] Where an investigating officer forms the view that there has been a breach in respect of any matter which he or she is investigating or that the broadcaster concerned has failed to co-operate with the investigation, the officer must report this to the Compliance Committee. The threshold for making a finding that there has been such a breach is that there has been a serious or repeated failure by a broadcaster to comply with the obligations that are the subject-matter of the investigation.[301] What will constitute a serious failure is unclear but it may include a repeated failure to comply with requests from the BAI or investigator, or the contravention of the relevant obligations after being warned by the BAI.[302] In addition, whereas the taking of steps to remedy a breach may mitigate its seriousness, a failure to make any effort to remedy the situation may constitute, in itself, a serious breach.[303] The report of an investigating officer in relation to an investigation to the Compliance Committee should include the investigating officer's findings in relation to the matter;[304] any response received from the relevant parties;[305] the details of any failure by the broadcaster concerned to comply with the investigator's requests under s 53(7) for documents and/or attendance;[306] and the recommendation of the investigating officer.[307] Where an investigating officer has formed a view that there has been a breach by the broadcaster concerned or a failure to co-operate, the broadcaster must be given the opportunity of making a submission to the Compliance Committee within 10 days of being notified of the investigating officer's views and recommendation.[308]

[8.153] Where the Compliance Committee, having considered the report and any submissions received, finds that there has been either a breach by the broadcaster concerned, or a failure to co-operate, the Committee may recommend to the BAI that it make a formal notification of that finding. The BAI must comply with that recommendation. This formal notification must set out the reasons for the notification; state that the BAI intends to apply to the High Court for a determination that there has been a breach or a failure to co-operate with an investigation unless the broadcaster requests in writing within 14 days that the BAI make a determination on the matter; indicate the amount of the financial sanction (not exceeding €250,000) that it proposes to deal with on its own determination. The notification may also indicate the amount of

299. Broadcasting Act 2009, s 53(7)(a).
300. Broadcasting Act 2009, s 53(7)(b).
301. Broadcasting Act 2009, s 52.
302. *Radio One Limerick v IRTC* [1997] 2 IR 291.
303. *Radio One Limerick v IRTC* [1997] 2 IR 291.
304. Broadcasting Act 2009, s 54(1)(b)(i).
305. Broadcasting Act 2009, s 54(1)(b)(ii).
306. Broadcasting Act 2009, s 54(1)(b)(iii).
307. Broadcasting Act 2009, s 54(1)(b)(iv).
308. Broadcasting Act 2009, s 54(2).

the financial sanction (not exceeding €250,000) that it intends to recommend to the court if the matter is dealt with by the court.[309] It should also comply with the instructions on communication of the notification set out in s 57.

[8.154] Where a request for the BAI to make a determination is made, the BAI must give the broadcaster the opportunity to make submissions before determining the matter. Any member who was a member of the Compliance Committee that appointed the investigator or made the recommendation may not take part in the hearing. Where the BAI determines that there has been a breach or a failure to co-operate with an investigation by the broadcaster, it may direct that the broadcaster shall pay the BAI a financial sanction not exceeding the amount proposed in the notification.[310] A broadcaster may appeal to the High Court against the BAI's determination to make a statement of findings or to impose a financial sanction, or both.[311]

[8.155] Although the intention of the Oireachtas may have been to provide for a procedure under which the BAI would be able to discourage broadcasters from having recourse to the High Court, there are potential dangers which this twin-track approach. In particular, the fact that the BAI must provide a provisional indication of its proposed sanction before receiving submissions raises the possibility of an argument that it may have prejudged matters at the final hearing.[312] By requiring the BAI to take a position before holding a hearing, it obliges it, in effect, to impose some fetters on its own discretion. It also creates a potential practical incentive for the BAI to impose a lesser sanction at the hearing in order to demonstrate that it has taken account of any submissions made.

[8.156] Where an application is made to the High Court, it may make a determination that there has been a breach or a failure to co-operate with an investigation by the broadcaster; direct, having regard to any amount the BAI recommends, that the broadcaster shall pay to the BAI a financial sanction not exceeding €250,000; and make such order it considers appropriate;[313] or may dismiss the application.[314] The court may also make such order as to costs as it thinks fit in respect of the application.

[8.157] In considering the amount (if any) of any financial sanction to be imposed on a broadcaster the BAI and the High Court are directed to take into account the circumstances of the breach or the failure to co-operate with an investigation in question, as the case may be, and must, where appropriate in the circumstances, also have regard to:[315]

    (a)   the need to ensure that any financial sanction imposed—

        (i)   is appropriate and proportionate to the breach or the failure to co-operate with the investigation, and

---

309. Broadcasting Act 2009, s 54(4).
310. Broadcasting Act 2009, s 55(3).
311. Broadcasting Act 2009, s 55(5).
312. See, for example, *P v Judge McDonagh* (7 July 2009, unreported), HC.
313. Broadcasting Act 2009, s 55(1)(a).
314. Broadcasting Act 2009, s 55(1)(b).
315. Broadcasting Act 2009, s 56.

        (ii)   will act as a sufficient incentive to ensure future compliance in respect of the requirement breached;

(b)   the seriousness of the breach;

(c)   the turnover of the broadcaster in the financial year ending in the year previous to the breach and the ability of the broadcaster to pay the amount;

(d)   the extent of any failure to co-operate with the investigation;

(e)   any excuse or explanation by the broadcaster for the breach or failure to co-operate with the investigation;

(f)   any gain (financial or otherwise) made by the broadcaster or by any person in which the broadcaster has a financial interest as a consequence of the breach;

(g)   the appropriateness of the time when the programme material concerned was broadcast;

(h)   the degree of harm caused or increased cost incurred by audiences, consumers or other sectoral or market participants as a consequence of the breach;

(i)   audience expectations as to the nature of the programme material;

(j)   the duration of the breach;

(k)   repeated breaches by the broadcaster;

(l)   continuation by the broadcaster of—

        (i)   the breach, or

        (ii)   the broadcasting of the matter to which an investigation relates after being notified of the investigation under s 53(3)(a);

(m)   the extent to which—

        (i)   the management of the broadcaster knew, or ought to have known, that the breach was occurring or would occur, and

        (ii)   any breach was caused by a third party, or any relevant circumstances beyond the control of the broadcaster;

(n)   the absence, ineffectiveness or repeated failure of internal mechanisms or procedures of the broadcaster intended to prevent breach by the broadcaster;

(o)   the extent to which the broadcaster had taken steps in advance to identify and mitigate external factors that might result in a breach;

(p)   the extent and timeliness of any steps taken to end the breach in question, and any steps taken for remedying the consequences of the breach;

(q)   submissions by the broadcaster on the appropriate amount of a financial sanction;

(r)   whether a financial sanction in respect of similar conduct has already been imposed on the broadcaster by the court or Authority; and

(s)   any precedents set by the court or Authority in respect of previous breaches or failures to co-operate with an investigation.

Public service broadcasters

[8.158] The 2009 Act also makes extensive provision for the regulation and governance of public service broadcasters – namely RTÉ and TG4 – in Ireland.

Governing boards

[8.159] The public service broadcasters operate under the oversight of their governing boards. Members of the board are required to ensure that each performs his or her functions in such a manner as to represent the interests of viewers and listeners; ensure that the activities of the corporation in pursuance of its statutory objectives performed efficiently and effectively; ensure that the gathering and presentation by the corporation of news and current affairs is accurate and impartial; and to safeguard the independence of the corporation, as regards the conception, content and production of programmes, the editing and presentation of news and current affairs programmes and the definition of programme schedules from State, political and commercial influences.

[8.160] Each public service broadcaster also has a director general whose function it is to carry on and manage, and control generally, the administration of the corporation; to act as editor-in-chief in respect of content; and to perform such other functions (if any) as may be determined by the board.[316]

[8.161] These provisions reflect the importance of ensuring independence of public service broadcasters from the influence of the State, or other persons. This is underlined by the statutory obligation imposed by s 98 on RTÉ and TG4 to be independent in the pursuance of their objects. With that in mind, although the 2009 Act makes some improvements to the appointments process, it is still somewhat disappointing that the Government retains significant control over the appointment of the vast majority of board members.

Members of boards

[8.162] Section 81 specifies that the boards of these public service broadcasters will be comprised of six government appointees, four members appointed by the Minister following consultation with the relevant Joint Oireachtas Committee, the director general of the broadcaster and one member of staff who is elected to the position. At least five members of the board must be of each gender, and members are appointed for no more than five years.

[8.163] Members must have experience suitable to qualify them to oversee a public service broadcaster in the following areas:[317]

    (a)   media affairs;

    (b)   public service broadcasting;

    (c)   broadcast content production;

---

316.   Broadcasting Act 2009, s 89.
317.   Broadcasting Act 2009, s 82.

  (d)   digital media technologies;

  (e)   trade union affairs;

  (f)   business or commercial affairs;

  (g)   matters pertaining to the development of the Irish language;

  (h)   matters pertaining to disability;

  (i)   arts, music, sport or culture;

  (j)   science, technology or environmental matters;

  (k)   legal or regulatory affairs; and

  (l)   social, educational or community activities or Gaeltacht affairs.

In addition, an appointee to the board of TG4 must be proficient in the Irish language.

[8.164] Members may at any time be removed from membership of the board by the Government if, in the Government's opinion, the member has become incapable through ill health of performing his or her functions, or has committed stated misbehaviour, or his or her removal appears to the Government to be necessary for the effective performance by the corporation of its functions. This may only occur where resolutions are passed by each House of the Oireachtas calling for the member's removal.[318]

[8.165] Members may also be removed by the Minister with the consent of the Government where the member fails to make a declaration in accordance with the requirements of s 17 of the Ethics in Public Office Act 1995. This requires the member to furnish the Standards in Public Office Commission[319] with a statement in writing of the member's interests and the interests of his or her spouse or child of which the member has actual knowledge.[320] The Minister must lay the order before each House of the Oireachtas, whereupon it may be annulled within 21 days by a vote of either House. This procedure may also be used by the Minister to remove a member where the member fails to comply with the disclosure requirements laid down by s 93,[321] or where a member fails to attend a meeting of the board for a consecutive six-month period.[322] In the latter situation, the Minister may not exercise his or her power of removal if the member can demonstrate to the Minister's satisfaction that the failure to attend was due to illness.

[8.166] A member of the board of a corporation will, however, be automatically disqualified from being a member of the corporation if he or she is adjudicated a bankrupt, makes a composition or arrangement with creditors, is convicted on indictment by a court of competent jurisdiction and is sentenced to a term of imprisonment, is convicted of an offence involving fraud or dishonesty, or is disqualified or restricted from being a director of any company.[323]

---

318. Broadcasting Act 2009, s 84(5).
319. Standards of Public Office Act, 2001, s 2.
320. Broadcasting Act 2009, s 84(8)(c).
321. Broadcasting Act 2009, s 84(8)(b).
322. Broadcasting Act 2009, s 84(8)(a).
323. Broadcasting Act 2009, s 84(6).

[8.167] If a member of the board of a corporation appointed by the Government, on the nomination of the Minister dies, resigns, becomes disqualified or is removed from office or for any other reason ceases to be a member of the board of the corporation, the Government on the nomination of the Minister, may appoint a person to be a member of the board of the corporation to fill the casual vacancy so occasioned for the unexpired period of the term of membership.[324] Where the member was appointed following consultation with the Joint Oireachtas Committee, that Committee must also be consulted on his or her replacement.[325]

[8.168] As with the BAI, individuals with a non-creative or non-educational interest in a contract with RTÉ or TG4, or candidates for election to, or members of the Oireachtas or the European Parliament may not be members of the Board.[326] Similarly, board members are also subject to the same sort of disclosure rules which also apply to the BAI.[327]

Audience council

[8.169] Provision is also made in the Act for the establishment of an audience council. The principal function of an audience council is to represent to the board the views and interests of the general public with regard to public service broadcasting by the corporation.[328] The audience council consists of 15 members appointed by its corporation[329] for no more than a five-year period.[330] One board member must be appointed to serve as a member of its audience council.[331] In appointing the members of its audience council, a corporation must endeavour to ensure that the audience council is representative of the viewing and listening public and, in particular, of Gaeltacht communities and persons with a sight or hearing disability.[332] The council may require the corporation to carry out relevant surveys and hold public meetings. An audience council must also make an annual report to the Minister, the board of its corporation and the BAI, of its proceedings and may, if requested to do so by the Minister, make special reports to the Minister during any year.[333]

Public service broadcasting under EU law

[8.170] The provision of government and state support for public service broadcasters raises issues from the point of view of EU rules on competition and, in particular, state

---

324. Broadcasting Act 2009, s 84(10).
325. Broadcasting Act 2009, s 84(12).
326. Broadcasting Act 2009, s 86.
327. Broadcasting Act 2009, s 93.
328. Broadcasting Act 2009, s 96(10).
329. Broadcasting Act 2009, s 96(2).
330. Broadcasting Act 2009, s 96(7).
331. Broadcasting Act 2009, s 96(3).
332. Broadcasting Act 2009, s 96(4).
333. Broadcasting Act 2009, s 96(16).

aid. The EU recognised the particular value of public service broadcasting in the Treaty of Amsterdam by incorporating Protocol 29, which provides that:

> The provisions of the Treaties shall be without prejudice to the competence of Member States to provide for the funding of public service broadcasting and in so far as such funding is granted to broadcasting organisations for the fulfilment of the public service remit as conferred, defined and organised by each Member State, and in so far as such funding does not affect trading conditions and competition in the Union to an extent which would be contrary to the common interest, while the realisation of the remit of that public service shall be taken into account.[334]

Nonetheless, the fact that public service broadcasters typically receive funds from government means that the Commission remains careful to scrutinise the funding and commercial activities of public service broadcasters so as to ensure there is no breach of the state aid rules set down by the Treaties. This has become a particularly sensitive issue in relation to new media forms where public service broadcasters have been accused by some of using their resources and reputation to cross-subsidise their involvement in matters beyond their public service remit.[335] The Commission, which has initial decision-making responsibility on this issue, has thus regularly been asked by rival broadcasters to investigate the conduct of public service broadcasters on state aid grounds.[336]

[8.171] The rules on state aid are laid down by Arts 106 to 108 of the Treaty on the Functioning of the European Union. For state aid to be present, several conditions must be satisfied:

1. There must be an intervention by the State or by way of State resources;[337]

2. The intervention must be liable to affect trade between Member States;

3. It must confer an advantage on the recipient;[338] and

4. It must distort or threaten to distort competition.[339]

[8.172] The existence of state aid is an objective matter which is based on a consideration of the effect of state intervention, rather than its intended purpose. In its most recent Communication on the Application of State Aid Rules to Public Service

---

334. See also the Council Resolution concerning public service broadcasting which stated that 'Broad public access, without discrimination and on the basis of equal opportunities, to various channels and services is a necessary precondition for fulfilling the special obligation of public service broadcasting', 25 January 1999.

335. See, for example, 'BBC's commercial activities face investigation' (2008) *The Daily Telegraph*, 18 July; 'ITN's David Mannion blasts BBC video-sharing deal' (2009) *The Guardian*, 28 August.

336. Marton, 'The impact of EU competition law on the financing of public service broadcasters' (2001) 6 Communications Law 56.

337. Case C–52/97 *Viscido v Ente Poste Italiano* [1998] ECR I–2629; *DB v Commission* [2006] ECR II–1047.

338. Case C–251/97 *France v Commission* [1999] ECR–I 6639; Case C–6/97 *Italy v Commission* [1999] ECR–I 2981.

339. Case C–173/73 *Italy v Commission* [1974] ECR 709.

Broadcasting in 2009, the Commission identified several aspects of public service broadcasting which could have such an effect. These included the fact that the state may directly invest in or otherwise financially support public service broadcasters. In addition, the Commission expressed the view that such state financing has cross-border effects given the international nature of the marketplace for television rights, the global reach of public service broadcasters' online operations, the cross-border nature of broadcast ownership and the potential impact on advertising where broadcasters transmit across national boundaries.

[8.173] However, the European Court of Justice held in *Altmark*[340] that public service compensation may be permissible where it is provided to offset public service obligations, such that the recipients 'do not enjoy a real financial advantage'. This has obvious relevance for public service broadcasters. However, the court also held that four conditions had to be satisfied if a measure was to avoid being classified as state aid on this ground. These are:

1.   The recipient undertaking must actually have public service obligations to discharge, and the obligations must be clearly defined.

2.   The parameters on the basis of which the compensation is calculated must be established in advance in an objective and transparent manner.

3.   The compensation cannot exceed what is necessary to cover all or part of the costs incurred in the discharge of the public service obligations, taking into account the relevant receipts and a reasonable profit.

4.   Finally, where the undertaking which is to discharge public service obligations, in a specific case, is not chosen pursuant to a public procurement procedure which would allow for the selection of the bidder capable of providing those services at the least cost to the community, the level of compensation must be determined on the basis of an analysis of the costs which a typical undertaking, well run and adequately equipped so as to be able to meet the necessary public service requirements, would have incurred in discharging those obligations.

[8.174] There is provision under Art 107 for derogations on the grounds, inter alia, of promoting culture, but the Commission will only allow this to apply where the aid is clearly aimed at culture only and does not, for example, extend to other social, democratic or educational means. As public service broadcasters typically have such wider remits, this is why they cannot usually rely on Art 107.

[8.175] The criteria laid down in *Altmark* have been strictly applied by the Commission when considering possible state aid to public service broadcasters. In particular, the Commission has laid very heavy emphasis on the importance of establishing each criterion by clear, transparent and verifiable means. Thus, it is not sufficient to simply fund a public service broadcaster to fulfil a public service remit. It is necessary, for example, to provide for a clear and precise definition (with due allowance for the editorial independence of broadcasters) of what that role involves and for effective

---

340.   Case (C–280/00) [2003] ECR–I 7747.

supervision of whether the obligations are being fulfilled. This is necessary to allow the Commission to review the matters as well as to allow other broadcasters to organise their affairs on the basis of an understanding of how and where state support will operate.

[8.176] The Commission is also alert to ensure that there will not be any distortion of competition beyond that necessary to perform the public service and to provide for its funding. In particular, it seeks to avoid any disproportionate effects from public funding, overcompensation and cross-subsidisation. As noted, this is a particular concern for the Commission at present in relation to the exploitation of new media opportunities by broadcasters. Thus, Austria was required to establish a new media authority to which public broadcasters would apply for approval for new media services[341] and Ireland was warned in relation to the lack of precision over its public service broadcasters' role in providing non-broadcast services.[342] By contrast, the use of licence fee income to establish a 24-hour public service news channel by the BBC was deemed acceptable as meeting clear standards of public service broadcasting.[343]

[8.177] It may also arise in respect of the way in which public service broadcasters are funded and generate commercial revenue. The Commission's communication permits either a 'single-funding' (public funds only) or 'dual-funding' (public funds and commercial revenues) system. In the latter situation, which applies in Ireland under the 2009 Act, the Commission requires a clear and precise definition of the public service remit and of the separation between public service activities and non-public service activities. This may include a requirement for a clear separation of accounts and an obligation to ensure commercial transactions are carried out on an arm's length basis. The Commission tends to scrutinise funding and accounting matters in detail so that, for example, funding by way of a specified loan given on commercial rates[344] may be permissible, whereas funding by indirect taxes that will raise an uncertain amount may not be.[345]

[8.178] Following an investigation by the Commission after a complaint was made by TV3, the Irish Government agreed to introduce remedial measures in the Broadcasting Act 2009. The Commission had been particularly concerned that the previous Irish legislation did not provide a precise definition of the public service functions of RTÉ and TnaG (as it then was) in respect of non-broadcasting services. It also indicated that compensation was not objectively calculated. This meant, in turn, that it could not be said that compensation was no more than was necessary to discharge the broadcasters' public functions. The Commission also expressed itself to be unconvinced with the adequacy of supervision under the Irish regime. The investigation was ended after commitments were given by the Government in relation to the new Act.

---

341. E 2/2008 – Austria – State funding for Austrian public service broadcaster ORF.
342. E 4/2005 – Ireland – State aid financing of RTÉ and TNAG (TG4).
343. NN 88/98 – United Kingdom – BBC 24 hours news channel.
344. N 287/2008 – Denmark; Rescue aid to TV2 Danmark A/S.
345. No C38/2009 (ex NN 58/2009) – Spain: New tax based funding system for public broadcasting in Spain.

[8.179] These are evident in several provisions of the Act. The obligations of RTÉ and TG4 are discussed elsewhere but are now provided for by statute. Objective factors for the assessment of the level of public funding provided are set out in s 124. Furthermore, the two broadcasters are also required to make annual statements of their performance commitments, and report on the extent to which they were fulfilled in the previous year.[346]

[8.180] In addition, the concerns about cross-subsidisation and entry into new markets are addressed by a number of provisions. Section 108(2) of the 2009 Act requires that all transactions or arrangements entered into by RTÉ or TG4 as between the activities arising from its public service objects, and its exploitation of commercial opportunities object, shall be made at arm's length and on commercial terms, while s 108(1) allows RTÉ and TG4 to engage in commercial activities for the purpose of using such commercial activities to subsidise its public service objects. Section 103 also requires the bodies to obtain ministerial consent to engage in new or ancillary services.

Obligations of RTÉ

[8.181] The Act makes specific provision for particular obligations in relation to both RTÉ and TG4. This provides some indication of the nature of the public service broadcasting function which each corporation is intended to provide.

[8.182] The objects of RTÉ are stated to be:

(a) to establish, maintain and operate a national television and sound broadcasting service which shall have the character of a public service, be a free-to-air service and be made available, in so far as it is reasonably practicable, to the whole community on the island of Ireland;

(b) to establish and maintain a website and teletext services in connection with the services of RTÉ;

(c) to establish and maintain orchestras, choirs and other cultural performing groups in connection with the services of RTÉ;

(d) to assist and co-operate with the relevant public bodies in preparation for, and execution of, the dissemination of relevant information to the public in the event of a major emergency;

(e) to establish and maintain archives and libraries containing materials relevant to the objects of RTÉ;

(f) to establish, maintain and operate a television broadcasting service and a sound broadcasting service which shall have the character of a public service, which services shall be made available, in so far as RTÉ considers reasonably practicable, to Irish communities outside the island of Ireland;

(g) subject to the consent of the Minister, the Minister having consulted with the BAI, to establish, maintain and operate, in so far as it is reasonably practicable, community, local, or regional broadcasting services, which shall have the character of a public service, and be available free-to-air;

---

346. Broadcasting Act 2009, s 102.

(h)   subject to the consent of the Minister, the Minister having consulted with the Authority, to establish and maintain non-broadcast non-linear audiovisual media services, in so far as it is reasonably practicable, which shall have the character of a public broadcasting service;

(i)   to establish, maintain, and operate one or more national multiplexes;

(j)   so far as it is reasonably practicable, to exploit such commercial opportunities as may arise in pursuit of these objects.[347]

In pursuit of these objectives, RTÉ is also required to:

(a)   be responsive to the interests and concerns of the whole community, be mindful of the need for understanding and peace within the whole island of Ireland, ensure that the programmes reflect the varied elements which make up the culture of the people of the whole island of Ireland, and have special regard for the elements which distinguish that culture and in particular for the Irish language;

(b)   uphold the democratic values enshrined in the Constitution, especially those relating to rightful liberty of expression; and

(c)   have regard to the need for the formation of public awareness and understanding of the values and traditions of countries other than the State, including in particular those of other Member States.[348]

RTÉ is further directed to ensure that its broadcast services:

(a)   provide a comprehensive range of programmes in the Irish and English languages that reflect the cultural diversity of the whole island of Ireland and include programmes that entertain, inform and educate, provide coverage of sporting, religious and cultural activities and cater for the expectations of the community generally as well as members of the community with special or minority interests and which, in every case, respect human dignity;

(b)   provide programmes of news and current affairs in the Irish and English languages, including programmes that provide coverage of proceedings in the Houses of the Oireachtas and the European Parliament; and

(c)   facilitate or assist contemporary cultural expression and encourage or promote innovation and experimentation in broadcasting.[349]

TG4 is subject to very similar requirements under s 118.

Broadcasting fund

[8.183] One of the innovations of the 2009 Act was that it makes provision for the establishment of a Broadcasting Fund. The purpose of this Fund, which is to be operated by the BAI and funded by up to 7 per cent of the net receipts from the payment of

---

347.   Broadcasting Act 2009, s 114(1).
348.   Broadcasting Act 2009, s 114(2).
349.   Broadcasting Act 2009, s 114(3).

television licences,[350] is intended to offer an independent source of funding for high-quality original or public service programming.

[8.184] Specifically, the objects of the Fund are to develop high-quality programmes based on Irish culture, heritage and experience; develop these programmes in the Irish language; increase the availability of such programmes to audiences in the State; to represent the diversity of Irish culture and heritage; to record oral Irish heritage and aspects of Irish heritage which are disappearing, under threat, or have not been previously recorded; and to develop local and community broadcasting.[351]

[8.185] The Fund may provide support for new television or sound broadcasting programmes, including feature films, animation and drama on Irish culture, heritage and experience; new television or sound broadcasting programmes to improve adult or media literacy; new television or sound broadcasting programmes which raise public awareness and understanding of global issues impacting on the State and countries other than the State; or the development of archiving of programme material produced in the State.[352] The Fund may only fund programmes which are broadcast on a free television service which provides near-universal coverage in the State, or as part of a community content provision contract. The programmes in question must also, with the exception of programmes for children or educational programmes or programmes in the Irish language, be broadcast during peak viewing times.[353] Funding cannot be provided for programmes which are produced primarily for news or current affairs. Any scheme produced by the BAI and approved by the Minister must be laid before each House of the Oireachtas and either House may, within 21 sitting days after the day on which a scheme was laid before it pass a resolution annulling the scheme.[354]

Coverage of major events

[8.186] Part 11 of the Act replaces the Broadcasting (Major Events Television Coverage) Act 1999 and Broadcasting (Major Events Television Coverage) (Amendment) Act 2003 with a new system for designating particular events as ones which must be covered on free television services that have near-universal coverage in Ireland. The power to designate major events was first introduced under Art 3A of the Television Without Frontiers Directive. It is not provided for by Art 14 of the Audiovisual Media Services Directive which allows for the designation of such events, and obliges other Member States to ensure that broadcasters within their jurisdiction do not frustrate the purpose of that designation.[355]

---

350. Broadcasting Act 2009, s 156(2).
351. Broadcasting Act 2009, s 155.
352. Broadcasting Act 2009, s 154(1).
353. Broadcasting Act 2009, s 154(2).
354. Broadcasting Act 2009, s 154(10).
355. See also Broadcasting Act 2009, s 165.

[8.187] The obligations imposed on Member States were considered by the House of Lords in *R (TVDanmark) v Independent Television Commission*.[356] The case was taken by a UK broadcaster who, having successfully bid in Denmark for the rights to Denmark's World Cup matches, was refused consent by the UK's Independent Television Commission to televise that event. The Lords held that English authorities were bound to ensure that the exercise by broadcasters subject to their jurisdiction of exclusive rights would not allow a substantial proportion of the public in another Member State to be deprived of the possibility of watching an event designated in that state. While the domestic authorities were was not bound by the decisions of the Danish authorities, they were obliged to take account of that state's system of regulation in exercising their powers so as to give effect to the system of reciprocal enforcement created by the Directive. The Directive was clear that regulation should as far as possible be harmonised so that the rights of the public to watch an event of national importance in a Member State should not be affected by whether the broadcaster was situated in that or another Member State.

[8.188] This has been a highly controversial area, both in Ireland and in other European countries. This is a consequence of the competing interests at work in this area, especially with regard to the rights to broadcast sporting events.[357] While the public expect to have free access to events of social importance, broadcasters and sports organisations may have a mutual interest in the sale of the rights to broadcast such events to subscription-based channels:

> [T]he relationship between sport and media [is] clear: both industries gained benefits from the complementary nature of their interests. On the one hand, sport provides valuable content and audiences for media operators and, on the other hand, the media is a revenue source and promotional tool for sport. More specifically, the sale of exclusive broadcasting rights is an important, if not the principal, source of revenue for sports organisations and clubs while sports content is decisive for media operators to create an attractive 'bouquet' of programmes for their audience.[358]

[8.189] The House of Lords has held that the Directive (or more accurately, the previous Directive) strikes a balance between these commercial considerations and the public interest in access to major events:.

> The result which Article 3a requires member states to achieve is perfectly clear. It is to prevent the exercise by broadcasters of exclusive rights in such a way that a substantial proportion of the public in another member state is deprived of the possibility of following a designated event. The obligation to achieve that result is in no way qualified by considerations of competition, free market economics, sanctity of contract and so forth. The fact that reference is made to these matters in

---

356. *R (TVDanmark) v Independent Television Commission* [2001] UKHL 42; [2001] 1 WLR 1604.
357. Although these are not explicitly mentioned by the Directive, the vast majority of events designated in Member States have been sporting occasions.
358. Lefever & Weekers, 'Digital sports content: the rise of new media players and the legal consequences in terms of obligations and liability risk' (2010) Ent L R 215.

the recitals to the Directive explains why the scope of Article 3a is limited in the way it is. Its terms represent a compromise between the policies in question and the interests of the general public in being able to watch sporting events for free. Member states are limited in the sporting or other events they may reserve for their public broadcasters. Only those of 'major importance for society' can qualify. Premier League football matches, for example, are subject to a free market. Furthermore, national measures enacted pursuant to Article 3a(1) must be approved by the Commission under paragraph (2) as 'compatible with Community law'. So the balance between the interests of sports organisers and pay-TV broadcasters in maintaining a free market and the perceived interest of the citizen in being able to watch important sporting events has already been struck in the terms in which Article 3a has been framed.[359]

[8.190] Challenges have also previously been brought at European level to the exercise of powers by Member States in this area, with the Court of First Instance finding in *Infront WM v EC Commission*[360] that the Commission's decision to accept the United Kingdom's designations should be annulled on procedural grounds. A more substantive challenge to the power of the EU to act in this way is currently before the European courts with the football authorities, UEFA and FIFA, questioning the designation of their events.[361] However, the increasing recognition by the EU of the social and public importance of sport,[362] culminating in the acquisition by the Union of a new competence in this area under Art 165 of the Treaty on the Functioning of the European Union, mean that sporting authorities may find it difficult in the long term to avoid continued regulation by the EU of the allocation of exclusive broadcasting rights. Indeed, it has been argued by some that there may be a right of access to such broadcasts as matters of public interest under Article 10 of the European Convention on Human Rights.[363]

[8.191] The power to designate under the 1999 Act was first exercised by the Minister in 2002 after a public outcry when the rights to screen live coverage of the Republic of Ireland's home international football matches over a four-year period were sold to the subscription-based channel, Sky Sports.[364] More recently, there has been controversy from the opposite perspective in relation to the Minister's proposal to designate certain rugby competitions as major events, with the result that the television rights in relation to those matches could only be sold to free-to-air broadcasters.

---

359. *R (TVDanmark) v Independent Television Commission* [2001] UKHL 42; [2001] 1 WLR 1604, para 33.
360. *Infront WM v EC* Commission (Case T–33/01).
361. *UEFA v Commission* (T–55/08); *FIFA v Commission* (T–68/08). See further Geay & Ward, 'UEFA and FIFA challenge EU approved listed TV events' (2008) 6 World Sports Law Report 3.
362. This has been referred to at European level as the 'specificity of sport'. For an in-depth treatment, see Parrish & Miettinen, *The Sporting Exception in European Union Law* (TMC Asser Institute, 2008).
363. See Lefever, Cannie & Valcke 'Watching live sport on television: a human right? The right to information and the list of major events regime' (2010) EHRLR 396.
364. See Cox, 'Legal regulation of the broadcasting of sporting events in Europe' (2004) 11(1) DULJ 146.

[8.192] Under s 162, the Minister may designate events as events of major importance to society. The result of this is that only a qualifying broadcaster – defined as one that provides near-universal coverage (which, in most situations, is coverage to 95 per cent of the population – will have the right to provide coverage of these events. Coverage must be provided on a free basis and it is for the Minister to also determine whether the coverage should be available on a live, deferred or both live and deferred basis, and in whole, in part or both in whole and in part.[365] In this regard, it should be noted that Art 14 of the Directive appears to indicate a presumption in favour of live broadcasts by providing that deferred coverage is permitted where 'necessary or appropriate for objective reasons in the public interest'.

[8.193] In considering whether to designate an event, the Minister must have regard to all the circumstances and in particular to the extent to which the event has a special general resonance for the people of Ireland, and the extent to which the event has a generally recognised distinct cultural importance for the people of Ireland.[366] In considering these criteria, the Minister may also consider whether the event involves participation by a national or non-national team or by Irish persons, and what past practice or experience with regard to television coverage of the event or similar events has been.[367] The Minister must also consider the nature of the event, the time within the State at which the event takes place, and practical broadcasting considerations.[368]

[8.194] Before making a designation order, the Minister must make reasonable efforts to consult with the organisers of the event and with broadcasters who are under the jurisdiction of the State for the purpose of the Council Directive, and must publish a notice of the event which the Minister intends to designate under that section on a website maintained by him or her and where appropriate in a newspaper circulating in the State, and invite comments on the intended designation from members of the public.[369]

[8.195] Where it is proposed to make, revoke or amend an order designating particular events, a draft of the order must be laid before each House of the Oireachtas and the order shall not be made until a resolution approving the draft has been passed by each House.

[8.196] The Minister is also obliged to review the designated list at least every three years.[370] The list is currently under review but at present includes:

- the Summer Olympics;

- the All-Ireland Senior Football and Hurling finals;

---

365. Broadcasting Act 2009, s 162(2).
366. Broadcasting Act 2009, s 162(2).
367. Broadcasting Act 2009, s 162(3).
368. Broadcasting Act 2009, s 162(4).
369. Broadcasting Act 2009, s 163.
370. Broadcasting Act 2009, s 173(2).

- Ireland's qualifying games in the European Football Championship and World Cup;

- the opening games, semi-finals and the final of the European Football Championship Finals and the FIFA World Cup Finals;

- Ireland's games at the Rugby World Cup Finals;

- the Irish Grand National and the Irish Derby;

- the Nations Cup at the Dublin Horse Show;

- Ireland's games in the Six Nations Rugby Football Championship (deferred coverage).

The proposed amendments announced by the Minister as part of a public consultation were to add the following events to the list:

- the provincial finals in the GAA Senior Football and Hurling Championships;

- the All-Ireland Championship Senior Football and Hurling quarter-finals and semi-finals;

- Ireland's games in the Six Nations Rugby Football Championship to move from a deferred to a live basis;

- European Rugby Cup (qualifiers – pre-quarter final stages – quarter finals, semi finals and final when an Irish team is participating);

- the Cheltenham Festival.

Where a broadcaster under the jurisdiction of the State who is not a qualifying broadcaster acquires exclusive rights to broadcast a designated event, that broadcaster may not broadcast the event unless it has first been made available to a qualifying broadcaster on request and the payment of reasonable market rates by the qualifying broadcaster.[371] A dispute as to reasonable market rates may be referred to the High Court.[372] Where a qualifying broadcaster acquires the right to broadcast a designated event, the broadcaster must broadcast the event on a free television service providing near-universal coverage. This obligation to broadcast addresses one of the concerns which have been expressed in other jurisdictions with similar systems where qualifying broadcasters have been accused of hoarding rights.[373]

[8.197] The Act provides for various other matters to be brought to the High Court under the designation system. Under s 166, a broadcaster who is concerned with a past or apprehended breach of the Act by another broadcaster may apply to the High Court for an order restraining the offending broadcaster from carrying on or attempting to carry on the prohibited conduct.[374] The broadcaster may also seek a declaration that the

---

371. Broadcasting Act 2009, s 164(1).
372. Broadcasting Act 2009, s 167(1).
373. See Lefever, Cannie & Valcke 'Watching live sport on television: a human right? The right to information and the list of major events regime' (2010) EHRLR 396.
374. Broadcasting Act 2009, s 166(1)(a).

contract under which the other broadcaster received exclusive rights to the designated event is void;[375] damages from the other broadcaster;[376] and a direction that the right to provide television coverage of the event shall be offered to the applicant broadcaster at reasonable market rates.[377]

[8.198] Where an event has been designated and no arrangement has been made between the event and a qualifying broadcaster by the time the event is 56 days away (or some other period set by the Minister), a qualifying broadcaster may make a summary application to the High Court for an order directing the event organiser to give rights to the qualifying broadcaster on reasonable market rates.[378] Where more than one broadcaster applies, the event organiser may choose between them.[379] The court may also direct the event organiser to provide the rights on terms fixed by the court where all terms and conditions have not been agreed. However, an event organiser is also entitled to notify the Minister of his or her intention not to broadcast the event, in which case this jurisdiction will not be available.[380]

[8.199] A more unusual procedure is provided for by s 168(2). This allows an event organiser to request the High Court to invite qualifying broadcasters to make an application for the rights in question. While this is obviously intended to address the situation where no broadcaster applies for a designated event (such as, for example, occurred in Belgium when no Flemish broadcaster sought to acquire the rights to the Belgian team's qualifying matches for the 2010 World Cup), it is not clear what role the High Court is envisaged to have on such an application.

Audiovisual Media Services Directive

[8.200] The EU has exercised an increasingly significant influence on broadcasting policy across the continent in recent decades. Although it was originally argued that broadcasting was outside the scope of the Community as a cultural matter, the ECJ regarded it as a form of service in *Saachi*,[381] which could accordingly be subject to regulation with a view to ensuring the free movement of services. Thus a Dutch restriction on the broadcasting of advertisements into Holland from another Member State was held to contravene Community law in *Bond van Adverteerders*.[382] With its competence to act in this area confirmed, the Community sought to move beyond negative prohibitions to also enact positive harmonisation measures which were

---

375.   Broadcasting Act 2009, s 166(1)(b).
376.   Broadcasting Act 2009, s 166(1)(c).
377.   Broadcasting Act 2009, s 166(1)(d).
378.   Broadcasting Act 2009, s 168(1). The question of reasonable market rates can be referred to an arbitrator under sub-s (5). This is also available where the organiser and broadcaster agree to an arrangement but cannot agree on the rates to be paid.
379.   Broadcasting Act 2009, s 168(8).
380.   Broadcasting Act 2009, s 168(3).
381.   *Saachi* [1974] ECR 409.
382.   *Bond van Adverteerders* (Case 352/85) [1988] ECR 205.

designed to provide a level playing field for broadcasters across the Community. This led to the enactment of the Television Without Frontiers Directive[383] in 1989.

[8.201] The most recent revision of this Directive is the Audiovisual Media Services Directive which Member States were obliged to give effect to by December 2009. The Directive has been implemented in Ireland by the Broadcasting Act 2009 and by the European Communities (Audiovisual Media Services) Regulations.[384]

[8.202] The Directive is a very important measure in that it establishes a relatively extensive set of rules in relation to the regulation of broadcasting in Europe. The main impetus for the introduction of this revised Directive was to respond to the significant technological changes which had occurred since the previous revision of the Television Without Frontiers Directive in 1997. As discussed further below, the Directive addresses this issue of technological change by adopting a technology-neutral or platform-neutral approach, in accordance with which it is the television-like nature of the content, rather than the way in which it is delivered, which will attract regulation. It has been described as an attempt to deal with 'the converging and ever-fluid global media environment' by 'playing an essential although non-exclusive role in both the regulation and governance of traditional and new media services and providers through the use of different and often hybrid modes of content regulation'.[385]

[8.203] The key aspects of the Directive are discussed further below. However, it might be useful to note at the outset that the Directive reflects the somewhat fragmented nature of EU broadcasting policy. While the EU now has competence to take action on cultural issues,[386] its policies in the broadcasting field have continued to be influenced by both economic and cultural factors. This means that the Directive, in general, operates in two ways. One the one hand, it aims to protect media service providers against over-regulation or unfair regulation at national level by establishing limits to the national power to regulate certain matters. These restrictions tend to reflect the economic objectives of ensuring free movement and facilitating an increase in commercial revenue for broadcasters. On the other hand, the Directive also imposes obligations and minimum standards on broadcasters in respect of a number of public policy objectives, such as the promotion and protection of cultural heritage and the protection of children and consumers. The difficult balance which the Directive attempts to strike between these often competing considerations is evident in many of the Directive's more controversial provisions.[387]

---

383. Directive 89/552/EEC on the coordination of certain provisions laid down by law, regulation or administrative action in Member States concerning the provision of audiovisual media services
384. European Communities (Audiovisual Media Services) Regulations (SI 258/2010).
385. Dizon, 'Looking beyond the linear/non-linear horizon: content regulation in the converging multilayered contours of the European audiovisual media landscape' (2010) Ent LR 185.
386. Treaty on the Functioning of the European Union, Art 167.
387. The Directive has provoked a great deal of academic comment, much of it critical. See, for example, Burri-Nenova, 'The New Audiovisual Media Services Directive: Television Without Frontiers, Television Without Cultural Diversity' (2007) 44 Common Market Law Review 1689; (contd \...)

[8.204] It should also be noted that the Directive does not prevent Member States from imposing more detailed or stricter rules, provided those rules comply with EU law.[388] This underlines the reality that the Directive should not be regarded as an end in itself. In many situations, it will operate alongside domestic regulations in the European broadcasting sphere. In practice, the country of origin provision of the Directive may somewhat limit Member States' freedom to introduce stricter provisions by facilitating the possibility of forum-shopping by broadcasters. However, the Directive marks a possible improvement over its predecessors in this regard in that it now allows Member States with stricter laws to take steps to limit the ability of service providers to broadcast material which contravenes domestic rules into that State from another Member State.

Scope of the Directive

[8.205] The Directive adopts a technology-neutral approach to the notion of what constitutes a media services provider. However, many of its provisions are strikingly ambiguous, employing a mixture of everyday and industry terms. It seems likely that litigation will be required to clarify some of these matters. Bearing that in mind, an audiovisual media services provider is defined by Art 1.1 as:

> [A] service defined by Articles 49 and 50 of the Treaty which is under the editorial responsibility of a media service provider and the principal purpose of which is the provision of programmes in order to inform, entertain and educate, to the general public by electronic communications networks within the meaning of Article 2(a) of Directive 2002/21/EC. Such an audiovisual media service is either a television broadcast as defined in point (e) of this Article or an on-demand audiovisual media service as defined in point (g) of this Article; and/or audiovisual commercial communication'.

[8.206] 'Television broadcast' is defined as 'an audiovisual media service provided by a media services provider for simultaneous viewing of programmes on the basis of a programme schedule',[389] while 'programme' is defined as:

> ... a set of moving images with or without sound constituting an individual item within a schedule or a catalogue established by a media service provider and whose form and content is comparable to the form and content of television broadcasting. Examples of programmes include feature-length films, sports events, situation comedies, documentaries, children's programmes and original drama.[390]

---

387. (contd) Good & Goldberg, 'European reaction to the proposed new Audiovisual Services Directive' (2006) 11 Comms L 183; Geach, 'Converging Regulation for Convergent Media: an overview of the Audiovisual Media Services Directive' (2008) 1 JILT 10. Jan Willem van den Bos, 'No frontiers: the new EU proposal on audiovisual media services' [2006] Ent LR 109, 111 and 113; Lutz, 'The distinction between linear and non-linear services in the new proposal for an audiovisual media directive'.

388. Directive is Directive 97/36/EC (Audiovisual Media Services Directive), Art 4.

389. Directive 97/36/EC (Audiovisual Media Services Directive), Art 1.1(e).

390. Directive 97/36/EC (Audiovisual Media Services Directive), Art 1.1(b).

The Directive also draws a distinction between linear services like traditional television broadcasting and non-linear or 'on demand' services. As explained below, different obligations are applied in certain instances to each under the Directive. An 'on-demand' service is one which is 'provided by a media service provider for the viewing of programmes at the moment chosen by the user and at his individual request on the basis of a catalogue of programmes selected by the media service provider'.[391] The latter could cover delivery methods such as online streaming services or webcasting.[392] This has been explained as distinguishing between 'push' content (where the provider determines when and how the material is made available) and 'pull' content (where it is the viewer who decides when and how to access the service).[393]

[8.207] Despite suggestions to the contrary, however, this does not mean that the Directive represents an attempt to regulate the internet.[394] Rather, it is capable of applying to internet material where it is sufficiently television-like and meets the other relevant criteria. In particular, the Directive exempts service providers who do not have editorial responsibility for the material supplied. Editorial responsibility is defined as 'the exercise of effective control both over the selection of the programmes and over their organisation either in a chronological schedule, in the case of television broadcasts, or in a catalogue, in the case of on-demand audiovisual media services'. This has generally been explained as intended to exempt many online providers, such as YouTube for example, who simply provide the framework for the publication and dissemination of material by third parties. It should be noted in this context that the Directive specifies in Art 4.8 that this Directive does not affect the continued application of the E-Commerce Directive.[395]

[8.208] For the Directive to apply, therefore:

- the service must be operated by a media service provider which exercises 'editorial responsibility';

- the media service provider must be based in the European Union;

- the service must consist of 'programmes';

- the principal purpose of the programmes must be to inform, entertain or educate;[396]

---

391. Directive 97/36/EC (Audiovisual Media Services Directive), Art 1.1(g).

392. See Onay, 'Regulating webcasting: an analysis of the Audiovisual Media Services Directive and the current broadcasting law in the UK' (2009) 25 Computer and Security Law 335.

393. On the implications of this approach for the individual's right of access, see Helberger 'The 'right to information' and digital broadcasting – about monsters, invisible men, and the future of European broadcasting regulation' (2006) Ent L Rev 70.

394. For a discussion of this debate, see Castendyk & Bottcher, 'The Commission's proposal for a new Directive on audiovisual content–a feasible solution?' (2006) Ent LR 180.

395. Directive 2000/31/EC. However, the Audiovisual Media Services Directive will prevail in a case of conflict unless it provides otherwise.

396. Wardale has argued that 'it is hard to see how these subjective criteria will ever operate to remove a service from the regulatory remit of the AVMS Directive'. Wardale, 'The new frontier – the Audiovisual Media Services Directive' (2009) European Intellectual Property Review 336, 338.

- the service must be mass media, meaning that 'it is intended for reception by and could have a clear impact on a significant proportion of the general public';

- in the case of an on-demand service, the service must be television-like. This means that the on-demand service 'competes for the same audience as television broadcasts and the nature and means of access to the service would lead the user to reasonably expect regulatory protection'.[397]

The Directive establishes a number of common rules which apply to all media services providers. The most significant are considered below:

Country of origin

[8.209] Article 2 sets out the principles governing the application of the country of origin principle under the Directive. This means that service providers must comply with the laws of the Member State where the service is established rather than those of the state or states where the service can be received. Article 2 indicates that the jurisdiction of a provider is a matter which is capable of being determined as a matter of fact based on, inter alia, an assessment of the location of the provider's head office, editorial decision-making and/or a significant part of its workforce.[398]

[8.210] Where none of these considerations apply, a provider may still be regarded as based in a Member State where it uses a satellite uplink or satellite capacity in that state.[399]

[8.211] The Directive does, however, provide for a procedure under which a Member State into which a service is provider may contact the Member State in which a service provider is based to consider a 'mutually satisfactory solution to any problems posed'. Where such a request is made, the Member State with jurisdiction over the provider is obliged to request the broadcaster to comply with 'the rules of general public interest in question'.[400] Where no solution is reached, a Member State is ultimately entitled after due notification and consultation with the other Member State and the Commission to take action against the broadcaster in question.

Freedom of transmission

[8.212] Article 3 obliges Member States to ensure freedom of reception and to refrain from restricting retransmissions on their territory of audiovisual media services from other Member State. This has been a fundamental principle of European broadcasting regulation for decades. Member States may derogate from this obligation where the provider in question has manifestly, seriously and gravely infringed the provisions of the

---

397. Ridgeway, 'The Audiovisual Media Services Directive – what does it mean, is it necessary and what are the challenges to its implementation?' (2008) Computer and Telecommunications Law Review 108.
398. Directive 97/36/EC (Audiovisual Media Services Directive), Art 2.3.
399. Directive 97/36/EC (Audiovisual Media Services Directive), Art 2.4.
400. Directive 97/36/EC (Audiovisual Media Services Directive), Art 4.2.

Directive on incitement to hatred or protection of children. However, this can only apply after the third infringement in a 12-month period, and after the Commission and government of the Member State in which the provider is based have been notified.

General obligations

[8.213] Member States are required to ensure that broadcasters do not engage in particular forms of conduct. This includes the broadcast of material containing any incitement to hatred on the grounds of race, sex, religion or nationality[401] or any interference with cinema copyright.[402] Broadcasters should also be encouraged to gradually make their services available to those with a visual or hearing disability.[403]

Advertising

[8.214] Articles 9 to 11 of the Directive lay down a number of quantitative and qualitative rules relating to advertising that apply to all service providers. Many of these are reflected in the terms of the 2009 Act, as discussed in more detail above. Subliminal and surreptitious advertising is prohibited, as are all forms of tobacco advertising and alcohol advertising aimed at children. Advertisements also may not prejudice respect for human dignity; include or promote any discrimination based on sex, racial or ethnic origin, nationality, religion or belief, disability, age or sexual orientation; encourage behaviour prejudicial to health or safety; or encourage behaviour grossly prejudicial to the protection of the environment.

[8.215] Product placement is also prohibited, with a limited power to derogate in certain circumstances. Ireland has exercised this power to derogate so that product placement is admissible for on-demand services that are cinematographic works, films and series made for audiovisual media services, sports programmes or light entertainment programmes (but not children's programmes); or where there is no payment for the placement of the product but only the provision of certain goods or services free of charge with a view to their inclusion in a programme. Any such placement must be appropriately identified and cannot influence the content of a programme in such a way as to affect the responsibility and editorial independence of the media service provider. Placements also may not directly encourage the purchase or rental of goods or services, in particular by making special promotional references to those goods or services, and may not give undue prominence to the product in question.[404]

Articles 19 to 25 provide for further restrictions in relation to television advertising.

Protection of minors

[8.216] Although the protection of minors is referred to as an important public policy objective throughout the Directive, it is notable that it imposes different obligations in

---

401. Directive 97/36/EC (Audiovisual Media Services Directive), Art 6.
402. Directive 97/36/EC (Audiovisual Media Services Directive), Art 8.
403. Directive 97/36/EC (Audiovisual Media Services Directive), Art 7.
404. Regulation 8 of the European Communities (Audiovisual Media Services) Regulations 2010.

this regard on linear and non-linear providers. Non-linear services are subject to less onerous requirements, which reflects the user-controlled nature of on-demand services.

[8.217] For on-demand services Member States must take appropriate measures to ensure that on-demand audiovisual media services provided by media service providers under their jurisdiction which might seriously impair the physical, mental or moral development of minors are only made available in such a way as to ensure that minors will not normally hear or see such on-demand audiovisual media services.[405]

[8.218] For television broadcasts, Member States are obliged to take appropriate measures to ensure that broadcasts do not include any programmes which might seriously impair the physical, mental or moral development of minors. Programmes that involve pornography or gratuitous violence are specifically identified by the Directive as programmes which may give rise to such concerns. The Directive allows for this obligation to be modified on the basis of the time of broadcast or by reference to some method for controlling access. However, it specifies that where such programmes are broadcast in an un-encoded form, Member States must ensure that they are preceded by an acoustic warning or are identified by the presence of a visual symbol throughout their duration.[406]

Access to exclusive rights

[8.219] The Directive regulates the ability of domestic laws to allow for the acquisition by particular broadcasters of exclusive rights to broadcast major events. This has an obvious importance to ensuring a level playing field between broadcasters based in different Member States. Thus, as discussed in more detail above, Member States are obliged to ensure that a broadcaster over whom they have jurisdiction does not frustrate the designation of an event as one of major importance by another Member State.[407]

[8.220] In addition, the Directive also requires Member States to ensure that any broadcaster established in the Union is allowed access on a fair, reasonable and non-discriminatory basis to events of high interest to the public which are transmitted on an exclusive basis by a broadcaster within their jurisdiction for the purpose of providing short news reports.[408] The Directive appears to indicate a preference for allowing this to occur by permitting other broadcasters to take such reports freely from the relevant broadcaster's transmission.[409]

Quotas

[8.221] Finally, the Directive also makes relatively extensive provision for quotas in relation to the broadcast of independent and European works. In general, it requires a

---

405. Directive 97/36/EC (Audiovisual Media Services Directive), Art 12.
406. Directive 97/36/EC (Audiovisual Media Services Directive), Art 27.
407. Directive 97/36/EC (Audiovisual Media Services Directive), Art 14.
408. Directive 97/36/EC (Audiovisual Media Services Directive), Art 15.
409. Directive 97/36/EC (Audiovisual Media Services Directive), Art 15.3.

majority of broadcast time excluding the time allotted to news, sports events, games, advertising, teletext services and teleshopping to be reserved for European works with 10 per cent of broadcast time or programming budgets to be reserved for European works from independent producers.

Chapter 9

REGULATION OF THE PRESS

SELF-REGULATION V STATUTORY REGULATION

[9.01] In addition to the laws covered elsewhere in this book which govern matters like defamation and privacy, newspapers and periodicals in Ireland are also regulated by the Press Council and Press Ombudsman. The regulation of the press is a common feature of media governance systems in most European countries. By and large, press regulation in these jurisdictions has taken one of two forms – self-regulation or statutory regulation. However, both versions have been subject to considerable criticism.

[9.02] On the one hand, self-regulatory systems like the Press Complaints Commission in the United Kingdom have been accused of being ineffective and unduly sympathetic to the interests of journalists and editors. In an era where it is demanded – not least by the press themselves – that commercial, professional and social bodies be subject to some degree of outside scrutiny, self-regulation by the press would appear as something of an anomaly.

[9.03] However, the traditional alternative of statutory regulation has also been criticised on the grounds that it allows government and the legislature to determine 'appropriate' forms of press coverage. It should be recalled that press regulation is concerned with the penumbra between reporting which is contrary to some legal principle and reporting which is clearly protected by the constitutional and Convention guarantees of media freedom of expression. For political actors to interfere in this area and dictate what will be regarded as acceptable coverage raises obvious concerns about censorship.

[9.04] The respective weaknesses of these models have been the subject of much discussion in the English context. The level of regulation provided by the Press Complaints Commission there has long been regarded by many as inadequate. The 1993 Calcutt Report concluded that self-regulation had failed and should be replaced with a statutory model.[1] The House of Commons Committee on Culture, Media and Sport noted in its most recent report that 'the general effectiveness of the PCC has been repeatedly called into question'[2] in the evidence presented to it. One lawyer suggested to the Committee that the PCC 'not only lacked power, but also nerve', explaining that:

> It cannot award damages. It cannot force apologies. As soon as there is any dispute of fact between the newspaper and the victim of the libel, the PCC backs off and says, 'This needs to go to law.'

---

1. Department of National Heritage, Review of press self-regulation (1993)
2. House of Commons Committee on Culture, Media and Sport, Second Report on press standards, privacy and libel (The Stationary Office Ltd, 2010), para 513.

Similarly, another law firm submitted that:

> It cannot: make findings of fact or declarations of falsity of allegations; make a
> monetary award of compensation in appropriate cases; compel witnesses or order
> disclosure; deal effectively with pre-publication disputes. There is also a general
> public perception that the Press Complaints Commission is too favourable to the
> media; accordingly there is a lack of public confidence in using this route to
> resolve serious complaints against the media.

[9.05] The Committee itself expressed its 'deep misgivings' about the self-regulatory
system. These comments echoed earlier academic criticisms of the self-regulatory
model:

> [It has been said that] a statutory regulator for the press would represent a very
> dangerous interference with the freedom of the press. This is altogether too
> alarmist. If freedom of the press means no more than our collective rights
> performed on our behalf by those daily engaged in news-gathering, we (the public)
> should determine how far we should restrict our collective rights. The freedom of
> the press, if it means nothing more than freedom of speech deployed through
> multifaceted, corporate bodies, should be kept alive and vigorously supported by
> controls which can be intrinsically justified, such as are the laws of libel, copyright
> and contempt of court. Article 10(2) needs as much constant public vigilance as
> does its primary sub-article. Hence there is no earthly reason why the legislature
> should not intervene in pursuance of Article 10(2) qualifications, so long as the
> legislation does not infringe the basic ingredients of Article 10(1). Statutory
> regulation of the media – we already have it for broadcasting and television – can
> be entirely acceptable if it observes the basic tenet of freedom of expression.[3]

The Committee's report also, however, provides a useful overview of the problems of a
system of statutory regulation. In an earlier report, the Committee had concluded that:

> We do not believe that there is a case for a statutory regulator for the press, which
> would represent a very dangerous interference with the freedom of the press. We
> continue to believe that statutory regulation of the press is a hallmark of
> authoritarianism and risks undermining democracy. We recommend that self-
> regulation should be retained for the press, while recognising that it must be seen
> to be effective if calls for statutory intervention are to be resisted.[4]

Despite its misgivings about self-regulation, it still favoured retaining it over replacing it
with a system of statutory regulation:

> We remain of the view that self-regulation of the press is greatly preferable to
> statutory regulation, and should continue. However for confidence to be
> maintained, the industry regulator must actually effectively regulate, not just
> mediate. The powers of the PCC must be enhanced, as it is toothless compared to
> other regulators.

---

3. Blom-Cooper, 'Press freedom: constitutional right or cultural assumption? (2008) PL 260, 275–276.
4. Culture, Media and Sport Committee, Seventh Report on self-regulation of the press (2007).

A HYBRID MODEL OF REGULATION

[9.06] Ireland has, however, recently developed a hybrid model of press regulation which combines elements of both statutory and self-regulation. This aims to avoid the main dangers associated with the traditional models by establishing a system which is independent of government in its funding and design but which has a certain level of statutory force. The system is still in its infancy and it would be premature to conclude that it represents a successful or effective middle ground between these competing models. Nonetheless, it is an interesting experiment which seems likely – if successful – to be incorporated in some form into other jurisdictions in the future.

Background

[9.07] The main impetus for the creation of the Press Council and Ombudsman was the publication by the Legal Advisory Group on Defamation in 2003 of a report recommending the establishment of a system of statutory regulation in Ireland. As part of its terms of reference, the Group had been asked 'to consider the nature and extent of any statutory intervention which might attach to the establishment of any entity concerned with the regulation of the press, to examine the particular modifications in the law which the establishment of such an entity might warrant, and, to make specific proposals in this regard'.[5] Having reviewed the arguments set out above and taken account of the way in which it had been possible for the Broadcasting Complaints Commission to subject the broadcast media to statutory regulation, the Group concluded that a similar statutory model should be introduced in Ireland. It felt that 'it should be possible to construct a statutory model which would respect fully the autonomy of the press while, at the same time, providing an important element of independence and transparency which would secure public confidence in any process which might be established',[6] and there was, accordingly, a compelling case for a statutory press council.

[9.08] This prompted the press industry to establish a regulatory system for itself in an effort to forestall statutory intervention in the industry. A Press Industry Steering Committee, made up of the National Newspapers of Ireland, the Regional Newspapers Association of Ireland, the Periodical Publishers Association of Ireland, the National Union of Journalists, and the Irish Editions of UK Titles was established with the aim of agreeing a model for an independent press complaints mechanism. Consultations were held with the Minister for Justice, Equality and Law Reform in relation to the Defamation Bill which was then making its way through the Oireachtas. Ultimately, the work of all parties led to the creation of the current system, under which the Press Ombudsman and Press Council exist as independent bodies which enjoy a specific statutory status under the Defamation Act 2009. The bodies are funded by the press industry and apply a Code of Practice which was originally drawn up by the Press Industry Steering Committee, based on several other codes and on the work of Professor Kevin Boyle and Ms Marie McGonagle. Because of the direct input of the industry into

---

5.   Report of the Legal Advisory Group on Defamation (2003), para 2.
6.   Report of the Legal Advisory Group on Defamation (2003), para 25.

the content of the Code of Practice and the funding of the Ombudsman and Council, the model bears distinct traces of the self-regulatory model and cannot truly be described as independent. The bodies also cannot fine errant publications, which has been one of the main criticisms levelled at the Press Complaints Commission in the United Kingdom.

[9.09] Concerns over the bodies' independence have been expressed:

> While the Ombudsman has been at pains to stress the independence of the Press Council and the concerted efforts to avoid the significant shortcomings and 'alarming procedural opaqueness' of the United Kingdom's PCC, in reality, there is really only a lay majority of one in the Irish Press Council (and an independent chairman) so it is hoped that the United Kingdom's 'structural bias in favour of the press' which 'permits it to ride rough shod over the rights of individuals to privacy and reputation' will not develop in Ireland.[7]

These concerns were further raised when it was decided by the Council that the publication of dissenting judgments or the fact that members of the Council had dissented would not be permitted. Given the narrow balance between lay members and industry insiders on the Council, this undermines its independence, especially if – as might be expected – the industry members tend to adopt a similar stance. This decision led one of its members to resign in protest at this 'façade of unanimity'.

[9.10] However, these factors are balanced by the fact that the courts can have regard to the Code and to the decisions of the Ombudsman and Council in defamation cases. This is the novel element of the hybrid system which has the most radical potential as it creates the possibility that a finding that a newspaper or periodical has breached the Code may ultimately have adverse legal consequences for the publication in question. Depending on how this is dealt with by the courts, this may create a significant incentive for publications to comply with the Code and to resolve any complaints by mediation rather than adjudication.

COMPOSITION OF THE PRESS COUNCIL AND OMBUDSMAN

[9.11] Professor John Horgan was appointed as the first Press Ombudsman in August 2007 and has remained in that post up to the present time. Professor Horgan's appointment was widely welcomed, in part because of his past experience as a journalist, politician and academic.

[9.12] The Press Council is comprised of 13 members with a majority from outside the newspaper and periodical industry. Seven members, including the Chairman, are drawn from what are described as 'suitably qualified persons representative of a broad spectrum of Irish society'. The other six members are appointed from within the industry. The first Chairman was former Provost of Trinity, Professor Tom Mitchell. He was recently replaced by Mr Dáithí O'Ceallaigh, who was previously a diplomat with the Department of Foreign Affairs.

---

7. Nagle, 'Keeping its own counsel: the Irish Press Council, self-regulation and media freedom' (2009) Ent LR 93.

COMPLAINT PROCESS

[9.13] The complaint process operated by the Ombudsman and Council is intended to operate as a free and speedy mechanism for resolving disputes. Parties are entitled to legal representation during the process but this is discouraged on the basis that the process 'becomes more complex and unnecessarily drawn out'.[8] The Ombudsman has previously indicated that he will not consider complaints that are already the subject of legal proceedings.

Complaint to the Ombudsman

[9.14] A complaint can be made against any newspaper or periodical which is covered by the Code of Practice, or against any journalist subject to the Code. At present, the publications covered are:

- *Evening Herald*;
- *Irish Daily Mail*;
- *Irish Daily Mirror*;
- *Irish Daily Star*;
- *Irish Daily Star Sunday*;
- *Irish Examiner*;
- *Irish Farmers Journal*;
- *Irish Independent*;
- *Irish Mail on Sunday*;
- *Irish News of the World*;
- *Irish Sun*;
- *Irish Sunday Mirror*;
- *Irish Times*;
- *Sunday Business Post*;
- *Sunday Independent*;
- *Sunday Times*;
- *Sunday Tribune*;
- *Sunday World*.

[9.15] Complaints may only be made by the individual who is personally affected by the impugned publication, or by a third party acting with the written consent of the person affected. Affected persons can include family members of the person who was the subject of the publication, where appropriate.[9]

---

8.   See www.presscouncil.ie/making-a-complaint.24.html.
9.   See, for example, *Ennis and the Sunday World* (3 December 2009).

[9.16] A complainant is directed to contact the editor of the publication involved in writing before making a complaint to the Ombudsman. The Ombudsman will consider a complaint if the editor fails to respond within a reasonable period, or responds in a manner which the complainant regards as unsatisfactory.

[9.17] Complaints must be made to the Ombudsman within three months of the conduct or publication about which the person wishes to complain. Complaints must be in writing and must contain a copy of the publication which is the subject-matter of the complaint, all correspondence with the editor, and a statement identifying the alleged breaches of the Code of Practice. A complaint can be communicated in written or electronic form.

[9.18] When a complaint is made to the Ombudsman, it is subject to an initial assessment of whether the complaint is valid. The Ombudsman will not consider complaints which do not present prima facie evidence of a breach of the Code of Practice, are the subject-matter of legal proceedings, are brought outside the three-month time limit, or are made by a person or persons not affected by the article who do not have the written consent of the relevant parties.

[9.19] If it is determined that the complaint is a valid one, the Ombudsman's office sends a copy of the complaint, together with any supporting information included by the complainant, to the editor of the publication involved. This is done with a view to facilitating a mediated and confidential resolution of the complaint. The office of the Ombudsman have indicated that the conciliation process typically takes about six weeks but that this may be extended where detailed or lengthy exchanges take place between the parties. In 2008 almost 25% of complaints were successfully mediated, with this number rising to almost 30% in 2009.

[9.20] If no mediated agreement is reached, the complaint is then subject to examination by the Press Ombudsman himself. This review is based on the complaint and on all of the circumstances surrounding it, which include any offers made by the editor as part of the pre-complaint or mediation process. The Ombudsman has frequently rejected complaints on the basis that sufficient remedial offers were made by the editor in question but rejected by the complainant.[10] However, where the publication is prominent, a clarification may not be sufficient and an apology or retraction may be required.[11] In adjudicating upon a complaint, the Ombudsman's decision may uphold the complaint, reject the complaint, determine that an offer made by the publication is, in all the circumstances of the particular complaint, sufficient remedial action by the publication concerned to resolve the complaint, or decide that there is insufficient evidence available to him to make a decision on the complaint. Reasons are given for any decision made.

---

10.   See, for example, *Crown and the Evening Herald* (30 June 2010); *McDaid and the Irish Sunday Mirror* (15 August 2010); *A Doctor and the Irish Daily Mail* (18 June 2010).
11.   *Geraghty and the Sunday Independent* (29 January 2010).

[9.21] If the Press Ombudsman upholds the complaint, the publication concerned is obliged to publish that part of his decision upholding the complaint. A copy of the decision is also published on the Ombudsman's website. Publications are required to publish decisions in accordance with the Publication Guidelines laid down by the Press Council. These require that decisions be published in full, promptly, on the same page and same day of the week as the original article, and with similar prominence. The rules also prohibit any editorial commentary being included with the publication of the decision. Decisions will normally identify the parties, but a complainant can request that he or she retain his or her anonymity.

[9.22] However, the rules in relation to prominence are qualified by an important exception. Where a complaint has been upheld in relation to an article published on the front page of a publication, the decision need only be published with due prominence on one of the first four editorial pages. This is a qualification which seems motivated by commercial considerations on the part of the industry. It is clear that a requirement to publish a decision on the front page of a newspaper could have an adverse impact on the publication in question by potentially reducing its sales on the date in question. Obliging newspapers to publish decisions on the front page might also, over time, have an effect on the reputation of those publications which are found to have been in breach of the Code on several occasions. However, a strong argument can be made that this qualification undermines the effectiveness of the Ombudsman system. It has already been noted that the Ombudsman cannot fine publications, which removes one obvious option for encouraging compliance with the Code. The risk of being obliged to publish a decision on the front page could have provided a significant alternative incentive to publications to adhere to the Code precisely because of the adverse consequences identified above. It is also questionable whether this system is adequate to protect the complainant's interest. Front page headlines, by virtue of their prominence, reach a readership beyond those who actually purchase a newspaper. A publication which breaches the Code on the front page will reach many more people than those who might see the decision of the Ombudsman several weeks later on the inside of the publication. Furthermore, even amongst those who do buy the publication in question, the impact of the decision is likely to be less than that of the original story. As the Court of Appeal observed in *Flood v Times Newspapers*, there is a danger for the affected party that the fact that 'a person is accused is generally of far greater interest than his or her subsequent triumphant acquittal' such that '[o]nce an accusation is dismissed, the blaring headline of accusation on page 1 becomes a tepid reference in the graveyard of page 2'.[12]

Appeal to the Press Council

[9.23] Either party can appeal a decision of the Press Ombudsman to the Press Council within 10 working days of the date of the decision. An appeal must state grounds and show reasonable cause, either in relation to significant new information, or to any error in procedure or in the application of the Principles of the Code of Practice. Mere

---

12. *Flood v Times Newspapers* [2010] EWCA Civ 804, para 119.

disagreement with the Press Ombudsman's decision cannot be grounds for appeal. The Press Council of Ireland determines whether appeals are admissible.

[9.24] If an appeal is admissible, the Council will consider the matter on the basis of the documentation relating to the complaint only. However, it may in certain circumstances forward details of any significant new information furnished by an appellant to the other party involved, should it regard this as necessary and appropriate, and consider any response by the other party to such new information, as part of the appeal process.

[9.25] The Ombudsman is also entitled to exercise a power to refer complaints directly to the Press Council where they involve complex or significant matters.

THE CODE OF PRACTICE

[9.26] The Code of Practice was originally adopted by the Press Industry Steering Committee. It is, however, open to revision and has been subject to minor amendments already since its publication in 2007. This should be borne in mind when reading this section as the provisions set out below are likely to be further amended in the future.

Preamble

The freedom to publish is vital to the right of the people to be informed. This freedom includes the right of a newspaper to publish what it considers to be news, without fear or favour, and the right to comment upon it.

Freedom of the press carries responsibilities. Members of the press have a duty to maintain the highest professional and ethical standards.

This Code sets the benchmark for those standards. It is the duty of the Press Ombudsman and Press Council of Ireland to ensure that it is honoured in the spirit as well as in the letter, and it is the duty of publications to assist them in that task.

In dealing with complaints, the Ombudsman and Press Council will give consideration to what they perceive to be the public interest. It is for them to define the public interest in each case, but the general principle is that the public interest is invoked in relation to a matter capable of affecting the people at large so that they may legitimately be interested in receiving and the press legitimately interested in providing information about it.

Principle 1 • Truth and Accuracy

1.1 In reporting news and information, newspapers and periodicals shall strive at all times for truth and accuracy.

1.2 When a significant inaccuracy, misleading statement or distorted report or picture has been published, it shall be corrected promptly and with due prominence.

1.3 When appropriate, a retraction, apology, clarification, explanation or response shall be published promptly and with due prominence.

Principle 2 • Distinguishing Fact and Comment

2.1 Newspapers and periodicals are entitled to advocate strongly their own views on topics.

2.2 Comment, conjecture, rumour and unconfirmed reports shall not be reported as if they were fact.

2.3 Readers are entitled to expect that the content of a publication reflects the best judgment of editors and writers and has not been inappropriately influenced by undisclosed interests. Wherever relevant, any significant financial interest of an organization should be disclosed. Writers should disclose significant potential conflicts of interest to their editors.

Principle 3 • Fairness and Honesty

3.1 Newspapers and periodicals shall strive at all times for fairness and honesty in the procuring and publishing of news and information.

3.2 Publications shall not obtain information, photographs or other material through misrepresentation or subterfuge, unless justified by the public interest.

3.3 Journalists and photographers must not obtain, or seek to obtain, information and photographs through harassment, unless their actions are justified in the public interest.

Principle 4 • Respect for Rights

Everyone has constitutional protection for his or her good name. Newspapers and periodicals shall not knowingly publish matter based on malicious misrepresentation or unfounded accusations, and must take reasonable care in checking facts before publication.

Principle 5 • Privacy

5.1 Privacy is a human right, protected as a personal right in the Irish Constitution and the European Convention on Human Rights, which is incorporated into Irish law. The private and family life, home and correspondence of everyone must be respected.

5.2 Readers are entitled to have news and comment presented with respect for the privacy and sensibilities of individuals. However, the right to privacy should not prevent publication of matters of public record or in the public interest.

5.3 Sympathy and discretion must be shown at all times in seeking information in situations of personal grief or shock. In publishing such information, the feelings of grieving families should be taken into account. This should not be interpreted as restricting the right to report judicial proceedings.

5.4 Public persons are entitled to privacy. However, where a person holds public office, deals with public affairs, follows a public career, or has sought or obtained publicity for his activities, publication of relevant details of his private life and circumstances may be justifiable where the information revealed relates to the validity of the person's conduct, the credibility of his public statements, the value of his publicly expressed views or is otherwise in the public interest.

5.5 Taking photographs of individuals in private places without their consent is not acceptable, unless justified by the public interest.

Principle 6 • Protection of Sources

Journalists shall protect confidential sources of information.

Principle 7 • Court Reporting

Newspapers and periodicals shall strive to ensure that court reports (including the use of photographs) are fair and accurate, are not prejudicial to the right to a fair trial and that the presumption of innocence is respected.

Principle 8 • Prejudice

Newspapers and periodicals shall not publish material intended or likely to cause grave offence or stir up hatred against an individual or group on the basis of their race, religion, nationality, colour, ethnic origin, membership of the travelling community, gender, sexual orientation, marital status, disability, illness or age.

Principle 9 • Children

9.1 Newspapers and periodicals shall take particular care in seeking and presenting information or comment about a child under the age of 16.

9.2 Journalists and editors should have regard for the vulnerability of children, and in all dealings with children should bear in mind the age of the child, whether parental or other adult consent has been obtained for such dealings, the sensitivity of the subject-matter, and what circumstances if any make the story one of public interest. Young people should be free to complete their time at school without unnecessary intrusion. The fame, notoriety or position of a parent or guardian must not be used as sole justification for publishing details of a child's private life.

Principle 10 • Publication of the Decision of the Press Ombudsman / Press Council

10.1 When requested or required by the Press Ombudsman and/or the Press Council to do so, newspapers and periodicals shall publish the decision in relation to a complaint with due prominence.

10.2 The content of this Code will be reviewed at regular intervals.

APPLICATION OF THE CODE

[9.27] The Ombudsman and Council's decisions applying the Code are published and remain available on their websites. While the majority of the decisions involve the simple application of the terms of the provisions then in force to the complaints made, there are a number of specific aspects of the Code, and its interpretation, that are worthy of comment. These are particularly relevant to the question of whether the courts, in having regard to the Code and decisions of the Ombudsman under the Defamation Act 2009, are likely to place significant reliance on the decisions or, in the alternative, to consider whether the Code and decisions diverge from the relevant legal principles.

Preamble

[9.28] The Preamble sets out the objectives of the Code and presents a vision of press freedom which broadly accords with that favoured by the Irish courts[13] and by the European Court of Human Rights.[14] In particular, the Preamble emphasises the relationship between the freedom of the media to publish and the right of the people to be informed. This suggests the sort of instrumentalist democratic theory of media expression which was discussed in more detail in Chapters 1 and 2, where the protection of media freedom is primarily premised on the interests of its audience. Thus, the Preamble echoes recent European Court of Human Rights jurisprudence in acknowledging the responsibilities and duties of the press as well as its freedoms.[15] In many ways, of course, it is this recognition of responsibilities and duties which ostensibly justifies the establishment of a system of press regulation.

[9.29] One aspect of the Preamble which may be subject to comment is its recognition of the 'the right of a newspaper to publish what it considers to be news, without fear or favour, and the right to comment upon it'. It is unclear whether this is intended to indicate that a newspaper should have an absolute entitlement to publish any material it considers to be news without sanction, or whether it ought to be entitled in the first instance to publish what it considers to be news and bear the consequences of any decision in that regard. It is clear from the case law on matters such as defamation or privacy that, while the courts recognise the primary role of editors and journalists in determining what constitutes newsworthy journalism,[16] they also recognise that the industry is not the final arbiter of what is in the public interest.[17] The Preamble itself appears to acknowledge this by referring to the public's 'legitimate' interest in receiving information. The latter reading of this 'right' thus seems the more appropriate one.

Fact and comment

[9.30] This principle has been invoked on a relatively regular basis by the Ombudsman in his decisions in relation to complaints concerning an alleged breach of Principles 1 and 2. Where he is satisfied that a matter is not reported as fact, he has tended to provide considerable leeway to the press in the way in which they report material. The distinction between fact and comment in the jurisprudence of the European Court of Human Rights was developed in order to provide appropriate protection for statements of opinion and comment. The focus of the distinction is to protect comment. The Ombudsman's approach tends to focus on the other side of the equation by holding that, provided something is not reported as fact, the lower principles of truth and accuracy apply.

---

13. *Irish Times v Ireland* [1998] 1 IR 359; *Mahon v Post Publications* [2007] 3 IR 338.
14. See, for example, *Lingens v Austria* (1986) 8 EHRR 407; *Bladet Tromso v Norway* (1999) 29 EHRR 125; *Editions Plon v France* [2004] ECHR 58148/00.
15. See, for example, *Stoll v Switzerland* (2007) 24 BHRC 258.
16. *Charman v Orion Publishing Group* [2008] 1 All ER 750, 773.
17. *Jameel v Wall Street Europe* [2007] 1 AC 359, 408.

[9.31] The Ombudsman has accordingly distinguished between statements that are reported as statements of fact, and statements that are attributed to sources. In *Foley and the Evening Herald,*[18] he relied on this distinction to find that statements which were not attributed to sources breached this principle. In *Dwyer and the Irish Sun,*[19] he rejected a complaint in relation to an article which was headlined 'DWYER WAS INVOLVED IN CARDINAL BOMB PLOT – New Bolivia terror claims' on the basis that it made clear that the report concerned an allegation rather than a statement of fact. However, the family's complaint was upheld in relation to a headline 'Assassin hired by drug lord' because it reported unconfirmed assertions from anonymous sources as fact.

[9.32] A similar approach was taken in *A Man v Sunday World,*[20] where the Ombudsman rejected a complaint that an individual had been identified as the subject of allegations of child sexual abuse in part on the grounds that the allegation had not been presented as fact. This approach was summarised by the Ombudsman in *Hogan and the Sunday World*[21] when he stated that 'insofar as any of the statements complained of are comment, conjecture, rumour or unconfirmed reports, directly or indirectly attributed to a source, the freedom of newspapers to publish such matter is protected under the Code of Practice as long as their attribution to a source is clear.'

[9.33] It is submitted that this is highly questionable both as a matter of logic and of principle. It does not seem accurate to say that reporting that an allegation has been made is not a statement of fact, as it would seem to be a statement of fact about the existence of the allegation. More generally, simply because a statement is not presented as fact does not automatically make it comment. Similarly, the fact that a statement is not presented as fact does not mean that the publication may automatically invoke the greater degree of latitude which newspapers enjoy in publishing comment. The addition of the qualification that 'it is alleged' or 'sources indicate' should not confer carte blanche on the press in reporting matters as, from the affected person's perspective, this is unlikely to significantly reduce any damage caused to their reputation or good name. This is reflected to an extent in decisions like that in *McCamley and the Irish Sun*[22] where the Ombudsman upheld a complaint in part on the grounds that the inclusion of the term 'reportedly' in the body of the piece did not counteract the less qualified allegations made in the headline of the report.

[9.34] The difficulty with the approach adopted to decisions like that involving the Daily Mail is well illustrated by the decision of the Court of Appeal in *Flood v Times Newspapers*[23] where the court rejected the argument that the publication of details of an allegation and the identity of the person who had been the subject of the complaint was protected as factual and neutral reportage. The court pointed out that it would not

---

18. *Foley and the Evening Herald* (23 March 2010), upheld by Press Council 16 April 2010.
19. *Dwyer and the Irish Sun* (4 September 2009).
20. *A Man v Sunday World* (8 June 2010).
21. *Hogan and the Sunday World* (6 July 2009).
22. *McCamley and the Irish Sun* (25 January 2010).
23. *Flood v Times Newspapers* [2010] EMLR 26.

protect the rights of persons to their reputation and good name to allow newspapers the freedom to publish the details of allegations on the basis that they were not taking any position on the truth of the allegations.

[9.35] Support for this view is also provided by the recent decision of the European Court of Human Rights in *Ruokanen v Finland*[24] where it was held that it was not contrary to Article 10 to prosecute and criminally convict an editor and journalist for aggravated defamation where they had reported that an allegation of rape had been made against certain individuals in a form from which specific individuals could have been identified. The court held that the reporting of allegations was a statement of fact and that, having regard to the presumption of innocence and the right to reputation of third parties, it had been appropriate for the Finnish authorities to prosecute those responsible for publication.

Privacy

[9.36] As befits an area where the developing jurisprudence in Strasbourg and in the English courts has been subject to considerable criticism by the press,[25] there are a number of areas where it is arguable that the provisions of the Code concerning privacy may not fully accord with the case law under Article 8 of the European Convention on Human Rights. In particular, principle 5.5 conspicuously fails to address the question of whether photographs of individuals in public places which are taken without their consent would be a breach of the Code. Decisions like *Von Hannover v Germany*,[26] *Peck v UK*,[27] *Campbell v MGN*,[28] *Murray v Big Pictures Ltd*[29] and *McKennitt v Ash*[30] indicate that the taking and publication of such photographs will, in some situations, constitute a breach of an individual's Article 8 rights. However, the Ombudsman has held in *Foley and the Irish Daily Star*[31] that rule 5.5 will only apply where photographs are taken in private places.

[9.37] In applying this rule, the Ombudsman has applied a relatively broad conception of what constitutes legitimate public interest. In *Treacy and the Irish Daily Mail/Sunday Independent/Irish Independent*[32] he commented that:

> The journalistic publication of personal information about an individual is not, in itself, evidence of a breach of the Code of Practice, which defines the right to privacy in terms of the 'private and family life, home and correspondence' of citizens. In the very specific circumstances and context of the court case

24. *Ruokanen v Finland* (Application 45130/66) 8 April 2010 (Fourth Section).
25. See, for example, 'Max Mosley case: bend over, free speech, this is going to hurt' (2008) *The Sunday Times*, 13 July.
26. *Von Hannover v Germany* (2005) 40 EHRR 1.
27. *Peck v UK* (2003) 36 EHRR 41.
28. *Campbell v MGN* [2004] 2 AC 459.
29. *Murray v Big Pictures Ltd* [2008] EMLR 399.
30. *McKennitt v Ash* [2006] EMR 10.
31. *Foley and the Irish Daily Star*, 27 May 2010. This was upheld by the Press Council.
32. *Treacy and the Irish Daily Mail/Sunday Independent/Irish Independent*, 13 Jul 2010.

concerned, there was a legitimate journalistic interest in providing additional information about the complainant.

It is not clear from the Ombudsman's decision what the specific circumstances he took into account were. *Egeland v Norway*[33] indicates that the fact that someone is involved in court proceedings does not automatically establish a public interest in publishing additional photographs or material relating to them. However, as the court case referred to concerned, in part, the witness's private life, it seems likely that the decision was based on that particular aspect of the case rather than on a general principle that the private life of anyone involved in court proceedings thereby becomes a legitimate subject-matter of public interest. This is supported by the fact that in *Parents and the Daily Star*, the Ombudsman held that the publication of a photograph of a child who was involved in a civil action was a breach of principle 5, together with principle 9.

[9.38] The Ombudsman and Council have also confirmed that matters that are known to some other persons may still be subject to a successful complaint for breach of privacy. In *Fahy and the News of the World*, the publication of details relating to the complainant's place of work was held to breach his right to privacy despite the newspaper's argument that this was information which would have been known to others.

[9.39] The Ombudsman has held that it is not a breach of the right to privacy to use material, including photographs, placed into the public domain by an individual via services like Facebook or Twitter or freely available online.[34] However, the obtaining of private photographs for publication in and by a newspaper different from that for which permission was originally sought has been adjudged to be a breach of principle 3.2.[35]

[9.40] There is also a question as to whether it can be stated as an absolute principle that 'the right to privacy should not prevent publication of matters of public record'. Although the courts have not had to directly address this question in Ireland, there may be scope to argue that the right to privacy may preclude the publication of some information even where that information is contained in a public record. For example, where information is in a public record but relates to events in the very distant past, it may be arguable that a person may have acquired privacy rights which could limit the re-publication of that material. This reflects the fact, as acknowledged by the United States Supreme Court in *Department of Justice v Reporters Committee for Freedom of the Press*[36] that there may be a 'practical obscurity' in some form of public records which should be taken into account in assessing whether the disclosure of the information contained therein is justifiable. The Ombudsman has referred to this matter in a non-privacy context when he observed, in respect of the publication of material and allegations relating to criminal convictions 18 years previously, that 'publication in these

33. *Egeland v Norway* [2009] ECHR 34438/04.
34. *Mr Everett Bopp and the Irish Mail on Sunday* (18 Aug 2010); *O'Donoghue v Sunday World* (17 June 2010).
35. *Fitzpatrick and the Irish Sun* (30 April 2009).
36. *Department of Justice v Reporters Committee for Freedom of the Press* 489 US 749 (1989).

circumstances of comments about the complainant's criminal past is, eighteen years after his release from prison, of dubious relevance to a discussion of his activities or capabilities as a playwright.'[37] However, in *O'Donoghue and the Sunday World*, the Ombudsman expressed the view that the re-publication of matters of public record from the complainant's criminal trial five years later was not a breach of his right to privacy.[38]

[9.41] The decision of Hedigan J. in *Tolan v An Bord Pleanála*[39] also provides an example of a situation in which the public record may contain false or defamatory material. A *Florida Star v BJF*-type[40] situation could also arise where material identifying a rape victim should not have been included in the record in the first place. This highlights the fact that there may be some scope to argue in limited circumstances that, contrary to what rule 5.2. implies, the right to privacy may preclude wider publication of matters of public record.

THE DEFAMATION ACT 2009

[9.42] The Press Council and Ombudsman were formally recognised by the Minister for Justice[41] in 2010 as institutions for the purposes of the 2009 Act, having met the minimum requirements set out in s 44. The significance of this is that, under the new s 26 defence of fair and reasonable publication on a matter of public interest, the court is directed by sub-s (2) to have regarded, inter alia, to:

(f)   in the case of a statement published in a periodical by a person who, at the time of publication, was a member of the Press Council, the extent to which the person adhered to the code of standards of the Press Council and abided by determinations of the Press Ombudsman and determinations of the Press Council;

(g)   in the case of a statement published in a periodical by a person who, at the time of publication, was not a member of the Press Council, the extent to which the publisher of the periodical adhered to standards equivalent to the standards specified in paragraph (f);

[9.43] It is plain that this aspect of the Defamation Act 2009 is intended to create an incentive for publications to both become members of the Press Council, and to abide by its Code of Practice and adjudications. This is perhaps the most radical element of Ireland's new 'hybrid' model in that it confers statutory recognition on the Council without interfering with the content of its Code or its determinations. The industry is allowed to set its own standards but there is the potential for a legal penalty to apply where a publication fails to conform to these self-imposed standards. This represents a

---

37.   *Gantley and the Evening Herald* (19 October 2009).
38.   *O'Donoghue and the Sunday World* (17 June 2010, unreported).
39.   *Tolan v An Bord Pleanála* [2008] IEHC 275.
40.   *Florida Star v BJF* 491 US 524 (1989). The Supreme Court held that publication could not be prevented on First Amendment grounds.
41.   Defamation Act 2009 (Press Council) Order 2010 (SI 163/2010).

compromise between the criticisms of self-regulation as ineffective and of statutory regulation as overbearing.

[9.44] At present, the courts have not yet had the opportunity to consider the influence which factors (f) or (g) may have in its assessment of whether an allegedly defamatory statement was fair and reasonable publication on a matter of public interest. It seems reasonable to expect, however, that the courts may be inclined to attach considerable emphasis to the conclusions of the Ombudsman and Council in this area. One of the major issues which has always confronted judges who are asked to consider allegations of unlawful, irresponsible or unjustifiable journalistic conduct has been an understandable reluctance on their part not to interfere, or be seen to interfere, with the exercise by the press of its constitutional role. Lord Hoffman's words in *R v Central Independent Television*,[42] as cited by Fennelly J in *Mahon v Post Publications*,[43] reflect this view:

> Newspapers are sometimes irresponsible and their motives in a market economy cannot be expected to be unalloyed by considerations of commercial advantage. Publication may cause needless pain, distress and damage to individuals or harm to other aspects of the public interest. But a freedom which is restricted to what judges think to be responsible or in the public interest is no freedom. Freedom means the right to publish things which government and judges, however well motivated, think should not be published. It means the right to say things which 'right thinking people' regard as dangerous or irresponsible. This freedom is subject only to clearly defined exceptions laid down by common law or statute.

As against that, however, the fact that there are difficulties inherent in regulating or supervising a particular activity does not justify a failure to regulate it at all. Thus, the courts have been required to deal with actions which allege wrongdoing on the part of the press and which require them to subject the actions and intentions of journalists and editors to scrutiny, while being aware of the courts' limitations in undertaking that exercise. The establishment of a Press Council and Ombudsman provides an opportunity to strike a balance between these influences by subjecting the actions and decisions of the press to a preliminary level of scrutiny on the basis of the industry's own standards. If a newspaper, when judged according to this effective process of peer review, has been found to fall short of the standards expected, it appears less objectionable for a court to also conclude that there has been unfair or unreasonable conduct on the part of the publisher concerned.

[9.45] However, this highlights a number of potential pitfalls which the courts and the Ombudsman/Council will have to consider in operating this system. The first is that it is more logical for the courts to place particular emphasis on the decisions of the Ombudsman and Council where they uphold a complaint against a publication. Where a publication has been found to breach the industry's own standards, there is a certain logic in the court finding that the publication was also not fair and reasonable. However, the fact that a publication did not breach industry standards does not necessarily mean

---

42.   *R v Central Independent Television* [1994] Fam 192; [1994] 3 WLR 20.
43.   *Mahon v Post Publications* [2007] IESC 15.

that it is not contrary to what the law would regard as fair and reasonable conduct. This is especially the case given the potential divergences discussed above between the Code of Practice and the Ombudsman and Council's interpretation of it and, on the other hand, the decisions of the European Court of Human Rights on Arts 8 and 10 in particular. In several respects, the Code of Practice seems to allow journalists and editors more leeway than may be permissible under the Convention jurisprudence. It may be that it would be preferable for the industry to incorporate stricter standards into the Code where that is justified by the Strasbourg case law as this may make it more likely that the courts will be able to attach particular importance to decisions of the Ombudsman and Council when considering a s 26 defence. If the two diverge in a significant way, the industry's own understanding of its standards is likely to have reduced influence in the legal sphere.

[9.46] This question of the legal status to be attached to situations where a complaint is upheld by the Ombudsman or Council also gives rise to a second potential difficulty with the relationship between decisions of the Ombudsman and Council and s 26. If it becomes the case that the courts will generally conclude that a publication which has been found to breach the Code cannot be covered by s 26, this may undermine the speedy and conciliatory character of the Ombudsman process. In the first place, it could prompt more litigation by encouraging a successful complainant to initiate a defamation action. In addition, it could also mean that a newspaper would come to regard the Ombudsman process as an extension of a potential legal action and therefore engage with it in a much more cautious and defensive manner than would otherwise be the case. While this latter danger is reduced somewhat by the changes introduced by s 24 of the 2009 Act, it is still something which should be borne in mind as the case law on s 26 is developed by the courts.

[9.47] Finally, it may also argued that the decisions of the Ombudsman and Council may have limited utility in a s 26 context as a result of the relatively brief terms in which they tend to be delivered. In many instances, the decisions of the Ombudsman and Council recite the details of the complaint and then conclude that there has or has not been a breach of the Code in the specific or particular circumstances of that case. In general, the specific circumstances in question are not identified and there is little scope to understand precisely how the Ombudsman or Council came to its conclusion. O'Dowd has suggested that this will undermine these aspects of s 26:

> One may contrast the telegraphic nature of the Irish Press Ombudsman's and Press Council's determination with the closely reasoned and highly analytical decision of the Swiss Press Council upon which the European Court of Human Rights placed such weight in Stoll v Switzerland. In that context, it must be doubtful how useful it will be to refer the court (and particularly a jury) to 'the extent to which the [defendant] adhered to the code of standards of the Press Council and abided by determinations of the Press Ombudsman and determinations of the Press Council' for the purpose of assessing whether or not it was fair and reasonable to publish.[44]

---

44. O'Dowd, 'Ireland's new Defamation Act' [2009] 2 Journal of Media Law 173, 186.

[9.48] If the reasoning of the Ombudsman and Council were clearer, it would be open to the courts to take a more case-specific approach to s 26. If the courts were able to understand and review the reasoning of the Ombudsman and Council, they could adopt an approach under which they would recognise the expertise of the Ombudsman and Council on matters of journalistic conduct but intervene where persuaded that the reasoning applied was incorrect. This could also mitigate the other problems identified above by increasing the importance for s 26 of the reasoning applied by the Ombudsman and Council which would thereby remove some of the significance from the result alone. If a court is able to consider and, if necessary, reverse a decision on the basis of its reasoning, this takes some of the focus off the outcome of the complaint and breaks any suggestion of an automatic equivalence of outcomes. Of course, this can still be done even where relatively short reasons are provided. The court may simply conclude that the facts of the case warrant a particular result. However, in the absence of more detailed reasoning, it will be difficult for the courts to identify why a particular decision was reached, and to thus take that into account in considering what was fair and reasonable in the circumstances.

Chapter 10
MEDIA OWNERSHIP

INTRODUCTION

[10.01] Public discourse about freedom of expression and the media tends to operate on the assumption that the greater the freedom of the press, the greater the contribution to the marketplace of ideas. The proliferation of media service providers in a globalised economy might be thought a positive development in this context as it produces an increased volume of contributions. There are, however, increasing concerns about protecting diversity of media content and plurality of ownership.[1] As noted by the Advisory Group on Media Mergers:[2] 'Concern has been expressed about the extent to which media businesses do not generate their own original sources of news but rather feed off one another.'[3] It is common practice for newspapers, for example, to carry similar if not identical articles.[4] It has been noted that while digital television may result

---

1. See Komorek, 'European attempts to regulate media concentrations. Persisting conflict of interests' (2004) Hibernian Law Journal 53. The protection of plurality in the media has been recognised as a valid justification for measures that might otherwise fall foul of the fundamental freedoms under the EC Treaty. See *Gouda* [1991] ECR 1–4007; *Commission v Netherlands* [1991] ECR 1–4069; *Veronica Omroep* [1993] ECR 1–487; *TV10* [1994] ECR 1–4795; *Familia Press* [1997] ECR 1–3689. The position under the European Convention on Human Rights is somewhat unclear. While the court recognises the value of plurality of the media as an important aspect of Art 10, its early approach was to justify licensing restrictions on the basis of the protection of the 'rights of others' (ie other broadcasters) in *Groppera Radio AG* (1990) 12 EHRR 321. There is some support for the proposition that media plurality is required by Art 10 in the Commission decisions in *De Geillustreerde Pers NV v Netherlands* [1976] 8 DR 5 and *Verein Alternatives Lokalradio Bern v Switzerland* [1986] 49 DR 126. See also *Verein Gegen Tierfabriken v Switzerland* (2002) 34 EHRR 159 discussed in Jones, 'Television Without Frontiers' in Eeckhout and Tridimas (eds), *Yearbook of European Law 1999–2000* (Clarendon Press, 2000), 306–307. The Council of Europe has been a strong policy advocate for increased media pluralism. See Van Loon, 'Media Freedom versus Access Rights in a European Context' in Marsden and Higgott (eds), *Regulating the Global Information Society* (Routledge, 2000) and see also Komorek, 'Is media pluralism? The European Court of Human Rights, the Council of Europe and the issue of media pluralism' [2009] European Human Rights Law Review 395.
2. In March 2008, the Minister for Enterprise, Trade and Employment announced the establishment of an advisory group to review the current legislative framework regarding the public interest aspects of media mergers in Ireland. The group was asked to examine the provisions of the Competition Act 2002 in relation to media mergers – particularly the 'relevant criteria' in the Act which the Minister refers to when considering media mergers. It made a number of recommendations about the reform of the law relating to media mergers and these are considered in detail below.
3. *Report of the Advisory Group on Media Mergers* (June 2008), para 3.13.
4. See observation to similar effect in *Report of the Advisory Group on Media Mergers* (June 2008), para 3.11. Syndication arrangements have been found by the Competition Authority to be consistent with competition in the relevant market. See the decision of the Competition Authority of Ireland in *Newspaper Publishing/Irish Times* [1995] IECA 420 (Decision No 420) 12 September 1995 and Notif CA/531/92E.

in more channels and more services, 'it is difficult to ascertain whether this will be matched by a corresponding rise in the pluralism of content.'[5]

[10.02] The increasing flow of cross-border media services as a result of globalisation has led to a situation where the media market in the State is 'larger and more complex that could have been imagined even 25 years ago.'[6] Concerns have been expressed, however that:

> Notwithstanding the multiplication of platforms and channels, there is a view amongst some respondents that media diversity is in effect being reduced for those citizens who lack either the means or the time or the inclination to seek out alternative viewpoints on the Internet or elsewhere.[7]

[10.03] One of the ways in which this problem has been addressed is to regulate concentrations of ownership of media undertakings. The dangers of concentrated ownership in the media sector were highlighted by Mary Harney, then Tánaiste, introducing the Competition Bill (now the Competition Act 2002):

> The products or services offered by the mass media of newspapers, radio and television are different from the generality of consumer products and services in at least one vital respect. We depend on them significantly for information and views about the world in which we live. The material they provide influences how we see the world, how we interpret events and, to a significant extent, our attitudes and even our behaviour. This has a particular relevance to the operation of our political system. The proper functioning of our democratic system depends ultimately on liberty of expression and all that entails. Excessive concentration of media ownership and control involves risks that go beyond those involved in the case of ordinary goods and services.[8]

[10.04] A focus on ownership alone is insufficient to protect diversity of content and other measures may also be required.[9] Competition law in and of itself does not have all the answers. As Harrison and Woods have pointed out in the context of broadcasting:

> [T]here are problems which arise when taking a standard competition-law-based approach to cases in the broadcasting sector. These problems arise from the

---

5.   *Report on Media Pluralism in the Digital Environment*, Council of Europe Steering Committee on the Mass Media (October 2000). www.humanrights.coe.int/media/documents/other/PL-Report(EN).doc.
6.   *Report of the Advisory Group on Media Mergers* (June 2008), para 3.1.
7.   *Report of the Advisory Group on Media Mergers* (June 2008), para 3.15.
8.   Dáil Éireann Reports 550 (28 February 2002). See also Power, *Competition Law and Practice* (Bloomsbury Professional, 2001), paras 53.01–2.
9.   As has been noted: 'The maintenance of plurality and diversity in the digital environment will require an array of different measures. A combination of competition law, media ownership rules and other measures will be necessary to meet the public interest objective of media pluralism and diversity. Competition law alone will not be sufficient as it is primarily concerned with the operation of economic markets rather than with pluralism objectives. Media ownership rules alone will not suffice either to ensure pluralism.' *Report on Media Pluralism in the Digital Environment*, Council of Europe Steering Committee on the Mass Media (October 2000), para 65. www.humanrights.coe.int.

particular characteristics of the sector and the nature of competition law. In general terms, competition law is based on an economic perspective on the world, based on an assumption that companies will indulge in profit-maximising behaviour and that consumers make choices about what they want to buy on a rational basis, and assumes that they have full knowledge about products available. Central to this analysis is a rational transactional view of the world, based on a willingness to pay a price.[10]

This ignores the fact that 'what the consumer would choose is not necessarily what is required for the creation of a well-functioning public sphere, the representation of minorities and other public interest considerations.'[11]

[10.05] The increasing alliances between media businesses including those between 'old media' and 'new media' also renders assessment and regulation of the state of the market more difficult. The matter of ownership might be addressed by means of merger regulation but cross-ownership is only one issue. As has been noted: 'Acquisitions of share ownership will usually be publicly known, since many of the companies involved are present on different stock exchange markets. However, certain types of alliances or agreements on common business strategies might not be equally so transparent.'[12]

[10.06] The issue of ownership, nonetheless, remains significant if for no other reason than that changes in ownership provide a point of regulatory intervention and an opportunity to explore issues regarding diversity of content. As noted below, the current regime for merger regulation in Ireland does not make effective use of this opportunity. This is partly due to flaws in the procedure under the legislation and partly due to a distinct lack of clarity as to the criteria to be applied when assessing media mergers. As discussed below, the Competition Act 2002 contains special provisions for certain mergers involving the media in an attempt to address the particular concerns raised by concentrated ownership in this sector. Criticisms have been made of this regime and legislative reform has been proposed by the Advisory Group on Media Mergers in its report issued in June 2008.[13] The background to the current legislative provisions is discussed before an explanation of the current procedures for merger approval in the media sector and the recommendations for change made by the Group. This chapter goes on to set out the provisions in the Broadcasting Act 2009 which impact on media ownership as well as the EC Merger Regulation[14] and its application to media mergers.

---

10. Harrison and Woods, *European Broadcasting Law and Policy* (Cambridge University Press, 2007), 148.

11. Harrison and Woods, *European Broadcasting Law and Policy* (Cambridge University Press, 2007), 148.

12. *Report on Media Pluralism in the Digital Environment*, Council of Europe Steering Committee on the Mass Media (October 2000), para 56. www.humanrights.coe.int.

13. The Advisory Group on Media Mergers is referred to throughout the remainder of this chapter as 'the Group'.

14. Council Regulation (EC) No 139/2004 of 20 January 2004 on the control of concentrations between undertakings (the EC Merger Regulation).

Before considering these matters, the concentration of ownership in the Irish media sector is discussed briefly.[15]

OWNERSHIP OF IRISH MEDIA

[10.07] The report of the Group included statistical data concerning the levels of ownership of Irish media. It noted the strong position of some players in the Irish market, notably RTÉ in the public sector and Independent Newspapers in the private sector. It noted, however, that local newspapers and local radio were also strong in Ireland. In this context, the Group pointed out the difficulties that could arise in defining the market where media services are concerned.[16] The data compiled on behalf of the Group give a useful overview of the levels of concentration of ownership in the Irish market across the newspaper, radio and television sectors.

Newspapers

[10.08] Regional papers were not found by the Advisory Group to have a problematic concentration of ownership.[17] As far as daily newspapers were concerned, the Group found that there were no serious concerns relating to plurality of ownership.[18] For Sunday papers, the picture was different with Independent News Media's wholly owned publications constituting 48% of market share measured as including Irish titles or Irish editions of UK titles. If the broadsheet market alone was taken, the share rose to 54.5%. Where Irish titles only were counted, Independent News Media's share was 75%. The inclusion of publications which Independent News Media had an interest in[19] (as opposed to wholly owned publications) pushed the percentage market share among Irish titles up to 92.2% of the market for Sunday newspapers.[20]

Radio

[10.09] The Group found that RTÉ had almost 70% of the market in national radio. Communicorp accounted for the other 30%. The inclusion of local radio stations in the calculations reduced these shares to 36% and 16% respectively. Local radio in Dublin was assessed as having balanced ownership. In Cork, one undertaking controlled 82% of the market. Local radio in other areas typically held 100% of the local radio market

---

15. For a more extensive discussion of the history of the Irish media market see McGonagle, *Media Law* (Sweet & Maxwell, 2003), 43–63.
16. *Report of the Advisory Group on Media Mergers* (June 2008), para 3.41.
17. *Report of the Advisory Group on Media Mergers* (June 2008), para 3.46. While Independent News Media owns 14 local papers, this has not given rise to concern from the Competition Authority that plurality in this market is compromised. See Komorek, 'Legal Protection of Media Pluralism at National Level. An Examination of the United Kingdom and Ireland' (2010) 10(1) Hibernian Law Journal 92, fn 28.
18. *Report of the Advisory Group on Media Mergers* (June 2008), para 3.45–7.
19. The *Irish Daily Star on Sunday* (50%) and the *Sunday Tribune* (29%).
20. *Report of the Advisory Group on Media Mergers* (June 2008), para 3.48.

share in those areas. The overall share of most of such stations dropped to around 50% if national stations were included.[21]

Television

[10.10] Ireland currently has three national television channels that receive public funding through an annual licence fee payable by those in possession of a television receiver. Radio Telefís Éireann (RTÉ), the public service broadcaster, was the only supplier of terrestrial television in Ireland up until the late 1990s. It currently operates two channels: RTÉ 1 with an audience share of about 30% and RTÉ 2 with an audience share of around 11%.[22] RTÉ also cooperates with the Irish language channel Teilifís na Gaeilge (TG4). The Radio and Television Act 1988 introduced commercial broadcasting to Ireland by providing for a system of licensing. The first commercial television station in Ireland was launched in 1998 under the name TV3. Its main shareholders are Can West Global Communications and Granada Media and it enjoys audience share of around 12%.[23] British terrestrial television channels are also available to approximately 70% of the population, mainly through cable services. BBC reaches a market share of around 13% and Channel 4 – around 4%.[24] BSkyB is the sole provider of digital satellite television services in Ireland through Sky Digital. The Irish cable market has recently altered dramatically. Previously, there were two main cable operators: Éire (NTL) and Chorus Communications. In 2004 Chorus was fully taken over by Liberty Media's affiliate, UGC Europe (since renamed Liberty Global Europe).

Cross-ownership issues

[10.11] The Advisory Group recognised, in its report, that economic realities may require substantial cross-ownership across different media and noted the particular need to ensure that mergers of this type were accompanied by 'robust mechanisms to measure and to report on relative levels of internal diversity at the consolidated enterprise.'[25]

[10.12] Cross-ownership issues were considered by the Competition Authority and the Broadcasting Commission of Ireland (BCI)[26] in the radio and press sectors due to

---

21. *Report of the Advisory Group on Media Mergers* (June 2008), para 3.50–52.
22. AGB Nielsen Media Research 2008, referred to by Komorek, 'Legal Protection of Media Pluralism at National Level. An Examination of the United Kingdom and Ireland' (2010) 10(1) Hibernian Law Journal 92, fn 20. The Advisory Group cited slightly different figures whereby RTÉ accounted for almost 70% of the market share enjoyed by Irish licensed broadcasting stations, with Tullamore Alpha accounting for a further 23.5%. Other smaller undertakings had relatively smaller market shares. Once all the television stations broadcasting in Ireland were taken into consideration, however, RTÉ's overall share was 37.1% of the all day and 43.7% of the peak viewing audiences. *Report of the Advisory Group on Media Mergers* (June 2008), para 3.53.
23. *Report of the Advisory Group on Media Mergers* (June 2008), para 3.53.
24. *Report of the Advisory Group on Media Mergers* (June 2008), para 3.53.
25. *Report of the Advisory Group on Media Mergers* (June 2008), para 3.27.
26. This body was abolished under Broadcasting Act 2009 which established the Broadcasting Authority of Ireland.

developments in the Irish market between 2007 and 2009. The issue arose in 2007 when Communicorp, a company controlled by Denis O'Brien, which owned two Dublin radio stations (98FM and Spin FM), one national radio station (Newstalk) and a 26% stake in Independent News and Media, acquired national radio station Today FM and Dublin station FM104 from Emap.[27] This acquisition would result in Communicorp having control over almost 25% of all commercial radio licences in Ireland and over 53% audience share in Dublin.

[10.13] The Competition Authority ordered Communicorp to divest FM104 due to concerns about both stations' similar programming format which made them the closest competitors in the Dublin area.[28] Communicorp then sold FM104 to UTV.[29]

[10.14] In 2008 the Broadcasting Commission of Ireland (BCI) investigated the cross-ownership concern between Communicorp and Independent News and Media arising out of the increased shareholding of O'Brien who held over 27% by May 2008. It concluded that the interests of Communicorp in Independent News and Media were not substantial.[30] In March 2009 three of O'Brien's long-term associates were appointed to the board of Independent News and Media.[31] In May 2009 the BCI started a review of the new development. It stated that the agreement giving Communicorp a number of seats in Independent News and Media provided O'Brien with the ability to influence the strategic direction of the publishing company. The BCI also noted that the change of ownership gave Communicorp, Independent News' second-largest shareholder, a 'substantial interest' in the newspaper group and raised issues about O'Brien's control of other media in Ireland. [32] In July 2009 the BCI concluded again that Communicorp does not control an 'undue' share of the country's media market.[33]

BACKGROUND TO THE COMPETITION ACT 2002 PROVISIONS ON MEDIA MERGERS

[10.15] Prior to the introduction of the Competition Act 2002, mergers were dealt with under the Mergers, Take-Overs and Monopolies (Control) Act 1978 as subsequently amended by the Competition Act 1991. Under this legislative framework, mergers were notified to the Minister for Industry and Commerce and could be referred by him to the Competition Authority for investigation.

[10.16] One such referral was made by the Minister in the *Independent Newspapers/ Tribune* case.[34] In that case, the Minister referred a proposal between Independent

---

27.   O'Brien bidding to rule the airwaves' (2007) *The Irish Times*, 24 July.
28.   Determination of Merger Notification M/07/040, Communicorp/SRH, 7 December 2007
29.   Determination of Merger Notification M/07/069, UTV/FM104, 17 January 2008.
30.   Reuters, 'Irish regulator reviews O'Brien's media empire', 12 May 2009.
31.   Reuters, 'Irish regulator clears O'Brien media empire', 28 July 2009.
32.   Reuters, 'Irish regulator reviews O'Brien's media empire', 12 May 2009.
33.   Reuters, 'Irish regulator clears O'Brien media empire', 28 July 2009.
34.   See Competition Authority, Annual Report 1992, paras 3.1–.5.

Newspapers and the *Tribune* to the Competition Authority for investigation pursuant to s 7(b) of the Mergers, Take-Overs and Monopolies (Control) Act 1978. According to the terms of the proposal, Independent Newspapers would increase its shareholding in the *Tribune* to 53.09%. In March 2002 the Competition Authority presented its report to the Minister, having decided by a majority that the proposal between the two entities would distort competition and would operate against the public good. The Authority found that, in terms of readership, while 'no newspaper is a perfect substitute for any other newspaper', there were still some newspapers which cluster together. It found that Irish Sunday newspapers constituted a distinct market from daily newspapers and that in that market, the proposed acquisition would increase the bidder's share from 59.9% to 71.2%. In terms of advertising, the acquisition would increase the bidder's coverage from 70% to 73.6% of all adults. The Authority was also not satisfied that the proposed editorial charter would ensure editorial independence between the two entities.

[10.17] The Authority acknowledged the Tribune Group's financial difficulties and the fact that it would be insolvent but for the financial support from the bidder. It accepted that the *Tribune* would probably close if the bid were not allowed to proceed but took the view that if that did occur, the titles would be likely to be purchased by another party and that this would be to the benefit of competition.

[10.18] On the basis of the Authority's report, the Minister made an order prohibiting the acquisition of further shares in Tribune Group by the *Independent*.[35]

[10.19] In *Blockbuster/XtraVision (Ardnasillagh)*,[36] the Competition Authority considered a proposed merger in the video outlet market. Blockbuster proposed to acquire shares in Ardnasillagh (an investment holding company) and thereby acquire the Xtravision chain of video shops. The notification of the proposed merger went to the Minister who in turn referred the take-over to the Competition Authority for investigation.

[10.20] Blockbuster was a subsidiary of Viacom which was an entertainment and publishing company with broadcasting, entertainment, video, theme park and publishing operations. Viacom had a 50% interest in CIC Video which was a video distributor which supplied movies by Paramount and Universal Studios. The agreement provided that, for the most part, the vendors (other than the financial institutions) would not compete with Ardnasillagh in Ireland or the UK for the two years following completion.

[10.21] The Authority defined the relevant product market as:

> [t]he market for video rental in the State … A narrow definition of the market is applicable in this case. The market is local in that consumers are unlikely to travel outside a geographic area in order to rent a video …

---

35.   An appeal of this decision was lodged by the Independent pursuant to s 12 of the 1978 Act but they did not proceed with it.

36.   See Power, paras 53.57–59.

The Authority found that a broader definition of the market as a home entertainment market which would encompass television and video was not applicable because such a broad definition was 'neither appropriate in the analysis of this particular transaction nor at this time in the State, in what could best be described as the relatively early stage in the development cycle of a home entertainment market in Ireland'.

[10.22] The Authority commented that:

> [T]hreats to consumer welfare may, in certain cases, arise from a merger. Such concerns are most likely to arise where there are significant horizontal effects. Concentration concerns are most likely to arise where there are significant horizontal effects. Concerns about horizontal effects generally relate to increased concentration in the market, possibly leading to monopolization and/or price collusion.

In the present case there were:

> ... no horizontal effects as a result of the merger as the acquirer, Blockbuster was not active in the Irish video rental or retail market. On trading, its market share in the rental market would be the same as is currently held by Xtra-Vision.

Ultimately the Authority recommended that the Minister approve the take-over as it was in the common good, according to the criteria laid down in the 1978 Act.

Suir Nore Relays Ltd/Princes Holdings Ltd; Aringour Ltd/CMI /Liberty (Ireland) Ltd

[10.23] In 1999 the Minister for Enterprise, Trade and Employment referred two proposed mergers to the Authority, the proposed acquisition of the entire issued share capital of Suir Nore Relays Ltd by Princes Holdings Ltd and the proposed acquisition of the entire share capital of Aringour Ltd/CMI by Liberty (Ireland) Ltd. The Authority's report noted that the market in which the companies operated was television transmission but went on to find that the telecommunications market was also of relevance to the transaction. The Authority noted that 'telecommunications and broadcasting, which have traditionally been separate markets, will overlap in the future'. The Authority agreed with the notifying parties that competition in the market for television transmission occurs among as opposed to within platforms. It noted that in the broadcasting sector, the different cable and MMDS companies did not compete with each other because of regulatory restraints. The effect of these was such that a customer, if unhappy with one provider, could not seek supply from another provider. While the proposals would reduce the number of substantial participants in the cable MMDS market to two, the Authority did not think this would have any effect on competition.

[10.24] The Authority considered the Irish telecommunications market which it found to be still at an early stage of development. It noted that the acquisition by Liberty of Aringour/CMI would mean that existing customers of CMI would be able to avail of digital and interactive services more quickly than if CMI was to remain a stand-alone entity. The Authority found that the consolidation of a number of cable/MMDS companies with relatively small geographically dispersed subscriber bases into a single entity with a larger and more integrated subscriber base could have a beneficial impact on competition in the telecommunications sector.

[10.25] The Authority found that the proposal did not raise any competition or broader cultural concerns in relation to concentration in the media generally. It considered that the transactions would have no effect on continuity of services or supplies, level of employment, rationalisation of operations in the interests of greater efficiency, research and development, increased production, access to markets or employees. It found that there could be a positive impact on regional development as the proposals would make advanced television and telecommunications services available outside Dublin. This was likely to be a positive development for consumers.

[10.26] The Authority recommended that the mergers be allowed to proceed without conditions and this was accepted by the Tánaiste.

The Commission on the Newspaper Industry

[10.27] The special provisions in the Competition Act 2002 dealing with media mergers have their origins in the Report of the Commission on the Newspaper Industry. This Commission was established in 1995 to review the 'state-of-play' of the newspaper industry in Ireland. The Competition Authority had been requested to investigate the industry after Independent Newspapers acquired a 29% holding in the Irish Press Group. According to its *Interim Report of Study on the Newspaper Industry*,[37] the Authority was concerned with two primary issues: (1) the question of transfrontier competition in the industry; and (2) the issue of dominance.

[10.28] In its 1996 report, *Report of the Commission on the Newspaper Industry*,[38] the Commission identified a number a concerns and made a number of recommendations with regard to competition law. Its primary concerns were (a) the fact that 'further concentration of ownership in the indigenous industry could severely curtail the diversity requisite to maintain a vigorous democracy and (b) the powerful position of Independent Newspapers.'[39]

[10.29] The investigation found that the acquisition by Independent Newspapers of a stake in the Irish Press Group was designed to prevent a rival acquiring control of the newspapers belonging to the Irish Press Group. The report concluded that this had prevented more intense competition in the market and therefore amounted to an abuse of a dominant position,[40] in breach of ss 4 and 5 of the Competition Act 1991.[41]

---

37. *Interim Report of Study on the Newspaper Industry* (The Stationery Office, Dublin, 1995).
38. Pn 2841 (The Stationery Office, Dublin, 1996).
39. The Commission noted that the size of the group was not indicative of anti-competitiveness in itself. The actions of Independent Newspapers in relation to its acquisition of 29.9% share in the *Sunday Tribune* which was operating at a loss and continued to operate so being supported by loans from the Independent Newspapers, did, however, raise concerns.
40. *Interim Report of Study on the Newspaper Industry* (The Stationery Office, Dublin, 1995), paras 8.53–55.
41. The Competition Act 1991 was repealed and replaced by the Competition Act 2002.

[10.30] The Commission made three recommendations with competition law/mergers implications. These were that (a) the Minister in assessing changes in the ownership in the newspaper sector should assess the implications of any changes in relation to plurality and diversity criteria, (b) the existing Irish merger regime should be amended in respect of activities in the newspaper industry resulting in a widening of the powers to regulate not only the acquisition of shares but also the acquisition of control over newspapers by other means and (c) any issue of concentration of ownership on the media should be the subject of cross-media as well as mono-media considerations.

The Competition and Mergers Group

[10.31] Following this report, the Competition and Mergers Review Group (the CMRG) was established in 1996 to review and make recommendations on (i) mergers legislation; (ii) effectiveness of competition legislation and associated regulations; (iii) cultural matters in the context of the Competition Act 1991 and in particular, s 4(2) of that Act; and (iv) appropriate structures for implementing the proposed new legislation. In its 2000 Report[42] the CMRG recommended that provision be made for media mergers in competition legislation. This recommendation was reflected in the provisions of the Competition Act 2002.

THE COMPETITION ACT 2002 – MERGER PROVISIONS

[10.32] The Competition Act 2002 regulates mergers and acquisitions under Pt 3.[43] Section 18(1) provides for the notification of certain mergers and acquisitions to the Competition Authority where they are over a certain threshold. This provision applies to all mergers and is capable of capturing mergers involving media undertakings also. There are special additional provisions made for media mergers under s 23 (discussed below).

---

42. Competition and Mergers Review Group, *Final Report* (Pn 8487, Department of Enterprise, Trade and Employment, Dublin 2000). See www.dete.ie/publications/commerce/2002/cmrg1.pdf.

43. The Mergers, Take-Overs and Monopolies (Control) Act 1978 was the first merger-specific legislation in the State. While it did not specifically make reference to 'media mergers', s 2(5) of the Act provided that the Minister for Enterprise and Employment could declare that a specific class of proposed mergers or take-overs would be subject to the 1978 Act. Such an Order could be made by the Minister where the 'exigencies of the common good so warranted'. In 1979, the Minister made an Order which related to 'proposed mergers or take-overs of the following class, namely, proposed mergers or take-overs involving enterprises where at least one of which is engaged in the printing and/or publication of one or more than one newspaper'. Under this regime, proposed mergers or take-overs in the newspaper sector fell within the scope of the Mergers Act regardless of whether the financial thresholds set out therein were met. The Order did not apply to broadcast media (radio or television) as prior to the enactment of the Radio and Television Act 1988, no commercial broadcasting was licensed in the State. The 1978 Act was later amended by the Competition Act 1991 which provides for a role for the Competition Authority in assessing mergers and acquisitions. See the *Independent Newspapers/Tribune* case discussed above.

Procedure for mergers generally

[10.33] Mergers or acquisitions must be notified where, in the most recent financial year:[44]

(i)   the world-wide turnover of each of 2 or more of the undertakings involved in the merger or acquisition is not less than €40,000,000,

(ii)   each of 2 or more of the undertakings involved in the merger or acquisition carries on business in any part of the island of Ireland, and

(iii)   the turnover in the State of any one of the undertakings involved in the merger or acquisition is not less than €40,000,000.[45]

This provision captures any media mergers which meet the criteria. There is also provision in s 18(5) of the Act for the Minister to specify by order a class of mergers or acquisitions to require notification. The relevant order is considered in detail below as it is pursuant to this that media mergers which do not meet the threshold are subject to the requirement of notification.

[10.34] The Act defines the terms 'merger' and 'acquisition'[46] in s 16(1) which provides that for the purposes of the Act, a merger or acquisition occurs where:

(a)   2 or more undertakings, previously independent of one another, merge, or

(b)   one or more individuals or other undertakings who or which control one or more undertakings acquire direct or indirect control of the whole or part of one or more other undertakings, or

(c)   the result of an acquisition by one undertaking (the 'first undertaking') of the assets, including goodwill, (or a substantial part of the assets) of another undertaking (the 'second undertaking') is to place the first undertaking in a position to replace (or substantially to replace) the second undertaking in the business or, as appropriate, the part concerned of the business in which that undertaking was engaged immediately before the acquisition.

---

44.   The point in time at which the notification requirement is triggered is where a merger or acquisition is agreed or will occur if a public bid that is made is accepted.

45.   Competition Act 2002, s 18(1). It has been pointed out that there is no definition in the Act as to the meaning of the phrase 'carries on business' and the Competition Authority has been said to treat mergers as notifiable in situations where the business concerned has only a tenuous connection with the State. The reference in Competition Act 2002, s 18(1)(a)(2) to 'the island of Ireland' as opposed to 'the State' has also been the subject of adverse comment: *Report of the Advisory Group on Media Mergers* (June 2008), para 4.5. (The critical comments referred to are attributed to another source).

46.   As the procedure relating to mergers and acquisitions is the same, the term 'mergers' is used in places throughout this chapter for the sake of simplicity to cover both types of arrangement.

In the context of s 16(1)(b), 'control' essentially means the ability to exercise decisive influence over the activities of an undertaking.[47] Control is measured in all the circumstances of the matter and not simply by reference to the legal effect of any instruments.[48] There are also provisions in the Act which set out situations in which a merger or acquisition will be deemed not to occur.[49]

---

47.   Competition Act 2002, s 16 provides in relevant part as follows:

(2) For the purposes of this Act, control, in relation to an undertaking, shall be regarded as existing if, by reason of securities, contracts or any other means, or any combination of securities, contracts or other means, decisive influence is capable of being exercised with regard to the activities of the undertaking and, in particular, by – (a) ownership of, or the right to use all or part of, the assets of an undertaking, or (b) rights or contracts which enable decisive influence to be exercised with regard to the composition, voting or decisions of the organs of an undertaking.

(3) For the purposes of this Act, control is acquired by an individual or other undertaking if he or she or it–

(a) becomes holder of the rights or contracts, or entitled to use the other means, referred to in subsection (2), or

(b) although not becoming such a holder or entitled to use those other means, acquires the power to exercise the rights derived therefrom.

(4) The creation of a joint venture to perform, on an indefinite basis, all the functions of an autonomous economic entity shall constitute a merger falling within subsection (1)(b).

(5) In determining whether influence of the kind referred to in subsection (2) is capable of being exercised regard shall be had to all the circumstances of the matter and not solely to the legal effect of any instrument, deed, transfer, assignment or other act done or made.

48.   See Competition Act 2002, s 16(1)(5) set out above.

49.   Section provides in relevant part as follows:

(6) For the purposes of this Act, a merger or acquisition shall not be deemed to occur if – (a) the person acquiring control is a receiver or liquidator acting as such or is an underwriter or jobber acting as such, or (b) all of the undertakings involved in the merger or acquisition are, directly or indirectly, under the control of the same undertaking, or (c) control is acquired solely as a result of a testamentary disposition, intestacy or the right of survivorship under a joint tenancy, or (d) control is acquired by an undertaking referred to in subsection (7) in the circumstances specified in subsection (8).

(7) The undertaking mentioned in subsection (6)(d) is an undertaking the normal activities of which include the carrying out of transactions and dealings in securities for its own account or for the account of others.

(8) The circumstances mentioned in subsection (6)(d) are that the control concerned is constituted by the undertaking's holding, on a temporary basis, securities acquired in another undertaking and any exercise by the undertaking of voting rights in respect of those securities, whilst that control subsists, is for the purpose of arranging for the disposal, within the specified period, of all or part of the other undertaking or its assets or securities and not for the purpose of determining the manner in which any activities of the other undertaking, being activities that could affect competition in markets for goods or services in the State, are carried on.

(9) In subsection (8) 'specified period' means – (a) the period of 1 year from the date on which control of the other undertaking was acquired, or (b) if in a particular case the undertaking shows that it is not reasonably possible to effect the disposal concerned within the period referred to in paragraph (a), within such longer period as the Authority determines and specifies with respect to that case.'

[10.35] The procedure once a notification is made is dealt with in s 20 of the Act. The Competition Authority is required to cause notice of the notification to be published within seven days of receiving it and must consider all submissions made, whether in writing or orally, by the undertakings involved in the merger or acquisition or by any individual or any other undertaking.[50] This obligation does not apply where the circumstances involving the merger or acquisition are such that the Competition Authority considers it would not be in the public interest to cause the notice to be published. It is not clear what those circumstances might be and the Authority is given no guidance as to how it might exercise this discretion.[51]

[10.36] Once a merger or acquisition is notified to it, the function of the Authority is to form a view as to whether the result of the merger or acquisition would be to substantially lessen competition in markets for goods or services in the State.[52] The Authority may enter into discussions with the undertakings involved, or with any individual or other undertaking with a view to identifying any measures which might ameliorate the effects of the merger or acquisition on competition in markets for goods or services.[53] Where the undertakings concerned in the merger or acquisition submit proposals with regard to the manner in which the merger or acquisition may be put into effect or to the taking, in relation to the merger or acquisition, of any other measures which would ameliorate any effects of the merger or acquisition on competition in markets for goods or services, these can become binding on the undertaking(s) concerned. Such proposals become binding where the Authority states in writing that they form part of the basis of its decision to clear a merger or acquisition under ss 21 or 22 of the Act.[54] The Authority must consider any submissions made to it orally or in writing by the undertakings involved, any individual or any other undertaking.[55] The undertakings concerned in the merger or acquisition can be required to provide specified information if the Authority considers it necessary for the assessment of the merger or acquisition under Pt 3.[56]

[10.37] The Competition Authority assessment of a proposed merger or acquisition can be divided into two phases. On receipt of a notification, the Authority has one month[57] to decide either that (a) the result of the merger or acquisition would not be to substantially lessen competition in markets for goods or services in the State so that it can be put into effect; or (b) that it should conduct a full investigation. The Authority must inform the undertakings concerned of its decision and has two months within which to publish the determination. This is often referred to as Phase 1.

---

50.   Competition Act 2002, s 20(1)(a).
51.   The Group commented that it considered it to be important that a notice of notification of all media mergers be published: *Report of the Advisory Group on Media Mergers* (June 2008), para 4.10.
52.   Competition Act 2002, s 20(1)(c).
53.   Competition Act 2002, s 20(1)(b).
54.   Competition Act 2002, s 20(3).
55.   Competition Act 2002, s 20(1)(a)(ii).
56.   Competition Act 2002, s 20(2).
57.   This can be extended to 45 days.

[10.38] If the Authority decides to enter into a full investigation (Phase 2), it has three options at the end of that investigation process. It may either clear the merger, decide that the merger cannot be put into effect or it can provide that it may be put into effect subject to specified conditions. A Phase 2 decision must be made within four months of the notification of the proposed merger to the Authority.[58]

Provisions specific to media mergers

[10.39] As mentioned above, there are special provisions to deal with media mergers. These concern both the types of arrangements that have to be notified and the procedure once notification of a media merger is made.

Notification of media mergers

[10.40] Under s 18(5), where the Minister is of opinion that the exigencies of the common good warrant it, he may, after consultation with the Competition Authority, specify a class or classes of merger or acquisition for the purposes of the notification requirements. Such classification is effected by ministerial order. The media were formerly classified under this provision by virtue of the Competition Act 2002 (Section 18(5)) Order 2002 which effectively required the notification of all media mergers.[59]

[10.41] This order was revoked and replaced in 2007 by the Competition Act 2002 (Section 18(5) and (6) Order 2007 (the 2007 Order).[60] The 2007 Order specifies two classes of merger or acquisition for the purposes of s 18(1)(b) of the Act as follows:

(a)   the class of each merger and each acquisition in which at least one or more of the undertakings involved carries on a media business in the State, and

(b)   the class of merger and each acquisition where at least one of the undertakings involved carries on a media business in the State and one or more of the undertakings involved carries on a media business elsewhere.

[10.42] Section 23(10) of the Act defines a media merger as '[a] merger or acquisition in which one or more of the undertakings involved carries on a media business in the State.' That subsection goes on to provide for a number of other important definitions.[61]

---

58.   This can be extended where there is a need for further information from the undertakings concerned.

59.   Competition Act 2002 (Section 18(5)) Order 2002 (SI 622/2002). The Competition Authority was critical of this provision, pointing out that 'it had the effect of causing many mergers to be notified that have no nexus with the State, and in some cases, no practical link with media business at all'. See Competition Authority, *Annual Report 2006*, 35.

60.   Competition Act 2002 (Section 18(5) and (6) Order 2007 (the 2007 Order) (SI 122/2007). The Order came into effect on 1 May 2007.

61.   It has been noted that the lack of a definition of the word 'publication' in this context has given rise to difficulties in practice. *Report of the Advisory Group on Media Mergers* (June 2008), para 4.29.

[10.43] Under s 23(1):

'[M]edia business' means:

(a)   a business of the publication of newspapers or periodicals consisting substantially of news and comment on current affairs,

(b)   a business of providing a broadcasting service, or

(c)   a business of providing a broadcasting services platform.

'Broadcasting service' means a service which comprises a compilation of programme material of any description and which is transmitted or relayed by means of wireless telegraphy, a cable system or a multipoint microwave distribution system, a satellite device or any other transmission system, directly or indirectly for reception by the general public, whether that material is actually received or not, and includes a sound broadcasting service within the meaning of the Radio and Television Act 1988. The definition excludes any such service (whether involving audio-visual material or audio material) that is provided by means of the system commonly known as the Internet.

'Providing a broadcasting service' is to be construed as a reference to doing either or both of the following: (a) supplying a compilation of programme material for the purpose of it being transmitted or relayed as a broadcasting service, or (b) transmitting or relaying as a broadcasting service programme material.[62]

'Providing a broadcasting platform' is to be construed as a reference to the transmitting or retransmitting of programme material by means of wireless telegraphy, a cable system or a multipoint microwave distribution system, a satellite device or any other transmission system.[63]

[10.44] Media mergers which meet the thresholds set out in s 18(1) or mergers which fall within the definition of a media merger set out in the ministerial order described above[64] will require notification. It has been pointed that the there may be some mergers involving the media which are not subject to any requirement of notification under the Competition Act. Examples have been given such as the acquisition of a media business in the State (of any turnover) by a foreign non–media business (of any turnover) where the foreign business does not carry on business in any part of the island of Ireland or the acquisition of a media business in the State with a turnover of less than €40m by a Northern Ireland non-media business that has less than €40m turnover in the State regardless of its worldwide turnover.[65]

The Minister's role

[10.45] Where media mergers are notified to the Authority, the Minister for Enterprise, Trade and Employment takes on a role in deciding whether to clear them or not. It is the Minister's involvement and the additional criteria that apply to media mergers that are

---

62.   Competition Act 2002, s 23(10) and (11).
63.   Competition Act 2002, s 23(10) and (12).
64.   Competition Act 2002 (Section 18(5) and (6) Order 2007 ('the 2007 Order') (SI 122/2007).
65.   *Report of the Advisory Group on Media Mergers* (June 2008), fn 56.

intended to address the special features of the media sector considered above. Where a media merger is notified to the Authority, it is required to notify the undertakings within five days that it considers the merger to be a media merger. It must also forward a copy of the notification to the Minister within the same time limit.[66] If the Authority decides to clear the merger it must, immediately after doing so, inform the Minister of that fact. The Minister may, within 10 days of being informed of the Authority's determination, direct the Authority to carry out a Phase 2 investigation in relation to the merger.[67] The undertakings must be informed of this decision to carry out a Phase 2 investigation.[68] To facilitate the special procedure for media mergers, decisions to clear such mergers at Phase 1 do not take effect until the expiry of 10 days.[69] If the Minister directs the Authority to conduct a Phase 2 investigation, the initial decision to clear the merger does not operate so as to allow the merger to take effect.[70]

[10.46] Where the Competition Authority conducts a full (Phase 2) investigation of a media merger either by Direction from the Minister[71] or by its own determination[72] and concludes at the end of that investigation that the merger may be put into effect or that it may be put into effect subject to conditions, then it must immediately inform the Minister of this determination.[73] The Minister may by order and having regard to the 'relevant criteria' clear the merger (with or without conditions) or refuse to clear it.[74] The Minister must publish, with due regard for commercial confidentiality, a statement of the reasons for his or her making such an order within two weeks after the date on which the order is made.[75] In making his decision, the Minister may consider such submissions or observations from persons claiming to be interested in the matter as the Minister thinks proper.[76]

[10.47] Where, on the other hand, the Authority conducts a Phase 2 investigation of a media merger – either pursuant to s 23(2) or under s 21(2)(b) and concludes at the end of that investigation that the merger in question should be prohibited, the Minister has no further role.

[10.48] Where the Authority decides following a Phase 2 investigation whether at its own initiative or by ministerial direction to clear a media merger or to clear it subject to conditions, it must immediately inform the Minister. The Minister then has 30 days within which to clear the merger, refuse to clear the merger or clear it subject to

66. Competition Act 2002, s 23(1).
67. Competition Act 2002, s 23(2).
68. Competition Act 2002, s 23(3)(b).
69. Competition Act 2002, s 23(9)(a).
70. Competition Act 2002, s 23(3)(a).
71. Competition Act 2002, s 23(2).
72. Competition Act 2002, s 21(2)(b).
73. Competition Act 2002, s 23(4).
74. Competition Act 2002, s 23(4).
75. Competition Act 2002, s 23(5).
76. Competition Act 2002, s 23(6).

specified conditions.[77] In making his determination, the Minister must have regard only to the 'relevant criteria'.[78]

The relevant criteria under s 23(10)

[10.49] The definition of relevant criteria[79] is set out in s 23(10) as meaning:

    (a)   the strength and competitiveness of media businesses indigenous to the State,

    (b)   the extent to which ownership or control of media businesses in the State is spread amongst individuals and other undertakings,

    (c)   the extent to which ownership and control of particular types of media business in the State is spread amongst individuals and other undertakings,

    (d)   the extent to which the diversity of views prevalent in Irish society is reflected through the activities of the various media businesses in the State, and

    (e)   the share in the market in the State of one or more of the types of business activity falling within the definition of 'media business' in this subsection that is held by any of the undertakings involved in the media merger concerned, or by any individual or other undertaking who or which has an interest in such an undertaking.

The Competition Authority is required, under s 23(7), to form an opinion as to how the application of the relevant criteria should affect the exercise by the Minister of his or her powers in relation to a media merger. If the Minister requests it, the Authority must inform the Minister of this opinion.[80]

Supervision by the Oireachtas

[10.50] The Minister is subject to the supervision of the Oireachtas in the exercise of his powers under s 23. Section 25 provides that any order of the Minister (including an order that a media merger be put into effect) must be laid before each House of the Oireachtas as soon as may be after it is made. If a resolution annulling the order is passed by either of the Houses within 21 days on which that House has sat following the laying before the House of the order, it is annulled accordingly. The effect of such annulment is to give effect to the determination of the Competition Authority. This is without prejudice to the right of appeal to the High Court from the Authority's decision. The Advisory Group on

---

77.   Competition Act 2002, s 23(4). The determination by the Authority does not take effect until 30 days have expired. At that stage it may take effect if the Minister has not made an order relating to the merger or has indicated in writing that he does not intend to make an order.

78.   Competition Act 2002, s 23(4).

79.   The criteria were drawn from the *Report of the Commission on the Newspaper Industry* (1995) and the *Report of the Competition and Mergers Review Group* (2000). See discussion in the *Report of the Advisory Group on Media Mergers* (June 2008), pp 62–64.

80.   Competition Act 2002, s 23(8).

Media Mergers was critical of the provision for Oireachtas supervision on the basis that it was too lengthy a process and recommended its abolition.[81]

[10.51] The replacement of the 2002 Order in 2007 has led to a decline in the number of media mergers notified to the Authority. In June 2008 the number notified since the Act came into effect on 1 January 2003 was 89.[82] In 2008 itself, five were notified and only two were notified in 2009.[83] The vast majority of media mergers notified to the Authority have been cleared under Phase 1.[84]

THE ADVISORY GROUP ON MEDIA MERGERS – RECOMMENDATIONS FOR REFORM

[10.52] The Advisory Group on Media Mergers was established by the Minister for Enterprise, Trade and Employment in March 2008 to review the existing legislative framework regarding the public interest aspects of media mergers in Ireland. Its report considers how the existing mechanism for the approval of media mergers under s 23 of the Competition Act 2002 might be amended to reflect the relationship between the media and the public interest in media plurality in the State.[85]

[10.53] The Group was critical of the current framework, noting:

> ... concerns about the role of the Competition Authority, lack of clarity in the relevant criteria as currently defined and the absence of clear statutory mechanisms to enable the Minister to protect the public interest in media plurality.[86]

The role of the Competition Authority in media mergers

[10.54] In its analysis of the procedure for merger clearance, the role of the Competition Authority in the application of the 'relevant criteria' was criticised by the Group. The obligation to 'form an opinion' which may never be requested by the Minister was

---

81. *Report of the Advisory Group on Media Mergers* (June 2008), paras 7.17–20.
82. *Report of the Advisory Group on Media Mergers* (June 2008), para 4.45.
83. Competition Authority of Ireland, *Annual Report 2009*, 35. See www.tca.ie.
84. Of the 89 media mergers that had been notified as of June 2008, 86 had been cleared under Phase 1. See *Report of the Advisory Group on Media Mergers* (June 2008), para 4.45. In 2005 the Competition Authority entered into a Phase 2 investigation of the proposed acquisition of MS Irish Cable Holdings BV (trading as NTL) by UPC Ireland Ltd. UPC Ireland Ltd was ultimately owned by Liberty Global Inc which also owned the Irish cable provider, Chorus. Following the Phase 2 investigation, the Authority had concerns about cross-ownership interests held by a number of directors of Liberty Global including the leading shareholder in Liberty Global. The Authority was specifically concerned about cross-ownership interests linked to NewsCorporation and BSkyB and imposed 19 conditions on the transaction. The Minister approved the transaction subject to the same conditions. See the Competition Authority *Annual Report 2005*, 27–28.
85. *Report of the Advisory Group on Media Mergers* (June 2008), para 2.2.
86. *Report of the Advisory Group on Media Mergers* (June 2008), para 2.3.

described as 'anomalous'.[87] One of the issues considered by the Group was whether the Competition Authority should play a greater role in applying the relevant criteria to media mergers. The Group decided against this on the basis that the Authority's expertise lay in the economics of markets, not in issues of plurality or diversity.[88] It was recommended that the Competition Authority's role in the context of media mergers should be focused on the application of competition criteria.[89] The Group also noted that the function of applying criteria relating to plurality and diversity was 'one essentially of political judgment as to how the public interest is best protected as a result of a particular media merger.'[90] It recommended that the Minister for Enterprise, Trade and Employment remain the Minister with responsibility for the area but it also recommended that there should be a duty on him to consult with the Minister for Communications, Energy and Natural Resources in the case of mergers involving holders of broadcasting licences.[91]

The desirability of a statutory test for the Minister

[10.55] One of the other recommendations made by the Group was that a clearer statutory test be introduced by legislation to clarify the objective of any ministerial intervention as being to protect the plurality in media business in the State.[92] In the same vein, it was recommended that there should be a statutory definition of 'plurality' and that it should include both diversity of ownership and of content. The suggested definition of 'diversity of ownership' was:

> ... the spread of ownership and control of media businesses in the State amongst individuals and other undertakings linked to the market share of those media businesses as measured by listenership, readership or other appropriate methods.[93]

It was noted that '[d]iversity of ownership in this sense gives a weighting to the power of the media business in which a share or control is held. It thus refers to the extent to which ownership or control of the "ability to influence" or "opinion forming power" of media businesses is spread'.[94]

[10.56] In respect of diversity of content, the suggested definition was:

> ... the extent to which the broad diversity of views and cultural interests prevalent in Irish society is reflected through the activities of media businesses in this State, including their editorial ethos, content and sources. 'Views' includes but is not limited to, news and current affairs.[95]

---

87. *Report of the Advisory Group on Media Mergers* (June 2008), para.7.7.
88. *Report of the Advisory Group on Media Mergers* (June 2008), para 5.10.
89. *Report of the Advisory Group on Media Mergers* (June 2008), paras 7.8–16.
90. *Report of the Advisory Group on Media Mergers* (June 2008), para 5.11.
91. *Report of the Advisory Group on Media Mergers* (June 2008), para 5.13.
92. *Report of the Advisory Group on Media Mergers* (June 2008), para 6.55.
93. *Report of the Advisory Group on Media Mergers* (June 2008), para 6.55.
94. *Report of the Advisory Group on Media Mergers* (June 2008), para 6.55.
95. *Report of the Advisory Group on Media Mergers* (June 2008), para 6.55.

This definition was intended to refer to Irish culture rather than just referring to views.

[10.57] Bearing in mind these definitions, the Group proposed a new statutory test to guide the Minister in the application of criteria as follows:

> Whether the result of the merger is likely to be contrary to the public interest in protecting plurality in the media in the State.[96]

Analysis of the existing 'relevant criteria'

[10.58] As well as setting out a statutory test, the Group also analysed the 'relevant criteria' as set out in s 23(10).

[10.59] In respect of the first criterion, '(a) the strength and competitiveness of media businesses indigenous to the State', the report noted that this was the only criterion that could be viewed as a competition criterion. The use of the word 'indigenous' was criticised on the basis that it generated a lack of clarity. The use of the word in the Competition Act 'reflected public and industry concern about the ambitions of foreign media organizations in respect to the Irish market, as well as a fond appraisal of a home-grown media'.[97] The *Report of the Commission on the Newspaper Industry* had viewed the contribution to diversity made by imported titles, including those that had 'Irish editions' to be of a lesser value than that of the indigenous press.[98] The Group also noted the lack of any definitions of 'competitiveness' or 'strength' in the provision.

[10.60] The group considered (b) and (c) together. Paragraph (b) refers to the extent to which ownership and control of media businesses in the State is spread amongst individuals and other undertakings. Paragraph (c) is similar, save that it refers to 'particular types of media business'. The Group noted the difference in wording between the two provisions in that (b) refers to ownership 'or control' whereas (c) refers to ownership 'and control'. The Group did not see any difference of substance between the two and queried the need for separate criteria.[99]

[10.61] Criterion (d) – 'the extent to which the diversity of views prevalent in Irish society is reflected through the activities of the various media businesses in the State' was recognised as creating difficulties of application. Nonetheless, as the Group noted, 'for so long as society wishes to regulate media mergers in order to avoid a reduction in diversity, it will be necessary for the responsible body – in this case the Minister – to

---

96. *Report of the Advisory Group on Media Mergers* (June 2008), para 6.53. The Council of Europe has taken a similar approach, viewing media pluralism as referring to the scope for a wide range of social, political and cultural values, opinions and interests to find expression through the media. See Council Recommendation on measures to promote media pluralism, 19 January 1999; Council Recommendation on media pluralism and diversity of content, 31 January 2007.
97. *Report of the Advisory Group on Media Mergers* (June 2008), para 6.20.
98. *Report of the Advisory Group on Media Mergers* (June 2008), para 6.20.
99. The Group hypothesised that there may have been a reason for the distinction in that (b) may have been meant to translate the Commission on the Newspaper Industry's formula 'plurality of ownership' whereas (c) may have been intended to capture 'plurality of titles'. In the Group's view, this aim was not realised by the wording used (para 6.32).

make such decisions.'[100] The report did recommend, however, that the Minister use certain concrete indicators that would help him make rational and objective decisions in this area.[101]

[10.62] The Group also considered criterion (e): 'the share in the market in the State of one or more of the types of business activity falling within the definition of 'media business' in this subsection that is held by any of the undertakings involved in the media merger concerned, or by any individual or other undertaking who or which has an interest in such an undertaking'. Media business is defined as: '(a) a business of the publication of newspapers or periodicals consisting substantially of news and comment on current affairs, (b) a business of providing a broadcasting service, or (c) a business of providing a broadcasting services platform'. The omission from this definition of any reference to the internet, or associated technologies and undertakings was criticised given developments in the market for newspapers and television which make use of this resource in various ways. The Group noted that this could give rise to editorial issues as well as the capacity for internet sites to close advertising deals that might have knock-on effects in taking advertising revenue from other media. This was seen as a potentially important factor given the ability of media conglomerates to offer package deals across platforms and media. The Group also noted the relevance of gaming to diversity and plurality in the media given the growing impact of online gaming in the field of culture.[102]

[10.63] The Group noted that (e) was the only one of the 'relevant criteria' which focused specifically on the merger or acquisition in question. The report noted that (e) addressed only the pre-merger shares and not the post-merger shares. It also seemed to require the Minister to take account of the market share of individual shareholders having an interest in one of the undertakings no matter how small that undertaking may be.

New 'relevant criteria' proposed

[10.64] In light of the proposed statutory test, the Group advocated new criteria to replace the 'relevant criteria' in s 23(10). These were:

(a)   The likely effect of the media merger on plurality which includes both diversity of ownership and diversity of content.

This criterion was proposed to be placed first as the most important of the list. The Group recommended that when examining diversity of ownership, the Minister would look at both the spread of ownership and control and the market share. When assessing the diversity of content, the Minister should examine the overall level of choice for

---

100. *Report of the Advisory Group on Media Mergers* (June 2008), para 6.42.
101. *Report of the Advisory Group on Media Mergers* (June 2008), para 6.42.
102. *Report of the Advisory Group on Media Mergers* (June 2008), para 6.46–51.

citizens as well as the balance between the three media strands of commercial, state-owned and community-based media:

> (b)   The undesirability of allowing any one individual or undertaking to hold significant interests within a sector or across different sections of media business.

The Group felt that this criterion 'enables the Oireachtas to put down a marker' on this point. It recommended that the Minister set out in guidelines what might constitute 'significant interests' in this context.

> (c)   The consequences for the promotion of plurality in media business in the State of intervening to prevent the media merger or attach conditions to the approval of the media merger.

This criterion is intended to cover, for example, the situation where the immediate effect of a merger between one undertaking and another failing undertaking might be to reduce plurality in the market but a decision to prohibit it might ultimately have a more significant adverse effect.

> (d)   The adequacy of other mechanisms to protect the public interest in plurality of the media if the Minister was not to intervene.

This is intended to enable the Minister to have regard to regulation by eg the BCI or voluntary codes of conduct which might suffice to protect the public interest in plurality if the merger was allowed to proceed.

> (e)   The commitments that the undertakings are willing to offer and which are capable of being effectively incorporated into any decision by the Minister.
>
> (f)   The extent to which the public interest can be secured by the imposition of any conditions in any decision by the Minister to approve the merger.

Criteria (e) and (f), like (d), enable the Minister to assess whether it is necessary or proportionate to prohibit a merger where other means of protecting the public interest in plurality may be possible.

Proposal for additional matters to which the Minister must have regard

[10.65] As well as suggesting the replacement of the relevant criteria, the report also recommends that certain matters should be identified as matters to which the Minister should have regard. These additional matters were any guidelines issued by the Minister on media plurality in the State, the decision of the Competition Authority (which the Group recommended should be binding on the Minister in so far as it determines the issue of substantial effect on competition in the market, the decision of the BCI, the opinion of a consultative panel to be set up by the Minister,[103] any submissions received in public consultation and finally, a catch-all provision for such other matters relevant to the relevant criteria as the Minister sees fit.[104]

---

103. *Report of the Advisory Group on Media Mergers* (June 2008), paras 7.34–39.
104. *Report of the Advisory Group on Media Mergers* (June 2008), paras 6.58–60.

Indicators of diversity of content and spread of ownership

[10.66] The Group also considered concrete indicators of diversity of content and spread of ownership.[105] It did not recommend including these in the 'relevant criteria' or as matters to which the Minister must have regard. Instead, the Group suggested that the indicia might usefully be incorporated into guidelines to be issued by the Minister or any questionnaires that might be used in the context of media merger clearance.

[10.67] The Group pointed out that the need to protect diversity of content cannot be achieved by addressing ownership and competition between undertakings alone. Some monitoring of content is required. It considered a number of indicia for diversity of content:

(a) Independent and objective demographic data on the audience/readership for particular media businesses, as a general indicator of the type of taste and content to which a particular media business caters.

(b) Records of any breaches of relevant codes of good practice, especially but not exclusively relating to fairness and honesty, respect for rights and incitement to hatred, in so far as such breaches imply bias or exclusion. Codes in this context might include the Code of Conduct of the Press Council or the NUJ. The BCI also undertakes compliance activity and the results of this could be useful indicator also.

(c) Policies and practice is respect of the recruitment and/or training of persons of a diverse range of cultural, ethnic, social or other backgrounds as company directors or as editors and other professional media workers within a media business.

(d) Employment levels and standards.

[10.68] These were seen as relevant because the media require sufficient resources to ensure the breadth and depth of coverage appropriate to a diverse and multicultural society. The Group did not, however, see security of employment as a key issue.

(e) Data on financial support from non-commercial sources for media content and on the criteria for its expenditure.

(f) A record of truthful, accurate and fair reporting on topics of public importance or controversy of directors, editors and large shareholders in any media business.

---

105. In this context, the Commission Task Force for Co-ordination of Media Affairs has also compiled a Media Pluralism Monitor. See the Final Report of the Task Force (2008). The Task Force also commissioned and independent study of each Member State's media plurality (including diversity of content): *Independent Study on Indicators for Media Pluralism in the Member States – Towards a Risk-Based Approach*. The report and study are both available from: http://ec.europa.eu/information_society/media_taskforce/pluralism/study/index_en.htm.

(g) 'Level of trust in' and 'contribution to being "informed by"', each media outlet by age, sex, socio-economic group and geographical location. The Group had reservations about using this criterion (which was proposed by the Competition Authority) on the basis that this could be difficult to measure objectively.

[10.69] The Group also considered indicia of spread of ownership as follows:

(a) Independent and objective demographic data on the audiences/readership for particular media businesses, as a general indicator of the control of flow of information to any particular sector, be it a geographic community or some other community of interest.

(b) Independent and objective data on the various market shares enjoyed by particular media businesses. The Group noted that criterion (e) of the relevant criteria set out in s 23(10) referred only to market share in the State. This was viewed as a constraint on the Minister which failed to address the realities of the global economy in that, for example, the Minister could consider the significance of a potential purchase by an undertaking having massive media interests outside the State but none within it even in the case of competition between that foreign undertaking and an indigenous one.

(c) Annual reports of media businesses in respect to shareholdings, where these are reliable and accurate. The report noted that the BCI already requires these. It suggested that the laws relating to banking secrecy and company disclosures may need amendment to ensure greater transparency in respect of financial holdings and activities in media businesses. The Group noted the powers enjoyed by the US Securities and Exchange Commission in respect of media mergers and suggested that similar powers might be considered here.

(d) Other information disclosed by parties to a merger or by citizens with an interest in that merger.

(e) Information concerning any safeguards for the editorial integrity of undertakings that are proposed to be merged.

(f) Data relating to the strengths and weaknesses of companies that will remain in any relevant market after a merger or take-over.

Reform of the current statutory procedure for merger clearance

[10.70] As well as proposing a statutory test to be applied by the Minister in the event of intervention, the Group also considered in detail the mechanism by which the Minister exercises his powers. The Group was critical of the current provisions on the basis that it was:

> ... anomalous that when a specialist body such as the Competition Authority concludes that, in its opinion, the result of the merger or acquisition will not be such as to substantially lessen competition in markets for goods and services in the State that the Minister should have power to direct the Competition Authority to

proceed to a full investigation, the object of which is to determine that exact same issue.'[106]

The effect of this was to delay mergers by up to three months while the Competition Authority applies the same test during Phase 2 as it applied during Phase 1.

[10.71] The Group was also critical of gaps in the legislation which potentially allowed for media mergers to go ahead without ministerial scrutiny.

[10.72] One such loophole identified by the Group was the fact that if the Competition Authority fails to inform the undertakings concerned of its determination under Phase 1 within the time limit, the result is approval by default with no opportunity for the Minister to engage with the issues raised. A similar point can be made in respect of Phase 2 investigations where the Authority fails to make a determination within the time period.[107]

[10.73] Another major flaw in the procedure under s 23 identified by the Group is the fact that the Minister's power to intervene arises only where the Competition Authority clear a merger (with or without conditions). The Group was critical of the limited 10-day time period the Minister has to direct a Phase 2 investigation. If the Minister fails to intervene during this time period, his power to protect the public interest in plurality and diversity is lost. The brevity of this period is compounded by the fact that it starts at the time the Competition Authority makes its determination, not at the time if informs the Minister thereof. As the Group pointed out, it was possible that a situation could arise where the Authority through administrative oversight or otherwise omitted to inform the Minister promptly or at all.

[10.74] The Group noted that the Act had not been amended to take account of the possibility that a media merger might be notified to the Commission under the ECMR rather than to the authority. Where the ECMR opted not to refer the matter back to the Authority (under Arts 4 or 9 of the ECMR), the Minister's power to intervene could not arise.[108]

[10.75] The Group recommended that the role of the Oireachtas be excluded from any reform of the procedure, leaving ministerial accountability to the corrective mechanism of judicial review.[109]

[10.76] It also recommended that the current mechanism regarding notification of mergers in s 18 should remain and that the Competition Authority should be the arbiter of competition aspects of mergers. In this regard, it recommended that the findings of the Authority as regards the impact of a merger on competition should be binding on the Minister. It also recommended that the Minister should be given the power to seek

---

106.   *Report of the Advisory Group on Media Mergers* (June 2008), para 7.2.
107.   Competition Act 2002, s 19(1)(c). See Competition Act 2002, ss 19(1)(d) and 23(4); discussed in the *Report of the Advisory Group on Media Mergers* (June 2008), para 7.5.
108.   *Report of the Advisory Group on Media Mergers* (June 2008), para 7.6.
109.   *Report of the Advisory Group on Media Mergers* (June 2008), para 7.20.

commitments from undertakings which could then be made binding on them in the event of merger clearance.[110] He should also be required to invite submissions from undertakings[111] and members of the public where he proceeds to a Phase 2 investigation.[112] The Minister should also, according to the Report, be required to give reasons for decisions to the undertakings concerned in the context of s 23(5).[113]

[10.77] Under the proposed new arrangements, Phase 1 would involve the Minister considering whether in view of the Competition Authority's determination and any commitments offered by the undertakings, the proposed transaction gives rise to real concerns that it might be contrary to the public interest in the preservation of plurality and diversity in the media business in the State. At Phase 2, the Minister would consider the proposed merger by applying the statutory test having regard to the relevant criteria as reformed. The Minister at this point would reserve the right to conclude at any point that he no longer has concerns, thus terminating Phase 2 and allowing for earlier clearance.[114]

[10.78] In respect of time limits, the Group recommended a 30-day time limit for Phase 1, to commence at the time the Minister is notified or at the time of the determination of the Authority – whichever is latest. The four-month time limit for Phase 2 should start from the date of the Phase 1 decision by the Minister.[115]

Interaction with the public

[10.79] In addition to the recommendations described above, the Group recommended the publication of information on plurality in the media sector[116] and that the role of the media in a democracy be recognised by statute – ideally in the long title to the Act which provides for media mergers.[117] It also proposed that there should be an addition to s 23(5) to require the Minister to invite submissions from members of the public generally as well as the undertakings concerned in situations where he decides to proceed to a Phase 2 investigation.[118]

THE BROADCASTING AUTHORITY OF IRELAND

[10.80] Mergers and acquisitions of undertakings providing broadcasting services are subject to the Competition Act 2002.[119] In addition to the controls thereunder, the

---

110. *Report of the Advisory Group on Media Mergers* (June 2008), paras 7.22–29.
111. And members of the general public – see discussion below.
112. *Report of the Advisory Group on Media Mergers* (June 2008), paras 7.47–52.
113. *Report of the Advisory Group on Media Mergers* (June 2008), para 7.53.
114. *Report of the Advisory Group on Media Mergers* (June 2008), para 7.32.
115. *Report of the Advisory Group on Media Mergers* (June 2008), para 7.34.
116. *Report of the Advisory Group on Media Mergers* (June 2008), paras 7.42–46.
117. *Report of the Advisory Group on Media Mergers* (June 2008), para 8.22.
118. *Report of the Advisory Group on Media Mergers* (June 2008), paras 7.47–52.
119. See the definition of 'media business' in the Competition Act 2002, s 23(1), discussed above.

Broadcasting Authority of Ireland's regulatory powers also bear on the spread of ownership and diversity of content in the broadcasting sector. The Broadcasting Authority of Ireland was established under the Broadcasting Act 2009.[120]

Granting of licences

[10.81] The Broadcasting Authority is responsible, through its Contracts Award Committee, for the licensing of television and radio broadcasting services under the Broadcasting Act 2009. Section 25 sets out the objectives of the Authority and provides in s 25(1) that in the performance of its functions, it shall endeavour to ensure: (a) that the number and categories of broadcasting services made available in the State by virtue of the Act best serve the needs of the people of the island of Ireland, bearing in mind their languages and traditions and their religious, ethical and cultural diversity; (b) that the democratic values enshrined in the Constitution, especially those relating to rightful liberty of expression, are upheld; and (c) the provision of open and pluralistic broadcasting services.

[10.82] There is a further obligation on the Broadcasting Authority to stimulate the provision of high quality, diverse and innovative programming by commercial, community and public service broadcasters and independent producers, promote diversity in control of the more influential commercial and community broadcasting services and to promote and stimulate the development of Irish language programming and broadcasting services.[121]

---

120.   It replaced the Broadcasting Commission of Ireland. Which was itself the new name given to the Independent Radio and Television Commission under the Broadcasting Act 2001. The Independent Radio and Television Commission was established by the Radio and Television Act 1988 to license and oversee the operation of independent radio and television broadcasting in Ireland. The Broadcasting Act 2009 repealed both the Radio and Television Act 1988 and the Broadcasting Act 2001. The Broadcasting Act 2009 is considered in detail in **Ch 8**.

121.   Broadcasting Act 2009, s 25(2). There are other obligations in this subsection which provides in full as follows: 'Without prejudice to the generality of subsection (1), the Authority, and the statutory committees, shall– (a) stimulate the provision of high quality, diverse and innovative programming by commercial, community and public service broadcasters and independent producers, (b) facilitate public service broadcasters in the fulfilment of their public service objects as set out in this Act, (c) promote diversity in control of the more influential commercial and community broadcasting services, (d) provide a regulatory environment that will sustain independent and impartial journalism, (e) provide a regulatory environment that will sustain compliance with applicable employment law, (f) protect the interests of children taking into account the vulnerability of children and childhood to undue commercial exploitation, (g) provide a regulatory environment that will facilitate the development of a broadcasting sector in Ireland that is responsive to audience needs and in particular is accessible to people with disabilities, and (h) promote and stimulate the development of Irish language programming and broadcasting services.'

[10.83] Under s 25(3):

> The Authority and the statutory committees, in performing their functions, shall seek to ensure that measures taken–
>
> (a)   are proportionate having regard to the objectives set out in this section,
>
> (b)   are applied across the range of broadcasting services taking account of the degree of influence that the different types of broadcasting services are able to exert in shaping audience views in the State,
>
> (c)   are mindful of the objects, functions and duties set for public service broadcasters in Parts 7 and 8,[122]
>
> (d)   will produce regulatory arrangements that are stable and predictable, and
>
> (e)   will readily accommodate and encourage technological development, and its application, by the broadcasting sector.

[10.84] Section 66 of the Act requires the Broadcasting Authority to consider whether awarding a licence to a particular person or a company could operate against the public interest. In particular, the BAI must have regard to the desirability of allowing any person, or group of persons, to have control of, or substantial interests in, an undue amount of the communications media in the area[123] and the desirability of having a diversity of services in the area catering for a wide range of tastes including those of minority interests.[124]

Terms and conditions of licences

[10.85] As well as applying these provisions to the granting of licences, the Authority may also impose licence terms and conditions which impact on ownership and control. The relevant provisions of the Broadcasting Act 2009 are contained in ss 66 and 69. Section 69(2) provides in relevant part that:

> ... the Authority may specify in a broadcasting contract all or any of the following terms or conditions ...
>
> (c)   a condition prohibiting the assignment of the contract or of any interest in it;
>
> (d)   if the broadcasting contractor is a company, a condition prohibiting any alteration in the Memorandum or Articles of Association of the company or in so much of that Memorandum or of those Articles as may be specified or prohibiting any material change in the ownership of the company...

---

122.   These provisions have a bearing on content and the spread thereof. The Act includes both general provisions and provisions specific to certain licensed undertakings eg the requirement of Irish language programming placed on TG4 in Broadcasting Act 2009, s 118.
123.   Broadcasting Act 2009, s 66(2)(i).
124.   Broadcasting Act 2009, s 66(2)(f).

[10.86] Where the Broadcasting Authority does not insert such terms or conditions, s 69(3) provides for certain statutory conditions to apply as follows:

    (a)   a broadcasting contract, or any interest in a broadcasting contract, shall not be assignable, nor shall any alteration be made in the Memorandum or Articles of Association of any company which is a broadcasting contractor, nor shall there be any material change in the ownership of such a company, without the previous consent in writing of the Authority, and the Authority may, if it considers it reasonable so to do, refuse such consent;

    (b)   in considering whether to grant its consent to an assignment of a broadcasting contract, a change in the Memorandum or Articles of Association of a company which is a broadcasting contractor, or a material change in the ownership of such a company, the Authority shall have regard to the criteria specified in section 66(2) and, where applicable, section 66(4).

This effectively requires licence holders to notify changes in ownership or control to the Broadcasting Authority for its consideration. In its consideration of such a proposed change, the Broadcasting Authority must have regard to certain criteria.

[10.87] The criteria set out in s 66(2) are:

    (a)   the character, expertise and experience of the applicant or, if the applicant is a body corporate, the character expertise and experience of the body and its directors, manager, secretary or other similar officer and its members and the persons entitled to the beneficial ownership of its shares,

    (b)   the adequacy of the financial resources that will be available to each applicant and the extent to which the application accords with good business and economic principles,

    (c)   the quality, range and type of the programmes proposed to be provided by each applicant or, if there is only one applicant, by that applicant,

    (d)   the quantity, quality, range and type of programmes in the Irish language and the extent of programmes relating to Irish culture proposed to be provided,

    (e)   the extent to which the applicant will create within the proposed broadcasting service new opportunities for talent in music, drama and entertainment and in particular in respect of Irish culture,

    (f)   the desirability of having a diversity of services in the area specified in the notice catering for a wide range of tastes including those of minority interests,

    (g)   the desirability of allowing any person, or group of persons, to have control of, or substantial interests in, an undue number of sound broadcasting services in respect of which a sound broadcasting contract has been awarded under this Part,

    (h)   the desirability of allowing any person, or group of persons, to have control of, or substantial interests in, an undue number of sound broadcasting services in the area specified in the notice,

(i)   the desirability of allowing any person, or group of persons, to have control of, or substantial interests in, an undue amount of the communications media in the area specified in the notice,

(j)   the extent to which the service proposed–

   (i)   serves recognisably local communities and is supported by the various interests in the community, or

   (ii) serves communities of interest,

(k)   any other matters which the Contract Awards Committee considers to be necessary to secure the orderly development of broadcasting services, and

(l)   where directed by the Authority, any of–

   (i)   the amount of a single cash sum payment, as specified by the applicant during the course of his or her application, which the applicant is willing to pay to the Authority in respect of the award of the broadcasting contract,

   (ii) the amount of a periodic cash sum payment, as specified by the applicant during the course of his or her application, which the applicant is willing to pay to the Authority in respect of the award of the broadcasting contract, and

   (iii) the amount of a periodic cash sum payment determined by reference to a variable, as specified by the applicant during the course of his or her application, which the applicant is willing to pay to the Authority in respect of the award of the broadcasting contract.

[10.88] Section 66(4) sets out the following criteria:

(a)   the overall quality of the performance of the applicant with respect to the provision by him or her of a broadcasting service under any broadcasting contract held by him or her at, or before, the date of the making of the application, and

(b)   reports of the Compliance Committee.

[10.89] The criteria at s 66(2)(c)–(f) (and perhaps (i)) are all related to diversity of content. The provisions at s 66(2)(g)–(i), on the other hand, address diversity of ownership. The phrase 'undue number' in this context, is not defined in the Act. The predecessor of the Broadcasting Authority, the Broadcasting Commission, set out its view of what constituted an 'undue amount of communications media' under the Broadcasting Act 2001[125] in a policy document issued in 2005 in which it specified that one investor should not hold more than 25% of the licences. Up to 15% of the total number of licences was deemed 'acceptable'. Up to a further 10% ownership of the total number required 'more careful consideration by the Commission'.[126] In the absence of

---

125.   Independent Television and Radio Act 1988, s 6(2)(h) and the Broadcasting Act 2001, s 38(6).
126.   Broadcasting Commission of Ireland 'Ownership and Control Policy' (2005), 13. www.bci.ie/documents/o&c_policy_05.pdf.

any new policy documents emanating from the Broadcasting Authority, it seems likely that this policy will continue.[127]

THE EC MERGER REGULATION AND MEDIA MERGERS

[10.90] The EC Merger Regulation[128] replaced the 1989 Merger Regulation[129] which was based on the 'one-stop shop' principle, which gave the Commission sole control over all major cross-border mergers. The new Regulation similarly seeks to ensure that the same merger need not be notified to several competition authorities in the European Union but also adopts the principle of subsidiarity, whereby a merger is examined by the judicial authority best placed to do so.

[10.91] Under the Regulation, the general rule is that mergers and acquisitions with a Community dimension[130] are subject to the exclusive jurisdiction of the Commission under Art 1(1). While Member States may not apply national competition law to those mergers and acquisitions,[131] Art 21(4) provides that:

> Member States may take appropriate measures to protect legitimate interests other than those taken into consideration by this Regulation and compatible with the general principles and other provisions of Community law.
>
> Public security, plurality of the media and prudential rules shall be regarded as legitimate interests within the meaning of the first subparagraph.

---

127. The Broadcasting Authority had not, as of 24 September 2010, published any additional policy documents addressing the issue of ownership.
128. Council Regulation 139/2004/EC of 20 January 2004 on the control of concentrations between undertakings. This repealed and replaced Regulations 4064/89/EC and 1310/97/EC. See also Commission Regulation 802/2004/EC of 7 April 2004 implementing Council Regulation 139/2004/EC. On the role of the EU in promoting media pluralism, see the Commission's issues paper, 'Media Pluralism– what should be the European Union's role?' *Issues Paper for the Liverpool Audiovisual Conference* (July 2005). http://ec.europa.eu/avpolicy/docs/reg/modernisation/issue_papers/ispa_mediaplur_en.pdf, accessed 23 September 2010.
129. Regulation 4064/89/EEC.
130. A concentration has a Community dimension where (under Art 1(2)) (a) the combined aggregate worldwide turnover of all the undertakings concerned is more than €5000 million; and (b) the aggregate Community-wide turnover of each of at least two of the undertakings concerned is more than €250 million, unless each of the undertakings concerned achieves more than two-thirds of its aggregate Community-wide turnover within one and the same Member State. A concentration that does not meet the thresholds laid down in Art 1(2) has a Community dimension under Art 1(3) where: (a) the combined aggregate worldwide turnover of all the undertakings concerned is more than €2500 million; (b) in each of at least three Member States, the combined aggregate turnover of all the undertakings concerned is more than €100 million; (c) in each of at least three Member States included for the purpose of point (b), the aggregate turnover of each of at least two of the undertakings concerned is more than €25 million; and (d) the aggregate Community-wide turnover of each of at least two of the undertakings concerned is more than €100 million, unless each of the undertakings concerned achieves more than two-thirds of its aggregate Community-wide turnover within one and the same Member State.
131. Regulation 139/2004/EC, Art 21(3).

Article 21(4) operates in tandem with the Commission's review of the concentration on competition grounds. The Commission maintains contact with the domestic competition authorities who may be examining the transaction in light of relevant 'legitimate interest'. This means that a Member State can prohibit a transaction under Art 21(4) which was cleared by the Commission on pure competition grounds.

[10.92] Under Arts 4(4) and 9(1), a merger or acquisition which may significantly affect competition in a market within a Member State and which presents all the characteristics of a distinct market may be examined, in whole or in part, by that Member State.[132]

[10.93] The Merger Regulation itself contains no detailed provisions to deal with media mergers. The Commission has adopted a 'public interest' test when examining media mergers notified to it which seeks to accommodate concerns over media plurality.[133]

[10.94] It has been argued that the current view in Brussels 'that the combination of national legislation, EU competition law and EU legislative instruments provides a perfect and balanced solution for the protection of both structural and internal media pluralism in Europe' fails to adequately address the current threat to media pluralism in the EU.[134] Given that only six of the 27 Member States have special rules for media mergers, the criticism seems justified.[135]

---

132. Council Regulation 139/2004/EC, Art 4(4) provides for a procedure whereby a person or undertaking acquiring the whole or part of another undertaking may seek to have the merger or acquisition dealt with by the authority of a Member State. Under Council Regulation 139/2004/ EC, Art 9(1), the Commission may refer a concentration to a Member State authority on its own initiative. This is designed to address the situation where a merger with a Community dimension may significantly affect competition in a market within a Member State which presents all the characteristics of a distinct market. There is also provision in Council Regulation 139/2004/EC, Art 2 for a Member State to refer to the Commission a concentration which does not have a Community dimension under the Regulation but which affects trade between Member States and threatens to significantly affect competition within the territory of the Member State or States making the request.

133. For a critique of this, see Nitsche, *Broadcasting in the European Union – the Role of Public Interest in Competition Analysis* (Springer, 2001). Examples of Commission decisions on media mergers include *AOL/Time Warner* (11 October 2000); *Lagardère/Natexis/VUP* (Case M.2978) (2004); *Sony/BMG* (Case M.3333) (2007).

134. Komorek, 'Legal Protection of Media Pluralism at National Level. An Examination of the United Kingdom and Ireland' (2010) 10(1) Hibernian Law Journal 92.

135. See European Commission, DG Information Society and Media, 'Media Pluralism – what should be the European Union's role?' *Issues Paper for the Liverpool Audiovisual Conference*, July 2005. http://ec.europa.eu/avpolicy/docs/reg/modernisation/issue_papers/ispa_mediaplur_en.pdf, accessed 23 September 2010. For a discussion of the approaches taken to media pluralism in the various Member States, see Cavallin, 'European Policies and Regulations on Media Concentration' [1998] 1 International Journal of Communications Law and Policy. Available from www.ijclp.net.

MEDIA OWNERSHIP IN THE INTERNET ERA

[10.95] One of the striking developments in the media sector is the increasing role of the internet as a source of and delivery mechanism for information. The Advisory Group noted the contribution of the internet to plurality in the Irish media sector which makes it possible, for example, to access newspapers from all over the world,[136] but called for greater transparency of mergers involving Internet based services.[137]

[10.96] The current provisions of the Competition Act 2002 do not address the increasingly important role of the internet in this context. There is a striking gap in the context of broadcasting services. Under s 23(10) of the Competition Act 2002, the term 'broadcasting service' (which in turn is included in the 'media business' regulated by the provision, specifically excludes 'the provision of a broadcasting service whether involving audio visual or audio material provided by means of the system commonly known as the Internet.' The Advisory Group on Media Mergers suggested that this exclusion should be removed and a provision inserted which would include the broadcasting of certain audiovisual material over the internet.

[10.97] As far as the traditional print media is concerned, the definition of 'media business' simply refers to 'publication of newspapers or periodicals consisting substantially of news and comment on current affairs'. The Group recommended that the definition be amended to specifically include the publication of newspapers and periodicals over the internet.[138] Such an amendment would bring clarity to the issue although the current wording of that provision relating to the press seems capable of catching publication via the internet. The specific exclusion of in the context of broadcasting service supports such an interpretation.

[10.98] One of the difficulties with bringing the internet into the ambit of media merger regulation is the fact that services accessed online do not always fit easily into traditional media categories. Some will – for example the online publication of newspapers. Other forms of online media which such as gaming and related tie-ins are more difficult to conceive of in this way.[139] Further, as the Advisory Group itself recognised, there are many resources of news and information on the Internet which are posted privately or which simply aggregate material already published with no editorial responsibility. These include content sharing platforms such as www.youtube.com and news aggregation sites such as http://news.google.com.[140] While websites containing publisher-controlled content such as www.rte.ie seem to mirror their traditionally

---

136. *Report of the Advisory Group on Media Mergers* (June 2008), para 3.67.
137. *Report of the Advisory Group on Media Mergers* (June 2008), para 2.4.
138. *Report of the Advisory Group on Media Mergers* (June 2008), paras 2.6 and 8.20.
139. The Audiovisual Media Services Directive 2007/65/EC of the European Parliament and the Council of 11 December 2007 attempts this. For an account of some of the flaws with this approach, see Dizon, 'Looking beyond the linear/non-linear horizon: content regulation in the converging multilayered contours of the European audiovisual landscape' [2010] Entertainment Law Review 185.
140. *Report of the Advisory Group on Media Mergers* (June 2008), para 2.6.

broadcast forerunners, these other sources of information do not seem appropriate targets of merger regulation.

[10.99] To address this, the Group proposed a number of principles which should apply when considering the extent to which the law relating to the control of media mergers should apply to internet-based activity. These were: (a) Editorial content or responsibility. This recognises that where individual users post material this is not really 'media content'. Neither is news aggregation; (b) The scale of the potential impact on the public. This reflects the reality that much of the material on the internet is only of interest to a small number of people; (c) Private websites and e-mails should not come within the regulatory regime for media mergers; and (d) Services which are primarily of a non-economic nature should be excluded.[141] These principles, which accord with the approach taken in the Audiovisual Media Services Directive,[142] recognise that not all internet media require the same scrutiny.

[10.100] For the same reason, the Group recommended that any amendment of the definition of a broadcasting service should only cover the provision of audio-visual material over the internet which is under the control of the service provider delivering the service; primarily economic in nature; intended for reception by or could have a clear impact on, a significant proportion of the general public; in competition with or akin to newspapers or periodicals or broadcasting services transmitted or relayed by the means specified in the existing definition.[143] The inclusion of internet-based services within the context of merger regulation raises the prospect of over-inclusiveness in that material that is only incidentally published or broadcast in the State could be caught. The Group recommended that the idea of carrying on a business in the State be revised and amended to address this.[144]

---

141. *Report of the Advisory Group on Media Mergers* (June 2008), para 3.71.
142. Directive 2007/65/EC of the European Parliament and the Council of 11 December 2007. See Arts 17–19 of the recitals thereto. This Directive was implemented into Irish Law by the European Communities (Audiovisual Media Services Regulations) 2010 (SI 258/2010).
143. The Group also recommended that the Oireachtas should take a consistent approach to the issue in the context of the regulation of broadcasting and the regulation of media mergers. *Report of the Advisory Group on Media Mergers* (June 2008), para 3.73.
144. *Report of the Advisory Group on Media Mergers*, June 2008, para 8.21.

APPENDIX

DEFAMATION ACT 2009

Number 31 of 2009

ARRANGEMENT OF SECTIONS

PART 1
PRELIMINARY AND GENERAL

PART 2
DEFAMATION

PART 3
DEFENCES

PART 4
REMEDIES

PART 5
CRIMINAL LIABILITY

PART 6
MISCELLANEOUS

SCHEDULE 1
STATEMENTS HAVING QUALIFIED PRIVILEGE

PART 1
Statements Privileged Without Explanation or Contradiction

PART 2
Statements Privileged Subject to Explanation or Contradiction

SCHEDULE 2
Minimum Requirements in Relation to Press Council

AN ACT TO REVISE IN PART THE LAW OF DEFAMATION; TO REPEAL THE DEFAMATION ACT 1961; AND TO PROVIDE FOR MATTERS CONNECTED THEREWITH.

[*23rd July*, 2009]

BE IT ENACTED BY THE OIREACHTAS AS FOLLOWS:

PART 1
PRELIMINARY AND GENERAL

1 Short title and commencement

(1) This Act may be cited as the Defamation Act 2009.

(2) This Act shall come into operation on such day or days as the Minister may appoint, by order or orders, either generally or with reference to any particular purpose or provision, and different days may be so appointed for different purposes and different provisions.

2 Definitions

In this Act—

"Act of 1957" means the Statute of Limitations 1957;

"Act of 1961" means the Defamation Act 1961;

"cause of action" means a cause of action for defamation;

"correction order" has the meaning assigned to it by section 30;

"declaratory order" has the meaning assigned to it by section 28;

"defamation" shall be construed in accordance with section 6 (2);

"defamation action" means—

(a) an action for damages for defamation, or

(b) an application for a declaratory order,

whether or not a claim for other relief under this Act is made;

"defamatory statement" means a statement that tends to injure a person's reputation in the eyes of reasonable members of society, and "defamatory" shall be construed accordingly;

"defence of absolute privilege" has the meaning assigned to it by section 17;

"defence of qualified privilege" has the meaning assigned to it by section 18;

"defence of truth" has the meaning assigned to it by section 16;

"electronic communication" includes a communication of information in the form of data, text, images or sound (or any combination of these) by means of guided or unguided electromagnetic energy, or both;

"Minister" means the Minister for Justice, Equality and Law Reform;

"periodical" means any newspaper, magazine, journal or other publication that is printed, published or issued, or that circulates, in the State at regular or substantially regular intervals and includes any version thereof published on the internet or by other electronic means;

"plaintiff" includes a defendant counterclaiming in respect of a statement that is alleged to be defamatory;

"Press Council" has the meaning assigned to it by section 44;

"Press Ombudsman" has the meaning assigned to it by paragraph 8 of Schedule 2;

"qualified offer" has the meaning assigned to it by section 22;

"special damages" has the meaning assigned to it by section 31 (7);

"statement" includes—

    (a)   a statement made orally or in writing,

    (b)   visual images, sounds, gestures and any other method of signifying meaning,

    (c)   a statement—

        (i)   broadcast on the radio or television, or

        (ii) published on the internet, and

    (d)   an electronic communication;

"summary relief" means, in relation to a defamation action—

    (a)   a correction order, or

    (b)   an order prohibiting further publication of the statement to which the action relates.

3 Saver

(1) A provision of this Act shall not affect causes of action accruing before its commencement.

(2) This Act shall not affect the operation of the general law in relation to defamation except to the extent that it provides otherwise (either expressly or by necessary implication).

4 Repeal

The Act of 1961 is repealed.

5 Review of operation of Act

(1) The Minister shall, not later than 5 years after the passing of this Act, commence a review of its operation.

(2) A review under subsection (1) shall be completed not later than one year after its commencement.

PART 2
DEFAMATION

6 Defamation

(1) The tort of libel and the tort of slander—

    (a)   shall cease to be so described, and

    (b)   shall, instead, be collectively described, and are referred to in this Act, as the "tort of defamation".

(2) The tort of defamation consists of the publication, by any means, of a defamatory statement concerning a person to one or more than one person (other than the first-mentioned person), and "defamation" shall be construed accordingly.

(3) A defamatory statement concerns a person if it could reasonably be understood as referring to him or her.

(4) There shall be no publication for the purposes of the tort of defamation if the defamatory statement concerned is published to the person to whom it relates and to a person other than the person to whom it relates in circumstances where—

(a) it was not intended that the statement would be published to the second-mentioned person, and

(b) it was not reasonably foreseeable that publication of the statement to the first-mentioned person would result in its being published to the second-mentioned person.

(5) The tort of defamation is actionable without proof of special damage.

7 Amendment of certain enactments

(1) Section 77 of the Courts of Justice Act 1924 is amended, in paragraph (i) (inserted by section 4(a) of the Courts Act 1991), by the substitution of "the tort of defamation" for the words "slander, libel".

(2) The Civil Liability Act 1961 is amended—

(a) in section 11, by—

(i) the substitution, in subsection (5), of "defamatory statement" for the words "libel or slander", and

(ii) the insertion of the following subsection:

"(7) In this section ' defamatory statement ' has the same meaning as it has in the Defamation Act 2009.",

and

(b) in section 14(6), by the substitution of "a defamation action under the Defamation Act 2009" for the words "an action for libel or slander".

8 Verifying affidavit

(1) Where the plaintiff in a defamation action serves on the defendant any pleading containing assertions or allegations of fact, the plaintiff (or in the case of a defamation action brought on behalf of an infant or person of unsound mind by a next friend or a committee of the infant or person, the next friend or committee) shall swear an affidavit verifying those assertions or allegations.

(2) Where the defendant in a defamation action serves on the plaintiff any pleading containing assertions or allegations of fact, the defendant shall swear an affidavit verifying those assertions or allegations.

(3) Where a defamation action is brought on behalf of an infant or a person of unsound mind by a next friend or a committee of the infant or person, an affidavit to which subsection (1) applies sworn by the next friend or committee concerned shall, in respect of assertions or allegations, of which he or she does not have personal knowledge, state that he or she honestly believes the assertions or allegations, to be true.

(4) Where the plaintiff or defendant in a defamation action is a body corporate, the person swearing the affidavit on behalf of the body corporate under subsection (1) or (2), as the case may be, shall, in respect of assertions or allegations, of which he or she

does not have personal knowledge, state that he or she honestly believes the assertions or allegations to be true.

(5) An affidavit under this section shall be sworn and filed in court not later than 2 months after the service of the pleading concerned or such longer period as the court may direct or the parties may agree.

(6) If a person makes a statement in an affidavit under this section—

    (a)   that is false or misleading in any material respect, and

    (b)   that he or she knows to be false or misleading,

he or she shall be guilty of an offence.

(7) A person guilty of an offence under this section shall be liable—

    (a)   on summary conviction, to a fine not exceeding €3,000, or imprisonment for a term not exceeding 6 months or to both, or

    (b)   on conviction on indictment, to a fine not exceeding €50,000, or imprisonment for a term not exceeding 5 years, or to both.

(8) An affidavit sworn under this section shall include a statement by the deponent that he or she is aware that the making of a statement by him or her in the affidavit that is false or misleading in any material respect and that he or she knows to be false or misleading is an offence.

(9) In a defamation action—

    (a)   the defendant shall, unless the court otherwise directs, be entitled to cross examine the plaintiff in relation to any statement made by the plaintiff in the affidavit sworn by him or her under this section, and

    (b)   the plaintiff shall, unless the court otherwise directs, be entitled to cross examine the defendant in relation to any statement made by the defendant in the affidavit sworn by him or her under this section.

(10) Where a plaintiff or a defendant fails to comply with this section, the court may make such order as it considers just and equitable, including—

    (a)   in the case of such a failure on the part of the plaintiff, an order dismissing the defamation action, and

    (b)   in the case of such a failure by the defendant, judgment in favour of the plaintiff,

and may give such directions in relation to an order so made as the court considers necessary or expedient.

(11) The reference to court in subsection (5) shall—

    (a)   in the case of a defamation action brought in the High Court, include a reference to the Master of the High Court, and

    (b)   in the case of a defamation action brought in the Circuit Court, include a reference to the county registrar for the county in which the proceedings concerned were issued.

(12)(a) References in this section to plaintiff shall, in the case of a plaintiff who is deceased, be construed as references to his or her personal representative.

  (b) References in this section to defendant shall, in the case of a defendant who is deceased, be construed as references to his or her personal representative.

(13) This section does not apply to an application for a declaratory order.

9 Imputation

A person has one cause of action only in respect of the publication of a defamatory statement concerning the person even if more than one defamatory imputation in respect of that person is borne by that statement.

10 Defamation of class of persons

Where a person publishes a defamatory statement concerning a class of persons, a member of that class shall have a cause of action under this Act against that person if—

  (a) by reason of the number of persons who are members of that class, or

  (b) by virtue of the circumstances in which the statement is published,

the statement could reasonably be understood to refer, in particular, to the member concerned.

11 Multiple publication

(1) Subject to subsection (2), a person has one cause of action only in respect of a multiple publication.

(2) A court may grant leave to a person to bring more than one defamation action in respect of a multiple publication where it considers that the interests of justice so require.

(3) In this section "multiple publication" means publication by a person of the same defamatory statement to 2 or more persons (other than the person in respect of whom the statement is made) whether contemporaneously or not.

12 Defamation of a body corporate

The provisions of this Act apply to a body corporate as they apply to a natural person, and a body corporate may bring a defamation action under this Act in respect of a statement concerning it that it claims is defamatory whether or not it has incurred or is likely to incur financial loss as a result of the publication of that statement.

13 Appeals in defamation actions

(1) Upon the hearing of an appeal from a decision of the High Court in a defamation action, the Supreme Court may, in addition to any other order that it deems appropriate to make, substitute for any amount of damages awarded to the plaintiff by the High Court such amount as it considers appropriate.

(2) In this section "decision" includes a judgment entered pursuant to the verdict of a jury.

14 Meaning

(1) The court, in a defamation action, may give a ruling—

    (a) as to whether the statement in respect of which the action was brought is reasonably capable of bearing the imputation pleaded by the plaintiff, and

    (b) (where the court rules that that statement is reasonably capable of bearing that imputation) as to whether that imputation is reasonably capable of bearing a defamatory meaning,

upon an application being made to it in that behalf.

(2) Where a court rules under subsection (1) that—

    (a) the statement in respect of which the action was brought is not reasonably capable of bearing the imputationpleaded by the plaintiff, or

    (b) that any imputation so pleaded is not reasonably capable of bearing a defamatory meaning,

it shall dismiss the action in so far only as it relates to the imputation concerned.

(3) An application under this section shall be brought by notice of motion and shall be determined, in the case of a defamation action brought in the High Court, in the absence of the jury.

(4) An application under this section may be brought at any time after the bringing of the defamation action concerned includingduring the course of the trial of the action.

PART 3
DEFENCES

15 Abolition of certain defences

(1) Subject to sections 17(1) and 18(1), any defence that, immediately before the commencement of this Part, could have been pleaded as a defence in an action for libel or slander is abolished.

(2) In this section—

"defence" shall not include a defence under—

    (a) statute,

    (b) an act of the institutions of the European Communities, or

    (c) regulations made for the purpose of giving effect to an act of the institutions of the European Communities;

"European Communities" has the same meaning as it has in the European Communities Act 1972;

"statute" means—

    (a) an Act of the Oireachtas, or

    (b) a statute that was in force in Saorstát Éireann immediately before the date of the coming into operation of the Constitution and that continues to be of full force and effect by virtue of Article 50 of the Constitution.

16 Truth

(1) It shall be a defence (to be known and in this Act referred to as the "defence of truth") to a defamation action for the defendant to prove that the statement in respect of which the action was brought is true in all material respects.

(2) In a defamation action in respect of a statement containing 2 or more distinct allegations against the plaintiff, the defence of truth shall not fail by reason only of the truth of every allegation not being proved, if the words not proved to be true do not materially injure the plaintiff's reputation having regard to the truth of the remaining allegations.

17 Absolute privilege

(1) It shall be a defence to a defamation action for the defendant to prove that the statement in respect of which the action was brought would, if it had been made immediately before the commencement of this section, have been considered under the law in force immediately before such commencement as having been made on an occasion of absolute privilege.

(2) Subject to section 11(2) of the Committees of the Houses of the Oireachtas (Compellability, Privileges and Immunities of Witnesses) Act 1997, and without prejudice to the generality of subsection (1), it shall be a defence to a defamation action for the defendant to prove that the statement in respect of which the action was brought was—

(a) made in either House of the Oireachtas by a member of either House of the Oireachtas,

(b) contained in a report of a statement, to which paragraph (a) applies, produced by or on the authority of either such House,

(c) made in the European Parliament by a member of that Parliament,

(d) contained in a report of a statement, to which paragraph (c) applies, produced by or on the authority of the European Parliament,

(e) contained in a judgment of a court established by law in the State,

(f) made by a judge, or other person, performing a judicial function,

(g) made by a party, witness, legal representative or juror in the course of proceedings presided over by a judge, or other person, performing a judicial function,

(h) made in the course of proceedings involving the exercise of limited functions and powers of a judicial nature in accordance with Article 37 of the Constitution, where the statement is connected with those proceedings,

(i) a fair and accurate report of proceedings publicly heard before, or decision made public by, any court—

   (i) established by law in the State, or

   (ii) established under the law of Northern Ireland,

(j) a fair and accurate report of proceedings to which a relevant enactment referred to in section 40 of the Civil Liability and Courts Act 2004 applies,

(k) a fair and accurate report of proceedings publicly heard before, or decision made public by, any court or arbitral tribunal established by an international agreement to which the State is a party including the Court of Justice of the European Communities, the Court of First Instance of the European Communities, the European Court of Human Rights and the International Court of Justice,

(l) made in proceedings before a committee appointed by either House of the Oireachtas or jointly by both Houses of the Oireachtas,

(m) made in proceedings before a committee of the European Parliament,

(n) made in the course of proceedings before a tribunal established under the Tribunals of Inquiry (Evidence) Acts 1921 to 2004, where the statement is connected with those proceedings,

(o) contained in a report of any such tribunal,

(p) made in the course of proceedings before a commission of investigation established under the Commissions of Investigation Act 2004, where the statement is connected with those proceedings,

(q) contained in a report of any such commission,

(r) made in the course of an inquest by a coroner or contained in a decision made or verdict given at or during such inquest,

(s) made in the course of an inquiry conducted on the authority of a Minister of the Government, the Government, the Oireachtas, either House of the Oireachtas or a court established by law in the State,

(t) made in the course of an inquiry conducted in Northern Ireland on the authority of a person or body corresponding to a person or body referred to in paragraph (s),

(u) contained in a report of an inquiry referred to in paragraph (s) or (t),

(v) made in the course of proceedings before an arbitral tribunal where the statement is connected with those proceedings,

(w) made pursuant to and in accordance with an order of a court established by law in the State.

(3) Section 2 of the Committees of the Houses of the Oireachtas (Privilege and Procedure) Act 1976 is amended by the insertion of the following subsection:

"(3) In this section 'utterance' includes a statement within the meaning of the Defamation Act 2009;".

(4) A defence under this section shall be known as, and is referred to in this Act, as the "defence of absolute privilege ".

18 Qualified privilege

(1) Subject to section 17, it shall be a defence to a defamation action for the defendant to prove that the statement in respect of which the action was brought would, if it had been made immediately before the commencement of this section, have been considered under the law (other than the Act of 1961) in force immediately before such commencement as having been made on an occasion of qualified privilege.

(2) Without prejudice to the generality of subsection (1), it shall, subject to section 19, be a defence to a defamation action for the defendant to prove that—

    (a) the statement was published to a person or persons who—

        (i) had a duty to receive, or interest in receiving, the information contained in the statement, or

        (ii) the defendant believed upon reasonable grounds that the said person or persons had such a duty or interest, and

    (b) the defendant had a corresponding duty to communicate, or interest in communicating, the information to such person or persons.

(3) Without prejudice to the generality of subsection (1), it shall be a defence to a defamation action for the defendant to prove that the statement to which the action relates is—

    (a) a statement to which Part 1 of Schedule 1 applies,

    (b) contained in a report, copy, extract or summary referred to in that Part, or

    (c) contained in a determination referred to in that Part.

(4) Without prejudice to the generality of subsection (1), it shall be a defence to a defamation action for the defendant to prove that the statement to which the action relates is contained in a report, copy or summary referred to in Part 2 of Schedule 1, unless it is proved that the defendant was requested by the plaintiff to publish in the same medium of communication in which he or she published the statement concerned, a reasonable statement by way of explanation or a contradiction, and has refused or failed to do so or has done so in a manner that is not adequate or reasonable having regard to all of the circumstances.

(5) Nothing in subsection (3) shall be construed as—

    (a) protecting the publication of any statement the publication of which is prohibited by law, or of any statement that is not of public concern and the publication of which is not for the public benefit, or

    (b) limiting or abridging any privilege subsisting apart from subsection (3).

(6) A defence under this section shall be known, and is referred to in this Act, as the "defence of qualified privilege".

(7) In this section—

"duty" means a legal, moral or social duty;

"interest" means a legal, moral or social interest.

19 Loss of defence of qualified privilege

(1) In a defamation action, the defence of qualified privilege shall fail if, in relation to the publication of the statement in respect of which the action was brought, the plaintiff proves that the defendant acted with malice.

(2) The defence of qualified privilege shall not fail by reason only of the publication of the statement concerned to a person other than an interested person if it is proved that the statement was published to the person because the publisher mistook him or her for an interested person.

(3) Where a defamation action is brought against more than one defendant, the failure of the defence of qualified privilege in relation to one of the defendants by virtue of the application of subsection (1) shall not cause the failure of the defence in relation to another of the defendants unless that other defendant was vicariously liable for such acts or omissions of the first-mentioned defendant as gave rise to the cause of action concerned.

(4) Section 11(4) of the Civil Liability Act 1961 is repealed.

(5) In this section "interested person" means, in relation to a statement, a person who, under section 18(2)(a), had a duty or interest in receiving the information contained in the statement.

20 Honest opinion

(1) It shall be a defence (to be known, and in this section referred to, as the "defence of honest opinion") to a defamation action for the defendant to prove that, in the case of a statement consisting of an opinion, the opinion was honestly held.

(2) Subject to subsection (3), an opinion is honestly held, for the purposes of this section, if—

    (a) at the time of the publication of the statement, the defendant believed in the truth of the opinion or, where the defendant is not the author of the opinion, believed that the author believed it to be true,

    (b) (i) the opinion was based on allegations of fact—

        (I) specified in the statement containing the opinion, or

        (II) referred to in that statement, that were known, or might reasonably be expected to have been known, by the persons to whom the statement was published,

        or

      (ii) the opinion was based on allegations of fact to which—

        (I) the defence of absolute privilege, or

        (II) the defence of qualified privilege,

        would apply if a defamation action were brought in respect of such allegations,

    and

    (c) the opinion related to a matter of public interest.

(3) (a) The defence of honest opinion shall fail, if the opinion concerned is based on allegations of fact to which subsection (2)(b)(i) applies, unless—

      (i) the defendant proves the truth of those allegations, or

      (ii) where the defendant does not prove the truth of all of those allegations, the opinion is honestly held having regard to the allegations of fact the truth of which are proved.

    (b) The defence of honest opinion shall fail, if the opinion concerned is based on allegations of fact to which subsection (2)(b)(ii) applies, unless—

      (i) the defendant proves the truth of those allegations, or

(ii)   where the defendant does not prove the truth of those allegations—

(I)   the opinion could not reasonably be understood as implying that those allegations were true, and

(II)   at the time of the publication of the opinion, the defendant did not know or could not reasonably have been expected to know that those allegations were untrue.

(4) Where a defamatory statement consisting of an opinion is published jointly by a person ("first-mentioned person") and another person ("joint publisher"), the first-mentioned person shall not fail in pleading the defence of honest opinion in a subsequent defamation action brought in respect of that statement by reason only of that opinion not being honestly held by the joint publisher, unless the first-mentioned person was at the time of publication vicariously liable for the acts or omissions, from which the cause of action in respect of that statement accrued, of the joint publisher.

21 Distinguishing between allegations of fact and opinion

The matters to which the court in a defamation action shall have regard, for the purposes of distinguishing between a statement consisting of allegations of fact and a statement consisting of opinion, shall include the following:

(a)   the extent to which the statement is capable of being proved;

(b)   the extent to which the statement was made in circumstances in which it was likely to have been reasonably understood as a statement of opinion rather than a statement consisting of an allegation of fact; and

(c)   the words used in the statement and the extent to which the statement was subject to a qualification or a disclaimer or was accompanied by cautionary words.

22 Offer to make amends

(1) A person who has published a statement that is alleged to be defamatory of another person may make an offer to make amends.

(2) An offer to make amends shall—

(a)   be in writing,

(b)   state that it is an offer to make amends for the purposes of this section, and

(c)   state whether the offer is in respect of the entire of the statement or an offer (in this Act referred to as a "qualified offer") in respect of—

(i)   part only of the statement, or

(ii)   a particular defamatory meaning only.

(3) An offer to make amends shall not be made after the delivery of the defence in the defamation action concerned.

(4) An offer to make amends may be withdrawn before it is accepted and where such an offer is withdrawn a new offer to make amends may be made.

(5) In this section "an offer to make amends" means an offer—

(a) to make a suitable correction of the statement concerned and a sufficient apology to the person to whom the statement refers or is alleged to refer,

(b) to publish that correction and apology in such manner as is reasonable and practicable in the circumstances, and

(c) to pay to the person such sum in compensation or damages (if any), and such costs, as may be agreed by them or as may be determined to be payable,

whether or not it is accompanied by any other offer to perform an act other than an act referred to in paragraph (a), (b) or (c).

23 Effect of offer to make amends

(1) If an offer to make amends under section 22 is accepted the following provisions shall apply:

(a) if the parties agree as to the measures that should be taken by the person who made the offer to ensure compliance by him or her with the terms of the offer, the High Court or, where a defamation action has already been brought, the court in which it was brought may, upon the application of the person to whom the offer was made, direct the party who made the offer to take those measures;

(b) if the parties do not so agree, the person who made the offer may, with the leave of the High Court or, where a defamation action has already been brought, the court in which it was brought, make a correction and apology by means of a statement before the court in such terms as may be approved by the court and give an undertaking as to the manner of their publication;

(c) if the parties do not agree as to the damages or costs that should be paid by the person who made the offer, those matters shall be determined by the High Court or, where a defamation action has already been brought, the court in which it was brought, and the court shall for those purposes have all such powers as it would have if it were determining damages or costs in a defamation action, and in making a determination under this paragraph it shall take into account the adequacy of any measures already taken to ensure compliance with the terms of the offer by the person who made the offer;

(d) no defamation action shall be brought or, if already brought, proceeded with against another person in respect of the statement to which the offer to make amends applies unless the court considers that in all the circumstances of the case it is just and proper to so do.

(2) Subject to subsection (3), it shall be a defence to a defamation action for a person to prove that he or she made an offer to make amends under section 22 and that it was not

accepted, unless the plaintiff proves that the defendant knew or ought reasonably to have known at the time of the publication of the statement to which the offer relates that—

    (a) it referred to the plaintiff or was likely to be understood as referring to the plaintiff, and

    (b) it was false and defamatory of the plaintiff.

(3) Where the defendant in a defamation action made a qualified offer only, subsection (2) shall apply in relation to that part only of the action that relates to the part of the statement or the meaning, as the case may be, to which the qualified offer relates.

(4) A person who makes an offer to make amends is not required to plead it as a defence in a defamation action.

(5) If a defendant in a defamation action pleads the defence under this section, he or she shall not be entitled to plead any other defence in the action, and if the defence is pleaded in respect of a qualified offer only he or she shall not be entitled to plead any other defence in respect of that part of the action that relates to the part of the statement or the meaning, as the case may be, to which the qualified offer relates.

24 Apology

(1) In a defamation action the defendant may give evidence in mitigation of damage that he or she—

    (a) made or offered an apology to the plaintiff in respect of the statement to which the action relates, and

    (b) published the apology in such manner as ensured that the apology was given the same or similar prominence as was given to that statement, or offered to publish an apology in such a manner,

as soon as practicable after the plaintiff makes complaint to the defendant concerning the utterance to which the apology relates, or after the bringing of the action, whichever is earlier.

(2) In a defamation action, a defendant who intends to give evidence to which subsection (1) applies shall, at the time of the filing or delivery of the defence to the action, notify the plaintiff in writing of his or her intention to give such evidence.

(3) In a defamation action, an apology made by or on behalf of a defendant in respect of a statement to which the action relates—

    (a) does not constitute an express or implied admission of liability by that defendant, and

    (b) is not relevant to the determination of liability in the action.

(4) Evidence of an apology made by or on behalf of a person in respect of a statement to which the action relates is not admissible in any civil proceedings as evidence of liability of the defendant.

25 Consent to publish

In a defamation action it shall be a defence, to be known as the "defence of consent", for a person to prove that the plaintiff consented to the publication of the statement in respect of which the action was brought.

26 Fair and reasonable publication on a matter of public interest

(1) It shall be a defence (to be known, and in this section referred to, as the "defence of fair and reasonable publication") to a defamation action for the defendant to prove that—

(a) the statement in respect of which the action was brought was published—

    (i) in good faith, and

    (ii) in the course of, or for the purpose of, the discussion of a subject of public interest, the discussion of which was for the public benefit,

(b) in all of the circumstances of the case, the manner and extent of publication of the statement did not exceed that which was reasonably sufficient, and

(c) in all of the circumstances of the case, it was fair and reasonable to publish the statement.

(2) For the purposes of this section, the court shall, in determining whether it was fair and reasonable to publish the statement concerned, take into account such matters as the court considers relevant including any or all of the following:

(a) the extent to which the statement concerned refers to the performance by the person of his or her public functions;

(b) the seriousness of any allegations made in the statement;

(c) the context and content (including the language used) of the statement;

(d) the extent to which the statement drew a distinction between suspicions, allegations and facts;

(e) the extent to which there were exceptional circumstances that necessitated the publication of the statement on the date of publication;

(f) in the case of a statement published in a periodical by a person who, at the time of publication, was a member of the Press Council, the extent to which the person adhered to the code of standards of the Press Council and abided by determinations of the Press Ombudsman and determinations of the Press Council;

(g) in the case of a statement published in a periodical by a person who, at the time of publication, was not a member of the Press Council, the extent to which the publisher of the periodical adhered to standards equivalent to the standards specified in paragraph (f);

(h) the extent to which the plaintiff's version of events was represented in the publication concerned and given the same or similar prominence as was given to the statement concerned;

(i) if the plaintiff's version of events was not so represented, the extent to which a reasonable attempt was made by the publisher to obtain and publish a response from that person; and

(j) the attempts made, and the means used, by the defendant to verify the assertions and allegations concerning the plaintiff in the statement.

(3) The failure or refusal of a plaintiff to respond to attempts by or on behalf of the defendant, to elicit the plaintiff's version of events, shall not—

    (a) constitute or imply consent to the publication of the statement, or

    (b) entitle the court to draw any inference therefrom.

(4) In this section—

"court" means, in relation to a defamation action brought in the High Court, the jury, if the High Court is sitting with a jury;

"defamation action" does not include an application for a declaratory order.

27 Innocent publication

(1) It shall be a defence (to be known as the "defence of innocent publication") to a defamation action for the defendant to prove that—

    (a) he or she was not the author, editor or publisher of the statement to which the action relates,

    (b) he or she took reasonable care in relation to its publication, and

    (c) he or she did not know, and had no reason to believe, that what he or she did caused or contributed to the publication of a statement that would give rise to a cause of action in defamation.

(2) A person shall not, for the purposes of this section, be considered to be the author, editor or publisher of a statement if—

    (a) in relation to printed material containing the statement, he or she was responsible for the printing, production, distribution or selling only of the printed material,

    (b) in relation to a film or sound recording containing the statement, he or she was responsible for the processing, copying, distribution, exhibition or selling only of the film or sound recording,

    (c) in relation to any electronic medium on which the statement is recorded or stored, he or she was responsible for the processing, copying, distribution or selling only of the electronic medium or was responsible for the operation or provision only of any equipment, system or service by means of which the statement would be capable of being retrieved, copied, distributed or made available.

(3) The court shall, for the purposes of determining whether a person took reasonable care, or had reason to believe that what he or she did caused or contributed to the publication of a defamatory statement, have regard to—

    (a) the extent of the person's responsibility for the content of the statement or the decision to publish it,

    (b) the nature or circumstances of the publication, and

    (c) the previous conduct or character of the person.

PART 4
REMEDIES

28 Declaratory order

(1) A person who claims to be the subject of a statement that he or she alleges is defamatory may apply to the Circuit Court for an order (in this Act referred to as a "declaratory order") that the statement is false and defamatory of him or her.

(2) Upon an application under this section, the court shall make a declaratory order if it is satisfied that—

    (a) the statement is defamatory of the applicant and the respondent has no defence to the application,

    (b) the applicant requested the respondent to make and publish an apology, correction or retraction in relation to that statement, and

    (c) the respondent failed or refused to accede to that request or, where he or she acceded to that request, failed or refused to give the apology, correction or retraction the same or similar prominence as was given by the respondent to the statement concerned.

(3) For the avoidance of doubt, an applicant for a declaratory order shall not be required to prove that the statement to which the application concerned relates is false.

(4) Where an application is made under this section, the applicant shall not be entitled to bring any other proceedings in respect of any cause of action arising out of the statement to which the application relates.

(5) An application under this section shall be brought by motion on notice to the respondent grounded on affidavit.

(6) Where a court makes a declaratory order, it may, in addition, make an order under section 30 or 33, upon an application by the applicant in that behalf.

(7) The court may, for the purposes of making a determination in relation to an application under this section in an expeditious manner, give directions in relation to the delivery of pleadings and the time and manner of trial of any issues raised in the course of such an application.

(8) No order in relation to damages shall be made upon an application under this section.

(9) An application under this section shall be made to the Circuit Court sitting in the circuit where—

    (a) the statement to which the application relates was published, or

    (b) the defendant or one of the defendants, as the case may be, resides.

29 Lodgment of money in settlement of action

(1) In an action for damages for defamation the defendant may, upon giving notice in writing to the plaintiff, pay a sum of money into court in satisfaction of the action when filing his or her defence to the action.

(2) A payment to which this section applies shall be deemed to be a payment under such rule of court for the time being in force as provides for the payment into court of a sum of money in satisfaction of an action for damages for defamation.

(3) Where a payment to which this section applies is made, the plaintiff in the action concerned may accept the payment—

    (a)   in accordance with the rule referred to in subsection (2), or

    (b)   inform the court in which the action was brought, on notice to the defendant, of his or her acceptance of the payment in full settlement of the action.

(4) The defendant shall not be required to admit liability in an action for damages for defamation when making a payment to which this section applies.

30 Correction order

(1) Where, in a defamation action, there is a finding that the statement in respect of which the action was brought was defamatory and the defendant has no defence to the action, the court may, upon the application of the plaintiff, make an order (in this Act referred to as a "correction order") directing the defendant to publish a correction of the defamatory statement.

(2) Without prejudice to the generality of subsection (1), a correction order shall—

    (a)   specify—

        (i)   the date and time upon which, or

        (ii)   the period not later than the expiration of which,

        the correction order shall be published, and

    (b)   specify the form, content, extent and manner of publication of the correction,

and shall, unless the plaintiff otherwise requests, require the correction to be published in such manner as will ensure that it is communicated to all or substantially all of those persons to whom the defamatory statement was published.

(3) Where a plaintiff intends to make an application under this section, he or she shall so inform—

    (a)   the defendant by notice in writing, not later than 7 days before the trial of the action, and

    (b)   the court at the trial of the action.

(4) An application under this section may be made at such time during the trial of a defamation action as the court or, where the action is tried in the High Court sitting with a jury, the trial judge directs.

31 Damages

(1) The parties in a defamation action may make submissions to the court in relation to the matter of damages.

(2) In a defamation action brought in the High Court, the judge shall give directions to the jury in relation to the matter of damages.

(3) In making an award of general damages in a defamation action, regard shall be had to all of the circumstances of the case.

(4) Without prejudice to the generality of subsection (3), the court in a defamation action shall, in making an award of general damages, have regard to—

    (a)   the nature and gravity of any allegation in the defamatory statement concerned,

    (b)   the means of publication of the defamatory statement including the enduring nature of those means,

    (c)   the extent to which the defamatory statement was circulated,

    (d)   the offering or making of any apology, correction or retraction by the defendant to the plaintiff in respect of the defamatory statement,

    (e)   the making of any offer to make amends under section 22 by the defendant, whether or not the making of that offer was pleaded as a defence,

    (f)   the importance to the plaintiff of his or her reputation in the eyes of particular or all recipients of the defamatory statement,

    (g)   the extent (if at all) to which the plaintiff caused or contributed to, or acquiesced in, the publication of the defamatory statement,

    (h)   evidence given concerning the reputation of the plaintiff,

    (i)   if the defence of truth is pleaded and the defendant proves the truth of part but not the whole of the defamatory statement, the extent to which that defence is successfully pleaded in relation to the statement,

    (j)   if the defence of qualified privilege is pleaded, the extent to which the defendant has acceded to the request of the plaintiff to publish a reasonable statement by way of explanation or contradiction, and

    (k)   any order made under section 33, or any order under that section or correction order that the court proposes to make or, where the action is tried by the High Court sitting with a jury, would propose to make in the event of there being a finding of defamation.

(5) For the purposes of subsection (4)(c), a defamatory statement consisting of words that are innocent on their face, but that are defamatory by reason of facts known to some recipients only of the publication containing the defamatory statement, shall be treated as having been published to those recipients only.

(6) The defendant in a defamation action may, for the purposes of mitigating damages, give evidence—

    (a)   with the leave of the court, of any matter that would have a bearing upon the reputation of the plaintiff, provided that it relates to matters connected with the defamatory statement,

    (b)   that the plaintiff has already in another defamation action been awarded damages in respect of a defamatory statement that contained substantially the same allegations as are contained in the defamatory statement to which the first-mentioned defamation action relates.

(7) The court in a defamation action may make an award of damages (in this section referred to as "special damages") to the plaintiff in respect of financial loss suffered by him or her as a result of the injury to his or her reputation caused by the publication of the defamatory statement in respect of which the action was brought.

(8) In this section "court" means, in relation to a defamation action brought in the High Court, the jury, if the High Court is sitting with a jury.

32 Aggravated and punitive damages

(1) Where, in a defamation action—

    (a) the court finds the defendant liable to pay damages to the plaintiff in respect of a defamatory statement, and

    (b) the defendant conducted his or her defence in a manner that aggravated the injury caused to the plaintiff's reputation by the defamatory statement,

the court may, in addition to any general, special or punitive damages payable by the defendant to the plaintiff, order the defendant to pay to the plaintiff damages (in this section referred to as "aggravated damages") of such amount as it considers appropriate to compensate the plaintiff for the aggravation of the said injury.

(2) Where, in a defamation action, the court finds the defendant liable to pay damages to the plaintiff in respect of a defamatory statement and it is proved that the defendant—

    (a) intended to publish the defamatory statement concerned to a person other than the plaintiff,

    (b) knew that the defamatory statement would be understood by the said person to refer to the plaintiff, and

    (c) knew that the statement was untrue or in publishing it was reckless as to whether it was true or untrue,

the court may, in addition to any general, special or aggravated damages payable by the defendant to the plaintiff, order the defendant to pay to the plaintiff damages (in this section referred to as "punitive damages") of such amount as it considers appropriate.

(3) In this section "court" means, in relation to a defamation action brought in the High Court, the jury, if the High Court is sitting with a jury.

33 Order prohibiting the publication of a defamatory statement

(1) The High Court, or where a defamation action has been brought, the court in which it was brought, may, upon the application of the plaintiff, make an order prohibiting the publication or further publication of the statement in respect of which the application was made if in its opinion—

    (a) the statement is defamatory, and

    (b) the defendant has no defence to the action that is reasonably likely to succeed.

(2) Where an order is made under this section it shall not operate to prohibit the reporting of the making of that order provided that such reporting does not include the publication of the statement to which the order relates.

(3) In this section "order" means—

    (a) an interim order,

    (b) an interlocutory order, or

    (c) a permanent order.

34 Summary disposal of action

(1) The court in a defamation action may, upon the application of the plaintiff, grant summary relief to the plaintiff if it is satisfied that—

    (a) the statement in respect of which the action was brought is defamatory, and

    (b) the defendant has no defence to the action that is reasonably likely to succeed.

(2) The court in a defamation action may, upon the application of the defendant, dismiss the action if it is satisfied that the statement in respect of which the action was brought is not reasonably capable of being found to have a defamatory meaning.

(3) An application under this section shall be brought by motion on notice to the other party to the action and shall be grounded on an affidavit.

(4) An application under this section shall not be heard or determined in the presence of a jury.

PART 5
CRIMINAL LIABILITY

35 Abolition of certain common law offences

The common law offences of defamatory libel, seditious libel and obscene libel are abolished.

36 Publication or utterance of blasphemous matter

(1) A person who publishes or utters blasphemous matter shall be guilty of an offence and shall be liable upon conviction on indictment to a fine not exceeding ?25,000.

(2) For the purposes of this section, a person publishes or utters blasphemous matter if—

    (a) he or she publishes or utters matter that is grossly abusive or insulting in relation to matters held sacred by any religion, thereby causing outrage among a substantial number of the adherents of that religion, and

    (b) he or she intends, by the publication or utterance of the matter concerned, to cause such outrage.

(3) It shall be a defence to proceedings for an offence under this section for the defendant to prove that a reasonable person would find genuine literary, artistic, political, scientific, or academic value in the matter to which the offence relates.

(4) In this section "religion" does not include an organisation or cult—

    (a) the principal object of which is the making of profit, or

    (b) that employs oppressive psychological manipulation—

        (i) of its followers, or

        (ii) for the purpose of gaining new followers.

37 Seizure of copies of blasphemous statements

(1) Where a person is convicted of an offence under section 36, the court may issue a warrant—

    (a) authorising any member of the Garda Síochána to enter (if necessary by the use of reasonable force) at all reasonable times any premises (including a dwelling) at which he or she has reasonable grounds for believing that copies of the statement to which the offence related are to be found, and to search those premises and seize and remove all copies of the statement found therein,

(b) directing the seizure and removal by any member of the Garda Síochána of all copies of the statement to which the offence related that are in the possession of any person,

(c) specifying the manner in which copies so seized and removed shall be detained and stored by the Garda Síochána.

(2) A member of the Garda Síochána may—

(a) enter and search any premises,

(b) seize, remove and detain any copy of a statement to which an offence under section 36 relates found therein or in the possession of any person,

in accordance with a warrant under subsection (1).

(3) Upon final judgment being given in proceedings for an offence under section 36, anything seized and removed under subsection (2) shall be disposed of in accordance with such directions as the court may give upon an application by a member of the Garda Síochána in that behalf.

PART 6
MISCELLANEOUS

38 Limitation of actions

(1) Section 11 of the Act of 1957 is amended—

(a) in subsection (2), by the substitution of the following paragraph for paragraph (c):

"(c) A defamation action within the meaning of the Defamation Act 2009 shall not be brought after the expiration of—

(i) one year, or

(ii) such longer period as the court may direct not exceeding 2 years,

from the date on which the cause of action accrued.",

and

(b) the insertion of the following subsections:

"(3A) The court shall not give a direction under subsection (2)(c)(ii) (inserted by section 38(1)(a) of the Defamation Act 2009) unless it is satisfied that—

(a) the interests of justice require the giving of the direction,

(b) the prejudice that the plaintiff would suffer if the direction were not given would significantly outweigh the prejudice that the defendant would suffer if the direction were given,

and the court shall, in deciding whether to give such a direction, have regard to the reason for the failure to bring the action within the period specified in subparagraph (i) of the said subsection (2)(c) and the extent to which any evidence relevant to the matter is by virtue of the delay no longer capable of being adduced.

(3B) For the purposes of bringing a defamation action within the meaning of the Defamation Act 2009, the date of accrual of the cause of action shall be the date upon which the defamatory statement is first published and, where the statement is published through the medium of the internet, the date on which it is first capable of being viewed or listened to through that medium.".

(2) Section 49 of the Act of 1957 is amended by the substitution of the following subsection for subsection (3):

"(3) In the case of defamation actions within the meaning of the Defamation Act 2009, subsection (1) of this section shall have effect as if for the words 'six years' there were substituted the words 'one year or such longer period as the court may direct not exceeding two years'.".

39 Survival of cause of action on death

(1) Section 6 of the Civil Liability Act 1961 is amended by the insertion of the following definitions:

"'Act of 2009' means the Defamation Act 2009;

'aggravated damages' has the same meaning as it has in the Act of 2009;

'punitive damages' has the same meaning as it has in the Act of 2009.".

(2) Section 7 of the Civil Liability Act 1961 is amended by—

(a) the insertion of the following subsection:

"(1A) On the death of a person on or after the commencement of section 39(2)(a) of the Act of 2009, a cause of action for defamation vested in him immediately before his death shall survive for the benefit of his estate.",

and

(b) the insertion of the following subsection:

"(2A) Where by virtue of subsection (1A) of this section, a cause of action for defamation survives for the benefit of the estate of a deceased person, the damages recoverable for the benefit of the estate of that person shall not include general damages, punitive damages or aggravated damages.".

(3) Section 8 of the Civil Liability Act 1961 is amended by—

(a) the insertion of the following subsection:

"(1A) On the death of a person on or after the commencement of section 39(3)(a) of the *Act of 2009* a cause of action subsisting against him shall survive against his estate.",

(b) by the insertion of the following subsection:

"(2A) Where by virtue of subsection (1A) of this section, a cause of action for defamation survives against the estate of a deceased person, the damages recoverable against the estate of that person shall not include general damages, punitive damages or aggravated damages.".

40 Agreements for indemnity

An agreement to indemnify any person against civil liability for defamation in respect of the publication of any statement shall be lawful unless at the time of the publication that person knows that the statement is defamatory, and does not reasonably believe that there is a defence to any action brought upon it that would succeed.

41 Jurisdiction of courts

The Third Schedule to the Courts (Supplemental Provisions) Act 1961 is amended by—

(a) the insertion, in column (2) at reference number 6, of "a defamation action within the meaning of the Defamation Act 2009," between "other than" and "an action", and

(b) the insertion of the following:

| "7A A defamation action under the Defamation Act 2009. | Where the amount of the claim does not exceed €50,000. | At the election of the plaintiff— (a) the judge of the circuit where the tort is alleged to have been committed, or (b) the judge of the circuit where the defendant or one of the defendants resides or carries on business.". |

42 Malicious falsehood

(1) In an action for slander of title, slander of goods or other malicious falsehood, the plaintiff shall be required to prove that the statement upon which the action is founded—

(a) was untrue,

(b) was published maliciously, and

(c) referred to the plaintiff, his or her property or his or her office, profession, calling, trade or business.

(2) In an action for slander of title, slander of goods or other malicious falsehood, the plaintiff shall be required to prove—

(a) special damage, or

(b) that the publication of the statement was calculated to cause and was likely to cause financial loss to the plaintiff in respect of his or her property or his or her office, profession, calling, trade or business.

43 Evidence of acquittal or conviction

(1) Where a person has been acquitted of an offence in the State, the fact of his or her acquittal, and any findings of fact made during the course of proceedings for the offence concerned, shall be admissible in evidence in a defamation action.

(2) Where a person has been convicted of an offence in the State, the fact of his or her conviction, and any findings of fact made during the course of proceedings for the offence concerned, shall be admissible in evidence in a defamation action.

44 Press Council

(1) The Minister may by order declare that such body as is specified in the order shall be recognised for the purposes of this Act, and a body standing so recognised, for the time being, shall be known, and in this Act is referred to, as the "Press Council".

(2) Not more than one body shall stand recognised under this section for the time being.

(3) No body (other than a body that stands recognised under this section for the time being) shall be known as, or describe itself as, the Press Council.

(4) The Minister shall not make an order under subsection (1) unless he or she is satisfied that the body in respect of which he or she proposes to make the order complies with the minimum requirements specified in Schedule 2.

(5) If the Minister is of the opinion that a body for the time being standing recognised by order under this section no longer complies with the provisions of Schedule 2, he or she may revoke that order.

(6) The Minister shall, before making an order under subsection (5), allow the body for the time being standing recognised under this section to make representations to him or her.

(7) Whenever an order is proposed to be made under this section a draft of the order shall be laid before each House of the Oireachtas and the order shall not be made unless a resolution approving of the draft has been passed by each such House.

SCHEDULE 1
Statements having Qualified Privilege

Section 18

PART 1
Statements Privileged Without Explanation or Contradiction

1. A fair and accurate report of any matter to which the defence of absolute privilege would apply (other than a fair and accurate report referred to in section 17(2)(i) or (k)).

2. A fair and accurate report of any proceedings publicly heard before, or decision made public by a court (including a court-martial) established under the law of any state or place (other than the State or Northern Ireland).

3. A fair and accurate report of the proceedings (other than court proceedings) presided over by a judge of a court established under the law of Northern Ireland.

4. A fair and accurate report of any proceedings in public of a house of any legislature (including a subordinate or federal legislature) of any state other than the State.

5. A fair and accurate report of proceedings in public of any body duly appointed, in the State, on the authority of a Minister of the Government, the Government, the Oireachtas, either House of the Oireachtas or a court established by law in the State to conduct a public inquiry on a matter of public importance.

6. A fair and accurate report of proceedings in public of any body duly appointed, in Northern Ireland, on the authority of a person or body corresponding to a person or body referred to in paragraph 5 to conduct a public inquiry on a matter of public importance.

7. A fair and accurate report of any proceedings in public of any body—

(a) that is part of any legislature (including a subordinate or federal legislature) of any state (other than the State), or

(b) duly appointed in a state other than the State, on the authority of a person or body corresponding to a person or body referred to in paragraph 5,

to conduct a public inquiry on a matter of public importance.

8. A fair and accurate report of any proceedings in public of an international organisation of which the State or Government is a member or the proceedings of which are of interest to the State.

9. A fair and accurate report of any proceedings in public of any international conference to which the Government sends a representative or observer or at which governments of states (other than the State) are represented.

10. A fair and accurate copy or extract from any register kept in pursuance of any law which is open to inspection by the public or of any other document which is required by law to be open to inspection by the public.

11. A fair and accurate report, copy or summary of any notice or advertisement published by or on the authority of any court established by law in the State or under the law of a Member State of the European Union, or any judge or officer of such a court.

12. A fair and accurate report or copy or summary of any notice or other document issued for the information of the public by or on behalf of any Department of State for which a Minister of the Government is responsible, local authority or the Commissioner of the Garda Síochána, or by or on behalf of a corresponding department, authority or officer in a Member State of the European Union.

13. A fair and accurate report or copy or summary of any notice or document issued by or on the authority of a committee appointed by either House of the Oireachtas or jointly by both Houses of the Oireachtas.

14. A determination of the Press Ombudsman referred to in paragraph 9(2) of Schedule 2.

15. A determination of the Press Council referred to in paragraph 9(4) of Schedule 2 or a report of the Press Council relating to the past performance of its functions.

16. Any statement published pursuant to, and in accordance with, a determination of the Press Ombudsman or the Press Council.

17. Any statement made during the investigation or hearing of a complaint by the Press Ombudsman in accordance with Schedule 2.

18. Any statement made during the hearing of an appeal from a determination of the Press Ombudsman in accordance with Schedule 2.

19. Any statement published by a person in accordance with a requirement under an Act of the Oireachtas whether or not that person is the author of the statement.

PART 2
Statements Privileged Subject to Explanation or Contradiction

1. A fair and accurate report of the proceedings, findings or decisions of an association, or a committee or governing body of an association, whether incorporated or not in the State or in a Member State of the European Union, relating to a member of the association or to a person subject, by contract or otherwise, to control by the association.

2. A fair and accurate report of the proceedings at any public meeting, held in the State or in a Member State of the European Union, being a meeting held for a lawful purpose and for the discussion of any matter of public concern whether the admission to the meeting is general or restricted.

3. A fair and accurate report of the proceedings at a general meeting, whether in the State or in a Member State of the European Union, of any company or association established by or under statute or incorporated by charter.

4. A fair and accurate report of the proceedings at any meeting or sitting of any local authority or the Health Service Executive, and any corresponding body in a Member State of the European Union.

5. A fair and accurate report of a press conference convened by or on behalf of a body to which this Part applies or the organisers of a public meeting within the meaning of paragraph 2 to give an account to the public of the proceedings or meeting.

6. A fair and accurate report of a report to which the defence of qualified privilege would apply.

7. A copy or fair and accurate report or summary of any ruling, direction, report, investigation, statement (including any advice, admonition or censure given or administered by the Irish Takeover Panel under section 20 of the Irish Takeover Panel Act 1997) or notice made, given, prepared, published or served by the Irish Takeover Panel.

SCHEDULE 2
Minimum Requirements in Relation to Press Council

Section 44

1. The Press Council shall be a company limited by guarantee.

2. The principal objects of the Press Council shall be to—

    (a) ensure the protection of freedom of expression of the press,

    (b) protect the public interest by ensuring ethical, accurate and truthful reporting by the press,

    (c) maintain certain minimum ethical and professional standards among the press,

    (d) ensure that the privacy and dignity of the individual is protected.

3. The Press Council shall be independent in the performance of its functions.

4. The owner of any periodical in circulation in the State or part of the State shall be entitled to be a member of the Press Council.

5. (1) The number of directors of the Press Council shall be 13, of whom—

    (a)   7 shall be directors (in this Schedule referred to as "independent public interest directors") who represent the public interest,

    (b)   5 shall be directors who represent the interests of owners and publishers of periodicals,

    (c)   one shall be a director who represents the interests of journalists.

(2) One of the independent public interest directors of the Press Council shall be appointed as chairperson of the Press Council.

6. (1) The independent public interest directors shall—

    (a)   be persons who are of standing in the community,

    (b)   be persons who are independent of—

        (i)   the interests of owners and publishers of periodicals, and

        (ii)   the interests of journalists,

    and

    (c)   be selected for appointment as independent public interest directors—

        (i)   by a panel of persons who are, in the opinion of the Minister, independent of the interests referred to in paragraph 5(1)(b) and (c),

        (ii)   in accordance with a selection process that is advertised to members of the public in a manner that the Minister considers to be sufficient.

(2) The criteria for selecting persons for appointment as independent public interest directors shall be published in such manner as will enable them to be inspected by members of the public.

7. (1) The Press Council shall be funded from subscriptions paid by members of the Press Council calculated in accordance with such rules as the Press Council shall make for that purpose.

(2) The Press Council shall not accept gifts or funding from any person other than subscriptions referred to in subparagraph (1).

8. (1) The Press Council shall have authority to receive, hear and determine complaints concerning the conduct of its members.

(2) The Press Council shall appoint a person (in this Act referred to as the "Press Ombudsman") to investigate, hear and determine complaints made to the Press Council concerning the conduct of its members.

9. (1) The procedures for investigating, hearing and determining a complaint to the Press Ombudsman shall—

    (a)   where appropriate, provide for the expeditious and informal resolution of the matter between the complainant and the member of the Press Council in respect of whom the complaint was made,

    (b)   provide for the determination of the matter by the Press Ombudsman, where all reasonable efforts made in accordance with clause (a) in relation to the matter have failed,

(c) provide for the taking of remedial action by the member of the Press Council in respect of whom the complaint was made consisting of any or all of the following:

    (i) the publication of the decision of the Press Ombudsman by such members of the Press Council as he or she directs and in such form and manner as he or she directs;

    (ii) the publication of a correction of inaccurate facts or information relating to the complainant in a manner that gives due prominence to the correction in the publication concerned;

    (iii) the publication of a retraction in respect of the material complained of; or

    (iv) such other action as the Ombudsman may, in the circumstances, deem appropriate.

(2) A determination of the Press Ombudsman in relation to a complaint may be appealed to the Press Council.

(3) Where an appeal is brought against the determination of the Press Ombudsman it shall be determined by the directors of the Press Council.

(4) A determination of the Press Council, upon an appeal from a determination of the Press Ombudsman, shall be published by such members of the Press Council as the directors of the Press Council direct and in such form and manner as they direct.

10. The Press Council shall adopt a code of standards which shall specify the standards to be adhered to, and the rules and practices to be complied with by the members of the Press Council including—

(a) ethical standards and practices,

(b) rules and standards intended to ensure the accuracy of reporting where a person's reputation is likely to be affected, and

(c) rules and standards intended to ensure that intimidation and harassment of persons does not occur and that the privacy, integrity and dignity of the person is respected.

INDEX

Trespass to land
protection of privacy, action for,
7.221–7.223

Truth
pursuit of, 1.08–1.13

Unborn
right to life, 3.65

Video games
prohibited, 3.86

Video recordings
censorship and classification, 3.81–
3.83
fitness for viewing, 3.83
incitement of hatred, refusal of
certificate on grounds of, 3.29
refusal of certification, 3.84
religious advertising as to, 3.21–3.28

Vulnerable adults
private information relating to,
7.60–7.61

***Wilkinson v Downton*, rule in**
emotional harm, intentional infliction
of, 7.229–7.232